Sociology and Social Life

THIRD EDITION

AMERICAN SOCIOLOGY SERIES

Sociology and Social Life

THIRD EDITION

KIMBALL YOUNG · RAYMOND W. MACK

Northwestern University

AMERICAN BOOK COMPANY · *New York*

Preface to the Third Edition

The third edition of *Sociology and Social Life* follows closely the design of the first and second editions. It is neither an encyclopedia of sociological facts nor a cursory examination of major social problems. Our intention is to provide the student with a systematic interpretation of the major elements of sociology.

We have prepared new study materials at the end of each chapter. The interpretative summaries have been rewritten. New and more demanding questions have been written, in keeping with the increasingly high quality and high level of preparation of beginning college students. We are grateful to Mrs. Merle Kaminsky for her editorial and secretarial help in improving these study aids.

We have added annotated bibliographic references to recent publications and used material from new journals, such as *Transaction* and *New Society*. Graphs and tables from recent research and from 1960 Census tabulations have been added, and we have noted, in the text and in footnotes, contributions to research and theory which have been published since the second edition.

Sociology provides one way of examining social life. As an aid to this examination, sociology has developed a set of concepts making possible the ordering of the features common to a series of observations of human groups, their culture, and their interrelations.

Our study of man's social life is built around four concepts basic to all modern-day science: *structure*, *function*, *pattern*, and *process*. Within this systematic framework, the fundamental data of social relations (Part I), social organization (Part II), social institutions (Part III), and social dynamics (Part IV) are analyzed.

After an opening chapter on science, social science, and sociology as areas of study, Part I begins with a discussion of the nature and scope of group life and with the precipitates of man's social living which we call culture. Then follow chapters on the extent of cultural variability, on man's values and norms, and on the universal structures, functions, and processes to be found in all human societies. While our central interest is group life, we do introduce data from psychology insofar as it is pertinent to an understanding of how personality develops within a matrix of society and culture.

Part II begins with a discussion of status, role, and differentiation—concepts vital to the treatment of social organization. Then follow discussions of class structure and its functions, social mobility, racial and ethnic aspects of stratification, the demographic components of social structure and related demographic processes, folk and urban communities, human ecology and, finally, a chapter on the metropolis, the suburb, and the region.

The opening chapter of Part III gives a broad overview of the structure and function of social institutions. There follow separate chapters dealing with each of the major social institutions: familial, educational, religious, economic, and political. Each chapter is organized around four phases: (1) the various structures that result in the necessary functions; (2) the functions—both manifest and latent —that are the consequences of these structures; (3) the patterns of behavior associated with particular institutions in the United States; and (4) the set of norms integrated around the given functions and processes.

Part IV treats the process of change, factors that induce it, and its consequences. Chapter 25, "Deviant Behavior," helps provide a bridge to what is often the student's second course in sociology: Social Problems. The chapter examines one force for change: patterned deviation from accepted social norms. Chapter 26, "Social Change," deals with invention, diffusion, and factors affecting rates of change in social structure and culture. The final chapter, "Social Trends," should help the student place what he has learned about human groups and human society in the context of his own time, and should help him understand some of the forces at work in an industrial culture.

One aim of this text is to provide the fundamentals of sociology for the student who wishes to pursue advanced work in the field. But a second aim is to give the student who will take only one sociology course the familiarity with sociology that any liberally educated person should have. It will furnish him a body of knowledge as well as the major conceptual tools of sociological analysis.

Kimball Young

Raymond W. Mack

Evanston

Contents

List of Tables

List of Figures

Sociology and Social Life

CHAPTER 1

Sociology and the Social Sciences

Sociology is the scientific study of the social aspects of human life. It is a body of knowledge, compiled by the scientific method, about human interaction. By interaction we mean reciprocal stimulation and response between two or more people. Sociologists, therefore, are concerned with man, the social context, the human group.

People everywhere deal with one another as members of groups. Only in the most exceptional cases do individuals survive in isolation, and such isolation is never absolute. Even a hermit has some social experience. Every human being is born into a group and spends his lifetime in patterned social relations. Everything he does—crossing the street, naming a boat, choosing a wife, throwing a spear—is closely bound up with what he wants from others and with what others expect and accept from him. Each of us expects certain behaviors from his relatives, friends, and even other human beings seen only casually at, say, a traffic intersection; and we are aware that others expect certain behaviors from us in given situations. Thus group life is patterned. Social life—the way in which groups are put together and the way in which they function—is the subject matter of sociology.

Sociology is the youngest of the social sciences. If we are to understand the material that sociology covers, what sociologists do, and how they do it, it is first necessary to understand what is meant by *science* and by *social science*.

THE METHOD OF SCIENCE

When a student says he is "taking science this semester," he means that he is learning (or being exposed to the opportunity for learning) some of the content of a body of knowledge. The body of knowledge may be labeled physics, or chemistry, or biology. A science, then, is a body of knowledge. But this is an extremely inadequate definition. English literature, philosophy, and eighteenth-century painting are bodies of knowledge, too, but we do not classify them as sciences. People tend to think of science as a laboratory pursuit, but a body of knowledge need not be compiled by using test tubes and Bunsen burners in order to be a science. The data of political science, anthropology, and several other sciences were not gathered in laboratories, but they are sciences nonetheless.

Articles and advertisements in popular periodicals tempt one to equate science with control. The Sunday supplement generally has a feature telling the reader how to make his fellow men (and women) do what he wishes by "using psychology" on them. Other columns assure him that scientists have made it possible for him to control his environment in myriad ways: he can drive to town on tires that will not endanger his life by blowing out; a new device allows him to steer his automobile comfortably with one hand so that, with the other, he can light a cigarette from which scientists have removed the ingredient that used to stain his teeth; and finally, having arrived at the drugstore, he can purchase a scientifically compounded toothpaste which will remove any stains the other scientists missed. But we can point to sciences that do not offer us control of either our social or our physical environment. Astronomy, for example, is a body of knowledge which we classify as a science; but the astronomer does not exercise any control over the courses or rates of movement of the heavenly bodies he studies.

What, then, is the common factor that leads us to classify certain bodies of knowledge as science? It is the way in which the knowledge is obtained; the identification of a field of knowledge as a science rests on the method used to acquire that knowledge. Knowledge obtained by what we call the *scientific method* is referred to as *scientific;* those who utilize this method to add to a body of knowledge we call *scientists;* and knowledge compiled by the method is designated a *science*.

The Scientific Method The scientist seeks and organizes knowledge in three ways. He does not say that other data cannot be true or useful but he does claim that only knowledge gained in this manner is scientific.

(1) Sense Experience The most reliable method of gaining knowledge is through the senses: sight, hearing, taste, smell, and touch. When a person "just

has the feeling, deep inside him," that the Chicago Cubs will win the World Series, he does not have scientific knowledge. When Aristotle assumed that a horse had a certain number of teeth because that seemed a reasonable number of teeth for a horse to have, he did not add to scientific knowledge. Had he looked inside the mouths of a sample of horses to find out how many teeth were there, or reached inside to touch and count them, he would have had a scientific datum—straight, indeed, from the horse's mouth!

To be sure, scientists often use instruments in gathering data, but these are really only devices that serve the senses in making perceptions. The most refined gauge must be read by a human eye if it is to contribute to the storehouse of human knowledge. The thermometer does not feel temperature; the ruler does not measure distance; the stethoscope does not hear a heartbeat. These are only auxiliary to the human senses; it is the eye and ear of the person using the devices that make of their sensitive indications a scientific observation.

(2) Reason The best method of organizing knowledge is through the use of reason. There is a widespread belief that scientists are persons who "let the facts speak for themselves." Facts never speak for themselves. Facts have no meaning unless they are seen in relationship to other facts. During our lives we all acquire a considerable store of information which we may bring to bear upon each new fact we learn. We are unaware that our brains are cataloging the newly presented information by reference to other knowledge which we already possess.

If, for example, a friend tells us that the temperature outside today is

Sociologist at work: gathering data from students.

74, we are inclined to think that this fact is meaningful by itself. Actually, it would take pages to list all the facts to which we relate this one. Here are a few. Obviously, each word in our friend's sentence has a meaning for us because we were reared in a society where English is the standard language. Then too, we are familiar with a Fahrenheit scale for measuring temperatures and know that in ordinary conversation we refer to this scale rather than to the centigrade scale. We know that water boils at 212, that it freezes at 32, that normal room temperature in our society is about 70. Our conclusion—that it is unseasonably warm or cool today, or about what one would expect—indicates a knowledge of the time of year, the geographic location, and some information about temperatures in this area at this season in previous years. This simple illustration points up what we mean when we refer to a science as a body of knowledge: it is a body of knowledge because it consists of facts which have been organized with relation to one another by reason.

(3) *Agreement Among Observers* The best method of checking knowledge is through the independent conclusions of a number of competent observers. The reason we sometimes have to wait so long to gain access to a medical discovery is that a relationship between facts which seems apparent to one competent observer from his sense experience has not been validated by others, and hence is not yet accepted by scientists as part of scientific knowledge. It is not unknown in human experience for one observer to see small winged beings descending from the

Sociologist at work: visiting transitional neighborhood.

clouds, to hear them speak to him, and even to touch them. But because other competent observers cannot see, hear, or touch them, their existence cannot be accepted and treated as a scientific datum.

In summary, then, when (1) an observer gains knowledge through one or more of his senses and (2) he uses his reason to interpret his observations —that is, to relate them to other facts— and (3) other persons sufficiently well trained in the area being studied see, hear, touch, smell, or taste the same things as the first scientist and, using their reason, organize the knowledge

they have gained in the same way as the first observer—that is, reach the same conclusions as that first observer— then we have a scientific fact arrived at by the scientific method.[1]

Incidentally, method should not be confused with technique. Administering a questionnaire is a technique which sociologists use, just as making a microscopic slide is a technique which biologists use. A technique is a tool for

1 · For a list of facts in social science which have been validated by agreement among observers, and a study of the nature of such facts, see Robert C. Hanson, "Evidence and Procedure Characteristics of 'Reliable' Propositions in Social Science," *American Journal of Sociology*, 1958, 63:357–370.

Monkmeyer

Sociologist at work: analyzing data which has been processed by electronic computer.

gathering or analyzing data. So too, interviewing is a technique; but science is an overall method of gaining knowledge.

THE NATURE OF SCIENCE

We can see that the scientific method is an attempt to be completely objective. In other words, the scientist tries to separate his own wishes and values from the process of observation. His own conditioning influences his choice of problems to study, of course, but he tries not to let what he wants to discover affect what he actually does find. He has learned from his society its values, its norms, and its way of thinking. That is exactly why he utilizes the scientific method: to attempt to get outside himself and his milieu in order to see his physical and social environment as he would if he had not been taught a whole set of notions concerning the way it ought to be. There are many jokes about scientists, such as the story of the man on the train who commented to his seatmate, a scientist, "The sheep in that field have just been sheared," and the scientist: "They seem to have been, on this side."

The reluctance to overcommit himself is the caution of a man who does not want to let his preconceived ideas bias his observations. The stereotype of the absent-minded professor is perhaps not so derogatory as we sometimes assume; it is a portrait of a man who removes himself from the ordinary human world of prejudice and emotion, who strives during his working hours as a scientist to be an objective, unbiased, rational person.

It is important to understand that,

although its method is strict, science as a body of knowledge is ever-changing. It is not that facts are disproved; it is that they are added to or modified. The body of scientific knowledge is cumulative. Einstein's theory of relativity does not show that Newton's scientific facts were wrong; it adds to them; it explains more.

Finally, scientists generally assume that knowledge *per se* is worthwhile. The scientist does not assume that only facts about people are important and that facts about animals are not; or that only facts about economics are worth gathering and that information about religion is not; or that only data for which some immediate practical use can be found is worth pursuing and that study in other areas is useless. If the last assumption were held, for example, we would not be able to generate power to heat, light, and operate large factories with atomic energy; for when Einstein worked out the formula which led eventually to the splitting of the atom, his research had no immediate practical use. He was pursuing knowledge for its own sake because, as a scientist, he valued the idea of giving mankind more knowledge than it previously possessed.

The ideal model for scientific research is the controlled experiment.[2] Here two groups are measured: an experimental group, where some change is introduced; and a control group, which is similar to the experimental group but in which no change is deliberately effected. The two groups, experimental and control, are identical, except that some change is induced in the experimental group. The control group is used so that we can tell what change takes place normally with the passage of time, without the introduction of the experimental variable. The effect of an experiment can be measured by looking at the change in both groups, and then subtracting, as it were, the control group change from the experimental group change. (See Figure 1.)

Actually, of course, scientists do not always follow this ideal model. Sometimes they simply describe one cell (b) of the diagram in Figure 1. Sometimes they compare a "before" and "after" situation in an experimental group (a minus b) without having a control group. It is not unusual to compare two matched groups at one point in time (b and b'). And some research is based on observations of one group at one time and a different group at another time (a and b').

While it is not always possible to meet the ideal model of a controlled experiment, the least we can do is be aware of the goal and keep it in mind, so that we know the weaknesses of our conclusions when we only approximate the ideal.

We have discussed science in general; let us now narrow our focus.

SOCIAL SCIENCE

By *social science* we mean those bodies of knowledge compiled through the scientific method which deal with the forms and contents of man's interaction. To be social is to interact, to participate in group life. It is true that textbooks in the social sciences sometimes discuss the social interaction of living beings other than people, such as ants or apes, but they do so usually for the purpose of illustrating, drawing

2 · See Samuel A. Stouffer, "Some Observations on Study Design," *American Journal of Sociology*, 1950, 55:355–361.

FIGURE 1 · The Experimental Model

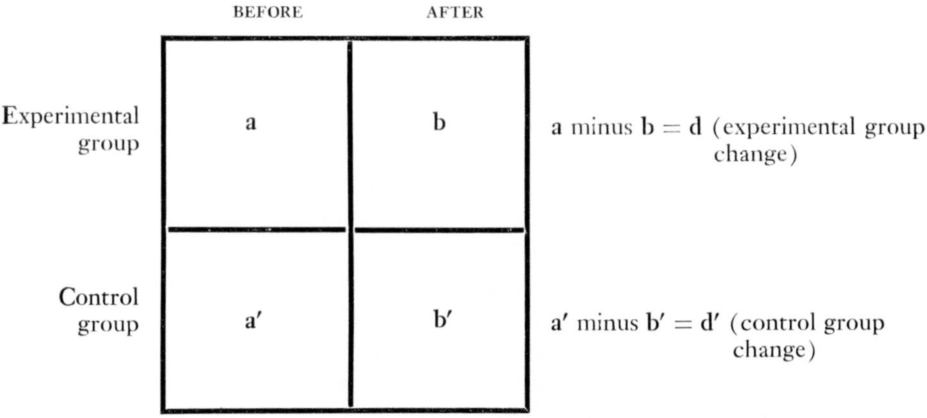

	BEFORE	AFTER	
Experimental group	a	b	a minus b = d (experimental group change)
Control group	a′	b′	a′ minus b′ = d′ (control group change)

d minus d′ equals the difference induced by the experimental variable

analogies, or in some other way attempting to interpret the social behavior of human beings.

Social Environment All human beings are social. People have to interact with other people in order to survive. Since all human beings live in a society—which is to say that every person is a member of some human group—it is just as reasonable to speak of a social environment as to speak, as people more often do, of their physical environment. People are profoundly influenced by their social as well as their physical surroundings. The three-year-old son of a steel mill laborer in Pittsburgh who is taken from his home and reared by foster parents in a steel mill laborer's family in Birmingham, England, not only will talk and act differently than he would have had he remained in Pittsburgh, but will think differently as well. The change in his physical environment will have been minimal; the alteration in his behavior will be traceable to the difference in the two social environments. As the physicist, the chemist, the astronomer, and the biologist study the universe in which we live and the elements of which it is composed in an attempt to understand our physical environment and to predict what will happen in a given set of circumstances, so the social scientist studies the social environment in which we live in an attempt to understand human society and to predict how people will interact in a given set of circumstances.

Social Sciences and Academic Disciplines It should be emphasized that not everything called science *is* science. Just as there was alchemy before there was a science of chemistry, so there were political philosophers who attempted to convert the lead of their opinions into the gold of facts before there were political scientists willing to employ the scientific method to learn about man's political behavior. Even today it is easy to find people calling themselves economists, sociologists, and political scientists whose primary concern is to reform the world in keeping with their own values or to gain recognition as experts by speculating about the course which society is taking, and who have no intention of risking their pet notions by subjecting them to empirical tests. During the past half-century, however, a larger and larger proportion of people have been interested in utilizing the scientific method in order to learn more about the various forms of behavior of human beings in social groups.

Some social scientists concentrate their study on one aspect of man's social behavior. Political scientists utilize the scientific method to compile information about the interaction which occurs as people attempt to maintain order in their societies. Economists attempt to assemble a body of knowledge about what takes place in the production and distribution of goods and services. Cultural anthropologists seek to learn the relationships between the political, economic, religious, and familial behaviors of persons within a given society, or to contrast the ways in which people in different societies come to fulfill the same needs.

Other social scientists are concerned primarily with social phenomena which are relatively unique; they observe, record, and attempt to interpret interactions that are not recurrent. A historian may draw parallels between the French Revolution and happenings in other times and places, but his business is the uniqueness of his subject matter; that is why a historian is more likely to be known as an authority on eighteenth-century France than as an expert on revolutions. The field of sociology is different from history in this respect. Its major concern is not with the unique in human events but with the similarities among social structures and the recurring nature of patterns of social interaction.

SOCIOLOGY

The difference between the generalizing focus of sociology and the more specialized focus in fields such as economics and political science is well stated by Pitirim A. Sorokin.[3] Sorokin suggests that the interactions which the economist studies be represented by the letters a, b, c, n, m, and f. The human behavior of interest to the political scientist can be called a, b, c, h, d, and j. Another social science might have as its subject matter those interactions represented by the letters a, b, c, g, i, and q. The first concern of the sociologist would be those social elements and relationships found among human beings whether they are acting as familial groups, say, or as political groups, or in economic pursuits: a, b, and c. Sociologists, then, study human interaction *as such*. They try to learn the likenesses among people in groups, no matter what the particular orientation of the group may be.

Specialties Within Sociology The general sociologist devotes himself to understanding universal social structures, such as groups and publics, and universal social processes, such as competition and co-operation. Much of what is synthesized into general sociological principles, however, is learned from research carried out in specialized sociologies, such as the sociology of the family, of war, of crime, of education. Scholars work in these more restricted areas in order to narrow their field of observation. They attempt to gain new insights by exploring one area of interaction intensively instead of making a

3 · Pitirim A. Sorokin, *Society, Culture, and Personality* (New York: Harper & Brothers, 1947), pp. 6–18.

broad survey of all human groups. This gives them an opportunity to make certain kinds of contributions to general sociology. First, they may uncover previously unnoted social phenomena of the type represented by *a*, *b*, and *c* in the Sorokin formula. For example, a specialist studying family organization may note that, as the family loses some of its functions to schools, public recreational facilities, and government agencies, it becomes less stable. Second, they may add to the body of knowledge about such interactions. Other sociologists may conclude from the findings of the family specialist that as any group loses functions, it loses stability. Third, specialization permits sociologists to note cases where some variation, say, in *b*, *d*, or *f* is accompanied by variation in *g*, *i*, or *q*. Thus the sociologist doing research in family organization may find that wherever families are decreasing in size, the literacy level of the population is increasing. This poses the question of whether one of these happenings is causing the other, or whether both are traceable to a third factor or variable.

Just as the delimitation of the scientist's field of observation through specialization has proved a fruitful procedure in the development of many disciplines, such as physics, chemistry, biology, and psychology, a number of the best-established principles in sociology have been derived from research in the fields of population, criminology, industry, the family, and so on.

BASIC MODES OF ANALYSIS

In examining man's social life, we shall build our analysis around four concepts which are shared by all contemporary sciences: structure, function, pattern, and process. All modern sciences, whether physical, biological, anthropological, or whatever, use these four abstractions as their basic framework for describing their data.

By *structure* we mean the way in which the thing we are analyzing is put together, the relationship of its parts to one another. A botanist will describe the structure of a leaf, the way it is put together. A chemist is concerned with the structure of a compound, the relationship of the elements in the compound to one another. The sociologist examines the structure of human society, the relationship of the positions in a human group to one another: of husband to wife, of employee to employer, of white to Oriental, and so on.

A *function* is the consequence of a structure. If we change the way in which a thing is put together, we get different functions. Contemporary American society is so structured that most people between the ages of six and sixteen years attend school. One function of our social structure is that most young adults are literate; another function of this structure is that relatively few people under sixteen years of age are in the labor force. If we lived in a social structure which provided no schools, one function of this structure would be to put most of the burden of education on the family, the church, the employer, or some other agency in the society.

It would not be possible to generalize in any science if the structures and functions being studied were not shared and repeated over and over in an orderly fashion. This repetitiveness which allows us to make predictions is called *patterning*. In sociology, patterns of behavior are those characteristics of life in a society which regularly recur and which are shared by many members of the society.

Process is a series of changes taking place in a definite manner. When we speak of the structure of a group, we are describing it as though we had taken a flash picture of it, had stopped it at a point in time. When we speak of the functions of that structure, we are describing the consequences of the way it is put together at a given moment. When we refer to a pattern of behavior, we sound as if its recurrence in its present form and meaning were permanent. Actually, we are aware that the phenomena included under these three concepts—structure, function, and pattern—are in a constant state of flux. It is the concept of process that permits us to maintain a dynamic view of our material. Social life, like all other life, is constantly undergoing modification. Terms such as co-operation, differentiation, or conflict, which describe social processes, allow us to summarize in a word certain patterns of change in social structures and their functions.

HANDICAPS TO SOCIOLOGY

Science is man's most fruitful way of observing, classifying, and interpreting his physical and social environments. We are all aware of the great strides in the physical and biological sciences which have made possible modern industry and agriculture, rapid transportation and communication, and the control of disease. Yet we find that man is often loath to take an objective viewpoint and apply the empirical method of science to his personal and social problems. We would ridicule a man who, if his automobile did not start, would say that the engine was evil or curse the steel from which it was made. We consider ignorant, at best, the person who attempts to set a broken leg with magic incantations. Many people, however, who consider the scientific method a useful device for establishing the principles on which an automobile is built or a leg is set nevertheless resist with great emotion the suggestion that the same method might establish universal principles about how husbands select wives or why some persons in a society become criminals. There are at least four reasons why such negative attitudes exist.

Resistance to Social Change The ways of men are hedged in by inertia. Human beings stubbornly resist innovations which exert pressure on them to alter their socially shared values and beliefs. We need not go back to Galileo or other medieval examples; it was during the present century in this country that a schoolteacher was tried in court for teaching his students the theory of evolution.

Social facts are considerably more emotion-laden, of course, than physical facts. When physicists announce that they have learned something new about the way atoms behave, most people are not very much excited about the discovery. They are not personally acquainted with any atoms; their parents did not teach them that good, moral atoms behave in a certain way; and they feel no obligation to revise their day-to-day thinking or behavior because of the physicists' discovery. But when sociologists announce that they have learned something new about how human groups behave, many people are likely to be agitated. They feel that their own observations of their acquaintances are just as valid as the studies of social scientists. Since their parents have taught them that good, moral human beings behave in a certain way, new scientific knowledge about human beings may threaten to make them feel obligated to revise their own day-to-day thinking and behavior. It takes a considerable amount of conscious effort to abandon ways of thinking to which one has become accustomed, and most people will resist new knowledge, even though rationally arrived at, in favor of old superstitions or prejudices. If we have long believed that people who live in the country are happier than those who live in the city, or that white people are more intelligent than Negroes, or that contact between groups of persons who resent and distrust each other will get rid of their hostility, then it is easier to reject the social scientist who informs us that these beliefs are prejudices and superstitions than it is to abandon our beliefs because the scientific evidence runs counter to them.

That people do resist facts which will force them to alter their thinking can be observed in any college classroom where such material is being presented. The phenomenon has been called the "my Aunt Emma" response: the demonstration of a preference for one's personal experience over many observations of many scientists when one's own observations run counter to theirs. The instructor in a sociology class, for example, reads from a United States Census report, "On the basis of interviews with millions of people, we conclude that the average high-school teacher has a larger annual income than the average factory laborer." A student replies, "Well, I don't think that's true, because my Aunt Emma is a teacher and her husband works in a factory and

his income is higher than hers." That his personal observation may be perfectly accurate without disproving the census-based generalization does not occur to Aunt Emma's nephew. He is looking for some evidence that will excuse him from having to reorient his thinking, that will help him avoid the effort which accompanies change.

Ethnocentrism Throughout history, man everywhere has displayed an interest in himself and his fellows. Enthusiasm for observing human behavior is, of course, a long first step toward social science. This enthusiasm is accompanied, however, by an attitude that is a serious deterrent to the development of social science. Members of any society tend to believe that their way of thinking and doing things is not only the best but the only right way. This belief that the ways of one's own group are superior to all others we call *ethnocentrism*. The Navaho of the southwestern United States refer to themselves in their native tongue as "Dineh" —"The People." Germans refer to *das Ausland*, collecting all countries outside Germany into a single noun. The ancient Jews classified themselves as "the Chosen People"; in ancient Greece there were only Greeks and barbarians. When the Greenland Eskimos first had white visitors, the highest compliment they could pay a white man was to say that he was, or soon would be, as good as a Greenlander. We in America have a tendency to lump all persons who are not members of our own society into one inferior category: foreigners.

It is easier, of course, for us to see ethnocentrism among other peoples. The following letter to the editor of a London newspaper may serve as a contemporary example:

"Sir,—It will be a tragic thing indeed if Britain ever changes over to driving on the right hand side of the road. At the risk of sounding like the Irish juryman (who 'had never met 11 more obstinate people in his life') I am prepared to assert that we left-drivers are right and that all the rest are wrong.

And I can prove it.

First of all, upon historical grounds. It was pretty perilous for pedestrians when right-handed coachmen (and most people, let's face it, are right-handed) wielded long whips on the right hand side of the road. We in Britain *thought* about the people on foot, and we were right then.

Now that we use steering wheels instead of coach whips we are *still* right. Because pulling down is easier than pushing up, it follows that the camber of the road naturally makes our *right* arms carry most of the work. When you take your car over the Channel, the first thing you notice is the effort transferring over to your *left* arm.

To change our proven right habits into others that are manifestly wrong would be a humiliating blow to our national rightful pride. I am, Sir, yours faithfully.

PHILIP HARBEN
Savage Club, 1, Carlton House Terrace, London, S.W.1." [4]

It is easy for us to see that this is ethnocentrism. But when we read in the newspapers that free enterprise is the best possible economic system, most of us do not recognize this statement as an illustration of ethnocentrism. We accept it as "right" and "true" (It may indeed be true, but we accept it not because of the evidence—which most of us don't know—but because we are ethnocentric). No category of persons, not even scientists, are free from ethnocentrism. That is why it is so difficult for an American scientist to evaluate objectively an experiment con-

4 · *The Times* (London, England), July 23, 1963, p. 11.

trasting democratic and authoritarian leadership.

Science as a way to knowledge does not serve the purposes of one political group better than those of another. There is no such thing, scientifically speaking, as Methodist sociology, or Italian physics, or what the leaders of the Soviet Union call "bourgeois genetics." Until people free themselves from this mode of thinking, ethnocentrism will be an obstacle to the development of science.

Closely linked to ethnocentrism is the widespread tendency to see personal and social problems and their possible solutions as either good or bad, or right or wrong. We assign facts, situations, and people that we fear or do not like or understand to the category of the evil or dangerous. That with which we agree or with which we feel comfortable is, we say, "all right."

Confusion of Engineering with Science
Scientists assume that any knowledge, whether or not it is "practical," is worthwhile. There is a crucial difference between the scientist, who discovers knowledge, and the engineer, who applies it. The physicist discovers the laws of mass and volume; the engineer applies these laws in constructing a bridge. Sir Alexander Fleming, a bacteriologist, discovered penicillin; the physician who injects penicillin into a patient is acting, not as a scientist, but as an engineer applying knowledge discovered by a scientist. The social worker does not test hypotheses in order to evaluate a scientific theory; he applies the knowledge furnished him by sociologists and psychologists. In other words, he is a social engineer. No invidious comparison between scientists and those who apply scientific knowl-

edge is implied. It is important, however, to understand the differences in what they are attempting to do and how they are attempting to do it. Much of the contemporary criticism of the social sciences stems from the fact that some amateur social engineers try to apply knowledge which social scientists have not yet validated.

The goal of the engineer forces him to be concerned with what will work, with principles that are immediately applicable. The goal of the scientist causes him to pursue with equal curiosity projects the results of which the engineer is eagerly awaiting and other projects which have no obvious applicability. If there is a possibility that observations of two sets of physical or social phenomena may lead to the understanding of some significant relationship between them, then the scientist is interested in those observations, whether or not they seem to offer a way to control disease, build bridges, or make money. He is aware that much of the most valuable information in the storehouse of science, such as that about atomic structures cited earlier in this chapter, had no immediate or obvious applicability at the time research leading to it was initiated. Pressures on scholars to engage in "useful" research can do much to deter the development of science.

Inefficiency of Terminology Words are the essential tools of thought, scientific or otherwise. All sciences require a clear and unambiguous terminology. The physical and biological scientists have solved this problem by creating complex technical vocabularies, as any freshman struggling with memorization of biological terms well knows. In most of the social sciences, however, the an-swer has not been so simple. First, many of the terms of the social sciences are words also found in everyday speech, and words in general usage are notoriously vague. Thus the word "instinct" once had a rather technical meaning in psychology and biology but, because of its literary and everyday meaning as any more or less learned but automatic response, it has been abandoned by scientists. Second, the language of sociology and psychology, because it is also the language of everyday speech, tends to be emotionally charged. Thus, if a sociologist asks on a questionnaire, "Are you a political conservative?" he may get an incoherent torrent of rage or affirmation instead of an answer, and even if the interviewee tries to answer honestly, there is no assurance that he and the scientist will be using the term *conservative* in the same way. Thus the sociologist must constantly try to prune his speech of even remotely emotionally charged words, re-teach common words to reluctant students, and guard against his own human reaction to connotative language.

Compare the following descriptions of one aspect of our society:

A

People sometimes have special feelings about strangers. In some cases this feeling makes them dislike people that are different or opposed to them and in other cases it does not.

B

In the broad sense, all persons who are not members of our in-group constitute an out-group, but one caution is necessary. The social order does not consist entirely of the in-group *vs.* out-group patterning. As an organizing feature of social life, in-groups and out-groups emerge when groups are in opposition—that is, in competition or conflict. But there are also groups that have no feelings of opposition to outsiders. For example, the congeniality

Science is not the only method for getting "knowledge": religion identifies faith and knowledge.

Episcopal Church Photo

group does not necessarily embody any attitudes of hostility toward an out-group. Whether any association becomes for us an out-group to which we are hostile depends on the relation of this group to some particular group of which we ourselves are a member.

Perhaps the second paragraph seems unnecessarily technical and obscure. By the time you have read Chapter 2, however, the terminology will be meaningful and the intricacies of the in-group-out-group distinction will be detailed. You will be able to understand what happens when newcomers come to a neighborhood, when traders come to a new territory, when the "Alligators" challenge the "Crocodiles" to a fight.

Science and Religion In addition to the four handicaps to sociology which we have discussed—resistance to social change, ethnocentrism, the confusion of engineering with science, and terminological inefficiency—there is a traditional block for some persons to the acceptance of the scientific method: the notion that science is opposed to religion.

Science and religion have come into conflict in the past over matters of dogma, not ethics. The famous religion-versus-science dramas of history have occurred when scientists have turned up evidence which made some theological dogma seem extremely unlikely —for example, the contention of ecclesiastical authorities in the time of

Copernicus and Galileo that the sun moved around the earth. Science does not challenge the rules of morality of any religion, because such guides for living are outside the province of science.

The dogma that all species of life were created in their present form and have not changed since, scientists can disprove; but they can neither prove nor disprove the moral principle expounded in the Golden Rule, which is a statement of what one *should* do. There is no way for science to determine what one should or should not do;

science at its most sophisticated stage can only predict what will happen if one does or does not do a certain thing. A scientific law says, "If *a* occurs, then *b* will result." It can never say, "*A should* occur, because that will be better for most people."

Some people object to social science on the ground that God did not intend us to understand man and that it is therefore evil to attempt to do so. Science does not offer a method for proving that there is or is not a God, much less for fathoming His wishes or intentions.

INTERPRETATIVE SUMMARY

Science is distinguished from other fields of learning by its commitment to the scientific method, its insistence upon objectivity, and its interest in knowledge *per se*. Social science applies the scientific method to the study of human interaction. The social scientist wants to form accurate generalizations about how people behave in groups and thus be able to predict how they will behave in the future.

Scientific method seeks knowledge on the basis of three assumptions. The scientist assumes that the most valid way of getting, organizing, and testing the reliability of knowledge is through (1) the use of man's sensory-perceptual experience, aided by instruments, (2) the use of logic or human reasoning, and (3) agreement among a number of independent observers.

The social sciences are broken down into academic disciplines, some scholars studying certain important systems which appear, with variations, almost universally, others concerning themselves with the unique event or system. Sociology is the social science dealing with human interaction as such. General sociologists attempt to find universal truth about human interaction. Of course, many sociologists specialize, dealing with particular institutions and phenomena existing at particular times and places. Sociologists are likely to cut across the lines of the academic disciplines; the difference between sociology and, say, economics or political science, is one of emphasis, the political scientist's emphasis being on the system being studied and the sociologist's being on the complex of attitudes and behavior of the people being studied.

Sociology is a science, embracing scientific objectives and employing scientific techniques. Sociology also shares, to some extent, scientific terminology; for example the terms *structure*, *function*, *pattern*, and *process* are used by all sciences to describe an object of study at a given time and in a state of flux.

The study of sociology has been handicapped in several ways, not the least of which has been the deprecation of it as a science; people tend to think that their own ethnocentric, religious, or hastily formed personal opinions are as valid as any developed in sociological research. Another handicap to sociology resulting from the failure to see it as a pure science is the notion that sociologists ought to obtain practical results. Again, the sociologist is interested in information for its own sake; the social *worker* may be compared to the engineer who applies the findings of science to practical problems.

Two additional handicaps to the unhampered pursuit of sociology exist. First, people fear and thus resist new ideas, especially threatening ideas about people. Second, the terminology of sociology, which should be as precise as that of the other sciences, is too often vague and emotionally charged.

REVIEW AND SUGGESTED READINGS

A • VOCABULARY

Concept	Pattern	Sociology
Datum (pl. data)	Process	Structure
Ethnocentrism	Sample	Variable
Experiment	Scientific method	
Function	Scientific technique	

B • QUESTIONS AND TOPICS FOR REVIEW

1. The unity of all sciences is said to lie in their common use of the scientific method. Would you classify the following as sciences?
   a. grammar
   b. geometry
   c. any areas of literary study
2. Under what circumstances might a control group be abandoned?
3. You've probably heard someone say, "Oh, she's an old maid" or, "They have three children; I doubt if they'll have any more." The speaker is illustrating what phenomenon about the *structure* of society?
4. Can you think of any "truths" that have been proven false or questionable in the past few years, as a result of sociological research? Think of such areas as
   a. the "proper" way to educate preschool children, or any particular age group
   b. the attitudes or behavior of any of the following: adolescents, college students, old people, Republicans, farmers, any particular religious group
5. How willing have people been to accept the findings you pinpointed in question four? In cases where you found reluctance, to what specifically do you attribute it: fear? habit? laziness?

C • SUGGESTIONS FOR FURTHER READING

F. Stuart Chapin. *Experimental Designs in Sociological Research.* New York: Harper & Brothers, 1947.

> Contains examples of experimental designs in sociology, as well as a discussion of *ex post facto* or quasi-experimental research models.

James B. Conant. *Modern Science and Modern Man.* New York: Columbia University Press. 1952. (Reprinted, Garden City, N.Y.: Doubleday & Co., Inc., 1955.)

> An excellent brief history of the development of science in this century. There is also a thoughtful discussion of the relationship between science and human morals and conduct.

Alex Inkeles. *What Is Sociology: An Introduction to the Discipline and Profession.* Englewood Cliffs, NJ.: Prentice-Hall, Inc., 1964.

A discussion of the major areas of sociological concern, approaches to sociological work, and the relation of sociology to values, to action, and to other academic disciplines.

Marie Jahoda, Morton Deutsch, and Stuart W. Cook, eds. *Research Methods in Social Relations*, 2 vols. New York: The Dryden Press, 1951.

Although especially designed to aid in the study of social prejudice, these volumes give good coverage of important phases of social research.

Abraham Kaplan. *The Conduct of Inquiry.* San Francisco: Chandler Publishing Company, 1964.

A detailed analysis of values, concepts, laws, measurement, and methodology in social science.

Paul F. Lazarsfeld and Morris Rosenberg, eds. *The Language of Social Research.* Glencoe, Ill.: The Fress Press, 1955.

An invaluable collection of papers on research methodology for the social scientist by a distinguished array of scholars.

George A. Lundberg. *Can Science Save Us?* New York: Longmans, Green & Co., Inc., 1947.

A stimulating essay indicating the prospects and difficulties of using social science to help present-day man solve some of his most pressing problems.

Robert S. Lynd. *Knowledge for What?* Princeton: Princeton University Press, 1939.

An essay in defense of the idea that social science should give more aid in the solution of contemporary social problems. Notes the conflict of values in the United States.

C. Wright Mills. *The Sociological Imagination.* New York: Oxford University Press, 1959.

A contention that sociologists work at the intersection of biography and history. There is a fascinating commentary on intellectual craftsmanship.

Thomas C. McCormick and Roy G. Francis. *Methods of Research in the Behavioral Sciences.* New York: Harper & Brothers, 1958.

A good brief treatment of the choice of social problems, study design, and the gathering and analysis of data.

NOTE ON FURTHER READING

For many of the topics discussed in this volume, the reader will find the *Encyclopedia of the Social Sciences* extremely valuable. (Almost all college or university libraries have at least one set of this publication.) Examples of the sociological concepts that are covered in this encyclopedia are the following: "Change, social," "Class," "Competition," "Conflict, social," "Control, social," and "Functionalism." Also valuable is the annual *Review of Sociology*, which contains summary reviews of research in various fields of sociology.

In addition, research and theoretical papers pertinent to the topics covered in each chapter of this book can be found in the following periodicals. These journals will not be cited in the *Suggestions for Further Reading* at the end of every chapter; the student should bear them in mind as useful references.

American Anthropologist
American Journal of Sociology
American Sociological Review
Annals of the American Academy of Political and Social Science
Behavioral Science
British Journal of Sociology
Current Sociology
Journal of Abnormal and Social Psychology
New Society
Pacific Sociological Review

Phylon
Rural Sociology
Social Forces
Social Problems
Sociological Abstracts
Sociological Inquiry
Sociological Quarterly
Sociology and Social Research
Southwest Social Science Quarterly
Trans-action
UNESCO *International Social Science Bulletin*

SOCIAL RELATIONS

PART I

SOCIAL RELATIONS

CHAPTER 2

Human Society and Social Groups

Interaction is the basic concept in sociology. When the action of one person stimulates a response in another, we have interaction. The activity may be physical movement or contact; it may be some expression of emotion; it may be verbal communication. A change in facial expression by one person may stimulate a change in attitude on the part of another. "John scowled heavily at Margaret's joke, causing her to revise her estimate of him" is a description of interaction.

Social interaction can take place in three different kinds of situations: person-to-person; person-to-group; and group-to-group. The first is illustrated by a prizefight or a conversation, the second by a preacher giving a sermon or a politician haranguing a crowd, the third by a football game or a battle in wartime.

There are two types of interaction: *direct* or bodily, and *symbolic* or communicative. The former is characterized by the movement and contact of persons or groups in space, the latter by gestures and speech.

Two or more persons in interaction constitute a group. Each of us is a member of many groups. With parents and brothers and sisters we make up a family. Many of us are tied also to a wider kinship group of aunts, uncles, and cousins. Most young people belong to school groups; many belong to so-

cial, athletic, and other special-interest clubs. More than half the people in the United States belong to churches; many are affiliated with lodges; others are members of occupational organizations. In addition to such regularized associations of people, we interact from time to time as members of shopping crowds, concert audiences, or other temporary collectivities in which the members interstimulate and respond to one another. Whenever two or more persons interact, whether in the intimacy of a family picnic or in the roar of a bargain sale, they are a group.

Of the variety of social structures in which we interact, some are closely knit and persistent in time, while others are loosely organized and temporary. In an attempt to communicate with some ease and precision, sociologists have set up a classification of the more common forms of social life.

RELATIVELY PERMANENT GROUPS

Because the term *group* covers such a wide range of human associations, we have more specific terms for classifying groups according to the intensity, frequency, duration, and focus of the interaction.

Family The human family is the basic and universal group. It had its origins in prehuman societies, and prototypes of many of its functions are to be found in such related species as monkeys and apes. The family in western societies usually consists of parents and their children, our interactions with grandparents, aunts, uncles, and cousins tending to be less intense. Among many nonliterate tribes a more extended kinship unit is the basic social structure. The family assumes the primary responsibility for providing for and rearing the child. The group's intense interaction normally lasts until the child marries.

As is true of other recurrent human groupings, the family is directed and controlled by rules and regulations which come down from the past and are seldom greatly modified in any given generation. We shall deal with the family in more detail in Chapter 20.

Congeniality Groups Some groups are formed and persist simply because friendships arise out of repeated association and shared interests or experiences. Such groups lack formal organization, rules, charters, or officers; they proceed on informal mutual agreement. The members of a congeniality group ordinarily share several activities: they may attend the movies, play cards, discuss politics, and ride to work together. A congeniality group is characterized by interaction of fairly high intensity, frequent contacts, and a broad general focus resting on sympathetic, affectionate relationships and persisting only so long as the members are in direct contact with one another.

Clubs A club is a formally organized congeniality group. Most of us gain our first experience as club members in grade school. Having learned a few things, however inaccurate, about formal organization, we may decide to convert our neighborhood or classroom play group into a club by establishing a few rules and electing or appointing officers. The rules may be no more complex than a stated meeting time and a decision to be known as the "Alligators," but the existence of rules or set procedure transforms the congeniality group into a club. The purpose may be nothing more than "to keep Johnny Harper out." (This example gives us some insight into one of the motivations for club formation, whether the clubs be college fraternities and sororities or country clubs.) Examples of adult clubs are lodges and many so-called "social and athletic" societies. Like congeniality groups, clubs generally are multi-purpose, depend on direct contact among the members for continuity, and involve interaction which is fairly intense as compared with the low intensity of interaction which usually occurs in chance encounters. Club meetings may be less frequent than the meetings of a congeniality group, but they will be formalized, and new members will be acquired by conscious decision rather than haphazardly and informally.

Organizations Organizations, too, are formally ordered, but they differ from clubs in that they are not multi-purpose. Organizations are formed to accomplish a specific objective—thus they are often referred to as special-interest groups. Most organizations cannot be described as exhibiting a very high intensity of interaction, because many of the members may never experience any direct interaction with most of the other members. Most members of the Democratic Party, for instance never meet most other members of the organization; they affiliate themselves with the Democratic Party because they share a goal with its members, and are kept informed of its activities (and its need for funds) largely by bulletin, letter, or other impersonal forms of communication.

The duration of an organization varies according to its success in winning adherents or in achieving its stated purpose. The Roman Catholic Church has persisted for centuries, while some organizations die a few days after being founded. The frequency of interaction also varies with the organization: a member may be kept posted by a daily bulletin, or he may hear from a central office only once a year, when it pleads for his continuing support.

It is often difficult to distinguish between an organization and a club. Most veterans groups are founded as organizations with the single purpose of protecting the rights of veterans, but most of them also become clubs, at the local level at least, which serve many purposes: recreation, business contacts, the encouragement of patriotism, and so on. The same is often true of labor unions: they are organizations at the national level, clubs at the local level. Groups based on a shared occupation, or on a shared set of values and beliefs, whether religious or political, are usually organizations.

These social structures—the family, the congeniality group, the club, and the organization—are the more permanent forms of group life. Social relations also occur in much less permanent forms. This is especially true in modern urban communities. Mobs milling through streets, crowds at department store sales, and audiences at rallies are groups, but they are transitory.

IMPERMANENT FORMS OF ASSOCIATION

Relatively impermanent forms of human association can also be classified according to the intensity, frequency, duration, and focus of the interaction occurring among the members of the group.

Audiences An audience is a number of persons in physical contiguity (that is, in the same place at the same time) all of whom are subject to the same stimulus. It is therefore proper to speak of a theater audience, a football audience, or, during a sermon, a minister's audience. It is not correct, in sociological language, to refer to everyone in the United States who is watching a play on Saturday night as a television audience, because the viewers are not in physical contiguity. And even though one member of the group attending a football game is gazing into his girl friend's eyes instead of focusing on the stimulus being shared by the others, this group is still a football audience, just as a group can still be a club even though one member is absent from a meeting.

The intensity of interaction among the members of an audience is, in general, fairly low. On occasion, the wild screaming of others in a stadium may stimulate someone to a like response. But most of the time the members of an audience interact only at the level of being aware that others are there, and hence modifying their behavior to the extent, say, of not removing their shoes at a concert, as they might if they were not in interaction with the rest of the audience.

The focus of an audience is the common stimulus of the play, concert,

These delighted people constitute an audience.

baseball game, or whatever its members came to see. Because of this focus, the duration is usually relatively brief. Ordinarily, the members of an audience interact as such on only one occasion, an obvious exception being the audience with concert series tickets or season passes to sports events.

As we have seen, the forms of group structure overlap on occasion. One frequently finds several congeniality groups in an audience. At a benefit performance, a whole club or organization may *be* the audience.

Crowds A crowd is a number of persons interacting on only one occasion, and at a very low level of intensity. A crowd is of brief duration. The members of the group are in physical contiguity, but they seldom have a shared and definite focus; hence they are char-

acterized by relatively random activity, or milling. After the common stimulus has been withdrawn, a group which has been an audience becomes a crowd. The people leaving a football stadium or a theater are a crowd. People standing on a street corner waiting for a bus are a crowd. A number of persons pushing past one another in a department store constitute a crowd. They are aware of one another's presence, but their level of interaction is not at all intense. They certainly are not organized with relation to one another in a manner comparable to a club. They do not have a focus, as an audience does. Each member of the crowd may have a purpose, as in the case of a shopping crowd, but the members are not subject to a common stimulus in the same sense as are people attending a concert.

Life Magazine

Korean crowd on the threshold of mob behavior.

Mobs Like crowds, mobs usually interact on only one occasion, and ordinarily for a brief time. Unlike crowds, however, mobs pitch their interaction at a high level of intensity; they are characterized by a display of emotion, usually accompanied by violent behavior. Mobs usually have a leader or leaders who help them focus their emotions and violence on a goal or target.

On a typical night in a college town, you can find an audience at the movie theater. Here is a group of persons in physical contiguity, together temporarily to focus on a common stimulus, *The Defense Rests.* Their interaction is not very intense; each person there is scarcely aware of the others. Yet this awareness will inhibit each person in some of his behavior: if the music on the sound track were on the radio at home, a couple might get up and dance to it; they will not do so here. On the other hand, being a group member encourages some behavior: one is more likely to laugh if the rest of the audience laughs than if he were alone.

Suppose the film breaks. Some members of the audience will whistle; others will shout. A few will throw their empty popcorn boxes at others' heads. Most people will turn to chat with their companions. Some will leave to get a drink of water or buy more popcorn. The common focus for the group is gone; people mill around. The audience has been transformed into a chattering and very loosely structured crowd.

Suppose at this point the lights go on, and the theater manager appears and says, "We can't repair the film, so there will be no movie tonight. We're sorry, but we can't give you your money back." A sophomore jumps up on his seat and shouts, "Let's fix him!" and with a roar the group surges toward the stage to revenge themselves on the theater manager. The crowd has become a mob.

Any relatively impermanent group, such as an audience, crowd, or mob, is composed of individuals who are also members of more permanent social structures, such as families, congeniality groups, and organizations. This seems obvious enough, but we sometimes forget it when emotion dims rationality. It is easy to hate a lynch mob by thinking of it as composed of bestial persons who are full-time lynch mob members. It is more difficult to try as a social scientist to understand it, remembering that its members spend the greatest portion of their social lives as parts of families and congeniality groups.

HUMAN AGGREGATES

Let us not fall into the error of thinking that any word used to describe two or more persons is a word describing some kind of group. People can be classified together without being a group. For people who are classified together because they share some characteristic but who are not in interaction, sociologists use the word *aggregate*. *Males* is a word describing a number of persons who, though they share common characteristics, do not all interact with one another.

Race The races of mankind are often thought to be the largest, most inclusive human groups. Actually, races are not groups at all; they are aggregates: people classified as alike because they share common characteristics.

Strictly speaking, race is a biological rather than a sociological term. It refers to a system of classifying human beings according to physical features, such as eye color, head form, chin prominence, and stature. Race has come to be of sociological importance, however, because people in some societies believe that these physical characteristics are correlated with patterns of behavior. If people believe that intelligence or morality or cleanliness is determined by one's eye color or head form or hair type or skin color, then these biological features will become sociological variables, because they will affect the likelihood that interaction will occur in certain situations; they will influence the social structuring of groups.

Social Categories A social category is made up of a number of persons sharing some innate characteristic which is socially defined and which therefore alters their life chances. A thing is *socially defined* when the people in a group believe that it has some consequences, and, since they believe so, act as if it did. In the United States, for example, many people believe that there are differences in administrative ability between the sexes. Because they believe this, they act as if it were true, despite the fact that there is no scientific evidence to support such a belief. The term *life chances* refers to the likelihood that given events will happen to a person. Being born to poverty-stricken parents helps determine one's life chances; for example, fewer poor people's children get to go to college than rich people's children. This is not a result of something the children themselves do; it is a matter of life chances.

Because people believe that women have less administrative ability than

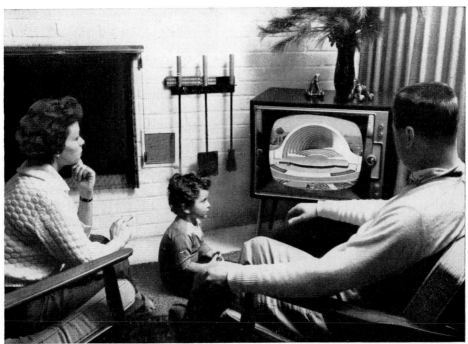

New York University photo by William Simmons

A family group which is also a small portion of a public.

men, they are less likely to vote for a woman for President of the United States or for Chairman of the Board of Directors of General Motors. This alters the life chances of a woman. Any girl, at the moment she is born in contemporary United States, because of an inborn characteristic which she cannot change (femaleness), has less chance of becoming President than any boy born at the same moment.

In some societies, race is a social category. Science has found no evidence of innate differences between races. Nonetheless, some people believe that such differences exist. Because they believe this is true, they act as if it *were* true. This alters the life chances of Portuguese in Hawaii, Negroes in the United States, Englishmen in Kenya, and others wherever race is a social category.

Publics A public is composed of a number of persons who are subject to a common stimulus but are not in physical contiguity. A public, then, is an aggregate rather than a group, because its members do not interact with one another. A speaker in an auditorium addresses an audience; a speaker on a radio broadcast addresses a public. Not all the readers of a newspaper interact with one another; a newspaper public is therefore not a group. Saying that public opinion favors Henry Jones for alderman does not mean that the voters have decided in interaction with one another that Jones is their man. It means that the voters have been exposed to information about Jones, that they have been subject to common stimuli. That is why they are called a public.

One should speak, then, of a concert *audience*, a lecture *audience*, a movie *audience*, but of a newspaper *public*, a radio *public*, and a television *public*.

Society In everyday language, *society* refers to every kind and degree of social relationship among human beings. We speak of one man enjoying the society of another, and we speak of the Temperance Society. Usually sociologists do not use the term *society* in this broad sense, but speak of *a* society as a number of persons with a locus (that is, who occupy a definite geographic area), some permanence, and a history.

A society refers to the broadest grouping of people who share a common set of habits, ideas, and attitudes, live in a definite territory, and consider themselves a social unit. One can make an argument, then, for the case that a society is the largest social group. A society is a number of persons in interaction to the extent that they are aware of one another's existence and think of themselves as a unit. On the other hand, one can argue that many modern societies are aggregates. They are composed of a number of persons who share a language and a notion of unity and who live within a specified territorial boundary, but who, for the most part, never interact. Actually, this is strictly a matter of how far one wants to stretch the definition of interaction. If being aware that others share one's feeling of being French, say, modifies one's behavior enough so that this can be termed interaction, then Frenchmen are a group. If we take the position that most Frenchmen are French by accident of birth and because they live within a specified territorial boundary, and that most of them do not stimulate or respond to most of their fellow-Frenchmen, then Frenchmen form an aggregate.

Most small, nonliterate tribal societies are groups. But it seems more realistic sociologically to consider many contemporary urban-industrial societies as aggregates.

Community Much of what we have just said about a society applies to the concept of community. By *community* is usually meant a collectivity of persons of all ages and both sexes who share a common culture and reside in a relatively limited space or locality. Thus we shall later discuss rural and urban communities. Some writers use the terms *society* and *community* synonymously, as when they speak of the national community. So too, it is used in a figurative sense as an organization when we speak of a community of scholars or scientists.

TYPOLOGIES OF GROUPS

For purposes of analysis, scientists often set up what they call typologies: descriptions of two opposite extremes, with a range of possible types between the poles. They talk of urban society and rural society, for example, knowing that no society is a perfect "rural" type and that no society is completely "urban." They can say, however, that Germany is more urban than Guatemala, and one scientist will know what another means because he is familiar with the typology. In other words, a typology is a classificatory scheme which alerts us to gross differences between groups.

Primary and Secondary Groups The most frequently used typology of

Life Magazine

Children at play: a primary group.

groups in sociology is that of primary and secondary groups.[1]

The primary group is characterized by intimate, face-to-face contacts and direct interaction made possible by common locality. The social stimuli are distinctly personal: voice, facial and other gestures, touch, smell, taste, and sight. Primary groups are the first groups into which the individual is inducted. The features of the primary group will be made clear if we note briefly certain of its more specific types.

With few exceptions, the *family* is the first group into which the infant is introduced. In the family the child acquires all his fundamental habits—those of bodily care, speech, determina-

tion of right and wrong, obedience, and so forth. He learns submission to authority and practices rivalry and co-operation with his brothers and sisters. Affections and dislikes are deep within the family. The family is thus *primary* not only as to its form but also in time, since it is the first group to which the child is exposed and the one in which he gets his fundamental training.

The *play group* arises out of contact between children of the same family or neighborhood. It is more or less spontaneous in its formation, developing out of new situations not necessarily found in the family. The children in the play group meet other children of like age. Parental authority is ordinarily not present. In these associations the child learns to give and take. There may be quarrels and division, but there are also co-operation and teamwork.

1 · The original discussion of primary groups can be found in C. H. Cooley, *Social Organization* (New York: Charles Scribner's Sons, 1909), pp. 23–31.

When the child enters the group, his play habits are often influenced by his home training. His aggressiveness or docility may be reflections of habits he has learned at home. The play group affords him early training in meeting his equals, learning to co-operate and to compete, and struggling to express his own will—things not always fully expressed or permitted within the family.

Another primary group is the *neighborhood*, where also there is a direct, face-to-face relationship. Neighborhoods are characterized by such things as borrowing and lending, social control through gossip, and the recreational activities which often accompany congeniality groups.

Secondary groups are characterized by much more deliberate and conscious formation than primary groups. Almost always they represent partial and specialized interests or needs. In fact, they are sometimes called "special-interest" groups. They do not necessarily depend on face-to-face contacts. A scientific association may exist for years without the members ever meeting one another. Secondary associations include the nation, the political party, the religious body, the employers' association, and the international labor union. Obviously, they are often coterminous with organizations.

Another feature of secondary groups is that they often outlast any given generation. Too, since the particular interests or needs they represent may persist through time, more organization is required than is found in primary groups. There develop traditions, codes, special offices, and fixed methods of carrying out the group's activities. The congeniality group is a primary group; the organization, in contrast, is a secondary group.

Primary and secondary groups represent opposite poles in a typology, and many groups do not conform precisely to the definition of either. A few will seem almost as much like one as the other. This is no cause for distress. Typology is an analytic tool. It sharpens our observation and helps us see obvious differences in the structuring of groups, such as the family and congeniality group, on the one hand, and special-interest organizations, on the other. We are then able to note different functions—that is, consequences for the members—which accompany the different types of structures.

In-groups and Out-groups The primary and secondary associations represent a basic structural and functional classification. Another important division, chiefly of functional nature, is that between the in-group and the out-group. This separation is found in all societies, primitive and modern.

The *in-group* is any association—either primary or secondary—in which we have a sense of solidarity, loyalty, friendliness, and co-operation. It is characterized by the expressions "we belong," "we believe," "we feel," and "we act." Toward the other members of our group we have a definite feeling of obligation, especially in a critical situation which would threaten them and us. We would protect them, as they would protect us. In the in-group we express our deepest sentiments of love and sympathy. We feel at home with those around us. We are familiar with their manner of acting and thinking, and they with ours. We understand their gestures; their words are our words. Often the vocabulary and accent are unique and themselves a badge of common membership. In short, our

*In-groups exclude
outsiders.*

Monkmeyer

lives center largely around the in-groups to which we belong. The degree to which one's life centers around any particular in-group depends, of course, on whether such a group satisfies the principal needs and interests of the individual.

The out-group consists of those persons, whether formally organized or not, toward whom we feel a sense of indifference, avoidance, disgust, competition, or outright conflict. We have no feeling of loyalty, sympathy, or co-operation toward such persons. Rather, we are often prejudiced against the members of the out-group. We may think the family on the next street is inferior to our own, or that our neighborhood is better than the one "across the tracks," or that our race or religion is much superior to another's. One's antagonisms, prejudices, and hatreds are usually focused on out-groups. The trade union, for example, opposes the employers' association. Toward other members of the union the individuals feel a sense of solidarity, loyalty, helpfulness, and co-operation. Toward the employer and (especially) toward the strikebreaker, there is intense bitterness.

In ordinary times within the larger national community, the attitudes toward out-groups are somewhat milder and more restrained than in time of war, when another nation or state becomes the out-group. It then becomes even virtuous to plunder, enslave, or kill the members of an out-group.

The pattern of in-group *vs.* out-group is a widespread feature of social organization wherever opposition or aggression comes into play. As we noted in Chapter 1, ethnocentrism is as common among civilized as among nonliterate peoples. Each society or smaller group nourishes its own importance, believes itself superior to all others, exalts its own gods, and derides the gods of other peoples. Certain symbols of common unity emerge, such as a tribal name and, with civilized societies, national or state name, maps, flags, insignia, songs, myths, and legends.

In the broad sense, all persons who are not members of our in-group constitute an out-group, but one caution is necessary. The social order does not consist entirely of the in-group *vs.* out-group patterning. As an organizing feature of social life, in-groups and out-groups emerge when groups are in opposition—that is, in competition or conflict. But there are also groups that have no feelings of opposition to outsiders. For example, the congeniality group does not necessarily embody any attitudes of hostility toward an out-group. Whether any association becomes for us an out-group to which we are hostile depends on the relation of this group to some particular group of which we ourselves are a member.

INTERPRETATIVE SUMMARY

Sociologists distinguish between groups and aggregates. They further classify groups according to the frequency, intensity, duration, and focus of the interaction involved. Among groups that are relatively persistent in time, families and close friendship groups have, obviously, highly intense interactions, though their focuses are broad and their structures informal. Clubs and organizations have formalized, verbalized structures, while their members usually interact with low intensity. Organizations are more formal, more single-minded than are clubs.

Among relatively impermanent groups, an audience is distinguished by its unity of focus, a crowd by its lack of focus. A mob is a crowd become intense or even violent.

An aggregate consists of people who do not interact yet have something in common biologically, socially, or both. Race is, at least ostensibly, a biological aggregate. A social category is an aggregate of people whose innate characteristics have social consequences. Societies and communities are socially and biologically defined aggregates with much in common, communities existing spatially within societies.

Sometimes it is difficult to classify a given collectivity as a group or aggregate, crowd or mob, primary or secondary structure, and so on. It should be remembered that such polar classifications (typologies) have been set up for purposes of easy communication between scientists, and that reality usually lies somewhere between the two extremes. Then too, classification of a group or aggregate may change as relations among its members change.

REVIEW AND SUGGESTED READINGS

A • VOCABULARY

Aggregate	In-group	Secondary group
Club	Interaction	Social category
Community	Organization	Typology
Congeniality group	Out-group	
Group	Primary group	

B • QUESTIONS AND TOPICS FOR REVIEW

1. Identify the following with a sociological term: (a) pedestrians waiting for a green light, (b) fans seeking a movie star's autograph, (c) the Navaho, (d) people with flat feet, and (e) Frank Sinatra and his friends.
2. Can an in-group ever technically be an aggregate?
3. List the chief primary and secondary groups in which you now participate. Rearrange your list (a) with reference to your degree of interest in the groups; (b) as to degree of continuity and permanence; and (c) as to the degree to which each group is definitely oriented toward an out-group.
4. Discuss some ways in which people try to overcome the handicap of being members of a *social category*.
5. Can you think of any people who probably consider themselves *lucky* to belong to a certain social category? Discuss.
6. Can you think of any instances in which a certain kind of group became in the course of its interaction another kind of group? Discuss.
7. Sociologists frequently redefine or modify the meanings of everyday words. Which of the following sociological terms conform most closely to their common meaning? Which must be relearned?
   - a. in-group
   - b. organization
   - c. group
   - d. mob
   - e. society
   - f. audience
   - g. family

C • SUGGESTIONS FOR FURTHER READING

C. H. Cooley. *Social Organization: A Study of the Larger Mind*. New York: Charles Scribner's Sons, 1909.

A classic study of the major forms of group life, but oriented almost completely to Euro-American societies and their cultures.

Scott A. Greer. *Social Organization*. New York: Random House, 1955.

A brief and highly competent analysis, including a model of the social group from the point of view of the functional interdependence of its members.

A. Paul Hare, Edgar F. Borgatta, and Robert E. Bales, eds. *Small Groups: Studies in Social Interaction*. New York: Alfred A. Knopf, Inc., 1955.

A wide range of papers on both theory and research; also an extensive annotated bibliography.

George C. Homans. *The Human Group*. New York: Harcourt, Brace & Co., 1950.

Deals almost entirely with various forms of human primary groups. The author reviews critically and systematically some of the important research in this field.

Michael S. Olmstead. *The Small Group*. New York: Random House, 1959.

Some case studies of group behavior, an analysis of the structure and functions of groups, and a paradigm for group analysis.

John W. Thibaut and Harold H. Kelley. *The Social Psychology of Groups*. New York: John Wiley & Sons, Inc., 1959.

A review of the literature on small groups ("group dynamics") and the presentation of a theory of social interaction, especially as it emerges from a considerable number of experiments on two-person groups and like relationships of small numbers of individuals.

Ralph H. Turner and Lewis M. Killian. *Collective Behavior*. Englewood Cliffs, N.J.: Prentice-Hall, Inc., 1957.

A systematic treatment of human groups and aggregates governed by emerging or spontaneous norms. Good analyses of crowds, publics, public opinion, and social movements.

Kimball Young. *Social Psychology*, 3rd ed. New York: Appleton-Century-Crofts, Inc., 1956.

Chapter 10, "The Human Group," and Chapter 12, "Behavior of Crowds," cover pertinent material.

CHAPTER 3

Group Behavior:
the Patterned Ways of Men

All sciences deal with structures, functions, patterns, and processes. The structure of basic interest to the sociologist is the human group. In the preceding chapter we examined various forms in which groups and aggregates are structured. We turn now to the *patterns* of behavior associated with social structures.

In any human collectivity, whether a family or a national society, there are certain recurrent, accepted, and expected ways of thinking and acting. Such patterns of behavior common to a society or other group we call *culture*.

CULTURE

In popular speech we sometimes hear a person referred to as "cultured" if he demonstrates erudition in the arts or an appreciation of gracious living. As used by social scientists, however, the term *culture* refers to considerably more than appreciation of the opera or an awareness of how to act at a reception.

Culture Defined The classic characterization of culture identifies it as "that complex whole which includes knowledge, belief, art, morals, law, custom, and any other capabilities and habits acquired by man as a member of society." [1] Culture, then, consists of commonly accepted and expected ideas, attitudes, values, and habits which individuals learn in connection with social living. For the individual in the early years of life, culture is an enormous aid in learning to get on more effectively in the world. The members of each new generation do not have to begin "from scratch," but benefit from the older generations around them, who, in turn, learned how to adjust to the physical and social world largely from their progenitors. Later, this new generation passes on to the next generation what it has learned from the previous generations and what it has added to the cultural whole.

Culture may be defined briefly as shared learned behavior. Let us look at the three crucial words in this definition.

It must be remembered that *behavior* in the sense in which we use it includes thinking and feeling, as well as overt acts. Any behavior is part of a culture only when it is *shared* by most members, or by specifically designated members, of the group. If you are the only person in the country who parts his hair with a wire brush, then this behavior is not part of American culture. Most Americans arrange their hair with

1 · E. B. Tylor, *Primitive Culture* (New York: Brentano's, 1924), p. 1. First published in 1871.

Culture is learned: acquiring skill for future farming.

a comb after they get up in the morning; this behavior is shared; it is a part of American culture. Most Americans believe that the United States is the best place in the world to live. As social scientists, we may describe both these beliefs as instances of ethnocentrism, but we will realize that these beliefs are part of the American culture. Most American women use cosmetics on their faces. Since this behavior is shared by a designated category of members of the society, it may be considered part of the culture.

By *learned* behavior we mean more than attitudes and ways of acting which are formally and consciously taught. Any behavior which is socially acquired (that is, which comes through participation in a human group) is learned. Certain behavior is determined, of course, by heredity; such behavior is not cultural. If a stone is thrown in your face, you will blink. This is shared behavior, but it is not learned; it is inherited. Therefore, blinking caused by an approaching missile is not part of the culture. Hunger pangs are not culturally learned, but the thought of fried chicken as satisfying, or of fried beetles

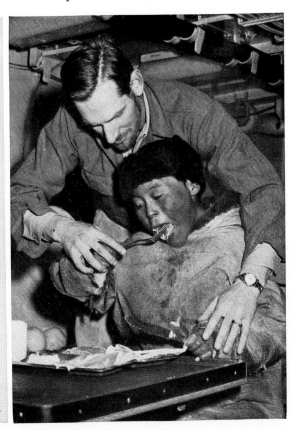

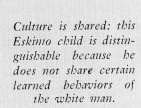

Culture is shared: this Eskimo child is distinguishable because he does not share certain learned behaviors of the white man.

Monkmeyer

as repulsive, is acquired, and hence is part of the culture.

It is difficult to exaggerate the importance of culture as a determinant of human behavior. We are much more likely to overemphasize the effects of heredity or of the physical environment than we are to recognize how large a proportion of our behavior is composed of shared ways of doing things learned in a social environment. Each of us likes to think of himself as a quite unusual individual. Yet we need only look about us at the types of clothing we wear, the kinds of food we eat, the forms of greeting we use, and thousands of other components of culture to see that we are not unique. The differences we note are small ones, and well within the ways of

behaving expected and accepted in our society. It is not unusual to see two American businessmen in suits of different colors, but people would gather to look if one of them were in a loin-cloth and the other in a flowing white robe. Our taste in clothing, like most of our behavior, is shared and learned; we are, in large part, creatures of our culture.

The Background of Culture Culture could not exist if man were not a social animal. Social species are those whose very existence depends on interaction among their members. These social essentials are not peculiarly human but are a basic fact in the existence of some insects, such as bees, and of all mammalian species, especially the primates: monkeys, apes, and man. Thus it is not man's social qualities that set him apart from all other animals. Rather, it is his capacity to invent and maintain a culture.

The first evidences of culture are found in the last phase of the Pliocene or earliest part of the Pleistocene—that is, in geologic deposits laid down about one million years ago. This long stretch has been divided into three major cultural periods: (1) the Old Stone Age, or Paleolithic, itself divided into Lower and Upper; (2) the New Stone Age, or Neolithic; and (3) the Metal Ages, comprising the Copper, Bronze, and Iron Ages. We live in an extension of the Iron Age.

At first the advancement of culture was halting and slow. This is evidenced in the fact that the Lower Old Stone Age occupied about 950,000 years, or 95 percent of man's total existence. The Upper Old Stone Age began about 50,000 years ago, and the Neolithic probably 13,000 years ago. The first phases of the Metal Ages appeared about 5,500 years ago.

The uncertainty of dating these gross epochs is worth noting. The farther back we go, the less certain the estimates are. In the past few decades, estimates among scholars of how long *hominidae* (the family of primates to which man belongs) have existed have ranged from 500,000 to nearly 2,000,-000 years. The beginning of the Neolithic is dated from 7,500 to 13,000 years ago. Not only are the approximations of these periods or stages variable; they are also somewhat arbitrary. Obviously, there is considerable overlapping between one period and another. For instance, there is ample evidence that even after man had begun the domestication

of plants and animals, he continued to supplement his food supply with hunting and fishing. So too, during at least the early stages of the Metal Ages, man continued to use some stone implements. There is a considerable overlap of cultural elements which persist from one era into another, even in such dramatic changes as the Industrial Revolution, which, unlike the shift from Paleolithic to Neolithic, did not require thousands of years.

The beginnings of culture were made not by members of the race to which modern man belongs, *Homo sapiens*, but by other, related races. To provide background for our discussion of the development of culture, in the Old Stone Age in particular, we must digress briefly to give some basic facts about the evolution of *hominidae* — the general concept for all human races.

Prehistoric Races of Man   The biological history of man is long and tortuous. Yet, as an examination of Figure 2 will show, in the total span of plant and animal life on the earth, the existence of man occupies but a very short period, only one or possibly two million of the nearly 2,000 million years of total geologic history. The initial step toward man came with the appearance of the first mammals, some 150 to 165 million years ago.

Like many lower animal forms, the mammals are divided into male and female sexes, so that any offspring draws on two, not one, hereditary strains for his basic physical traits. But more important, the female mammals, unlike females of lower forms, carry their young for given periods of time within their own bodies. This gestation period permits the growth of structures which prepare the new individual for more ef-

FIGURE 2 · Estimated Geologic Time and Forms of Life *

GEOLOGIC TIME			TIME IN YEARS Determined by the disintegration of radioactive minerals	STRUCTURAL STAGES	DOMINANT LIFE
CENOZOIC	Quaternary	Recent		Modern Man ↑	AGE OF MAN
		Pleistocene	? 1,000,000	Primitive Man ↑	
		Pliocene		Man-like Apes ↑	
	Tertiary	Miocene			AGE OF MAMMALS
		Oligocene		First Anthropoids ↑	
		Eocene		First Primates (Lemuroids & Tarsioids) ↑	
		Paleocene	60,000,000		
MESOZOIC		Cretaceous (Upper Cretaceous)		Early Placental Insectivorous Mammals ↑	AGE OF REPTILES
		Comanchean (Lower Cretaceous)	135,000,000		
		Jurassic		First Mammals ↑	
		Triassic	180,000,000	Mammal-like Reptiles ↑	
PALAEOZOIC		Permian		Primitive Reptiles ↑	AGE OF AMPHIBIANS
		Pennsylvanian (Up. Carboniferous)		First Amphibians	
		Mississippian (Lo. Carboniferous)		First True Fishes ↑	AGE OF FISHES
		Devonian			
		Silurian		Earliest Fish-like Vertebrates (Ostracoderms) ↑	
		Ordovician	450,000,000		
		Cambrian	550,000,000	Unknown Invertebrate Ancestry of the Vertebrates	AGE OF INVERTEBRATE LIFE
PROTERO-ZOIC		Pre-Cambrian			
ARCHAEO-ZOIC		Time	+1,850,000,000 Years		

* From H. F. Osborn, *The Hall of the Age of Man, Chart I.* Guide Leaflet Series of the American Museum of Natural History, No. 52. Revised by W. K. Gregory and G. Pinkley (New York: American Museum of Natural History, 1938). Reprinted by permission.

fective adaptation to his physical and social environment after birth.

It would take us too far afield to trace in detail the evolution of the human family. In addition to bisexuality, the preparatory gestation period, and the social care of the newborn through nursing, the most striking changes which mark the evolution of man are (1) the development of the cerebral cortex, making possible language and higher forms of learning and thinking;

(2) erect posture and bipedal locomotion; (3) prehensile (grasping) hands, made possible by the freeing of the forepaws; (4) the recession of the snout and the reduction of dentition and facial skeleton; and (5) changes in the mouth and throat parts which made possible the development of the mechanical means for speech.

Sometime about 30–35 million years ago the first simian, or apelike, forms and the first hominid, or manlike, forms began to diverge from some generalized and common ancestors of both apes and man. The simian line led to the gibbon, orangutan, chimpanzee, and gorilla species. From the hominid came a number of human species, of which modern man, *Homo sapiens*, is the only one extant. The cause of the divergence of simian and hominid forms is not known. We can guess that it resulted from a combination of mutations making for specializations in one direction or the other.

The Coming of Man Physical anthropologists believe that the earliest manlike forms appeared in Asia and Africa, in the Miocene or even perhaps in the Oligocene period. However, it is not till the Pleistocene—covering the last million years or so of geologic history—that we find fossil evidences of truly human forms.

For our purposes it is not necessary to review the evidence regarding these developments. Suffice it to say that most physical anthropologists today believe that the variational tendency in nature resulted in the emergence of a number of different species of the biological family *hominidae*.

The many discoveries of fossil remains of manlike forms which began a little more than a century ago have en-

abled archaeologists to give us the evidence of an advancing order of development of the *hominidae*, culminating in modern man. The first of these is Java Man (scientific name: *Pithecanthropus erectus*), found in 1891–1892 on the island of Java. A closely related genus, found in 1926 in China, is known as Pekin Man (*Sinanthropus pekinensis*). A more advanced form, Neanderthal Man (*Homo neanderthalensis*) was found in Germany in 1856. Specimens of this genus have since been discovered in widely scattered areas of Europe, North Africa, the Near East, and Asiatic Russia. In 1868 a still more advanced form, Cro-Magnon, was found in France. Many physical anthropologists regard this genus as an early form of modern man. In 1959 another "missing link" in this chain of development was found by L. S. B. Leakey in East Africa (*Zinjanthropus boisei*). Leakey at first suspected that this genus was directly ancestral to modern man (*Homo sapiens*). But another specimen of *Zinjanthropus* was found about fifty miles from the first. Despite its being roughly 200,000 years younger than the *Zinjanthropus* skull discovered in 1959, it matched the earlier find perfectly. This suggests that *Zinjanthropus* was an evolutionary dead end.[2]

Modern man is classified into three major races: white or caucasoid, yellow or mongoloid, and black or negroid. (See Chapter 13 for some details re-

2 · See the *New York Times*, April 4, 1964. Leakey now believes that subsequent discoveries in the Olduvai Gorge in Tanganyika (where *Zinjanthropus* was found) are directly ancestral to modern man. These specimens, called *Homo habilis*, had an arched foot and opposed thumb and walked erect. Wherever *Homo habilis* has been found, tools have been found also. Some of these specimens are more than 1,750,000 years old, pushing man's history back 1,250,000 years further than previous estimates.

garding physical differences.) Within each of these are a number of subracial aggregates. Thus the American or red Indian is classified as a large branch of the mongoloid race. In addition there are several mixed or composite aggregates made up of racial and subracial blends. The Polynesians are regarded as a racial mixture, as are the native peoples of Indochina, the East Indian islands, and the Philippines. Other mixtures are the Dravidians of India, the Papuans of New Guinea, and probably the native tribes of Australia.

With this review of man's racial history in mind, let us briefly tell the story of man's cultural history.

The Prehistoric Periods The beginnings of human culture occur in what is called the Lower Old Stone Age, or Early Paleolithic. The oldest stone implements were found in Africa. "These include pebble-choppers, core-choppers, rough but retouched flakes, and quantities of fractured and utilized pebbles." [3]

While no human artifacts have been found on the site of the first apeman, Java Man, crude stone implements have been found on the sites of Pekin Man. The stone tools consisted chiefly of rude core implements with chipped edges, used for cutting, scraping, and boring holes. And while only such stone artifacts remain, we can guess that the races of the earliest Paleolithic also used wood for spears and digging sticks, and bone for making points. Man must have learned the use of fire fairly early. We know, too, that early Paleolithic man must have eaten both

animals and plants, if we are to judge by the bones of deer and the seeds of the hackberry found there.

These early people must also have worn crudely fashioned garments, probably of skin. Anthropologists believe that family and kinship groupings formed the main basis of their social organization. Such groups may have moved from place to place according to the availability of food, and sometimes to a completely new locality as food resources declined.

The major economy, however, was foraging—gathering seeds, roots, and other plant foods—and fishing, trapping, and otherwise securing fish and game. It is well to recall that for a good 95 percent of mankind's sojourn on this planet, his survival has depended on this "gathering economy," as Childe calls it. [4]

From these beginnings man gradually learned to improve his implements and to invent additional ones, such as bone anvils. He also learned how to fasten a stout stick to his stone ax, thereby extending his manual control by a foot or more and enabling him to strike a much more forceful and accurate blow in attacking an enemy or a wild animal and in cutting or splitting a tree. Toward the end of this period the use of fire apparently became widespread, probably as a result of the need to keep warm in what had become a cold climate. Religious practices must have arisen, since archaeologists find evidence of formal burials. So too, the first remains of man's art are found in the Lower Paleolithic.

The Upper Old Stone Age Sometime between 35,000 and 50,000 years ago

3 · S. L. Washburn and F. Clark Howell, "Human Evolution and Culture," in Sol Tax, ed., *Evolution After Darwin* (Chicago: University of Chicago Press, 1960), p. 38.

4 · V. Gordon Childe, *What Happened in History* (London: Cobbett Press, 1947), p. 17.

came the end of the fourth glaciation of the northern hemisphere. This marks the beginning of the Upper Paleolithic, by which time the slowly accelerating rate of cultural growth was beginning to yield important advances. There was considerable specialization in both bone and stone tools and implements. The decorative arts were elaborated; personal adornment must have meant a great deal, if we can judge by the collections of rings, beads, bracelets, and the like.

Yet, despite notable advances, man throughout most of this period did not have polished tools, the bow and arrow, agriculture, or domesticated plants and animals. He was still a food-gatherer, a forager, a fisherman, and a hunter. Nevertheless, mankind was astir, both in migrations and in inventiveness. In the transition to the next stage, the bow and arrow, canoes, netting, and basketry appear. The first animal to be domesticated, the dog, was tamed during this period.

By the end of the Upper Paleolithic in Europe, the Near East, and North Africa about 13,000 years ago, there was a good deal of regional variation, as well as a variety of racial types.

The New Stone Age The Neolithic Revolution marked one of the greatest changes in human culture, one matched only, perhaps, by the Industrial Revolution. The Neolithic began in the Near East and the Nile Valley about 13,000 years ago. It spread to central and western Europe three or four thousand years later. During this period men began to polish some of their stone tools, giving them a sharper cutting edge, and they invented the arts of pottery and weaving. But these were not the most important changes: it was the

domestication of plants and animals that laid the foundation of man's subsequent history.

The first development of village life associated with the domestication of plants and animals seems to have taken place in the hilly flanks of the Fertile Crescent, an area in the upper reaches of the Tigris and Euphrates valleys in what is now Iraq. From here this type of economy spread westward to Syria and thence to Egypt and southeastward toward the Persian gulf.

The development of agriculture greatly altered man's social life and culture. Man's control of the planting, growth, harvesting, and use of cereals, root crops, and other plants, and his domestication of cattle, pigs, and, later, sheep gave him a more abundant food supply. The domestication of plants meant farming; that of animals led, in some cases, to herding, or pastoralism. Often there was a mixture of agriculture and the use of such domesticated animals as pigs, cows, goats, and sheep.

This new economy made possible a more rapid growth in population. It meant also, as agriculture came to dominate his economy, that man finally had to establish a more settled abode. He founded villages and thereby created the need for new forms of social control, especially as his numbers increased. And while the distinguishing features of civilization—the wheel, trade, writing, mathematics, and science—did not appear until later, in the Bronze Age, these inventions and discoveries would have been impossible without agriculture, settled life, and the consequent leisure. Man had begun to alleviate the grim struggle for survival.

The next great cultural step occurred about 5,000 years ago, when man learned how to smelt certain minerals: first copper, then tin, then an alloy of copper and tin to make bronze, and finally iron. The Age of Metals was born. During this period came the invention of writing and the wheel, and the extension of trade in surplus goods. By this time the major features of culture and social organization with which we are acquainted from the written history of our ancestors had appeared.

The Importance of Language Running through the evolution we have indicated above and an integral part of it was man's greatest tool, language. Without the ability to communicate ideas easily and accurately, man could not have developed the patterns of behavior which we call culture. Some animals do have a limited social heredity, but they lack the language needed to develop a culture. One ape, for example, may imitate another in using a stick to knock down a stem of bananas that is out of reach, but he cannot tell his offspring about it. Language enables man to transmit ideas about situations which are not present. Further, it allows him to communicate judgments concerning the proper behavior in such situations.

Most persons in our society, on entering a hotel for the first time, would not go directly to a room without stopping at the desk, nor would they go behind the desk and pick out a room key. They would not do such things because the patterns of behavior expected under such circumstances have been communicated to them by someone else in their generation or a preceding one who knew the proper procedure. The information, attitudes, ideas, and values of each generation can be passed on to the succeeding generation by means of language, and individuals can be pre-

pared for unusual as well as ordinary events.

Since language makes culture possible, it is largely responsible for the difference in complexity between the social life of human beings and the social life of animals, such as ants or chimpanzees, which interact socially but have no culture.

Language itself, of course, is part of culture. When the individuals in a group have learned to associate the same sounds with the same ideas, they have a language; they also have a set of shared, learned behaviors. Indeed, language is so vital a characteristic of any culture that a difference in language between groups is one of the more reliable means of differentiating between cultures—for example, between the cultures of France and Britain. One of the most obvious things an observer will notice as he moves from one society to another is the change in language, although other differences are also soon discernible.

To a considerable degree, language shapes the rest of the culture. An extreme example will make this clear. There are tribes which have no word for the color gray and, since man thinks with words, members of such a society are unable to think of gray. It is often noted that the English and American cultures are quite similar, though by no means identical. The languages spoken in the United States and in England differ somewhat, in content as well as pronunciation. Both are very different, however, from the language spoken in Japan, and the cultures show a similarly marked difference. While this does not imply a direct cause-effect relationship, it does seem generally true that linguistic similarities are found between cultures which share many other patterns, and radical differences in language accompany radical differences in other aspects of culture.

Complexity of Culture Ralph Linton has summarized the expanding nature of culture in the following words:

With language, it is possible for one individual to transmit practically the whole of his experience to another individual. However, this in itself would never have made possible the incredible richness of the human heritage. There are limits to the learning ability of any one person. Cultures can attain their wealth of content because they are carried by groups of individuals, i.e., societies. It has been said that Aristotle was the last man to be familiar with the sum total of the human knowledge of his time. After him, the accumulation became too great. Such a statement is absurd on its face, for by the time of Aristotle there were already thousands of cultures extant, and the existence, let alone the content, of most of these was unknown to him. He certainly did not know how to throw a boomerang or how to call a moose. Even if we take the total of human knowledge to mean simply the total knowledge embodied and transmitted in his own particular line of social heredity, the Greek, it is still impossible. Aristotle may have known all about Greek philosophy, literature, and art, but he probably did not know how to forge and temper a sword, or set a wolf-trap, or where mullet were thickest. The knowledge of these things was as much a part of Greek culture as were the plays of Euripides or the speculations of Plato, yet each of them was known, in complete and usable detail, to only a small part of the population which shared that culture. Society, then as now, was made up of groups of specialists, each group using and transmitting certain elements of the culture and leaving other elements to other groups.[5]

5 · Ralph Linton, *The Study of Man* (New York: Appleton-Century-Crofts, 1936), p. 84. Reprinted by permission of the publisher.

As we have seen, the word *culture* is used to refer to the total social inheritance of mankind. In this sense, the term designates all human behavior which is socially learned rather than biologically inherited and which is shared by most human beings or by specifically designated sets of them. In addition to this general use of the term, we use it more specifically to refer to the shared learned behaviors of a certain group of human beings.

Because of the complexity of any culture, it is often useful, for purposes of description and analysis, to examine a culture piece by piece, looking at one part, or a combination of related parts, at a time.

THE FORM AND CONTENT OF CULTURE

One way to examine a culture is to note the observable individual acts connected with it, cataloging each behavior which has been learned and is shared by the people in the society.

Traits Some anthropologists break down the larger totalities of culture into small elements or units, called *culture traits*. Psychologically these represent single combinations of acts and ideas related to a particular need or situation. For instance, fire-making may be thought of as a culture trait involving the use of certain implements and skills. For a nonliterate man this may be the device of rubbing two dry sticks together over a small pile of tinder. For civilized man it may mean the use of matches or a mechanical lighter. So too, ways of saluting another person—such as a man's lifting his hat to greet a lady—or parts of a ritual illustrate single traits.

Yet an analysis of culture by traits is open to the same criticism as is the attempt to understand an individual by listing and correlating sets of personality traits, such as tactfulness, honesty, punctuality, and the like. While useful up to a point, such a way of studying either a culture or a person fails to take into account that both a culture and a person operate as totalities.

Patterns   A culture pattern is an organization of traits or elements into an interrelated whole. Plow agriculture, so important a step in the history of man, is a pattern consisting of many culture traits: the way the plow is made, the manner in which the animals or machines that draw it are harnessed or driven, the use of the plant that is domesticated and harvested, how the seeds are put into the ground, and so on through a wide range of activities. The belief in and worship of one god, which we call monotheism, is another complex pattern made up of a wide variety of specific ideas, emotions, and habits. In civilized society, what the economists call the "market" is a somewhat systematic patterning of a wide variety of separate acts and ideas: buying, selling, lending, transporting, and so on.

Culture patterns form, in turn, even larger configurations of culture. Among the North American Indians, for example, patterns of maize culture were tied up with the making and use of pottery. There is no sound reason for this association of habits. Willow or grass baskets might have been used for holding and cooking maize, and, indeed, other Indian tribes did successfully cook their food in this way. In our own society, machine production is linked to capitalistic ownership, but in Soviet Russia machine production is associated with state ownership. Sometimes these linkages of culture patterns seem to have a certain logical basis in experience, but many of them are mere accidents.

Ethos   Those patterns of culture of a particular society which most distinguish it from other societies we call the *ethos*. Sumner, a pioneer American social scientist, defined ethos as "the totality of characteristic traits by which a group [i.e., a society] is individualized and differentiated from others." Thus Sparta and Athens, Judea, India, China, and the industrialized, capitalistic United States represent distinctive patterns and values. Moreover, as Sumner says, "The ethos of one group furnishes the standpoint from which it criticizes the ways of any other group." [6]

The ethos of any great body of people, therefore, becomes a clue to many matters of importance to sociology and the social sciences, especially those that are concerned with cultural change. The ethos is the heart of any culture.

Universals, Alternatives, and Specialties
An analysis of the place of a culture in the life of an individual or of a group of individuals in a given society reveals wide ranges of participation. Even in small societies, differences in thought and conduct are linked to age, sex, and occupational differences. In a complex industrialized society it is quite impossible for any one person to participate actively in all the many phases of the culture. The way in which the demands of the culture play upon an in-

6 · W. G. Sumner, *Folkways* (Boston: Ginn and Company, 1906), pp. 70, 73.

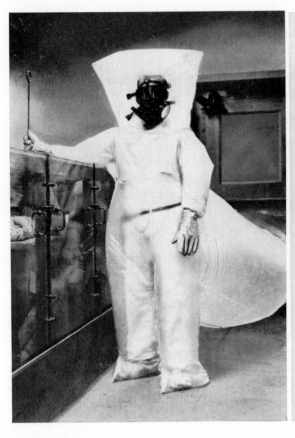

An occupational special- ty often requires special equipment: plastic suit for worker in atomic energy plant.

General Electric Company

dividual will vary. Three levels of participation in a culture may be distinguished.[7]

Universals are those core features of a culture which are widely accepted and required by the society. They are learned behaviors so widely shared that, without them, one is obviously "different" or an outcast. Examples of universals are the language spoken in the society, the standard patterns of social relationships (such as monogamy in our society), and the deep-seated moral values. In general, ethnocentric beliefs are universals. The term *universal* refers to behaviors associated with a particular culture; a pattern may be universal within one culture and unheard of in another. For example, in some Arabian societies, men wear robes, and the wearing of trousers is confined to women and serves as a mark of femininity.

Alternatives are activities in which individuals are allowed a choice. For instance, a universal in our culture demands legalized marriage for couples who wish to live together with the approval of the community; however, they are offered certain alternatives: they may be married at home, in a church, or at the city hall, by a minister, priest, rabbi, or justice of the peace. Alternatives are different activities allowed and accepted for achieving the same end.

7 · Linton, *The Study of Man*, pp. 272–274.

Specialties are learned behaviors shared by the members of certain social categories but not by most people in the society. The doctor, for example, knows things most of us do not know and performs certain activities in which most of us do not participate. In general, specialties are a consequence of the division of labor, and are shared according to sex, age, class, or occupation.

Subcultures Particularly in large industrial societies, there are groups of persons who share the total culture but also have a set of behaviors peculiar to the group. Anyone who has listened to a discussion among a group of medical students knows that they have a special language and a set of values of their own. Such shared learned behaviors which are common to a specific group or category are called *subcultures*. Specialties lead to subcultures. Railroaders, for further example, share in the general ethos; but in addition, they have a special language, they place a peculiar value on time, they know things and have ideas which are not shared among most members of the society. In other words, people who share occupational specialties can be said to participate in the same occupational subculture.[8]

Ethnic groups—persons who have entered our society from another one, such as Polish-Americans or Chinese-Americans—also have subcultures. In addition to the set of words, feelings, traditions, and rituals shared by most members of American society, they have a second set of behaviors which they have brought with them from their previous homes and which are now subcultures. All sorts of "societies" or "clubs"—German-American, Italian-American, and so on—help perpetuate some of the symbols and values of the countries and world regions from which their families came to the United States.

In this chapter, we have examined the form and content of culture. In the next we turn to the differences between cultures.

8 · See Howard S. Becker, *Outsiders: Studies in the Sociology of Deviance* (New York: Free Press of Glencoe, 1963). For other examples of research on occupational subcultures, see W. F. Cottrell, *The Railroader* (Stanford, California: Stanford University Press, 1940); S. Kirson Weinberg and Henry Arond, "The Occupational Culture of the Boxer," *American Journal of Sociology*, 1952, 57:460–469; William Bruce Cameron, "Sociological Notes on the Jam Session," *Social Forces*, 1954, 33:177–182; and Raymond W. Mack, "Occupational Ideology and the Determinate Role," *Social Forces*, 1957, 36:37–44.

INTERPRETATIVE SUMMARY

Culture is shared, learned behavior. Animals learn to a small extent by copying from one another, but only man knows how to transmit complex skills and abstract ideas to his fellows and to future generations. Thus we say that only man has the ability to have a culture.

Actually, the beginnings of culture were made not by man but by *hominidae*, earlier members of the family of primates to which man belongs. We think certain *hominidae* developed crude cultures about one to two million years ago.

Man's basic tool for transmitting culture is language. Even with this great aid, most aspects of a culture cannot be transmitted from person to person, since no one is an expert on a whole culture. Rather, we learn from specialists.

We speak of *cultures*, plural. A culture may be identified geographically. For example, the United States has a culture, its people having a common way of answering basic needs, a moral and artistic heritage, and so on. In analyzing a particular culture, the sociologist notes patterns of answering both basic and secondary needs. Especially important for his purpose are those patterns which most distinguish that culture from the cultures of other societies. The sociologist is interested also in noting which behavior is absolutely required by the culture, and in which cases an individual is allowed some choice. Finally, he studies occupational, ethnic, and other subcultures within the culture.

REVIEW AND SUGGESTED READINGS

A • VOCABULARY

Alternatives	Old Stone Age (Paleolithic)	Subculture
Culture	Patterns of culture	Universals
New Stone Age (Neolithic)	Specialties	

B • QUESTIONS AND TOPICS FOR REVIEW

1. What is meant by *ethos?* What are the distinctive features of the ethos of Western man?
2. Discuss each of the following as it exists in the United States, according to universals required and alternatives allowed: (a) the family, (b) dating, and (c) education.
3. Which culture patterns in the United States have changed or been modified over the years? Which have remained essentially the same?
4. Choose a culture pattern, such as the belief that girls should or should not attend college, and analyze its component traits.
5. List and discuss three subcultures in which you participate.

C • SUGGESTIONS FOR FURTHER READING

Ralph L. Beals and Harry Hoijer. *An Introduction to Anthropology*, 2nd ed. New York: The Macmillan Co., 1959.

A general introductory textbook with considerable space devoted to racial origins and distribution of modern races.

Robert J. Braidwood. *Prehistoric Men*, 3rd ed. Chicago: Chicago Natural History Museum Press, 1957.

A sound and well-written account designed for the layman.

Lyman Bryson, ed. *An Outline of Man's Knowledge of the Modern World*. New York: McGraw-Hill Book Co., 1960.

A magnificent book which succeeds in living up to its title. Part IV, "Man in Society," contains, among others, chapters by William F. Albright on archaeology, Margaret Mead on the modern study of mankind, and Seymour Martin Lipset on trends in American society.

Theodosius Dobzhansky. *Evolution, Genetics, and Man*. New York: John Wiley & Sons, Inc., 1955.

The topic of man's evolution approached from the standpoint of genetics.

Walter Goldschmidt, ed. *Exploring the Ways of Mankind*. New York: Holt, Rinehart and Winston, Inc., 1960.

A collection of 72 papers divided into 13 chapters covering the major topics in cultural anthropology. Each chapter opens with an introductory interpretation.

Melville J. Herskovits. *Cultural Anthropology*. New York: Alfred A. Knopf, Inc., 1955.

A general introductory text. Parts I and III are particularly pertinent to the material discussed in this chapter.

E. Adamson Hoebel. *Man in the Primitive World: An Introduction to Anthropology*, 2nd ed. New York: McGraw-Hill Book Co., 1958.

A well-written, general text covering both physical and cultural aspects of the field.

Felix M. Keesing. *Cultural Anthropology*. New York: Rinehart & Company, Inc., 1958.

A general introductory text with a good balance between factual materials and theoretical interpretations.

A. L. Kroeber, ed. *Anthropology Today: An Encyclopedic Inventory*. Chicago: University of Chicago Press, 1953.

A collection of papers which summarizes and interprets data from both physical and cultural anthropology.

Ralph Linton. *The Study of Man, An Introduction*. New York: Appleton-Century-Crofts, Inc., 1936.

This book, excellent in both content and style, has become a classic in anthropology. Chapters 5 and 6 are especially pertinent to the discussion here.

Ralph Linton. *The Tree of Culture*. New York: Alfred A. Knopf, Inc., 1955.

Contains chapters on cultural origins, cultural changes, and on various aspects of culture in all the major regions of the world.

Harry L. Shapiro, ed. *Man, Culture, and Society*. New York: Oxford University Press, 1956.

Sixteen chapters, each written by a specialist, presenting the basic materials of anthropology: physical, archaeological, and cultural.

George Gaylord Simpson. *The Meaning of Evolution*, revised edition and abridged. New York: The New American Library, 1952.

An incisive analysis of present interpretations of evolution and especially of the place of modern theory of genetics in this consideration.

CHAPTER 4

The Range of Cutural Variation

Every society of men possesses a culture. No matter how diverse the social structures, within each we find shared, learned behavior patterns. Each society has its universals, its alternatives, its specialties. Yet a pattern that is universal in one culture may be alternative in another, and not exist at all in a third. In Chapter 3 we presented the uniformities of human culture. We turn now to the topic of cultural variability.

FACTORS IN CULTURAL VARIATION

The uniformities of culture are more easily explained than the variations in time and place. The elements common to cultures everywhere stem, in part, from the fact that all human beings are basically the same biologically, so that their need for survival leads to certain commonalities in behavior. For example, all human beings must eat a certain amount of nourishing food, and a group must reproduce in order to survive as a society. But the patterns of acquiring and consuming food vary greatly from place to place, and the rules regarding who is supposed to have children, how often, and under what circumstances may differ from culture to culture. An analysis of certain factors should help us understand this variability.

Geography One explanation for the range of variation among cultures is the diversity of materials provided by the environment, and the effect of climate and landscape on the inhabitants. Certain effects of the physical environment on man are self-evident. The rigors of winter demand more clothes and warmer houses. To build shelters, man ordinarily has had to use materials near at hand: mud for huts in some places, stone in others, and ice or snow in still others. So too, living in places of rich soil and adequate rainfall produces social effects different from those produced by living on a rainless and windy desert or in the hot and humid regions of the tropics.

These daily and seasonal effects of the weather, water supply, and soil are obvious enough. Out of such repeated experiences arose popular and often erroneous folklore and pseudo-science about the impact of geography on human thought and action. For example, we often hear people argue that the Latins, living in warm climates as they do, have "hot blood" and are given to quick anger and impetuous behavior. In contrast, the Finns and Swedes, who live in cold latitudes, are said to be stolid in temperament and slow to action. These notions illustrate, in fact, the place of widely accepted but faulty beliefs which we noted in Chapter 1 when discussing pseudoscientific explanations of conduct.

But the fallacy of these and similar views must not mislead us. Geographic factors *do* play an important part in individual and group living. While there is no evidence that, unaided by culture, the desert makes for the invention of religious mysticism or the tropics for an inferiority of racial stocks, we cannot ignore the influence of climate, topography, and natural resources on man's existence. Especially is this true of elements in his material culture, such as food-getting, housing, manufacturing, and transport. *Yet even in these matters the geographic factors are chiefly limiting rather than directly causative.* The following illustrations bring out the manner in which cultures may vary even when the geographic conditions are the same.

Cultural Differences within Similar Geographic Environments The Eskimo represents a remarkable adaptation to a highly unfavorable environment; and if his were the only arctic culture we knew, we might assume that all arctic inhabitants followed much the same pattern. Take housing: is anything more natural than that the arctic dweller should build huts from the bountiful supply of snow at hand? Yet if we look across the Bering Sea to the Chuckchee of northeastern Siberia, in a similar climate, we find these people in winter months living not in snow houses but in large, clumsy tents of hide stretched over heavy supports. Furthermore, the Chuckchee use the domesticated reindeer for draft purposes, while the Eskimos use dogs to draw their sleds. The Chuckchee apparently borrowed the use of the domesticated reindeer from their neighbors, the Tungus, living to the south of them.

The Eskimos domesticated this convenient animal themselves only recently.

Or since the Pacific Northwest Indians have developed woodworking into a high art, why haven't the northern California tribes, with equally ample woodlands, done so? The answer lies not in the natural environment but in cultural divergences.

The American Southwest offers another striking contrast. The Hopi are intensive farmers; the Navahos do little farming, living a pastoral life. The Hopi live in terraced sandstone or adobe houses; the Navahos live in conical earth huts. The Hopi possess high art in pottery making; the Navahos show very crude ceramics workmanship. The Hopi men do the weaving; the Navaho women handle the loom. The Hopi are strictly monogamous; the Navahos permit polygyny. The family organization of the Hopi has strong mother-in-law taboos and gives the maternal uncles great power over their sisters' sons, whereas the Navahos have no such rigid taboos and have a different form of family organization. There are also marked differences in religious and magical practices. Finally, the Navahos, like the Plains tribes, have been warlike, while the Hopi have a relatively peaceful history.

The Negroid African Bushmen are seed-gatherers and hunters, live in crude windbreaks or caves, and use the bow and arrow. In contrast, their neighbors in the same sections of South Africa, the Hottentots, are a pastoral people, living in mat-covered portable huts and using the spear as their principal weapon, although they have the bow and arrow. While these tribes have many myths and other features of culture in common, the differences in material traits are striking. Once more we

*Cultural Adaptations
To Harsh
Environments*

Black Star

*The Eskimo builds his home from readily available
materials.*

*The North African
nomad finds the camel
the most efficient beast
of burden.*

Black Star

Black Star

The Arizona farmer makes dry land productive with irrigation ditches.

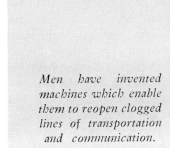

Men have invented machines which enable them to reopen clogged lines of transportation and communication.

Ewing Galloway

must seek the explanation largely in the history of their cultures and not in the physical environment.

The Paiutes, or "Digger Indians," living on the edge of the Great American Desert, considered the Rocky Mountain locust a particular delicacy. The locusts infested these areas periodically in great numbers, and the Indians drove them into brush enclosures to roast and eat them. When the Mormon colonists settled the Great Basin, beginning in 1847, they were greatly troubled during the first decade by plagues of these insects, which devoured every blade of grass, wheat, or corn. The Mormons did what they could to destroy the pests, but were unable to bridge the cultural chasm between themselves and their Indian friends and bring themselves to take up a new dietary habit. Had their own food taboos been less severe they, like the Indians, might have made something of a blessing out of what was to them a curse.

Geography and Contemporary Culture The above examples show that culture is perhaps the crucial determinant of social behavior. Yet the effects of natural environment, though often indirect and secondary, are nonetheless ever-present. Even with modern technology, agriculture is limited by soil, climate, and topography. If one wishes to grow bananas, he has his best chance of success in the rainy tropics. If he tries it in a semiarid section of the tropics, he will find it economically impractical. And in a humid, continental temperate zone one simply could not raise bananas at all, because killing frosts would destroy the crop. Similarly, coal miners are found in western Pennsylvania, with steel workers near by, but no such division of labor is found in central Texas. So too, in the developing air age, air currents and degrees of cloudiness and storminess in various regions will affect air transportation and, as a result, the location and function of certain cities.

In general, however, we may say that primitive man was more closely dependent on his immediate geographic conditions and resources than is modern man living in an industrialized society. As man has advanced to more complex forms of culture, he has overcome many of the handicaps of the "natural landscape." Not only has he changed the face of the earth itself and devised new and more rapid means of communication and transportation, but he has partially overcome poor soil by fertilization, provided more adequate water supply for crops by irrigation, insured himself against changes in temperature and humidity and, by the use of refrigeration in transporting and storing foodstuffs, removed earlier restrictions on the use of seasonal foods. In brief, cultural history runs a course from the most rudimentary societies, isolated and tied rather closely to their immediate physical environment, to modern times, in which there is little left in the environment of the ordinary man that has not been altered by his culture.

Race There persists a widespread be-belief that nonliterate peoples have powers of sight, hearing, smell, taste, and touch that far exceed those of civilized man. There is a concomitant belief that nonliterates lack the capacity to reason clearly and logically. The first notion has been thoroughly disproved by a long series of studies by psychologists who measured the sensory and motor capacities of nonliterates. Interestingly enough, it has also been shown that, even in these apparently simple psychological processes, cultural training may influence the responses. What members of a race or group see, hear, or otherwise sense is determined not only by their inherited capacities but also by what they have been taught by others in their group and culture.

Yet the recognition that in the simpler mental and motor responses nonliterates and modern man do not differ has not destroyed the other conviction, that in the higher mental functions there are sharp differences. This latter belief has been used by many writers who take the position that the high civilization of present-day European and American peoples rests on an inherent intellectual superiority of members of the white race. It is often asked why, if the colored races are equal in ability to the whites, the African tribes did not develop a high culture, such as emerged not far from them, first in the Fertile Crescent and later in Greece, Rome, and modern Europe. Or why, if the Mongolians are as intelligent as the whites, the inventions that make modern technology possible did not occur in the Far East.

To the student of prehistory and history, such questions are naïve for a number of reasons. For one thing, they completely ignore the fact of the slow cumulation of the important elements in a culture. As noted earlier, many fundamental features of culture, such as the use of fire, making of tools, development of language and thought forms, weaving, art, and religion, were initiated by races now extinct. Even the important advances of the Neolithic may have come, in part, from races that no longer exist. True, the beginnings of civilization, including the use of metals, the wheel, written language, money, commerce, and complex art, religion, philosophy, and early science, were developed largely from certain ancestors of present Mediterranean peoples. Yet there is every reason to believe that other races also played a part. And certainly the Nordic or Slavic subraces remained in the Neolithic cultural stage long after the Mediterranean people had made great advances in culture. In fact, the Nordics and Slavs are beneficiaries in modern times of the vast cultural contributions of other races and subraces.

Another factor influencing cultural growth is the degree to which a race is isolated. For example, the barriers of the sea long insulated the Australians from the main streams of Asiatic culture. So too, during the period of high Mediterranean culture, the African tribes south of the Sahara were cut off from that culture. They had learned the art of metallurgy, had developed a rather complex social organization, and had created some distinctive art forms; nonetheless, their isolation prevented them from participating in the European culture until very recent times. By the time this contact was made, the cultural divergences of Europe and Negroid Africa were sharp.

A third factor which affects the advancement of culture is its *directionality*. In the Western world, concern with physical welfare led to an increasing body of skills and knowledge centering on mechanical and scientific inventions and discoveries. Such a cultural base has in turn largely determined the interests—the "run of attention"—of those who are its beneficiaries. Modern Euro-American culture is heavily loaded on the side of science, technology, and activities involving material goods and services. In contrast, the Oriental peoples followed philosophic and artistic lines. Only in relatively recent times have they begun to show an interest in technology. Yet there is no evidence that the Mongoloid peoples are *innately* more given to mystic philosophy or moral searching than members of the white or Negro race. Nor can an objective student of comparative cultures discern any particular moral superiority of one race over another. If there were anything to the notion that races do have distinctive moral capacities (and there is not), one could chalk up a host of low scores for the white race, whose history has been marked by bloody and almost continuous conflict.

In short, no competent student of race, culture, and history now holds that racial differences have had any particular place in the building, cumulation, and continuity of human culture. Peoples of varying racial extraction have participated and do participate differentially in culture in accordance with what they have received from other peoples, what their own ancestors invented and passed on to them, or what those of any given generation invented and used. The striking variability in human culture has nothing to do with the physical features that mark one race or subrace off from another.

While racial type does not have any relationship to the various patternings of behavior found in different societies, another set of factors has, like geography, at least a limiting effect on the course of cultural development.

Invention The first of these factors, invention, apparently occurs haphazardly. There is no scientific evidence that a specific breed of people is in-

nately more inventive than any other collectivity. As a result, there would be an equal chance, within the limitations imposed by the geographic environment, of the occurrence of any given invention anywhere at any time if ability to invent were the only other variable. Actually, of course, the geographic environment is an extremely important item. Desert dwellers, for example, will not invent an improved fishhook, much less an outboard motor. The physical environment provides a further limiting feature simply in the number of people which it can support. If inventive ability is distributed among human beings on a random basis, or according to the law of averages —and it seems to be—then the larger the population of a society, the more inventions its members are likely to produce.

Invention is an even more determining factor than it might appear, since most inventions depend on previous inventions. The more you have, the more you are likely to get. Until someone discovered the principle of the wheel, no one could invent the pulley, much less the modern steam shovel. Until a way of striking fire was found, the idea of smelting iron was out of the question. Nowhere is the fact of the cumulative nature of culture made more dramatic than in the history of invention, reflected in Newton's statement, "If I have seen farther [than other men], it is by standing on the shoulders of giants." Try to imagine the hundreds of human beings through the centuries who had to contribute original ideas, or shape several already created implements into new combinations, before one could produce a modern automobile, with its springs, combination air- and water-cooled engine, upholstery made of synthetic fibers,

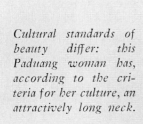

Cultural standards of beauty differ: this Paduang woman has, according to the criteria for her culture, an attractively long neck.

Black Star

chromium plating, sprayed-on paint, and countless other features far removed from the invention of the piston.

Isolation and Culture Contact If a major invention is announced in England tomorrow morning, Americans will hear of it on newscasts and read about it in the papers tomorrow evening. The rapid and extensive contact between these two societies makes it likely that they will become more and more similar as time goes by. It is as difficult to find an Italian town where one cannot buy Coca-Cola as it is to locate an American town where no restaurant serves spaghetti. Culture contact makes for uniformities in behavior.

This fact provides a clue for explaining the wide variation among cultures. Throughout most of human history, most societies have had no contact with outside societies other than their immediate neighbors. Only in the past few thousand years have men gained extended contact with cultures markedly different from their own.

Just as interaction between people who participate in different cultures makes for similarities between the cultures through the exchange of traits and patterns, so does a long period of isolation contribute to cultural variability. Since there are virtually infinite possibilities for variation in the ways man is capable of meeting his needs, the longer two societies are isolated from each

Cultural standards of beauty differ: by having her feet bound, the Manchu woman on the right has been crippled, according to our culture; according to her culture, she has been made more desirable.

other, the more likely they are to display different patterns of behavior. In one society, an inventive female will put a metal ring around her neck, and others will copy the fashion. Women with more leisure to make necklaces or more wealth to buy them will wear more than one. Eventually, the number of necklaces a woman wears will become such a standard way of indicating her wealth and position in the society that families will invest as much wealth as they can spare in metal rings to place around the necks of their daughters. Indeed, this can reach the point where the attractiveness of a female is judged partly by the length of her neck, with the result that parents place metal hoops around the necks of their young daughters to stretch them.

In ancient China, tiny feet were looked on as a mark of daintiness and femininity. Parents bound the feet of their girl children so tightly that the feet could not grow normally. This resulted, from the point of view of our culture, in young women who were crippled and deformed; but from the viewpoint of the other culture, the result was lovely, attractive, small-footed ladies. In fact, small feet became a mark of upper-class standing in China because, much as they may have admired small feet, poorer families recognized that tiny feet meant less ability to work, and girls were needed to aid in the family labors.

So long as there is no contact between the society where a long neck is a criterion of femininity and position and the society where tiny feet are a similar indication, there will be no opportunity for the values of the one culture to have any impact on the values of the other. The tendency will be for them to continue to develop along different lines. Female deities in one will have long necks; in the other, they will have small feet.

This is only one small example of cutural variability: differences in patterns of behavior aiming at artificial beautification. When one considers that there are opportunities for different lines of cultural development in every area of human behavior, it becomes apparent that variation between cultures, far from being just a quaint possibility, is virtually inevitable. Given the range of available choices, it is hardly possible that two societies isolated from each other would make the same selections. Furthermore, as cultures develop in relative isolation from one another, they are likely to become more and more divergent, each new trait and pattern having to fit in with those previously developed, as well as with the ethos or general value system. For example, a certain culture, esteeming men more than women, may provide that men should be the property owners and that no woman can hold land. Because of this the culture cannot develop an inheritance system which provides for daughters to inherit property or which prohibits sons from inheriting anything from their fathers. In other words, a culture must have some internal consistency.

EXAMPLES OF CULTURAL VARIATION

Having been reared within the framework of our own ethos, we are likely to think of our own culture patterns as "normal" or as a reflection of "human nature." It is instructive to examine a few instances of the many ways in which a society can organize some of its activities. The following passage from a study by Ruth Benedict points out cultural variations in attitudes toward adolescence and war, based largely on a study of several primitive societies.

Adolescence. The case of adolescence is particularly interesting, because it is in the limelight in our own civilization and because we have plentiful information from other cultures. In our own civilization a whole library of psychological studies has emhasized the inevitable unrest of the period of puberty. It is in our tradition a physiological state as definitely characterized by domestic explosions and rebellion as typhoid is marked by fever. There is no question of the facts. They are common in America. The question is rather of their inevitability.

The most casual survey of the ways in which different societies have handled adolescence makes one fact inescapable: even in those cultures which have made most of the trait, the age upon which they focus their attention varies over a great range of years. At the outset, therefore, it is clear that the so-called puberty institutions are a misnomer if we continue to think of biological puberty. The puberty they recognize is social, and the ceremonies are a recognition in some fashion or other of the child's new status of adulthood. This investiture with new occupations and obligations is in consequence as various and as culturally conditioned as the occupations and obligations themselves. If the sole honourable duty of manhood is conceived to be deeds of war, the investiture of the warrior is later and of a different sort from that in a society where adulthood gives chiefly the privilege of dancing in a representation of masked gods. In order to understand puberty institutions, we do not most need analyses of the necessary nature of *rites de passage*; we need rather to know what is identified in different cultures with the beginning of adulthood and their methods of admitting to the new status. Not biological puberty, but what adulthood means in that culture conditions the puberty ceremony.

Adulthood in central North America means warfare. Honour in it is the great goal of all men. The constantly recurring theme of the youth's coming-of-age, as also of preparation for the warpath at any age, is a magic ritual for success in war. They torture not one another, but themselves: they cut strips of skin from their arms and legs, they strike off their fingers, they drag heavy weights pinned to their chest or leg muscles. Their reward is enhanced prowess in deeds of warfare.

In Australia, on the other hand, adulthood means participation in an exclusively male cult whose fundamental trait is the exclusion of women. Any woman is put to death if she so much as hears the sound of the bull-roarer at the ceremonies, and she must never know of the rites. Puberty ceremonies are elaborate and symbolic repudiations of the bonds with the female sex; the men are symbolically made self-sufficient and the wholly responsible element of the community. To attain this end they use drastic sexual rites and bestow supernatural guaranties.

The clear physiological facts of adolescence, therefore, are first socially interpreted even where they are stressed. But a survey of puberty institutions makes clear a further fact: puberty is physiologically a different matter in the life-cycle of the male and the female. If cultural emphasis followed the physiological emphasis, girls' ceremonies would be more marked than boys'; but it is not so. The ceremonies emphasize a social fact: the adult prerogatives of men are more far-reaching in every culture than women's, and consequently, as in the above instances, it is more common for societies to take note of this period in boys than in girls.

Girls' and boys' puberty, however, may be socially celebrated in the same tribe in identical ways. Where, as in the interior of British Columbia, adolescent rites are a magical training for all occupations, girls are included on the same terms

as boys. Boys roll stones down mountains and beat them to the bottom to be swift of foot, or throw gambling-sticks to be lucky in gambling; girls carry water from distant springs, or drop stones down inside their dresses that their children may be born as easily as the pebble drops to the ground.

In such a tribe as the Nandi of the lake region of East Africa, also, girls and boys share an even-handed puberty rite, though, because of the man's dominant role in the culture, his boyhood training period is more stressed than the woman's. Here adolescent rites are an ordeal inflicted by those already admitted to adult status upon those they are now forced to admit. They require of them the most complete stoicism in the face of ingenious tortures associated with circumcision. The rites for the two sexes are separate, but they follow the same pattern. In both the novices wear for the ceremony the clothing of their sweethearts. During the operation their faces are watched for any twinge of pain, and the reward of bravery is given with great rejoicing by the lover, who runs forward to receive back some of his adornments. For both the girl and the boy the rites mark their *entrée* into a new sex status: the boy is now a warrior and may take a sweetheart, the girl is marriageable. The adolescent tests are for both a premarital ordeal in which the palm is awarded by their lovers.

Puberty rites may also be built upon the facts of girls' puberty and admit of no extension to boys. One of the most naïve of these is the institution of the fatting-house for girls in Central Africa. In the region where feminine beauty is all but identified with obesity, the girl at puberty is segregated, sometimes for years, fed with sweet and fatty foods, allowed no activity, and her body rubbed assiduously with oils. She is taught during this time her future duties, and her seclusion ends with a parade of her corpulence that is followed by her marriage to her proud bridegroom. It is not regarded as necessary for the man to achieve pulchritude before marriage in a similar fashion.

The usual ideas around which girls' puberty institutions are centered, and

University of Detroit

Different cultures have varying definitions of recreation: baseball, America's "national game."

which are not readily extended to boys', are those concerned with menstruation. The uncleanness of the menstruating woman is a very widespread idea, and in a few regions first menstruation has been made the focus of all the associated attitudes. Puberty rites in these cases are of a thoroughly different character from any of which we have spoken. Among the Carrier Indians of British Columbia, the fear and horror of a girl's puberty was at its height. Her three or four years of seclusion was called "the burying alive," and she lived for all that time alone in the wilderness, in a hut of branches far from all beaten trails. She was a threat to any person who might so much as catch a glimpse of her, and her mere footstep defiled a path or a river. She was covered with a great headdress of tanned skin that shrouded her face and breasts and fell to the ground behind. Her arms and legs were loaded with sinew bands to protect her from the evil spirit with which she was filled. She was herself in danger and she was a source of danger to everybody else.

Girls' puberty ceremonies built upon ideas associated with the menses are readily convertible into what is, from the point of view of the individual concerned, exactly opposite behaviour. There are always two possible aspects to the sacred: it may be a source of peril or it may be a source of blessing. In some tribes the first menses of girls are a potent supernatural blessing. Among the Apaches I have seen the priests themselves pass on their knees before the row of solemn little girls to receive from them the blessing of their touch. All the babies and the old people come also of necessity to have illness removed from them. The adolescent girls are not segregated as sources of danger, but court is paid to them as to direct sources of supernatural blessing. Since the ideas that underlie puberty rites for girls, both among the Carrier and among the Apache, are founded on beliefs concerning menstruation, they are not extended to boys, and boys' puberty is marked instead, and lightly, with simple tests and proofs of manhood.

The adolescent behaviour, therefore, even of girls was not dictated by some physiological characteristic of the period itself, but rather by marital or magic requirements socially connected with it. These beliefs made adolescence in one tribe serenely religious and beneficent, and in another so dangerously unclean that the child had to cry out in warning that others might avoid her in the woods. The adolescence of girls may equally, as we have seen, be a theme which a culture does not institutionalize. Even where, as in most of Australia, boys' adolescence is given elaborate treatment, it may be that the rites are an induction into the status of manhood and male participation in tribal matters, and female adolescence passes without any kind of formal recognition.

These facts, however, still leave the fundamental question unanswered. Do not all cultures have to cope with the natural turbulence of this period, even though it may not be given institutional expression? Dr. Mead has studied this question in Samoa. There the girl's life passes through well-marked periods. Her first years out of babyhood are passed in small neighbourhood gangs of age mates from which the little boys are strictly excluded. The corner of the village to which she belongs is all-important, and the little boys are traditional enemies. She has one duty, that of baby-tending, but she takes the baby with her rather than stays home to mind it, and her play is not seriously hampered. A couple of years before puberty, when she grows strong enough to have more difficult tasks required of her and old enough to learn more skilled techniques, the little girls' play group in which she grew up ceases to exist. She assumes woman's dress and must contribute to the work of the household. It is an uninteresting period of life to her and quite without turmoil. Puberty brings no change at all.

A few years after she has come of age, she will begin the pleasant years of casual and irresponsible love affairs that she will prolong as far as possible into the period when marriage is already considered fitting. Puberty itself is marked by

no social recognition, no change of attitude or of expectancy. Her pre-adolescent shyness is supposed to remain unchanged for a couple of years. The girl's life in Samoa is blocked out by other considerations than those of physiological sex maturity, and puberty falls in a particularly unstressed and peaceful period during which no adolescent conflicts manifest themselves. Adolescence, therefore, may not only be culturally passed over without ceremonial; it may also be without importance in the emotional life of the child and in the attitude of the village toward her.

Warfare is another social theme that may or may not be used in any culture. Where war is made much of, it may be with contrasting objectives, with contrasting organization in relation to the state, and with contrasting sanctions. War may be, as it was among the Aztecs, a way of getting captives for the religious sacrifices. Since the Spaniards fought to kill, according to Aztec standards they broke the rules of the game. The Aztecs fell back in dismay and Cortez walked as victor into the capital.

There are even quainter notions, from our standpoint, associated with warfare in different parts of the world. For our purposes it is sufficient to notice those regions where organized resort to mutual slaughter never occurs between social groups. Only our familiarity with war makes it intelligible that a state of warfare should alternate with a state of peace in one tribe's dealings with another. The idea is quite common over the world, of course. But on the one hand it is impossible for certain peoples to conceive the possibility of a state of peace, which in their notion would be equivalent to admitting enemy tribes to the category of human beings, which by definition they are not even though the excluded tribe may be of their own race and culture.

On the other hand, it may be just as impossible for a people to conceive of the possibility of a state of war. Rasmussen tells of the blankness with which the Eskimo met his exposition of our custom. Eskimos very well understand the act of killing a man. If he is in your way, you cast up your estimate of your own

French Embassy Press and Information Division

Different cultures have varying definitions of recreation:
Basque dancers

strength, and if you are ready to take it upon yourself, you kill him. If you are strong, there is no social retribution. But the idea of an Eskimo village going out against another Eskimo village in battle array or a tribe against tribe, or even of another village being fair game in ambush warfare, is alien to them. All killing comes under one head, and is not separated, as ours is, into categories, the one meritorious, the other a capital offence.

I myself tried to talk of warfare to the Mission Indians of California, but it was impossible. Their misunderstanding of warfare was abysmal. They did not have the basis in their own culture upon which the idea could exist, and their at-tempts to reason it out reduced the great wars to which we are able to dedicate ourselves with moral fervour to the level of alley brawls. They did not happen to have a cultural pattern that distinguished between them.

War is, we have been forced to admit even in the face of its huge place in our own civilization, an asocial trait. In the chaos following the World War all the wartime arguments that expounded its fostering of courage, of altruism, of spiritual values, gave out a false and offensive ring. War in our own civilization is as good an illustration as one can take of the destructive lengths to which the development of a culturally selected trait may go.

If we justify war, it is because all peoples always justify the traits of which they find themselves possessed, not because war will bear an objective examination of its merits.[1]

Implications of Cultural Variability

Illustrations such as the foregoing indicate that a considerable proportion of the behavior often attributed to instinct or to man's original nature is actually cultural. It is behavior that is shared within a given society, not by all hu-

1 · Ruth Benedict, *Patterns of Culture* (New York: The New American Library, 1946), pp. 22–29. First published by Houghton Mifflin Co., 1934. By permission.

man beings, and it is behavior that is learned, not innate.

The tendency to regard the patterns of behavior in our own society as "right" and all others as strange and improper stems from ethnocentrism, the disposition to evaluate other cultures on the basis of the values prevalent in our own. The perspective gained by examining the cultures of other societies is basic to a liberal arts education. Knowledge of the ethos of other times and places provides the ground for a more rational attitude toward other societies and a better understanding of our own.

INTERPRETATIVE SUMMARY

What factors are responsible for the differences among cultures? First, geography is important; people develop different cultures as they attempt to survive in their particular physical environments. Geography as a factor was particularly crucial during primitive days, when man had not yet conquered his environment. Race itself is not a factor, since no race is inherently superior to any other. Isolation of a race, however, will slow its growth and tend to keep it "different," while culture contact will make it more like its neighbors and more advanced.

Each of the above factors limits rather than determines the course a culture will take. For example, geographically similar cultures will frequently find different ways of adjusting to their environments and will hold different values. The only explanation we can give is that the "directionalities" of the cultures are different—in other words, the cultures differ because they were presented with alternatives and happened to choose differently.

Examples of cultural variability abound. For example, the terms "adolescence" and "adulthood" do not have universal meaning. Adulthood carries different obligations and privileges in various societies, and its advent is hailed in numerous ways. Even the adolescent turmoil which generally precedes adulthood in our society is not universal! Another example is war. Some societies never have war, others are *always* literally in a state of war, and yet others alternate between states of war and peace.

REVIEW AND SUGGESTED READINGS

A • VOCABULARY

Cultural variability   Cultural isolation   Ethnocentrism

B • QUESTIONS AND TOPICS FOR REVIEW

1. Consider the terms "Eastern man" and "Western man." What cultural phenomenon is illustrated by the fact that we find the terms useful?

2. In the United States, is there a definite time at which adult status is considered achieved? What privileges and obligations accompany recognition of adult status here?
3. Discuss the unique ideas of any of the subcultures in the United States (perhaps one to which you belong) about (a) what adult status means; (b) when it occurs; (c) who should celebrate it and how it should be celebrated.
4. Discuss the following statement: "Cassius Clay is a reflection on the Negro race."
5. Which problems in the controlling of the physical environment have proved most persistent in our country?
6. Consider Ruth Benedict's discussion of adolescence. In the societies described, which attitudes and acts seemed to stem from needs of the culture? Which seemed to be arbitrarily chosen?
7. Imagine three young men and three young women from six different societies being marooned on an island. What do you think would happen as they built up a shared culture?

C · SUGGESTIONS FOR FURTHER READING

Albert K. Cohen. *Delinquent Boys: The Culture of the Gang.* New York: The Free Press of Glencoe, 1955.

A brilliant attempt to understand the behavior of juvenile delinquents through sociological analysis. It demonstrates that the boys from different class strata get different kinds of social rewards from participation in gang life.

Yehudi A. Cohen. *Social Structure and Personality: A Casebook.* New York: Holt, Rinehart, & Winston, Inc., 1961.

Through the analysis of thirty-seven case studies the author examines the ways in which particular personality constellations influence the social structure.

F. L. K. Hsu, ed. *Psychological Anthropology.* Homewood, Ill.: The Dorsey Press, Inc., 1961.

A systematic analysis and critique of culture and personality.

Bert Kaplan, ed. *Studying Personality Cross-Culturally.* New York: Harper and Row, 1960.

An interdisciplinary text in culture and personality produced by thirty scholars.

Oscar Lewis. *The Children of Sanchez.* New York: Random House, 1961.

An intimate and powerful account of a family living in the slums of Mexico City, told in their own words.

CHAPTER 5

Cultural Values and Social Norms

Every society operates under some set of rules. Every group has certain regulations which its members learn. On the basis of what they have learned, individuals are usually able to predict the behavior of their fellows.

Most people learn the basic rules so well that, under ordinary circumstances, they are not even aware of them. One example of a relatively minor set of expectations will serve to illustrate the fact that societies could not operate if their cultures did not provide grounds for anticipating the behavior of the members in specific circumstances. When you approach a traffic light that is green, you proceed, confident that people traveling at right angles to your course are facing a red light and will stop. You do not *know* that the light in other directions is red at this place and at this time; you *assume* it. You are not acquainted with the people approaching you at ninety-degree angles; you have never personally made arrangements with them assuring you that they will stop at red traffic signals. But you have learned that you have a right to expect the city street department to keep the light in proper repair, to wire it so that when it is red in one direction it will be green at right angles to that direction. You have learned that you have a right to expect people to stop when the signal is red in their direction, that you have

an obligation to stop when it is red in your direction, and that you or others who violate these expectations will be punished.

This chapter will examine such expectations. It will define cultural values, discuss the social norms that grow out of those values, and explore the means used to assure that people abide by the norms.

VALUES

Values are assumptions, both conscious and unconscious, of what is right and important. Some set of values forms the core of every culture. The ethos—that is, the fundamental characteristics—of any culture is a reflection of its basic values. Let us take America, for example. During its tremendous industrial and population growth from 1870 to the present, American society became characterized by a number of culture features, among them the following: (1) belief in individual material success and general national progress; (2) faith in universal literacy and education as a means of solving social and personal problems; (3) belief in the virtue of sheer size, witnessed in ever-larger skyscrapers, school and industrial plants, and corporations; (4) rapid movement through space, seen in increased mobility of population and improved means of communication and transportation; (5) love of novelty—constant change to something new and more exciting, as in sensational news, exciting drama, speed racing, crazes, and fads; and (6) the craving for domination—the booster and the "bigger and better" spirit in almost every important aspect of public life.

In contrast to this, in the Orient, at least before Western civilization and its values reached there in the nineteenth century, men's thinking and acting took quite different patterns. There was no belief in progress in our sense. Mere physical size had no special merit. Certainly no virtue inhered in rapid movement. The ideal, rather, was the calm deliberation of the scholar or sage. In India, among large numbers of the population, instead of desire for personal material success and continued identification of the self with individual striving and "getting ahead," the fundamental desire expressed in religious life was renunciation of self, the abandoning of personal desire, and the elimination of the ambition to be important.

Such radical differences in cultural values result, of course, in widely divergent social structures and patterns of expectations in social interaction.

SOCIAL NORMS

By norms we mean group-shared expectations. A set of expected behaviors can be associated either with a certain situation or with a given position in the social structure. Examples of the former are "Who ever heard of eating peas with honey?" "A Scout is courteous," "A gentleman pays his debts," or, more generally, "He shouldn't have done that." One is supposed to be quiet, respectful, and not to interrupt others in a house of worship. On the other hand, one's trust that his lawyer need not and thus will not give the court damaging evidence against him is an expectation associated with the lawyer's position in the social structure.

Of course, not everyone in any society abides by all the norms all the time, and no norm is always obeyed. If everyone always did the "right" thing at the "right" time and place, there would be no need to have rules or laws.

It should also be obvious that not all norms—or even most of them—are written or legalized. Most of the understandings we share with other members of society are informal. There is no law saying that one should not eat peas with a knife, that men should hold doors open for women, that one should lend money to friends but not to strangers, or that one shakes hands when introduced. Yet we have all learned these expectations; they are part of our culture, and most of us conform to them most of the time.

Sociologists classify norms into folkways and mores, according to the degree of importance attached to the rules by the society.[1] As we shall see, law grows, in large part, out of the folkways and mores.

Folkways The most obvious way to determine the importance of a norm for the members of a society is to observe how severely they punish those who violate it. Norms which are not

1 · William Graham Sumner introduced the concepts of folkways and mores in *Folkways* (Boston: Ginn and Company, 1906), pp. 78–108. In his writing, *folkways* is the more general term; *mores* are folkways deemed especially important by the society. We believe that greater clarity can be maintained by reserving the term *folkways* for the less crucial norms, violations of which are not severely punished, and separating these from the morally judged norms, or mores, violations of which bring more stringent penalties.

looked on as extremely important—or, to state it another way, <u>norms which can be violated without severe punishment—are called folkways.</u>

Adult males should wear a coat and tie to church. People should arrive on time for appointments. Men may wear their hair crew cut; ladies should not. Professors should not serve whiskey in their offices. People should not park their automobiles in zones labeled "No Parking." School children should not call teachers by their first names. One should not persistently make loud noises late at night in a residential area. People should not smoke in a chapel. One should bathe frequently enough so that others are not conscious of his bodily odors. A man should not strike a woman. People should eat three meals a day. A person should respect his parents.

Each of the sentences in the preceding paragraph is a statement of a group-shared expectation, or norm, in contemporary American society. Some norms are covered by formal laws; others are not. Violations of some would be met by fines, imprisonment, or dismissal from one's job; failure to abide by others would be punished only by verbal statements of disapproval or by ostracism. All the listed norms have one thing in common, however: the fact that they are not looked on by most people as moral matters. People who smoke in chapel are regarded as crude, but not as immoral. People who are persistently late for appointments are considered thoughtless; they are not viewed as sinners. People who disturb the peace are a nuisance, not lost souls. We may avoid people who do not bathe frequently, but we do not judge them wicked. You may get fined for leaving your car in a no-parking area,

but nobody will think the Devil inspired you to park there.

Folkways are rules which most people in the society expect most other people in the society to obey most of the time. They are deemed the "right" way, and "normal" people accept most of them unquestioningly. One can, however, challenge a folkway and suggest that it would not really hurt anything to alter it, without being judged a menace to his society. Herein lies the difference between folkways and mores.

Mores The <u>mores are not open to question.</u> In learning his culture, the individual so thoroughly internalizes the mores that he seldom thinks of them consciously as rules. The professor may be so irked at his warm academic robes that he toys with the idea of going to commencement in a T-shirt, but it will not occur to him to go in the nude. Law enforcement agencies might take seriously a suggestion from a traffic authority for a set of graduated penalties for parking offenses: only a warning the first time, a small fine the second, a larger fine for the third violation, and suspension of the driver's license for the fourth offense. No one would take seriously a similar plan for dealing with wanton murderers: let them off the first time, and then gradually crack down on them. Murder is a violation of the mores, and there is no disposition either to treat it lightly or, for that matter, to discuss whether or not it should be considered a violation of the mores.

Probably the best evidence of how thoroughly we internalize the mores is the difficulty most people would have in thinking of examples. Many generalized maxims that spring to mind are not mores. Taking a human life, for instance, is not necessarily a violation of the mores—it depends on who does it and under what circumstances. On some occasions our society gives medals, rewards, and public acclaim to those who take human lives. In wartime, we decorate the man who has shot down more enemy planes than any other flier, and parades are given in honor of the soldier who single-handedly has slain a great number of enemy soldiers. A hero's treatment is accorded the policeman who kills a dangerous criminal in a gun battle. A sizable portion of our movies have heroes who, in the course of the story, violate the injunction "Thou shalt not kill." A person who has killed under the "unwritten law" is usually punished lightly—sometimes not at all. Apparently our society feels that the "wronged" spouse in an adultery case should not be punished as severely for taking his revenge as another murderer would be. A storekeeper will not be punished for shooting a burglar in his store. Neither the law nor the mores prohibit killing in self-defense. Unintentional killing is not criminal unless it is the result of negligence on the part of the killer. In other words, saying that our society prohibits the taking of a human life is far too broad a statement; it must be modified by a lengthy list of exceptions and qualifications.

While we have laws to deal with wanton murder, some of our mores are assumed to be so well learned that no law is needed to enforce them. The rare violations are met by community rejection and expressions of loathing of the participants and, if legally cataloged at all, are treated as "indecency" or "disturbance of the peace." Moral imperatives of this magnitude are so deeply impressed upon the members of

society that the average person cannot remember when or how he came to learn that certain behavior is wrong. Incest is such a prohibition. Most of us do not know when or from whom we learned that incest is morally evil, but a father who had sexual relations with his own daughter would arouse in us feelings of revulsion and contempt.

Similarly, if we were asked to cite a major prohibition of our society, most of us would not think of mentioning the sharing of public toilet facilities at the same time by men and women. That is to say, the prohibition is so efficient that the thing is literally unthinkable. If challenged, the ordinary citizen could not give a brief, rational explanation of why such behavior is wrong in the way that he would explain that it is wrong to violate a traffic regulation because it endangers the lives of others. He would be more likely to say, "It's wrong because it's evil," "Just because," or "Everybody knows it's wrong." It is, in other words, part of the mores.

Law In most relatively complex societies, some kind of political order serves as an overall seat of power and authority in which law becomes an important norm of control. Laws are laid down to establish or maintain the rights, duties, and liberties of the members of the state. Rights imply a two-sided relationship, in which one person owes the other a duty and the other person benefits thereby. A person has rights only insofar as others have duties toward him. One's rights set limits on other people's liberties. Freedom and responsibility always go together. In complex societies, the law represents the most certain of all the social norms.

In modern democracies, the law

usually falls into three categories: constitutional, statutory, and judge-made. The first sets out the basic features of the political order. The second is the product of legislative bodies and covers a wide range of individual and group activities. The third is the product of the courts—it consists of judicial decisions which are used as the basis of adjudication of subsequent cases.

To adjudicate cases involving legal disputes, courts are set up. The judicial system usually has two levels: courts of original jurisdiction and those for appeal.

Most courts fall into two legal categories: criminal law and civil law. Criminal law deals with such offenses against the public peace, morality, and order as misdemeanors and the more serious offenses, such as murder, treason, rape, housebreaking and entering, and arson. Civil cases are suits at law between persons or between duly constituted associations, such as corporations. These relate to such matters as enforcement of contract, titles to property, collections of debts, torts (which have to do with injuries of person to person that may lead to recovery of damages), guardianship of children, marriage and divorce, and many other matters not strictly related to the public peace.

The definition of what constitutes a criminal and what a civil case depends on the culture. In many primary-group communities, homicide or feuding is treated as a private, not a public, matter. In urban society these are considered crimes.

Folkways, Mores, and Cultural Variability It is precisely the quality of unquestioning acceptance that makes it difficult for people with diverse cultures to explain to one another the normative structure of their own societies. "Why can't you kill cattle?" an American asks a Hindu. "*We* do, and it doesn't hurt anything." And the only answer is, "Because it's wrong; everybody knows that." Or a Samoan asks an American, "Why do you get so disturbed about premarital intercourse? Our boys and girls engage in it, and go on to be happy husbands and wives." Again the reply is, "We don't think it's right."

Nowhere is ethnocentrism more easily seen than in the attempts of people from different societies to understand one another's mores. The reason is that the normative structure of a society is a set of interrelated parts. The patterned behavior, or culture, of any society is a function, or consequence, of that structure. A major change in any one part of the structure is certain, therefore, to bring about changes elsewhere. To facilitate the examination and analysis of the structure of a society, sociologists usually look at the norms governing its principal functions.

Institutions An institution is a set of folkways and mores integrated around a principal function of the society. For example, every society must provide for the production and distribution of goods and services. If it did not, people would starve and the society would no longer exist. The goods and services used, the ways in which they are produced, and the manner in which they are distributed all differ from society to society. But in some way, the society must be ordered so that one consequence of its structure is the production and distribution of goods and services; this is one major function of any society. The norms which are integrated around the production and distribution of goods and services are called the *economic institution*. In contemporary American society, these norms include many folkways, such as exchanging one's labor for money instead of bartering; the belief that most economic enterprises need not produce or distribute goods or services at night, on Sundays, or on holidays; the feeling that a normal adult male ought to be engaged in some kind of work; the belief that a man should save enough money to be prepared for an emergency; the idea that people should not engage in the production and distribution of goods and services until they reach a certain age; and so on. Like folkways in other areas of social life, some of those governing economic activity are supported by law and others are not. In addition to these folkways, there are mores regarding economic behavior. Slavery is prohibited; a healthy father is obligated to support his young children; a person is not allowed to appropriate another person's property by force. All the folkways and mores which control the behavior of people in the production and distribution of goods and services make up the economic institution.

There are other institutions—familial, political, educational, religious—which will be discussed in the chapter on universal social structures and functions. The importance of institutions for sociological analysis lies in the fact that the total social structure of a society and its functions can be seen efficiently in an examination of its major institutions and the relationships among them.

Integration of Institutions The basic values of a society pervade all its institutions. That is, there is an integra-

tion of values. This integration is never perfect. It is in a constant state of readjustment as the operation of social processes causes minor changes in the structure. However, there must be some degree of integration of institutions or the society will collapse.

An instance of integration among the institutions of our own society will illustrate this point. The social process of competition is stressed as a positive cultural value in the American economic institution. "Free enterprise" is spoken of favorably; men are urged to strive to "get ahead"; competitive examinations are held for promotion in many jobs; we admire the poor boy who works harder than his fellows and becomes a "success"; we pass legislation to prevent monopoly because "competition is good for the market." In such a society it would be silly to draw lots for high posts in government, or to discourage school children from learning to compete. And in fact, we do neither of these things. Our political and educational institutions are integrated with our economic institution: men compete for high political office; children are taught to compete for grades, for athletic honors, for fraternity bids, for scholastic prizes. While there is not a perfect meshing of values (it is sometimes bad taste to compete, as for the last piece of candy in the box), our institutions, in general, like those of any other going society, are so integrated that the norms of one institution support those of another.

SANCTIONS

Sanctions are the rewards or punishments used to establish *social control*—that is, to enforce the norms in a society. Sanctions may be applied in various ways, ranging from the use of physical force to symbolic means, such as flattery. Sanctions are used to force or persuade an individual or group to conform to social expectations.

Informal and Formal Sanctions Sanctions may be either informal or formal. Informal sanctions are illustrated by customs, the mores, and public opinion. The formal sanctions are those worked out by the state through law and administrative devices, those consciously developed within organizations for their own regulation, or those developed between or among organizations to regulate their relations.

When standardized codes of conduct are set down to be managed by special groups and passed on from generation to generation by special agencies, we have the beginning of formal sanctions. In the rise of the political state, formal lawmaking and the invention of writing, which made possible the keeping of records and the preservation of codes, were especially important. In a modern, complex, social-economic society we could not get along without the formal sanctions, because personal, intimate relations have largely been replaced by more impersonal and indirect contacts. For example, in the primary community, barter and direct dealing in produce were possible. Today, in an intricate economic organization, such relations are possible only in a limited way, and all sorts of controls have been evolved to meet the needs of buyers and sellers, of producers and consumers, of merchants, bankers, shippers, manufacturers, farmers, and others who have a part in the complex web of economic life.

It must be borne in mind that the formal and informal aspects of control are intertwined. In respect to the more loosely organized features of community life, the informal tends to outweigh the formal. But in the more highly institutionalized groups, although the informal is not unimportant, the major controls flow through formal channels.

As societies and their cultures become heterogeneous and as secondary groups arise, the whole problem of social control changes. Not only is there increased complexity of interaction, but everywhere there are crosscurrents of warring factions. Employers get at odds with labor unions over hours of work, rates of pay, and conditions of labor. Racial groups conflict with one another over jobs and social standing. Sectarian groups argue theological differences. Professional classes are in competition and conflict: physicians and surgeons against fakirs and magicians. There arises a need to regulate and delimit the expression of these narrower interests. There is always a danger that strong special-interest groups in conflict may disrupt the larger community and so threaten the existence of all its groups.

The application of regulatory or manipulative devices of any sort implies the use of power, the forms and intensity of which may vary greatly. The simplest meaning of power is one's ability to make another do one's bidding. More abstractly, power means the possession of some influence or force that may be used to oblige another to conform to some expectation. The sanctions through which power is exercised may be, as we have noted, either informal or formal, and they may be either physical or psychological. At least four aspects of power must be taken into account: (1) its amount or quantity; (2) its distribution among individuals or groups; (3) the purposes for which it is used; and (4) the means by which it is applied.

Amount of Power In simple interpersonal relations, the *amount* of power depends, in the last analysis, on physical strength. Yet effective relations do not rest entirely on strong muscles. If two men, A and B, are of the same weight and physical strength, neither may dominate or control the other. But if A has a stone or a club or a machine gun or an atom bomb and B has none, the control of A over B is apparent at once. To apply this to the group situation, it is clear that a group which has added mechanical power has tremendous advantages over one which has not. The mastery of the white man over native tribes or that of a highly armed and efficient nation over others less well-equipped are contemporary examples.

Power need not take mechanical form. Men have long used verbal magic, flattery, promises, indoctrination, and other forms of persuasion and suggestion to increase their management of others.[2] Patrice Lumumba once was able to talk his jailers into setting him free!

Distribution of Power Basically, those who can best satisfy the wants of a society will exercise control in that society. Since the physical and psychological wants of men expand faster than the means of fulfilling them, holders of power must exercise constant efforts to manipulate and control other persons. In the most elemental instances of dis-

tribution, to go back to our hypothetical situation of A and B, the one who possesses more force would also be in a position to effect its distribution among persons or groups. In more advanced societies, the distribution of power is correlated variously with such matters as age, sex, skills, knowledge, and class or caste, and with economic, religious, magical, political, esthetic, and other institutionalized features of social life. Of course everyone, no matter how low in the social system, has some degree or power over others in some situations. In our society, the basic distribution of power derives from the political state. At this point all we need to note is that, since power in some amount will always be present (in view of the very nature of man in society), a crucial problem will always be *who* is to have it—that is, how it is to be distributed.

Basic Aim of Sanctions The basic purpose of sanctions is to bring about conformity, solidarity, and continuity of a particular group, community, or larger society. Sanctions may be needed to achieve a balance of power among contending social units, or to deal with the threatened exploitation of a larger body by a smaller. Or deviant individuals who endanger solidarity and continuity may need to be forced into line.[3]

To control behavior means to bring about regular and recurrent actions or responses. Such regulation makes possible the prediction of behavior. We can anticipate what an individual will do or what his punishment will be if he fails to act. For example, a contract en-

2 · For an excellent discussion of power, see Robert Bierstedt, "An Analysis of Social Power," *American Sociological Review*, 1950, 15:730–738.

3 · See Eugene Litwak, "Three Ways in Which Law Acts as a Means of Social Control: Punishment, Therapy, and Education," *Social Forces*, 1956, 34:217–223.

Police Department of New York City

Negative sanctions are imposed on people who violate the mores: patrolman searching two suspects who are being booked.

ables the parties involved to know in advance what to expect and what each party will do. There is no changing of intention from day to day, and the obligation is binding for the time set. Personal whims may be permitted in informal relations, but they have no place in an established order. Furthermore, control, especially by some overall power, makes for equilibrium between warring factions or groups by obliging them to accommodate themselves to one another and to the needs and values of the larger society. Sanctions thus foster solidarity and integration. So too, sanctions make possible continuity. They form a part of the culture that is passed along from generation to generation. Thus each generation gets a pattern of control which keeps the social order running smoothly. If each

generation had to develop its own code, there obviously would be waste of effort.

Yet, in a rapidly changing society like our own, this continuity is disturbed, with the result that new codes have to be developed, often coming into conflict with old ones. New conditions demand new definitions, and behavior often far outruns the forms of control. For example, the present growing sense of insecurity, anonymity, impersonality, and dissociation in the individual in mass society is definitely related to the breakdown of the codes and rules of the more traditional social order.

Types of Sanctions By *types of sanctions* we mean the particular devices which are brought into play by those

Expressions of contempt are negative sanctions.

who have power and who aim at some particular objective. As we have noted, power may take the form of either overt force or manipulation of symbols. As manifestations of power, sanctions extend along a continuum from the most extreme use of force—the death penalty—to such verbal controls as flattery. Sanctions may also be thought of as negative or positive. Sanctions which inflict pain or threaten to do so are negative; those which elicit response by rewards are positive. Moreover, individuals invoking both formal and informal sanctions may employ a wide variety of means. Figure 3 provides a graphic arrangement of the chief sanctions, ranging from linguistic and gestural to those which consist of overt force.

Let us examine the symbolic sanctions first. It is well to recall that the bulk of all social interaction takes the form of words and gestures rather than bodily contact. One can push and shove another or withdraw from him; or strike, bite, punch, or kick him; or fondle, caress, and make love. But the range of interaction possible through talk and writing is enormous. The child soon learns that words are a substitute for overt sanctions. Children and adults also learn that verbal communication often will turn the trick of group regulation without recourse to more direct coercive measures. In most cases it is easy enough to bring about a desired result in behavior by the verbal approach. Overt bodily action we reserve for extreme cases. The sophistication of either an individual or a society is indicated in part by the degree to which it substitutes symbolic for overt sanctions.

So far as results go, the verbal method may be either negative or pos-

itive. That is, some language appeals may be directed toward stopping on-coming or anticipated behavior; other language stimuli may impel action in the desired direction. From the stand-point of the recipient, pleasant and positive verbal methods are chiefly praise, flattery, suggestion and persua-sion, some forms of education, slogans, and propaganda. Negative means are gossip, satire, name-calling, threats, and commands. Let us briefly examine the nature of these devices.

FIGURE 3 · A Classification of the Chief Sanctions

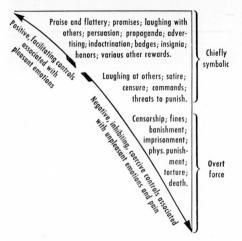

Praise is a reward in words, espe-cially from someone in a higher social stratum. It induces social amenability and conformity. *Flattery* is exaggerated and somewhat false praise, often used for ulterior purposes in dealing with others, especially those in an upper or superior social position. Flattery ap-peals directly to the ego and is a par-ticularly effective weapon in a society dominated by individualism and desire for material goods, though it can be effective in any society where prestige plays a part in control. *Indoctrination,* *advertising*, and *propaganda*, though

often different in motive, all condition persons to act along lines which they like or imagine they like. Individuals come to want to do the things suggested to them. *Persuasion* as a form of sug-gestion plays a part in all three of the above, as well as in less formal situa-tions. *Slogans* help define situations and direct behavior along desired lines. They are the verbal signposts which guide a group toward its objectives.

Closely associated with praise and flattery are rewards, badges, or other tangible objects drawn from a limited supply. *Rewards* are often unexpected benefits—for example, a reward for re-turning a purse one has found. *Badges* are external symbols conferred on offi-cials or on members of a group to desig-nate honor and authority. *Medals* granted for meritorious action not only confer prestige but have a valuable control effect on the recipient and, vicariously, on others. Other material symbols are *uniforms* and *insignia*.

While some *gossip* may be innocu-ous, that related to social control is largely critical in tone. Gossip helps make myths and legends and is effective in formulating public opinion.

Satire, a combination of humor and critical logic put in a sarcastic way, is a highly intellectual and hence distinctly limited means of control. It is a method of exposing the foibles and weaknesses of persons and making them squirm under the verbal lash. It is unpleasant, though the more genial satire may not sting deeply. *Laughing at others* is doubtless one of the oldest sanctions. It bespeaks superiority and is highly effec-tive, since it tends to mark off and isolate its target from his fellows, a very effective punishment. If a person loses his sense of belonging to a group, of participating in common enterprises,

Medals, badges, titles, and acclaim of achievement are positive sanctions:
Junior Achievement Award.

even though he is not bodily removed, he feels lonesome, unattached, and insecure.

Name-calling, or hurling epithets at those whom one dislikes, is an old control device. It is closely bound up with the still-prevalent notion that words have some peculiar magical power of their own to do damage to those against whom they are cast. To call names is also an aid in giving the recipient a lower position: it has the effect of downgrading a person. A "wop" or a "red" is beneath us socially. A "moron" is stupid, and a "Bohemian" is wild. Name-calling is a common device in propaganda.

Commands are a direct verbal form of ordering and forbidding—the oldest means of negative control through words. The command may be a positive order to do something or an inhibitory statement forbidding an action.

Commands represent direct power. They have much more the sense of exterior authority than do satire, laughter at others, or calling names. In our society the most effective commands in secondary groups are those issued by the government, the military, industry, and the church.

Threats are the most severe form of verbal sanctions. Yet to be fully effective they must be backed by physical force or the appearance of power to deny action. If the threat does not inhibit, then the person threatened must be made to suffer injury, pain, or punishment. Threats are distinctive carriers of emotion and accordingly have great potential power. A threat puts but two alternatives before the person threatened: there are only two ways out of the dilemma, and he must choose between them.

Closely related to commands and

Let us help put your family in a home of their own!

Picturing your family in a house is fun . . . but the real pleasure is having a home of your own. Your nearby Insured Savings and Loan Association can help you achieve this goal. Insured Savings and Loan Associations are specialists in home financing and make more home loans than all other financial institutions combined. If buying or building a home is close to your heart, why not act now?

Insured Savings and Loan Associations

©1961 The Savings and Loan Foundation, Inc., 1111 E Street N.W., Washington 4, D.C.

Illustration by the Savings & Loan Foundation

Advertising as a means of social control.

Under Japanese law, a man who has been arrested is allowed to cover his face to hide his shame.

Wide World

threats is <u>censorship</u>, which is also complementary to propaganda. It <u>is a restraint on the expression of opinion</u>, whereas <u>propaganda guides opinion and action along predetermined lines.</u> Censorship is usually a command of someone in authority, often a representative of the government or the church, to stop an expression of fact or opinion. It is often physical, as in burning tabooed books, in which sense it becomes an overt sanction. In fact, it may be considered a combination of the use of external force and symbolic controls.

The method of *overt action* is the final sanction when no other way remains open. This means of control has historically been largely negative and restrictive. It includes fines, imprisonment, whipping, mutilation, torture, banishment, and death. Commands and threats indicate that overt action is imminent, and that is why they are uniquely powerful when they are believed. Control by gross overt action appears in both primary and secondary groups, though in more sophisticated societies the right to inflict severe punishment on the individual is usually reserved by the state.

Sanctions as Norms In closing our discussion of norms and their enforcement, we should note that the sanctions themselves become norms. Spanking a child for behaving disrespectfully toward his mother is not only a negative sanction imposed for the violation of a norm, but is itself a folkway. In other cultures, the behaviors governing such a situation might be very different indeed.

Expressions such as "An eye for an eye and a tooth for a tooth," or "Make the punishment fit the crime" are not simply statements of suggested sanctions; they are reflections of the normative structure of the society.

We have dealt in this chapter with the integration of a society's values through its institutionalized norms and the preservation of the normative order through sanctions. In the next chapter, we turn to an analysis of the impact of society and its cultural values on personality.

INTERPRETATIVE SUMMARY

The written and the tacit rules of a society are called norms. A society's most important rules, such as those governing morality, are called mores. Mores may not be challenged, and defiance of them will elicit severe punishment. Folkways are less important, more flexible norms. An institution is a set of mores and folkways having the common goal of facilitating a particular function of a society.

Although some norms may be violated successfully some of the time, in general norms must be obeyed or a society will not be able to function. Sanctions are the rewards and punishments employed to enforce a society's norms. Everyone in a society has some power over other individuals, though those in the higher social strata and those who are for other reasons best able to satisfy society's needs will of course be most powerful. Sanctions may be informally invoked or codified by law, may be physical or psychological, and positive or negative. Positive sanctions involve ego-bolstering or manipulating of the minds of those who are to be controlled, while negative sanctions involve derision or the threat or actual use of physical and emotional pain. Sanctions themselves become norms when a society decides that a much-used manner of teaching a norm is the "right" way.

REVIEW AND SUGGESTED READINGS

A · VOCABULARY

Ethos	Institution
Folkways	Mores

B · QUESTIONS AND TOPICS FOR REVIEW

1. Which sanctions would probably work best for the following?
   a. neighborhood with one member who won't cut his grass and weeds
   b. substitute teacher with unruly class
   c. college fraternity with one member who won't help build a float for the homecoming celebration
   d. college professor with an average class
   e. journal of political opinion
2. People learn the norms of their society as they grow up. Find some examples of children's lack of understanding of their society's folkways and mores.

3. As is the case with many sociological terms, the terms *folkways* and *mores* are typologies, with reality frequently somewhere between the two. Look on page 66 at the folkways listed as being part of our American economic system. Which are most cherished by our society? How is each enforced?
4. Why has satire lost some power as a sanction in our century?
5. Why is a command called a negative sanction?

C · SUGGESTIONS FOR FURTHER READING

Richard C. Donnelly, Joseph Goldstein, and Richard D. Schwartz. *Criminal Law.* New York: Free Press of Glencoe, 1962.

A sociological approach to legal sanctions, edited by two law professors and a sociologist.

Florence R. Kluckhohn and Fred R. Strodtbeck. *Variations in Value Orientations.* New York: Harper and Row, 1961.

A cross-cultural study of values and norms in five communities in the Southwest. Actually a report on five subcultures.

Robert K. Merton and Robert A. Nisbet, eds. *Contemporary Social Problems.* New York: Harcourt, Brace & World, Inc., 1961.

Papers on patterned deviation by Clausen, Coleman, Gibbs, Greer, and others, organized around the theme that social organization generates tendencies toward deviance and disorganization, as well as toward conformity.

David Riesman. *Individualism Reconsidered.* Glencoe, Ill.: The Free Press, 1954. (Reprinted, Garden City: Doubleday & Co., Inc., 1955.)

In this collection of essays, two are pertinent to the material in this chapter: "Values in Context" and "New Standards for Old: From Conspicuous Consumption to Conspicuous Production."

Gresham M. Sykes. *The Society of Captives.* Princeton, N.J.: Princeton University Press, 1958.

A study of a maximum security prison as an example of the interplay of social forces when the exercise of power nears its extreme in a system of total social control.

William F. Whyte. *Street Corner Society: The Social Structure of an Italian Slum,* rev. ed. Chicago: University of Chicago Press, 1955.

An excellent description and analysis of the behavior of youth in a slum community during the depression of the 1930's. There are good discussions of norms and their supporting sanctions.

William H. Whyte, Jr. *The Organization Man.* New York: Simon and Schuster, Inc., 1956. (Reprinted, Garden City: Doubleday & Co., Inc., 1957.)

A study of the shift in values which is accompanying the bureaucratization of American society. Chapter 2, "The Decline of the Protestant Ethic," is a particularly good analysis of changing social norms.

CHAPTER 6

The Foundations of Personality

Two girls in the dormitory may say of a friend, "Poor Hortense hasn't had a date all semester; she just doesn't have any personality." What they mean, more precisely, is that the personality Hortense has does not conform to the desires and expectations of the men who are asking other girls for dates. A personality is a patterned body of inherited traits, learned habits, attitudes, and ideas as an individual has organized them to meet the daily requirements of social life. Every human being has a personality. When we speak of a "good" or "bad" or of a "strong" or "weak" personality, we are referring to how well a person's patterned habits, traits, attitudes, and ideas equip him to meet the expectations of a given social group.

A long-standing discussion concerns the relative importance of heredity and environment in shaping the personality. At one extreme are those who attribute almost all variation among human personalities to differential heredity: "He has his grandfather's surly attitude toward people"; "they've all been poor and lazy for years—there's bad blood in that family"; "She inherited her mother's instinct for dealing with people." At the opposite pole are those who assume that hereditary differences are so slight that any variations in behavior observed among normal people can only be accounted for as re-

sulting from different environments, social or physical: "He's very restless—got that way from being around such nervous people all the time"; "I'd be a great artist, too, if I'd had the training he has"; "His father made him practice throwing the discus every afternoon—he couldn't help but be a champion." Actually, the evidence does not support either one of these extreme positions.

HEREDITY AND PERSONALITY

Heredity is the transmission of genetic characteristics from parents to their offspring. Hereditary traits, then, are innate; they are present at birth. Obviously, no trait can be both cultural—learned behavior—and hereditary, or inborn. By *environment* we mean those stimuli—forces, situations, and so on—that affect the individual from outside. Environment includes the *physical* world external to the individual: the constant threat of starvation facing someone in an arctic setting might contribute to a personality organization different from that likely on a lush tropical island. The *social* environment also helps mold the personality: a child reared by loving, indulgent parents will probably organize his hereditary impulses and learned ideas into a personality different from that of a child with similar inherited characteristics who

82

grows up in a relatively regimented, impersonal orphanage.

Heredity The essential characteristics inherited by all human beings can be classified as follows:

(1) physical structure (how tall or short one is, whether one has a long or short nose, large or small feet—briefly, how one is put together)

(2) reflexes (direct responses to stimuli, such as withdrawing from a pinprick, blinking when something approaches the eye)

(3) innate drives (impulses to act based on physiological tensions; but these must be linked through learning with activities which will reduce the tensions)

(4) intelligence (the capacity to learn, to modify responses)

(5) temperament (patterned and recurrent responses associated with basic emotional make-up—for example, imperturbability, excitability, or lethargy)

Of the categories above, that of innate drives is probably subject to the greatest misunderstanding. The source of the confusion is the tendency to equate the drive with the activity that reduces the tension. Activity that will reduce tension must be learned. It stems, in other words, from the environment. The innate drive does not need to be learned; one is born with it. The walls of the stomach will contract in a newborn baby; the hunger drive is present. What to do about hunger must be learned, and is hence subject to a certain degree of cultural control. Whether one learns to relish fried chicken or fried crickets depends on the society in which he is reared; either can reduce the hunger drive.

Human beings do have acquired drives, or motives, but these are rooted in social learning, not in heredity. Desires for a college education or for a new car are tensions in the organism as definite as innate drives, but social life, not genes, creates these tensions.

Heredity has a limiting influence on personality development. We see evidence of this in the child whose inherited mental capacity is so restricted as to make it impossible for him to become a fully participating member of society. He simply cannot learn enough to enable him to organize his personality. The limiting nature of heredity is nowhere more dramatically illustrated than in the observations which were made of an ape and a child reared in an American home as if they were brother and sister.

The Story of Gua and Donald In June, 1931, Professor and Mrs. W. N. Kellogg, then at Indiana University, brought into their home a female baby chimpanzee $7\frac{1}{2}$ months old, which they named Gua. Their plan was to rear this ape in company with their own 10-month-old son, Donald.[1] The ape and the child lived in the same household and were exposed to more or less the same daily training and kindly care until March, 1932. The regimen included training in postural and body habits, in walking and feeding, play, and all the other habits which a young child in our American society acquires. There was little punishment in connection with their training, but a persistent effort was made by word and deed on the part

[1] · It would have been a sounder procedure had the ape and the child been reared together from birth. Furthermore, the presence of other children in the family might have modified some of the effects on both the chimpanzee and the child.

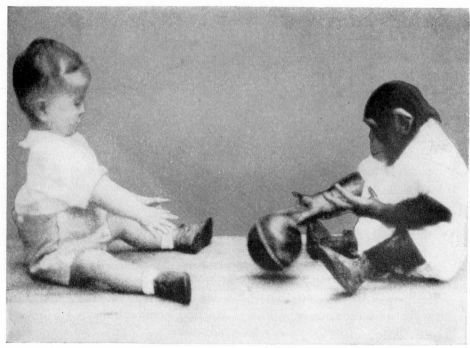

From The Ape and the Child, *W. N. & L. A. Kellogg. By permission.*

Donald and Gua at play.

of the adults to facilitate development. In connection with the daily routine, the Kelloggs made systematic tests, observations, and comparison of Gua's and Donald's capacities, traits, and activities. They measured their physical growth and strength, their hearing, seeing, and other senses, and their social-emotional development; and they put them through a number of critical learning tests involving manual skill, memory, recognition, and language.

A full appreciation of this interesting study can be had only by reading the Kelloggs' book.[2] Here we shall summarize the chief likenesses and differences between child and ape.

While Gua and Donald had similar reflex organization, Gua was more ma-

2 · See W. N. Kellogg and L. A. Kellogg, *The Ape and the Child* (New York: McGraw-Hill Book Co., 1933).

ture than the child in a number of items, such as strength of the grasping and rejecting responses. In motor dexterity the ape was in many ways far superior to the child, especially in climbing, in pulling open drawers, and in escaping danger. At $7\frac{1}{2}$ months the ape easily climbed into a high chair; the child was $18\frac{1}{2}$ months before he could do so. Gua learned to walk erect on her hind feet some time before Donald managed walking alone; she learned early to run and to skip, whereas Donald did not learn to skip during this period.

In our society, the fundamental training in habits of elimination ordinarily begins toward the end of the first year, and both ape and child were put on regular schedules shortly after Gua's arrival. From the outset the child was superior to the ape in bladder control.

This was probably due in part to the fact that the water intake of the ape was much larger, so that her frequency of urination was about one-third greater than the child's. In bowel control the child was at first superior to the ape, but the latter—after four months—equalled the child's record of success, even though the ape eliminated from four to seven times in 24 hours, whereas the child's usual reaction was but twice in the same span.

In a number of sensory-perceptual responses, also, the ape and the child were much alike. Both reacted vigorously to tickling, and the observers reported not only smiling on the part of the ape but a whimpering sound which they termed laughter. Gua, however, disliked too-bright illumination, had remarkable visual acuity, and was much more responsive to noises—slight or loud—than the boy.

At play the ape and child were much alike in handling, biting, and exploring their toys. From the outset, however, Donald showed more interest in examining and manipulating things in the environment. At first their play was of the solitary sort, but later simple social games and mutual examination and exploration began. Both were intrigued by the face; they tried kissing and tactile interplay. They became quite protective of each other, holding on to each other, for instance, while riding in a play wagon.

Yet significant differences were early apparent. Gua never got accustomed to older children or to strange adults. In contrast, as Donald grew older he showed increased concern with both children and grownups in the neighborhood. One of the most telling reactions was the growing intensity of the emotional dependence of the ape on Professor and Mrs. Kellogg. She ran to them when frightened, and from the beginning showed much stronger fear responses than the child. As time went on, Gua revealed increasing anxiety whenever they left the house without her. Jealousy also was more evident in Gua than in Donald. Her craving for affection and attention from others was much stronger. Donald at 15 months showed distinct bashfulness—an evidence of emerging sense of self. Gua never did reveal such an attitude.

To test their intelligence, a large number of the Gesell infant tests were used. In many of these the ape showed a more rapid rate of learning. In many rudimentary memory tests the ape was superior to the child, but in matters requiring minute manual dexterity, the ape was inferior. In age of walking erect and alone and in showing interest in its own reflection in the mirror, the ape was superior. Gua learned to eat with a spoon at 13 months, a habit Donald did not acquire until he was $17\frac{1}{2}$ months old. The ape also managed to drink from a glass at an earlier age, and she was more successful in using a toy to get at objects placed behind an obstruction. Yet, taking all the Gesell tests together, the learning of the two was closely parallel.

In vocal communication and the beginning of higher mental powers as seen in the beginnings of language, the child was clearly superior. Both soon learned to follow correctly all sorts of vocal commands to perform simple motor tasks, and Gua early showed great sensitiveness to vocal indications of approval or disapproval from adults. Surprisingly enough, the ape was at first more correctly responsive to human commands than was the child. She learned to comprehend simple verbal responses by pointing to a picture of a dog on the command "Show me a bow-wow," and she learned to utter certain distinctive bark-like sounds to indicate "Yes" when asked "Do you want an orange?" Later the child surpassed the ape in verbal comprehension.

However, in spite of nine months of living with human beings and being exposed to kindly and patient teaching, *Gua never acquired a single human word.* That is, she could not use names for objects. Donald, on the contrary, before the first year began using words for objects. He called Gua "Gya" and acquired the usual vocabulary and simple sentences for a child of his age. There is little doubt that, had the ape remained in the Kellogg home, her human companion would soon have outstripped her in acquiring the essential habits of communication and conduct which so sharply distinguish the *Homo sapiens* from the anthropoid. These involve such characteristics as true language and the use of concepts, memory expressed in symbolic form, the skilled use of tools and other material objects, and, above all else, the self-image which plays such an important part in human personality.

ENVIRONMENT AND PERSONALITY

The comparison of Gua with Donald exemplifies how no amount of training can overcome the limitations imposed by heredity on mental capacity. We know too, however, that inherited capacity alone cannot produce a human personality. No matter how impressive the capacities an individual may inherit, he can learn ideas and attitudes and organize them into a personality only by learning the content of culture from his

society. Just how essential the social environment is to the development of personality can be seen in the records of children kept in almost total isolation. In the words of one writer, these show "what happens when the social environment of a child approaches zero." [3]

Folk tales and history provide accounts of individuals reared by animals. These range from the alleged founders of Rome, Romulus and Remus, to the much-publicized Amala and Kamala, the "wolf children" of India.[4] In recent years some more carefully authenticated instances of isolation of young children have been reported. We shall review two of these.

The Case of Anna On February 6, 1938, the *New York Times* carried a story of a child aged 5 who had been confined in an attic room of a farmhouse in Pennsylvania for nearly the whole of her life. She lacked any of the ordinary traits of a child of her age. She was removed to a county old-folks home and then to a foster home. Later she was placed in a private school for defectives. She died on August 6, 1942. The following summary is based on a variety of observations made by experts.

Anna was the second of two illegitimate children of a young woman in her twenties. After six months of being moved from place to place, she was brought into the household of her mother's parents. Because of the anger and aversion of the maternal grand-

3 · Francis N. Maxfield, "What Happens When the Social Environment of a Child Approaches Zero," unpublished manuscript, quoted in Kingsley Davis, *Human Society* (New York: The Macmillan Company, 1948), p. 206.

4 · For a summary account of feral (undomesticated, wild) man, see J. A. L. Singh and R. M. Zingg, *Wolf Children and Feral Man* (New York: Harper & Brothers, 1942)

father, Anna was hidden away in an upper room. She was fed almost entirely on a milk diet; she was not bathed, trained in any personal habits, or caressed or given any but the scantiest attention. She spent most of her time in a crib or half-reclining, half-sitting in a chair tilted and braced against a coal bucket.

Observations made at the county home and later in the foster home show some of the effects of such extreme isolation. At first Anna reclined in a supine position, immobile, indifferent to those around her, and completely apathetic. She appeared to be deaf and dumb. Her social contacts were either purely perfunctory or "openly antagonistic." As a result of a sound diet and massages, her physical condition improved rapidly. Gradually she began to develop some mental and social traits normal for very young children. She acquired visual discrimination as to color and improved in posture and motor co-ordination, including the ability to chew food. Yet after four months she had not learned to speak. By the end of six months, however, she began to walk. In time she learned to control her elimination. She also gradually showed interest in the people around her.

After nine months in the county home, she was placed in the care of kindly and understanding foster parents. Within a month following this, definite progress was evident.

In August, 1939, she was placed in a private school for defectives. Although she could now walk, could feed herself, was fairly neat, and could recall people and understand simple commands, she could not speak. She had, in general, the mental and behavioral characteristics of a child under two years of age.

Even two months after her arrival at the special school, she had not learned any words. Five months later, in April, 1940, a clinical psychologist reported that she was large for her age, normal in hearing and vision, now able to climb stairs, and had reached the "babbling stage" of speech reactions, with some promise of further linguistic development. On the Merrill-Palmer scale she had a mental score of 19 months; on the Vineland Social Maturity scale, a score of 23 months.

On July 1, 1941, the school reported that she had grown in height and weight, could bounce and catch a ball, and had made progress in adjustment to group life with other children. Finally, she had begun to talk. The report concluded that "there was nothing peculiar about her except that she was feeble-minded—'probably congenital in type.'" [5] Two months before her death, another report indicated further progress. She could talk, mainly in phrases, and would repeat words and try to carry on a conversation. She was tidy in her personal habits; walked and ran fairly well; and, while somewhat excitable, was good-natured.

It is evident that the child's development was adversely affected by isolation. But her failure to make much headway after she was placed in more normal social circumstances does raise the question as to whether or not she was feeble-minded. Before taking up this and related matters about her case, let us pause to see what happened to Isabelle.

The Case of Isabelle Isabelle was about Anna's age and was also an illegitimate child who had been kept away

5 · Davies, *Human Society*, p. 134.

from society. She was found in November, 1938, in Ohio, nine months after Anna was discovered. Her mother was a deaf-mute who, with her child, had been secluded in a dark room away from the rest of the family. Isabelle was removed from this environment and placed in the hands of child specialists. The essential facts of her story are these:

When found at six years of age, Isabelle was rachitic, probably from improper diet and lack of sunshine. She could not speak but made certain croaking sounds. Her communication with her mother had been by simple gestures. Her reaction toward strangers, especially men, was almost that of a wild animal, revealing much fear and hostility. At first it was thought that she was deaf. Later, when it was found that she could hear, she was given various intelligence tests and pronounced feeble-minded. Her first score on the Stanford-Binet was 19 months, practically a zero point on the scale. On the Vineland Social Maturity scale her initial score was 39—an age level of $2\frac{1}{2}$ years.

The individuals who had taken charge of Isabelle began a systematic program of training, beginning with pantomime and dramatization. Within a week Isabelle progressed to her first try at verbalization. From a slow start, she picked up speed in her rate of learning and in a few weeks passed through the usual stages of learning for a normal child from ages one to six years. That is, within two years she acquired knowledge and skills that ordinarily take six years to attain.

Kingsley Davis, who reported this case as well as that of Anna, says that Isabelle at age fourteen was in the sixth grade and doing well both in her schoolwork and in her social-emotional adjustment to her classmates.[6]

Interaction of Heredity and Environment

We have looked at Gua, a case of hereditary limitations on the ability to learn from the social environment, and at Anna and Isabelle, who had not developed their innate capacities because of lack of contact with the social environment. What can we conclude about the relationship between heredity and environment? It is clear that heredity is not some factor acting independently of environment, but that the genes are organic chemical agents which determine the appearance of various traits, some of which may be profoundly altered after birth, while others, like eye color, hair color, skin color, and facial features, vary little or not at all. The essential point is that he-redity is not just a force which determines skin color or the presence or absence of any given trait. Rather, it helps determine *"the way an individual reacts in various environments."*[7]

On the other hand, it is difficult to overemphasize the part environment plays in the development of an individual. Even in the period of embryonic and foetal growth, environmental factors within the womb are important—pressures, temperature, gravity, and chemical influences playing a part. There is no evidence that the ideas and attitudes of the mother during pregnancy will carry over to the foetus, as

6 · The material on Anna and Isabelle is from Kingsley Davis' two articles: "Extreme Isolation of a Child," *American Journal of Sociology*, 1940, 45:554–565, and "Final Note on a Case of Extreme Isolation," *American Journal of Sociology*, 1947, 52:432–437.

7 · From L. D. Dunn and Th. Dobzhansky, *Heredity, Race and Society* (New York: Penguin Books, 1946), p. 17. Italics added.

the superstitious believe, but the physiological environment of the womb is certainly important in development. After birth, external physical and social-cultural factors come more and more into play. Hence we must realize that the individual is the joint product of heredity and environment.

The studies of Donald and Gua, Anna, and Isabelle indicate the importance of inherited capacity in the development of the organism. But they show, too, that learning lies within a frame of social contact. Anna and Isabelle each had a capacity to learn. Certainly they were physically like other human beings. Yet neither developed full human traits in the absence of human contacts. As for Gua, who was clearly a normal ape so far as learning ability goes, after more than nine months of constant exposure to human society and culture, she failed to develop the distinctive traits of a human being.

Apparently much of Gua's adaptation was due to the fact that biologically the ape is prepared for a fairly complex social life. She learned from human society up to a certain point. Anna and Isabelle, though having some differences in potential intelligence, had no adequate stimulation to develop their capacities. In other words, *nature* put a limit on Gua's mental and social-emotional growth, and *environment* blocked that of the girls. Anna and Isabelle had the potentialities to acquire culture but failed to do so because they were not given an opportunity.

MATURATION AND SOCIALIZATION

Let us now examine the processes through which heredity and environment interact to shape personality.

Maturation   Maturation involves changes in the tissues and organs of the body which take place as the individual gets older and which occur without learning or conscious effort. Since they need not be learned and do not depend on the environment for initiation, these changes can be considered a part of heredity. They are predetermined because the individual is a member of the human species.

The differences which began to appear between Donald and Gua during their final months together were the result of maturation. Gua did not develop the ability to speak, and no amount of training would give her this neuromuscular capacity because she did not inherit the equipment. Donald did not learn to walk until the maturation process had made him ready to learn his skill. Isabelle learned in two years what it takes most children six years to acquire because adequate maturation had taken place. Despite the fact that, as an isolated child, she had not been exposed to the opportunities to learn many things, her body had been growing and developing. When the opportunity arose for her to learn, she did not have to wait for maturation in order to be able to do so.

Socialization   As we have learned, the process of inducting the individual into the social world is called *socialization*. It consists of teaching the person the culture which he must acquire and share, of making him a participating member in society and its various groups, and of persuading him to accept the norms of his society. Socialization is a matter of learning, not of biological inheritance. In the socialization process the individual learns the folkways, mores, sanctions, and other pat-

Elders teach culture patterns to the next generation: old man teaches folklore to children in the Blue Ridge Mountains.

Monkmeyer

terns of the culture, as well as the skills, ranging from language to manual dexterity, which will enable him to become a participating member of society.

All that the individual must learn he learns from other members of the society: consciously, from being told what to do by his parents, brothers and sisters, friends, or teachers; or unconsciously, by picking up incidental information while observing other people, reading books, watching television, or hearing people discuss the behavior of others. In all these situations, the learning is social. The whole process of socialization falls within the scope of interaction. It is within the structure of the human group that the individual acquires culture.

Forms of Social Learning There are two types of social learning. The first, called cultural conditioning, is the process by which the individual learns the fundamental culture patterns of the society in which he will live. Through cultural conditioning one learns to walk, talk, handle social obligations, develop the attitudes approved by the society regarding religion, sex, older people, work, recreation, social control, and anything else governed by social norms. For example, cultural conditioning teaches a child to defer to those in positions of power and to dominate children younger and smaller than he is.

Cultural learning is not all there is to socialization, however. In learning to live in society the individual invari-

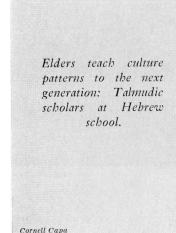

Elders teach culture patterns to the next generation: Talmudic scholars at Hebrew school.

Cornell Capa

ably has social experiences which influence his personality without influencing anybody else's. Obviously, behavior so acquired is socially learned; it is one result of the socialization process. It is not, however, a shared pattern, and hence cannot be considered cultural. Such socialization is called *personal-social learning.*

Personal-social learning is probably best seen in an extreme example. A small girl who is badly frightened by a red-headed man may always fear red-headed men. She has learned this in interaction, but it is not part of American culture to fear red-headed men. This cannot, therefore, be considered cultural conditioning; it is personal-social learning.

Socialization and the Personality The case histories of Anna and Isabelle show that, with virtually no socialization, there developed nothing we can call personality. That is, there is no organized body of traits, habits, attitudes, and ideas without social learning.

Another question of interest to the student of personality is this: Given similar inherited capacity in two persons and assuming no interference with the process of maturation, how much difference is there likely to be between them if they are socialized differently? In other words, to what extent will different experiences in social learning mold different personalities from the same raw materials?

In this connection, studies of iden-

Learning through imitation.

tical twins are most enlightening. Since identical twins come from the same fertilized egg, they are presumed to possess identical genes. The following brief summaries of six pairs of identical twins socialized in quite different surroundings illustrate some of the important findings:

Case I A pair of twin young women, one with very much more formal education than the other but the other with a much more varied social experience. After twenty-odd years of separation, they were practically identical physically and in intelligence, but were extremely different in temperament—in personality.

Case II A pair of twin young women, one reared in London, England, and the other in a small Ontario town. They had about the same amount and kind of education. When tested, the Canadian girl was very much more intelligent and in much better physical condition. In temperament-personality they were extremely similar.

Case III Two twin young women, separated over twenty years, reared in about the same social and physical conditions, but one with far more education than the other. Physically and temperamentally they were extraordinarily similar, but the more educated twin was strikingly more intelligent.

Case IV Two twin young men, separated over twenty years, one reared in cities of some size, the other reared in country villages, both with high-school education. The city boy was in much better physical condition and was slightly more intelligent. In temperament-personality they were as different as two persons chosen at random.

Case V Two twin girls, separated

for twenty-eight years but visiting each other from time to time. One had always lived on a farm; the other had lived in a small town and had spent most of her time indoors. The farm girl stopped school after the grades; the town girl went through high school and studied music for 20 years. These girls differed equally strongly in all three respects: physically, intellectually, and temperamentally. They showed the most pronounced effects of environmental differences of all of the pairs studied.

Case VI Twin girls, separated for thirty-seven years, both having almost a high-school education, both married and with four and six children respectively. One married a man who had always made a good deal of money; the other married a poor man. The life of one was easy, that of the other very hard. There was very little difference between them in IQ, only minor differences in temperament, but a very striking difference in physical condition. The twin who had an easy life seemed hardly over thirty, while the one who had a hard life seemed eight or ten years older.[8]

It is clear from these cases, as it is from similar data, that there is just about as much deviation in identical twins reared apart as among nonrelated members of the population.

Studies of foster children also confirm this relationship between socialization and personality development. The intelligence, social-emotional traits, and attitudes of foster children reflect their training at the hands of the foster parents, particularly when the chil-

dren are placed under foster care at an early age.[9]

ORIGIN OF THE SELF IN INTERACTION

For the infant at birth there is no distinction between self and not-self. This distinction has to be learned. There is no self prior to interaction. The self is social, and arises out of interaction with an awareness of others.

To develop a sense of self, the individual must learn to view himself as an object. He must, in popular parlance, "see himself as others see him." For example, learning to conform to the demands of others involves learning the distinction between those others, or potential need-satisfiers, and the self, whose needs must be met. From such beginnings the sense of selfhood emerges. Shortly after he is born, an infant is aware only of innate drives. His stomach contracts; he cries. His skin is pierced by a sharp object on the edge of his bed; he withdraws. Soon he learns to notice other people, and to expect certain things from them. The approach of someone to his bed may mean the disturbing process of diaper-changing, and he cries.

The Rise of the Self in Interaction It is only when he perceives that others expect certain behaviors from him and learns to act as he thinks they want him to act that the person develops a social self. When a child knocks over a vase and has learned to say to himself some-

8 · H. H. Newman, "Identical Twins," *Scientific Monthly*, 1932, 34:171. By permission. See also H. H. Newman, *Multiple Human Births* (New York: Doubleday & Co., Inc., 1940).

9 · For a thorough review and comment on studies of twins and foster children, see Robert S. Woodworth, "Heredity and Environment: A Critical Survey of Recently Published Material on Twins and Foster Children," Social Science Research Council, *Bulletin*, No. 47 (New York: Social Science Research Council, 1941).

thing like, "Mother will think I should be sorry; I'll apologize," he is becoming a self. This is <u>the major process in the emergence of human personality.</u>[10] <u>The development of the sense of self</u> enables one to take a place in a social structure, to learn cultural behaviors, to expect positive sanctions when he conforms and negative ones when he deviates, to become a socialized, fully participating member of society.

The child's learning to act as others anticipate he will act is the process of socialization. The process is mostly unconscious—the child finds it fascinating to try out new roles while, unknown to him, some of these roles become reorganized into his own system.

Specific Role-taking One of the fundamental processes that come into play during socialization is identification, which is a learned reaction. In identification, the act of one person serves as the stimulus for another, whose response is similar to the stimulating act of the first person. Identification makes it possible for one person to take over or accept ideas, attitudes, or habits of another. Psychologically this mechanism depends on imagination—on the capacity to develop within the internal subjective world the image of another. Identification is the key process in imitation. It is the basis of sympathy, and mixed in it are large elements of the emotion of love.

The process of identification or imitation may be regarded as a form of role-taking or "role practice," as R. R. Sears calls it.[11] The mother or some other adult serves as a model whom the child imitates. Thus he may play the role of the mother, assuming her voice, gestures, attitudes, and actions. At another time he may identify with his father, an uncle, or a neighbor. Moreover, in this process of interaction the mother or others come to expect or anticipate the child's taking certain roles and not others.

In this manner the child associates his own actions with the demands or responses of others, thereby building up habits and attitudes or roles concerning what he should do in their presence. C. H. Cooley referred to this as "the reflected looking-glass self." [12] <u>The self arises when the individual takes the view and action toward his own act and thoughts which he learns or infers that others take toward them.</u> Put otherwise, the sense of selfhood develops out of social interaction at that point where the individual is capable of considering his whole congeries of habits, thoughts, feelings, and emotions as an *object* to himself.

The Integration of the Self The generalized sense of self is really the organization of generalized attitudes, traits, and ideas which become co-ordinated into the total sense of selfhood. In time the various specific roles of the child begin to get organized or inte-

10 · It is this interactional component that Baldwin was alluding to in his reference to the development of self-feeling as the "dialectic of personal growth." See J. M. Baldwin, *Mental Development in the Child and Race*, 1895, rev. ed., 1906 (New York: The Macmillan Company) and *Social and Ethical Interpretations in Mental Development*, 1897, rev. ed., 1906 (New York: The Macmillan Company).

11 · R. R. Sears, Eleanor E. Maccoby, and Harry Levin, *Patterns of Child Rearing* (Evanston, Ill.: Row, Peterson & Company, 1957), pp. 369–376.
12 · See C. H. Cooley, *Human Nature and the Social Order* (New York: Charles Scribner's Sons, 1902). This book provides one of the important descriptions and interpretations of the social-cultural origin of the self.

grated into larger patterns of response. That is, out of a wide range of specific roles of "others" which he has played, there emerges a generalized and more or less total role of the child. The child assumes this role in all areas of his life—play, school, family. Later he will be pupil, comrade, industrial worker, religious participant, voter, and the like, carrying into his new roles certain elements of the first roles.

Any social group or the larger community which gives the individual his unity of self may be called "the generalized other." The "generalized other" is as broad as the child's contacts.

Most people have a more or less integrated central self and a series of partially deviant selves that serve them in adapting to varied situations.[13] In any case, it is the generalized self that makes possible consistency, continuity, and hence predictability of behavior in an individual. The uniformities of needs, situations, and cultural expectancies all operate together to produce some sort of unity in the personality. What the moralists call "character" illustrates the matter. Honesty, truthfulness, integrity, dependability, fidelity, and all the other virtues are but traits of a certain ideal person who is consistent and predictable in his interactions with his fellows.

The integration of the personality is made possible by the relation of the individual to persons and symbols of the in-group and the out-group. We can love our fellow members of the in-group and co-operate with them, and at the same time despise and be hostile toward members of the out-group.

Society supports integration of the personality by permitting certain impractical or even antisocial traits to be indulged on occasion. Thus, for example, a person need not forever inhibit all his aggressive and destructive impulses, risking that these impulses will become more insistent and "take over" his personality. Certain groups—comradeship or congeniality groups, criminal gangs, religious cults fostering intense emotionalism, or mobs—may afford the individual a chance to express his elementary personal desires rather fully. The hostility to the out-group, the hatred and even physical violence permitted with moral approval of the in-group, afford one an opportunity to express aggressive impulses. This is exactly what intense conflict does for us. War, labor-employer disputes, religious controversy, even sports—all afford an opportunity to strike a balance between two otherwise opposite tendencies within us. Figure 4 shows how an individual can indulge conflicting impulses in primary and secondary groups and still maintain a reasonably integrated, efficiently functioning personality.

In contrast, pathological dissociation, as in split personality, occurs when a segmented organization of roles—that is, separately co-ordinated ideas, habits and attitudes—come to dominate the organism.[14] As Mead puts it, dissociation "is a process of setting up two sorts

---

13 · On the whole topic of the rise of the self, see G. H. Mead, *Mind, Self, and Society* (Chicago: University of Chicago Press, 1934). The literature on dissociated personalities is enlightening, since it gives us some clue to the wide range of potential self-organization. Most of us probably possess potentialities for quite different selves from those we expose to our fellows under ordinary circumstances. On this topic consult Kimball Young, *Personality and Problems of Adjustment*, 2nd ed. (New York: Appleton-Century-Crofts, Inc., 1952), pp. 174–178.

14 · For a review of the important known cases of dissociation, see William Taylor and M. Martin, "Multiple Personality," *Journal of Abnormal & Social Psychology*, 1944, 39:281–300.

of communication which separate the behavior of the individual." [15] It is clear that dissociation is linked to the processes of memory and forgetting, and

15 · George H. Mead, *Mind, Self, and Society* (Chicago: University of Chicago Press, 1934), p. 143. By permission.

Mead, like James, emphasizes time and again the high importance of memory as fundamental to the continuity and consistency of role-taking. Dissociation is also characterized by a breakdown of the inhibition discussed above as necessary to group living.

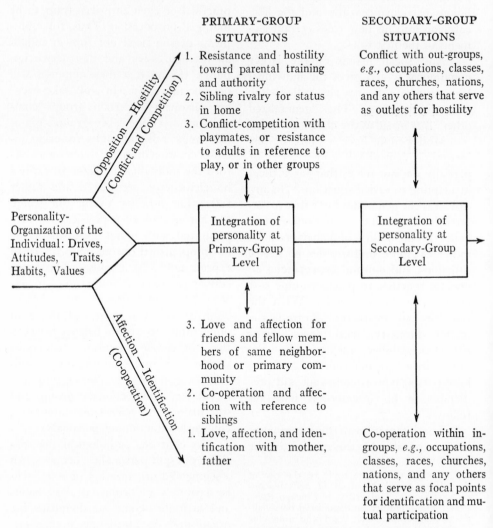

FIGURE 4 · Social Groups, Social Processes, and Integration of the Personality

INTERPRETATIVE SUMMARY

Numerous studies have shown that personality is a product of both heredity and environment. Research has basically been of two types: studies of individuals with widely different heredities who were reared together or in similar environments, and studies of individuals with identical or similar hereditary make-up who were reared in different environments. In all studies, both heredity and environment were seen to have a limiting effect on intelligence, temperament, and physical condition.

Personality is developed through the process of socialization. In the early months of life, the maturing child learns that he is an entity. From this point on he will be avid to learn the attitudes and skills he will need in order to exist in his society. To this extent his personality will be similar to everyone else's. At the same time, however, his social experiences will lead him to develop certain opinions and patterns of behavior which set him off from other individuals. He will undoubtedly experiment with entire roles, discarding parts of roles as inimical to his idea of self and retaining others. Desires which conflict with his self-image and with what he thinks others expect of him will be inhibited or channeled into socially acceptable outlets; his personality will be integrated. The entire process of developing an integrated personality will be largely unconscious.

REVIEW AND SUGGESTED READINGS

A · VOCABULARY

Cultural learning	Personality	Integration
Dissociation	Personal-social learning	Maturation
Drive	Environment	Socialization
Emotion	Heredity	Social self

B · QUESTIONS AND TOPICS FOR REVIEW

1. Which of the inherited traits show the widest range of variation among individuals?
2. In Case VI involving identical twins (page 93), what factors might account for the fact that after thirty-seven years of separation the girls did not differ markedly in temperament and IQ?
3. Which sociological or psychological concepts are involved in the following?
   a. An author writes a novel having the theme that man is inherently evil.
   b. A mother spanks her year-old child who won't respond to toilet-training.
   c. A young man writes, "The very rich are different from you and me."
   d. A newcomer to a big city learns he can't contact the mayor just by telephoning him.
   e. A college student is impressed and influenced by some words he reads: "Work, for the night will come in which no man worketh."
   f. A nine-year-old buys a Coke in a coffee shop and leaves a ten-cent tip.
   g. A child sees a white man contemptuously call a Negro "boy," sees the pain on the Negro's face, and decides *he* will never act that way.
4. At about what age does role-playing as a conscious game generally stop? Why?
5. A man in an airplane has a sudden impulse to jump out. Is he "normal"?

6. Name some impulses which "integrated" personalities usually submerge. How many of these impulses are associated with feelings of hostility or craving for affection?

C · SUGGESTIONS FOR FURTHER READING

G. W. Allport, *Pattern and Growth of Personality.* New York: Holt, Rinehart and Winston, 1961.

Personality viewed as characteristically organized to promote intra-individual consistency and patterning. Little about the place of social interaction in personality growth and functioning.

Erving Goffman, *The Presentation of Self in Everyday Life.* Garden City, N.Y.: Doubleday & Co., 1959.

A provocative description analysis of social interaction, with considerable attention to the function of role expectation and role performance.

George C. Homans, *Social Behavior—Its Elementary Forms.* New York: Harper & Brothers, 1961.

An incisive discussion of personality, with some attention to social and cultural factors as they bear on its development and function.

M. R. Jones, ed. *Nebraska Symposium on Motivation.* Lincoln: University of Nebraska Press, 1960.

A collection of rather technical papers on various facets of motivation by competent psychologists.

Weston La Barre. *The Human Animal.* Chicago: University of Chicago Press, 1954.

A witty and sound presentation of the interplay of man's biological make-up and his cultural environment.

Gardner Lindzey, ed. *Handbook of Social Psychology.* Reading, Mass.: Addison-Wesley Publishing Co., 1954.

From volume 2, Chapter 16, "Social Motivation," by Gardner Murphy and Chapter 18, "Socialization," by Irvin L. Child, are excellent reviews of the literature on these two topics, both important in the discussion of personality.

David C. McClelland, ed. *Studies in Motivation.* New York: Appleton-Century-Crofts, Inc., 1955.

A series of papers which provide wide coverage of the topic. Considerable attention is given to cross-cultural materials.

Robert R. Sears, Eleanor E. Maccoby, and Harry Levin. *Patterns of Child Rearing.* Evanston, Ill.: Row, Peterson & Company, 1957.

An analysis of data collected through interviews of 379 American mothers on how they reared their children from birth to kindergarten age.

Neil J. Smelser and William T. Smelser, eds. *Personality and Social Systems.* New York: John Wiley & Sons, 1963.

Selected articles, both theoretical and empirical, showing the interplay of personality and environment.

Chalmers L. Stacey and Manfred F. DeMartino, eds. *Understanding Human Motivation.* Cleveland: Howard Allen, Inc., 1958.

A wide selection of papers on motivation and such related topics as ego-formation, frustration and aggression, and perception.

Maurice Stein, Arthur J. Vidich, and David M. White, eds. *Identity and Anxiety, Survival of the Person in Mass Society*. New York: The Free Press of Glencoe, 1960.

A collection of forty-two papers the basic aim of which is to explore "the threats to authentic identity" in mass society; also has material on the potentials of developing "personal styles" in the contemporary world.

Allen Wheelis. *The Quest for Identity*. New York: W. W. Norton & Company, Inc., 1958.

An insightful discussion of the significance for personality of the vast changes in our way of life: technological and ideological.

John W. M. Whiting and Irvin L. Child. *Child Training and Personality: A Cross-Cultural Study*. New Haven: Yale University Press, 1953.

The authors have made comparison among a wide range of nonliterate peoples with regard to such matters as socialization, fixation, and the origins of fear and guilt.

CHAPTER 7

Universal Social Structures
and Functions

All societies have certain basic survival tasks in common. We should be able to pinpoint these universal functions if we are careful to distinguish tasks that are really basic from those that are culturally defined. We must be even more careful in naming universal social structures, since societies have many ways of meeting their needs. However, if we use the universal functions, the tasks necessary to any society, as guides, we ought not to be surprised to find that each society has *some* structure with which to meet each of the basic needs; to this extent we can generalize. A family may be monogamous or polygamous; a government may be democratic or totalitarian; an economy may be capitalist or socialist. The nature of these specific structures varies from society to society, but there will always be some structures performing the functions, because the functions are universal.

Therefore, we shall discuss first the functions that must be performed by a society if it is to continue, and then the structures that carry out these functions.[1]

1 · There are several good discussions of universal structures and functions. Two of the best are from Davis, who calls them "societal necessities," and Bennett and Tumin, who refer to them as "functional prerequisites of continuous social life." See Kingsley Davis, *Human Society* (New York: The Macmillan Company, 1949), pp. 28–31; and John W. Bennett and Melvin M. Tumin, *Social Life*

UNIVERSAL SOCIAL FUNCTIONS

In every human society, some set of social structures must be organized to provide five functions necessary for survival: (1) replacement of population, (2) socialization of new population, (3) maintenance of a sense of purpose, (4) production and distribution of goods and services, and (5) preservation of order. Some sociologists consider as basic functions also such things as provision of nutriment or maintenance of biologic adequacy, but since these matters are not strictly *social* in the same sense as the functions listed above, we shall not treat them here.

Replacement of Population Sexual reproduction is not, it is true, the only method of bringing new members into a society. Annexation, the acquisition of slaves, and immigration are means of recruiting people. (Each of these three modes of population expansion has occurred in the United States during its history.) Theoretically, it would be possible for a society to fill the positions of its dying members by recruiting replacements in one or more of these three ways from people born into other societies. The practical difficulty lies

(New York: Alfred A. Knopf, Inc., 1949), pp. 41–59.

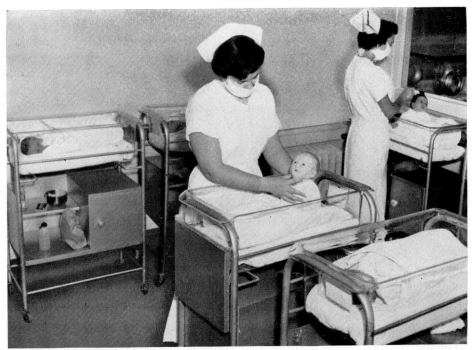

Courtesy Mountainside Hospital, Montclair, N.J.

Every society has some responsibility for replacement of population: one standard procedure.

less in the recruitment than in the knowledge and loyalty required to maintain the social order. Teaching new members the basic cultural values and norms of a society is a task most readily accomplished when those new members are born into the society. Being entirely dependent for their survival on the adults in their primary group, small children are much more easily socialized into the accepted behaviors and attitudes than are adult immigrants or captives. American Indians, aware of this fact, in the days of frontier warfare ordinarily took captive for induction into their society only young children, seldom adults.

For the bulk of its new members, therefore, generation after generation, a society depends primarily on sexual reproduction.

It is generally believed that reproductive behavior is merely a natural biological phenomenon. Actually, the behavior patterns of human beings as they propagate their kind, like their behavior in any other area of social life, are shaped and modified by the culture through which they have been socialized. The basic act of procreation is influenced by the norms of the society concerning size of family, form of marriage, whether the sex act itself is considered exalted or shameful, age at which people marry, and economic obligations parents are expected to fulfill toward their children. There is no society which does not have a set of norms governing reproduction. Every culture contains some set of prohibitions, expectations, and rewards having to do with who should have children and the circumstances under which reproduction should occur.

The cultural values patterned around reproduction are enforced by both positive and negative sanctions. For example, we are critical of people whose families are notably larger than the norm, who "breed like animals," or who "just had another child and can't support the ones they have now." But we esteem people who, able to afford families, have them and hence have met their responsibility to society: "They gave two sons to the Church"; "The Bells had four boys in service during the war." There is a definite feeling in American society that married couples are obligated to have children; people can be heard to speak disapprovingly of a couple with a big house and plenty of money who are "too selfish to have a family."

The emphasis societies place on the reproductive function and the elaborate cultural regulations with which they surround it can be related to the historical circumstances wherein the likelihood of survival for any group or tribe was directly related to the size of the society. When physical safety depended on the number of able-bodied warriors a tribe or nation could put into the field, every additional child was important in the struggle for power. Although modern technology has resulted in many more variables in the balance of power between nation-states, the number of persons who can be mustered for a military organization or for military production is still an important element in a society's international position. So too, size of population is a significant economic consideration. Mass production depends on a mass market; a larger population means more consumers.

Socialization of New Population In any on-going society there must be some structure which has as its function or consequence the teaching of new members. Merely having replacements is not sufficient; the replacements must learn the culture of the society. They must be taught the basic values, or ethos, around which the normative system is organized. They must learn all the thousands of little behavior patterns that are accepted as normal in the society where they are born: what to eat, how to eat it, where to eat it, when to eat it; what to wear, how to wear it, where to wear it, when to wear it; what to say, how to say it; and so on. Each new member must develop, sooner or later, a sense of self. He must learn to curb his own desires when they interfere with the reasonable expectations of others. He must, in short, adjust to social living.

It would be difficult to overstress how essential this function of socialization is to the continuity of society, or what an enormous task it is. Bennett and Tumin put it well:

. . . The newborn has no values or norms of right and wrong, nor any developed techniques. He may reasonably be conceived of as a self-seeking biologic organism whose drives and needs have to be socially channeled if they are to be satisfied with what the society has to offer. He must, moreover, learn to discriminate, in the pursuit of his needs, that point at which any further pursuit will generate opposition which may undermine his later capacity to satisfy his own needs.[2]

Socialization is carried on both formally and informally. Going to school is part of the socialization process, but so is going to the movies, or

2 · Bennett and Tumin, *Social Life*, p. 51. By permission.

overhearing a conversation in which someone is criticized and hence learning that one can avoid criticism by avoiding the behavior of the person under discussion. Socialization is a continuous process; when, at the age of eighty-two, a person learns something new about getting along in society, he is still being socialized. Socialization is cumulative: learning to recognize the letters of the alphabet lays the groundwork for learning to comprehend written words, and reading written words enables one to learn still other things. Whenever we ask someone to give us new information in terms with which we are familiar—what a thing tastes like, what it feels like, what it is similar to—we are demonstrating the cumulative nature of socialization.

A society would cease to be, and its culture would be lost, if some agency did not perform the function of socializing its new members.

A Sense of Purpose A major portion of the time and effort expended in socializing a new member of a society is invested in teaching him what the beliefs and goals of that society are, and in indoctrinating him with the idea that these are good and are worthy of his practice and defense. But there is a further function which must be universally met. Societies must in some way motivate their members to *maintain* the conviction that life is good and worthwhile. In other words, people must be imbued with a sense of meaning. They must be convinced that fitting into the social structure as they have been taught to do—that meeting the expectations of the culture—is worth the effort.

Obviously, a society could not continue to exist if everyone decided

that it was easier to quit than to go on. A French sociologist, Emile Durkheim, made a fascinating study [3] of one category of people who decide to quit, in which he concluded that what he called "anomic suicide" occurs most frequently in situations of *anomie*, a French word best translated as "without rules." A society lacking definite norms to regulate morals and social conduct is called anomic. In an anomic situation, such as a sudden economic depression, when the old rules no longer seem to apply and no new ones are immediately forthcoming, people do not know what is right and wrong or what the social expectations are, and they lose their sense of purpose. At such a time, suicide rates soar.

More recent research on sense of purpose as an essential social function has been summarized by the eminent neurologist Harold G. Wolff as follows:

Most physicians have seen sudden and unexplainable death come to those who are overwhelmed or filled with despair. There is good evidence that "bone pointing," "hexing," and excommunication of transgressors of tribal mores may remarkably shorten life if not immediately kill a man. Suitable studies have not been made until now to explain such deaths. However, it has been shown that wild rats

3 · Emile Durkheim, *Le Suicide*, trans. John A. Spaulding and George Simpson (Glencoe, Ill.: The Free Press, 1951). Originally published in France in 1897. For other studies of suicide see Ruth S. Cavan, *Suicide* (Chicago: University of Chicago Press, 1928); Calvin F. Schmid, *Suicides in Seattle, 1924 to 1925: An Ecological and Behavioristic Study* (Seattle: University of Washington Publications in the Social Sciences, Vol. 5, October, 1928); Louis I. Dublin and Bessie Bunzel, *To Be or Not To Be, A Study of Suicide* (New York: Harrison Smith and Robert Haas, 1933); Andrew F. Henry and James F. Short, Jr., *Suicide and Homicide* (Glencoe, Ill.: The Free Press, 1954); Paul J. Bohannan, ed., *African Homicide and Suicide* (Princeton, N.J.: Princeton University Press, 1960).

capable of swimming for ninety or more hours may, nevertheless, when terrified and then plunged into water die in a few minutes. Careful study of the heart in these creatures reveals that death results from a depressive action of the nervous system, gradually slowing and ultimately arresting the heart's beat. Moreover, if lifted out of the water just before the heart stops the rat promptly recovers, and on subsequent immersion swims as it did before this crisis.

Early information from Japan, as yet statistically unsupported, indicates that those who experienced the catastrophe of the atom bomb at Hiroshima, but who suffered no burns or direct effects of irradiation, have had a shorter life span than other Japanese. Death has resulted from the usual and varied terminal illnesses. It is as though they had grown twenty years older than their age.

Though we lack definitive support for this early impression, we do have precise information from our own records of the war concerning the effect on life span and health of prolonged adverse life experience. Thus, of approximately 6,000 United States prisoners of war captured by the North Koreans, about one third died. Medical observers reported that the cause of death in many instances was ill defined, and was referred to by them as "give-up-itis." Occurring as it did in a setting of serious demoralization, humiliation, despair and deprivation of human support and affection, the prisoner became apathetic, listless, neither ate nor drank, helped himself in no way, stared into space and finally died.

A recently completed study of the effects of imprisonment on Americans during World War II tells us that approximately 94,000 United States prisoners of war were taken in Europe. These men were imprisoned about ten months. Less than 1 per cent of them died before liberation. In contrast, in the Pacific theater, about 25,000 Americans became prisoners of war. They remained in prison four times as long as those captured in Europe, and suffered far more than any others the effects of threats, abuse and humiliation. Their demoralization was often extreme. Over one third died before liberation.

Six years after liberation, those who survived the Japanese prison experience were re-examined. In the first place the total number of deaths in this group during these six years was more than twice the expected incidence for a similar group of persons not so exposed, and three times as great as in the group of United States prisoners of war in Europe. The causes of death included many diseases not directly related to confinement or starvation. Thus, nine times the expected number died of pulmonary tuberculosis, twice the expected number died of heart disease, more than twice the expected number of cancer, more than four times the expected number of diseases of the gastrointestinal tract, twice the number from suicide, and most striking of all, three times the expected number of deaths as a result of accidents.

What happened to those who survived? What was the incidence of illness during the six years after their liberation? It was found that the admission rate to veterans' hospitals of the former prisoners of war of the Japanese was closely related to the amount of stress endured by the former soldier during his imprisonment. Those who had experienced less duress had admission rates only slightly more than the European prisoners of war, whereas those who had suffered greatly had far the greatest number of admissions, amounting to seven times as many as did those who had not been prisoners, and "very poor health" interfered with work in one half. Interestingly enough . . . those who were in "very poor health" had many different diseases including those which did not appear to be immediately related to incarceration, i.e., hernia, deafness, and diseases of bones, muscles, and heart. There were ten times as many "impairments" as among the European prisoners of war group.

What about the rest who neither died nor became sick or disabled? Again facts run out. But a study of a few of the survivors who have since become unusually effective citizens is suggestive. Despite exposure to many stressful conditions, the imprisonment for them was a painful but temporary interruption in a life viewed as a continuum. They were convinced that they would come out alive and that they would not be imprisoned long. They were able to extract a few satisfactions even while enduring deprivations. New interests were cultivated (one man raised rabbits for food and began breeding them for increased size). Mind and spirit were mainly focused on life as it was to be lived in the future. The immediate distress seemed less real, the future more substantial. Plans were made for occupation, marriage, family, children, often with meticulous and obsessive detail, including domicile, city or town education for self and kin, entertainment, the kind of food and where it would be eaten. Among these prisoners academic courses were organized, teaching carried out, seminars and discussions led. These men formed tightly knit groups, believed in, helped each other, and even laughed together. Immediately after liberation, a few had transient illnesses, but there is little to indicate that their vitality has been sapped. Indeed, a few have assumed major responsibilities.

In short, prolonged circumstances which are perceived as dangerous, as lonely, as hopeless, may drain a man of hope and of his health; but he is capable of enduring incredible burdens and taking cruel punishment when he has self-esteem, hope, purpose, and belief in his fellows.[4]

Production and Distribution of Goods and Services

A society without division of labor would be one in which each individual worked to satisfy his own wants and no one worked to produce anything for anyone else. No such society exists. The fact that new members born into a society are at first unable to provide for their own needs would in itself make such an arrangement impossible if the society were to survive. Actually, of course, the division of labor extends far beyond what is necessitated by differences in age and sex. The cumulative nature of cul-

ture results in the assignment of certain tasks to certain social categories and these, in time, become institutionalized. But basic culture patterns trace ultimately to biological characteristics. For instance, it is biologically necessary that the tasks of child-bearing and nursing children be performed by women. It is also true that, during the late stages of pregnancy, women are not as able as men to stalk game in the hunt, move swiftly in battle, or lift heavy objects in construction work. Out of this complex of biological imperatives emerges a cultural situation in which it is not customary in most societies for women to be hunters, warriors, or construction laborers. It is not that it is biologically impossible for most women most of the time to perform the work of a hunter, a warrior, or a construction laborer (both of the latter two roles have been performed in our own era by women in the Soviet Union); it is that the specialization surrounding motherhood—a direct result of biological equipment—tends to result in a further division of labor between the sexes. This social specialization on the basis of sex is culturally defined by norms and sanctions. People do not expect a girl to be a construction laborer; it just wouldn't be right. Who would want to marry a girl bricklayer?

The economic structure and the set of values governing it differ radically from society to society, but everywhere people have some set of norms ordering their activities so that the function of producing goods and services and distributing them will be performed. In even the most favorable environment, some such social arrangements are necessary: even where socially defined needs are minimal and natural resources are abundant, some-

4 · Harold G. Wolff, "A Scientific Report on What Hope Does for Man," *Saturday Review*, 1957, 11:44–45. By permission.

Gary Wagner Associates

Every society has some responsibility for maintaining order:
Thanksgiving Day Parade.

one has to be assigned the responsibility of picking the coconuts or berries for those unable to pick their own.

Preservation of Order We have seen that if a society is to survive, it must reproduce new members, socialize them, provide them with a continuing sense of purpose, and insure their biological well-being by arranging for the production and distribution of goods and services. Finally, some structure within the society must result in the preservation of order. Two facets of order are essential: the society must not destroy itself from within, and it must not allow itself to be destroyed from the outside, by some other society.

We noted in Chapter 5 that the folkways and mores which serve to order a society internally are enforced through formal and informal sanctions. Obedience is essential to the continuity of a society. If a society were to reach the stage where most of its members failed to abide by the basic rules, it would be doomed. If people killed each other wantonly, refused to honor agreements, failed to fulfill social responsibilities, and meted out no punishment to those who ignored the social norms, the society would soon cease to exist. Anarchy may be a fit topic for philosophical speculation but it is not a possible condition for social life.

It is equally necessary that a society protect itself from outside attack. This is hardly debatable: there are historical instances of societies which have perished through inability to maintain an order capable of resisting external pressures or attacks. Ancient Carthage was destroyed by the Romans; in more recent history, because the Tasmanian aborigines could not maintain order in the face of the English onslaught, they disappeared.

In small, nonliterate tribal societies, internal order is almost entirely the result of folkways and mores. That is, order is not formalized, but is ordinarily maintained by such informal sanctions as gossip, ridicule, and ostracism. This is possible because such societies are virtually primary groups. In large societies, such as our own, which are spread over thousands of miles and are composed of millions of people most of whom never see or interact directly with most of their fellow "tribesmen," formal sanctions are necessary to maintain order. We have, therefore, elaborate bodies of written laws and regulations, and impersonal systems of police and courts to enforce the rules.

In the same way, order for the handling of external relations is, in complex societies, more than simply a matter of whether or not a hunter crosses the path of someone from the out-group. We maintain intricate webs of formal relations with representatives of other societies through full-time officials in a Department of State, the United Nations, and other secondary groups devoted to the function of the preservation of order.

The Interdependence of Functions As can be seen on careful examination, each of the five universal functions discussed in this chapter is an abstraction made for the analysis of social organization. Each is by no means separate from the others. If any one of these functions is not performed, the society, and hence all the other functions, come

to an end. The functions are an interlocking system which makes the maintenance, stability, and continuity of social life possible.

The reproduction of new members for the society, like their socialization, takes place within the framework of the norms, which are there to perform the function of maintaining order. The function of socialization is necessary in order to teach a new member his obligations in each of the other functions: reproduction, production and distribution of goods and services, and preservation of order. So too, it is through socialization that one acquires his sense of purpose, which motivates him to do his part in maintaining social order, producing goods, and so on.

It is because of this interrelationship among the functions that a change in any one of them is certain to have repercussions in the others. This is a topic which we shall treat at greater length in Part III, SOCIAL INSTITUTIONS.

Having outlined the universal functions, we shall look briefly now at the structures which produce them.

UNIVERSAL SOCIAL STRUCTURES

The universal functions, abstract as they may sound, are very real; they are the consequences of observable group structures: families, schools, churches, governments, and businesses. The nature of the group or groups responsible for each function varies with the organization of the society and the values of its culture. But in every human society there are some social structures resulting in reproduction, socialization, a sense of purpose, the production and distribution of goods and services, and the informal and formal preservation of order.

The Family Throughout human history, the family has been the group primarily responsible for most of these functions. Even today, in small, relatively isolated societies, the family is the basic primary group around which the major tasks of social life are organized.

In all societies, ancient or modern, small or large, the family is the structure which provides for the reproduction of new members for the society. Families may be organized with one husband, one wife, and their children; one husband, multiple wives, and their children; one wife, multiple husbands, and their children. Or they may consist of great-grandparents plus all their male children and spouses for four generations. And so on. Regardless of the kind of family organization called for by the culture, all societies have some provision for a family structure, and it is that structure which results in the function of reproduction.

Educational Structures The family always participates in socialization as well, but the extent varies considerably from society to society. In a totalitarian state, children may be taken from their parents at a very early age and indoctrinated in state schools. In very small, nonindustrial, isolated societies, the family may serve the function of the "school," having almost the entire responsibility for inducting the child into the ways of his society.

People are socialized as a result of participation in many social structures. One learns something about his society by interacting with his fellows in religious groups, whether they are Sunday School classes or tribal ceremonials. Membership in a congeniality group of playmates is a source of socialization; the child here comes in contact with the values of the culture which surrounds him and learns to conform to group expectations. Clubs, organizations, and even audiences offer experiences which help mold the individual into a socialized member of society.

Our own society sponsors tax-supported secondary groups, the public schools, to carry out an important part of the function of socialization. Some societies do not have schools, but all societies have some set of social structures in which their members learn the norms.

Religion As in the case of socialization, the sense of purpose is taught to people and maintained in them by a variety of groups. Because of the range of cultural variability, sociologists use the word *religion* in a considerably broader sense than that in which it is ordinarily defined. For one person, a belief that the scientific method offers the possibility for a better life in this world may serve this function; for another person, the belief that service to a supernatural being promises a blissful and eternal afterlife may serve the same function.

Some structures in all societies have as a secondary or even latent function the fostering of a sense of purpose. Groups such as Senior Citizens' Clubs, community centers, and Marine Corps platoons are not religious structures, but are like religious structures insofar as they offer the individual something to participate in and believe in, and allow him to convince himself that his behavior is purposive, that his efforts are not in vain.

STRUCTURES

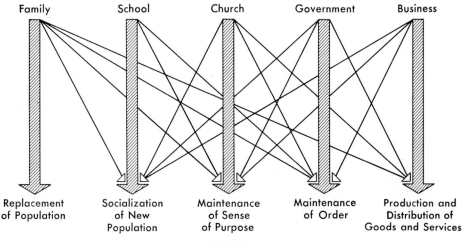

FIGURE 5 · The Interrelationship of Social Structures and Functions

Economic Structures In the simplest tribal societies, the family is the basic economic group. This was so also in the days of the frontier in the United States. Father, mother, and children worked the fields together, producing most of what they consumed. Now father may work for one company, mother for another, and brother and sister for a third and fourth. The corporation has become the major economic organization in our economy; secondary groups perform the functions of producing goods and services formerly carried out by primary groups.

Whatever the economic organization of a society—corporate and industrial or primary and agricultural—some groups exist which produce and distribute goods and services. They may specialize in economic activity, as does a steel company, or they may meet this need in addition to others,

as does a family. But in all societies there are structures which carry out this function.

Government Like other social structures, those which preserve order vary greatly in their complexity, depending in general on the complexity of the rest of the society. A tribe may be composed of half a dozen families, with the head of one serving as chief. He will settle disputes within the group and lead the warriors in battle against other tribes. At the other extreme are the large nations of the mid-twentieth century, each of which has an enormous formal governmental structure, with a military branch, a foreign relations branch, a taxation branch, and police and courts at various levels to maintain order within the society.

It is necessary only to note that, as in the cases of reproduction, socialization, and so on, all societies must have some particular structures which will result in such control or norm-enforcing functions.

The Interdependence of Structures While each structure has a function for which it is primarily responsible, it also has other, supplementary functions. Conversely, a function may derive from more than one structure. This is graphically shown in Figure 5. The crucial nature of these social structures is indicated by the tight balance which obtains among them. A change in the economy, for example, from a homestead agricultural system to a mass-production factory system necessitates a change from an all-relatives-under-one-roof familial group to an immediate family. This, in turn, will alter the early socialization of the child, and so on. As with the functions which they produce, universal structures are so closely interrelated that an alteration in one has repercussions throughout the social system.

The treatment of these fundamental structures has been quite brief. No further detail is given them here because Part III, SOCIAL INSTITUTIONS, devotes a chapter to each of the universal structures, their functions, and a description of the behavioral patterns which we find associated with them.

INTERPRETATIVE SUMMARY

Several universal social functions may be pinpointed, since all societies must perform certain basic tasks in order to survive. Each society must replenish its population, must produce and distribute food and other necessities, and must guard against destruction from within or without. Furthermore, each society must teach new members the values, knowledge, and skills of the society, and must convince each individual that life on his society's terms is worthwhile.

Generalizations about universal social structures are of necessity broad: each society must develop *some* structure or groups of structures for renewing itself, for distributing goods and services, and so on. Specific structures vary with the complexity, physical limitations, and directionality of the society. For example, primitive societies assign multiple functions to one or two simple structures. More complex cultures have many specific structures, each having a basic function, each having secondary functions which reinforce the work of other structures. In any society, structures and functions are interdependent: if one basic structure drops or gains a task, another structure gains or drops that same task; and the structure with the new responsibility may do its job better, worse, or just differently.

REVIEW AND SUGGESTED READINGS

A · VOCABULARY

Anomie	Function	Structure

B · QUESTIONS AND TOPICS FOR REVIEW

1. Which develops first in a society, the need for a certain basic structure or the need for a certain basic function? Which is more likely to undergo change, a basic structure or a basic function?

2. Discuss a socialization experience of a specific adult.
3. A sense of purpose is necessary for an individual's well-being and for society's survival. What aggregates in our society seem most "lost"? In each case, why has the problem of finding a sense of purpose been especially difficult to solve?
4. Those in opposition to groups such as the American Civil Liberties Union, the White Citizens Councils, the John Birch Society, or the National Association for the Advancement of Colored People say that such groups are undermining what function of the society? What is the answer given by such groups?
5. Give an example from our culture in which the change in a structure or even in one of the rules of a structure brought changes throughout the society's structures and functions.

C • SUGGESTIONS FOR FURTHER READING

Howard Becker and Alvin Boskoff, eds. *Modern Sociological Theory*. New York: The Dryden Press, 1957.

Chapter 8, "Structural-Functional Analysis in Modern Sociology," by Walter Buckley, is pertinent to the discussion in this chapter.

Bernard Berelson and Gary A. Steiner. *Human Behavior: An Inventory of Scientific Findings*. New York: Harcourt, Brace & World, Inc., 1964.

An attempt to summarize what is scientifically known about human behavior. Where they find adequate research evidence, the authors present general theoretical statements.

Edgar F. Borgatta and Henry J. Meyer, eds. *Sociological Theory*. New York: Alfred A. Knopf, Inc., 1956.

Parts IV and V, on social structures and their persistence, contain essays relevant to our material on universal social structures and functions.

Lewis A. Coser and Bernard Rosenberg, eds. *Sociological Theory: A Book of Readings*. New York: The Macmillan Company, 1964. (Second Edition)

Chapter 14 contains essays which are milestones in the development of structure-function theory by such scholars as Spencer, Durkheim, Malinowski, and Pareto.

Amitai Etzioni, ed. *Complex Organizations. A Sociological Reader*. New York: Holt, Rinehart and Winston, Inc., 1961.

A collection of papers by 46 specialists in organizational analysis, with particular reference to the structure and function of large and complex organizations.

CHAPTER 8

Universal Social Processes

The discussion of social structures and their functions concerns a cross section of patterned behavior at a given moment. A description of a social structure is a sort of theoretical snapshot: we know that in real life the subjects move, but for analytic convenience we describe their interrelationship as a set of statics at a point in time. Sociologists also deal, of course, with the analysis of social dynamics: the study of change, modification, or alteration in social relationships through time.

INTERACTION

Interaction is the key element in all social life. Hence the concept is crucial to any study of the dynamics of society and culture. Without interaction there would be no social or group life. The mere placing of individuals in physical proximity, although it usually results in at least a modicum of interaction, does not weld them into a social unit or group. It is when persons work or play or talk together with a common end, or when they compete or quarrel with one another, that associative life, properly speaking, exists. We underline the point, then, that interaction is the basic social process, the broadest term for describing dynamic social relationships.

Basic to man's survival is his struggle for material goods and other rewards culturally defined as desirable. The chief forms of such struggle, or *opposition*, are competition and conflict. Yet not all life consists of striving against another individual or in a physical situation. People may combine to gain a goal or reward. This we call *co-operation*, or mutual aid. Then too, the individual learns a variety of distinguishing behaviors, which set him off from others according to his age, sex, occupation, and class. This process is *differentiation*. In fact, opposition, co-operation, and differentiation constitute a base line from which still other more specialized forms of interaction arise, such as accommodation, stratification, and assimilation. We shall examine first the universal processes of opposition, co-operation, and differentiation, and then turn to the processes derived from them.

OPPOSITIONAL PROCESSES

Opposition, as well as co-operation, occurs in every society, although its form and direction are modified by the culture of the time and place. Opposition may be defined as a struggle *against* another or others for a good, goal, or value; co-operation as joint striving *with* another or others for a good, goal, or value. *Felt scarcity* or desire for a good or value—money, power, affection, and so on—is basic to both opposi-

112

tion and co-operation. This felt necessity is defined not only biologically but also culturally. Indeed, what men fight for, or co-operate together for, is determined in large measure by their learning.

For purposes of analysis, opposition may be divided into competition and conflict. _Competition is a form of opposition in which two or more persons or groups struggle for some end or goal but in the course of which attention is focused chiefly on the reward rather than on the competitor._ In _conflict_ the person or group thwarts, injures, or destroys the opponent in order to secure a goal or reward. That is, in conflict interest is often directed initially toward frustrating the opposing individual or group and then toward the ultimate end. It is a two-step process. It is assumed or expected that once the opponent is _hors de combat_, the reward will fall to the victor.

Obviously, in real life, competition sometimes shades into conflict. For example, rivals for the hand of a girl may resort to fisticuffs in their efforts to secure the maiden's favor, and for the moment they are more interested in knocking each other about than in courting. Or a business firm unable to compete with another under the usual "rules of the game" may employ gangsters to beat up the competitor's workmen or to destroy his goods with a view to forcing the opposing firm to withdraw from the struggle.

The source of competition and conflict appears to be the frustration which comes into play when quick attainment of a goal or reward is denied. Not only are drives accompanied by emotions, but the blocking of the movement from drive to consummation sets up intense emotional states that serve to stimulate further the individual's striving toward his goal. Rage, fear, and love are emotions that are particularly linked to man's efforts to get what he wants.

If the individual is blocked in his efforts to secure the wanted reward, he may proceed in various ways to avoid, offset, overcome, or get around the interference. He may make a highly emotionalized direct attack on the object or situation which blocks his way. If this fails, he may set about acquiring the skill and knowledge needed to attain the goal. And in this learning he may seek and obtain help from others. If he fails to learn the requisite techniques or does not try to acquire them, he may find a substitute for the original goal. This is well illustrated in compensation, which may be expressed in overt behavior or in daydream or fantasy. The individual may, of course, give up the effort either to reach the original reward or to secure a substitute. Rather, he may regress to an earlier state or avoid the situation. When confronted by a serious or prolonged crisis, some people make no effort to adapt themselves to the situation. Perhaps the most striking illustrations occur among the low-grade feebleminded and in certain forms of mental disorder, especially in severe cases of schizophrenia, which are often marked by regression to infantile reactions. Yet even normal people occasionally revert to childish means of dealing with their problems.

Rudimentary forms of social struggle are evident among the lower mammalians; among human beings, opposition is shaped at most points by cultural learning, including early personal-social learning. For example, a child who in his earliest months was deprived

Monkmeyer

In American society, people compete in recreation.

of either sustenance or affection or both might well develop patterns of reactions to, say, parental authority, or to situations offering the alternative between dominance and submission—might become a little "tiger" or little "mouse." When he becomes an adult, the way he handles competition and conflict will be culturally determined in the broad sense, in that he will follow his society's rules governing these processes, and in the narrower sense in that he will always be something of the "tiger" or "mouse" he learned to be in his early social relationships.

Culture and Competition While culture itself is rooted in man's basic drives and interactions, the particular goods—material or nonmaterial—for which he strives vary greatly because of historical factors, accidents or circumstance of the time and place, and local adaptation to resources. In our own society we take competition and conflict so much for granted that it is difficult for us to understand that a tribe or nation can have little of them.

In fact, however, an examination of the far-ranging variabilities of culture makes it clear that whether whole societies become generally conditioned to competitive or to co-operative forms of economic and community life depends on the nature of the central ethos or value system of the society. An excellent illustration of such variability is found in the survey of the cultures of thirteen widely separated native tribes, prepared under the direction of Margaret Mead.[1] Although in interpreting

1 · See *Co-operation and Competition Among Primitive Peoples*, Margaret Mead, ed. (New York: McGraw-Hill Book Co.,

these surveys Mead found that the suggested division of social systems into competitive or co-operative is not entirely feasible, her analysis is helpful in indicating the relation of these two basic processes to the tribal structure and to the life organization of the individuals within these societies. Among other significant findings of this survey we may note the following:

(1) No matter what the nature of the cultural system, strong self-esteem and a sense of power can be found in some members of the society. (2) There is no relationship between the form of the culture and the local problems of sustenance and material resources. For example, there is no reason to assume that lack of food necessarily makes for either competition or co-operation. (3) The concept and valuation of personal success are determined more by the broad and general group emphasis on either competition or co-operation than by the degree of technology or the plenitude of food. (4) "There is a correspondence between: a major emphasis on competition, a social structure which depends upon the initiative of the individual, a valuation of property for individual ends, a single scale of success, and a strong development of the ego" [social self].[2] This is the sort of pattern that characterizes our own society. (5) "There is a correspondence between: a major emphasis upon co-

operation, a social structure which does not depend upon individual initiative or the exercise of power over persons, a faith in an ordered universe, weak emphasis upon rising in status, and a high degree of security for the individual."[3]

It must be emphasized that in none of these tribes do we find either competition or co-operation wholly lacking. Such fundamental processes are correlative to each other. As economists long ago pointed out, competition itself rests on certain implicit agreements to follow certain rules in the oppositional relations. Yet when a society tends to stress one process, the other process may be found to be less institutionalized and hence less recognized.

Ralph Linton and Abram Kardiner cite a striking example of the effects of a basic change in economy on social organization and individual traits.[4] Among the Tanala of Madagascar, the Betsileo tribe found it necessary, because of soil erosion and other changes, to shift from the cultivation of dry rice to that of wet rice. The system of dry-rice farming was marked by communal ownership of land, a high degree of co-operation, and equal distribution of produce under an extremely authoritarian rule of the fathers. Under this somewhat rigid but paternalistic control, the individual, though passive and obedient to authority, was well-adjusted.

The shift to an economy of wet-rice farming brought in its wake some startling changes. Communal ownership gave way to individual ownership. There was a mad rush for fertile acres in nearby valleys. The individual be-

1937). For a critical review of the psychological, sociological, and anthropological treatment of opposition and co-operation, see M. A. May and L. W. Doob, "Competition and Co-operation," *Bulletin*, No. 25 (New York: Social Science Research Council, 1937). The latter, however, makes no adequate distinction between competition and conflict.

2 · Mead, *Co-operation and Competition*, p. 511. This and the following quotation by permission of McGraw-Hill Book Company.

3 · *Ibid.*

4 · See Abram Kardiner, *The Individual and His Society*, Chapters 7, 8 (New York: Columbia University Press, 1939).

Better Living, *E.I. du Pont de Nemours & Co., Inc.*

In American society, people compete for their livelihood.

came important, and he soon began to feel in sharp competition with his fellows over rights, as well as duties. The former family organization broke down, and there was a sharp increase in such deviant conduct as crime, homosexuality, black magic, and neuroticism. In time a whole new social organization emerged, including a rigid class structure of king, nobles, commoners, and slaves. This rapid shift in a basic feature of the culture illustrates clearly how much institutions influence the life organization of individuals.

It is clear, then, that competition may take a wide variety of forms. It may be central to some aspects of a cultural system and not to others. Moreover, under the impact of invention, political revolution, or shifts in the resource base of an economy, striking changes may occur in the interrelations of competition and other social processes.

Conflict Conflict is characterized by emotionalized and violent opposition, in which the major concern is to overcome the opponent as a means of securing a goal or reward. It is direct and openly antagonistic struggle of persons or groups for the same object or end. The aim of conflict is the defeat, subjugation, or annihilation of the other person or group as a means of obtaining the goal. In the struggle to overcome the other person or group, the goal is often temporarily relegated to a level of secondary importance. In contrast to competition, which, at least in its stricter impersonal aspects, is more or less continuous and unconscious, conflict is an intermittent but highly conscious process. Of course, in many situations competition and conflict are interrelated, the conflict often arising at critical points in the more prolonged competitive process.

Conflict is affected by the nature of the group and its particular culture. The objects of conflict may be property, power and status, freedom of action and thought, or any other desired value. When economic interests loom large and there are many individuals or groups striving for material gain and power, conflict of economic interests may supplement the competitive process. If sectarianism is rife, we can expect conflict to occur in religion. In other words, the culturally determined values of a society will set the stage for its struggles.

Not only is the form of conflict modified by the particular societal order and its culture, but everywhere there arise regulations to govern it. In feuds, for example, there are certain accepted methods of killing the other fellow. Lynching follows a certain tradition. When the conflict is infrequent and when no adequate techniques have been worked out, more violent and unpredictable sorts of conflict arise, such as race riots. In war, of course, there are all sorts of rules more or less agreed upon by the belligerents during the interludes of peace.

At its most rudimentary level, conflict results in the removal or annihilation of the opponent. In human society, however, most conflict ends in some sort of agreement, or accommodation, or in the fusion of the two opposing elements.

CO-OPERATION

Co-operation, like opposition, is a basic feature of human interaction. These ambivalent patterns, we have noted, appear to underlie all other more specialized social processes. As Albion W. Small, one of the founders of sociology in America, put it, "Struggle and co-operation are correlates in every situation"—that is, there is either "conjunction" or "conflict" of interests.[5] Yet the interplay of these two processes is not always understood. Some writers consider opposition the fundamental form of interaction; others believe that co-operation is the basic social process. For example, some use the term *co-operation* as a synonym for almost all social contact, holding that opponents in fighting must "co-operate" in order to exchange blows, or that traders "co-operate" in their market relations, or that the compromise of disputes between laborers and employers represents a form of co-operation. Such broad and loose use of the term makes it practically identical with our terms *interaction* and *social*, and thus too vague for effective description and analysis. We limit the term *co-operation* to a more specific aspect of human intercourse, one having to do with mutual aid or an alliance of persons or groups seeking some common goal or reward—in short, as some kind of conjoint rather than opposing action.

Patterns of mutual aid are found among all human groups. Such habits and attitudes begin in infancy and childhood within the family and the congeniality group. Upon the basis acquired in these primary groups, the individual develops co-operative behavior patterns as an adult.

Yet for rudimentary mutual helpfulness to develop into more deliberate form, people must first of all be directly

5 · Albion W. Small, *General Sociology* (Chicago: University of Chicago Press, 1905), pp. 357, 203.

Life Magazine

Co-operation: African oarsmen.

motivated to seek a goal that may be shared. Second, they must acquire some knowledge of the benefits of such activity—hence the need for education to foster co-operation. Third, they must acquire a favorable attitude toward sharing both the work and the rewards involved. And finally, they need to equip themselves with the skills necessary to make the co-operative plan work.[6]

Like opposition, co-operation arises from the orientation of the individual to the in-group and the out-group. While competition, rivalry, and conflict may arise in the in-group, it is evident that an in-group could not persist were it not for co-operation. The solidarity of the in-group is expressed most strongly in mutual aid, helpfulness, and

6 · See M. A. May and L. W. Doob, "Competition and Co-operation."

loyalty to the group-accepted symbols. Such co-operation is most in evidence when the in-group stands in sharp opposition to some other body of persons, an out-group. The very strength of the in-group feeling of solidarity rests in part on the fact that hostile feelings are directed toward some out-group. The intensity of the in-group feelings seems correlated, indeed, with the intensity of antagonism toward the out-group.

Co-operation imposes various forms of restraint on the participant. The self cannot have its way entirely if it is to work co-operatively with another self. If a self-assertive trend becomes too strong, co-operation will be replaced by struggle. Co-operation always implies inhibition of certain ego-centered drives. A child in team play cannot always assume the chief role. As we advance to higher—that is, to more conscious and complex—forms of co-operation, this fact becomes even more evident. From the restraint so imposed there arises a moral control which stands in contrast with the impulsiveness and lack of self-control found in uninhibited conflict. In the struggle of one group against another, this moral order is highly important, as it is also in controlling the relations of persons to one another within the group itself.

The function of co-operation is well summarized in the following words of C. H. Cooley: "Co-operation . . . arises when men see that they have a common interest and have, at the same time, sufficient intelligence and self-control to seek this interest through united action: perceived unity of interest and the faculty of organization are the essential facts in intelligent combination." [7]

Culture and Co-operation We need not posit an instinct of sociability or gregariousness in order to explain co-operation. The instances of interaction simply within the family would furnish sufficient ground upon which to construct the co-operative social order which we find everywhere. Beyond the family the neighborhood, the play group, and the whole set of secondary groups call for co-operation. If we say that human co-operation is a form of interaction between two or more persons or groups striving toward some goal or reward which may be shared in material goods, in prestige and power, or in some other accepted satisfaction, we can also say that *culture is what gives co-operation pitch and direction*.

In our own society there appears to be far more teaching of the child, youth, and adult in competitive and conflictive attitudes, habits, and ideas than in those involving co-operation. Yet our society is not given entirely to conflict or to competitive individualism. Within the social class, the team, the trade union, the employers' association, the religious confraternity, interdependence and mutual aid are absolutely essential. Nevertheless, in all these the fundamental and persisting values are frequently those of the competitive-conflictive *ethos*.

An illustration of a different cultural attitude toward co-operation will be instructive. S. D. Porteus, a psychologist, tells of his difficulty in getting certain natives of Australia to work individually and competitively on intelligence tests. The natives turned to him for help to do the task and were clearly upset when he refused. Porteus had earlier been adopted as a tribal brother, and the natives simply could not understand how a person in such a relationship to them could refuse to co-operate in a task put before them.[8]

From an ethnocentric standpoint, forms of co-operation found in other societies may strike us as being absurd and the individuals therein as lacking in ambition and initiative. Some societies, like the one just mentioned, emphasize co-operation as a cultural value much more than we do. Other societies set less value on co-operation than we. But co-operation, like competition and conflict, is a universal characteristic of human societies; in no society is it completely lacking. Among men as among animals, there is a good deal of non-

7 · C. H. Cooley, *Sociological Theory and Social Research* (New York: Henry Holt & Co., Inc., 1930), p. 176. By permission.

8 · See S. D. Porteus, *The Psychology of a Primitive People* (New York: Longmans, Green & Co., 1931), pp. 308–309.

deliberate mutual aid, especially in time of grave danger. Even in our highly individualistic, competitive world men have also been conditioned, in primary-group situations especially, to interdependence and mutual aid in time of stress. Certainly such patterns are distinctly culturized for us through our Judeo-Christian religion. Again, it must be recalled that competition and conflict are closely related. For example, in one situation members of a group may be highly co-operative with one another and definitely conflictive toward other groups. The ethos of the culture will define the nature and degree of such co-operation and conflict.

DIFFERENTIATION

Another universal process is differentiation. It emerges in a society when specialties are developed and assigned on the basis of variations in age, sex, capacity, and other elements. Again, there are certain prototypes of this process among the lower animal forms. The social training of young monkeys and apes by the mother rests on age differences. So too, the sexual behavior of these species demonstrates specialization in activity, the male being in general more aggressive, the female more passive.

Certainly all human societies show variations in conduct, especially in role and status. However, some universals exist. All societies give a place to childhood different from the one they give to maturity or old age. Everywhere women bear children and care for them, while the fathers and husbands carry on certain strenuous activities remote from the home. Everywhere we find some individuals who dominate others in varying social situations. Even

in the most rudimentary societies, there is always some division of labor.

DERIVED SOCIAL PROCESSES

From opposition, co-operation, and differentiation emerge several other social processes. These *derived* processes are also universal in human societies. Out of differentiation grows *stratification*. Co-operation among varied groups may lead to *assimilation*. Since conflict is not usually continuous between groups, some working arrangement, or *accommodation*, arises. This section will describe the processes derived from opposition, co-operation, and differentiation.

Accommodation The word *accommodation* has been used in two related senses—to indicate a condition of institutional arrangement, and to indicate a process. As a *condition*, accommodation is the fact of equilibrium between individuals and groups and the "rules of the game" which have been developed. Etiquette, or the "proper" way of acting socially, the "agreements" developed between conflicting economic groups, treaties between nations, and the techniques, traditions, and arrangements which define the relations of persons and groups are forms of accommodation.

As a *process*, accommodation has to do with the conscious efforts of men to develop such working arrangements among themselves as will suspend conflict and so make their relations more tolerable and less wasteful of energy. It concerns the movement toward the accommodated state. It is a means of resolving conflict without the complete destruction or absorption of the opponent—that is, without either party's entirely losing its identity. It takes place at a conscious—though not necessarily rational—level, and for the most part is in the nature of formal and external regulations or arrangements.

The effects of accommodation may vary somewhat with the circumstances. Accommodation may act to reduce the conflict between persons or groups as an initial step to synthesis of differences into a new pattern—in other words, it may lead to assimilation. It may serve to postpone outright conflict for a specific period of time, as in a treaty between nations or a labor-management agreement. It may permit groups separated by sharp social-psychological distance to get along together. In this function it is closely related to stratification as seen in class or caste systems. It may prevent what the culture considers an undesirable amalgamation or biological inbreeding of two groups and their subsequent assimilation.

Sometimes the accommodation is viewed by the parties involved as mutually beneficial. In other instances the arrangements are imposed on one group by another with superior power and prestige.

Forms of Accommodation Accommodative arrangements between groups or individuals take a variety of forms, from coercion through compromise and conciliation to toleration.

Coercion is a type of accommodation in which action and thought in social relationships are determined by constraint, compulsion, or force. Coercion implies the existence of the weak and the strong in any conflict. It takes two forms—physical or direct application of force; and psychological, or indirect application of force. For example, slavery is an arrangement in which

the basic social interaction is one of domination by master and subjection of slave. Slavery involves absence of political rights for the slave, compulsory labor, and property rights of the master with regard to the slave as an individual.

Various political dictatorships are coercive accommodations in which a strongly disciplined minority seizes power and inflicts its control on whole populations. It is a mistake to assume that such despotism is never welcome as a means of settling conflicts. When older values and practices are lost and a struggle rages between multiple warring interests, the masses come in time to look for a strong man who will bring peace and order. Such a person was Napoleon Bonaparte, who stabilized France after its bloody revolution. Benito Mussolini did something of this sort for Italy after World War I. It was the case with Adolf Hitler and the rise of Nazism in Germany. And under Nicolai Lenin, Joseph Stalin, and others, the Communist Party unified a discordant Russia and in time welded it into a powerful nation-state.

Coercion is not confined, of course, to slavery, conquest, revolution, and international relations; it occurs also in situations involving racial, religious, industrial, and other conflicts.

Compromise, unlike coercive accommodation, implies a fair degree of equality in bargaining power of two contestants or willingness of the stronger party to substitute justice for strength as the basis for agreement. Compromise may be defined as a conscious method of settling a conflict in which all parties agree to renounce or reduce some of their demands in the interest of peace. Readiness to compromise means that groups and individuals are able to view themselves somewhat objectively, and to see themselves as others see them. Intransigent attitudes generated in the heat of conflict give way to more reasonable thinking. Certain international agreements and management-labor agreements on wages, hours of work, and other conditions of employment are examples of compromise. In a political democracy, too, parties or factions resolve their differences by compromise. This is especially true when they are about evenly matched in voting power.

Arbitration is a special device for bringing about compromise when the contending parties themselves are unable to resolve their differences. Disputes are settled by a third party, who may be chosen by the opposing sides or appointed by some larger agency of power, as in legalized compulsory arbitration of labor disputes. _Mediation_, which is closely akin to arbitration, is the introduction into a conflict of a neutral agent whose efforts are directed toward bringing about a peaceful settlement. The mediator has no power to settle the conflict; his function is advisory only. The use of arbitrators or mediators is common in industrial and religious disputes in our society.

Closely related to compromise and sometimes involving compromise is _conciliation_, which is an attempt to reconcile disputants as a means of bringing about an agreement. In our modern industrial system certain forms of conciliation have grown up as a permanent program for settling disputes between owners and workers. Such organizations, called "works councils" or "shop committees," may or may not exist independently of trade unions. In these organizations representatives of the owners and workers set up institu-

tional devices for handling disputes over wages, hours, and working conditions. Conciliation has also been used in racial and religious struggles. Conciliation always connotes a milder response to an opponent than coercion. In the end, conciliation, like toleration, opens the door to assimilation.

While some strain may remain after an accommodative arrangement has been made, and while neither party ever gets everything he wanted, the art of accommodation is important in a world of temporizing. In our earliest social relations, all of us learn to get along with half measures. To operate in the social world on an all-or-none principle is extremely difficult, if not impossible. We soon discover that doing so will not get us the things we want. In a world of contending wishes and interests and a limited supply of goods, material or otherwise, accommodation seems inevitable.

In any case, discussion between the parties to a conflict is an essential aspect of accommodation as it is expressed in compromise, arbitration, mediation, and conciliation. Deliberation as a means of settling differences is linked to the culture patterns of democracy, individualism, liberalism, and the scientific attitude. It means that conflict is reduced in intensity from overt force to the level of verbal give-and-take. Since deliberation permits an objective consideration of many phases of a struggle, in the end it should lay the foundation for a consensus of attitudes and opinions essential to any agreement that is to be effective. One of the problems of international relations is the continuing difficulty of reducing coercion to some milder form of accommodation.

Another form of accommodation

is *toleration*, or better, *tolerant partici-pation*. It is an outgrowth of the live-and-let-live policy just noted. It is a form of accommodation without formal agreement. Sometimes it is not entirely deliberate and conscious, but grows up from long-continuing avoidances developed to soften hostilities. There have been many instances of this type of arrangement, such as among various language and nationality groupings in central Europe and among the Navajo and Pueblo Indians.

Stratification Differentiation takes place universally on the basis of age, sex, and other factors, such as intelligence. Out of differentiation comes what is called division of labor, or assignment of various tasks to categories of people sharing different characteristics. But still another process is derived from differentiation. Social categories are ranked on the basis of what they do. This grading or ranking is called *social stratification*.

The concept of stratification includes both the process of ranking differentiated categories into classes and the resultant hierarchy of classes. As a process, stratification has to do with the forms of interaction involved in the ranking of, for example, wealthy people above poor people, or people who abide by the folkways and mores above deviants, or people whose tasks are considered important for the welfare of society above those whose work is less highly valued.

When sociologists deal with stratification from the point of view of hierarchy of power and activity, they are concerned with the structure of social classes and the functions which result from the structure. These functions include norms, sanctions, rights, duties, and symbols of identification and difference which define the class structure.

Since an entire chapter will be devoted to the structure and functions of class systems, we shall not treat the subject in greater detail here.

Assimilation If person-to-person, person-to-group, or group-to-group relations remained at the level of accommodation, there would occur no fusion of groups and their cultures. *Assimilation* is the fusion or blending of two previously distinct groups into one. Obviously, assimilation requires more fundamental changes than the "antagonistic co-operation" which we call accommodation. When the process of assimilation takes place, the people in two distinct groups do not just compromise or otherwise agree to get along with each other; they become so much like each other that they are no longer distinguishable as separate groups.

Assimilation occurs only when there is relatively continuous and direct contact. It is a comparatively slow process, though the history of human societies is full of examples of such merging of groups and their cultures. Among the more striking cases was the assimilation of the Anglo-Saxon and Norman societies in Britain in the two centuries after 1066, when the Normans invaded England. The so-called American "melting pot" is a recent instance of assimilation. It is not usually possible today to tell the descendants of Englishmen or Germans who came here in the eighteenth century from the descendants of Scotsmen who emigrated at about the same time. Previously distinct groups have become fused into one, or assimilated. A factor which helps complete the process of assimilation is amalgamation, the intermarrying of members of different groups.

Amalgamation We sometimes say that a person is partially assimilated, or that Italian-Americans, for example, are not as fully assimilated as Irish-Americans. The fact that assimilation is not an all-or-nothing condition but rather a matter of degree is simply an indication that it is a process that occurs through time. Complete assimilation always implies amalgamation—that is, accepted intermarriage between the originally divergent groups. Without biological amalgamation, complete assimilation is not possible. If the two groups are still differentiated by the provision that their members shall not intermarry, then they are, *ipso facto*, not fully assimilated.

Mere intermixture of groups to a limited degree does not guarantee assimilation. Amalgamation must be accepted in the mores; it must become a part of the institutional structure before assimilation exists. For instance, in the United States there has been considerable racial crossing between whites and Negroes, but there has been little true amalgamation, despite the fact of a common culture. No observer of the contemporary American scene would contend that Negroes and whites have become fused into one indistinguishable whole. For purposes of most interaction, accommodation and stratification rather than assimilation have been the rule. On the other hand, the rate of intermarriage among our European immigrant groups is a definite indication of the fusion of persons from many societies into one new one. The United States is a case study of a society composed, through assimilation and amal-

gamation, of a variety of social and biological elements.

In Chapter 13 we shall say more about assimilation, the factors that affect its rate, its effect on the stratification structure, and the factors that impede it.

Acculturation When two or more cultures come into contact, the subsequent intermixture of shared, learned behavior patterns is called *acculturation.* This process may involve the almost complete absorption of one culture by another, or a relatively equal merging of traits and patterns from both cultures. Acculturation can occur with or without assimilation. The accommodative relations of Christian and Moslem societies through the centuries have resulted in acculturation. Christians have adopted some of the behavior patterns of Moslems, and Moslems have adopted some of the behavior patterns of Christians; but the members of the two societies have not assimilated.

The blending of Oriental and Occidental elements in contemporary Japanese culture is another instance of acculturation without assimilation of two groups. The Japanese way of life has changed considerably in a relatively short time under the impact of Western culture. Not only is there more Western-style clothing in Japan, as well as other evidences of acculturation, such as increased use of telephones, television, and subways, but there are alterations in such basic culture patterns as food consumption and formal education. (See Table 1.)

Again, the hybrid patterns of Latin-American societies have sprung from the acculturation of Spanish and American Indian cultures, characterized by a degree of both assimilation and amalga-

TABLE 1 · Some Examples of Twenty Years of Acculturation in Japan *

	1935	1955
Per cent which rice is of total diet	85.5	69.3
Grams of protein in average daily diet	52.4	66.0
Number of students registered in high schools and universities	186,000	3,201,000

* Data from "Japanese Habits Undergo Change," the *New York Times*, July 8, 1956.

mation. Large portions of Greek and Roman culture have become acculturated with Hebraic and Germanic patterns, and have, in turn, contributed to our own culture.

The whole question of the degree of acculturation and the interplay of accommodation and assimilation is crucial in the contemporary world, not only in the relations of nation-states with one another in peace and war but in the relations of stratified classes to one another within societies. It is often noted that the social distance between the most privileged classes and the least educated, lowest-paid classes in our society is considerably narrower than it was a generation or two ago. When we speak of the existence of "mass society," we are referring to the fact that Mrs. Astorbilt and Joe Doakes saw the same television program last night, that both are members of the Book-of-the-Month Club, and that their sons at the Old English Finishing School and Corner High, respectively, are dressed in remarkably similar clothes. We are referring, in other words, to acculturation between classes within a society.

Socialization Socialization, as we have seen, is interaction by means of which the individual learns the social and cultural requirements that make him a functioning member of his society. This interaction teaches him habits, ideas, attitudes, and values. He learns to conform to the cultural expectations expressed as mores, folkways, traditions, and sanctions. He develops a sense of self and learns to identify with culturally defined in-groups. He acquires his in-group's attitudes toward out-groups —attitudes of opposition, avoidance, or indifference. The initial socialization occurs in the child's contacts with his parents, siblings, and playmates. But all through life the individual continues to feel the impact of his society upon him.

Since we discussed socialization in some detail in Chapter 6, we shall not pursue the subject further here. It is mentioned at this point only to emphasize the fact that, like the other concepts dealt with here, it is a universal process. We shall return to the topic when we deal with the family in Chapter 20 and with educational institutions in Chapter 21.

INTERPRETATIVE SUMMARY

The word *process* describes people interacting: fighting, helping one another, teaching their young, and so on. Like structures and functions, certain processes are universal. One such process is opposition, or struggle over a goal which cannot be shared or which the antagonists refuse to share. They may calmly concentrate on attaining the goal, they may see destruction of their enemy as absolutely essential to their own success, they may be able to "see his side" and be willing to give up part of their demands so that he will not suffer, or they may not even be conscious that a struggle is going on in the first place. The form of the struggle will also be dependent on how each antagonist assesses his relative strength; a powerful force may insist on having all its demands met, while equal sides will probably settle for some sort of compromise.

Co-operation, the process of working together for a common goal, is the opposite of competition and conflict. Co-operation leads to acculturation, in which cultures or subcultures adopt behavior patterns from one another, and finally to assimilation, the state in which two groups actually blend into one.

All societies condone both opposition and co-operation under some circumstances. However, a given society may stress one more than the other, depending on the ethos of the society. Furthermore, goals themselves and the rules concerning how one may go about attaining them will differ from society to society.

Two intra-society processes are differentiation and socialization. In assigning specialties, or differentiating, a culture must take into account certain broad biological limitations which members of all societies have in common; beyond this, the culture may follow its own course in dividing necessary labor and deciding how groups should be ranked socially. Socialization is the process in which an individual is taught the ways of his culture, including its ways of carrying out the other processes.

The terms used to describe universal processes are also used in describing the states resulting from those processes. The process of stratification results in a society that is stratified, the process of assimilation results in partial or total assimilation, socialization of a child results in an adult who is reasonably socialized.

REVIEW AND SUGGESTED READINGS

A · VOCABULARY

Accommodation	Competition	Interaction
Acculturation	Conflict	Mutual aid
Amalgamation	Co-operation	Stratification
Assimilation	Differentiation	

B · QUESTIONS AND TOPICS FOR REVIEW

1. Are elections in your state and city usually competitions or conflicts? Discuss the most recent one, or one you remember well, in the light of these two concepts.
2. The following illustrate what social processes?
   a. A French child is heard saying, "C'est o.k.!"
   b. A magazine article reports that college-educated Jewish people are tending increasingly to marry outside their religion.
   c. A group of American technologists goes to an underdeveloped country to help out for a year.
   d. An old woman declares, "I can't remember when the 'old country's' special holidays are anymore, and none of you young people ever knew."
3. A teacher and a high-school student are at odds after the student has declared contemptuously that the teacher's class is worthless. Discuss various ways in

which the bad feelings between them might be altered. Use specific terms you have learned in this chapter.

4. In Chapter 2, we introduced several typologies, such as in-group and out-group. What are some typologies discussed in this chapter?
5. The statement "Let's agree to disagree" illustrates what social process?
6. How do subcultures in our society try to resist assimilation?
7. What arguments can you think of to support the idea that wars are usually competitions, not conflicts?

C • SUGGESTIONS FOR FURTHER READING

R. F. Bales. *Interaction Process Analysis: A Method for the Study of Small Groups.* Reading, Mass.: Addison-Wesley Co., Inc., 1950.

One of the accounts of the development of a system of categories for classifying interactions in a small group. Tentative hypotheses are presented concerning the character of interaction and the development of norms.

Stuart Chase. *Roads to Agreement: Successful Methods in the Science of Human Relations.* New York: Harper & Brothers, 1951.

A survey of various means of accommodating conflict, such as "worker-participation" in industrial relations, the Quaker meeting, and group dynamics.

Lewis A. Coser. *The Functions of Social Conflict.* New York: The Free Press of Glencoe, 1956.

The author discusses the consequences of conflict which are adaptive for, or which contribute to, the social structure.

E. Franklin Frazier. *Race and Culture Contacts in the Modern World.* New York: Alfred A. Knopf, Inc., 1957.

A summary on a global basis, covering the past two centuries, of racial and cultural conflict, its accommodation, and the assimilation process.

Milton M. Gordon. *Assimilation in American Life.* New York: Oxford University Press, 1964.

An excellent analysis of the process of assimilation of racial, religious, and national minorities, and of the pressures for and against assimilation in an urban industrial society.

Joyce O. Hertzler. *Society in Action: A Study of Basic Social Processes.* New York: The Dryden Press, 1954.

Chapter 1 contains a good discussion of the significance of the idea of process. The book has an extensive bibliography.

Arthur Kornhauser, Robert Dubin, and Arthur M. Ross, eds. *Industrial Conflict.* New York: McGraw-Hill Book Co., 1954.

Forty papers on industrial conflict, including two on its origins and several on its accommodation and control.

Robert E. Park and E. W. Burgess. *Introduction to the Science of Sociology,* 2nd ed. Chicago: University of Chicago Press, 1924.

Chapters 4–6 and 8–11 contain pertinent source materials and good theoretical discussions. This is still the classic discussion in English of social processes.

SUMMARY OF PART I

In Chapter 1, science was defined and sociology's place as a social science was explained. Since sociology was defined as the social science dealing with interaction as such, Chapter 2 presented a method for classifying groups and for distinguishing between groups and aggregates.

Chapters 3, 4, and 5 dealt with culture. Chapter 3 presented a brief history of culture and introduced some terms useful in describing the form and content of all cultures. Chapter 4 discussed why cultures vary and provided two extended examples of cultural variation. Chapter 5 dealt with the rules which societies impose on their members so that their culture will not disintegrate, and with the ways in which societies' members are brought to conform.

Chapter 6 paused to deal with concepts generally considered the province of psychology, yet important for our further study of the individual in society. The chapter concerned personality, especially the development of personality through interaction. The relative importance of heredity and environment, particularly social environment, was discussed. The concept of the self was introduced, and the development of the self was traced from its roots in childhood role experimentation to its graduate emergence in the self-conscious, integrated personality.

Chapters 7 and 8 examined four concepts previously described as crucial for all scientific analysis: structure, function, pattern, and process. Jobs which all societies must perform in order to survive and the universal structures which perform the jobs were discussed in Chapter 7. The universal processes of opposition, co-operation, differentiation, and socialization were studied in Chapter 8.

In Part II, we shall discuss in more detail the social process of differentiation, analyze stratification structures and their functions, and study urban structures and their consequences for social life.

PART II

SOCIAL ORGANIZATION

CHAPTER 9

Status and Role

When an architect speaks of the "structure" of a building, he is talking about three things: (1) the materials of which it is composed (brick siding, asphalt shingle roof); (2) the relationship between the parts (the porch floor rests on a foundation; from the porch floor rise four pillars which support the porch roof); and (3) the building as a unit or whole (a split-level house, a Southern colonial dwelling). When a sociologist speaks of the "structure" of a society, he is talking about the same three sets of features which concern the architect in describing a house: (1) the building materials (number of males and females or of adults and children in each occupational category, and so on); (2) the interrelationship of the parts (what husbands expect from wives, how employees interact with employers, how parents and children treat one another); and (3) the nature of the society as a whole—that is, the result of the materials of which it is built and the way they are put together. For example, the Russian Communists expect identification with the collectives and put great stress on the obligations which each person has toward his fellows; Americans, in contrast, encourage each person to develop his own talents, and they think highly of one who has achieved a great deal in this individualistic, competitive society.

BASIC UNITS OF SOCIAL STRUCTURE

The building blocks of which a social structure is composed are called *statuses*. A status, then, is a position in a social structure. Whenever we describe a position without regard to the individual who is occupying it, we are talking about a status.

Status An infantryman is issued one winter uniform, one summer uniform, and a rifle. He must be between certain age limits. He must have an I.Q. score of 70 or above. He has authority over enemy civilians. Commissioned officers and military police have authority over him. Note that these sentences describe the *status* of infantryman; they do not describe a specific person. It does not matter whether the infantryman is dull, jolly, or morose: the personality of the individual occupying the status is quite another variable. When Phil Talcott is discharged and Sam Kingsley is drafted to replace him, the status of infantryman remains unchanged. A status is an abstraction, a description of one's place in a social group relative to other positions in the group.

Role A *role* is the function of a status. When an individual occupies a given position, the placement of that position

Each Person
Plays
Many Roles

Monkmeyer

Husband and father

Monkmeyer

Church Board Member

Monkmeyer

Salesman

above some others and below still others will have consequences for his interaction in the group. The consequences of occupying that status are called his role. We can speak, then, of the status of foreman, which is a position in a work group above that of laborer and below that of shop superintendent. The role of the foreman is the result of his status in the group: he is expected to give orders to laborers and to take orders from the shop superintendent. Like status, role is an abstraction; it remains the same even if the expectations are being met by different individuals. Retiring one foreman and hiring a replace-

ment does not alter either the position, the status, or its consequences, the role.

Role Behavior The component of the social situation that *can* be altered is the *role behavior*, or the way a certain individual fulfills the expectations of his role. The status of surgeon ranks above that of nurse; the surgeon's role includes the expectation that he will tell the nurse what to do. But the role behavior of surgeons varies considerably. Dr. Merton gives specific orders in a pleasant voice, whereas Dr. Moore gives very general instructions in a harsh tone. The contrast between them stems from neither status nor role, but from role behavior.

Every person in a society occupies many statuses, of course. A person may be at one and the same time a citizen of the United States, an attorney, a member of the Episcopal Church, a Post Commander in the American Legion, a male, an adult, a husband, a father, an uncle, a son, a nephew, and a member of the local Board of Education. Each of these is one of his statuses. With each is associated a role, a set of expectations he is supposed to fulfill with respect to people in other related statuses, such as minister, wife, Chairman of the Board of Education, and so on. To each of these roles he brings his personality, which determines some of the patterns of his role behavior. Since, fundamentally, each role and status is derived from social norms, or group-shared expectations of what ought to be, people in the society will evaluate his role behaviors and pass judgment on how well he meets the expectations of each of his roles.

Prestige and Esteem Each status in a social structure has attached to it an evaluation. It is considered "good" or "important" or "difficult" or "routine" or "criminal" or "dirty." There is always some judgment in the norms of a society about how desirable a status is. This evaluation of the status is called its *prestige*. The evaluation of an individual's role behavior in a status which he occupies is called *esteem*. This is the judgment by one's fellows of how well he fulfills the expectations of his role. Most people in the United States believe that vice-president of a large corporation is a more desirable status than street sweeper. Thus, no matter who is

occupying the status or how well he is doing, it is proper to say that the status of corporation executive has higher prestige than the status of street sweeper. However, people may notice that Bob Simpson does an excellent job of sweeping the street, while Dick McGinnis does not take his work seriously and leaves trash piled up at the curb. Simpson, then, has high esteem because of his role behavior, while McGinnis has low esteem, despite the fact that the two occupy the same status.

A person may be in a status which has high prestige and earn high esteem by his role behavior there, but prestige does not ensure esteem. The alcoholic attorney has low esteem even though he is in a status which has high prestige; the best cleaning woman in an office building occupies a status with low prestige but earns high esteem. The esteem accruing collectively to individuals in a status can in time alter the prestige of that status. If, over a period of years, only incompetent persons were made deans of colleges, the prestige of deanship would suffer. Each of us is usually proud to point to highly esteemed persons who occupy the same status as we, because we feel (perhaps without being aware of it) that their presence raises the prestige of our position.

The Reciprocal Nature of Roles Since a role is a set of expectations, it is impossible to define one role without referring to another. There cannot be a parent without a child, or an employer without an employee. There must be another role doing the expecting. In this sense, roles are but a series of rights and duties—that is, they represent certain reciprocal relations among individuals. To understand this interplay, we must define *right* and *duty*. A right is a privilege to act which is reciprocal to another's duty to permit the act. Of course, a duty is not always passive: a duty may sometimes be an obligation to act, reciprocal to another's right to expect the act. The rights of one are always qualified and limited by the obligations of another.

All societies reveal a wide range of such reciprocal relations. The economic structure *is* a structure because the interactions of men in the market express more or less widely accepted rights and duties. A legal contract to work or to deliver a product at a specified time and place is a pattern of reciprocal rights and duties supported by the law of contracts. In family life the interplay of sympathetic identification of parent and child is counterpoised by obligations to provide on the part of the former and by duties of obedience on the part of the latter. Power relations in the operations of government reveal the same pattern. The king and his subjects, the judge and the accused, the police and the citizen whose property he protects, the elected official and his constituency, all have reciprocal rights and duties.

Of the many patterns of such reciprocities, some operate quite independently of others. Some come into conflict with each other. Many rights and duties associated with family life or religion have little or nothing to do with those outside the home or the church. In contrast, a man's ethical code about killing may cause inner conflict regarding his rights and duties as citizen-soldier when he is called on to engage in war. Or the widely accepted relations of competitive business may, in time, come into conflict with one's humanitarian feelings. As related to the organization of the self, such conflicting roles, made up as they are of habits, attitudes, ideas, and values, may produce a rift in the personality. Yet in most societies we find that a cluster of roles may become the center around which an integrated personality is built up.

Forms of Status and Role   As we have said, each person in a human society occupies a number of statuses. Some of them are ascribed; others are achieved. By *ascribed statuses* we mean those positions which are assigned to an individual regardless of his abilities or performance. "Princess" is an ascribed status; where there is a hereditary royalty, a girl does not work her way up to being princess. She is *born* a princess, and whether she is pretty or ugly, tall or short, intelligent or stupid, a princess she remains. *Achieved statuses*, on the other hand, are not assigned at birth, but are left open to be filled by the persons who compete most successfully for them. Being male is an ascribed status. It is determined at birth; either you are male or you are not. Being a husband is an achieved status; it does not result automatically from one's being born a male but depends on a male's own behavior. Negro is an ascribed status. One cannot change his color to white. But policeman is an achieved status. One is not born a policeman; he becomes one through his own talent and choice.

ASCRIBED STATUSES AND ROLES

In some societies statuses have been largely of the ascribed sort. This was true of the ancient Incan Empire, where

An example of ascribed status: age.

The Chase Manhattan Bank

the newborn male infant was classified as "babe in arms," later as "able to stand," and still later as "under six." Then from six to eight years he was termed a "bread receiver," and so on, until at twenty years he became "almost a man," at twenty-five "able-bodied," at fifty "half an old man," and after sixty years "an old man asleep."[1] While no modern society draws such sharp distinctions as these, highly authoritarian cultures, both contemporary and ancient, often fix statuses rather rigidly. This was true in feudal Japan, for example, where individual and family status was regulated by mi-

nute rules. In contrast, one of the distinguishing features of democratic societies is the permission of individual choice and freedom. While ascription of certain statuses remains, in a wide range of activities status is acquired, not ascribed or fixed in advance.

In highly fixed societies the individual may not experience the fear and worry over his roles and statuses as much as one does in a society demanding continual struggle for role and status. In the latter, anxiety and a heavy sense of inferiority and guilt usually follow if one fails to "make good."

Age All societies recognize differences in role and status related to age. Adults have more physical strength and

1 · A. M. Tozzer, *Social Origins and Social Continuities* (New York: The Macmillan Company, 1925), p. 208.

more experience than adolescents. In old age, mental and physical powers decline, and dependence on others once more limits the range of thought and action. Yet variations in age are defined more by custom than by physiology. As Ralph Linton puts it, "In the case of age, as in that of sex, biological factors involved appear to be secondary to the cultural ones in determining the content of status." [2]

In most societies there are four major categories of age differences as related to role and status: infancy and childhood, youth, maturity or adulthood, and old age.

The Ascribed Status of Child The role and status of infant and child are always related to dependency on and guardianship by adults. Yet how societies regard babies varies among both primitive and civilized peoples, and may change with time and circumstance. In ancient Sparta, where there was heavy stress on the need for a strong body as well as a normal mind, sickly or deformed infants were done away with, usually by being abandoned in the hills. Among some primitive tribes, twins were thought to be a bad omen, and they were disposed of lest some evil descend upon the family and the tribe. In other societies, as in our own, babies are idolized and made much of by adults.

Among some peoples the child is regarded as a miniature adult, and is expected to act like "a little man" or "a little lady." Among others there is firm demand for silent conformity—children are expected "to be seen but not heard" when in the presence of their

"elders and betters." In still other societies a child may be given a very high status. This is so among the Marquesans, where the eldest son is considered the head of the family, regardless of his age. Ralph Linton reports seeing a nine-year-old Marquesan boy, son of a chieftain, drive all the adults out of the family house when he became angry over what seemed a trivial matter.[3] Sometimes there is little or no formal direction or discipline of the children until they are ready to pass into adult status, say, during adolescence.

In Western society, it is clear that the culturally defined period of dependency and immaturity has been markedly lengthened, largely as a result of these societies' complexity, their emphasis on occupational specialization, and their high standards of living. Indeed, this prolongation of the occupancy of the ascribed status of child is one measure of the complexity of a culture.

Since each role is defined by reference to another, there are certain reciprocal relations between parent and child. The major rights and duties in this relationship tend to take shape as norms. Obviously, the duties of the parent to the child cannot be enforced by the latter. But failure to provide for the child's care and training according to the group norms may be punished by the group. Failure of parents to live up to the norms of child care laid down by the culture usually results in some other group's taking over this obligation. In a primary community, serious neglect of children by their parents may lead to gossip as a device to stimulate the parents to do their duty, or neighbors may help the children. In urbanized society today we have a large number of

2 · Ralph Linton, *The Study of Man* (New York: Appleton-Century-Crofts, Inc., 1936), p. 119 By permission.

3 · *Ibid.*, p. 119.

agencies, both privately and publicly supported, which concern themselves with child welfare. In a society which places a high value on children, failure on the part of the parents to fulfill their duties leads to their punishment by sanctions decreed in the law and the mores and to the rise of substitute means replacing parental care.

The Ascribed Status of Youth The break between various "age" periods is determined by culture, as well as by birthdays. While some societies recognize changes from childhood to sexual maturity by special ceremonials and overt changes in social status and role, other societies make no such sharp division. In our society we recognize a certain age gradation in our division of schooling into elementary, secondary, and college. Confirmation ceremonies and high-school graduation symbolize a passage of the growing boy or girl into a new role and status. The long period of permissive and accepted preparation for adulthood is restricted, for the most part, to the urban, literate societies, largely as a result of their complexity, specialization, and high standards of living.

This transition from childhood to youth is associated with the coming of full sexual capacity and the appearance of those secondary sex characteristics which further distinguish the male from the female. There are also changes in height and weight, and other bodily modification which mark the shift toward adulthood. Since there are variations in the age at which the individual passes through puberty, the culture usually provides a certain latitude for fulfillment of the expected roles and statuses related to this phase.

A major expectation of the as-cribed role of youth is that one learn the essential skills that will prepare him for his adult role and status. In Western societies we tend to prolong this period of preparation, just as we tend to prolong the period of childhood. This is neatly reflected in the law. We have thrown added protection about young people by increasing the years of compulsory education, by prohibiting child labor, and by restricting early marriage.

We have, however, a curious inconsistency in our treatment of youth. True, the continued emotional and financial dependence of children on parents is evident. Nowhere else in the world is youth given such leisure and opportunity for education. In other societies individuals in this age group have ascribed adult roles. Yet our youth have greater freedom from parental control than formerly. Our adolescent boys and girls are more sophisticated and mature in many ways than their parents were in their youth. Opportunities for escaping from family, neighborhood, and community controls afford our young people forms of experience which their fathers and mothers often do not understand or approve of. Various factors have created a situation in which the role and status of youth, their rights and duties, and the responsibility of their elders for their future welfare are not always clearly defined. This very confusion reflects changing patterns of differentiation in our society.

The Ascribed Status of Adult In every society the adult takes over rights and duties not expected of children, youth, or old people. The age at which the individual comes to maturity will be determined by elements in the particular culture. Thus, among the American Plains Indians, acceptance as a member

of a war party marked arrival at adulthood. In our society political majority
is assumed when the person acquires
voting privileges. The capacity to hold
office, too, is assumed to be related to
age. In the United States, while most
local and state offices are open to any
qualified voter 21 years or over, the
holding of federal offices is restricted
to narrower age limits. A person under
25 years of age cannot hold office as a
Representative in the national Congress. One must be 30 years old to be
eligible for the United States Senate
and 35 years to be eligible for the
Presidency.

Voting privileges and eligibility to
hold office and perform jury service are
basic marks of adult political responsibility in a democratic country. With
these, of course, go all the obligations
of the good citizen, which are stipu-
lated, at least on the negative side, by
the legal codes and mores regarding
conduct, both private and public. Under a dictatorship the ordinary adult
may be accorded no voting or discussion privileges, but he will be ascribed
specific public roles as party member,
worker, taxpayer, or soldier—roles assigned only to those considered in this
society as adults.

The Ascribed Status of the Aged Old
age is determined not solely by the
physiological condition of muscles,
glands, and brain, but also by the culture. To cite our Plains Indians again,
loss of war prowess meant that the man
was ascribed a new status. But when
the old men of a tribe continued to
wield great influence far into the years
of physiological senility, old age in the
cultural sense was delayed, no matter
how feeble mentally or physically the
individual became.

In some primitive societies old age
carries with it a real distinction in prestige. In many tribes the elders are the
most powerful and revered members of
the group. In a country like ancient
China, where ancestor worship dominated family and community life for
centuries, the power of old age over
the social order was everywhere apparent. Deference to old age, to the patri-
arch of the family, and the desire for
sons to carry on ancestor worship long
retarded the rise of new ideas and new
ways of life.

Throughout the history of our
own European culture, old age has retained great power. In the patriarchal
family order, as in ancient Rome, the
oldest male in the family retained control over all other members. It is so
even today in the peasant areas of Europe. Where urbanization has taken
place and industry has developed, this
reverence for old age has been modified.

A large percentage of our old people become dependent on others for
economic support. Until recently, in
our individualistic society practically
all provision for old age rested on the
efforts of the person himself and on his
family. Only gradually are we assigning a certain responsibility to the community and state to provide for the
aged through pensions and insurance.

Age statuses are ascribed; they are
fixed for the individual at birth, regardless of his efforts in later years. No matter how hard he works at it, an eight-
year-old child cannot immediately enjoy the status of adult. And a thirty-
year-old man, whether he works at it
or not, whether he wants to be or not,
is considered an adult. He is an adult
because the norms of the society decree
that he is; the status is assigned him,
not achieved.

Sex Because it is a visible, unchangeable physical characteristic, sex is an obvious and convenient basis for ascribed status. All societies have a dual set of roles associated with the two sexes. The first set is necessitated, of course, by biological facts: the male and the female have different roles in the reproduction of children. But there are many other statuses ascribed on the basis of sex. It is a basic variable in the division of labor. Occupations, religious roles, intellectual pursuits, political responsibilities, and many other activities are differentiated according to sex. The interesting thing about sexually ascribed statuses, as we shall see, is the wide range of variation from society to society in the assignment of sex roles.

(a) Sex: Cultural Variability. People have often assumed that all male statuses and female statuses are so ascribed because of innate differences between the sexes. Women are described as having more musical ability than men, or less business sense, or as being physically weaker or more religious. Ralph Linton provides a nice perspective on this topic with descriptions of roles ascribed on the basis of sex in other societies.

The division and ascription of statuses with relation to sex seems to be basic in all social systems. All societies prescribe different attitudes and activities to men and to women. Most of them try to rationalize these prescriptions in terms of the physiological differences between the sexes or their different roles in reproduction. However, a comparative study of the statuses ascribed to women and men in different cultures seems to show that while such factors may have served as a starting point for the development of a division the actual ascriptions are almost entirely determined by culture. Even the psychological characteristics ascribed to men and women in different societies vary so much that they can have little physiological basis. Our own idea of women as ministering angels contrasts sharply with the ingenuity of women as torturers among the Iroquois and the sadistic delight they took in the process. Even the last two generations have seen a sharp change in the psychological patterns for women in our own society. The delicate, fainting lady of the middle eighteen-hundreds is as extinct as the dodo.

When it comes to the ascription of occupations, which is after all an integral part of status, we find the differences in various societies even more marked. Arapesh women regularly carry heavier loads than men "because their heads are so much harder and stronger." In some societies women do most of the manual labor; in others, as in the Marquesas, even cooking, housekeeping, and baby-tending are proper male occupations, and women spend most of their time primping. Even the general rule that women's handicap through pregnancy and nursing indicates the more active occupations as male and the less active ones as female has many exceptions. Thus among the Tasmanians seal-hunting was women's work. They swam out to the seal rocks, stalked the animals, and clubbed them. Tasmanian women also hunted opossums, which required the climbing of large trees.

Although the actual ascription of occupations along sex lines is highly variable, the pattern of sex division is constant. There are very few societies in which every important activity has not been definitely assigned to men or to women. Even when the two sexes cooperate in a particular occupation, the field of each is usually clearly delimited. Thus in Madagascar rice culture the men make the seed beds and terraces and prepare the fields for transplanting. The women do the work of transplanting, which is hard and backbreaking. The women weed the crop, but the men harvest it. The women then carry it to the threshing floors, where the men thresh it while the women winnow it. Lastly, the women pound the grain in mortars and cook it.

When a society takes over a new industry, there is often a period of uncertainty during which the work may be done by either sex, but it soon falls into the province of one or the other. In Madagascar, pottery is made by men in some tribes and by women in others. The only tribe in which it is made by both men and women is one into which the art has been introduced within the last sixty years. I was told that during the fifteen years preceding my visit there had been a marked decrease in the number of male potters, many men who had once practiced the art having given it up. The factor of lowered wages, usually advanced as the reason for men leaving one of our own occupations when women enter it in force, certainly was not operative here. The field was not overcrowded, and the prices for men's and women's products were the same. Most of the men who had given up the trade were vague as to their reasons, but a few said frankly that they did not like to compete with women. Apparently the entry of women into the occupation had robbed it of a certain amount of prestige. It was no longer quite the thing for a man to be a potter, even though he was a very good one.[4]

The notion that a division of labor with statuses ascribed on the basis of sex is rooted in biological differences simply does not make sense, for variations occur not only between societies but even within a society as large as ours. For example, in the Midwest, women were ordinarily assigned the job of husking corn, while men were trimmers. In the Far West, the arrangement was reversed: men were huskers and women were trimmers.

(b) Sex: Physical Differences. The ancient myth that women are innately the weaker sex is not supported by science. In fact, there is a mass of evidence that the female withstands the hazards of life better than the male. The most obvious illustration can be seen in the difference in life expectancy. As Table 2 shows, at birth the life expectancy

4 · Ibid., pp. 116–118. By permission.

TABLE 2 · Life Expectancy at Birth of White Males and Females in United States, 1900–1960 *

	LIFE EXPECTANCY	
Year	Male	Female
1900	46.6	48.7
1930	59.7	63.5
1950	67.3	72.6
1960	67.4	74.1

* Health, Education, and Welfare Trends (Washington, D.C.: U.S. Department of Health, Education, and Welfare, Government Printing Office, 1960), p. 3. The 1960 figures are from U.S. Bureau of the Census, Statistical Abstract of the United States, 1963.

of white females is nearly seven years greater than that of white males. More remarkable is the fact that the difference between the sexes has increased in the very period when life expectancy has been lengthened. The same kind of difference obtains in infant mortality figures. Although infant mortality in the United States has decreased about two-thirds since 1900, the ratio of male to female deaths has actually risen. It has been established that the relative weakness of the male is a condition existing even before birth. More male than female children are conceived, but the ratio of prenatal mortality is 127 males to 100 females.[5]

We should not overlook the possibility that some of the sharp differences between the sexes in mortality rates may be attributed to culture rather than to physiology. It is not unlikely that the stresses which men face in our society because of their sexually ascribed statuses contribute to a shorter life expectancy for them. At any rate, the idea that women are physically unable to perform heavy work cannot be accepted. They are unable to do heavy

5 · Amram Scheinfeld, Women and Men (New York: Harcourt, Brace & Co., 1944), p. 32.

labor in our society because our norms say that they should not, and their ascribed roles neither prepare them for it nor allow them to do it.

(c) Sex: The Division of Labor. The fact that the roles most directly related to childbearing and child rearing tend to be ascribed on the basis of sex has an effect on the whole set of economic statuses. Even where economic statuses are, within sexual categories, achieved statuses, there will be differences between the roles of males and females in those statuses ascribed according to sex.

From what we know of the natural separation of the reproductive function and from observations of nonliterate tribes, it is clear that, for the most part, a certain basic division of labor had its source in sex differences. An elaborate cross-comparison of occupations and sex among nonliterate peoples made by G. P. Murdock showed that males are concerned either "exclusively" or "predominantly" with such matters as pursuit of sea mammals, hunting, trapping, and fishing. In contrast, females are "predominantly" or "exclusively" occupied with such activities as gathering fruit and nuts, preserving meat and fish, gathering herbs, roots, and seeds, and cooking.[6]

While there are some variations, warfare and the chase seem the more usual habits of the male, while sedentary occupations are more often assigned to the female, who must remain near home in order to attend to the young children. As W. I. Thomas long ago put it, "The primitive division of labor among the sexes was not in any sense an arrangement dictated by the men, but a habit into which both men and women fell, to begin with, through their difference of organization—a socially useful habit whose rightness no one questioned and whose origin no one thought of looking into."[7] Moreover, so accepted was this view that a man who did woman's work was looked on with scorn and contempt, not just by men but by women too.

Modern peasant and farm households, until the introduction of industrial devices, were not greatly different from those of more primitive societies. It was not until the commercial and industrial changes of the modern world took women out of the home that their economic functions changed. The emancipation of women—both mothers and grown daughters—from the household economics illustrates again how culture patterns give the direction to social processes.

Women in increasing numbers have gone into vocations outside the home, gaining money wages of their own and freedom of residence, and experiencing changes in their personalities which influence other relations of the sexes as well. Yet, in spite of great changes, there remain many inequalities between the sexes in rates of pay, hours of labor, control of working conditions, and types of work. Table 3 shows that women usually earn less than men even when they have the same occupational statuses.

The common defense of lower pay for women is that they are not as efficient as men, which is perhaps true in many cases, not from less innate ability so much as from lack of adequate training. In the whole public reaction to the newer economic role of women there

6 · See G. P. Murdock, "Comparative Data on Division of Labor by Sex," *Social Forces*, 1937, 15:551–553.

7 · W. I. Thomas, *Sex and Society* (Boston: Richard G. Badger, 1907), p. 140.

TABLE 3 · Income Differences Between Male and Female Year-round Full-time Workers in Selected Occupational Categories, Measured by Median Income of Females as Percentage of Median Income of Males, 1959 *

OCCUPATIONAL CATEGORIES	MEDIAN INCOME		FEMALE INCOME (as a Percentage of Male Income)
	Male	Female	
Professional, technical, and kindred workers	$7,122	$4,342	61.0
Nonfarm managers, officials, and proprietors	6,471	3,528	54.5
Clerical and kindred workers	5,129	3,500	68.2
Sales workers	5,544	2,324	41.9
Operatives and kindred workers	4,731	2,890	61.1
Service workers, except private household	4,023	2,187	54.4

* *Current Population Reports*, Series P-60, No. 35, January 5, 1961, Table 27, p. 45.

is a curious paradox. On the one hand, much so-called "social legislation" aimed at control of hours, wages, working conditions, and kinds of work for women rests on the ancient attitude toward women as the "weaker sex." On the other hand, many advocates of women's complete equality with men, especially in economics and politics, demand that they be given the freedom allowed men to enter any vocation and receive equal wages, and that they have complete equality before the law.

Race Since we shall devote an entire chapter to racial and ethnic aspects of stratification, we shall note here only that, in the United States and some other societies, race is an ascribed status. Like age and sex, race can have a modifying effect on the prestige of an achieved status and can affect the esteem which one receives for his behavior, even in an achieved role.

ACHIEVED STATUSES AND ROLES

All societies have some ascribed statuses, though some use ascription more than others. Age and sex are uni-

versally used in human societies as a basis for ascription. All societies also have some achieved statuses. Again, the proportion of statuses which are open to achievement varies widely around the world.

No matter how much emphasis a society places on its ascribed statuses, there will be some individuals who will alter the place they are assigned in the structure because they have special talents or ambitions. Societies therefore always make at least minimum provisions in their normative structures for the orderly change of status. In effect this allows a society to capitalize on the deviant instead of punishing him. Furthermore, by making certain changes of status legitimate, a society may recruit members with unusual abilities for statuses where average ability is just not enough. The leader of combat teams, the artist, and the inventor are examples of statuses which a society may find it worthwhile to throw open to achievement rather than assigning on the basis of birth.

The more complex a society is— the more specialized its division of labor—the higher the proportion of achieved statuses it is likely to have. An

Ewing Galloway

An example of an achieved status: college graduate.

elaborate division of labor offers the individual who is extremely talented a competitive advantage. If every male in a society does his own hunting, his own house-building, and his own toolmaking, a talent for toolmaking in one man or house-building in another is of little importance. But once the society is so structured that one man specializes in house-building and another in toolmaking, allowing these statuses to be achieved offers dividends both for the specialists and for the society. More and better houses can be built, and more and better tools can be made if each man is encouraged to perform the task at which he excels instead of being assigned a status because his father held it before him.

In a society such as ours, virtually all occupational statuses are achieved. The proliferation of secondary groups

means that most organizational memberships also are achieved statuses. Many primary group roles are achieved as well; that is what we are referring to when we say that one is free to choose his friends. They are not, in other words, assigned to him by something like clan membership. We are even allowed, in our society, to treat church membership as an achieved status, which makes our social structure unusual indeed, from either the historical or cross-cultural point of view. In most societies, one is born into his religious group; it is just as much an ascribed status as his family membership. To leave it is to be excommunicated from the tribe. But in the United States, religion, like occupation, education, marital status, and many other statuses, is left to the discretion of the individual.

In a society in which almost all

occupational statuses are achieved, individuals are absolutely interdependent. The very specialization which leads to a system of achieved statuses produces bonds of essential interaction. The woodworker is dependent on the toolmaker, the weaver is dependent on the shepherd, the grocer on the farmer, and the entrepreneur on the banker. A structure characterized by achieved statuses enhances competition for those statuses, but the specialization of roles also necessitates co-operation.

THE INTERRELATIONSHIP OF ASCRIBED AND ACHIEVED STATUSES

If all statuses were achieved, some of them might not get filled. All societies, therefore, ascribe some statuses, because it is better to be sure that the role will be performed, even in a mediocre fashion, than to take a chance on not having it done at all in the hope that it will be done extremely well. Too, the assignment of every individual

to some ascribed statuses provides a certain security; one does not have to face a life in which all his fellows are potential competitors for every bit of prestige and esteem which he may strive for and attain.

Within this framework of ascribed statuses are sets of achieved statuses. One can compete for some of these, but he does not have to compete for all of them. The ascribed status of male excuses one from competing for a whole set of statuses: seamstress, stenographer, and so on. The ascribed status of old man relieves one from competing for statuses such as quarterback, valedictorian, and others. In other words, ascription reduces some of the pressure involved in free choice. The existence of some statuses for which one is eligible to compete, on the other hand, accomplishes two things. It permits the individual some latitude in picking what he wants to do and is good at doing, and it contributes to the survival of the social structure by motivating people to seek statuses and ultimately fulfill their duties.

INTERPRETATIVE SUMMARY

Status, prestige, and role are abstractions dealing with society's tendency to differentiate, to evaluate the positions it thus creates as "high" or "low," and to demand certain behavior from individuals occupying the positions. Each individual occupies many statuses. To a certain extent, a person may "coast" on the prestige of a status he occupies; but his role behavior will always be watched by society, and he will lose esteem if he does not conform to expected patterns.

All societies assign some statuses on the basis of such natural categories as sex and age; in fact, all share this age breakdown: childhood, or the period of virtual dependence; youth, the time of increasing sexual maturity and of preparation for adult responsibility; adulthood, the time of broadest rights and full responsibility; and old age, the time of declining powers. The exact age at which an individual is considered an adult, the reverence or lack of it which children or old people receive, the chores youth is required to do will vary among societies, but each society will ascribe some statuses on the basis of age. Similarly, though physiological or psychological differences between the sexes are actually minimal, all societies ascribe some statuses, especially those involved with division of labor, on the basis of sex. Relatively simple societies tend to ascribe many statuses on such bases, while complex societies leave more statuses open to achievement; conversely, one reason the latter societies *are* complex is that unstifled achievement has led to specialization and thus efficiency.

The implications of status and role are important psychologically as well as sociologically. For example, while the reciprocal nature of roles gives the individual a certain security, role conflict may prove overwhelming. The competition for coveted statuses is particularly intense in complex, achievement-oriented societies.

REVIEW AND SUGGESTED READINGS

A · VOCABULARY

Achievement	Prestige	Social structure
Ascription	Role	Status
Esteem	Role behavior	

B · QUESTIONS AND TOPICS FOR REVIEW

1. How does the way an actor uses the term *role* differ from the way a sociologist uses it?
2. These two provocative statements from chapter 9 merit discussion and illustration:
   a. "In Western societies, it is clear that the culturally defined period of dependency and immaturity has been markedly lengthened, largely as a result of these societies' complexity, specialization, and high standards of living. Indeed, this prolongation of the occupancy of the ascribed status of child [and youth] is one measure of the complexity of a culture."
   b. "Race [or any other ascribed status] can have a modifying effect on the prestige of an achieved status."
3. What is the only absolutely accurate way of determining the status of various occupations in the United States?
4. Is Private in the army an ascribed or an achieved status? Explain.
5. Name three achieved statuses that are virtually closed to you and tell why each is closed.

C · SUGGESTIONS FOR FURTHER READING

R. F. Bales and P. E. Slater. "Role Differentiation in Small Decision-Making Groups," Chapter 5 in Talcott Parsons, R. F. Bales, *et al.*, eds. *Family, Socialization, and Interaction Process.* New York: The Free Press of Glencoe, 1955.

A report on empirical research in decision-making. "The evidence suggests that the degree of consensus on who stands where on various status orders is a critical factor in the structure and development of the group." (p. 296)

Joseph T. Drake. *The Aged in American Society.* New York: The Ronald Press Company, 1958.

Part I contrasts the status of the aged in agrarian and in urban industrial societies.

Neal Gross, Ward S. Mason, and Alexander W. McEachern. *Explorations in Role Analysis: Studies in the School Superintendency Role.* New York: John Wiley & Sons, Inc., 1958.

An attempt to develop a cluster of role concepts for the social sciences, supported by an empirical study of formal educational roles.

Robert W. Habenstein and Edwin A. Christ. *Professionalizer, Traditionalizer, and Utilizer.* Columbia, Missouri: The Institute for Research in the Social Sciences, 1955.

An interpretative study of the work of the general-duty nurse in nonmetropolitan general hospitals in central Missouri. Chapters 5 and 7 are particularly pertinent, since they deal with role and status in relation to the three sociological types of nurses which provide the title of this monograph.

Margaret Mead. *Male and Female. A Study of the Sexes in a Changing World.* New York: William Morrow & Co., Inc., 1949.

This book is the product of many years of field research and solid thinking on the relations of men and women in various societies.

Alva Myrdal and Viola Klein. *Women's Two Roles: Home and Work.* New York: Humanities Press, 1956.

A statistical analysis of the conflict between familial and professional roles as seen in American, Swedish, French, and British women.

William H. Whyte, Jr. *The Organization Man.* New York: Simon and Schuster, 1956.

A descriptive analysis of middle-class American men who work for large corporations, governmental bureaus, foundations, research establishments, or in the legal profession, revealing the inner conflict over social roles which their participation in such organizations induces.

CHAPTER 10

Differentiation and Leadership

All groups, large or small—except the most transitory—reveal some differentiation in the distribution and forms of power or dominance. In some instances, as in spontaneously developed play groups, the leader who emerges may be the strongest or most intelligent. Sometimes the leader is selected by someone of higher authority or position of power. The leader may persuade his followers, order them, or rely on his popularity or on some other appeal, such as the fact that the group considers him a father figure.

Before studying leadership itself, let us examine differentiation, the process responsible for the development of leaders and followers.

DIFFERENTIATION

Some type of specialization or differentiation of role is found in every society. Such differentiation is clearly related, as we shall see in the next chapter, to the rise and operation of social classes. In the economic order, for example, it occurs in the different roles of entrepreneur, manager, and skilled and unskilled laborers. It is self-evident in the professions. In the political order it is seen in the varying roles of public administrators, and in religion, in the distinctive roles of prophet, seer, and priest. In truth, some form of specialization of role is found in every associa-tion of people and, moreover, where such differentiation is linked to basic needs and goals it takes on the permanence and persistence of institutions.

Differences in age and sex are obvious foundations of specialization everywhere, although how the varied roles are defined depends, of course, on the particular culture. So too, different occupations create conditions for variation in roles and statuses while at the same time fostering interdependence. As Henry Clay, the British economist, once put it, "From the point of view of the individual, division of labor means *specialization;* from the point of view of society, it means *co-operation.*" [1]

While some specialization is found in tribal societies, highly integrated specialization is associated with extensive agriculture, handicrafts, the marketplace, writing, the political state, and other aspects of a more complex culture. The ancient world, even before the rise of Greece and Rome, witnessed differentiation in economic, political, military, religious, and other areas of human association. Professions and techniques evolved, with their particular knowledge, skills, language, and status. In fact, their development illustrates the emergence of variations in group participation called "specialties."

1 · Henry Clay, *Economics for the General Reader* (New York: The Macmillan Co., 1918), p. 21.

Economic Division of Labor In a society without economic specialization, each man would work to satisfy his own wants only. Division of labor did not go very far in any society until people began to produce goods or services in such quantity that the surplus could be exchanged for the goods or services of others. But specialization of economic roles depended not only on the level of technology and the needs of the tribe or society but also on the degree of sophistication in the marketing process. Man learned only gradually that division of labor benefits oneself as well as others.

While there was considerable specialization in the ancient world, it was the coming of the factory system that marked the great expansion in division of labor. The modern machine makes it possible to produce small parts that can be combined into a total product. This, of course, involves standardization and further simplification in the making of a particular part. Mechanization also makes for efficient production and fosters mergers and large-scale corporate ownership and control. Finance capitalism and machine-dominated division of labor grew up together.

Let us note some of the functions or consequences of a highly differentiated economic structure: (1) Specialization makes it possible to select workers according to their capacity to do a particular job. Both intelligence and temperament may be important. (2) It facilitates the acquisition of high skill in some one craft or phase of an operation. The "Jack-of-all-trades" is displaced by one who can learn the needed skill quickly and accurately. (3) It increases efficiency because it makes for concentration of attention and skill on single items of work, and this, in turn, is associated with (4) standardization of product, which makes mass production possible and often—though not always—results in a better product. (5) It saves time and human energy. This is the virtue of automation. (6) It permits classification of skills and products, making in turn for effective management.[2] And (7), to repeat, it promotes the factory system and the organization of large-scale units of production. This means the assembly of workers and many machines under one management, making supervision simpler, allowing concentration of raw materials at convenient points, and permitting urbanization with its more advantageous marketing.

Some of the alleged negative consequences of division of labor, especially in the machine age, are the following: (1) Factory work and machine production involve safety hazards and may produce ill-health if not properly regulated. (2) Overspecialization may so concentrate attention and skill on simple muscular responses as to make for monotony and fatigue, destroying incentive and creative interest in one's job. Critics of the modern factory system often contend that such work is unpleasant and disheartening and lowers the morale of the workers. They say that the artisan who made a total product—chair, house, pair of boots, piece of cloth—understood every step in the

2 · The extent of specialization is indicated in the listing of over 40,000 titles of particular jobs in the *Dictionary of Occupational Titles*, 2 vols., 2nd ed. (Washington, D.C.: U.S. Government Printing Office, 1949). Of this number approximately 9,000 are coded titles—that is, they fall into a number of more-or-less established job categories. The rest are uncoded but usually are related to some recognized job classification. Supplement 1 (published in 1955) contains 2,260 new and revised definitions and 1,322 new code numbers.

process, enjoyed putting the material together, and had genuine satisfaction in seeing the finished product. They argue that *the machine dominates the personality*. These critics tend to agree with Karl Marx, who defended the thesis that the machine—an objective, impersonal thing—controlled the spirit, initiative, and freedom of the operator. Instead of being the end or aim of the economic process, the individual, he said, becomes merely the means to production, an appendage to a system of machines that reduces him to a nonentity. The impersonality which characterizes much of modern life would thus be traceable not merely to the operations of the market and the wage system, but to the factory system itself. (3) The modern machine tends to destroy the skilled trades and to substitute semiautomatic and automatic machines, leaving the operator only simple movements to perform. (4) In a capitalistic society, such high specialization tends to make the worker increasingly dependent on the owner-manager. Moreover, the business cycle subjects the worker to seasonal and long-term periods of unemployment.

The features which we have just described are, of course, familiar. Efficient and advantageous as the factory system is for our economic welfare, it has not contributed to the larger society and culture without some human costs. Yet man's ability to make new adjustments is great; and when there is good health, adequate income with steady employment, and retirement benefits, many of the bad effects of overspecialization tend to disappear. In general, highly industrialized societies make possible a higher level of living than mankind ever experienced in the past.

Social Implications of Specialization
In studying the division of labor, we are concerned not only with differentiation of activities but also with how the various activities mesh or are interdependent. It is interesting that the individualism associated with a laissez-faire philosophy should produce a social structure so interdependent that the dislocation of any considerable section of it—say a key industry like steel-making or transportation—threatens the whole society. In other words, specialization promotes not only separateness but also the integration of group life.

Thus specialization fosters cooperation. The weaver is dependent on the sheep raiser for his wool, and both need a merchant or middleman to market their goods; the entrepreneur is dependent on the banker for capital; and so on. In fact, the economic order consists of a vast network of competition, co-operation, and differentiation.

In a society where all women gardened and cooked and all men hunted and fished, the total content of the culture would be little more than the combined knowledge of any two normal adults of opposite sex. A second consequence of elaborate occupational specialization, then, is an increase in the content of culture. Bushmen do not have much more to transmit to the next generation than any one Bushman can know. Americans have so much more to transmit than any one American could possibly know that the concept of the content of culture becomes staggering.

LEADERSHIP

Specialization has an important place in the creation of leadership. A person who can perform a certain act more efficiently and quickly can serve as a model for others to imitate and thus set the stage for others to attribute to him special qualifications even when he does not assume them. Then too, leaders can offset some of the disadvantages of specialization, such as impersonality.

The Origins of Leadership Observation of children in the home, on the playground, and in the school gives us some idea of how dominance arises. Difference in physical strength may permit one child to take a toy from another, but in the long run the most important element in dominance is intelligence, though strong drive or motive is also important.

The beginnings of differences in dominance and submissiveness first appear in the home. The parents may serve as a model through their aggressiveness or lack of it. Then too, family traditions may stimulate dominance. Parental talk of the high intelligence or exploits of a child may well stimulate aggressiveness in the child. Class distinctions may play a part, too, as when upper-class parents expect their children to assume leadership roles.

A variety of interpersonal situations may facilitate dominance. Let us cite two. Rejection by a parent may lead a child to acts of dominance as compensation or as demonstration of his worth or ability. Frustration likewise may set up acts of dominance, as in sibling rivalry. Actually, experience in conflict situations may provide effective training in leadership. From what a child learns at home or at school, he may go on to a role of dominance in his adolescent peer group. As scout leader or as captain of the ball team,

he gets further training for positions of dominance as an adult.

In any case, the broader cultural values will determine how, when, and where such childhood and adolescent experiences in dominance will be transmuted into adult behavior later. In a militaristic society, ambitious young men will compete for positions of leadership in the armed forces. When a business, money-making ethos is dominant, the stress will be on financial leadership and rewards. In contrast, a society controlled by religious and mystic values and norms will not ordinarily encourage either military or economic prowess.

All in all, leadership is a combination of ability and opportunity. When class structure is strong, dominance tends to be associated with a particular class or caste, and followership and submissiveness to go with membership in the lower ranks. In a democratic system, where class lines are somewhat vague and loose, leaders may and do arise from any class provided they follow the accepted patterns of the culture. Leaders in our society, however, are much more likely to be recruited from the upper than from the lower classes.[3]

Types of Leaders Many attempts have been made to classify leaders. Bernard M. Bass has a listing of nineteen typologies.[4] Some of these involve dimensions of personality, others social

3 · See W. Lloyd Warner and James Abegglen, *Big Business Leaders in America* (New York: Harper & Brothers, 1955).
4 · Bernard M. Bass, *Leadership, Psychology, and Organizational Behavior* (New York: Harper & Brothers, 1960), pp. 86–87. Bass drew the list from L. F. Fisher, *Philosophy of Social Leadership According to Thomistic Principles* (Washington, D.C.: Catholic University Press, 1948).

roles. An early effort using role categories was E. B. Gowin's distinction between the "intellectual" and the "executive." In the former he included scientists, authors, philosophers, and artists; in the latter, corporation presidents, governors of states, high religious officials, and top trade-union officials.[5] Similar was O. L. Schwarz's classification of "men of thought" and "men of action." [6] Sir Martin M. Conway, an English popularizer of social psychology, in discussing crowd behavior, used a three-fold classification: "crowd-representative," or group organizer; "crowd compeller," one who persuades or forces a group to follow him; and "crowd exponent," one who, perceiving the motives and frustrations of the masses, becomes their leader because he verbalizes and crystallizes their desires and shows them how to act.[7]

Another distinction was drawn by A. B. Wolfe, an economist, in his typology of conservative, radical, and scientist. Wolfe contended that, while they represent different roles, often the conservative and the radical are alike in personality make-up and reveal emotional and highly biased views in regard to the things they value most. Only the scientist, he claimed, retains his impartiality and impersonal attitudes.[8]

A contemporary writer has come up with a three-way typology of "Princes," "Heroes," and "Supermen." The first are men motivated to dominate others; the second are dedicated to great and noble causes; and the third are iconoclasts who break down old norms and values.[9]

Still another typology has been proposed by Charles M. Bonjean on the basis of an empirical study of community leaders in a medium-sized city. The data consisted of ratings by known leaders and nonleaders of a specified number of local "leaders." The author found that leaders fall into three categories: (1) *Visible leaders*," who are playing widely perceived and accepted roles in the community. (2) "*Concealed leaders*," who have more power or leadership function "within the leadership circle or power elite" than is commonly realized. And (3) "*symbolic leaders*," who do not wield "as much influence in the community as the community at large thinks they do." [10]

From studies of small groups, ranging in size from three-man to six-man groups, Robert F. Bales and his co-workers found that participants differentiate between "idea specialists" and "best-liked men." While the former are highly regarded for their aid in solving problems presented to the group, they are not, on the whole, the best-liked.[11]

In his discussion of political lead-

5 · E. B. Gowin, *The Executive and His Control of Men* (New York: The Macmillan Co., 1915), pp. 6–7.
6 · O. L. Schwarz, *General Types of Superior Men* (Boston: Richard G. Badger, 1916).
7 · Sir Martin M. Conway, *The Crowd in Peace and War* (New York: Longmans, Green & Co., Inc., 1915).
8 · A. B. Wolfe, *Conservatism, Radicalism, and Scientific Method* (New York: The Macmillan Co., 1923). Yet, as one of the present authors long ago pointed out, scientists are objective and impartial only in reference to their specialties. See Kimball Young, "The Need of Integration of Attitudes among Scientists," *Scientific Monthly*, 1924, 18:291–305.

9 · Eugene E. Jennings, *An Anatomy of Leadership* (New York: Harper & Brothers, 1960).
10 · Charles M. Bonjean, "Community Leadership: A Case Study and Conceptual Refinement," *American Journal of Sociology*, 1963, 68:672–81. Quotations are from page 678.
11 · See Robert F. Bales and Philip E. Slater, "Role Differentiation in Small Decision-making Groups," Chapter 5 in Talcott Parsons and Robert F. Bales, *Family, Socialization, and Interaction Process* (New York: The Free Press of Glencoe, 1955).

ership, H. D. Lasswell developed a five-fold typology: (1) The *bureaucrat*, or *administrator*, operates an institution or agency along precise, orderly, and fixed lines. (2) The *boss* is a hard-headed opportunist concerned with the manipulation of political power by direct or indirect means. (3) The *diplomat* is concerned with the manipulation of political power through suave manner, calmness, patience, and clever and sometimes insincere use of conversation and social graces. (4) The *agitator* strives for reform or revolution. He is adept in the use of programs, catchwords, and suggestive slogans. He paints the *status quo* as completely evil and decadent, the future as a new heaven on earth. And (5) the *theorist* makes a systematic analysis of his environment from which he formulates a logical and consistent picture of his world of men and events.[12]

None of these classifications of leadership is completely satisfactory. First, we know far too little about the causal sequences in the life course of leaders; second, we have no adequate criteria for determining types; and third, the divergent historical situations in which leaders operate are very hard to classify. Moreover, it is evident that the various classificatory schemes mirror both the culture and the personal experience and bias of those who construct them.

Thus, whether there are general traits of leadership remains a moot question. There is one generalization we *can* make. Followers may *ascribe* to those in positions of dominance over them personality traits and powers that the latter may not possess. This is a fa-miliar phenomenon: a distinguished natural scientist or engineer is expected by the masses to be expert also in international relations, labor-management problems, or the effect of comic books on children's conduct.

Once traits and powers are attributed to leaders, they may capitalize on these projections from their followers and assume knowledge, skill, and leadership in fields where they have no actual competence. Sometimes, too, individuals who are the beneficiaries of such projection of potency attain at least a modicum of capability in the areas in which wisdom has been attributed to them.[13]

Leadership in Mass Society While Lasswell's classification of leaders is by no means to be regarded as final, a modification of it seems applicable to modern mass societies, both democratic and authoritarian. The three most significant types of leaders today seem to be the administrator, the expert, and the agitator. The unprecedented expansion of large-scale industry and business has placed managerial personnel in a highly strategic position in the power structure of economic enterprise. So too, the extension of political controls over new areas of social life has resulted in an increase in administrative functionaries, with all this implies as to further power of the governmental bureaucracy.[14]

Our complicated industrial, political, and military systems cannot oper-

12 · See H. D. Lasswell, *Psychopathology and Politics* (Chicago: University of Chicago Press, 1930).

13 · See Robert K. Merton, *Social Theory and Social Structure*, rev. ed. (New York: The Free Press of Glencoe, 1957), pp. 421–436.

14 · For an analysis of the growing importance of the administrative role in our military establishment, see Morris Janowitz, *The Professional Soldier, A Social and Political Portrait* (New York: The Free Press of Glencoe, 1960).

Burton Berinsky for ILGWU "Justice"

Leaders crystallize the vague feelings and attitudes of their followers.

ate without the expert. His role as a specialist requires that he be completely objective, dispassionate, and unconcerned, in that role, with the moral implications of his function. While he occupies a position of control absolutely vital to the operation of our complex culture, as an expert he is set apart from the moral order. He symbolizes the highest degree of impersonality and segmentalization in our mass society.

On occasion the agitator will assume an important role in mass society, particularly in time of grave economic and political insecurity. In such situations the agitator easily changes into a would-be dictator and, with his appealing slogans and fine promises, may capture the support of the masses in his drive for power. If the agitator combines his talents with those of an organized revolutionary minority, he may become the agent for producing great changes, both political and economic. Often the mass of followers do not understand the changes that are brought about once the demagogue gets in power.

Relationship Between Leaders and Followers Our discussion of power distribution among leaders and heads of organizations in a mass society suggests the whole problem of the relationship of those in positions of power to their followers. In societies where there is wide participation of the masses in politics, economic life, and religion, the role of the persuasive and responsible leader is especially vital. Such a leader crystallizes the vague feelings and attitudes of the masses when they are confronted with situations they cannot handle.

The followers find in the leader and his program an image which they can follow. So too, in setting his role and giving him prestige, they project upon the leader many qualities they believe a leader should have. Then, by identification, the followers seem to themselves to share these qualities. Their projection affects the leader, of course, who to be successful must assume these roles and accept the attendant status. As George C. Homans puts it, "The leader is the man who, on the whole, best lives up to the standard of behavior that the group values." [15] Such a leader as a *symbol* provides a focus for feeling and acting conjointly. Around him followers build up patterns of response which yield results and give much satisfaction as well.

Of course, in every society the leader is separated from his followers only in degree. He shares with them their biological make-up and their participation in society and culture. Nevertheless, he embodies distinctiveness and variability in thought and action which the followers like and admire. The leader's behavior becomes a focus for the identification of the followers and hence makes for effective group activity and solidarity.

Leadership and Group Effectiveness
The interrelations of leader and followers will be qualified by the aim of the group, its organizational form, the already-existing patterns of control, and a variety of other factors. Commonsense observation, as well as research, shows how the values, attitudes, and output of a group are affected by the nature of the relationship of the mem-

bers to the leader and to one another. [16]

The dominance that an individual may exercise will vary according to cultural patterns. Many institutionalized groups have a hierarchical and rather fixed ordering of levels of authority. This is clearly seen in the military system, in churches with a formal priesthood, in government, in educational systems, and in our industrial order. The control that individuals have in such groups arises largely from ascribed status. These persons represent headship or *office*. They anticipate identification, obedience, and deference from the group members. However, it should not be imagined that because dominant individuals in these situations are not voluntarily chosen for their positions, their followers are less inclined to do as they say. Whether they are or not depends on their social-cultural training.

Studies of morale and leadership in the United States Army during World War II show that good morale among the troops was correlated with their having as officers men who were interested in them, understood their needs, recognized their abilities, were just in discipline, job assignment, and promotional policy, and kept them informed—insofar as security permitted—as to the nature of particular missions. The men did not greatly resent dominance and control, but they wanted to know "what the score was," as they put it. [17]

16 · For a review and discussion of the literature on these topics, see Ralph M. Stogdill, *Individual Behavior and Group Achievement* (New York: Oxford University Press, 1959); and Bernard Bass, *Leadership, Psychology, and Organizational Behavior* (New York: Harper & Row, 1960).

17 · See S. A. Stouffer, *et al., Studies in Social Psychology in World War II*, 4 vols. (Princeton, N.J.: Princeton University Press, 1949). For the discussion here, Vols. 1 and 2, *The American Soldier*, are the most pertinent.

15 · George C. Homans, *The Human Group* (New York: Harcourt, Brace & Co., 1950), p. 169.

Much the same reactions have been noted in industry and business. A wide range of studies of the interplay of productivity, supervision, and employee morale has shown the importance of a firm but understanding supervisory force. Such a force facilitates the workers' identification with their jobs and with the informal as well as formal organization in the factory or in the store. So too, as Morris S. Viteles remarks,

It appears that the supervisor who sees the problem of productivity exclusively in the technical terms of work methods and standards is less likely to motivate workers to increased production than one who sees the problem in terms of workers' status, characteristics, needs, and aspirations. The development of "employee-oriented" supervisors, adequately equipped for dealing with interpersonal relations on the job, therefore represents one promising approach to the solution of problems of motivation and morale in industry.[18]

To summarize, we may say that among other things important in making a work group or any other group effective are these: The individual wants to feel secure; he wants approval when it is pertinent; he wants to know what to do and what is expected of him; he wants a sense of participation; he wants consistent discipline; and he wants to be treated fairly and justly. If appropriate relations are maintained between the workers and their managers and supervisors, even rather authoritarian headship will be effective. But as a survey of the presidents of 171 of the largest corporations in the United States shows, although 50 percent of the top executives support an autocratic rather than a democratic management, they specify that "the autocrat must listen to the top management group he leads." [19]

Place of Informal Association In addition to the formal organization of such groupings, some kind of informal association and ordering of control often arises. Thus, in a military unit, government bureau, or factory section, voluntary leadership may grow out of the day-to-day interactions of the soldiers, the clerks, or the industrial workers. Sometimes, especially in periods of crisis, these informal leaders wield more power and influence than the formal heads of the operation. Productivity, morale, and sense of participation in the group are all greatly affected by such informal leadership.

The informal groupings that arise within the formal organization perform important functions not only in productive efficiency but in the matter of group morale. Cliques and friendships develop among the workers, and within these leaders emerge. Sometimes these congeniality groups have bearing on the work operations of the structure itself, and sometimes they deal only with recreational relationships. With regard to productivity, one important function of these informal groupings of workers is to protect themselves against practices which they consider a menace to their welfare. For example, in one plant, pressure by other employees was put on any worker who tended to exceed a certain minimum standard of output. This pressure con-

18 · Morris S. Viteles, *Motivation and Morale in Industry* (New York: W. W. Norton & Company, Inc., 1953), pp. 161–162. This book contains a review and discussion of a wide range of studies in the United States and elsewhere dealing with industrial morale.

19 · Joseph B. Marshall, "America's Best-Managed Companies," *Dun's Review and Modern Industry*, 1960, 75:38–40.

sisted of ridicule, name calling ("rate buster"), and even a certain amount of mild physical punishment. In this particular study, many of the men admitted to the research team that they could have turned out much more work but said they feared that if production were increased too much, the rates of pay would be cut.[20]

On the development of the informal organization, Stogdill has this to say:

Informal organization comes about as a result of the development of discrepancies (a) between work performances and responsibilities as defined and (b) between informal interactions and formally defined interactions. Thus leadership is ever confronted with the task of reconciling discrepancies—discrepancies between what ought to be done and what is being done, between goals and achievements, between organizational needs and available resources, between the needs of individual members and the requirements of organization, between formal lines of co-operation and informal patterns of co-operation.[21]

The form and nature of dominance, then, is always related to the situation. The voluntary leader or the appointed head must possess qualities that make for effective problem-solving. The members must identify themselves with the leader if they are to participate adequately. Finally, the situation and the members furnish the leader satisfying outlets for his intellectual and other abilities and for his need for recognition and power, and the leader gives the followers a feeling of protection and security—resembling, perhaps, that experienced earlier in life in the family.

20 · See F. J. Roethlisberger and W. J. Dickson, *Management and the Worker* (Cambridge: Harvard University Press, 1939); and their *Management and Morale* (same publisher, 1943).

21 · Ralph M. Stogdill, "Leadership, Membership, and Organization," *Psychological Bulletin*, 1950, 47:1–14. Quotation from p. 7. By permission of the author and the American Psychological Association, Inc.

INTERPRETATIVE SUMMARY

The emergence of leaders and followers is a natural result of the process of differentiation. Though the ethos of a culture will determine the forms leadership takes and, to some extent, who will be leaders, some generalizations may be made. Leadership everywhere is a combination of opportunity and ability, the latter having as its components strength, drive, and especially intelligence. Leaders are people who, having been supported in their early attempts to dominate, go on to establish patterns of dominance. They find positions of dominance satisfying and sometimes even challenging.

Many attempts have been made to classify leaders into types. For an industrial, highly specialized society like our own, the following system is at least a start: administrator, expert, and agitator. An administrator is a "man of action," a policy-maker in such areas as politics, business, education, and religion. The expert supplies the administrator with information on which to base his decisions. The agitator becomes prominent in time of social upheaval. If successful, he may later take an administrative position.

Followers everywhere do not care how their leader was chosen so much as how he treats them. They want above all to feel secure, which means that they want their leader to be fair, supportive, understanding, and interested in them. They will be more effective as a group if they have such a leader. This is particularly true in a highly specialized society where work is noncreative and relations impersonal; in fact, in such task-oriented groups workers will frequently band together defensively, informally choosing a leader who can fulfill needs their formal leader does not recognize. Followers feel secure with a leader who is like themselves, yet more knowledgeable and bolder.

REVIEW AND SUGGESTED READINGS

A · VOCABULARY

Division of labor	Headship	Morale
Dominance	Leadership	Specialization

B · QUESTIONS AND TOPICS FOR REVIEW

1. We have said, "Once traits and powers are attributed to leaders, they may capitalize on these projections from their followers and assume knowledge, skill, and leadership in fields where they have no actual competence." What groups, or even individuals, seem to be the worst offenders here?
2. List some specific complaints you have heard people make about their bosses.
3. Why do people enjoy informal television discussion shows? On what bases do the moderators of such shows probably choose guests for a given night?
4. Illustrate with contemporary examples: "Leadership is a combination of ability and opportunity."
5. Why are some people who are leaders early in life not leaders later?
6. Using concepts you learned in this chapter, give the plot of a film, play, or fictional work dealing with the theme of leadership. Which concepts figure most importantly in the story? Is the story credible?
7. With regard to an athletic team or a public school, discuss social differentiation, occupational specialization, and their consequences.

C · SUGGESTIONS FOR FURTHER READING

Bernard Bass. *Leadership, Psychology, and Organizational Behavior.* New York: Harper & Brothers, 1960.

A well-written discussion of a wide variety of topics related to leadership. The bibliography contains 1,155 titles.

Cecil A. Gibb. "Leadership," Chapter 24 in *Handbook of Social Psychology,* vol. 2, ed. Gardner Lindzey. Reading, Mass.: Addison-Wesley Publishing Company, 1954.

A good review of some of the more important papers and books on leadership. The author discusses leadership as a phenomenon within the matrix of interaction.

J. E. Hulett, Jr., and Ross Stagner, eds. *Problems in Social Psychology: An Interdisciplinary Inquiry.* Urbana, Ill.: University of Illinois Press, 1952.

A symposium of papers on a variety of topics. Those in Round Table III deal with leadership and morale.

David Riesman. *The Lonely Crowd: A Study of the Changing American Character.* New Haven: Yale University Press, 1950.

Chapter 11, "Images of Power," deals with the role of leaders in recent American history.

Melvin Seeman. *Social Status and Leadership: The Case of the School Executive.* Columbus, Ohio: Ohio State University, Bureau of Educational Research and Service, Monograph No. 35, 1960.

A report on research in the interaction of educational administrators with their teachers and their public. Excellent analysis and interpretation.

Ralph M. Stogdill. *Individual Behavior and Group Achievement: A Theory. The Experimental Evidence.* New York: Oxford University Press, 1959.

An attempt to build a theory of organization achievement. There is a clear recognition of the place of interaction, including leadership, in this process. This book, like the preceding one, is partly an outgrowth of the Ohio State Leadership Studies. The bibliography contains 794 titles.

Class Structure and Its Functions

In most societies people classify one another into categories, and rank these categories from higher to lower. The process of defining and ranking such categories is called *social stratification,* and the resulting set of ranked categories is called the *stratification structure.* The categories themselves, by analogy with the different layers of rock in a geological formation, are called *strata*. More popularly, we know them as *classes.*

The degree of definiteness or rigidity of the stratification structure varies considerably from society to society. In some societies, no member can change from the category into which he is born, he must marry a person born into the same category as he, and his category membership will be the prime determinant of his wealth, the amount of education he gets, the occupation in which he spends his life, and various other features of his social life. Strata as rigid as this are called *castes.* In other societies, the stratification structure is relatively vague and changeable. In such a situation, the son of an accountant may quit high school, never go to college, become a garage mechanic, and yet marry the daughter of his employer. Furthermore, there may be some disagreement among members of the society as to whether the accountant is upper class or middle class, and whether the garage mechanic is middle

class or lower class. Societies like this do not have classes which are discrete, well-defined units like castes; their classes are simply aggregates of statuses which have approximately the same prestige.

Finally, there are tribal societies which have virtually no class structure: they have a division of labor with specifications for hunting, child rearing, and other essential tasks based on age and sex, and are stratified only to the extent of having a chief or medicine man. The more complex the division of labor becomes, the more opportunity there is for a class structure to develop; therefore, settled communities are likely to have more complex stratification systems than nomadic tribes, and urban societies invariably have a class structure. Table 4 shows the differing degrees of stratification found among some 180 tribal bands and communities studied by anthropologists.

The process of stratification can lead to many different kinds of class structures. The stratification structure of a society will depend on the normative order of the culture, since this will determine the criteria upon which statuses are ranked: the power they have, the wealth associated with them, and so on. When we speak of a stratification structure, it is easy to sound as if it were a static, permanent thing. Actually, of course, stratification, like any

TABLE 4 · Types of Social Stratification Among Tribal Bands
and Settled Communities *

STRATIFICATION PATTERN	BANDS	SETTLED COMMUNITIES	TOTAL
Complex structure of social classes	0	31	31
Hereditary aristocracy and commoners	0	38	38
Social classes based directly on wealth	0	14	14
Wealth distinctions without formal classes	7	19	26
Social classes absent	27	44	71
TOTAL	34	146	180

* From George P. Murdock, *Social Structure* (New York: The Macmillan Co., 1949), p. 88. By permission. For another study by the same author, which includes a classification of 565 societies according to type of social stratification, see "World Ethnographic Sample," *American Anthropologist*, 59:664–687, 1957.

other feature of social organization, is constantly changing.

There are various ways in which one can define the class structure of a society. Karl Marx used "class" to mean persons sharing important characteristics in the system of economic production. He assumed that an individual's status in relation to the economic process—that is, whether he owned and controlled the means of production or worked for someone else—was the most relevant factor in determining the behavior of that person and others like him. Marx believed that people shared common interests determined by their relationship to the means of production, and that they would develop class consciousness as a result.[1]

Max Weber wrote of the stratification of societies on the basis of three variables: (1) the possession of economic goods and opportunities for income, (2) access to political power, and (3) prestige, or social honor.[2]

W. Lloyd Warner and his associates use "class" to mean a number of persons having in common an evaluation assigned to them by their fellows, whether or not they are aware of this evaluation or, if aware of it, are in agreement with it. In other words, a class is a number of people sharing a roughly equal level of prestige.[3]

None of these is the "right" or "wrong" definition of class. These different approaches are useful for viewing different dimensions of the functions of the stratification structure.

To achieve some perspective on the wide variation in types of class structures and the dynamics of the stratification process, we shall look briefly at stratification in various times and places.

A CROSS-CULTURAL VIEW OF STRATIFICATION

Class Systems Among Nonliterates

While extremely rudimentary societies have no class structure, some kind of class system is rather widespread among

1 · Karl Marx and Friedrich Engels, *Communist Manifesto* (1848). Reprinted in *Social Reformers: Adam Smith to John Dewey*, ed. Donald O. Wagner (New York: The Macmillan Co., 1934), pp. 421–451.

2 · Max Weber, *From Max Weber: Essays in Sociology*, translated and edited by Hans H. Gerth and C. Wright Mills (New York: Oxford University Press, 1946), pp. 180–195.

3 · W. Lloyd Warner, M. Meeker, and Kenneth Eells, *Social Class in America: A Manual for Procedure for the Measurement of Social Status* (Chicago: Science Research Associates, 1949).

nonliterate peoples. In North America the Kwakiutl had a rather rigid scheme, as did the warring Plains Indians. The Pueblo groups, on the other hand, had a somewhat flexible class structure. There were caste systems in both Peru and Mexico. In large parts of Africa, Asia, and Oceania, class organization is common. For example, in many parts of western Africa the king and his nobles make up a rigid, inheritable class rationalized as of divine sanction. Below them are various governmental ranks, specialized craftsmen, commoners, and slaves. There are other forms of class structure, as among the cattle-raising Wahuma of eastern Africa, who are the top class ruling the horticultural Bantu, whom they conquered.

In Polynesia we find an abundance of caste. The Maori nobility of New Zealand trace their descent through primogeniture back to the highest gods. Every man of distinction has to memorize his lineage so that on occasion he can recite his pedigree. There are five groups of freemen: chiefs, priests, landed gentry, large landholders, and commoners. Moreover, the gradations of rank within these castes are numerous. Complex forms of address and carefully detailed rituals are worked out to control the relations of the various castes and ranks to one another. Somewhat similar caste systems exist elsewhere in the South Pacific.

Caste in India The Hindu caste system has long been of great interest to Western peoples, and around it has grown up a host of myths and legends. In actuality it is more flexible, more dynamic, and more complex than is generally recognized.

The word *caste* comes from the Portuguese *casta*, meaning lineage; and its application to the system in India shows that the first Westerners to reach the region understood the central place which kinship has in the maintenance of the gradations. The Hindu word for caste is *varna*, meaning color, and there is little doubt that in India color and racial differences have had some part in setting up caste lines.

Hindu tradition relates that the major divisions were established about 600 B.C. The ancient Laws of Manu gave the four chief castes as follows: (1) the *Brahmans*, or priests, who were "assigned the duties of reading the Vedas [the sacred books], of teaching, of sacrificing, of assisting others to sacrifice, of giving alms if they be rich, and if indigent of receiving gifts"; (2) the military chieftains, or overlords, called the *Kshatriya*, whose duties were "to defend the people, to give alms, to sacrifice, to read the Vedas, to shun the allurements of sensual gratification"; (3) the agriculturists, herdsmen, and traders, called the *Vaisya*; and (4) the servile class of menials and industrial workers, or *Sudra*, whose duty it was "to serve the before-mentioned classes without depreciating their worth."[4]

Actually, the Laws of Manu mention 50 castes besides these major *varnas*. Outside these four orders, and outside the pale of Hinduism, is a varied mass of outcastes, the lowest of whom, the *Chandalas*, are regarded about on a par with such "unclean" animals as dogs and donkeys.[5]

The four divisions, indeed, are but the skeleton of a highly complex sys-

4 · Quoted material from F. Max Miller, Chapter 10, *The Laws of Manu*, Vol. 25, in *The Sacred Books of the East* (London: Oxford University Press, 1886).

5 · See L. S. S. O'Malley, *Indian Caste Customs* (London: Cambridge University Press, 1932), p. 13.

tem of castes and subcastes. The 1901 census of India listed over 800 castes and subcastes.[6] When the local difference in subcastes are taken into account, the number in fact reaches nearly 5,000. Castes and subcastes are constantly forming and reforming by division or unification. When we come to study the system closely, we find, not the static, stereotyped picture of fiction or popular legend, but a living, changing social organization. Although the Indian system of castes represents the most highly integrated system of social stratification that has arisen anywhere, its very dynamic character shows that, while the regulations are severe and of long standing, the actuality of social practice cannot be defined within narrow, unchanging limits. Moreover, caste or subcaste in India is not determined by any one standard. Castes are formed on the basis of occupations, sectarian groups, races, tribes, or other associations of people with distinctive cultural traits or social roles.

To people of Western culture, some of the regulations of caste seem extreme indeed. For example, one may not sit down to eat with another who is not of the same caste. All meals must be prepared by one of his own caste or by a Brahman. No man of inferior caste may touch the cooked rations of one of higher caste or, for that matter, enter into the latter's culinary quarters. No water or other liquid, once contaminated by the touch of one of inferior caste, may be used. (Tanks, rivers, and other larger bodies of water, however, are not considered capable of defilement.) Articles of dry food—for in-

6 · After the census of 1901, the tabulation of every tribe and minor caste was abandoned as not worth the time and effort. See O'Malley, p. 3.

stance, rice, wheat, or millet—are not made impure by passing through the hands of a man of lower caste, but they cannot be used if they become moistened or greased. Among the peoples of southern India, where the unclean castes are peculiarly offensive to the higher ranks, pollution may occur even without touching. For example, a Kaniyan pollutes a Brahman if he comes within 32 feet of him, and a Niar pollutes him at a distance of 24 feet.

The severity of social pressure on the man who has been put out of his caste is striking. When a Hindu is expelled from his caste, his friends, relatives, and fellow townspeople refuse to accept his hospitality; he is not invited to their houses; he cannot secure brides or bridegrooms for his children; his own married daughters scarcely dare visit him lest they also lose caste. His priest, barber, and washerman will not serve him. Fellow members of his caste even decline to assist at a funeral of one of his household. With group codes felt so strongly by the individual, it is no wonder that such a system persists even in the face of many forces that tend to disintegrate it.

Though the caste system remains dominant, many changes have weakened its hold on the population. (1) The urbanization of population affords the person who has lost caste a chance to change his identity in a great city, to take up another occupation, and perhaps to marry outside his caste. (2) Travel and mobility throw the castes together in situations that were not likely to arise before the coming of the railroad and the crowded conditions of large cities. (3) Schooling has helped alter the attitude toward caste, especially among those with a higher education. (4) Christianity and other foreign religions have gradually had some effect on attitudes toward caste. (5) The spread of nationalistic and democratic ideas has had a powerful influence on the attitudes toward some features of the caste structure. In fact, in the very first years of Indian independence, measures were introduced in the national legislature to abolish many features of the caste system.[7]

Yet the inertia of custom and tradition is powerful.[8] The village, the heart of Hindu social organization, is the seat of caste at its strongest. Family life, religion, and occupation still provide powerful support for the system.

Class and Caste in Mediterranean Societies The class structures of Babylonia, Egypt, Persia, Greece, and Rome were often rigid, though not as elaborate as that which developed in India. In Egypt there were two upper classes —warriors and priests. Besides these there were various lesser classes of professionals and artisans, all relatively fixed. Babylonia, as early as the time of Hammurabi (ca. 1950 B.C.), had a hierarchical feudal order in which class lines were strictly drawn.

Mesopotamia was apparently fairly free from anything approaching caste, but ancient Iran, or Persia, from which the Aryan conquerors of India are thought to have come, had, according to legend, four castes—priests, warriors, agriculturists, and artificers. In Greece we find variation. Sparta long retained what was in effect a caste system, with

a division of the population into spartiates, or full citizens; perioeci, those engaged in husbandry or trade; helots or serfs; and slaves. On the other hand, as Athens developed into a complex and cosmopolitan state, the ancient class structure there was greatly modified.

In Rome the story is an interesting one of relatively definite classes constantly being dissolved by changes in economic and political power and then re-established, until we get to the Empire, with its final crystallization of Roman society. With the gradual disappearance of the middle classes, the patricians formed a closed class, and the masses were rather thoroughly subjugated under a severe economic and political regime from which the individual could not escape.

Classes in Feudal Europe With the breakup of the Roman Empire following the barbarian invasions, society in western Europe was refashioned along somewhat different lines. The feudal order which emerged was a more or less legally fixed system of classes, sometimes called *estates*. There were various gradations: overlords, lesser lords, knights, burghers, guild members, freemen, and serfs. A shift from one level to another was difficult. Gradually economic and political changes came about, and the seeds were sown for the disintegration of the old order and the rise of more flexible classes.[9]

Classes in Modern Europe The Commercial and Industrial revolutions disrupted the feudal order and set in motion cultural and social changes that

7 · A 1955 law makes discrimination against untouchables (the lowest caste) a crime. In 1956 a law was passed permitting intercaste marriages.
8 · See Fred Greene, *The Far East* (New York: Rinehart & Company, Inc., 1957), p. 376; and Gerald D. Berreman, "Caste in India and the United States," *American Journal of Sociology*, 1960, 66:120–127.

9 · For an excellent discussion of the estate system of medieval Europe, see Kurt B. Mayer, *Class and Society* (New York: Random House, 1955), pp. 16–21.

not only produced a shift from primary to secondary organization of society but influenced Western class structure. While the landed aristocracy, the military class, and the ecclesiastical hierarchy remained in the upper brackets, new classes emerged: first, from the large industrial entrepreneurs, bankers, and merchants; second, from the petty business groups; and third, from the rapidly growing urban industrial masses. The last became increasingly numerous and socially more powerful than the peasant and gradually declining serf classes. The shift in the strength of the lowest class was slow. Serfdom did not disappear in France until shortly before the French Revolution, until Napoleon's time in Germany, and in Russia not until after the middle of the nineteenth century.

The most important elements in the modern world which tended to alter the class system were (1) the capitalistic business enterprise and its close associate, the factory system; (2) the political order, which stressed nationalism and, later, democracy; (3) the coming of religious tolerance and freedom following the Protestant Reformation; and (4) the expanding spirit and practice of free inquiry, which led to modern science and technology and had a marked effect on political democracy, business, and even religion. As we have already noted, these same forces led to many of the characteristic features of our mass society.

The liquidation of former social classes following a great political-economic revolution is well documented in history. For example, in contrast to Czarist days, the present pyramid of power in Soviet Russia follows the pattern of a dominant-party elite: a vast range of administrative officials at the top and below this the masses, within which there are some recognized gradations.[10] Wars, like revolutions, often bring about considerable shift in the class organization; World War I induced many such alterations in Europe, and World War II resulted in even more drastic changes.

Since the end of the Middle Ages—say from the fifteenth century to the present—there has been a gradual loosening of old patterns of class rule in the political field. The emergence of nationalism led within two centuries to the beginnings of democratic control. The movement of persons up and down the political ladder—like the movement in occupations or wealth—is accelerated in periods of rapid social change or revolution. During the last century, political changes in Great Britain and western Europe brought political power into the hands of the middle classes. In the present century there have been still further shifts toward parliamentary democracy, as in the Weimar Republic of Germany and in Czechoslovakia, and a shift toward fascist revolution, as under Hitler and Mussolini. In all these cases the class system was modified. After World War II, Russian influence on central Europe fostered imitation of the Soviet pattern. Elsewhere in Europe, liberal democratic forces often found themselves in conflict with conservative elements.

In religious activity, much the same thing has taken place. Although during the history of the Roman Catholic Church certain families sometimes

10 · For diagrams showing the shift in class structure in Russia, see David Dallin, *The Real Soviet Russia* (New Haven: Yale University Press, 1944), p. 97. See also Alex Inkeles, "Social Stratification and Mobility in the Soviet Union: 1940–1950," *American Sociological Review*, 1950, 15:465–470.

dominated the highest position, it is nevertheless true that the Church has always provided some opportunity for people of ability to move upward from the lower social classes. The Protestant Reformation especially made it more possible for persons of lower status to rise in importance. Moreover, the individualism stimulated by Protestantism has had an effect on political, economic, and intellectual life. Hence achieved status became an important factor in the class structure.

CLASS STRUCTURE IN THE UNITED STATES

The United States is the prime example of an open-class system, in which birth or lineage is only one element in the determination of class status. Despite regional variations in the degree to which ascribed status may be overshadowed by achieved status, the open-class system has been increasingly identified with the common man and the democratic process. Yet it would be a mistake to assume that the sense of class difference has ever completely disappeared.

An interesting aspect of our American stratification structure is the fact that, along with this open-class system, there existed human slavery, which later, under military-political pressure, gave way to a caste system based on color. The persistence of the white-Negro caste relationship not only is an intriguing cultural paradox but continues to present the United Sates with one of its most serious and pressing local and national dilemmas.[11]

11 · For a full and incisive analysis of this problem, see Gunnar Myrdal, *et al., An American Dilemma: The Negro Problem and Modern Democracy*, Second Edition. (New York: Harper and Row, 1963.)

It is the purpose of this section to discuss the general aspects of the American class system. Chapter 13 will take up color-caste and other minorities in the United States.

"Looseness" of the American Class Structure [12] The criteria by which people assign prestige to a status in modern urban-industrial societies are vague and shifting. Consequently, classes are not clearly delineated, but tend to overlap and blur into adjacent strata. For example, there is consensus in the United States that it is better to make much money than little, that it is better to be educated than ignorant, that professional statuses have higher prestige than unskilled statuses. But it is not so easy when more criteria than one are involved. Who ranks higher in the class structure, the person with a moderate income and a great deal of education, or the one with a moderate amount of education and a high income?

Most Americans would agree that the top stratum of our society is composed of the highest professional and managerial people. It would generally be agreed, too, that there is an upper-middle class of smaller businessmen, junior executives in large corporations, lower-ranking professionals and semi-professionals, and people in the top reaches of sales and civil service. But there is no clear-cut point at which the upper class is divided from the upper-middle, because the strata are not ascribed; the statuses are not castes. Simi-

12 · For a more extended discussion of this phenomenon, see Talcott Parsons, "A Revised Analytical Approach to the Theory of Social Stratification," in *Class, Status, and Power*, Reinhard Bendix and S. M. Lipset, eds. (New York: The Free Press of Glencoe, 1953), esp. pp. 122–125.

larly, the lower-middle class is separated from the lower class roughly on the basis of lower white-collar jobs versus manual labor, but the highest paid skilled laborers earn higher incomes than the lowest paid office workers, and the point of distinction is often blurred.

In short, the prestige of categories can be ranked with sufficient precision for many research purposes, but one cannot say, "I know Homer Tinwiddle—he's upper-middle class," with the same sureness that one could have described the status of a given individual in the Hindu caste system. A nice illustration of this is a study of the stratification structure of Danielson, Connecticut, a textile-mill town of about 6,000 people.[13] A random sample of 150 families was drawn, and a list of their names was given to 24 raters, most of whom had lived in Danielson all their lives. The raters were asked to pick out all the families they knew from the list of 150 and make a class placement for each, but no instructions were given about the number of classes to be used. One rater divided the families into only three classes, some raters used four, and others distinguished between five, six, or seven classes. Since there was little agreement among the raters on the number of classes in the stratification structure, there was naturally not much agreement on which family belonged in which class, even though on the whole the raters agreed on the relative placement of families. Such variance among raters is a reflection of "looseness" in the stratification structure. True, the society is stratified, but class boundaries

are not sharp.[14] It is easier to describe a person's status than label his stratum.

Occupation and Stratification Given the "looseness" of the class structure in the United States, sociologists have tried to find indicators of an individual's class status. The most frequently used items are occupation, education, and income. Other items associated with or dependent on these variables have also been used: type of home, quality of neighborhood, monthly rental, and the like.

Research has shown that the best single indicator of class status in American society is occupation.[15] One reason is that someone familiar with our society can make an immediate and fairly accurate estimate of the other two important class indicators, educational background and education, just by knowing a person's occupation.[16] That is why the quickest, most economical answer one can ordinarily offer to the question "Who is he?" is to tell what the person's occupation is. Table 5

13 · Gerhard E. Lenski, "American Social Classes: Statistical Strata or Social Groups?" *American Journal of Sociology*, 1952, 58:139–144.

14 · For other research dealing with the same topic as Lenski's, see Thomas E. Lasswell, "A Study of Social Stratification Using an Area Sample of Raters," *American Sociological Review*, 1954, 19:310–313; S. Stanfeld Sargent, "Class and Class-Consciousness in a California Town," *Social Problems*, 1953, 1:22–27; Richard Scudder and C. Arnold Anderson, "The Relation of Being Known to Status Rating," *Sociology and Social Research*, 1954, 38:239–241; Scudder and Anderson, "Range of Acquaintance and of Repute as Factors in Prestige Rating Methods of Studying Social Status," *Social Forces*, 1954, 32:248–253; Werner S. Landecker, "Class Boundaries," *American Sociological Review*, 1960, 25:868–877; and C. Arnold Anderson, "A Skeptical Note on the Relation of Vertical Mobility," *American Journal of Sociology*, 1961, 66:560–570. (This issue contains five other papers on social stratification.)

15 · Warner, Meeker, and Eells, *Social Class in America*, Chapters 8–14.

16 · Joseph A. Kahl and James A. Davis, "A Comparison of Indexes of Socio-Economic Status," *American Sociological Review*, 1955, 20:317–325.

TABLE 5 · Distribution of Median Family Income by Occupation of Family Head, 1959 *

OCCUPATION OF FAMILY HEAD	MEDIAN INCOME
Self-employed professional and technical workers	$10,750
Salaried managers, officials, and proprietors	8,429
Salaried professional and technical workers	7,937
Sales workers	6,655
Self-employed managers, officials, and proprietors	6,416
Craftsmen, foremen, and kindred workers	6,324
Clerical and kindred workers	5,978
Operatives and kindred workers	5,376
Service workers, except private household	4,594
Laborers	4,259
Farmers and farm managers	2,423
Farm laborers	2,035
MEDIAN INCOME ALL OCCUPATIONS	5,417

* From *Current Population Reports*, Series P-60, No. 35, January 5, 1961, Tables 10 and 13, p. 30

TABLE 6 · Education and Income by Occupation in the United States *

OCCUPATIONAL CATEGORIES	MEDIAN SCHOOL YEARS COMPLETED	MEDIAN INCOME
Professional, technical, and kindred workers	16.2	$8,477
Nonfarm managers, officials, and proprietors	12.5	8,399
Clerical and kindred workers	12.5	6,218
Sales workers	12.5	6,949
Craftsmen, foremen, and kindred workers	11.2	6,500
Operatives and kindred workers	10.1	5,595
Farmers and farm managers	8.8	3,067
Private household workers	8.7	1,770
Service workers, except private household	10.8	4,839
Farm laborers, and farm foremen	8.5	2,398
Laborers, except farm and mine	8.9	4,479

* Median school years completed as of March, 1962. Source: U.S. Department of Labor, Bureau of Labor Statistics, *Monthly Labor Review*, May, 1963. Income in 1959 of families with heads in the experienced civilian labor force. Source: 1960 *Census of Population*, Volume 1, *Characteristics of the Population*, Part 1, United States Summary, Table 230, pp. 1–610.

shows the high correlation between total family income and the occupation of the head of the family. Table 6 shows the three-way association between occupation, education, and income.

Furthermore, there is considerable agreement among Americans about the relative prestige of various occupational statuses themselves. The National Opinion Research Center conducted a public-opinion poll in which a representative sample of people in the United States ranked 90 different occupations on a five-point scale: excellent standing, good, average, below average, and poor. From two-thirds to three-fourths of all people gainfully employed in the United States were in one of the 90 occupational statuses rated. The ratings were scored so that an occupation receiving exclusively "excellent" ratings would score 100, while one unanimously rated "poor" would score 20. Table 7 shows the findings of this research. Although there are a few minor

TABLE 7 · The Prestige of Occupations *

Occupation	Score
U.S. Supreme Court Justice	96
Physician	93
State Governor	93
Cabinet member in the federal government	92
Diplomat in the U.S. Foreign Service	92
Mayor of a large city	90
College professor	89
Scientist	89
United States representative in Congress	89
Banker	88
Government scientist	88
County judge	87
Head of a department in a state government	87
Minister	87
Architect	86
Chemist	86
Dentist	86
Lawyer	86
Member of the board of directors of a large corporation	86
Nuclear physicist	86
Priest	86
Psychologist	85
Civil engineer	84
Airline pilot	83
Artist who paints pictures that are exhibited in galleries	83
Owner of factory that employs about 100 people	82
Sociologist	82
Accountant for a large business	81
Biologist	81
Musician in a symphony orchestra	81
Author of novels	80
Captain in the regular army	80
Building contractor	79
Economist	79
Public schoolteacher	78
County agricultural agent	77
Railroad engineer	77
Farm owner and operator	76
Official of an international labor union	75
Radio announcer	75
Newspaper columnist	74
Owner-operator of a printing shop	74
Electrician	73
Trained machinist	73
Welfare worker for a city government	73
Undertaker	72
Reporter on a daily newspaper	71
Manager of a small store in a city	69
Bookkeeper	68
Insurance agent	68
Tenant farmer—one who owns livestock and machinery and manages the farm	68

TABLE 7 (continued)

Occupation	Score
Traveling salesman for a wholesale concern	68
Playground director	67
Policeman	67
Railroad conductor	67
Mail carrier	66
Carpenter	65
Plumber	63
Garage mechanic	62
Local official of a labor union	62
Owner-operator of lunch stand	62
Corporal in the regular army	60
Machine operator in a factory	60
Barber	59
Clerk in a store	58
Fisherman who owns his boat	58
Streetcar motorman	58
Milk route man	54
Restaurant cook	54
Truck driver	54
Lumberjack	53
Filling station attendant	52
Singer in a night club	52
Farm hand	50
Coal miner	49
Taxi driver	49
Railroad section hand	48
Restaurant worker	48
Dock worker	47
Night watchman	47
Clothes presser in a laundry	46
Soda fountain clerk	45
Bartender	44
Janitor	44
Share cropper—one who owns no livestock or equipment and does not manage farm	40
Garbage collector	35
Street sweeper	34
Shoe shiner	33
Average	69.8

* Cecil C. North and Paul K. Hatt, "Jobs and Occupations: A Popular Evaluation," *Opinion News*, 1947, 9:3–13. By permission.

differences among raters—priests rate higher in the East and lower in the Midwest, while farmers rate higher in the West—such differences are relatively unimportant in view of the overwhelming agreement among raters about the relative prestige of occupational statuses. It is important to note, too, that the individual occupational statuses rated cluster into occupational classes which are highly correlated with the distribution of income and education presented earlier. These occupational categories and their average prestige scores can be seen in Table 8.

In summary, then, occupation is

TABLE 8 · The Prestige of Occupational Categories *

OCCUPATIONAL CATEGORY	NUMBER OF OCCUPATIONS IN THAT CATEGORY	AVERAGE SCORE
Government officials	8	90.8
Professional and semiprofessional workers	30	80.6
Proprietors, managers, and officials, except farm	11	74.9
Clerical, sales, and kindred workers	6	68.2
Craftsmen, foremen, and kindred workers	7	68.0
Farmers and farm managers	3	61.3
Protective-service workers	3	58.0
Operatives and kindred workers	8	52.8
Farm laborers	1	50.0
Service workers, except domestic and protective	7	46.7
Laborers, except farm	6	45.8

* Ibid.

the best single indicator of class status in the American stratification structure, since it has a high correlation with other objective indicators of class status and since most Americans agree about the relative prestige of occupations themselves.

FUNCTIONS OF THE CLASS STRUCTURE

Research such as the nationwide public-opinion poll on the prestige of occupations offers us useful information about the existence of a class structure and the consensus among members of society about the criteria of status. But to understand the consequences, the functions, of the structure, we need research of more depth, such as descriptions of the variations in the way people live in the different strata.

Style of Life Various occupations, incomes, and amount of education lead people to share different norms and to behave differently. In other words, the existence of a class structure leads to the development of class subcultures. And in time, the patterns fostered in

the subculture themselves become criteria of placement in the class structure. Not just one's income, but the way he spends it; not just his occupational status, but his attitude toward it—these become factors partially determining his class status.

The most detailed descriptions of the styles of life of people in different classes are found in the work of W. Lloyd Warner and his associates.[17] One of the most exhaustive investigations was that of "Yankee City," a New England community of about 17,000. As we have seen, there are no specific, discrete classes in the United States; rather, there is a stratification hierarchy

17 · W. Lloyd Warner and Paul S. Lunt, *The Social Life of a Modern Community* (New Haven: Yale University Press, 1941); W. Lloyd Warner and Paul S. Lunt, *The Status System of a Modern Community* (New Haven: Yale University Press, 1942); W. Lloyd Warner and Leo Srole, *The Social Systems of American Ethnic Groups* (New Haven: Yale University Press, 1945); W. Lloyd Warner and J. O. Low, *The Social System of the Modern Factory* (New Haven: Yale University Press, 1947); Allison Davis, B. B. Gardner, and M. R. Gardner, *Deep South* (Chicago: University of Chicago Press, 1941); W. Lloyd Warner et al., *Democracy in Jonesville* (New York: Harper & Brothers, 1949); A. B. Hollingshead, *Elmtown's Youth* (New York: John Wiley & Sons, Inc., 1949).

the dividing lines in which depend on the criteria of class status utilized by the researcher. After 99 percent of the people in Yankee City had been classified on the basis of interviews by his staff of researchers, Warner described six categories which he felt were sufficiently different from one another to be called separate classes:

1. *Upper-upper:* the elite, based on inherited high family status and wealth, socialized in aristocratic etiquette, and comprising 1.4 percent of the population.

2. *Lower-upper:* families with patterns of income, occupation, and participation similar to the upper-uppers, but with more recently acquired wealth and hence lacking old-family prestige; professionals and businessmen; making up 1.6 percent of the total.

3. *Upper-middle:* moderately successful business and professional people without distinguished lineage; respected civic leaders but not "society people"; constituting 10.2 percent.

4. *Lower-middle:* small businessmen, white-collar workers, craftsmen and foremen, living in neat houses; conservative, self-conscious about respectability; comprising 28.1 percent.

5. *Upper-lower:* lower white-collar employees, semiskilled factory workers, and service workers; "poor but hardworking"; comprising 32.6 percent.

6. *Lower-lower:* not "respectable" people; unskilled workers, families on relief, transients; making up 25.2 percent.

Warner found numerous variations in style of life among the six classes. For example, some social clubs were exclusively upper-upper; upper-middle-class men belonged to luncheon clubs; fraternal lodges were primarily lower-middle; and labor unions were upper-lower. Similarly, members of the different classes attended different churches, read different magazines, and in general showed evidence of participating in a number of different subcultures.

There are striking similarities between the conceptions of the class structure held by the residents of Yankee City, with their assumptions of differences in morals and "respectability" between the classes, and the description of the stratification structure of Plainville, a rural community in Missouri studied by James West.[18]

An investigation of class structure in Burlington, Vermont, showed that nationality and religion in the subculture played important parts in the class system. In this community the top class is made up of families of old Yankee stock, although they are a definite numerical minority of the total population. The other broad category is made up of "foreigners" and "newcomers." The "foreigners" are not necessarily individuals or families born outside the country but rather those not of the Yankee tradition. The "newcomers" are families of perhaps acceptable New England background who have not yet been thoroughly assimilated into the local community. But within this wide division there is a "maze of classes and cliques" resting, for the most part, on three kinds of distinction: (1) economic, divided between professionals and proprietary versus laboring groups; (2) religious, with Protestants considering themselves better than Catholics; and (3) "ethnic" (or nationality) differences, "which serve to enhance the divisions based on religion or economic status and also to create division within

18 · *Plainville, U.S.A.* (New York: Columbia University Press, 1945), p. 117.

TABLE 9 · Fertility Differentials in the United States *

MONEY INCOME OF FAMILY, 1949	NUMBER OF CHILDREN UNDER 5 PER 1,000 MARRIED WOMEN 15–49 YEARS OF AGE
$5,000 and over	407
$4,000–4,999	476
$3,000–3,999	571
$2,000–2,999	580
$1,000–1,999	628
Under $1,000	677

* From *Current Population Reports*, Series P-20, No. 27, February 3, 1950, pp. 10–11.

the religious worlds or the economic levels." [19]

The study of Muncie, Indiana, by the Lynds divided the inhabitants into a two-class system: working people and professional-proprietary.[20]

All these investigations and many others show (1) a considerable flexibility in standards, which may include income, occupation, nativity, education, religion, and length of residence; (2) a patterning, at least in regions of older settlement, which gives the residents of long standing—provided they have some wealth and education—the highest ranking; (3) only a gradual acceptance into the top class of people of recently acquired wealth; and (4) moral values and style of life as frequently important standards of judgment, though these are often linked with religious and economic distinctions.

The evidence of differences in style of life includes variations by class in sexual behavior,[21] in family pattern (see Table 9), religious participation,[22] and many other culture patterns. We will not discuss these variations here, since they will be taken up in more detail in the chapters on familial, educational, religious, and political institutions.

Life Chances A person's class status, with its concomitant income, education, and style of life, affects greatly the likelihood that certain things will happen to him. As we have noted, the odds for or against one's having any given experience, as they are influenced by his class status, are called his *life chances.* Life chances include a vast array of variables. An individual's position in the class structure alters "everything from the chance to stay alive during the first year after birth to the chance to view fine arts, the chance to remain healthy and grow tall, and if sick to get well again quickly, the chance to avoid becoming a juvenile delinquent—and very crucially, the chance to complete an intermediary or higher educational grade." [23]

It is easy to dismiss many factors

19 · See E. L. Anderson, *We Americans: A Study of Cleavage in an American City*, (Cambridge: Harvard University Press, 1937). Quotations from p. 125.

20 · See R. S. Lynd and H. M. Lynd, *Middletown* (New York: Harcourt, Brace & Co., 1929).

21 · Alfred C. Kinsey, Wardell B. Pomeroy, and Clyde E. Martin, *Sexual Behavior in the Human Male*, Chapters 10 and 11 (Philadelphia: W. B. Saunders Co., 1948); and Alfred C. Kinsey *et al.*, *Sexual Behavior in the Human Female*, Chapters 7 and 8 (Philadelphia: W. B. Saunders Co., 1953).

22 · Liston Pope, "Religion and the Class Structure," *Annals of the American Academy of Political and Social Science*, 1948, 256:84–91.

23 · Hans Gerth and C. Wright Mills, *Character and Social Structure* (New York: Harcourt, Brace & Co., 1954), p. 313.

Black Star

Life chances are partly a function of economic status: a costly modern school building.

which are really life chances with the notion that the individual controls his own destiny: the statement, for instance, that class status influences one's chances to view fine art can be brushed aside with the retort that museums are free, and that if a person doesn't take advantage of them, it is his own fault. Such an attitude fails to take into account style of life and the power of subculture. A child reared in a slum area who does not even know about the existence of museums or who has been socialized to believe that painting is for "sissies" has different chances for art experience than one brought up in a wealthy home and taught that all respectable people know something about art.

The crucial effect of income on life chances is dramatically illustrated by the fact that the life expectancy of

infants born into high-income strata is nearly ten years greater than that of children born to parents in the lowest-income class.[24] Upper-class children are larger and grow faster than lower-class children, a fact apparently related to differences in diet, which depends on both income and style of life.[25]

As Table 10 shows, people in the lowest-income strata spend nearly three-fourths of their total income for food, while those in the higher strata spend less than one-fourth for food. Obviously, this leaves lower-class families with not only less money but a lower *proportion* of their total incomes

24 · Albert J. Mayer and Philip Hauser, "Class Differentials in Expectation of Life at Birth," in Reinhard Bendix and Seymour M. Lipset, eds., *Class, Status and Power* (Glencoe, Ill.: The Free Press, 1953), pp. 281–284.

25 · See Raymond W. Mack, "Housing as an Index of Social Class," *Social Forces,* 1951, 29:391–400.

TABLE 10 · Expenditures for Food by Urban Housekeeping Families of Two or More Persons *

1947 Income After Taxes	Average Weekly Income Before Federal Taxes	Amount Spent for Food	Per Cent of Weekly Income Spent for Food
All Families	$80.34	$25.57	31.8
Under $1,000	18.60	13.76	74.0
$1,000–$1,999	38.00	17.12	45.1
$2,000–$2,999	59.94	22.35	40.7
$3,000–$3,999	77.52	27.06	34.9
$4,000–$4,999	94.36	30.07	31.9
$5,000–$7,500	128.52	31.36	24.9
$7,500 and over	269.22	44.08	16.4

* From J. Frederic Dewhurst and Associates, *America's Needs and Resources* (New York: The Twentieth Century Fund, 1955), p. 128. By permission.

available for education and other expenditures that might improve their class position. The smaller amount of money available for purposes other than groceries is reflected in the figures of Table 11, which shows that a sample of lower-class people exceeded those in wealthier classes both in symptoms of illness and in the proportion of those symptoms which were not being treated by a physician. Lack of money is likely to be only one of the factors accounting for this situation; lower education levels would make it less

Monkmeyer

Life chances are partly a function of economic status: a one-room rural school.

TABLE 11 · Level of Health and Health Care of Individuals in Urban † Michigan
Families by Gross Income of Family, 1948 *

GROSS INCOME OF FAMILY	PERCENTAGE DISTRIBUTION					
	One or More Untreated Symptoms	No Positive Symptoms	All Positive Symptoms Treated		Total	Number
			by M.D.	by Non-M.D.		
Under $1,000	38.0	45.7	16.3	0.0	100	92
$1,000–1,999	21.5	62.7	15.4	0.4	100	241
$2,000–2,999	22.0	51.7	26.1	0.2	100	418
$3,000–3,999	14.3	71.5	14.2	0.0	100	323
$4,000–4,999	12.6	61.6	24.0	1.8	100	167
$5,000 and Over	8.5	70.1	20.7	0.7	100	140

† "Urban" is exclusive of Detroit and also of densely settled areas near a large city and designated by the 1940 Census as "metropolitan." A total of 153 households and 548 individuals residing in fringe areas are excluded from this table although tabulated in the survey.

* From Charles R. Hoffer, Duane L. Gibson, Charles P. Loomis, Paul A. Miller, Edgar A. Schuler, and John F. Thaden, *Health Needs and Health Care in Michigan*, Special Bulletin 365, Michigan State College Agricultural Experiment Station, East Lansing, 1950, pp. 82–83.

likely that the lower-income classes would be aware of the need for treatment of some symptoms.

Thus the class structure tends to perpetuate itself. People having high incomes and college educations are more likely to be in favor of having their children get college educations.[26]

26 · Herbert Hyman, "The Value Systems of Different Classes," in Bendix and Lipset, pp. 426–442.

And those who receive a college education are considerably more likely than those who do not to be able to afford to send their children to college, as an examination of Table 12 will show. But despite this tendency, as we shall see in the next chapter, some people do alter their class status, moving upward or downward in the stratification structure. In some societies it is more common than others.

TABLE 12 · The Influence of Education Upon Income *

AMOUNT OF EDUCATION	ESTIMATED LIFE-TIME INCOME RESULTING FROM PREVAILING 1949 INCOME LEVELS OF MALES
Average	$133,000
No school years completed	58,000
1–4 years elementary school	72,000
5–7 years elementary school	93,000
8 years elementary school	116,000
1–3 years high school	135,000
4 years high school	165,000
1–3 years college	190,000
4 years college or more	268,000

* Paul C. Glick, "Educational Attainment and Occupational Advancement," *Transactions of the Second World Congress in Sociology*, Volume 2: *Social Stratification and Social Mobility* (London: International Sociological Association, 1954), p. 192.

INTERPRETATIVE SUMMARY

Some simple tribal societies, particularly nomadic ones, have no complicated class structure; but most societies have either a rigid system called a *caste* system, or a more flexible system called a *class* structure. A particular hierarchy may be based on differences in race, tribe, occupation, religion, or a combination of these and other factors. The tendency is toward more flexible class systems. Broad changes occurring toward the end of the Middle Ages brought more social mobility to European societies and eventually even influenced such rigid societies as India. These changes—the rise of capitalism in the economic realm and, in the realm of thought, the emergence of scientific method, religious tolerance, nationalism — had in common the assumption that individuals and their achievements are supremely important.

The United States has a flexible class system, with the exception of its treatment of the Negro, who is held down in a virtual caste. Important indicators of class status in our society are income, education, and occupation. Occupation is especially important, since it usually reflects one's education and income, the other two important factors, and also since most people agree on the relative prestige of American occupations, tending to admire positions involving power and requiring intelligence. It is frequently difficult, however, to determine the social class of a particular individual, since in a given situation one factor may outweigh other usually important ones. Then too, regional differences in class structure exist, some communities placing emphasis on statuses which other communities minimize or do not even recognize.

Though a given individual's position in the hierarchy may be difficult to pinpoint, that position is not likely to change much in his or his children's lifetime. This is true because, first, his position will determine his style of life; and the behavior patterns he learns from others who share his style of life will in turn indicate his position and pinion him to it. Second, he will teach his children his own way of life, since it will be the only way he knows. Third, if he is poor, he will find it difficult to help his children find a better way of life even if he wants to.

REVIEW AND SUGGESTED READINGS

A • VOCABULARY

Caste	Estate	Stratification structure
Class	Life chances	Style of life

B • QUESTIONS AND TOPICS FOR REVIEW

1. In your community, what criteria are most important in the stratification structure?
2. Discuss the prestige and make an estimate of the social class of the following:
   a. writer of one little-known novel acclaimed by critics—presently a chicken farmer by choice
   b. lawyer from "good" state school, age 26, working for corporation at rather low salary, has wife and two children
   c. educated and intelligent "society girl" who married beneath herself

    d. your city's mayor

    e. Jack Paar

3. Which is more difficult to pinpoint, differences between lower- and middle-class behavior, or differences between middle- and upper-class behavior? Why?

4. One way of quickly gauging a person's class is by noting the language he uses. When doing this, however, one must remember that many grammatical forms once considered substandard have now passed into acceptable usage. What kinds of people use each of the following structures?

    a. "He don't ever listen to me."

    b. "So I says to him, 'Billy, you've got to settle down!'"

    c. "She had just left it laying there, for anyone to steal."

    d. "Yesterday I lay down the law to those kids of mine."

    e. "Mrs. Daley and myself had a wonderful time."

    f. "It's he who's responsible, and he'll pay, by George!"

5. How do you account for the fact that government officials as an occupational category have higher prestige in the United States than professional and semi-professional workers?

C · SUGGESTIONS FOR FURTHER READING

David Caplovitz. *The Poor Pay More: Consumer Practices of Low-Income Families*. New York: The Free Press of Glencoe, 1963.

    A carefully documented research study of low-income families in New York showing the inflated cost of living for the poor.

John F. Cuber and William F. Kenkel. *Social Stratification in the United States*. New York: Appleton-Century-Crofts, Inc., 1954.

    A textbook containing useful summaries of several research studies, such as those of Yankee City, Plainville, and Elmtown.

Art Gallaher, Jr. *Plainville Fifteen Years Later*. New York and London: Columbia University Press, 1961.

    A replication of West's Plainville study, concluding that the impact of the rapid social change in American society has produced a less caste-like structure in this community, with positions becoming more achieved and less ascribed.

Joseph A. Kahl. *The American Class Structure*. New York: Rinehart & Company, Inc., 1957.

    A highly literate discussion of class structure in the United States, with an especially good chapter on income, wealth, and style of life.

Kurt B. Mayer. *Class and Society*. New York: Random House, 1955.

    A very sound introduction to the topic of social stratification, with good illustrative data.

Leonard Reissman. *Class in American Society*. Glencoe, Ill.: The Free Press, 1959.

    A useful book for the student interested in the various theories of class structure, with a chapter on several methods for study stratification.

CHAPTER 12

Social Mobility

By *social mobility* we mean movement within the social structure. When a person leaves a job paying $5,000 a year to accept one paying $8,000, he has altered his position in the class structure. He has been socially mobile. Since one's class status is determined originally by the class status of his parents, when one acquires a different amount of education from that of his parents, or moves into a different occupational stratum, or adopts a different style of life, he has been socially mobile. Movement within the social structure may occur for a whole category of people; the ethnic minorities who were socially defined as foreign and inferior two generations ago but are now largely assimilated exemplify the social mobility of an entire category of people.

SOCIAL MOBILITY AS A PROCESS

Such movement is a change that takes place in the status of an individual, a group, or a category. It is, in other words, a process. The term *mobility* is used also to indicate the spatial movement, or migration, of a population, but we shall here restrict our use of the word to social mobility, or movement within a social structure.

Types of Mobility An alteration in status can be either upward or down-ward in the stratification structure, or it can be horizontal. Horizontal mobility is movement from one status to another when there is no difference between the ranks of the two statuses. A person who quits his job as an electrician to become a machinist is horizontally mobile: the two occupational statuses take about the same amount of training, pay about the same, and carry about the same prestige in the community (see Table 7, Chapter 11). A change in status has taken place; the process of social mobility has occurred, but the movement has been *horizontal*, within a stratum. On the other hand, a truck driver's son who wins a college scholarship and, on graduation, joins a law firm as an accountant has achieved upward *vertical* mobility from the status into which he was born. If he is then inefficient, loses the job, and goes to work as a waiter in a restaurant, he is downwardly mobile from his previous job.

An individual can experience vertical mobility by altering any one of the characteristics which determine his ranking in the stratification structure: his occupational status, the amount of education he has, his income, or his style of life. But he can also experience mobility simply by being a member of some social category if a change takes place in the prestige accorded that category. In time of war, for example, ca-

178

ONLY 35—BUT HE HAS EARNED IT!

Used to be you didn't see a young man at the wheel of a Cadillac very often.

Most of the proud and happy people driving Cadillacs showed at least a little gray at the temples.

But things are changing. In fact, it isn't at all unusual any more for a man in his thirties to move up to the "car of cars."

There are two basic reasons for this.

In the first place, success is coming earlier now to a greater group of young men than in years gone by.

Men are going into business and the professions with fine technical training which starts them off at levels they used to be years in attaining.

And, secondly, the news of Cadillac's remarkable economy is spreading far and wide.

Actually, once a man feels justified in making the initial investment, he is economically on sound ground when he selects a Cadillac.

First of all, he can keep it and drive it with pride for almost any period of years he may elect—for its endurance is beyond all practical measurement.

Upkeep is remarkably low—and few cars of any size or price will run farther on a gallon of gasoline.

Thus, it is small wonder that more and more people in a younger age bracket are making the move to Cadillac. It has become a logical and practical thing for them to do.

So, if *you* are ready for a Cadillac—remember that *achievement*—and not age—is the criterion.

Why not see your nearest dealer soon?

GM Photographic

American culture makes upward mobility an ethic, and offers both symbolic and material rewards to those who succeed.

reer military men, without any alteration in their education, income, or occupation, are suddenly more sought after as party guests, luncheon club speakers, and subjects of feature articles. The occupational status of soldier understandably holds more prestige for many people in war than in peacetime; hence incumbents of the status are automatically upwardly mobile.[1] Similarly, after the stock market crash of 1929 and during the depression of the 1930's, the prestige of bankers and brokers suffered. It was not necessary for an individual banker to alter his occupation or income or style of life to experience vertical mobility; the occupational status itself was downwardly mobile.

The Measurement of Mobility By far the most frequently used indicator of mobility in sociological research is change in occupation; the next most common indicator is change in income.[2] As we have seen, occupational status is closely correlated with educational status, income, style of life, and the other determinants of class status. Thus a change in occupation is probably the best single indicator of social mobility.[3]

Occupational mobility may be measured in either of two ways: (1) career mobility may be studied by charting a person's work history in order to see whether he has been upwardly mobile, stable, or downwardly mobile since he entered the labor force; or (2) a person's occupational status may be compared with that of his father to determine the direction and degree of intergenerational mobility.

Social Mobility and Social Structure Sociologists study social mobility in order to ascertain the relative "openness" of a social structure. In other words, they are interested in the relative difficulty which different persons, groups, or categories experience in acquiring the goods or statuses that are valued in the culture and hence are objects of competition. The more equal the opportunity for achieving such goods and statuses, the more social mobility there will be, and the greater the amount of social mobility, the more open the class structure.

In caste societies, the class structure is closed. There is virtually no vertical mobility, because statuses are ascribed at birth. The occupational status one will enter, the amount of education he will receive, his income, and his whole style of life are known when he is born. In an open-class society, these statuses are not ascribed, but are left to the individual to achieve. It is true that

1 · This is in keeping with the idea that social stratification is essentially a function of the division of labor, and that statuses are therefore differentially evaluated according to the scarcity of personnel qualified to fill them and the degree of importance assigned to the statuses by the normative structure of the society. For the classic statement of this position, see Kingsley Davis and Wilbert E. Moore, "Some Principles of Stratification," *American Sociological Review*, 1945, 10:242–249. For a discussion of this approach to stratification, see Melvin M. Tumin, "Some Principles of Stratification: A Critical Analysis," *American Sociological Review*, 1953, 18:387–394; Davis, "Reply," *American Sociological Review*, 1953, 18:672–673; Tumin, "Rewards and Task Orientations," *American Sociological Review*, 1955, 20:419–423; Richard D. Schwartz, "Functional Alternatives to Inequality," *American Sociological Review*, 1955, 20:424–430. For a critique of an extension to economic theory of the idea of functional importance as a criterion in the stratification of statuses, see Richard L. Simpson, "A Modification of the Functional Theory of Social Stratification," *Social Forces*, 1956, 35:132–137.

2 · Raymond W. Mack, Linton Freeman, and Seymour Yellin, *Social Mobility: Thirty Years of Research and Theory* (Syracuse: Syracuse University Press, 1957), p. 2.

3 · As Chinoy points out, occupational data are relevant to all theories of stratification utilized by contemporary sociologists, whether they define the class structure in

Marxian, Weberian, or "class-consciousness" categories. See Ely Chinoy, "Social Mobility Trends in the United States," *American Sociological Review*, 1955, 20:180–186. This is not to deny that mobility is multidimensional. For evidence that what we call mobility has a number of components, see Charles F. Westoff, Marvin Bressler, and Philip C. Sagi, "The Concept of Social Mobility: An Empirical Inquiry," *American Sociological Review*, 1960, 25:375–385.

the life chances of a street sweeper's son born in the slums differ considerably from those of a broker's son born in the suburbs, but the culture does not exclude the former from achievements equal to or greater than those of his contemporaries. On the contrary, the ethos of an open-class society will encourage him to try to achieve statuses carrying higher prestige than those into which he is born.

Just as there is some vertical mobility, even though very little, in India, so that it cannot be referred to as a perfect example of a caste structure, so there are some ascribed statuses in the United States and other open-class societies. Our own social structure is only relatively open; race, for example, is an ascribed status, and members of racial minorities are blocked in their attempts to achieve certain statuses. In general, however, our society emphasizes the open-class ideal, and people in the United States are socialized into a belief system which encourages them to try to be upwardly mobile. (See, for example, the advertisement reprinted on page 179.)

THE MOBILITY ETHIC

The emphasis on vertical social mobility in the American social structure is one of the most striking features of our class system. Mayer points out that

. . . the United States has placed greater emphasis on social mobility than any other large nation in modern times. Americans have firmly proclaimed the idea of equality and freedom of achievement and have acclaimed the large numbers of individuals who have risen from humble origins to positions of prominence and affluence. Indeed, the belief in opportunity is so strongly entrenched in the culture that most Americans feel not only that each individual has the "right to succeed" but that it is his duty to do so. Thus we are apt to look with disapproval upon those who fail or make no attempt to "better themselves." [4]

This mobility ethic, or cultural value attached to improving one's position, has roots both in a normative structure growing out of political revolution and frontier economics and in a religious heritage from the Protestant Reformation in Europe. We shall look first at the aspects of the mobility ethic which would seem to derive from our peculiar situation as a young nation offering the combination of enormous natural resources and the opportunity to gain refuge from tyranny.

Roots of the American Mobility Ethic
The relative importance of achieved status so characteristic of the open-class system has permeated the ethos of the United States for several reasons. First of all, this country afforded tremendous economic opportunities for the ordinary man—free land for settlement, other natural resources for easy exploitation, and a rapidly expanding business world. Second, political freedom was an essential tenet almost from the beginning of our country, and it became increasingly significant as our population expanded under favorable material conditions. Third, religious tolerance and freedom not only furnished an outlet for individual choice but gave our democracy a strong supporting noneconomic, nonpolitical ideology and practice. And fourth, freedom of research and invention, of personal migration, and other associated features of individualism and liberalism became

4 · Kurt B. Mayer, *Class and Society* (New York: Random House, 1955), p. 69. By permission.

Education is one route to upward mobility: the transition from farm laborer to college student

Monkmeyer

deeply and firmly embedded in our culture.

The Protestant Ethic The religious institutions of a society both influence and justify its social structure. The values associated with the Protestant Reformation and the rise of capitalism in Europe were most compatible with an open-class structure.[5]

5 · For a more detailed discussion of the relationship between Protestantism and capitalism, see Max Weber, *The Protestant Ethic and the Spirit of Capitalism*, trans. Talcott Parsons (New York: Charles Scribner's Sons, 1930); and R. H. Tawney, *Religion and the Rise of Capitalism* (New York: Harcourt, Brace & Co., 1936). The most damning indictment of the whole thesis of Weber, Tawney, Sombart, and others is Kurt Samuelsson, *Religion and Economic Action: The Protestant Ethic, the Rise of Capitalism, and*

The moral system of the Roman Catholic Church stressed otherworldliness; its emphasis was on rewards in the hereafter. The culturally established Catholic ethic of medieval times urged one to accept his lot—that is, to do the best possible job in the status in which he found himself. If a person were a serf, it was because God had intended him to be a serf, and he was as surely engaged in the Lord's work digging potatoes as he would have been ruling an empire. The rationale for the performance of worldly tasks was other-

the Abuses of Scholarship (New York: Basic Books, 1961). An excellent general summary of the literature on the functions of religious structure is Elizabeth K. Nottingham, *Religion and Society* (New York: Random House, 1954).

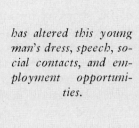

has altered this young man's dress, speech, social contacts, and employment opportunities.

Monkmeyer

worldly: reparation for sins and purification through humility. Like the Hindus, medieval Christians were encouraged to make the best of the ascribed statuses into which they were born, with the promise that they would be rewarded for the acceptance of their worldly lot when they were reborn into an afterlife.

The Protestant Reformation changed all this by emphasizing the importance of good works. Protestantism was a morality of individualism, and the individual was to be judged not on his humility but on the basis of what he accomplished. Luther and Calvin sanctified work; they made virtues of industry, thrift, and self-denial. Wesley preached that the fruits of one's labor

were the signs of salvation.[6] Favor with God no longer depended on trying, but on doing; a person was saved not for accepting his lot but for proving that he could better it. The culmination of the Protestant Reformation, then, according to Weber, was to give divine sanction to the drive to excel.

It should not be thought that the expression "Protestant Ethic" implies that people in contemporary American society who are reared in Protestant faiths are socialized to accept the mobility ethic, while American Roman Catholics and those of other religions

6 · A detailed analysis of the material here summarized can be found in Adriano Tilger, *Work: What It Has Meant to Man Through the Ages* (New York: Harcourt, Brace & Co., 1930).

are not. "Protestant Ethic" is simply a phrase applied to a cultural value associated historically with the Reformation and the rise of capitalism; the concept has become part of the American ethos, and research indicates that people of all faiths may internalize it.[7] The point is that, in the words of Nottingham,

In the same manner that religion has aided the Hindus to interpret the rigidities of their caste system, religion has provided moral justification to Americans for certain aspects of the American competitive class system—particularly the high premium placed on success and the consequent penalization of failure. Without this interpretation the successful might feel guilty about their success and the unsuccessful discouraged and resentful about their failures. Furthermore, given positive attitudes to the material world, it is not enough to claim that all moral imbalances will be rectified in heaven: it is crucial to interpret success as morally right—and failure as implying moral lack—here and now.[8]

Political, economic, and religious institutions—all buttress the idea in the United States that upward mobility is a good thing. But believing in mobility and personally experiencing it are two different things.

FACTORS CONTRIBUTING TO SOCIAL MOBILITY

There are several characteristics of the American social structure that account for the relatively high rate of upward mobility.

7 · See Raymond W. Mack, Raymond J. Murphy, and Seymour Yellin, "The Protestant Ethic, Level of Aspiration, and Social Mobility: An Empirical Test," *American Sociological Review*, 1956, 21:295–300.

8 · Nottingham, *Religion and Society*, p. 74. By permission.

Immigration The millions of immigrants who entered the United States in the late nineteenth and early twentieth centuries made a certain amount of upward mobility virtually automatic for the people already here. Mass immigration increased the size of the population dramatically, and thus contributed to a growth of the economy. Such growth meant that there was an increase in the number of occupational statuses to be filled at all levels in the stratification structure. The filling of the statuses at the bottom of the structure by immigrants working as low-paid unskilled laborers allowed native Americans and their sons to move up and fill some of the statuses higher in the structure.

As a factor in the rate of vertical mobility in the United States, immigration is less important now than it once was. Yet, even with legislation which has slowed greatly the rate of immigration, there is still a steady stream of people entering the United States from other countries. Furthermore, the internal migration from rural areas to urban centers, particularly the movement of Negroes from the South to the North, has much the same effect on the total stratification structure that immigration used to have.

Mechanization Some of this internal migration is symptomatic of another factor that has contributed to a high rate of upward mobility in American society: technological change. The constant trend toward replacing human muscular effort with machinery, culminating in what we call automation, has reduced the proportion of occupational statuses that call for unskilled labor and increased the number of semiskilled jobs. With this have come the growth of bureaucratic industrial organizations and the expansion of government services, both of which require more white-collar personnel. Finally, the freeing through mechanization of larger and larger proportions of the labor force has allowed the expansion of service industries.

We shall discuss these trends more fully in Chapter 23, "Sociological Aspects of the Economic Order." We need point out here only that the creation of new occupational statuses in the middle part of the stratification structure and the reduction in the number of occupations at the lower end of the structure necessitate some upward mobility. There is a tendency for the traditional stratification pyramid to become diamond-shaped as the economy becomes more mechanized and more bureaucratic. That is, there is a contraction at the bottom of the pyramid as fewer and fewer people are engaged in unskilled work and an expansion in the middle as more and more people enter semiskilled and lower white-collar statuses. This means that if every family had just enough children to take over the statuses the parents had occupied in the stratification structure, there would still be some upward mobility, since there would not be enough lower-class statuses for the children of lower-class people, and there would be more middle-class statuses than middle-class children to fill them.

Differential Fertility Actually, people in each class do not have exactly the number of children needed to replace them. As we saw in Table 9, page 172, there are marked differences in the birth rates in the various income classes, with the reproduction rate of the lowest income class being more than 50 percent higher than that of the top stratum. Professionals and other white-collar people typically do not have enough children to replace themselves in the labor force. Farmers and farm laborers, on the other hand, have as much as 50 percent more than enough children to take their places. This would be true even if there were no changes in the number of people needed to fill each occupational category from generation to generation. Actually, we know that the clerical and professional personnel have been an increasing proportion of the labor force, while unskilled laborers and farm laborers have become a smaller proportion of the total number of workers.

The openings created in the stratification structure by the low birth rates of the white-collar classes can be filled only by the children of farmers and manual workers. Thus differential fertility, like mechanization and immigration, induces a certain amount of vertical mobility.

In the section that follows we shall turn to the question of just how much mobility there is, and whether the American class structure is becoming more rigid or more open.

THE AMOUNT OF MOBILITY IN THE UNITED STATES

The mobility ethic, the belief that upward mobility is both possible and desirable in our society, has probably led to an exaggerated general notion of the number of cases in which the poor laborer's son becomes president of a corporation. A study comparing more than 8,000 top executives in the largest firms in the United States in 1952 with the top business leaders in 1928 shows that, in both periods, more than 50 percent of the business leaders were sons of owners or executives.[9] The following biographical sketch of a leading executive in an American metropolis illustrates the pattern:

Mr. Parks has one son, Mark, Jr., who is now the more active member of the team he and his father represent. He is an alert and capable man, as active in a variety of civic affairs as his father is said to have been some years ago. His rise in the company was from the bottom up. Several of the leaders in Regional City who have inherited businesses have followed the pattern of beginning at the bottom of the ladder in the company. The rise of these men has been meteoric, in many instances, but the newspapers in biographical accounts of the lives of such persons solemnly report that they have "worked their way to the top." The occupational ascent of Mark Parks, Jr., illustrates the rapidity of such a rise up the ladder of success. The pattern is in the American tradition, but most men find the ascent a longer process than did Mark, Jr.

Young Mark, upon graduation from college, came into his father's business as a shipping clerk. He became successively a stockroom clerk, a stock foreman, and an office manager for one of the branch warehouses. Two years after he started as shipping clerk, he was elected a director of the corporation and placed in charge of one of the major subsidiaries of the company. Three years later he was named treasurer of the company, and in three years more he became operations vice-president. After two years in this position he was made president. His father then became chairman of the board and has since gradually relinquished active control of the business in favor of his son. He still retains a firm control in matters of general policy, however. Mark, Jr., is the authority on administrative matters. So we see that within ten years this young man rose from stock clerk to company president. It

is claimed, and rightly so perhaps, that by dint of hard work he made good. Certainly it cannot be denied that so young a person as he was in the earlier years of his service in the business shouldered considerable responsibility and has continued to do so increasingly. It may be surmised, nevertheless, that his father's position in the company was extremely helpful in his business success.[10]

Intergenerational Mobility Not all occupations exhibit as high a rate of intergenerational continuity as business management. Most of the research on occupational mobility indicates that approximately two-thirds of the sons have been vertically mobile, either upward or downward, from the class strata of their fathers.[11] Occupational mobility, then, is more likely than occupational continuity, as Table 13 shows. More important in evaluating the "rags to riches" myth is the fact that, while many sons experience *some* mobility, very few experience *much*. They move, but not far. If one is not in the same occupational category as his father, the next most likely place for him is in the occupational category either immediately above or immediately below that of his father. If a semiskilled worker in a mass-production factory has a son who is mobile, that son is most likely to

9 · W. Lloyd Warner and James C. Abegglen, *Occupational Mobility in American Business and Industry*, 1928–1952 (Minneapolis: University of Minnesota Press, 1955), p. 45. See also F. W. Taussig and C. S. Joslyn, *American Business Leaders* (New York: The Macmillan Co., 1932).

10 · Floyd Hunter, *Community Power Structure: A Study of Decision Makers* (Chapel Hill: University of North Carolina Press, 1953), pp. 27–28. By permission.

11 · See, for example, P. E. Davidson and H. D. Anderson, *Occupational Mobility in an American Community* (Stanford, California: Stanford University Press, 1937); Richard Centers, "Occupational Mobility of Urban Occupational Strata," *American Sociological Review*, 1948, 13:197–203; Seymour M. Lipset and Reinhard Bendix, "Social Mobility and Occupational Career Patterns," *American Journal of Sociology*, 1952, 57:366–374, 494–504; Natalie Rogoff, *Recent Trends in Occupational Mobility* (Glencoe, Ill.: Free Press, 1953); Cecil G. North and Paul K. Hatt, "Jobs and Occupations: A Popular Evaluation," *Opinion News*, 1947, 9:3–13.

TABLE 13 · Occupational Mobility in a Representative Sample of the American Population *

FATHER'S OCCUPATION	SON'S OCCUPATION (PERCENTAGE IN EACH CATEGORY)							
	Pro-fessional	Busi-ness	White Collar	Skilled	Semi-skilled	Ser-vice	Farm	Non-farm labor
Professional	23	4	9	3	2	4	2	3
Business	24	31	23	7	11	6	2	12
White collar	10	9	15	4	6	3	2	0
Skilled	13	18	21	30	19	20	3	9
Semiskilled	5	8	10	14	19	12	4	17
Service	5	3	3	5	3	8	0	1
Farmers	17	25	16	29	32	28	84	32
Nonfarm labor	2	2	3	7	7	12	3	19

* From Cecil C. North and Paul K. Hatt, "Jobs and Occupations: A Popular Evaluation," *Opinion News*, 1947, 9:12. Columns will not total 100 per cent because some respondents did not know their father's occupation. By permission.

move one step down to unskilled work or one step up to skilled labor; it is unlikely that he will become an executive or a professional man. In summary, we can say that more sons are mobile than are not, but that most sons work at either the same occupational level or one immediately adjacent to that of their fathers.

In the light of the effects of immigration, mechanization, and differential fertility on the openness of the class structure, it is not surprising that there is more upward than downward mobility. One study of the mobility of a representative sample of white urban males showed that nearly 30 percent of the sons of manual laborers moved up into nonmanual occupational statuses, while fewer than 20 percent of the sons of fathers in nonmanual work were downwardly mobile into manual occupations.[12] The point that most mobility is into adjacent strata still holds: sons of manual laborers who move up into

white-collar work are more likely to become salesmen or clerical workers than professional men or business executives.

Despite the considerable mobility between white-collar and the so-called "blue-collar" occupational statuses, the line between them is the greatest hurdle in the class structure. There is more mobility within the manual strata and within white-collar categories than there is between the two.

Career Mobility Studies of the mobility experienced by individuals during the time they are in the labor force point in general to the same conclusions as intergenerational studies. They reveal more mobility than stability, but the bulk of the mobility is horizontal rather than vertical, occurring within occupational categories, not between them.[13] While it is not unusual for a person to change his occupation four or five times during his career, about

12 · Richard Centers, *The Psychology of Social Classes* (Princeton: Princeton University Press, 1949), p. 180.

13 · Lipset and Bendix, "Social Mobility"; Davidson and Anderson, *Occupational Mobility*.

half these moves are from one semi-skilled job to another, or from one managerial post to another, and so on. Those shifts which do involve vertical mobility are usually limited in extent, the most common pattern being a move to an immediately adjacent occupational category in the class structure. Career moves from the bottom to the top of the occupational hierarchy are as exceptional as intergenerational mobility of this type. Research on career mobility further confirms the studies of intergenerational movement in indicating that there is slightly more upward than downward mobility.

Trends in Social Mobility Many social scientists have speculated that the mobility ethic might become a norm inconsistent with the facts of American class structure. They have said that the rate of upward mobility has been declining, that "the strata are becoming more rigid; the holes in the sieve are becoming smaller." [14] Certainly one can cite arguments which suggest that the chances to work one's way up in American society are diminishing: the passing of the frontier days of free homesteading, the decline in immigration, the fact that the fertility rates of the different classes are not as disparate as they used to be. As early as 1948, however, Edward Shils pointed out that "In spite of the oft-asserted claim that

opportunities for ascent into the upper strata are diminishing in the United States, no conclusive evidence has been presented on either side of the issue by social research." [15]

Since that time, a considerable amount of research has been published on trends in rates of social mobility in the United States. These studies certainly offer no evidence that the American class structure is becoming more rigid. Indeed, even allowing for the expansion of opportunities for upward mobility as a result of the trend away from a class pyramid and toward a diamond-shaped class structure, Rogoff still concludes that the rate of upward mobility was about the same in 1940 as in 1910. [16] If the mobility rate was about the same in 1940 as in 1910 even if one does *not* count the mobility which is an automatic result of changes in the occupational structure, then the actual mobility rate would seem to be higher now than it used to be. The conclusions reached in the research comparing the social origins of American business leaders in 1928 and 1952 confirm this fact:

. . . American society is not becoming more caste-like; the recruitment of business leaders from the bottom is taking place now and seems to be increasing. Mobility to the top is not decreasing; in fact, for the last quarter century it has been slowly increasing. [17]

Undoubtedly a significant proportion of this mobility is traceable to the changes in the distribution of occupational statuses growing out of mechanization.

14 · The quotation is from J. O. Hertzler, "Some Tendencies Toward a Closed Class System in the United States," *Social Forces*, 1952, 30:313–323. For other arguments that the amount of upward mobility in the United States is decreasing, see Elbridge Sibley, "Some Demographic Clues to Stratification," *American Sociological Review*, 1942, 7:322–330; C. Wright Mills, *White Collar* (New York: Oxford University Press, 1951), p. 259; and W. Lloyd Warner, *Structure of American Life* (Edinburgh: The University Press, 1952), p. 76.

15 · Edward Shils, *The Present State of American Sociology* (Glencoe, Ill.: The Free Press, 1948).

16 · Rogoff, *Recent Trends*, p. 106.

17 · Warner and Abegglen, *Occupational Mobility*, p. 36.

Class Consciousness and Motivation
One more question should be considered before we leave the topic of social mobility. Not everyone is mobile. Who is mobile and why? In Chapters 11 and 12 we have looked at the class structure as it is seen by sociologists. We have examined the views of students of society regarding the way in which educational, occupational, racial, ethnic, and other statuses are stratified in the United States. One other factor, important in the study of class stratification, is especially meaningful in understanding social mobility patterns: how do most people, who are not professional students of society, perceive the class structure? How conscious are ordinary citizens of the differential prestige accorded to various statuses?

The fact that there is a high degree of consensus on such things as occupational rankings indicates that people have been socialized into the stratification structure. Research showing that children between the ages of 4 and 6 years have already learned to respond to racial differences as a criterion for evaluating people demonstrates that socialization concerning this part of the stratification structure is powerful and effective.[18] Yet, despite the evidence that Americans are aware of their stratification system, many polls indicate that the overwhelming majority of Americans consider themselves to be "middle class." [19] Part of the explanation for the fact that between 75 and 90 percent of the people polled in these studies identify themselves as middle class probably rests in the looseness of the class structure—in the fact that there are no sharp dividing lines between strata. Perhaps even more important is the mobility ethic itself, the norm which says that everyone is supposed to want to move up and which makes it self-derogatory to identify oneself as lower class. On the other hand, the American distaste for aristocracy makes it snobbish for one to claim that he is upper class.

Centers found, however, that there is more class consciousness in Americans than one would be led to think, given the number who claim to be middle class. He simply offered them a fourth choice: working class. In a nationwide poll using the more respectable term *working class*, he found that Americans saw themselves as follows: upper class—3 percent; middle class—43 percent; working class—51 percent; and lower class—1 percent.[20]

The significance of class consciousness for social mobility lies in the fact that attitudes and values have consequences in behavior patterns. If one believes he can be mobile, he will try to be. One's level of aspiration depends on what he has been socialized to believe about his present status and the chances and desirability of altering it.[21] Research has shown that manual workers are aware that most of them are not going to rise to managerial positions

18 · Mary Ellen Goodman, *Race Awareness in Young People* (Reading, Mass.: Addison-Wesley Co., Inc., 1952).

19 · See, for example, *Fortune* Survey, "The People of the United States—A Self-Portrait," *Fortune*, 1940, 21:21; George Gallup and S. F. Rae, *The Pulse of Democracy* (New York: Simon and Schuster, Inc., 1940); Hadley Cantril, "Identification with Social and Economic Class," *Journal of Abnormal and Social Psychology*, 1943, 38:74–80.

20 · Centers, *Psychology of Social Classes*, p. 180.

21 · For an analysis of the effects of working-class attitudes on striving for social mobility, see Herbert H. Hyman, "The Value Systems of Different Classes: A Social Psychological Contribution to the Analysis of Stratification," eds. Reinhard Bendix and Seymour M. Lipset, *Class, Status and Power: A Reader in Social Stratification* (Glencoe, Ill.: The Free Press, 1953), pp. 426–442.

and that, reconciled to the status in which they find themselves, they do not plan upward mobility for themselves but project their ambitions onto their children.[22] Of course, the ones most likely to be upwardly mobile are those who actively seek to achieve upward mobility.[23]

One reason for the high degree of occupational inheritance in business leadership statuses is that businessmen's sons are taught to expect to fill these occupational statuses and manual workers' sons are socialized to believe that there is little chance of their attaining such positions. Indeed, young people with approximately the same I.Q.'s show differences in their educational and occupational aspirations directly related to the occupational statuses of their fathers, a matter which we shall discuss further in our chapter on educational institutions.[24] The higher the prestige of the father in the hierarchy of occupational statuses, the more likely the son is to aspire to high occupational status himself.

Thus, just as race can become an ascribed status through the social defi-

nition imposed by the culture, so can class subcultures make education and occupation, and hence income, tend to be ascribed. Coates and Pellegrin, after comparing top-level executives with lower-level supervisors, conclude as follows:

The social origins and socio-cultural backgrounds of executives and supervisors are significantly different. These variations are basic factors in differential occupational opportunities and placement. Occupational placement and early career experiences lead individuals to adopt attitudes, values, and behavior patterns which function as important positive or negative influences in subsequent career progress and occupational mobility. . . . . Subjective factors, such as attitudes and values which affect occupational behavior patterns, are extremely important influences in determining comparative levels of occupational aspiration.

Levels of aspiration, as they result from attitudes and values, not only affect occupational behavior, but also determine occupational plans and goals and condition mobility drives.[25]

Class consciousness, then, although it is considerably less potent in our relatively open-class structure than in societies more rigidly stratified, is a factor in keeping the extent of vertical mobility limited, even though such mobility is common.

22 · Ely Chinoy, "The Tradition of Opportunity and the Aspirations of Automobile Workers," *American Journal of Sociology*, 1952, 57:453–459.
23 · Richard Scudder and C. Arnold Anderson, "Migration and Vertical Occupational Mobility," *American Sociological Review*, 1954, 19:329–334.
24 · William H. Sewell, Archie O. Haller, and Murray A. Straus, "Social Status and Educational and Occupational Aspiration," *American Sociological Review*, 1957, 22:67–73.

25 · Charles H. Coates and Roland J. Pellegrin, "Executives and Supervisors: A Situational Theory of Differential Occupational Mobility," *Social Forces*, 1956, 35:121–126. Quotation from p. 125. By permission.

INTERPRETATIVE SUMMARY

Open-class societies are, by definition, characterized by widespread social mobility. In our own society, people have had highly favorable, even unique conditions for upward social movement. Political freedom and democracy were held sacred from the beginning of our existence as a nation. Even earlier than this, the country afforded unprecedented opportunities for agricultural and industrial pioneering by ambitious individuals. The Protestant Ethic, embraced by most Americans, taught that achievement in this world is not only justifiable but morally obligatory. As our country developed, immigration and mechanization led to increasingly skilled and "important" jobs for people already here, while the tendency of the upper classes to have few children forced them to relinquish some prestigious jobs to members of lower classes. Even though many of these factors have become less important in our century, factors such as increasing mechanization have reinforced a tendency toward a diamond-shaped social structure.

Though horizontal mobility during one's lifetime is likely, vertical mobility is generally not dramatic. Many sons succeed in reaching the occupational category immediately above that of their father; few go higher, and some go lower. The most difficult gap to bridge in one generation is that between blue-collar and white-collar jobs. One reason for the lack of great intergenerational mobility is class consciousness. While class consciousness, combined with a good dose of the Protestant Ethic, may lead to a longing for a better life, it may also lead to a sound recognition of what is possible, based on what has generally been possible for members of one's class. Then too, class consciousness may lead to pride in one's class, and thus a father may socialize his child to want to put on a white or a blue collar.

REVIEW AND SUGGESTED READINGS

A · VOCABULARY

Career mobility	Mobility ethic	Social mobility
Intergenerational mobility	Protestant Ethic	

B · QUESTIONS AND TOPICS FOR REVIEW

1. Suppose you had known each of the last three Presidents of the United States at the time when each was sixteen years old. What would you have considered the likelihood that each would become President? On what factors would you base your judgment?
2. What professions have risen in prestige in your lifetime? What factors have contributed to their rise?
3. A TV drama series about a first-rate father-and-son legal team has been very successful. Assuming that most people are not in the professional class and are not greatly mobile, why have shows such as this, as well as TV "doctor" dramas and the like, become so popular?
4. How might a middle-class white housewife invoke the Protestant Ethic to justify her paying her Negro maid only $35 a week? How might a gangster use it to rationalize his activities and, perhaps, guilt?
5. What might be some possible explanations for a case of *downward* mobility from one generation to the next?
6. In what sense can you argue that even achieved statuses *tend* to become ascribed?

C · SUGGESTIONS FOR FURTHER READING

Bernard Barber. *Social Stratification.* New York: Harcourt, Brace & Co., 1957.

Chapters 13–16 provide a good summary of what sociologists know about social mobility.

Reinhard Bendix and Seymour M. Lipset, eds. *Class, Status, and Power: A Reader in Stratification.* Glencoe, Ill.: The Free Press, 1953.

A collection of papers covering a wide range of material on stratification, including social mobility.

Richard Centers. *The Psychology of Social Classes.* Princeton: Princeton University Press, 1949.

Good material on people's beliefs and attitudes on social stratification. There is some discussion of social mobility.

Seymour M. Lipset and Reinhard Bendix. *Social Mobility in Industrial Society.* Berkeley and Los Angeles: University of California Press, 1960.

A comprehensive, well-documented analysis of the rates of mobility in industrial society.

Natalie Rogoff. *Recent Trends in Occupational Mobility.* Glencoe, Ill.: The Free Press, 1953.

An intergenerational study of occupational mobility.

W. Lloyd Warner and James C. Abegglen. *Occupational Mobility in American Business and Industry, 1928–1952.* Minneapolis: University of Minnesota Press, 1955.

A study of social mobility among business executives.

CHAPTER 13

Racial and Ethnic Relations

People who are discriminated against (in other words, accorded differential treatment) because they are believed to be inherently different from the dominant members of the society are called a minority.[1] The word does not mean that they are necessarily a numerical minority: the Bantu natives of South Africa are a minority because, although there are fewer Europeans than Bantu in South Africa, the culture of the Europeans is normative for the society. The Europeans are in power; they control the society, and the Bantu, defined as belonging to a lower category, are excluded from full participation in the culture.

A Negro may be a college graduate and an experienced pilot in the United States Air Force and yet be rejected as a job applicant by a commercial airline needing pilots. A private club the membership of which is composed exclusively of wealthy businessmen who are graduates of New England universities may refuse to admit a wealthy businessman with whom some of its members attended college because he is Jewish. A political party caucus may decide that it is useless to run an intelligent, willing young attorney for the legislature because his name

is Colucci. Obviously, other factors may override income, occupation, and education in determining one's position in the class structure. It is not true that two men occupy equal class statuses merely because they have the same income and education and occupy similar occpational statuses—not true, that is, if one is of English ancestry and the other Italian, or if one is Protestant and the other Jewish, or if one is white and the other Negro. One's ethnic (cultural) background or his "race" can "cause" his achieved economic, educational, or occupational status to be reevaluated by the members of society. Indeed, they can place him in a separate class, or caste-like, structure.

MINORITIES AS SOCIAL CATEGORIES

If the members of a society are to exclude some of their fellows from full participation in the culture and define them as a minority, the people who comprise the minority must have some visible characteristic by which they can be identified. The Negroes of the Ituri Forest can treat the pygmies as a minority because they can tell by a man's stature that he is a pygmy.[2] New En-

---

[1] · Our definitions of "dominant" and "minority" follow closely those of R. A. Schermerhorn, *These Our People* (Boston: D. C. Heath, 1949), pp. 5–6.

[2] · Carleton S. Coon and Patrick Putnam, "The Pygmies of the Ituri Forest," *A Reader in General Anthropology*, ed. Carleton S. Coon (New York: Henry Holt & Co., Inc., 1948), pp. 323–325.

193

gland Yankees can treat local French-Canadians as a minority because the latter's speech and family names set them off from the dominant people. A minority's identifiability may result from speaking a different language, having a different skin color, possessing different eye color, or attending a different church from the people in the dominant category. In other words, minorities can either be different physically or behave differently, but one or the other is necessary if they are to be identifiable; and they must be identifiable if they are to be discriminated against as a minority. That was why the Nazis forced German Jews to wear arm bands—so that they could be more easily identified.

If it is his behavior that makes a person identifiable, he can become socialized into a new culture and be assimilated. But physical differences are more permanent; if it is one's skin color that identifies him, no amount of socialization into the culture of the dominant category will remove him from minority status. If physical differences such as skin color or hair type make a person identifiable, the only thing that will remove him from minority status is a change in the dominant group so that the entire minority is assimilated and becomes part of the dominant group. So-called racial minorities are therefore less able to lose their separate identity and shed their minority status than are ethnic minorities.

The most frequently used term for labelling identifiability of a minority is race. Race is a confusing word, however, because it means different things to different people. Mongoloids share certain physical characteristics, and we speak of the Mongoloid race. Some Jews are blond and blue-eyed, others

dark-haired and brown-eyed; all of them share a cultural heritage centered around a religion, and many people speak of the Jewish race. The English have a melting-pot history which includes Celts, Vikings, Angles, Saxons, Normans, Jutes, Hungarians, Turks, and even some African Negro genes via Mediterranean peoples; they share a language and political boundary, and one can read of the characteristics of the English as a race. *Aryan* is a term referring to the Indo-European languages (Latin, Germanic, Celtic, Slavonic, etc.), yet people discuss the differences between Aryan and non-Aryan *races*. Actually, the word *race* has one meaning to scientists and many other meanings in popular usage.

Race as a Biological Concept A race, as the concept is used by geneticists and physical anthropologists, is a number of people who share a set of innate physical characteristics. Nonscientists often assume that members of a race share an unchangeable set of physical characteristics that set them apart permanently from other races. This is not so; races are subject to the same processes of genetic change as all other living organisms.

All human beings belong to a single species. The races of man that today inhabit the earth probably developed through a combination of mutations (some of which permitted survival more easily in one environment than in another), long periods of relative isolation which facilitated inbreeding, and a selection resulting from various cultural standards of what were and were not desirable physical traits.[3] The

3 · For an excellent, readable discussion of genetics and the development of the races of man, see the Department of Mass Com-

major groups of races formed through mutation, isolation, adaptation, and selection have not remained unchanged, because the peoples have not remained absolutely isolated. Since the earliest period of human history, individuals, armies, traders, and whole tribes have migrated and have intermarried with other physical types, thus breaking up the distinctive hereditary patterns.

As a result, there are no pure races within the human species. It is there-

munication, UNESCO, *What Is Race? Evidence from Scientists* (Paris: United Nations Educational, Scientific and Cultural Organization, 1952).

fore impossible to devise a system of classification on the basis of inherited physical traits. Physical anthropologists have been trying for years to develop such a classification. The magnitude of their difficulties can be seen by noting the vagueness of the categories in Table 14. Loose as this three-way classification is, it does not cover all the races of man. African Bushmen-Hottentots, for example, have Mongoloid eyes. Australian aborigines have Negroid skin and Caucasoid hair. Some Polynesians have white skin and some dark brown skin; most of them have wavy hair, but there are many with straight

TABLE 14 · Physical Characteristics of the Three Main Races of Mankind *

TRAIT	CAUCASOID	MONGOLOID	NEGROID
Skin color	Pale reddish white to olive brown; some dark brown.	Pale yellow to yellow-brown; some reddish brown.	Brown to brown-black; some yellow-brown.
Stature	Medium to tall.	Medium tall to medium short.	Tall to very short.
Head form	Long to broad and short; medium high to very high	Predominantly broad; height medium.	Predominantly long; height low to medium.
Face	Narrow to medium broad; no projecting jaw.	Medium broad to very broad; cheekbones high and flat.	Medium broad to narrow; frequent projecting jaws.
Hair	Head hair: color light blond to dark brown; texture fine to medium, form straight to wavy. Body hair: moderate to profuse.	Head hair: color brown to brown-black; texture coarse; form straight. Body hair: sparse.	Head hair: color brown-black; texture, coarse; form light curl to woolly or frizzly. Body hair: slight.
Eye	Color: light blue to dark brown; occasional side eye-fold.	Color: brown to dark brown; fold of flesh in inner corner very common.	Color: brown to brown-black; vertical eye-fold common.
Nose	Bridge usually high; form narrow to medium broad.	Bridge usually low to medium; form medium broad.	Bridge usually low; form medium broad to very broad.
Body build	Slim to broad; slender to rugged.	Tends to be broad; occasional slimness.	Tends to be broad and muscular, but occasional slimness.

* Adapted from Wilton M. Krogman, "The Concept of Race," *The Science of Man in the World Crisis,* ed. Ralph Linton (New York: Columbia University Press, 1945), p. 50. By permission.

or kinky hair. Some have broad and short faces, others long and narrow features. Since there is no such thing as pure race among human beings, one obviously cannot set up a classification scheme for pure races and expect the data to correspond to the theory.

The most important thing to realize about racial classifications is that they do not correlate with either social structures or culture patterns. High cheekbones show some relationship to reddish-brown skin, and brown-black hair is associated with brown-black skin, but none of these characteristics is associated with intelligence, or a caste structure, or musical ability, or inventiveness, or a belief in one God, or the practice of polygamy, or anything else except other physical characteristics. Such an expression as "It's Arnold's Negro blood that makes him dance so well" is simply a holdover from the era before scientists discovered genes, when people believed that traits were transmitted through the blood.

Berry summarizes nicely the biological concept of race:

The term "race," as used by most biological scientists, refers to a set of categories rather than to discrete, invariable entities. Races are not so much real things which man has discovered as they are pigeon-holes which man has constructed. These categories, to be sure, are based upon clusters of hereditary, physical char-

acteristics. . . . The criteria upon which racial classification is based are non-adaptive, physical, secondary, and have little survival value. Certain societies, however, have come to attach great social significance to these biological trivia.[4]

Race and Culture We have seen in Chapter 6 that culture is one of the basic determinants of individual personality. What one has an opportunity to learn shapes his responses to situations and sets limits on his performance as a member of society. This was illustrated by the identical twins who had varying interests and attitudes and even different I.Q.'s because they were socialized in different environments.

The results of cultural environments have often been interpreted as innate racial differences. An example is the widespread belief that there are inherited differences between races in intelligence. It is easy to take the fact that Negroes are more often unskilled laborers than are whites or that whites are more often found in high economic or educational statuses than are Negroes as evidence of racial inferiority. It takes sociological sophistication to see these differences between the races as functions of the stratification structure.

Table 15 seems to indicate that

4 · Brewton Berry, *Race and Ethnic Relations*, 2nd ed. (Boston: Houghton Mifflin Co., 1958), p. 49. By permission.

TABLE 15 · Average Scores on Two Army Intelligence Tests of 1,750,000 Men During World War I *

CATEGORY	ALPHA TEST (for literates)	BETA TEST (for illiterates)
White	59	43
Northern Negro	39	32
Southern Negro	12	20

* Robert D. North, "The Intelligence of American Negroes," *Research Reports*, 1955, 3:2–8. Tables from p. 4. By permission.

TABLE 16 · Contrasts of Whites from Three Lowest Scoring States with Negroes from Three Highest Scoring States on Army Alpha Test of Intelligence During World War I *

| | WHITES | | | NEGROES | |
State	Number of Cases	Median Score	State	Number of Cases	Median Score
Arkansas	618	41.0	New York	850	44.5
Kentucky	832	41.0	Ohio	152	48.8
Mississippi	665	40.8	Illinois	578	46.9

* *Ibid.*, p. 4.

whites are more intelligent than Negroes. But the fact that the differences between Northern and Southern Negroes are even greater than those between Northern Negroes and whites raises a question: how much of the difference in intelligence test scores is attributable to differences in cultural experience? There is no evidence to support the theory that the more intelligent Negroes move North. How much of the Southern Negro's inferiority, then, is traceable to inferior schools, less well-educated teachers and parents, fewer years of formal education, and so on? The answer is apparent from Table 16, which contrasts Negroes from the three highest-scoring states with whites from the lowest-scoring states. Several other studies made at different times in various parts of the country indicate that differences in performance on intelligence tests by race, as well as differences by region, are attributable to environmental factors.[5] It should be stressed that differences in cultural experience make it just as difficult to prove that there are *not* inherited differences between races as to prove that there *are*. But there is no scientific evidence to support the

belief that such inherited differences exist. A group of distinguished social scientists has summarized the situation in a statement on race issued from a meeting in UNESCO House in Paris:

Whatever classification the anthropologist makes of man, he never includes mental characteristics as part of those classifications. It is now generally recognized that intelligence tests do not in themselves enable us to differentiate safely between what is due to innate capacity and what is the result of environmental influences, training, and education. Wherever it has been possible to make allowances for differences in environmental opportunities, the tests have shown essential similarity in mental characters among all human groups. In short, given similar degrees of cultural opportunity to realize their potentialities, the average achievement of the members of each ethnic groups is about the same.[6]

It is possible to marshal evidence that one race has produced a culture superior to that of the others, *if you ignore human history*. One can argue that, on the basis of industrialization and the present world balance of powers, Caucasoids are obviously superior to Mongoloids and Negroids. But this does not explain where this superiority was when Mongoloids under Attila or

5 · For an exhaustive review of such studies, see Robert D. North, pp. 2–8.

6 · Department of Mass Communication, UNESCO, *What Is Race?* p. 62.

Genghis Khan were overrunning Europe, or why the Chinese invented printing four centuries before Europeans did, or why Africans were smelting iron ore while Europeans were still living in caves.

School children brought up in a Western heritage do not know about the Zulu conqueror, Chaka, or about his heroic opponent, Moshesh, or about Shamba Bolongogo, king of the Bakuba, who after three centuries is still remembered for his great reforms and inventions and for his love of peace. Few people have heard of the Liberian prophet Harris or of Kamehameha, King of Hawaii, or of the Mandingo Emperor, Gongo Musa, who is said to have embellished his cities with buildings of a style still used in the mosques of the Western Sudan. These, and a score of others, may well have been prevented merely by their isolated environment from achieving recognition as "great" men in the Western sense of the term . . .

Cultures have flourished and waned in the past, undoubtedly they will continue to have their ups and downs in the future . . . All that science can say is that no connexion has been found between the biological constitution of the peoples and the level of their past or present culture; nor is there any hereditary or other biological reason for supposing that, just because White civilization is leading in the development of the present highly technical age, some races have less aptitude for learning technological skills. There is no reason, for example, why an African, because he is a Negro, cannot learn to drive a tractor or be a soil chemist, or any other of the tasks necessary for underdeveloped countries to help themselves. Such abilities cannot be considered racial ones.

Of course, children of a highly technical civilization have an enormous advantage over those who live in simple, isolated cultures. At an early age they learn the logic that two and two make four, they unconsciously learn the principle of cause and effect, they tinker with machines to see how they work. A Negro child born in the jungle of the Congo is brought up in a world with a different image of nature and its forces. If he is to adopt Western culture he has to learn, not only how a machine works, but also to interpret natural phenomena according to rigid laws which no longer permit the intervention of spirits or magic. But these are cultural, not racial, differences.[7]

The Social Definition of Race What we call "races" in the United States depends on social belief, not on biology. Whether or not one is a Negro depends on whether or not people think he is, not on any specific hair color, hair type, head form, or degree of darkness of skin color. It is obvious that the criteria of classification used are not biological, since the biological characteristics show overlap between the races—for instance, some people considered white have darker skins than some people considered Negro. What ultimately determines whether or not an American is Negro is whether or not he is believed to have any Negro ancestry, as the following news story illustrates:

Davis Knight had lived in Mississippi all of his twenty-three years, except for three years in the Navy. He married blonde, blue-eyed Junie Lee Spradley and farmed a poor piece of land. One night the county police arrested him. Knight was a Negro, they said; Junie Lee was white. In Mississippi that kind of marrying was against the law.

Knight said they were wrong. But a relative, irked by an old family feud, had dug up Davis Knight's genealogy. His great-grandfather had been Cap'n Newt Knight, who deserted the Confederate Army and set up "The Free State of Jones" in Jones County. Cap'n Newt had children by Rachel, a Negro slave girl. Rachel was Davis Knight's great-grandmother.

Through succeeding generations the Knights had married white men or women. Davis Knight's own parents had not

7 · *Ibid.*, pp. 62–63.

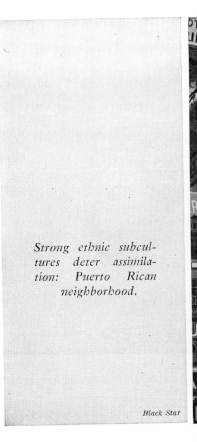

Strong ethnic subcultures deter assimilation: Puerto Rican neighborhood.

Black Star

known of the Negro strain in their ancestry. The story the relative dug up would affect a number of other families in the neighborhood, all sprung from the loins of Cap'n Newt and Rachel. Last week a court in Ellisville convicted Cap'n Newt's great-grandson of miscegenation, sentenced him to five years in jail.[8]

The social definition of race is recognized by the United States Census. Census enumerators are instructed that a person should be counted as an Indian if he is regarded as an Indian in the community where he lives. Social definition also decides whether or not one is a member of an ethnic minority. Suppose a man is the son of a family known in their community as Jews.

8 · *Time,* December 27, 1948. Copyright Time, Inc. By permission.

Even if their name is Smith and they do not attend a synagogue, their parents were Jewish and they are considered Jews. But what happens if the man moves to a new community and does not tell anyone that he is a Jew? He is no longer Jewish! He is the same person, but the social definition of his status has been altered. When we say that the descendants of nineteenth-century German-Americans are almost completely assimilated, we mean that most of them are identified by the members of American society not as Germans or as German-Americans but as Americans.

Minority status, then, is as changeable as the characteristic that makes the minority identifiable. If the only

Ewing Galloway

Negroes comprise over ten percent of the population of the United States, but seldom occupy upper-class status.

thing that confers minority status on a person is his surname, he can change the name and no longer be identifiable as a member of the category. If, however, it is his skin color that is the basis for discrimination, he is more permanently consigned to minority status because he is visibly different.

In either case, the definition of the status is social, and the members of the minority are a social category—that is, the characteristics associated with the minority are present because people *believe* they are present. Statuses are, after all, simply sets of rights and duties assigned to people by other people. A role is a set of expected behaviors, and this is as true of a minority role as of any other. By expecting certain social behaviors from members of a minority, therefore, the people in the dominant category tend to make their own beliefs come true.[9]

Let us look at a few examples. White Americans have believed for years that Negroes are less capable of learning than whites, that they are innately less intelligent. What, given this belief, is a rational course of action for the dominant whites? Provide inferior schools and inferior teachers for Negroes. Then compare the scores of white and Negroes on intelligence tests, and Negroes will average lower than whites. By the very fact of believing that Negroes cannot perform as well as

9 · An extremely interesting discussion of the process by which "social beliefs father social reality" can be found in Robert K. Merton, *Social Theory and Social Structure*, rev. ed., Chapter II, "The Self-fulfilling Prophecy" (New York: The Free Press of Glencoe, 1957).

whites, whites have made this true. Similarly, part of the stereotype of the Jew is that he is aggressive or "pushy." Because the members of the dominant category believe this, they set up extra hurdles for the Jew, such as quotas for admission to medical schools. Thus, if a Jewish boy wants to become a doctor, he has to be not only as good as his non-Jewish competitors, but better. He has to work hard enough and perform well enough to overcome discrimination. In other words, he *has* to be aggressive and "pushy."

Minorities, then, are social categories. By being born a member of a minority, one has his life chances altered. In this sense, minorities are subclasses in the stratification structure. In the total class structure, a businessman has higher prestige than a laborer, but a Protestant businessman has higher prestige than a Jewish businessman. Incidentally, discrimination is not instinctive; it is learned. It is not some inborn tendency to discriminate that explains the presence of racial and ethnic minorities; it is the process and resultant hierarchy of social stratification. Race is important when it is socially defined as a synonym for class.

MINORITIES IN THE SOCIAL STRUCTURE

As recently as 1910, racial and ethnic minorities accounted for more than one-fourth of the population of the United States, as can be seen from Tables 17 and 18. In recent decades the Negro population has remained a fairly constant tenth of the total, while the foreign-born population has diminished markedly. How do Negro and foreign-born people become minorities? What places some people in a society in racial or ethnic social categories? Ordinarily, a racial or ethnic population becomes defined as different and placed in a social category in one of four ways.

Patterns of Minority Emergence [10] A number of people may become a minority through annexation, colonialism, or migration, either involuntary or voluntary. Most European minorities, such as the Poles in Russia or the Greeks in Turkey, have acquired minority status because of political annexation. The only time a sizable minority was cre-

10 · For a more detailed discussion of these patterns, see Charles F. Marden and Gladys Meyer, *Minorities in American Society*, 2nd ed. (New York: American Book Company, 1962), Ch. 1.

TABLE 17 · Size and Proportion of Negro Population in the United States, 1850–1960 *

Year	Population (millions)	Percentage
1850	3.6	15.5
1870	4.9	12.3
1890	7.5	11.9
1910	9.8	10.7
1930	11.9	11.4
1950	15.0	10.0
1960	18.9	10.5

* *Statistical Abstract of the United States*, 1953, U.S. Bureau of the Census, Tables 2, 101, 102; *Historical Statistics of the United States, 1789–1945*, 1949, p. 25; *Seventeenth Census of Population* (1950), *Characteristics of the Population*, Table 35 (Washington, D.C.: U.S. Government Printing Office). 1960 data from preliminary census reports.

TABLE 18 · Size and Proportion of the Foreign-born Population in the United States, 1850–1960 *

YEAR	FOREIGN-BORN (White) (millions)	U.S. POPULATION (Census) (millions)	PERCENTAGE OF FOREIGN-BORN
1850	2.2	23.2	9.5
1870	5.5	39.8	13.8
1890	9.1	62.9	14.5
1910	13.3	92.0	14.5
1930	14.0	122.8	11.4
1950	10.2	150.7	6.8
1960	9.7	179.3	5.4

* *Statistical Abstract of the United States*, 1953, U.S. Bureau of the Census, Tables 2, 101, 102; *Historical Statistics of the United States, 1789–1945*, 1949, p. 25; *Seventeenth Census of Population* (1950), Vol. II, *Characteristics of the Population*, Table 35 (Washington, D.C.: U.S. Government Printing Office); 1960 *Census of Population*, Volume 1, Characteristics of the Population, Part 1, United States Summary.

ated in the United States through annexation was after the Mexican War, when the Mexicans in Texas, California, and the Southwest were taken into the United States.

The colonial pattern became common in Asia and Africa as European nations succeeded in dominating the political and economic lives of the natives in those regions. Relations between the dominant people in the United States and the American Indian have in general followed the colonial pattern of political and economic subordination of the native population, the maintenance of a color line, and minimal development of social services for the natives. Our relations in the past with the native populations of Cuba, Alaska, Puerto Rico, the Hawaiian Islands, and the Philippines have tended toward the creation of colonial minorities.

A third pattern for creating a minority is migration. The method by which our slaves were acquired is a case of involuntary migration. Taking slaves obviously creates a social category, since the slave population is assumed

to lack some of the rights of citizens of the society, and a pattern of dominance and submission is set up when the slaves are purchased or captured.

The vast bulk of the people who have occupied minority status in the United States came through voluntary migration. Over 36 million immigrants entered the United States during the past century. Fewer than one million of these came from Asia and Africa. More than three-fourths of them emigrated from Germany, Italy, Ireland, Poland, Great Britain, Austria, Hungary, and Russia.[11] Analyses of this immigration usually divide it into the "old" immigration, from northern Europe, most of which occurred before 1890; and the "new" immigration, from southern and eastern Europe after that time. In the decades around the turn of the century, immigration was nearly as great a factor as the birth rate in increasing the nation's population. Since the Immigration Act of 1924, the num-

11 · The figures in this paragraph are from the United States Immigration and Naturalization Service, *Annual Report*, 1948, Tables 1, 4 (Washington: U.S. Government Printing Office).

ber of people entering minority status in our society through voluntary immigration has decreased.

All immigrants enter a society as minorities. The reasons for this are stated well by Kahl:

It has been emphasized that men evaluate one another in terms of group values; individuals are considered worthy of deference if their behavior exemplifies the ideals of their culture. In ordinary circumstances a man cannot be a model citizen if he is not thoroughly familiar with the culture, and this is not possible if he has not grown up in it. Most groups distrust outsiders and even before they have observed them sufficiently, assume that they will not behave as well as group members. Consequently, outsiders are devalued and granted low prestige.

The outsider has other disadvantages. Not being familiar with all the intricacies of the local culture, he is less likely to have occupational skills that will earn him a high income. He will not have friends and relatives in high places who can assist his career. He will not have a family name that bestows prestige through the halo effect of noteworthy ancestors.

Each of those disadvantages can be great or small, depending upon the circumstances. If the outsider is a well-trained physician who comes to a backward community that desperately needs medical service, he is likely to be honored. If he is an ambitious farm boy who moves to a city in his own nation, and shows great ability in business and complete respectability in his personal behavior, he can, through time, earn high prestige among the city's successful people. But if he is an uneducated peasant, who comes to an advanced industrial nation and walks the streets behind a pushcart selling apples, and fails to master the language and the urban habits of the host culture, then he is relegated to a low position and may well be regarded as "that stupid, dirty foreigner." [12]

12 · Joseph A. Kahl, *The American Class Structure* (New York: Rinehart & Company, Inc., 1957), pp. 221–222. By permission.

Patterns of Dominant-Minority Relations A minority can cease to exist as a minority in one of two ways: it can be exterminated, or its members can be totally amalgamated and assimilated into the dominant category. As long as the minority exists, some kind of accommodation between these two extremes must operate. The accommodation may range from the acceptance of slavery by the minority to the acceptance by the dominant category of the minority's attempt to become assimilated, and even the offer by the dominant category of active assistance toward assimilation. Government schools to help immigrants learn the language and the ways of our culture exemplify dominant encouragement of assimilation.

In general, European immigrants have been encouraged to assimilate. Americans have been critical, indeed, of ethnic minorities that segregate themselves and retain their "foreign" institutions. The immigrant considered most desirable has been the one who socializes his children into his adopted culture patterns and becomes "Americanized." Racial minorities, on the other hand, have been discouraged from assimilating. Many states have laws against intermarriage between whites and Negroes or Mongoloids. All the culture patterns that keep racial minorities separate from the dominant category—segregated housing, schools, churches, and so on—are a deterrent to total assimilation.

Identifiability is the key to the rate and degree of assimilation of a minority. How recently the members of a minority have arrived in a society is usually indicated by how well assimilated they are. The reason for this is that the more recently they have arrived, the less time they have had to learn new culture patterns; and the less they act like dominant people, the more identifiable they are. The similarity of the culture in which they were socialized to the one where they have immigrated is a factor in the rate of their assimilation for the same reason: the more different they are, the more identifiable they are. An English factory laborer recently arrived in the United States is much less identifiable than a recently arrived Sicilian peasant; the Englishman speaks, dresses, and acts more like an American. And because he is less identifiable, he can be assimilated more rapidly.

Another factor that delays assimilation by making the minority more visible is population concentration. A large congregation of different people in one area is considerably more noticeable than a few such people would be. Because they are different and noticeable, there seems to be even more of them. They are more likely to inspire fear, to be singled out as a threat to the prevailing way of life, to have stereotypes built up about them, and to become the objects of prejudice and discrimination. Figure 6 shows the impact of concentration of a minority population on its status and prospects. The lowest proportion of eligible Negroes registered to vote is in states where they comprise more than 40 percent of the total population; the highest proportion registered to vote is in

FIGURE 6 · The Relationship Between the Concentration of Negroes in the Population, the Proportion of Negroes of Voting Age Registered, and the Protest Movement, February 1960 *

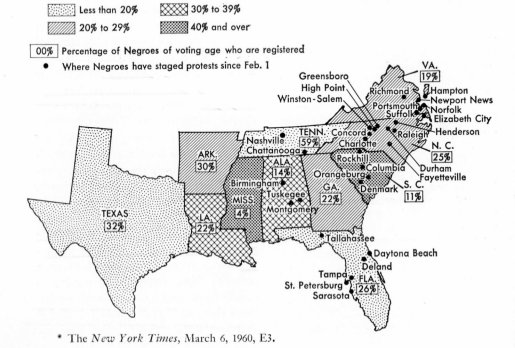

* The *New York Times*, March 6, 1960, E3.

states where they are less than 20 percent of the total.

The basic difference between European ethnic minorities and Asiatic and African racial minorities is the degree to which their identifiability is readily changeable. The Greek immigrant who learns English and changes his name will rear children who not only will not be identifiable as Greeks, but will indeed not *be* Greeks. Their identifiability as a minority depends on culture patterns; as American culture patterns are substituted for Greek, their identifiability is reduced to the vanishing point. But no matter how completely a Negro is American in his thoughts, language, and behavior patterns, he is identifiable as a member of a minority because his visibility depends on his physical features, not his cultural behavior.

Ascribed Status and Color Caste In many ways the position of the Negro in the United States is caste-like. His minority status is fixed by his physical identifiability and the social definition of race. A person may work his way up in the stratification structure from unskilled laborer to professional, but he cannot work his way up from Negro to white. The caste line is in effect an uncrossable barrier, separating the races into two distinct stratification structures, as in Figure 7. The highest status

FIGURE 7 · Color Caste and Class in the United States *

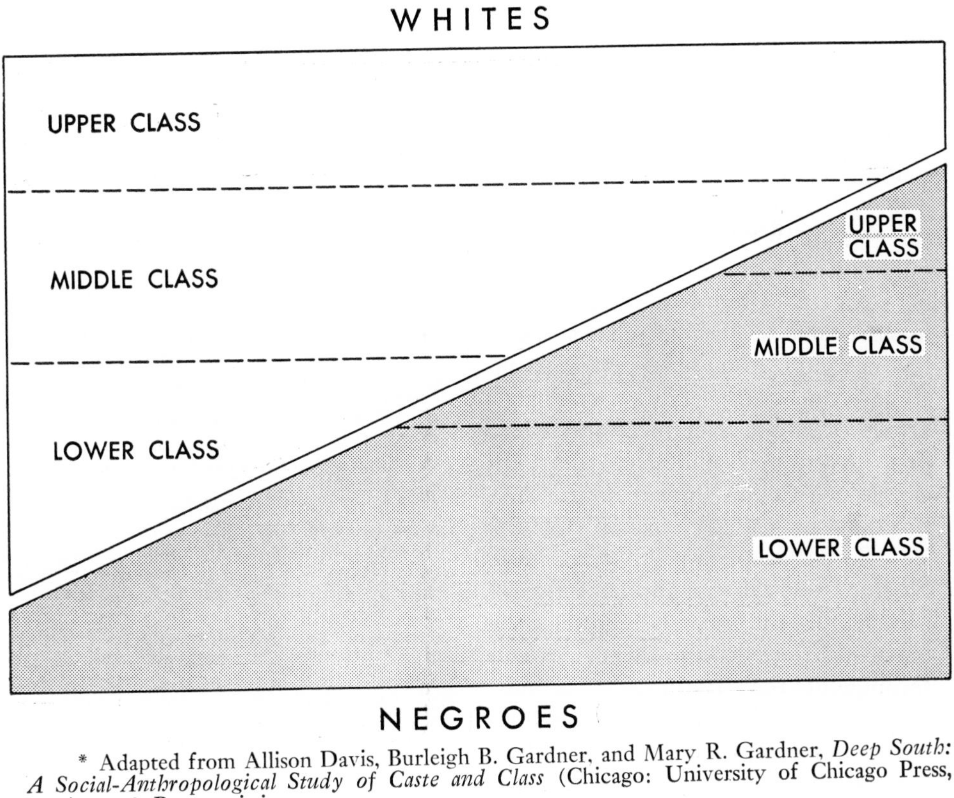

* Adapted from Allison Davis, Burleigh B. Gardner, and Mary R. Gardner, *Deep South: A Social-Anthropological Study of Caste and Class* (Chicago: University of Chicago Press, 1941), p. 10. By permission.

TABLE 19 · Maternal Mortality Rate, by Race (per 10,000 Live Births) 1936–1950 *

YEAR	ALL RACES	WHITE	NONWHITE
1936	56.8	51.2	97.2
1940	37.6	32.0	77.3
1945	20.7	17.2	45.5
1950	8.3	6.1	22.2

* *Maternal Mortality Statistics, United States, 1950,* National Office of Vital Statistics, U.S. Public Health Service, December 3, 1953 (Washington, D.C.: U.S.Government Printing Office), p. 368.

in the Negro structure is not as high as the highest in the white, and the lowest in the white structure is not as low as the lowest in the Negro. If American society were organized on a true caste basis, the line dividing the races would be horizontal, so that no Negro status could be as high as any white one. If there were "separate but equal" Negro and white stratification structures, the dividing line would be vertical. But if Negro and white were really equal, it would not occur to anyone in either category to draw any line anywhere.

There is abundant evidence that minorities occupy distinctive class statuses in the stratification system. Table 19 shows that race is a social category in which life chances differ radically. Even as medical advances have cut the maternal mortality rate to less than one-seventh of what it was a few years ago, nonwhites have changed from having a rate nearly twice as high as whites to one over three and a half times as great as whites. (In the 1950 census, the Census Bureau for the first time used the category of nonwhite for all colored people in the population. Negroes constitute approximately 90 percent of the nonwhite category.) Such variations in life chances extend throughout the stratification system: 16 percent of the white men in the labor force in 1950 were in unskilled labor and service jobs; nearly half the

Negro men were in these occupational statuses.[13] While 60 percent of the white families in the United States had incomes in 1955 of over $4,000 a year, only 25 percent of the nonwhite families were in this bracket.[14] These stratification factors are directly related, of course, to the educational life chances of the Negro, as can be seen in Figure 8.

The conflict between the cultural values of political equality and opportunity for economic advancement as opposed to the ascribed status of the Negro constitutes what Myrdal has called the "American dilemma." [15] Attempts to solve it have changed the class status of the Negro in the United States radically in the past few decades.[16]

13 · U.S. Department of Labor, *Negroes in the United States: Their Employment and Economic Status,* Bulletin 1119, December 1952 (Washington, D.C.: U.S. Government Printing Office), p. 44.
14 · U.S. Bureau of the Census, *Statistical Abstract of the United States,* Table 384 (Washington, D.C.: U.S. Government Printing Office, 1957), p. 313.
15 · Gunnar Myrdal, *An American Dilemma* (New York: Harper & Brothers, 1944).
16 · Five volumes documenting the status of the Negro in relation to housing were published in 1960 by the University of California Press, Berkeley and Los Angeles: Nathan Glazer and Davis McEntire, *Studies in Housing and Minority Groups;* Eunice and George Grier, *Privately Developed Interracial Housing;* Luigi Laurenti, *Property Values and Race;* Davis McEntire, *Residence and Race;* and Chester Rapkin and William G. Grigsby, *The Demand for Housing in Racially Mixed Areas.*

FIGURE 8 · Employment and Earnings Patterns of Non-whites in the United States *

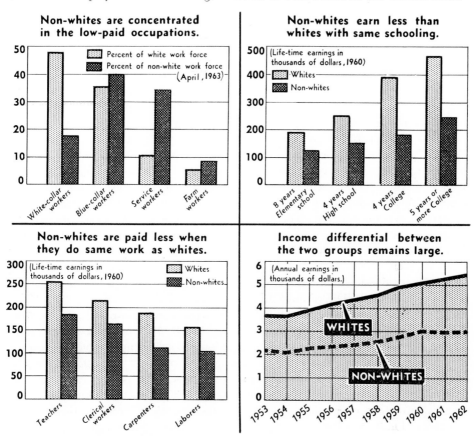

Non-whites are concentrated in the low-paid occupations.

Percent of white work force
Percent of non-white work force
(April, 1963)

White-collar workers · Blue-collar workers · Service workers · Farm workers

Non-whites earn less than whites with same schooling.

(Life-time earnings in thousands of dollars, 1960)
Whites
Non-whites

8 years Elementary school · 4 years High school · 4 years College · 5 years or more College

Non-whites are paid less when they do same work as whites.

(Life-time earnings in thousands of dollars, 1960)
Whites
Non-whites

Teachers · Clerical workers · Carpenters · Laborers

Income differential between the two groups remains large.

(Annual earnings in thousands of dollars.)

WHITES

NON-WHITES

1953 1954 1955 1956 1957 1958 1959 1960 1961 1962

* The *New York Times*, August 4, 1963, 10 E.

RAPID SOCIAL CHANGE IN AMERICAN RACE RELATIONS [17]

As recently as 1950, only eighteen states prohibited segregation in transportation and recreation facilities. Now the Interstate Commerce Commission has outlawed all racial barriers on trains and buses and in terminals.

In 1950 there were still more states in which segregation in the public schools was mandatory than there were states in which school segregation was prohibited. The Supreme Court outlawed public school segregation in 1954. Seven years later, there were only three states that had not begun to comply with the order. (One of them was the locus of the original lawsuit that resulted in the Court's decision.)

Twenty years ago the white primary kept most Negroes out of the elections in the South that counted. The Supreme Court struck at white primaries in 1954, and in 1957 Congress passed the first civil rights act in eighty years, empowering the Justice Department to bring suit to win the ballot for Negroes. Literacy tests and other de-

17 · Much of the material in this section is from Raymond W. Mack, "Desegregation and the Frustrated White Rats," *New Society*, 1963, 37:6–9.

vices used to exclude the Negro from the voting booth are under attack; thirty voting cases are pending in the courts, and the Justice Department is involved in seventy other investigations. The apportionment decision of March 1962 by the Supreme Court reduced the rural dominance in a number of Southern state legislatures.

The Presidential Committee on Equal Employment Opportunity is pressuring government contractors to employ Negroes in skilled jobs. The median income of Negro families is more than six times higher than it was twenty years ago.

In 1870, 80 percent of all American Negroes could neither read nor write. That illiteracy rate has been reduced to 7 percent. The proportion of college graduates among young Negro adults has tripled in the past twenty years.

Besides these objective changes in the status of the American Negro there is an emerging body of public opinion that is intolerant of intolerance. The National Opinion Research Center asked a national sample of white Americans in 1942 whether they believed that "Negroes are as intelligent as white people—that is, can they learn just as well if they are given the same education?" Only 42 percent of the whites said "Yes." But by 1956, the proportion answering "Yes" to the same question had risen to 77 percent. Another NORC survey asked white adults, "If a Negro with just as much income and education as you have moved into your block, would it make any difference to you?" In 1942, only a little over a third of the respondents said "No"; by 1956, the proportion who said that it wouldn't matter to them was over one-half.

Most striking for projecting what the future holds are research studies that tabulate responses according to amount of education and age. The American Institute of Public Opinion asked a national sample of Americans, "If your party nominated a generally well-qualified man for President, and he happened to be a Negro, would you vote for him?" Of those who had only a grade school education, 49 percent said "No." The percentage dropped to 39 percent for those who had completed high school, and among those with a college education, only 21 percent said they would reject a well-qualified candidate because of his race. A similar pattern emerges with age. Thirty-four percent of the voters 21 through 29 years of age said "No." The percentage rose to 37 among those aged 39 to 49. The highest negative response was among people 50 years of age and over—48 percent. Four out of five American youths now graduate from high school, and one-half of these go on to college. The youthful and the educated constitute a growing pressure group.

Research on desegregation by Melvin M. Tumin suggests that "the hard core" of Southern resistance to desegregation lies among the poor and uneducated.[18] The outstanding characteristic of those most willing to resort to violence to defy the law of the land is a below-average amount of schooling. The violence-prone, hard-core people are as stable in residence patterns as their neighbors; they belong to churches in about the same proportion and attend about as frequently. But

18 · Melvin M. Tumin, "Readiness and Resistance to Desegregation: A Social Portrait of the Hard Core," *Social Forces*, 1958, 36:256–263.

their earning power is significantly lower than that of their neighbors, partly because few of them have completed nine or more years of school. The wider society impinges much less directly upon them. They are less influenced by newspapers and magazines. They are less well prepared than their fellow citizens to adjust to rapid social change.

Desegregation of the South is of course especially difficult, since the South is characterized by the very factors that make resistance to change part of its way of life. The South remains predominantly agrarian, with a high birth rate and a low level of formal education. It is the most rural section of urban America, the least schooled region in a highly educated society, the unindustrialized portion of a technologically oriented nation.

But it is short-sighted to think of desegregation as a problem belonging only to the South. Remember that fifty years ago 90 percent of all American Negroes lived in the states of the old Confederacy. One measure of the swiftness of the change in the Negro's status is the fact that half our Negro population now live in the cities of the North and West. New York City is 14 percent Negro; Chicago is 24 percent; Philadelphia, 26 percent; Detroit, 29 percent; and Newark 35 percent Negro. The tremendous migrations northward have created problems at both ends of the line. Mississippi lost one-fourth of its total Negro population in the 1940's. While some Mississippians might laughingly claim that migration promises the ultimate solution of their problem at the North's expense, this is not so. It is the Negroes whom Mississippi can least afford to keep that stay at home. Those most likely to migrate are the young

people with better than average education. And every year these people are packing into already overcrowded Negro ghettoes in Northern cities, their residential segregation ensuring segregation in schools and other facilities.

In the long run, therefore, the problem of desegregation will hit the whole country. The South, at present, is particularly vulnerable to rapid change, for the Southern states depended for segregation on laws that have been declared unconstitutional. The North does not yet feel the same pressures, because its segregation is accomplished informally through residential patterns and is harder to strike at through the courts. But, again, race relations is not just a Southern problem; it is what Gunnar Myrdal called it—an American dilemma.

The upheaval of desegregation imposes strains on our social system far beyond the immediate results of human inertia and resistance to change. Within the span of a generation, we have projected into urban life the majority of one-tenth of our population, many of whom were brought up to live in feudal serfdom. While enormous strides are being made in education and other endeavors, an enormous price is also being paid for the suddenness of the change. As Philip M. Hauser points out, "Tossing an empty bottle on an asphalt pavement in the city has quite different consequences from tossing it into a cotton field. Using physical force, including a knife or gun, in the resolution of personal conflict receives much more attention and has a much greater impact on the community in the city than it has in the rural South. The patterns of family and sexual behavior that the Negro inherited as a product of his history and his share in the American way of life have created . . . many complications . . . in the urban setting." [19]

Other immigrant groups have reacted to urbanization with personal and social disorganization. But it is a foolish disservice to the minority and to the society to state that, or act as if, no special problem exists. There *is* a Negro problem. But it is a problem born of rapid social change, not of biology. And at the very moment when responsible Negro and white Americans are trying valiantly to cope with it, there is pressure for more and more rapid change.

Inequalities remain, and while they remain there will be continuing agitation for change. When the NORC asked a national sample of Americans, "Do you think most Negroes in the United States are being treated fairly or unfairly?" one-third of the whites and two-thirds of the Negroes answered "Unfairly." Together, these people constitute a sizable group of dissatisfied citizens.

They are dissatisfied because equality of opportunity is basic to the American ethic of self-realization and achievement, and the American Negro is denied equality of opportunity. Negro Americans learn the rules of the American way of life from the same textbooks as white Americans, but they find that many of the economic trails are blocked for them. Negro youths learn from books and movies and television that an American should work to get a better job and improve himself by study, but they are excluded from apprentice training by many craft unions.

19 · Philip M. Hauser, *Population Perspectives* (New Brunswick, N.J.: Rutgers University Press, 1960).

Negro median family income remains less than 60 percent that of whites. The mass media urge all America to get out and vote, but in 100 counties in eight Southern states, the United States Civil Rights Commission found that Negroes were prevented from voting by threats of physical harm or economic reprisal or by outright denial of the right to register.

American children are told that the Supreme Court is the law of the land, but it is over ten years since the Court ruled that separate facilities were inherently unequal, and there are seven states in which fewer than one percent of the Negroes share in white classrooms.

The South has no monopoly on racial discrimination. Americans are taught to work and earn recognition and the social rewards of success, but United Nations Under-Secretary Ralph Bunche has seen his son denied membership in a tennis club. Judge James C. Flanigan of Denver was turned away from the local golf course. The citizens of Deerfield, Illinois, voted to increase their taxes, and purchase as a park the land on which a builder has begun to construct 51 houses to cost about $30,000, twelve of them earmarked for Negro families.

What does the Negro American want? To answer that question, one need only strike out the word "Negro." He wants what other Americans want: a home, a car, good clothes, economic security, a friendly community. Above all, as an American citizen, he wants a fair chance to compete for a share in the American way of life.

INTERPRETATIVE SUMMARY

A minority is a category of people who are discriminated against because they have physical features and/or behavioral patterns which differ from those of the dominant culture. Minorities enter a society through colonialism, in which case the minority may well be numerically superior; through voluntary or forced migration; or through annexation. Treatment of a minority may range from attempts to exterminate the group to extreme persecution to some form of accommodation. If the minority is distinguished by its behavior rather than by some physical characteristic, members of the group may become assimilated in the new culture. Such assimilation will be accomplished more quickly if the dominant culture is willing to help and if the minority shows willingness to break away from its old ways and learn new. Of course, minorities whose old and new cultures are similar will generally have the easiest time in becoming assimilated.

Racial minorities find assimilation particularly difficult, since people identify them by physical characteristics. Though there is no pure race and no correlation between any physical trait and any innate ability, majorities continue to discriminate against individuals having imagined racial characteristics. Indeed, a majority may even place members of a minority in positions where they have no choice but to develop the imagined behavior patterns; the majority then considers its original opinion confirmed, and the minority is kept from assimilation indefinitely. Such a situation exists between Negro and white in our own society.

Though the Negroes in our society have historically been treated as a virtual caste, recently their position has changed rapidly. The Supreme Court, Congress, and Presidential committees have acted on the national level to integrate schools, transportation and recreational facilities, jobs, and elections. Studies show that attitudes of whites toward Negroes are changing, especially among young and educated whites from the South as well as the North; these attitudes will undoubtedly facilitate further changes.

REVIEW AND SUGGESTED READINGS

A • VOCABULARY

Assimilation	Identifiability	Race—biological, social
Caucasoid race	Minority	Visibility—social
Colonialism	Mongoloid race	
Ethnic group	Negroid race	

B • QUESTIONS AND TOPICS FOR REVIEW

1. Consider colonialism as it exists today in specific countries. Discuss the type of accommodation, stability of the accommodation, and comparative number of majority and minority.
2. How is the definition of *social category* that you were given in an earlier chapter broadened in this chapter?
3. What are some of the highest positions held by Negroes in the United States today? What factors were responsible for the achievement in each case?
4. How do you account for the difference between the I.Q. scores made by Negroes in the three highest-scoring states and whites in the lowest-scoring states? Why is the difference not greater?

5. What factors should be considered by an individual who is thinking of changing his name so that he will not be so easily identified as a member of a minority?

6. Are all out-groups minorities? Are minorities always out-groups?

7. Consider the five universal social functions discussed in Chapter 7. Under
which of these would you analyze the civil rights protest movement?

C · SUGGESTIONS FOR FURTHER READING

Milton L. Barron, ed. *American Minorities*. New York: Alfred A. Knopf, Inc.,
1957.

A book of readings that provides a wide coverage of the topics usually treated in
texts in race relations.

William Brink and Louis Harris. *The Negro Revolution in America*. New York:
Simon and Schuster, 1964.

A nationwide sampling of American Negroes as to what they want and how they
intend to get it. Also contains data gathered from 100 Negro leaders, and a section
on what whites think of Negroes.

John Burma. *Spanish-Speaking Groups in the United States*. Durham, North Car-
lina: Duke University Press, 1954.

An account of the adjustments of Spanish-speaking peoples to the dominant culture in this country.

E. Franklin Frazier. *The Negro in the United States*, rev. ed. New York: The
Macmillan Company, 1957.

The most complete analysis available of the historical backgrounds of the Negro
minority, racial conflict and its accommodation in the United States, and the institutional structure of the Negro community.

Everett C. Hughes and Helen M. Hughes. *Where Peoples Meet: Racial and Ethnic Frontiers*. Glencoe, Ill.: The Free Press, 1952.

Essays on ethnic subcultures and the assimilation process.

Raymond W. Mack, ed. *Race, Class, and Power*. New York: American Book
Company, 1963.

A collection of readings interpreting minority status within a stratification
framework.

Charles F. Marden and Gladys Meyer. *Minorities in American Society*, 2nd ed.
New York: American Book Company, 1962.

A good textbook on racial and ethnic relations in the United States.

George Eaton Simpson and J. Milton Yinger. *Racial and Cultural Minorities*, rev.
ed. New York: Harper & Brothers, 1958.

A complete treatment of both the sociology and social psychology of dominant-
minority relations.

Sister Frances Jerome Woods. *Cultural Values of American Ethnic Groups*. New
York: Harper & Brothers, 1956.

An original treatment of minority roles in the various social institutions.

CHAPTER 14

Population Pressures

Demography is the technical term for the study of population. This word comes from two Greek roots: _demos,_ meaning people, and _graphein,_ meaning to write. Thus, demography is a writing about people. More accurately, demography is the science of population. It consists chiefly of statistical analyses of such topics as birth and death rates, migration, marriage, health conditions, and the relationship of population to the social structure.

Certainly, for sociologists to understand the structure of any society, they must know about the number of people filling positions in that social structure, as well as facts about the social and cultural characteristics of those people.[1]

Among other topics, we are concerned with the actual and potential pressures of population on such resources as food, water, timber, and minerals. We want to know about the relation of population size to industrial and military manpower. There are matters of the quality of the population and the

1 · Students sometimes wonder why up-to-date textbooks occasionally quote or cite population figures derived from sources one, two, or more decades old. There are two reasons. First, a number of years elapse before detailed analyses of a census can be made, since such studies are usually expensive and demand high-level knowledge and skill. Second, statistical studies are introduced in sociology textbooks mainly to bring out a point in systematic theory or to provide pertinent illustrations rather than the latest data.

optimum population for a country in the light of problems of resources, manpower needs, and the like. In the next chapter we shall examine how such matters as income, occupation, class status, education, and religious affiliation influence population growth, size, and distribution.

Population may be studied from at least three points of view. First, it may be treated as a body of facts. Demographic data show (1) numbers and growth trends; (2) birth and death rates; (3) distribution—spatial and cultural; (4) composition and characteristics, such as age, sex, marital status, race, religion, and occupation; (5) movement—that is, in- and out-migrations; and (6) quality—that is, the degree of physical and mental adequacy. In short, these data give us the _what,_ the _when,_ and the _where_ of population.

Second, the study of population has to do with a dynamic aspect of human behavior which requires both psychological and sociological analysis and interpretation. For example, how is the character of a population influenced by fertility, mortality, and migration? How does the culture of the time and place affect demographic trends? What about birth control and its influences? And what about the attitudes, values, and habits that are the behavioral foundations of the facts of population?

Third, the facts of population may

be viewed in relationship to a program of social action or reform. Malthus, as we shall see, thought that one basic cause of human misery was the fact that populations tend to increase so rapidly as to put greater and greater pressure on food resources. What about controlled breeding for better human stock? How are problems of displaced populations best handled? These are but a few examples of the kinds of problems that arise when matters of public policy or programs of social action are considered.

FOOD AND POPULATION RESOURCES

The culture patterns of a society are always influenced by the size, composition, and distribution of its population.

Rapid Growth in Population Growth of population depends on the excess of births over deaths. In the eighteenth century, after centuries of only slight increase, the world experienced an enormous expansion in numbers. In the nineteenth and twentieth centuries the increase has been even greater.

In 1650 the estimated population of the world was between 465 and 545 million. Within the next 100 years it had risen to about 720 million. By 1850 it had reached 1.1 billion. Estimates for 1963 put the global population at about 3.2 billion—almost triple that of a century ago. It is worth noting, moreover, that nearly two-thirds of this latter increase has taken place since 1900. As Figure 9 shows, by 1960 the world had added one and one-half billion people since the turn of the century. And of the growth between 1950 and 1960, nearly one-half a billion—56 per-

cent of the total growth—took place in Asia.

This growth has not occurred uniformly over the earth. It was the white race that first showed the most striking changes. The total white population for the year 1000 A.D.—about the time of the First Crusade—is estimated at 30 million. By 1800 this had risen to 210 million, and by 1915 the figure was 645 million. In other words, in 115 years the white race increased 2.5 times as much as it had in the previous 800 years. Between 1850 and 1950 the population of Europe more than doubled, while that of the American continents and Oceania quadrupled. At the time of its founding, the United States had just under 4 million inhabitants. In 1890 it had 63 million, a nearly 15-fold increase in a little more than a century. Seventy-five years later it had increased 3 times more.

Similar upsurges have taken place elsewhere in the world, although not at such a marked rate. In fact, as the population in many industrialized countries of the Euro-American culture tends to become more or less stationary, the growth in other regions and countries accelerates. For example, at the present rate, India, now with 400 million, will more than double her numbers by the turn of this century unless limitations are imposed. Accurate figures for China are hard to come by, but a census taken in June, 1953, showed a total population of 602 million. It is quite likely that her numbers also may double by the year 2000. In 1954 Japan had a population of over 88 million, while in 1900 she had had considerably fewer than half this number. For a long time during the first half of this century, she had been adding more than a million people a year to her total. The Soviet

FIGURE 9 · The World's Population: Now and in the Future *

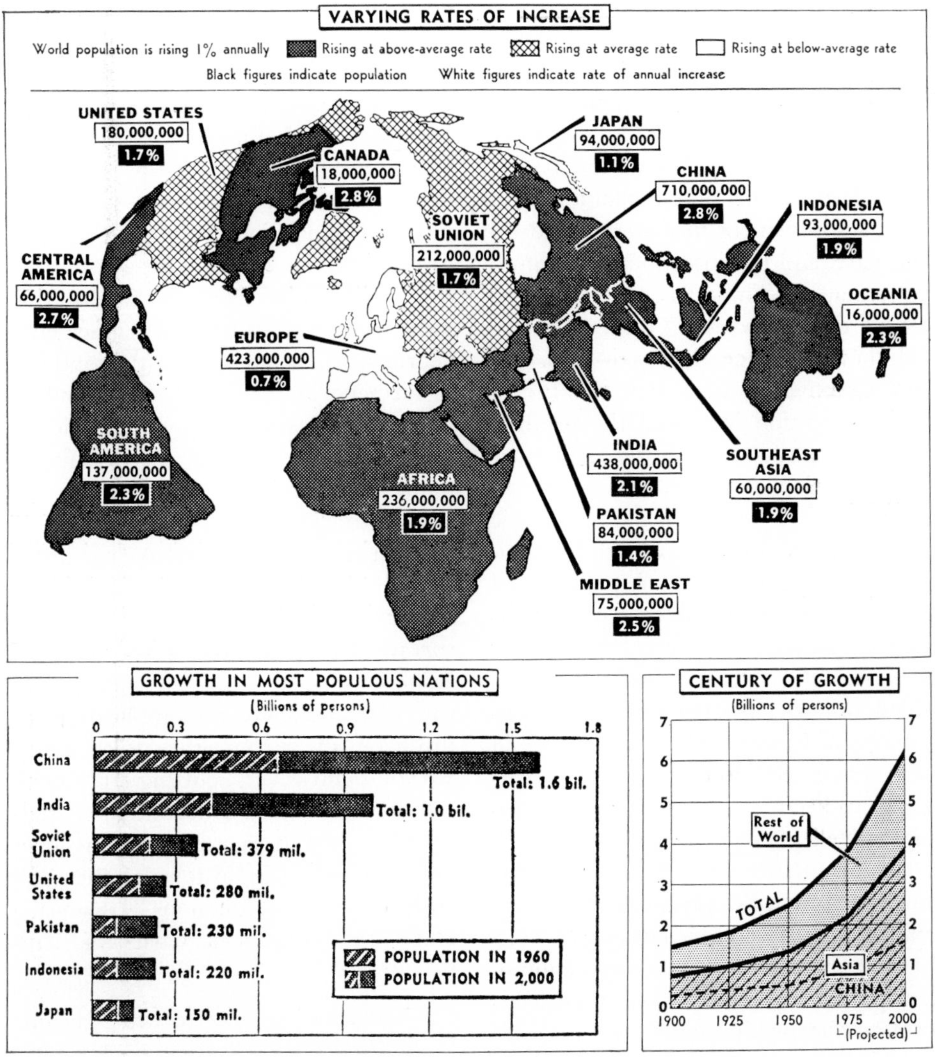

VARYING RATES OF INCREASE

World population is rising 1% annually ▓ Rising at above-average rate ▨ Rising at average rate ☐ Rising at below-average rate

Black figures indicate population   White figures indicate rate of annual increase

UNITED STATES 180,000,000 1.7%
CANADA 18,000,000 2.8%
JAPAN 94,000,000 1.1%
CHINA 710,000,000 2.8%
INDONESIA 93,000,000 1.9%
SOVIET UNION 212,000,000 1.7%
CENTRAL AMERICA 66,000,000 2.7%
OCEANIA 16,000,000 2.3%
EUROPE 423,000,000 0.7%
SOUTH AMERICA 137,000,000 2.3%
AFRICA 236,000,000 1.9%
INDIA 438,000,000 2.1%
SOUTHEAST ASIA 60,000,000 1.9%
PAKISTAN 84,000,000 1.4%
MIDDLE EAST 75,000,000 2.5%

GROWTH IN MOST POPULOUS NATIONS
(Billions of persons)

China	Total: 1.6 bil.
India	Total: 1.0 bil.
Soviet Union	Total: 379 mil.
United States	Total: 280 mil.
Pakistan	Total: 230 mil.
Indonesia	Total: 220 mil.
Japan	Total: 150 mil.

POPULATION IN 1960
POPULATION IN 2,000

CENTURY OF GROWTH
(Billions of persons)

Rest of World
TOTAL
Asia
CHINA
1900 1925 1950 1975 2000
(Projected)

* The *New York Times*, April 2, 1961, E7.

Union already has a population of 212,000,000. If the present trend continues, by 1970 the U.S.S.R. will have more people than all the rest of Europe combined.

For the world as a whole, not only have the total numbers increased, but the annual rates of increase have risen steadily. For 1750 it is estimated that the rate of growth was 0.29 percent per year. A century later that rate had nearly doubled, to 0.51 percent annually. In 1960 it was estimated at between 1.3 and 1.7 percent per year.[2]

Reasons for Population Growth Almost all this tremendous increase in the

2 · See Philip M. Hauser, *Resurgent National Population Growth: Challenge and Opportunity* (New York: Cyrus J. Lawrence & Sons, April, 1959), pp. 8–9. (A brochure.)

world's peoples is the result of <u>*a reduction in the death rate, not a rise in the birth rate.*</u> This cutting down of the death rate derives from numerous causes, among the most important of which are the following: (1) Advances in modern medicine led to the reduction of infectious and contagious diseases, improvement in maternal and infant care, and the introduction of public sanitation. These advances all acted to cut the death rate. Only indirectly did they influence the birth rate. (2) The Commercial and then the Industrial Revolution increased the production of manufactured goods and their transportation and distribution. Moreover, these changes in the economic patterns of culture provided jobs for an increasing number of people. All this, in turn, made for a higher standard of living. (3) New lands in the Americas and elsewhere not only provided an outlet for the expanding populations of Europe and Asia but also, in time, furnished foodstuffs and raw materials to keep the industrial system going as well as to provide a market for goods manufactured in Europe. (4) Because of scientific advances, plant and animal stocks have been greatly improved, while commercial fertilizers and power machinery have greatly increased the production of the world's foodstuffs and commodities useful in providing clothing and shelter, such as fibers and lumber.

Reasons for Variations in Population Increases If we examine the rates of increase by countries and world regions, we discover considerable variation. The most notable differences are those between highly industrialized regions and those that have not experienced an industrial revolution, the "un-derdeveloped" regions. Most of the countries of northwestern Europe seem to be approaching a relatively stable population. In these countries <u>the decline in rates of population growth was associated with rapid industrialization, which began about 1760. It is the underdeveloped areas that have shown the most striking increases in rates of growth.</u> Let us examine the reasons.

Unlike the historical situation in northwestern Europe in the nineteenth century, when industrialization and improvement in medicine went hand in hand, many present-day underdeveloped areas have reaped the benefits of modern medical care without, at the same time, going through industrialization. In other words, we have the diffusion of one set of cultural patterns—scientific medical care—without the spread of a second set of patterns that historically had been associated with the first. In fact, the application of medicine in cutting the death rate—without, however, cutting the birth rate—has produced a decline in mortality rates "much sharper than any ever experienced in the history of the presently industrialized nations."[3] Kingsley Davis thus describes what has happened:

The amazingly accelerated reduction of mortality has . . . been accomplished by international disease control, not by economic development in these areas themselves. It required no essential change in the customs and institutions of the people, no advance in general education, nor growth in per capital income. . . .

Since disease control has not involved basic changes in social institutions, education, and real income, fertility has re-

3 · Kingsley Davis, "The Unpredicted Pattern of Population Change," *Annals of the American Academy of Political and Social Science,* 1956, 305:53–59. Quotation p. 55. All quotations by permission.

mained high in nonindustrial regions. . . . The industrial countries began lowering their birth rates *before* their sharpest declines in mortality, but the backward areas will do so long *after* their mortality has reached a low modern level. As a result the densely settled and impoverished countries of the world are experiencing an unprecedented population growth which does not reflect economic development but in fact creates strong impediments to it.[4]

Davis doubts that "social modernization," as he calls it, can really "match the three percent population growth per year found in these areas, much less exceed it."[5] Yet there has grown up an ever-widening demand for an improved standard of living—a "world-wide 'revolution of expectations,'" as it has been called.[6]

Returning to the overall picture of world population growth, one may well ask: Can such rapid multiplication of numbers go on indefinitely until, in the words of E. A. Ross, who paraphrased Darwin, there is "standing room only"?[7] Are there no limits to the number of people the world can support? Let us examine the question more closely, first by reviewing how various social thinkers regarded the matter in the early days of the Industrial Revolution.

Theories of Population and Food Supply
Changes in commercial and eco-

nomic life and the spread of political democracy in the eighteenth century sounded a note of optimism in Europe and America that found ready expression in the doctrine of inevitable social progress. This optimism found even more vehement expression in the nineteenth century. As J. J. Spengler describes it,

. . . The common man, once looked upon as a creature of little dignity placed in the world for the service of the master classes, was coming into his own. A beneficiary, primary and secondary, of the redistribution of economic and political power under way, he was held in greater esteem than formerly; his wants, rights, and potentialities were receiving more attention than ever, and they would receive even greater attention as the democratic movement, and the values it stood for, gained in scope.[8]

Such men as the idealistic Marquis de Condorcet in France and William Godwin in England expressed the growing faith of the period in the steady march of mankind toward perfection. Once poverty, misery, vice, crime, and war were removed by proper social reforms, all would be well. Godwin went so far as to say, "Make men wise, and by that very operation you make them free . . . There will be no war, no crime, no administration of justice as it is called, and no government. Besides this, there will be neither disease, anguish, melancholy, nor resentment. Every man will seek with effable ardor the good of all."[9]

Others, seeing poverty and the sor-

4 · *Ibid.*, p. 57.
5 · *Ibid.*, p. 59.
6 · "Population: the Numbers Game," *Time*, January 11, 1960, 75:19–22.
7 · See E. A. Ross, *Standing Room Only?* (New York: Appleton-Century-Crofts, Inc., 1927) for an early but incisive recognition of the problem. Ross evidently took the title of his work from Darwin's remark, "Even slow-breeding man has doubled in twenty-five years, and at this rate, in a few thousand years, there would literally not be standing room for his progeny." See *Origin of Species*, 1859 (London: Humphrey Milford, 1902), p. 59.

8 · J. J. Spengler, "Malthus's Total Population Theory: a Restatement and Reappraisal," *Canadian Journal of Economics and Political Science*, 1945, 11:245. All quotations by permission. This entire article is a most thoughtful discussion of Malthus and his period.
9 · Quoted by J. O. Hertzler, *Social Progress* (New York: Appleton-Century-Crofts, Inc., 1928), pp. 46–47.

did conditions of the peasants and city masses, were not so optimistic about man's perfectibility. They realized "that man does not live in a boundless physical, social, and psychological universe; that limitations are imposed upon his behavior, and upon the outcome of this behavior, by this circumscribed physical milieu, by his restricted physiological and psychological make-up, and by the social and institutional controls which issue out of these physical and personal conditions." [10] In fact, there arose two divergent schools of thought about the whole problem, one of optimism, one of pessimism.

With reference to population, the controversy broke out with the publication of an answer to Godwin by an English clergyman, Thomas R. Malthus, entitled *An Essay on the Principle of Population as It Affects the Future Improvement of Society* (1st ed., 1798).[11] Malthus contended that Godwin was wrong in blaming circumstances for our social ills. It was man's original nature that was at fault. The sexual urges leading to reproduction tended to people the world more rapidly than man could increase his sustenance.

In a time when romantic reformers were preaching doctrines of unlimited human progress, Malthus had gone to work making calculations concerning the relation of food supply to population increase. He argued that there is a "constant tendency in all animated life

to increase beyond the nourishment prepared for it"—that is, animal life is endowed with the capacity for rapid reproduction, but the food supply has definite limits.

Applying this principle to human beings, Malthus worked out the following formula: "Population, when unchecked, goes on doubling itself every twenty-five years, or increases in geometric ratio." Food supply, which he calls "means of subsistence," under circumstances the most favorable to human industry, could not possibly be made to increase faster than in arithmetical ratio.[12] In other words, a population would increase every twenty-five years in the ratio of 1, 2, 4, 8, 16, 32, 64, 128, 256, and so on, while the food supply would increase, at best, in the ratio of 1, 2, 3, 4, 5, 6, 7, 8, 9, etc. According to this computation, unless checked, in two hundred years—assuming about 22 years to a generation—a population would stand, with reference to food, in the proportion of 256 to 9.

With this thesis before him, based as it was not on mere fantasy but on statistics of population and food production of his time, Malthus inquired as to the checks on population growth. These he saw as of two sorts: positive and preventive. The *positive* checks arise from want of adequate subsistence and its effects of poverty, misery, disease, and deterioration of morality. The *preventive* checks of Malthus's time were celibacy, deferment of marriage,

10 · Spengler, p. 245.
11 · The second edition, 1803, was called *An Essay on the Principle of Population, or a View of Its Past and Present Effects on Human Happiness with an Inquiry into Our Prospects Respecting the Future Removal or Mitigation of the Evils Which It Occasions.* There is an edition of Malthus available in Everyman's Library (New York: E. P. Dutton & Co., Inc.).

12 · Spengler, p. 245. Malthus confuses the reader by identifying food supply with subsistence. At times he discusses what we today call "level of living," which includes more than food. Elsewhere he uses "means of subsistence" to mean only food. For a most incisive discussion of the relation of population to food supply, see Edward S. Deevey, Jr., "The Human Population," *Scientific American*, 1960, 203:195–198, 200, 202–204.

and moral (that is, sexual) restraint, leading to reduction in the number of births.

Malthus argued that no devices of political or economic organization or of emigration would stop the positive checks from operating, but only moral restraint of the biological passions. This did not imply, so rationalized the pious Malthus, that God has not our welfare at heart, but rather that "natural and moral evil seems to be the instrument employed by the Deity in admonishing us to avoid any mode of conduct which is not suited to our being and will consequently injure our happiness." [13]

Above all else, the writings of Malthus were timely. His work gave a needed dash of cold facts to the glowing enthusiasm of the utopian dreamers of the period who seemed to ignore completely the natural and biological foundations of all human societies.

Although the doctrine of progress and man's perfectibility might be easy to scotch, it was hard to kill. Nineteenth-century enthusiasts arose on every hand to denounce Malthus. Significant expressions of optimism were found in the work of Karl Marx, who denied that population necessarily outruns the food supply. He held that the problem of feeding the population results from the exploitation of the masses by the capitalist class. Once the injustices of faulty distribution of wealth were remedied, there would be food enough for all. Henry George, best known for his theory of the single tax on land values, argued that "nowhere can want be properly attributed to the pressure of population against the power to procure subsistence in the then existing degree of human knowledge; that everywhere the vice and misery attributed to overpopulation can be traced to warfare, tyranny, and oppression, which prevent knowledge from being utilized and deny the security essential to production." He thought it was only a faulty economic and political order that "in the midst of wealth condemns men to want." [14]

Throughout the nineteenth century, while the theorists argued, population continued to increase at a rapid rate. And in spite of free land and increased industrial production, poverty, misery, crime, and vice persisted. With a view to improving the condition of the masses, there arose in England about 1880 a movement known as Neo-Malthusianism. It aimed to educate the masses consciously to cut down the number of births. The leaders, Annie Besant and Charles Bradlaugh, argued that the spread of contraceptive practices in order to reduce the birth rate would lead to an improvement in health, in family life, in the standards of living, and in morality.

But the critics of birth control were not far behind. As birth rates did decline, especially in the Western world, the cry of "race suicide" was heard. One of the most vocal exponents of large families and rapid increase of population was Theodore Roosevelt, who expressed the beliefs and attitudes of millions who saw in the declining birth rate a threat to man's very existence. Then too, they feared that the price of a Neo-Malthusian program might be loss of the white man's supremacy in the world.

The debate still goes on. In recent decades, the world has heard such dic-

13 · These quotations are from the 9th edition of Malthus's *Essay*.

14 · Quoted by E. A. Ross, *Tests and Challenges in Sociology* (New York: Appleton-Century-Crofts, Inc., 1931), p. 8.

220 · Sociology and Social Life

tators as Hitler and Mussolini in Europe and the militarists of Japan crying out for larger populations in their countries. Since their downfall and in the face of postwar problems, many serious students of the issue have stressed the dangerous implications of the continuing growth of population as it relates to food and other resources and to standard of living. In the face of some divergences of interpretation about the seriousness of the present-day population problem, and especially in view of some of the sharp differences in rates of growth in various areas of the world, let us examine some of the facts about the relation of population to resources.[15]

Food Supply and Population   Without doubt, population and food supply are related. But these are not the only factors to be taken into consideration in discussing the increase in world population. The densely crowded countries of northwestern Europe could not possibly have supported themselves on the food raised on their own land; they furnished goods and services to other regions which, in turn, provided them with foodstuffs and raw materials. Technological advances provided work for millions in the production, manufacture, and distribution of goods and services. So long as commerce between nations of the world went on freely, large massing of population in industrial centers was not serious.

Yet in spite of the tremendous improvement in agricultural production (most of which has come from mechanical devices and not from im-

15 · See Kingsley Davis, "The Theory of Change and Response in Modern Demographic History," *Population Index*, 1963, 29:345–366.

provement in natural fertility of land), in spite of the rising consciousness of the need to conserve water and forest and mineral resources, in spite of the possibility of synthetic foods produced by applied chemistry, and in spite of increased industrialization, the population in many parts of the world is still pressing on the means of subsistence: foods, timber, coal, iron, and oil. Clearly, land and climate distinctly limit the range of man's habitation. Of the total land surface of the earth, little more than one-third is available for raising food and other necessary articles of consumption. Yet the number of people that the world will support is, of course, definitely related to the standard of living. The earth would support at a bare subsistence level a great many more people than there are now.

There are two compatible possible courses. One involves improved use of present arable lands and their extension, for example, by the use of rich tropical lands in South America and of the semi-arid regions of Asia. The second course is to extend the belief in and practice of birth control. Those supporting the latter measure are up against great cultural inertia and face formidable opposition. The Roman Catholic prohibition of birth control has doubtless influenced attitudes and practices not only in western Europe and the United States, but in Latin America, the Philippines, Indonesia, Ceylon, and parts of Africa. In addition, in Moslem countries, where children are regarded as "a gift of Allah," there is strong resistance to the introduction of such a program. It is interesting to note that after a few years of propagandizing for birth control, the Communist masters of Red China have quietly dropped the campaign and returned to the Marxian view that if the means of production were justly distributed there would be no population problem.[16]

Culture and Cycles of Population Growth Will the growth in eastern Europe, the Orient, Africa, and South America be continued within reasonable limits? If the growth in the latter areas goes on at the present potentially explosive rate, the entire world will probably be forced in the direction of a lowered standard of living.

Students of population have shown that, so far as the Western world goes, there has been a cycle of rapid growth, followed by stabilization and, finally, by a trend toward decline in numbers. Will the rest of the world follow suit? In short, is there a generalization or "law" of human population in relation to resources and culture?

In considering this question, a number of factors must be taken into account. First of all, as noted above, there has been a rapid increase in population in a number of countries that as yet have not become industrialized. This is the result of the diffusion of modern medical care independently of any basic change in the economy and education of these areas. Moreover, conditions in these regions are not precisely like those that existed in the nineteenth century when the cycle began in western Europe and the United States. While far more efficient technologies for rapid industrialization are available today than in 1800, there is a dearth of resources and no new land for expanding agriculture.

16 · For accounts of resistance to the use of contraceptive devices, see Carl E. Taylor, John B. Wyon, and John E. Gordon, "Ecological Determinants of Population Growth," *Milbank Memorial Fund Quarterly*, 1958, 36:107–125.

As to voluntary restriction of births, the whole force of culture in those regions is contrary to such practices. It is doubtful that measures of birth control will be adopted before the industrialized culture patterns and demands for higher standards of life have become widespread in all classes and ancient and sacred folkways have largely disappeared.

DIFFERENTIAL RATES OF GROWTH

Let us examine the variations in absolute numbers of people and in the rates of increase.

Density of Population Population is by no means spread uniformly over the earth. Nor are all areas blessed with good climate, soils, and other resources that make them equally acceptable as places to live. For example, the wide steppes, the deserts, and the extensive mountainous sections of Asia make up at least half of its land mass. These regions support very few people. In contrast, the rich valleys of India and China support millions. In other regions—the United States, Canada, and the Soviet Union in Europe—there are ample soil and other resources but relatively few people.

A measure frequently used in studies of population is density of persons per square mile mass. (Table 20 lists some countries of low and high density.) Yet the figures for density do not tell the whole story. They must be interpreted in relation to the degree of industrialization, extent and kind of soil resources, and rates of growth. For example, Java and India are chiefly agricultural, and yet the pressure of numbers on the food supply is mounting

TABLE 20 · High and Low Population Density for Selected Countries *

Countries of High Density	Persons per Square Mile	Countries of Low Density	Persons per Square Mile
Java	1080	Australia	4
Belgium	769	Canada	5
Japan	644	Argentina	19
United Kingdom	548	Soviet Russia	26
Italy	418	Finland	34
India	324	United States	50

* Computed from census data in *The World Almanac, 1960* (New York: New York World-Telegram and Sun, 1960).

year by year. Not only is the pressure on the arable lands increasing, but cultural inertia evidently prevents some rational attempts at improvement. Sumatra, an island neighbor of Java, has rich untapped soil resources, but the Javanese for the most part do not look with favor on migration to Sumatra. So too, there are some excellent unused areas in parts of southern India, but the millions in the congested sections of the country are not interested in moving to these distant areas. Australia, long a target of expanding Oriental populations, has recently been stimulating immigration from Great Britain, but so far is unwilling to open her doors to her Far Eastern neighbors.

In contrast, highly industrialized countries, such as Britain and Belgium, are able to support very high concentrations of population per square mile because their economy rests on industry, not on agriculture. Both countries raise only a part of their own food, and export manufactured goods in exchange for a heavy amount of foods and raw materials. If they had to depend on their own farming, both these countries would soon feel the pinch of famine. For example, the density per square mile of arable land in Britain is about 2,500 persons, in Belgium about 2,200. A similar situation exists in Japan, whose growth in numbers has been possible only because she has been the only first-class industrial nation of the Far East. Her attempt to get more and more of the trade of that region was one reason for her entry into World War II. With a density of about 3,200 persons per square mile of arable land, she certainly could not provide her own food.

Thus, it is clear that the whole matter of density can be understood only in relation to the amount and nature of basic resources—agricultural and otherwise—and the extent of industrialization as these, in turn, are related to absolute numbers of people and rates of growth. Yet the future of many industrialized nations, especially in Europe, is not altogether certain, despite their relatively stable populations. Without external markets they may face a lowering of standards of living as soon as other nations become industrialized and no longer need their manufactured goods. England, in particular, faces this unpleasant prospect.

Birth Rates In discussing rates of growth, it is necessary to distinguish between fecundity and fertility. *Fecundity* is the full potential powers of reproduction in a population—the birth rate if every woman of childbearing age bore all the children she possibly could.

Fertility is the actual rate of reproduction. It is measured by the birth rate, but we must distinguish between the crude birth rate and the refined, or specific, birth rate. The *crude birth rate* is simply the number of births per 1,000 people at a given period. The *refined*, or *specific birth rate* is the births per 1,000 women of childbearing age, usually considered to be from 15 to 44 years. The crude birth rate gives an estimate of the fertility of any population, but it leaves out of account the age and sex distribution of the population.

For long-range comparisons of population growth or decline, the *net reproduction rate* is a better index than either crude or refined birth rates. Such a rate is based on the average number of daughters that will be born per 100 females starting life together if birth and death rates at different age levels remain constant. Thus a net reproduction rate of 1.00 means that, on the average, the survivors of a group of 100 females of the same age will give birth to 100 daughters. An index of 1.00 means that a given population is just replacing itself; anything less means that it is not.

As noted earlier, until the fourth decade of this century, there was a steady decline in the birth rate in countries of western Europe, in the British Dominions, and in the United States. In fact, in some countries the net reproduction rate fell to less than 1.00. But during World War II and subsequently, both the marriage rate and the birth rate have increased. As a result, the net reproduction rate in most countries of the same world areas has gone up. Unfortunately, data from Soviet Russia and her satellites is not easy to secure, but there are many indications that birth rates in these countries also rose after World War II.

Specific birth rates in any country are influenced by such factors as age, race, nativity, marital status, occupation, social class, religious affiliation, and type of community. Some of these specific factors will be examined in the next chapter.

Death Rates Mortality may be measured by the *crude death rate*, which is the ratio between the number of individuals who die in a given time and the median number of individuals alive during that interval, usually stated in thousands. Thus a death rate of 12 means 12 deaths per 1,000 of the population. Specific death rates may be computed for age, sex, and other factors.

Throughout history the births in many societies have just about balanced the deaths, so that the population remained practically stationary for generations. This was true for long periods in the Orient and, until three centuries ago, in Europe. In fact, until recently, in all countries outside western Europe, the United States, Canada, New Zealand, Australia, and the scattered European colonies, high death rates have accompanied high birth rates. Among nonliterate peoples the birth rates and the mortality rates are both unusually high by our standards.

Recent decades have witnessed a rapid decline in the death rate. This trend has been going on in Europe for well over a century. There has been a similar decline in the death rate in the United States, where the annual average in 1906–1910 was 15 per 1,000. The death rate has fallen off considerably since then, except in 1918, when it was

18 because of an influenza epidemic. By 1920 it had dropped to 13; by 1962, it was 9.5.

While the principal decline in the death rate has occurred among Western nations, the phenomenon is worldwide. Although birth rates are also falling, mortality rates in many regions are falling somewhat faster.

Medical science has most significantly influenced the death rate for the early years of life. A noteworthy decline in infant and child mortality is evident in every civilized country. Table 21 gives a few samples. In particular, note the high rates shown in the three right-hand columns.

The decrease in child mortality is usually attributed to the following causes: (1) improvement in child care at home, especially in feeding and sanitation; (2) decrease in the number of children born to the average mother, permitting more adequate care of those who are born; (3) improvement in economic status of large sections of the population; and (4) control of diseases of childhood and early adult life. Additional progress in the conquest of disease the world over makes for the reduction of death in all age groups.

With regard to the second factor, various studies in France, England, and the United States bear out the fact that infant mortality is much lower in small families than in large families. Since small families have higher economic standards, it is evident that mortality is closely related to social-economic status.

The reduction in infant and child deaths has increased the expectation of life, particularly at birth. For example, in 1900 for the United States the life expectancy at birth was 48 years for males and 51 years for females. In 1960 the corresponding ages were 67 and 74. Various studies have shown that the chief gains in life expectancy come from lowering the death rates of those under 10 years of age. Table 22 gives some comparative figures at various age levels for selected countries. It is clear that the sharpest differentials are in the younger age levels. Also noteworthy are the clear sex differences. Females everywhere have a greater life expectancy than males and, while the gap is narrowed as the groups move to higher age levels, the differentials are still clear at 60 years and over.

To repeat, the reduction of death

TABLE 21 · Infant Mortality in Selected Countries. Deaths Under One Year per 1,000 Live Births *

COUNTRIES	RATES FOR		AVERAGE RATES FOR APPROXIMATE PERIODS		
	1957–1959	1947	1936–1940	1921–1925	1885–1895
Chile	117	161	234	265	——
France	24	66	71	95	168
England and Wales	22	41	56	76	148
United States	26	32	52	74	——
Sweden	16	25	42	60	108

* Data for 1885–1895 from W. S. Thompson, *Population Problems*, 1st ed. (New York: McGraw-Hill Book Co., 1930), p. 140; for 1921–1925 from *Population Index*, 1938, 4:197–198. Computations are made on the basis of varying periods, so that in some instances only approximate periods are covered. The sources give the precise dates. Data for the United States before 1922 are not complete. Data for 1936–1940 and 1947 from *Population Index*, 1948, 14:275–276. For 1957, 1958, 1959, *Population Index*, 1960, 26:291–293. The rate for the United States for 1936–1940 is for both whites and nonwhites.

TABLE 22 · Expectation of Life at Various Ages in Selected Countries *

COUNTRY	YEARS	SEX	AGES			
			At birth	10	20	60
India	1941–50	M	32.4	39.0	33.0	10.1
		F	31.7	39.5	32.9	11.3
Mexico	1950	M	46.7	51.1	42.7	15.3
		F	49.8	54.4	45.8	16.0
Chile	1952	M	49.8	51.4	42.7	14.0
		F	53.9	55.7	47.1	16.4
France	1958	M	67.0	59.6	50.0	15.9
		F	73.4	65.7	56.0	19.5
England and Wales	1958	M	68.0	60.1	50.4	15.1
		F	73.7	65.5	55.7	19.0
Japan	1958	M	65.0	58.7	49.2	15.3
		F	67.6	63.0	53.5	18.4
United States	1958	M	67.2	59.5	50.0	15.7
Whites only		F	73.7	65.6	55.9	19.2

* Data from *Population Index*, 1960, 26: 383–387.

rates in some countries with no corresponding decline in the birth rates leads to intensive population pressure, and may be an important factor in encouraging nationalist expansion and ambition. The international aspects of population problems warrant our next consideration.

INTERNATIONAL RELATIONS AND POPULATION PROBLEMS

The survival of mankind has always rested on a somewhat precarious balance between numbers and subsistence. This balance is maintained largely by fluctuations in the death rate, as Malthus pointed out.

It is quite clear that at least half of the world's population is living at a mere subsistence level, if not below it. This is particularly true of the underdeveloped areas. Students of world affairs are increasingly aware that the future peace and welfare of the world are closely bound up with differences in rates of growth as they are related to food and other resources, health, and extent of industrialization.

Income, Food, and Death Rates While it is difficult to secure completely accurate information on the relation of death rates to standards of food consumption and income, careful estimates have been made. These give a rather grim picture.

The countries of high mortality are also those of low income and inadequate diet. The correlation of infant mortality rates, per capita income, and daily per capita calorie consumption is shown in Table 23.

The world is really separated into two great population pools: one is relatively contracting; the other is extending itself rapidly. In the one, the ratio of population to resources has been brought under control. In the other, the Malthusian factors continue to operate. The problem is how to reconcile this disparity. To meet the present difficulty, a number of changes would have to be made.

TABLE 23 · Correlation of Food, Income, and Infant Mortality Rates
in Selected Countries *

COUNTRY	INCOME †	INFANT MORTALITY RATE (Deaths Under One Year per 1,000 Live Births)	PER CAPITA CALORIES PER DAY
United States	1453	26.4	3100
New Zealand	856	23.4	3370
Sweden	780	15.8	2910
United Kingdom	773	22.5	3300
Denmark	689	23.4	3420
Australia	679	20.5	3200
Belgium	582	30.2	2920
Portugal	250	88.4	2430
Italy	235	44.9	2650
Mexico	121	80.8	2380
Honduras	83	67.4	2260
India	57	96.1	1890
Pakistan	51	100.9	2010
Philippines	44	109.2	1940

† Standardized to 1949 U.S. dollars.
* From computations of Edward G. Stockwell and Paul C. Glick, Bureau of the Census, 1960.

Increase in Food One crucial and immediate task is to increase the world production of foodstuffs to take care of the increasing and undernourished populations. Considerable advances have been made,[17] but in India, China, and Indonesia—to note three of the most needy regions—the race between people and production goes on apace. Cultural inertia, such as unwillingness to migrate, plays a part. India, for further example, with the highest per capita cattle population in the world, continues largely on a vegetarian diet because of the place of the sacred cow in religious ideology and practice.

It must be recalled that only 7 percent of the globe is under cultivation and that there are wide variations in the per capita density of land used for food production. In eastern and southern Asia there are, respectively, less than

17 · See, for example, Arthur Gaitskell, *Gesira: A Study of the Development in the Sudan* (London: Faber and Faber, 1959).

0.5 and 0.8 of an acre of cultivated land per person. Yet these are the very regions where the pressure of population on food resources is becoming most severe. By way of contrast, in North America there are nearly 4 acres of cultivated land per capita. Moreover, the yield in calories per acre is much higher. Thus the output of food per person is vastly greater in the advanced than in the poorer countries. Clearly, education and improved distribution are called for, though suggestions are easier to make than to implement.

Industrialization The development of industry is usually considered an important next step in relieving population pressures. The argument is that the vital revolution, or cycle of growth, which resulted in stabilization of population in the Western world, represents a pattern of change essential for the rest of the world. The Food and Agriculture Organization report states:

Depletion of resources: sheet erosion in a New Jersey spinach field.

The way out of this situation is to open up resources other than those of farming for the bulk of the population. . . .

This calls for rapid, large-scale development of industry and trade, and of educational and other services. For that purpose, large investments both of capital and of technical skill will be needed. The only alternative to this investment for the Western world is to restrict its own high production. The investment will be profitable because it will vastly increase the productivity and the purchasing power of millions of human beings. The improvement of agriculture in the less-developed countries will in itself result in large demand for tools, machinery, fertilizers, transportation equipment, processing equipment, and other material, as well as for consumer goods to meet the needs of more prosperous farm populations.[18]

18 · "World Food Appraisal, for 1946–1947," a report of the Food and Agriculture Organization of the United Nations (Washington, D.C., December 26, 1946).

A careful examination of the facts shows the limitations of such a program. Among other factors are inadequacy of resources for further industrialization and the constant need for new capital. Nor would the shift of large numbers of persons from peasant agriculture to skilled and semiskilled industrial occupations be easy. As has been demonstrated by the experience of Soviet Russia, it takes time to train the workers of a peasant economy to become factory hands. J. J. Spengler, studying the relations of economy to population and resources, has discussed this topic fully.

The evidence presented . . . lends no support to the easy optimism of those who see in industrialization a simple and ready solution for the overpopulation that already affects more than half the world. Countries marked by intense overpopula-

U.S. Department of Agriculture

Conservation of resources: strip cropping and contour plowing in Minnesota.

tion must virtually raise themselves by their own bootstraps. They lack land, capital, and the opportunity to make up this lack. They can get only limited relief through trade and capital imports.[19]

Migration of Excess Population One of the oldest proposals to alleviate, if not solve, the world's population difficulties is to get people to go somewhere else. Some contend that, instead of transferring capital goods and setting up new industries, excess peoples should emigrate to other, less crowded areas.

Almost all students of population today view with suspicion any scheme to stimulate the migration of large numbers of people from crowded to less crowded areas. It has been shown that, unless the country of origin is cutting its own birth and death rates at the time of out-migration, emigration will only temporarily relieve the pressure. The places of those who go somewhere else will be taken by the newborn of those who remain at home. As Notestein puts it, ". . . Emigration will not check growth in the most important areas of population pressure at the present stage of their demographic evolution. It would be unfortunate to waste the open spaces of the world in a fashion that could only intensify future problems of adjustment."[20]

This view is not, however, univer-

19 · J. J. Spengler, "Aspects of the Economics of Population Growth, Parts I and II," *Southern Economic Journal*, 1947, 14:123–147; and 1948, 14:233–265. Quotation from p. 265. By permission.

20 · Frank W. Notestein, "Problems of Policy in Relation to Areas of Heavy Population Pressure," in *Demographic Studies of Selected Areas of Rapid Growth* (New York: Milbank Memorial Fund, 1944), p. 150. By permission.

sally held. Radhakamal Mukerjee, a leading Hindu sociologist, believes that the contrasted areas of the world should develop "a complementary program of birth control and 'open door.'" The expanding and pre-industrial countries would practice birth control, but in the meantime the industrialized countries would permit immigration to relieve the present pressures, of the Orient especially.[21] While few American students would take this position, for a time there was renewed agitation in some quarters to get the United States and other relatively sparsely populated countries to permit rather extensive immigration again. But the persistence of relatively high birth rates in western Europe, in the British Commonwealth, and in the Americas has weakened the argument for inviting large numbers from more crowded areas.

Even if a limited quota program were set up for places such as the United States and the British Commonwealth, it could only result in temporary alleviation. Such a plan for international migration is not a simple solution. What is needed in most well industrialized countries is not common laborers but professionals, technicians, and highly skilled workmen. Yet these are the very people the emerging industrial areas want to keep.

Relation of Technical Modernization to Cultural Changes Any extensive program to modernize agriculture or develop industry in countries with population pressure will result in a variety of additional changes in their cultures. In the past, the declines in mortality, followed by declines in natality, meant

the rise of the small-family system, increased standards of living, better practices of health and sanitation, and a host of culture patterns associated with city life. The older moral and religious practices and controls gave way to more secular interests and habits. One of the most important of these changes has been the acceptance of birth control.

These are the familiar marks of a shift from primary-group to secondary-group organization of society. Yet the speed with which such changes occur varies greatly. Only in recent decades has the urban way of life reached the rural areas of the older industrialized countries of the West. The future courses elsewhere will depend on the directionalities of the cultures involved.

In this connection, the case of Japan and its shift from agricultural to industrial economy is worth noting. Since 1868, when it was opened up to trade and contact with Europe and the Americas, Japan has been going through a process of change in mortality and natality rates not unlike that of industrialized countries with relatively stable populations.

Yet there are some differences between the patterns of change in Japan and in the Western world. Large numbers of Japanese peasants who have moved to the cities have not as yet altered their ways of life as markedly as did the rural migrants in Europe and the United States. The Japanese "urban peasants," to use Talcott Parson's phrase,[22] keep much of their rural and feudal culture.

Irene B. Taeuber, an expert on the demography of Japan, has summarized

21 · See Radhakamal Mukerjee, "Population Theory and Politics," *American Sociological Review*, 1941, 6:784–793.

22 · Talcott Parsons, "Population and Social Structure," *Japan's Prospect*, ed. Douglas G. Haring (Cambridge: Harvard University Press, 1946).

changes in Japan and their possible relevance for the rest of Asia:

Japan constitutes one case study in the demographic correlates of modernization of a predominantly industrial type, albeit a peculiarly significant one. Japan's historic culture is Eastern. Her industrial and urban transformation was thus divorced from a base in the nonmaterial culture of the West except in so far as specific elements were deliberately selected for imitation or diffused through more informal mechanisms. . . .

The population growth that accompanies indigenous and comprehensive industrial development and the slowing of that growth through a progressive limitation of childbearing are alike products of the changes in ways of living and thinking that are precondition and product of industrialization. The relations of culture and demography proceed through the intermediation of the economic process itself. Political stability, a disciplined labor force, and rapid capital accumulation are necessary aspects of substantial industrialization. Cultural factors exert a major influence on the extent and speed of the economic transformation, for there are cultural preconditions to indigenous economic transformations and cultural limitations to imposed transformations. As industrialization extends over time and expands over wider segments of a nation, the demographic transition of declining mortality and declining fertility becomes a necessary consequence of the accompanying economic pressures and cultural stimuli. But industrialization regarded as economic, political, or social process is in turn modified by the changing dynamics of population. The relationships are complex; the particular constellation of factors that produced the population growth of Imperial Japan will not be duplicated in detail elsewhere. The fundamental fact, though, is that experience within the East corroborates the hypothesis deducible from Western experience: substantial increases in the size of the total population is a correlate of industrialization, but the social and psychological transformations implicit in industrialization result eventually in a lessened rate of reproduction and a slowing growth. Given the technologies and the basic values of the twentieth century, both population growth and the ultimate slowing of that growth are predictable consequences of the industrial and urban transformation of agrarian cultures.

If the experience of the one nation in Monsoon Asia that has achieved a substantial degree of industrialization can be transferred to project the future of the other cultures, industrialization and urbanization will lead eventually to declines in fertility that will first lessen and then eliminate the growth that accompanies modernization.[23]

The author goes on to indicate that the crucial factor is time. Whether public policy and social planning might facilitate the shift remains to be seen.

Population Pressures in War and Peace

The basic pressure of numbers on food resources has long been recognized. Only under the impact of modern science and technology has this pressure been eliminated among certain peoples. The optimism associated with betterment of living during the first flush of industrialization led to a belief in inevitable social-cultural progress. As we have seen, it was thought that mankind had really turned a corner, since science could offset nature's way of balancing births and deaths and the available food supply. A century and a half later, many students of world affairs are not so sure about these views, since more than half the world's peoples are still living under the Malthusian shadow, so to speak.

The highly industrialized countries have long since pre-empted the best

23 · Irene B. Taeuber, "Population and Labor Force in the Industrialization of Japan, 1850–1950," *Economic Growth: Brazil, India, Japan*, eds. S. Kuznets, W. E. Moore, and J. J. Spengler (Durham, N.C.: Duke University Press, 1955), pp. 358–359. By permission.

lands of the earth. Although similar imbalances of peoples and means of livelihood have been known in history, the present problem of disproportion between population and means of survival is particularly acute. The "have-nots" are pushing on the "haves" for a redistribution of resources, a threat which the latter resent and resist. As Thompson says,

In order for population pressure to become dangerous to peace, the people of a given country must feel this pressure and believe (rightly or wrongly) that something can be done about acquiring larger resources by force. . . . When . . . a people comes to feel that it is being kept from lands and resources it really needs by peoples who are not using them or are using them in only a limited way, we have a dangerous situation.[24]

The problem is psychological and cultural, rather than strictly biological. When disease, vice, poverty, and early death are taken for granted, people are not likely to bestir themselves to raise their level of living. The fatalism of the Orient bespeaks this, in part. It is when hope, not despair, is generated that pressures arise. Individuals and nations come to feel discriminated against because they do not have free access to the world's resources. They view with envious eye the great expanses of sparsely settled lands in Australia or the Americas. Or they resent the high level of productive efficiency in such countries as Germany, Britain, and the United States that permits a way of life beyond the wildest dreams of the common man in their own areas.

Actually, there are two main danger spots today: one in central, eastern Europe and the Middle East; the other in the Far East. For the next two or three generations, the former may be a greater threat to world peace than the latter. Thompson believes, however, that "the germs of another world war are inherent in the future development of the Pacific region, if this development is along the lines that have been followed in the past." [25] That is, if something is not done to plan and direct industrialization, population growth, and control of resources, conflict is pretty certain to arise.

It is clear that today's population imbalances and pressures are bound up with economic and political trends which bring us face to face with the political order. Strong nationalist states, many with imperialist ambitions, have dominated the world's resources and industrial development for more than 300 years. It is very doubtful that the world can continue, split into warring sovereign states which fluctuate between peace and war but never arrive at any long-time equilibrium.

What does the future hold? There are two important factors in the situation that must be borne in mind. First, what is the prospect of altering present political practices of the major nations in such a way as to limit the traditional extremes of nationalism and the doctrine of sovereignty? Certainly some modification is necessary in order to build an effective international organization for world peace. Second, any effective movement toward an international organization must take into account present differences between those large cultural systems that follow authoritarianism and those that try to act along the lines of democracy.

24 · W. S. Thompson, *Population Problems*, 4th ed. (New York: McGraw-Hill Book Co., 1953), pp. 359–360. By permission.

25 · Thompson, *Population and Peace in the Pacific* (Chicago: University of Chicago Press, 1946), p. 11.

INTERPRETATIVE SUMMARY

Since the eighteenth century, and particularly in our century, the world has experienced a rapid growth in population. In sophisticated industrial societies, the decline in the death rate as a result of medical progress and improved standards of living has been somewhat offset by the concomitant decline in the birth rate. More backward societies, however, have reaped the benefits of medical knowledge, which are relatively easy to administer as far as lowering the death rates is concerned, without managing to keep birth down.

The problem stemming from the population explosion in such countries is, of course, lack of food. Some theorists have argued that, since people are basically good and since some countries have more food than they need, eventually everyone will "share the wealth" and the problem will disappear. More practical suggestions have included sharing knowledge about improved methods of agriculture, conservation, and birth control; and migration of people in underdeveloped countries to places with extra resources. Those who see industrialization as essential to improved standards of living would lend money and technicians to help backward areas industrialize. All these suggestions have been tried and all have worked to some extent, though factors such as poor resources, cultural inertia, and widespread lack of education in the countries needing help have impeded improvement.

Local population pressures have international repercussions when the "have-not" nations gain hope and begin to demand more of the world's wealth, as they are finally starting to do in our century. Two present danger spots are central eastern Europe and the Middle East, and the Far East.

REVIEW AND SUGGESTED READINGS

A • VOCABULARY

| Demography | Fertility | Mortality |
| Fecundity | Malthusian doctrine | Neo-Malthusian program |

B • QUESTIONS AND TOPICS FOR REVIEW

1. Discuss one of the "trouble spots" of the world in relation to its population pressures. How well have various solutions to the problem worked there?
2. Give specific illustrations of how population pressures during the last decade have had international repercussions.
3. Why are "have-not" countries more truculent today than in the past?
4. What are some problems with diffusing birth control methods to backward populations, besides those mentioned in this chapter?
5. Can the population *increase* in the United States during the last few decades be interpreted as a natural part of our present "cycle of population growth"?
6. Cite two ways in which societies have maintained relatively stable numbers.
7. Can you think of other ways in which population stability might be maintained? Explain.

C • SUGGESTIONS FOR FURTHER READING

Roy G. Francis. *The Population Ahead.* Minneapolis: University of Minnesota Press, 1958.

A discussion of factors bearing on the quality of future populations.

Philip M. Hauser and Otis Dudley Duncan, eds. *The Study of Population: An Inventory and Appraisal*. Chicago: University of Chicago Press, 1959.

A review of the status of demography as a science. This "multiscience discipline" deals with the analysis of population-size, composition, variables, and change. It is also concerned with the interrelations of demography and other system variables in sociology.

William Petersen. *Population*. New York: The Macmillan Company, 1961.

In addition to the usual coverage of fertility, morbidity, mortality rates, and so forth, there is one chapter on the population of primitive peoples, another on that of pre-industrial civilizations, and one on population during the Industrial Revolution.

T. Lynn Smith. *Fundamentals of Population Study*. Philadelphia: J. B. Lippincott Co., 1960.

An introductory textbook treating conventional demographic considerations.

W. S. Thompson. *Population Problems*, 4th ed. New York: McGraw-Hill Book Co., 1953.

A general text combining sociological theory and the basic facts of demography. Has a selected bibliography.

W. S. Woytinsky and E. S. Woytinsky. *World Population and Production: Trends and Outlook*. New York: The Twentieth Century Fund, 1953.

A broad survey of the collective resources and of the economic performance and promise of the nations of the world.

Dennis H. Wrong. *Population*. New York: Random House, 1956.

A brief introduction to demography; particularly concerned with world population growth and distribution, with the continuing problem of people and food resources, and with problems of fertility, mortality, and migration.

CHAPTER 15

Differentials in Population

Certain aspects of community life reflect or are affected by variations in the sex and age composition of the population. If, for example, there are a great many more males than females, as was true in most pioneer communities, marriage rates will be affected, and there will be a high percentage of bachelors but few spinsters. If the proportion of children is high, as in residential suburbs, the problem of education will certainly be different than if there are very few children, as is true of certain sections of our major cities inhabited largely by adult males. Again, when the population has a disproportionate number of people in the older age groups, a host of conditions involving the labor force and social status may exist that are not found when the population is younger.

AGE AND SEX DISTRIBUTION

One way of showing certain basic facts about age and sex distribution is to classify the frequency of males and females by five- or ten-year age intervals. A graphic presentation of such a distribution is called a "population pyramid." In so-called "normal" populations, the sexes are about equal in number. (See Ceylon, in Figure 10.)

A population may grow by excess of births over deaths, by immigration, or by both means. The importation of foreign-born adults into a community produces problems of accommodation, acculturation, and assimilation that will not be found when the population is recruited from births within the community.

From about 1820 to the opening of World War I, this country experienced an increasing influx of foreigners. Because the chief call was for a vigorous labor force, the age and sex distribution of the foreign-born tended to be skewed in the direction of the males and concentrated in the middle range of age classes.

After World War I, severe restrictive laws were passed to reduce the number of immigrants to be admitted in any one year. In fact, the 1930's occasionally saw slight losses in numbers from out-migration. As a result, the distribution of the foreign-born has become further concentrated in the middle and upper age ranges. This portion of the American population represents an ever-smaller part of our total population.

The situation in the rural areas of the United States which are becoming increasingly more industrialized reflects shifting age distributions. There is a high proportion of children, but a distinct shrinkage in the 20–29 age group shows clearly how the cities are draining the country areas of young men and women. The American farm is over-

FIGURE 10 · Life Expectancy and Its Effect on Population *

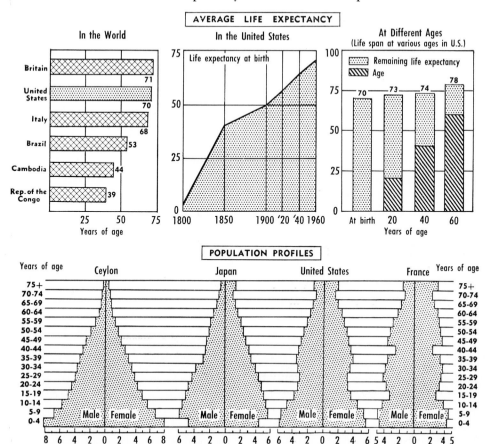

* The *New York Times*, January 15, 1961, E11. In underdeveloped Ceylon, where birth and death rates are high, the population is concentrated in the younger age brackets. In Japan, a society in transition, the birth rate is falling. In the U.S. and France, with lower birth and death rates, the population is spread more evenly through the lifespan. In France the population "gap" at ages 15–19 and 40–44 is due to the effects of two world wars.

crowded, and agricultural production exceeds our needs. Many young people see the city as a way out of their economic dilemmas.

Some Effects of an Aging Population

The populations of western Europe, the United States, and the British Dominions (described in Chapter 14) are growing older—that is, there is an increasingly higher ratio of individuals in the older age groups. A common mea-

sure of this shift is the increase in median age. (This is the age at which 50 percent of the population falls above and 50 percent below.) For the United States, to cite only one example, the median age in 1800 was 16 years; in 1850 it was 19 years; in 1900 it was 23 years; and in 1960 it was 30 years. A somewhat more telling indicator is the percentage of individuals under 20 years, as contrasted with the percentage of those 65 years and over. Table 24 re-

TABLE 24 · Percentage of Persons Under 20 Years and Over 65 Years
in Selected Countries *

| | PERCENTAGES OF TOTAL POPULATION | | MEDIAN AGE |
	Under 20 Years	Over 65 Years	
Mexico	52.0	3.4	19.2
Union of South Africa	51.0	3.5	19.6
India	47.6	3.6	21.4
Japan	44.8	5.0	23.0
United States	35.2	8.3	30.2
France	30.2	11.4	33.6
England and Wales	28.6	11.2	28.6

* From Donald J. Bogue, *The Population of the United States* (Glencoe, Ill.: The Free Press, 1959), p. 105. Data compiled from various issues of *United Nations Demographic Yearbook: 1948–1954.* By permission. For a discussion of trends and the social mechanics of aging, see Clyde V. Kiser, "The Aging of Human Populations: Mechanisms of Change," in Clark Tibbitts and Wilma Donahue, eds., *Social and Psychological Aspects of Aging* (New York: Columbia University Press, 1962), pp. 18–35.

veals some interesting differences in selected countries.

In industrialized countries there is a definite shift toward "older" populations, as can be seen in both Table 24 and Figure 10.

Age and Sex Factors and the Labor Force In many societies, particularly the agricultural, productive work begins fairly early in life: the child and the youth are put to certain tasks which induct them into the labor force. In our urban industrialized America, the work period tends to be confined to a rather limited part of the life cycle. With the extension of life expectancy, of course, the working period is much longer for the average man than it was in the past. But the age at which one enters the labor forces is also later than heretofore. In fact, viewed historically, the most striking changes in the age composition of the labor force have been in the youngest and the oldest age groups. Both male and female child labor increased steadily from 1870 to 1900, when the peak of children gainfully employed was 1,250,000. At the latter date, 26 percent of all boys 10 to 15 years old and 10 percent of all girls in this age bracket were in the nation's working force. By 1940 the gainful employment of younger children had practically ceased.

At the other end of the age scale, there has been a marked decrease—though less than in the case of children —in the percentage of men aged 65 and over in the labor force. This long-term trend is correlated with the changing nature and declining importance of farming, an occupation adapted to the capabilities of both young and old; with the decrease in self-employment; and with the substitution of semiskilled for skilled labor. Moreover, the old-age security program may have encouraged earlier retirement in recent decades.

One of the most significant features of the labor force in this country is the high number of persons in the 16–24 age group who are kept out of the working cohort because they remain in school. At no time in the history of mankind and in no other country has there been such a high proportion of individuals in this age bracket still engaged in getting an education. The situation reflects both our high prosperity and our great faith in the value of an education. (See Chapter 21.)

Associated with the progressive aging of the population is the fact that our labor force has come to consist more largely of individuals from 35 to 64 years old.

Our labor force itself has grown. A substantial factor in this has been the marked increase in the employment of women. In 1870 slightly less than 15 percent of the total working population was female; in 1960 the corresponding percentage was 32.1. More than twelve times as many women were gainfully employed in 1960 as in 1870. In contrast, the number of male workers has increased not quite fivefold. In addition, the proportion of married women gainfully employed is increasing. In 1890 fewer than 5 percent of all married women in this country were in the labor force. In 1960 one out of every three married women was working.

It may be that the increasing flow of women into the working force may offset, to some extent, the effects of male retirement or the inadequate intake of younger men. So far, however, women's work has been restricted to a rather limited number of occupations.

As the population grows older, there will be further pressure to make additional provisions for social security. Without change in the average number of years in the labor force, white men in this country at age 25 in 1956 had a life expectancy of seven years more than in 1900. It is clear that problems of old age and retirement will become increasingly serious.

The composition of a population is influenced by patterns of reproduction. Here we shall look at some of the important factors—regions, community, class, and so on—that make for differences in birth rates among various human groups and aggregates.

As we have noted in the preceding chapter, the specific factors affecting differential birth rates must be examined against the background of the long-range decline in fertility. Further, the interplay of fertility rates and death rates must always be considered. Neither rate by itself tells an accurate demographic story.

Rural-Urban and Regional Variations

On the average, city families have fewer children than farm families. Families who live in the rural nonfarm localities occupy an intermediate position between the city and the farm averages. Such variations in fertility rates are not a recent phenomenon. They seem to have appeared as early as the eighteenth century in Europe, and they became increasingly evident as the Industrial Revolution spread, first throughout Great Britain and then on the Continent. They have been characteristic of the United States for a long time.

Changes in net reproduction rates over a period of more than half a century are shown in Table 25. Note the recent increase in rates. Whether the high fertility of the years following World War II will continue, it is difficult to say. "The births in 1961 correspond to a rate of over 24 per 1,000 population in the United States. In every year of the 1950's, the birth rate was 24 per 1,000 or higher.[1]

There have been, in addition, important redistributions as a result of in-migration and out-migration, state by state. For the 1950–1960 decade, Oregon, California, Washington, Nevada,

1 · From "U.S.A. Population Changes: 1950–1960," *Population Bulletin*, 1963, 19:29,

TABLE 25 · Net Reproduction Rates, Region, and Urban or Rural Residence, 1905–1910 to 1961 *

Color and Area	1905–1910	1930–1935	1935–1940	1942–1947	1961
All classes	1.34	.98	.98	1.29	1.70
White	1.34	.97	.96	1.27	1.65
Nonwhite	1.33	1.07	1.14	1.46	2.10
Urban	.94	.75	.73	1.09	
Rural nonfarm	1.50	1.15	1.15	1.47	
Rural farm	2.02	1.63	1.66	1.86	

* *Statistical Abstract of the United States: 1955* (Washington, D.C.: U.S. Government Printing Office, 1955), p. 65. Data for 1961 from *Statistical Abstract of the United States: 1963* (Washington, D.C.: U.S. Government Printing Office, 1963), p. 56.

Arizona, and Florida had in-migrations of 8 million persons. Only three states lost population in this decade: Arkansas, West Virginia, and Vermont. The total loss was 226,000.[2]

Another indication of shifts in distribution is the shrinkage of the ratio of farm to nonfarm population. In 1900, 31 percent of the American people lived on farms; by 1960 this had declined to 12 percent.[3] With increasing mechanization and commercialization of agriculture, we may look for still further decreases.

Religious Differences Throughout Christian history, religious bodies have, on the whole, encouraged large families and opposed birth control. Now urbanization and secularization are undermining these traditional religious values. There have been a number of studies that reveal significant differences in the fertility rates of Protestants and Catholics, but for some time the true importance of the religious factor was veiled because other variables were not adequately controlled.

One of the first adequate studies

2 · From "Marked Population Growth in the United States and Canada," *Statistical Bulletin*, 1960, 41:3.
3 · From *The World Almanac*, 1961 (New York: New York World-Telegram and Sun, 1961), p. 464.

was made by Frank Notestein. A sample made up entirely of native-white urban women who had completed their child-bearing period showed differences were greatest in the business group and were least in the unskilled group.[4]

Another study of the relation of religious affiliation and fertility was made by Donald J. Bogue, who used 1957 data from the federal Bureau of the Census. Bogue found, among other things, "that no one of the religious groups is subject to uncontrolled fertility. . . . Although the fertility of every religious group is above the replacement level, no group is characterized by rates of children ever born that imply an average of 5 or 6 children per married woman. Thus, fertility control is a widely-accomplished fact throughout all major American religious groups."[5]

Baptists are the most fertile, but this is partially accounted for by the

4 · Frank W. Notestein, "Class Differences in Fertility," *The Annals of the American Academy of Political and Social Science*, 1936, 188:32. The data were collected from native white completed families (those in which the mothers are beyond childbearing age) in the 1930's from Columbus, Syracuse, Bushwick (Brooklyn), and in selected poor sections of Pittsburgh, Syracuse, Detroit, Baltimore, and Cleveland.
5 · Bogue, *The Population of the United States*, p. 696.

high percentage of Negroes in this church, as well as by the fact that a large percentage of the white Baptists were born in the rural sections of the South or reared in places where high birth rates were expected.

Among older women, the Roman Catholics are more fertile than any other group except the Baptists. But Bogue goes on to indicate that younger Catholic women have so fully accepted planned parenthood that "their age-standardized fertility measure in 1957 was only one per cent above that of the nation."[6]

The lowest birth rates are found among the Jewish and Presbyterian women. Lutherans have moderately low fertility rates, and the Methodists have average fertility. It has been pointed out, however, that these differential birth rates among denominations also reflect age, color, residential, and occupational variations. Yet Bogue claims that "there is . . . unmistakable evidence that differences in religious doctrines *do* stimulate fertility differences, independent of these other traits."[7]

A study of social and psychological factors affecting fertility of the white population of Indianapolis, Indiana, tends to confirm Bogue's views. This investigation of 6,551 completed families showed significant differences in fertility between Catholics and Protestants. Of the Protestant couples, 67 percent had only one or two children, while of the Catholic couples only 52 percent had this few. The average number of children in Protestant families was 2.19, in Catholic, 2.74. These differences were found at all economic levels except the very lowest, where the

size of the Protestant families slightly exceeded that of the Catholics.[8]

Earlier European studies showed that Catholics tend to have larger families than Protestants. Yet, because the probable effects of income, class, education, and locality were not carefully controlled, it is difficult to tell how much of the difference was due to such factors and how much to religious views alone. One cannot neglect the probability, however, that religious values do influence fertility. The high ratio of children to women in Utah, for instance, may be attributed to the emphasis the Mormon Church places on the desirability of large families.[9] It is generally assumed that as people "lose their religion" they become more inclined to use some means of restricting conception.[10]

As was expected, Kinsey found some differences in degree of sexual activity—as he defined it—among religious groups. The Orthodox Jews and devout Catholics were less sexually active than those Jews and Catholics who reported little interest in their traditional religious faiths. Similarly, there was some variation among Protestants in consonance with strength of religious belief. There is obviously some correlation between frequency of sexual intercourse and likelihood of pregnancy when contraceptives are not used.

6 · Bogue, p. 696.
7 · Bogue, p. 697.

8 · Clyde V. Kiser and P. K. Whelpton, "Social and Psychological Factors Affecting Fertility, II: Variations in the Size of Completed Families of 6,551 Native White Couples in Indianapolis," *Milbank Memorial Fund Quarterly*, 1944, 22:72–105.
9 · See Harold T. Christensen, "Mormon Fertility: A Survey of Student Opinion," *American Journal of Sociology*, 1948, 53:270–275.
10 · See A. C. Kinsey, et al., *Sexual Behavior in the Human Male* (Philadelphia: W. B. Saunders Co., 1948), pp. 479–487.

Social Status and Birth Rate Differential fertility is also associated with social status. In Western society at least, social status is compounded chiefly of such matters as occupation, income, education, place of birth, and place of residence, as these fall along a scale of social rating and consensus. Such external factors have their counterpart in the ideas, beliefs, attitudes, and values of the individuals concerned. There is an extensive literature on the relation of status to fertility rates; we shall review only selected examples of the more significant studies.

One of the first studies, published in 1899, was made by Jacques Bertillon, a French statistician. Bertillon compared the birth rates for six economic classes in the populations of Paris, Berlin, Vienna, and London. In all instances he found a steady increase in fertility rate as he arranged his data from the "very rich" to the "very poor." And, although the death rates were higher for the poorer than for the richer groups, his report showed definitely that the poor tend to reproduce themselves faster than the rich. In 1903 Sir Arthur Newsholme and T. H. C. Stevenson, two British investigators, made a further study in London and found much the same facts. Commenting on the long-range effects of such differences, they noted that the "very rich" produced less than 10 percent of any next generation, whereas the "very poor" produced 25 percent.[11]

A more adequate study was made on the basis of data from the census of 1911 for England and Wales. Rates were computed for completed families only. Such data gives a truer picture of what actually happens in families of different social classes. The results confirmed the previous findings. For example: 100 women of the upper and middle classes who were married between 1881 and 1886 and who were over 45 years of age in 1911 had borne 422 children, whereas 100 women of the unskilled class, of like marriage and age range, had given birth to 609 offspring. Between these extremes were wives of textile workers and of skilled artisans, for whom the comparable figures were 513 and 556. A like number of miners' wives had had 684 children, and 100 farmers' wives, 632. Analysis of marriages and children in the order of fertility further showed that the least fertile 25 percent of marriages of completed families produced only 2.1 percent of all births, whereas the most fertile 25 percent produced 52 percent of all births.[12]

A study by Jerzy Berent indicates that both class status and social mobility affect fertility. Table 26 shows that both upper-class position and upward mobility have a marked effect on lowering the birth rate. It is highly probable that a similar pattern is found throughout the industrialized Western world.

An analysis of the data of the 1950 census shows the persistence of differentials in fertility as related to occupation, income, and education. The following quotation from the Census Bureau brings out some of the significant

11 · Sir Arthur Newsholme and T. H. C. Stevenson, "The Decline in Human Fertility in the United Kingdom and Other Countries as Shown by Corrected Birth Rates," *Journal of Royal Statistical Society*, 1906, 69:34–87. These authors report the Bertillon data.

12 · Great Britain, Census Office: *Fertility of Marriage*, 2 vols. (London: H. M. Stationery Office, 1917). Some of the data from this report was taken from W. S. Thompson, *Population Problems*, 4th ed. (New York: McGraw-Hill Book Co., 1953), p. 182.

TABLE 26 · Number of Live Births to Families of Completed Fertility, by Social Class †
of Origin and Present Class Position, the United Kingdom, 1949 *

| SOCIAL ORIGIN OF HUSBAND | PRESENT SOCIAL CLASS | | | | |
	I	II	III	IV	AVERAGE
I	1.74	1.79	1.96	2.00	1.81
II	2.04	2.14	2.51	2.97	2.38
III	1.87	2.01	2.67	3.69	2.81
IV	2.40	3.20	3.22	3.68	3.44
AVERAGE	1.88	2.17	2.73	3.56	2.77

† Social Class defined as follows:

I. Professional, high administrative, managerial, and executive.
II. Inspectional, supervisory, other non-routine nonmanual.

III. Skilled manual and routine nonmanual.
IV. Semiskilled and unskilled manual.

* Jerzy Berent, "Fertility and Social Mobility," *Population Studies*, 1952, 5:244–260. Table from p. 247. By permission.

facts that account for the continuing differentials:

. . . In 1950, persons in the upper economic groups tended to postpone somewhat longer the birth of their first child and to have their last child after fewer years of marriage than persons in the lower economic groups.

Married women college graduates of childbearing age in 1950 who had been married ten years or more had about half as many children on the average (1,954 children per 1,000 women) as married women who had not completed the seventh grade of school (3,632 children per 1,000 women). . . . The . . . detailed statistics . . . show a generally consistent pattern of progressively higher fertility among groups with progressively lower

amounts of schooling. During the first two years of married life, the college graduates had 172 children per 1,000 women and those with less than seven years of school had 427 children per 1,000 women. In the marriage period "10 years or more," the college graduates gave birth to 261 children per 1,000 women and those with less than seven years of school gave birth to 1,242 children per 1,000 women. . . .[13]

Some clear-cut differences in fertility as related to occupation for couples married 10 years or more are brought out in Table 27.

13 · From 1950 *Census of Population*, Series PC–14, No. 22, "Fertility by Duration of Marriage: 1950" (Washington, D.C.: Bureau of the Census, 1956), p. 1.

TABLE 27 · Average Number of Children Ever Born per 1,000 Women by Selected Occupational Categories of the Husbands, for the United States: 1950 *

OCCUPATION	AVERAGE NUMBER OF CHILDREN EVER BORN PER 1,000 WOMEN
Professional, technical, and kindred workers	283
Clerical, sales, and kindred workers	371
Managers, officials, and proprietors, except farm	414
Craftsmen, foremen, and kindred workers	625
Operatives and kindred workers	722
Farmers and farm managers	932
Laborers, except farm and mine	989
All occupational groups	666

* *Ibid.*, p. 2. Data are for women 15 to 44 years old married once and husband present for period of marriage of 10 years or more.

Beginning in the last quarter of the nineteenth century and continuing to the present, there has been a steady decline in family size in all classes in Western industrialized countries. The rate of this decrease has not been uniform by class, however, as a number of students of differential fertility have indicated.

From an analysis of fertility trends in England and Wales from 1876 to 1934, J. W. Innes reports that, while there was a general decline in fertility throughout the last quarter of the nineteenth century, the decrease took place more rapidly in the upper than in the lower classes. This was true until 1911. From then on—at least for the next 20 years—there is some evidence that a lower limit of fertility had been reached with less absolute disparity than formerly between the birth rates of the various classes.[14]

In a further study for the decade from 1921 to 1931, Innes showed that, while the inverse relation between status and fertility did hold for the upper two classes, the divergence was slight. All classes declined in fertility, but the semiskilled did much more so than any others, and the two top classes were only slightly divergent from the skilled laborer and semiskilled in 1931.[15]

Some of the earlier generalizations about a universal and constant inverse ratio between socio-economic status and size of family must certainly be qualified. Small samples of urban areas in China and more extensive data from rural China, for instance, indicate a slightly higher fertility among the more prosperous classes.[16] K. A. Edin and others discovered a like trend in Stockholm beginning about 1919, and subsequent studies have tended to confirm this trend toward lessening the gap in fertility rates among the various classes.[17] In this country, at least in urban areas, similar changes are taking place. Clyde V. Kiser reports that married women of the highest socio-economic position in the United States are no longer characterized by the lowest birth rate. Wives of professional men now have a higher fertility rate than wives of businessmen. Similarly, the educational differential seems to be disappearing. For example, wives who report having some college have a birth rate almost as high as those with only a high-school education. Nor does the inverse relationship between fertility and income hold for those in the highest income brackets.[18]

Warren S. Thompson's thesis regarding the reasons for these differentials is pertinent.

The classes that first gained control over fertility lived predominantly in the cities and were of better than average socioeconomic status. However, the knowledge of conception control spread gradually—first, to other urban groups of lower socioeconomic status, and later, to rural groups. As this took place fertility declined in all classes, but for some time it continued to decline more rapidly in the upper socioeconomic classes. . . . Since it seems likely to the author that economic considerations are going to play a more and more important role in determining

14 · J. W. Innes, *Class Fertility Trends in England and Wales*, 1876–1934 (Princeton: Princeton University Press, 1938).

15 · J. W. Innes, "Class Birth Rates in England and Wales, 1921–1931," *Milbank Memorial Fund Quarterly*, 1941, 19:72–96.

16 · See Paul H. Landis and Paul K. Hatt, *Population Problems: A Cultural Interpretation*, 2nd ed. (New York: American Book Company, 1954), p. 266.

17 · For a review of these studies, see Thompson, *Population Problems*, pp. 191–194.

18 · See Clyde V. Kiser, *Group Differences in Urban Fertility* (Baltimore: Williams and Wilkins, 1942).

the size of the family as voluntary control increases, it seems not improbable that the less favored economic groups will soon have as small families as the more favored groups, or, perhaps, even smaller.[19]

Among the Western countries at least, the class differentials in fertility that have been present for at least three generations may tend to disappear. Meanwhile, differential fertility is developing among nations, and this creates problems in international affairs.

Psycological Factors Affecting Fertility

The shift from the large-family to the small-family pattern in Western society is not merely a matter of changes in the material aspects of culture. The objective facts which we have just reviewed have their counterparts in the ideas, attitudes, and values of the people themselves. During the 1930's it became rather commonly accepted that the downward trend in fertility rates would continue, but the upswing in birth rates during and after World War II has led to some revision of predictions about trends.

In the Indianapolis study noted earlier, Lois Pratt and P. K. Whelpton discuss data on the relation of number of children desired by the wife and husband at the time of marriage to actual fertility of the couple. Of interest is their data on relation of actual fertility to the number of children the wife and husband said they would like to have if they could begin married life over. The study finds

. . . a positive relation between the index of interest [in children] and the number of children wanted at marriage and also the number wanted if married life could

19 · Thompson, *Population Problems*, p. 195. By permission.

be relived. . . . This is true for all wives and husbands and also for their children. The number of children wanted at marriage is substantially smaller than the number wanted if married life could be relived for wives and husbands at all levels of interest. Among all couples the number wanted at either period is consistently larger than the number actually born, regardless of level of interest.[20]

The Indianapolis data also "point up the popularity of the two-child family. Over half the wives (54 percent) and husbands (55 percent) stated that at the time of marriage they had wanted two children. Among about one-third of the couples *both* wife and husband stated that they wanted two children." [21] For the section of the larger sample who said that they had definitely planned for a second child, the chief reason given was that an only child is handicapped by not having siblings. The "desire to insure against childlessness" was of minor importance; and interests of brothers and sisters in having additional siblings does not seem to be of any importance in this subsample.[22]

Not only is there a growing belief in the value of the small family, but there is evidence that planning for children has become more and more widespread. The Indianapolis survey

20 · Lois Pratt and P. K. Whelpton, "Social and Psychological Factors Affecting Fertility, XXIX: Interest in and Liking for Children in Relation to Fertility, Planning and Size of Planned Family," *Milbank Memorial Fund Quarterly*, 1955, 33:454–455. By permission.

21 · H. V. Muhsam and Clyde V. Kiser, "Social and Psychological Factors Affecting Fertility, XXXII: The Number of Children Desired at the Time of Marriage," *Milbank Memorial Fund Quarterly*, 1956, 34:312.

22 · Erwin S. Solomon, Jeanne E. Clarke, and Charles F. Westoff, "Social and Psychological Factors Affecting Fertility, XXXI: Fear of Childlessness, Desire to Avoid an Only Child, and Children's Desires for Siblings," *Milbank Memorial Fund Quarterly*, 1956, 34:160–177.

has given us the most complete analysis of the effects of planning for births. Whelpton has summarized the findings for couples selected according to certain demographic and other criteria: [23]

> . . . Approximately 90 per cent of all these couples had tried to plan the number and spacing of their children, and only 10 per cent had not tried. Among the latter, of course, are many of the couples who found that they were sterile or of low fecundity. If only the couples whose childbearing capacity appeared to be normal during most of their married life are considered, the proportion that tried to plan fertility rises to over 98 per cent. Classifying these couples according to the success of their efforts brings out important differences in family size. Only 40 per cent of the couples had "planned" their last child or had "planned" not to have any children; in this group there were 146 births per 100 couples. Over 30 per cent of the couples had not "planned" the last child but said they had no more children than they wanted; in this group there were 199 births per 100 couples. Finally, about 25 per cent of the couples said they had more children than they had "planned" or thought they ought to have; in this group there were 296 births per 100 couples. In contrast, there were approximately 700 births per 100 couples among the few couples that had not attempted to control family size. For the group as a whole, therefore, the attempts at the voluntary limitation of family size had reduced the gross reproduction rate to less than one third of what it otherwise would have been.[24]

23 · These criteria were "husband and wife native white; both Protestant; married in 1927, 1928, or 1929; wife under 30 and husband under 40 at marriage; neither previously married; residents of a large city most of the time since marriage; and both elementary-school graduates." See P. K. Whelpton and Clyde V. Kiser, "Social and Psychological Factors Affecting Fertility, VI: The Planning of Fertility," *Milbank Memorial Fund Quarterly*, 1947, 25:209–210, n. 2.

24 · P. K. Whelpton, *Forecasts of the Population of the United States, 1945–1975* (Washington, D.C.: U.S. Government Printing Office, 1947), p. 25.

While this part of the Indianapolis study did not include the Catholic and Jewish population, it does show that for this carefully controlled group, consisting of nearly all the couples in that community that met the criteria, the practice of contraception and voluntary parenthood is now nearly universal.

It has been suggested also that the hurry and stress of urban living leaves less energy for reproductive functions and even makes for neurotic reactions which unfavorably influence potency and fertility. Raymond Pearl has shown for one sample that the upper-urban classes report far less frequency of sexual intercourse per month than the rural-farm group.[25] Kinsey has also reported finding some class and educational differences in frequency.[26] In this connection, it is interesting to note that there are scattered instances in which the adoption of a foster child by a couple considered sterile has been followed by the birth of their own children. It may well be that a good deal of contemporary sterility is induced by emotional stress rather than by biological loss of sexual potency.

These considerations, tentative as they are, seem to indicate that in matters of reproductive behavior, not only biological but cultural and psychological factors are crucial. Individuals in any society are dominated by ideas and values that help determine fertility rates for them.

Birth rates, of course, are only part of the explanation for variations in population growth or decline. Equally relevant are death rates.

25 · Raymond Pearl, "Biological Factors in Fertility," *Annals of the American Academy of Political and Social Science*, 1936, 188:145–150.

26 · Alfred C. Kinsey, *et al.*, pp. 355–357.

DIFFERENTIALS IN THE DEATH RATE

During the past century, there has been not only a general decline in birth rates in Western countries but also a marked decrease in the mortality rates. For example, the crude death rate in Sweden during 1808–1812 was 33 per 1,000, and in France for the same period, 25.7. In 1950 the corresponding rates were 13.1 and 10.2. In 1848–1852 the crude death rate in England and Wales was 22.6; in 1950 it was 11.7. These rates vary widely from country to country, but in some countries they are dropping quite sharply. Unfortunately, comparable demographic data for some sections of the world are still inadequate. This is true for most of Africa, southeast Asia, China, and certain areas in the Near East. Nevertheless, what evidence we have seems to support the idea that in these regions, too, the death rate has been going down in recent decades.[27] For the United States as a whole, adequate mortality statistics were not available before 1910. In that year the death rate per 1,000 population was 14.7. It dropped steadily thereafter; by 1960 it had reached 9.4.

Trends in the reduction of the death rate in the United States since 1870 show these facts: (1) The mortality rate for children under five did not decline materially until after 1900, when the number of deaths per 1,000 for infants under one year was 162.4. By 1950 this had dropped to 33.0. For white males in the age-span of from one to four years, the toll in 1900 was 18.1 per 1,000; in 1960 it was only 1.1 per 1,000. The decrease among non-

whites is even more striking. For example, for nonwhite males one to four years of age, the mortality in 1900 was 39.3 per 1,000; in 1956 it was only 2.0 per 1,000.[28] (2) The death rate for individuals over four years but under middle life has moved slowly downward. And (3) the mortality rate for persons in the upper-age brackets has remained about the same.

A factor that long influenced the death rate was the high maternal mortality. This has been almost eliminated by advances in medical science. As late as 1935, for whites it was 53.1 per 10,000 live births and for nonwhites, 94.6. By 1957 it was 2.6 for whites and 11.3 for nonwhites.[29]

There is good reason to think that there may be a slight rise in the death rate, especially if the rising birth rate after World War II should level off. The current rate rests on the fact that the United States still has a high proportion of people at the childhood and early adult levels, periods of life when mortality is low.

Disease, Age, Sex, and the Death Rate

The influence of disease on the death rate is qualified in most instances by age. Some diseases, such as diarrhea, whooping cough, measles, diphtheria, and scarlet fever, occur chiefly in infancy and childhood. In addition, earliest infant mortality is affected by congenital defects. Other diseases, such as typhoid and pulmonary tuberculosis, attack middle life most frequently. Adults in the later years are most susceptible to pneumonia, cancer, diabetes, and to such organic breakdowns as heart and circulatory disorders, nephritis, and Bright's disease.

27 · See Thompson, p. 237.

28 · Bogue, p. 177.
29 · Bogue, p. 210.

With the decrease in infant and childhood mortality and the aging of the population, there has been a change in the relative seriousness of acute and chronic diseases. Modern medicine and sanitation have largely eliminated the incidence of the acute diseases of childhood and have restricted the incidence and spread of typhoid, diphtheria, smallpox, and other acute disorders that formerly attacked young and old alike. In contrast, chronic diseases—that is, those that persist or recur with such virulence as to need continued medical and nursing care—have become more prevalent in the last half century.

For the younger ages, the disasters of disease and death tend to be related to poor living conditions, improper maternal care, and infectious diseases due to lack of adequate public health measures. Death in the later years seems most often related to organic breakdowns, which may have various causes —earlier infections, congenital defects, the nature of occupations, low-quality medical care resulting from class position, and so on.

Changes in the causes of death are related not only to the advances of medical knowledge and skill, but also to shifts in the age distribution of the population and to improvement in levels of living. In the United States, there were more than four times as many people 65 years old or over in 1960 as there were in 1900, which means that disorders related to aging have become increasingly significant. At the beginning of the century, the leading causes of death were influenza and pneumonia, tuberculosis, and diarrhea and enteritis. Today nearly 40 percent of all deaths are due to diseases of the heart, about 16 percent to cancer and related malignancies, and 11 percent to vascular lesions affecting the central nervous system.[30]

There are also some sex differences in these matters. Disorders showing a higher incidence for men than women are arteriosclerotic heart disease, including coronary disease; cancer, especially of the mouth and respiratory system, and of the urinary organs. Women have a higher incidence of cancer of the genital organs and the breast, of diabetes, and of hypertension with heart disease.[31]

Race and Survival There are many misconceptions about differences in racial mortality. Wherever the differences appear, they seem so closely bound up with economic status, with sanitation, and with medical care that it is hard to discover any specific racial factors. As we have noted, for this country and others, the mortality rate for Negroes is higher than for whites. Yet with improved sanitation and improvement in living standards for Negroes, the earlier differences are lessening. Thus in the United States in 1900, while the death rate per 1,000 for whites was 17.0, for nonwhites (chiefly Negroes) it was 25. In 1957, for whites it was 9.5 and for nonwhites, 10.4— surely a significant change. Another way of indicating this is to cite life expectancy. The closing of the gap is shown by the fact that in 1919–1931 the life expectancy for white males was 59.1 years, for nonwhites, only 47.5; by 1961 that for white males at

30 · See J. Frederic Dewhurst and Associates, *America's Needs and Resources: A New Survey* (New York: The Twentieth Century Fund, 1955), pp. 299–300. Also Bogue. pp. 197–198.

31 · Bogue, pp. 197–198.

birth was 67 years, for Negro males, 61.[32]

Sex, Marital Status, and Mortality

Women are not the weaker sex, despite popular belief that they are. Both biology and demography show that women have a higher survival rate than men. Apparently a lethal selection begins almost from the start of life. First of all, more males are conceived than females, in a ratio of about 120 to 100. However, even prenatally, "the death toll is higher for males than for females. . . ."[33] Prenatal mortality "is inversely related to the socioeconomic class of parents and to adequacy of prenatal care and diet of mother."[34]

As a result of prenatal losses, by the time of birth the sex ratio is reduced to about 106 males to 100 females. But even this slight advantage does not last. Among infants under one year, death takes a higher toll of boys than girls. And right on through the age brackets, there is a persistent superiority in survival among females. Up to age 65, the female rate is about half that of the male rate; for 65 years and over, the female rate is about one-third lower.

Another differential is evident when we compare the mortality of single, married, and widowed persons. Studies both in Europe and in this country reveal the general fact that married persons live longer than single. In general, however, the single have a lower death rate than the widowed and divorced.[35]

Most of these facts of marital differences are not difficult to explain. Undoubtedly marriage acts as a selective agent. In general, it is the more vigorous men who marry and take on marital responsibilities. There may be some such selection among women also, but in the past it has been much less than among men. Greater regularity of living among the married, especially as it affects men, is also conducive to longevity. Thompson makes the point that, in general, marriage "apparently represents a better adaptation to life, physically and mentally, than does celibacy."[36]

Occupational Mortality

The kind of work a person does will determine in part his exposure to various kinds of illness or accidents, and thus play a part in affecting type and time of death. Obviously, construction workers, truck drivers, and miners are more exposed to hazards of working conditions than are bookkeepers or schoolteachers.

As one report puts it, "The disparity in mortality between the professional and managerial occupations and the semiskilled workers narrowed appreciably between 1930 and 1950. Similarly, agricultural workers no longer enjoy as marked an advantage in mortality as they did in the earlier period."[37] For example, from 1930 to 1950, whereas for people in managerial occupations the mortality ratio (ratio between number of deaths that

32 · Data from *Statistical Abstract of the United States, 1959* (Washington, D.C.: U.S. Government Printing Office, 1959), p. 63; and from *Population Bulletin*, 1963, 19:147–148.

33 · "Prenatal Mortality," *Statistical Bulletin*, 1956, 37:2–3.

34 · *Ibid.*, p. 3.

35 · See Thompson, pp. 247–248.

36 · Thompson, p. 248.

37 · From "Recent and Future Mortality Trends," *Statistical Bulletin*, 1960, 41:1.

actually occurred to number expected) remained constant at 85, for semiskilled workers it dropped from 113 to 100. For agricultural workers the ratio rose from 71 to 96.

In discussing various studies of occupational mortality made in Great Britain, Thompson points out a vicious circle.

Selection picks many of the poorer physical specimens of manhood for the worst-paid jobs, and then poor pay makes decent living impossible. The inevitable result of this combination of circumstance is an extremely high death rate in certain occupational groups. It is, perhaps, the living conditions enforced by poorly paid work, even more than the nature of the work itself, that cause the high death rates in many occupations.[38]

Urban-Rural Differences For many decades, rural communities have had lower death rates than urban communities. In the United States the rural areas still have lower rates, but with the extension of public health facilities, sanitation, and improved medical care in our cities, the differences are lessening.

An important element in the drop-

38 · Thompson, p. 254. By permission.

ping of the death rate has been the sharp decline in infant mortality. One Census Bureau report notes that "Between 1915, the first year for which a comparable figure is available, and 1953, the infant mortality rate dropped 72 percent."[39] The rural-urban differentials, however, continue. Thus for 1953, the mortality for urban white children under one year per 1,000 live births was 25.1; for nonwhites it was 42.6. The comparable rates for rural whites and rural nonwhites were 24.9 and 48.0, respectively. We may also compare rural-urban differentials in metropolitan counties with like differences in nonmetropolitan counties. Table 28 presents these contrasts for 1958.

Commenting on these facts, the Census Bureau report states that "The contrast in infant mortality rates between the metropolitan counties and the nonmetropolitan is greater than that between urban and rural areas. . . . The small cities show slightly lower rates than the large cities and the rural areas.[40]

39 · *Vital Statistics—Special Reports*, vol. 42, no. 15, January 4, 1956, p. 327.
40 · *Ibid.*, p. 329.

TABLE 28 · Rural-Urban Differentials in Infant Mortality in Metropolitan and Non-metropolitan Counties in the United States, 1958. Deaths under One Year per 1,000 Live Births *

METROPOLITAN COUNTIES		NONMETROPOLITAN COUNTIES	
Urban—white	23.7	Urban—white	25.4
Urban—nonwhite	42.4	Urban—nonwhite	49.4
Rural—white	21.7	Rural—white	24.4
Rural—nonwhite	42.6	Rural—nonwhite	51.2

* From "Infant Mortality: United States and Alaska, Hawaii, Puerto Rico, and the Virgin Islands (U.S.), 1958," *Vital Statistics—Special Reports*, vol. 52, no. 5, August 15, 1960, p. 127.

INTERPRETATIVE SUMMARY

Western industrial societies are experiencing a long-range decline in fertility. However, rates of fertility vary among different groups and social categories. In our own country, though several interrelated factors affect birth rates, differences among groups are declining. For example, though city families on the average still have fewer children than do farm families, the differential is decreasing. Though birth rates still vary considerably among religious groups, the number of individuals of all faiths who are apparently planning family size is increasing. Again, though our upper economic groups still tend to have fewer children, starting their families later and finishing earlier, this differential also has decreased markedly as contraceptive education has filtered down to the lower classes and secularization has become widespread.

The death rate in Western countries, as well as in many non-Western countries, is also declining. The most striking decrease has come in the lower age groups, as medical science has conquered or restricted the diseases of childhood. Medical advances have also increased life expectancy, the major cause of death among older people currently being organic breakdown. The fact that people are living longer has had consequences throughout our culture; for example, many individuals are working more years, yet can look forward to a long period of retirement, which they and their employers must provide for.

Differentials in death rates and causes of death among other aggregates exist. Almost from the start of life, the female survival rate is higher than that of the male, and certain causes of death are more frequent among members of one sex than the other. Married people tend to live longer than individuals without a mate, their conformity with this particular norm perhaps reflecting an overall adjustment to their culture. Though the mortality rate for members of one race in a given society may at first appear significant, any differentials are so closely related to other factors that generalizations are difficult. Death rates and causes vary, though decreasingly, among occupational groups; and rural communities still have lower death rates than urban, though here too differentials are lessening.

REVIEW AND SUGGESTED READINGS

A • VOCABULARY

Labor force	Longevity	Population pyramid
Lethal selection	Net reproduction rate	

B • QUESTIONS AND TOPICS FOR REVIEW

1. Discuss differential fertility rates as related to religion, education, socio-economic status, etc., in the following groups: (a) your parents' friends, (b) your local or national religious group, and (c) your married friends.
   In each group, do you note any trends concerning age differences between parents and children? What are they?
2. What are the norms in your subcultures concerning work for married women?
3. Discuss various retirement plans with which you are familiar. Which seem both adequate and fair to young people who must take salary deductions?
4. In the light of differential death rates in Western society for infants, children,

those of middle age, and those of old age, what do you think are the pressing challenges of modern medicine?

5. Playwright Edward Albee has been interested in the problems of our "aging" society. He describes old people as frequently leading lives of futility, though they are not senile, while vigorous middle-aged daughters and sons-in-law view them with impatience and occasional pity. He says that though the off-spring are scrupulous about "living up to their responsibilities" to their parents in material aspects, they are not respectful and may even be glad when the old people die.

Avoiding "my Aunt Emma" generalizations, discuss which portions of Albee's observations seem especially valid? Which seem inevitable in view of other culture patterns in our society?

C · SUGGESTIONS FOR FURTHER READING

(In addition to the following, see pertinent sections on differential fertility in the volumes listed at the end of Chapter 14.)

Donald J. Bogue, *The Population of the United States*. Glencoe, Ill.: The Free Press, 1959.

A basic reference which presents, clearly and comprehensively, a description of the social characteristics of the population of the United States, with an analysis of the trends altering this composition.

Frank Lorimer, ed. *Culture and Human Fertility*. Paris, France: United Nations Educational, Scientific and Cultural Organization, 1954.

Subtitled a "study of the relation of cultural conditions to fertility in non-industrial societies." Part I, by Lorimer, deals with the general theory of demography; Parts II, III, and IV present specific demographic studies of selected areas of Africa; and Part V deals with like studies of Brazil.

Joseph J. Spengler and Otis D. Duncan, eds. *Population Theory and Policy: Selected Readings*. Glencoe, Ill.: The Free Press, 1956.

Papers dealing chiefly with demographic data as related to social structure and socio-economic changes and to demographic theory.

Joseph J. Spengler and Otis D. Duncan, eds. *Demographic Analysis: Selected Readings*. Glencoe, Ill.: The Free Press, 1956.

A companion volume to the above, presenting basic demographic information and analysis of concrete problems, with some attention to research methodology and techniques.

CHAPTER 16

Folk and Urban Communities

The widespread and rapid urbanization of the world is one of the most significant trends of our time. Worldwide urban expansion is bringing about great changes in the major patterns of social organization and culture. In many ways it is as revolutionary in its effects on society and institutions as the domestication of plants and animals and the emergence of village life in the Neolithic.

The striking growth of cities in the nineteenth and twentieth centuries is a novel event in human history. Although cities existed five or six thousand years ago, the cities of the ancient world were generally small towns by modern standards. The largest of them contained only 1 or 2 percent of the total population of their society, and Davis estimates that it took from 50 to 90 farmers to produce the surplus needed to enable one man to live in an urban center.[1] In fact, it is here, in the ratio of farmers to urban dwellers, that the explanation can be found for the recency and suddenness of urbanization. Not until the Industrial Revolution, with its factory system, improvement of farming, and tremendous speed-up in the transportation of goods, was it possible for whole so-cieties to become urbanized. Only when one farmer can raise enough food for many people besides himself can a society exist in which the majority of the people live and work in cities.

WORLD URBANIZATION

Only in the past century and a half has the world known truly urban *societies*, in which a high proportion of the total population live in cities. Table 29 shows that as recently as 1800 only 2.4 percent of the world's population lived in cities of 20,000 or more; today more than one-fifth of the people live in such cities. Furthermore, as can be seen from Table 29, the proportion of people living in large cities has risen even more dramatically. By 1950 the proportion of people in the world living in cities was higher than that in even the most urbanized country before modern times.[2]

These figures are even more impressive when one realizes that the average is held down by Asia, Africa, and Latin America; the bulk of the urbanization, as Table 30 shows, has occurred in Oceania, Europe, and North America. Davis describes the trend as follows:

In 1800 there were apparently less than 50 cities with 100,000 or more in-

---

1 · Kingsley Davis, "The Origin and Growth of Urbanization in the World," *American Journal of Sociology*, 1955, 60:429–437. All quotations by permission.

2 · *Ibid.*, p. 433.

TABLE 29 · Percentage of World's Population Living in Cities *

	CITIES OF 20,000 OR MORE	CITIES OF 100,000 OR MORE
1800	2.4	1.7
1850	4.3	2.3
1900	9.2	5.5
1950	20.9	13.1

* Davis, p. 433.

TABLE 30 · Percentage of World's Population Living in Cities, by Regions *

	IN CITIES OF 20,000 PLUS	IN CITIES OF 100,000 PLUS
World	21	13
Oceania	47	41
North America (Canada and U.S.A.)	42	29
Europe (except U.S.S.R.)	35	21
U.S.S.R.	31	18
South America	26	18
Middle America and Caribbean	21	12
Asia (except U.S.S.R.)	13	8
Africa	9	5

* Davis, p. 434.

habitants. This was less than the number in the million class today and less than the number of 100,000-plus cities currently found in many single countries. By 1950 there were close to 900 cities of 100,000 or more people, which is more than the number of towns and cities of 5,000 or more in 1800.

As yet there is no indication of a slackening of the rate of urbanization in the world as a whole. If the present rate should continue, more than a fourth of the earth's people will be living in cities of 100,000 or more in the year 2000, and more than half in the year 2050. For places of 20,000 or more, the proportions at the two dates would be something like 45 per cent and 90 per cent. Whether such figures prove too low or too high, they nevertheless suggest that the human species is moving rapidly in the direction of an almost exclusively urban existence. . . . When . . . more than a third of the population of a country lives in cities of the 100,000 class (38.4 per cent in England and Wales in 1951), the country can be described as almost completely urbanized (81 per cent being designated as "urban"

in the English case in 1951). We thus have today what can be called "urbanized societies," nations in which the great majority of inhabitants live in cities. The prospect is that, as time goes on, a greater and greater proportion of humanity will be members of such societies.[3]

The trend toward an urban social order is of concern to sociologists because it brings with it drastic alterations in social organization and interactional patterns. We shall look first at the structure and culture of the folk or primary society and then at the changes that occur in social structure and culture with urbanization.

THE FOLK COMMUNITY

The family, band, clan, tribe, and small village long antedate urban society, with its masses of people divided

3 · Ibid., p. 434.

into many special-interest groups. The very first forms of human society and culture, however, can only be inferred. We know, of course, that the primary forms of human grouping are far older than the secondary.

Earliest men apparently lived in relatively small bands, formed on the basis of family and blood ties. Their economy consisted of seed and root gathering, and hunting and fishing. Their social organization must have been most rudimentary.[4]

The culture of present-day primary communities stems from the Neolithic Revolution. As noted in Chapter 3, the domestication of plants and animals and the development of agriculture made possible more permanent settlement. This in turn brought changes in social organization and division of labor, and laid the foundations of rural culture patterns which have come down into our own time.

Even today, from two-thirds to three-fourths of the world's people live in what may be called folk or peasant societies. Their culture stands intermediate between that of the band or tribe and urban patterns. Folk culture has much in common with tribal culture—solidarity of family life, importance of religion, forms of moral control, and simple social order generally.

Structure and Functions of Folk Society

The two outstanding characteristics of a folk or primary social structure are small size and isolation. "There are no more people in it than can come to know each other well, and they remain in long association with each other." [5] These structural features have functions, of course, for the culture.

Isolation means a limitation of the opportunities for stimulus and response. Our chief concern here is the effects on the primary community of spatial or geographical isolation, effects which in reality are largely cultural. The influences of isolation are evident in comparisons of the intelligence-test scores of urban and rural children. As a rule, school children in cities do better on the standard mental tests than their country counterparts. Moreover, there is a gradation in the test performance as one goes from larger cities to towns, to villages, to open country, and finally to sharply isolated communities.

While biologically inherited factors may be producing certain of these deviations, investigations tend to bear out the thesis that a large part of the difference is due to the cultural variability between rural and urban societies. Certainly the deviations along a continuum from highly isolated to city schools cannot be explained as a matter of biological heredity.

Cultural isolation induces variability in life patterns. As we observed in Chapter 13, if the segregation continues over long periods, certain distinctions may arise which mark off one society sharply from another. On a smaller scale, our own Southern mountain whites illustrate the effects of isolation. Living for generations undisturbed by changes going on around them, these people have continued a culture which still reflects many as-

4 · For a very readable and extended reconstruction of the life of early man, see George R. Stewart, *Man: An Autobiography* (New York: Random House, 1946).

5 · Robert Redfield, "The Folk Society," *American Journal of Sociology*, 1947, 52:293–308.

pects of the seventeenth and early eighteenth centuries. Their habits, attitudes, and ideas are similar to those of the colonist and pioneer, and they are generally suspicious of the outside world.[6]

Among the most interesting forms of isolation are the "cultural islands" of distinct groups that have persisted in the midst of highly secularized and technologically developed areas. By voluntary segregation the Amish, Mennonites, Dunkers, and other "plain people" who migrated from Europe have maintained certain cultural traits for generations. Their clothing, agricultural practices, vehicles, and certain social institutions have been carried down with little change from the time of the Protestant Reformation. These groups have regarded the "simple life" as the "good life," and have fought doggedly to keep their children from becoming "worldly." The more conservative sects, particularly the House Amish, shun all technological innovations except those absolutely necessary to their survival. Similarly, "agricultural islands," in which distinct occupational practices of bygone days have been retained, are found in several places in America.

Another structural feature of the folk community is a minimal division of labor. Except for the basic division

6 · See J. C. Campbell, *The Southern Highlander and His Homeland* (New York: Russell Sage Foundation, 1921); M. T. Matthews, *Experience-Worlds of Mountain People*, Teachers College Contributions to Education, no. 700 (New York: Teachers College, Columbia University, 1937). For comparison, see O. W. Junek, *Isolated Communities: A Study of a Labrador Fishing Village* (New York: American Book Company, 1937). Peter A. Munch, *Sociology of Tristan da Cunha* (Oslo, Norway: I Kommisjon hos Jacob Dybwad, 1945) is an invaluable study of community isolation on an inaccessible island in the south Atlantic.

by age and sex differences, there are few specialized roles. All women are gardeners, all weave their own cloth, all men fish and hunt, and so on. One function of this characteristic of folk social structure is the absence of secondary groups. Since there are few special interests, there is little need for special-interest organizations. Where everyone picks coconuts, there is no point in organizing an International Amalgamated Coconut-Pickers Union!

Of course, while the family and the neighborhood are the most primary of all associations, even primitive communities have some groups which serve the more special interests of their members. Tribal councils, secret societies, and formalized age and sex groups cut across the more elemental kinship and neighborhood contacts. Nevertheless, in primary communities the number of such organizations is relatively small, and among those which do exist the social contacts often tend to be informal.

One other result of small size, isolation, and lack of specialization is homogeneity of population. The different physical types, interests, occupational roles, values, religious groupings, and attitudes so obvious in an urban society are absent from the folk community. The people tend to be much alike, in body build as well as in culture patterns.

Folk Culture An examination of peasant culture in various areas of the world reveals a number of universal patterns, as well as many local variations. One striking feature, in contrast to the situation in urban life, is the great importance of the family, not only as a reproductive and child-rearing agency but as an economic unit. In many societies it is not the individual as such but the entire family as a group that tills the soil, plants and harvests the crops, and carries out co-operatively the other necessary farm functions. For the most part, too, the farm family is of the patriarchal type: the father is the final arbiter in most of the family's major decisions.

Forms of land ownership vary. Farmer-ownership and tenancy often exist side by side. In general, tenancy is associated with lower levels of living for the tenant than those of farmers who own their own property. In short, while variations exist, peasant societies are characterized by strong family and community solidarity and close ties to the soil.

We have already mentioned several of the main characteristics of folk culture as functions of the structure of a folk society: the lack of secondary groups, the homogeneity of values and behavior patterns. This homogeneity contributes to an outstanding feature of folk culture: the powerful sense of unity binding the people together. The members of a folk society exhibit a strong in-group feeling. Since the whole of their social lives is wrapped up in a society which is a primary group, they are inclined to view the entire outside world as an out-group. While most rural Americans participate extensively in urban culture, there is enough community solidarity remaining in isolated rural sections to make the urban visitor feel "left out."

Finally, folk cultures are notable for the extent to which social control is informal. Sanctions are imposed through gossip, ridicule, or ostracism. Behavior is governed by folkways and mores; there is little formal law. Where everyone knows everyone else intimately, the informal pressures of the community are sufficient to enforce the norms.

The Effects of Urbanization on the Folk Community In our time, however, rural culture is being influenced more and more by that of the urban, industrial world. The farmer typically produces surplus goods for a wider market, makes use of the money economy of urban society, and takes part in a larger political order by paying taxes, voting, and sending his children to intercommunity or consolidated schools.

The continued extension of commercial farming with an eye to profits, along with the introduction of machinery, has greatly influenced the social organization of primary communities. In those countries where agriculture has come to operate within the framework of a money and marketing economy, the self-sufficient farmstead, which still characterizes much of the world's agriculture, is disappearing. The introduction of commercialization and mechanization into agriculture has meant that the urban ways of life—level of living, secularization, and so forth—have infiltrated rural culture more and more.

Until rapid means of transportation and communication were introduced, with the consequent intrusion of urban culture into these rural and village areas, the small town and village communities were not very different from the farming regions around them. Contact for the most part was face-to-face. There was a strong sense of independence, on the one hand, and a kind of rural solidarity, on the other. There was a strong conservatism and

Belgian Information Service   Combine

In Africa, many folk communities are moving rapidly toward urbanism: contrast the ritual dance with the election broadcast in Ghana.

prejudice against new ideas and practices, except perhaps those bearing directly on economic techniques. The range of interaction was limited largely to the primary community. Contacts with the outside came through some reading of newspapers and through such institutions as the school, the political forum, and the church, although even these reflected the rural culture for the most part.

However, it was the towns in the farming areas which experienced the first breakdowns of primary-group organization. The initial impact was usually on their economic functions. The trend was from self-sufficiency to specialization, from a barter to a money economy, from independence to interdependence, with growing domination by the urban centers outside.

THE URBAN COMMUNITY

Urban communities differ from folk communities both in their structure and in their culture. The simplest summary of the differences between the two types of social organization is to say that they tend to be opposites: whereas the folk community is homogeneous, the urban is heterogeneous, and so on.

Structure and Functions of Urban Society Two features of any urban community are its size and the density of its population. There is, of course, no sharp dividing line for classification according to size or density of population. The Census Bureau somewhat arbitrarily says that a concentrated population of 2,500 or more is a city.

Ewing Galloway

In a folk society, the entire community may be a primary group: a kraal in Southern Rhodesia.

When a community becomes large enough that most of the residents are not able to know most of the others personally, some of the patterns of social relations typical of a folk society tend to disappear. One function of relatively large population size, then, is impersonality in interaction. A community as a whole cannot be primary when there are too many people in it for each to have personal knowledge of most of the others. In most rural communities in the United States, it is considered polite to speak to anyone you meet on the street. But if you tried to greet everyone you met as you walked across Times Square in New York City, you would find that you had set yourself an impossible task, and the people whom you addressed would be divided in their opinion as to whether you intended to fleece them of their money or were mentally unbalanced.

Neither can a sharp line be drawn between folk and urban communities simply on the basis of density of population. It is obvious, however, that many of the factors associated with urbanism are functions of the density of the population. While the average farm in the United States covers about 247 acres, the average density of cities of more than 100,000 is three families per acre. A farm family, then, occupies about 700 times as much land as a city family. Thus we see the necessity for farmers to be able to grow more food than they need before urbanization can take place. One characteristic of a city is that it has such a high density of population that it could not support

In an urban society, an entire isolated community may be a primary group: a village in Vermont.

itself by farming the land it occupies.

The city has a complex division of labor. Since, unlike mines or farms, cities are usually not places where raw materials are produced, the people living in cities depend entirely on noncity dwellers for these materials. City people thus must support themselves by manufacturing finished products from raw materials, marketing these products, or supplying services, which range from dry cleaning to the creation of symphony music. Such economic organization results from specialization for efficient production and service and leads to a more elaborate stratification system than is typical of folk communities.

Urban differentiation and stratification give rise to a great heterogene-ity in the population. The impersonality of urban life allows people with a different skin color or accent or religion to pass relatively unnoticed in a way that could never be possible in the primary organization of a folk community. In addition, the occupational specialities associated with the complex division of labor create differences in the population: variations in training, values, work hours, recreation patterns, and so on.

A final function of the size and heterogeneity of the population is the proliferation of secondary groups. Community-wide organizations to satisfy some of the needs for social contact have long been a part of urban life. Settlement houses, various youth groups, and other organizations aim to

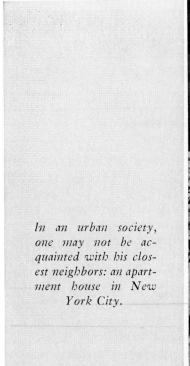

In an urban society, one may not be acquainted with his closest neighbors: an apartment house in New York City.

Black Star

provide socially healthful recreation and education for individuals who do not otherwise have these advantages. Some of their most effective work, moreover, is done at the neighborhood level. Civil Defense organizations and "drives" for the Red Cross and other organizations illustrate how a given crisis may serve to stimulate formal organizations and at least temporarily revive neighborliness in large cities. Sometimes out of these come primary-group relations which did not previously exist.

It should be remembered that in contemporary United States most of the people who live in rural places are in general part of an urban structure, not a folk one. They are closely linked to the city by the interdependence of roles in an urban society. The greater the impact of the metropolitan centers on their rural hinterlands, the less the visible difference between the rural and urban structures in an urban society. For instance, city populations used to be markedly younger than farm populations in the United States. By 1950, however, this characteristic had largely disappeared. Similarly, there is little difference between rural and urban areas in sex composition. Most structural differences seem to decrease as the rural community is linked more closely to the urban by improved transportation and communication. One structural difference remains: the urban population, as can be seen in

TABLE 31 · Education of the Population of the United States, 1950, by Urban and Rural Residence *

	PER CENT DISTRIBUTION		
Amount of Education: *Persons 25 Years or older*	*Urban*	*Rural-Nonfarm*	*Rural Farm*
No school completed	2.3	2.7	3.1
Grade school (1–8 years)	39.5	49.3	62.5
High school (9–12 years)	40.2	33.9	26.6
College (13–16 years)	15.2	10.9	6.3
Education not reported	2.7	3.2	1.5

* Adapted from Donald J. Bogue, "Urbanism in the United States, 1950," *American Journal of Sociology*, 1955, 60:471–486. Table from p. 482. The data summarized in the accompanying paragraph are from this article.

Table 31, has a considerably higher average educational attainment than the rural population. This rural-urban contrast continues because it is the rural people with high-school or college training who are most likely to migrate to the city.

Urban Culture We must not neglect the fact that the city also induces variability, inventiveness, and cultural change. Urban life may and does foster creativeness in basic as well as secondary situations, in personal life organization, and in social movements. Yet, on the whole, the larger the community, the more likely we are to find a sense of personal isolation, loss of intimacy with others, and similar marks of mass society. A central integrating set of values may be difficult to find. "Purchasability of services and things" tends to displace "personal relations as a basis of association." [7] The roles of the individual become so varied and so specialized that both competition and co-operation seldom involve the whole personality. One comes to feel himself but a combination of bits and pieces,

7 · See Louis Wirth, "Urbanism as a Way of Life," *American Journal of Sociology*, 1938, 44:17. This entire article is a classic statement of the social psychology of city life.

not an integrated participant in his society and its culture.

A superficial observer might imagine that modern cities are by all odds the most favorable places for social interaction. While it is true that city dwellers may talk superficially to many people, it has often been said that persons may feel more lonely in large cities than anywhere else. There is a vast difference between the incidental and temporary contiguity in urban mass society and the shared experience and interstimulation of members of a small community and its neighborhoods.

In rural and small-town life, the neighborhood continues to have a definite place. It is the area of borrowing and lending, of mutual aid, and of intimate gossip. In earlier periods it seldom had any very formal organizations. Yet urban influences affect both neighborhood and community life in rural and small-town areas. The rise of a secondary-group organization of society means the introduction of all sorts of formal associations having to do with agriculture, education, religion, and recreation where there were none before.

The city, especially as it grows larger, is characterized by the decline and even loss of neighborly interaction. A number of factors help account for the lessening of the importance of neighborhood contacts for the city-dweller. (1) There is a complex division of labor and an individualization of interest. (2) High residential mobility does not permit a sense of "settling down" in any one street or section of the city. (3) Easy availability of transit facilities for reaching work or friends reduces the need to seek contacts next door. (4) A wide variety of secondary groups outside the immediate area of one's residence provides outlets for one's interests.

Integration In spite of the dominance of secondary-group interests and of impersonal relations, many cities have community goals and common values in life. Edward L. Thorndike and Robert C. Angell have both made attempts to find factors leading to unity among such people who have different backgrounds and interests.[8]

A review of Angell's study of a sample of American cities will show a particular approach to this topic. For selected cities Angell collected sociological data on education, employment of women, ratio of native-born to foreign-born, recreation, and other items. He also set up certain indices of social integration based on such criteria as crime rates and existence of community welfare work. Angell tentatively

8 · See Edward L. Thorndike, *Your City* (New York: Harcourt, Brace & Co., 1939) and his *144 Smaller Cities* (New York: Harcourt, Brace & Co., 1940); Robert C. Angell, "The Social Integration of Selected American Cities," *American Journal of Sociology*, 1942, 47:575–592; and Angell, *Integration of American Society: A Study of Groups and Institutions* (New York: McGraw-Hill Book Co., 1941). See also Angell, "The Moral Integration of American Cities," *American Journal of Sociology*, 1951, 57, Part 2:1–140.

concluded that social integration in a city tends to be higher where (1) there is a long tradition of strong support of schools, libraries, and public recreation; (2) fewer mothers are gainfully employed; (3) there is a high proportion of native-white population; and (4) there is the least disparity among incomes by class groupings.

While Angell's findings are admittedly inconclusive, they suggest some ways of measuring the emergence of culture patterns of mass society. This is a vital matter in our present-day world, where the city has come more and more to dominate the entire culture.

Urban Decentralization Much has been written about the danger to our whole culture and society from the overwhelming dominance of the city, and there has been considerable talk about intentional decentralization. Some decentralization has already been effected. For example, electrical power permits the shifting of light machine industry into suburban and even rural areas. So too, improved facilities for travel have increased the growth of suburban centers around the larger cities, as one can see by contrasting the rapid rate of suburban population growth with the only gradual increase in city density shown in Table 32. However, these changes do not mean less urban domination, since by them the fundamental urban culture is actually extended.

Suburbanization The recent move toward what Fava has called "suburbanism as a way of life" presents an interesting sociological picture of people trying to cling to some of the values of rural living while participating in an

TABLE 32 · The Growth in City Living in America *

Year	Urban people (1000's)	Urban area (1000 acres)	Acres per person
1900	30,160	5,545	.184
1920	54,158	9,535	.176
1940	74,424	12,800	.172
1960	125,000	21,400	.171
1980	193,000	32,000	.164
2000	279,000	45,000	.160

Since 1900, people and land in cities have more than quadrupled and if present trends continue they will have doubled again by the year 2000. The small change in density reflects the continuing reach of metropolis into adjacent areas

* Data from Resources for the Future, Inc., *Resources in America's Future*, Baltimore: Johns Hopkins Press, 1963. These figures employ the 1950 U.S. Census definition of urban land for 1960 and for the projections. The general trends are not affected significantly by the change in definition.

urban social structure.[9] Suburbs are characterized by the availability of open space, which allows single-family dwellings and a relatively lower population density than cities. Structurally they are middle class and tend to contain proportionately more young married couples with children than do central cities. Culturally they emphasize neighboring and other primary values. Some of the pertinent problems of suburban living will be discussed in Chapter 18, but first, we shall see how physical space acquires social meanings through human use.

9 · A considerable research literature on the suburbs has grown up; see, for example, Sylvia Fleis Fava, "Suburbanism as a Way of Life," *American Sociological Review*, 1956, 21:34–37; Richard Dewey, "Peripheral Expansion in Milwaukee County," *American Journal of Sociology*, 1948, 54:118–25; Nathan L. Whetten, "Suburbanization as a Field for Sociological Research," *Rural Sociology*, 1951, 16:319–30; E. Gartly Jaco and Ivan Belknap, "Is a New Family Form Emerging in the Urban Fringe?" *American Sociological Review*, 1953, 18:551–57; and Wendell Bell, "Familism and Suburbanization: One Test of the Social Choice Hypothesis," *Rural Sociology*, 1956, 21:276–83.

INTERPRETATIVE SUMMARY

The folk community as a typology is characterized by small population, isolation, primary group contacts, and minimal division of labor. Some consequences of this structure are homogeneity of attitudes, interests, and even physical build of the population; minimal stratification; and control by informal sanctions. In contrast, the urban community contains many people within a small area, a situation leading to impersonal interactions and a complex division of labor and stratification system. Attitudes and interests are not city-wide, urban living frequently demanding individual creativity to a degree not necessary in a tight community, where a father or tribal chief maps out one's life. Sociologists have found a high degree of unity on basic issues among certain entire city populations, however, particularly when the populations were fairly homogeneous at the outset.

The last hundred and fifty years has seen a rapid growth in urban societies, societies in which the great majority of the population live in cities. Members of folk-type communities are moving to the larger cities; and the folk communities themselves, particularly those which have extensive contact with nearby cities, are adopting urban economic patterns and concomitant values and behavior.

While the United States still has a few areas which remain by choice virtual folk communities, most rural people in our country are part of an urban structure. City-reared people who move to the suburbs are spreading city culture still further.

REVIEW AND SUGGESTED READINGS

A • VOCABULARY

Cultural island	Folk society	Urbanism
Folk culture	Neolithic Revolution	Urbanization

B • QUESTIONS AND TOPICS FOR REVIEW

1. Consider the chances for a successful marriage between two Americans, one of definite farm background and the other of big city background. You should explore other variables that might influence the outcome, of course.
2. Discuss the probable validity of this statement: "I went to high school in a small town, but I'd pit its school system against that of any fancy suburb in the United States."
3. What is the most important typology you learned about in this chapter? Why?
4. If you live in a rural area or in a town with a large city nearby, discuss some patterns of city living that have emerged in your lifetime.
5. What are some frequent complaints about "big" universities? How relevant is each to the situation at your school? What are some of the things schools, and subgroups in the schools, intentionally do to offset the results of "bigness"?
6. In your area, do values seem integrated on an area-wide level, on the community level, or on some other basis?

C • SUGGESTIONS FOR FURTHER READING

Edmund de S. Brunner and W. C. Hallenbeck. *American Society: Urban and Rural Patterns*. New York: Harper & Brothers, 1955.

A textbook comparison of rural and urban communities. It covers a wide range of topics, including expansion of human relationships, kinds of communities, their function and structure, and community development and planning.

Noel P. Gist and Sylvia Fava. *Urban Society*, 5th ed. New York: Thomas Y. Crowell Company, 1964.

For years one of the standard books in the field, this edition introduces new discussions of leisure, migration, and the image of the city.

Paul K. Hatt and Albert J. Reiss, Jr., eds. Cities and Society: *The Revised Reader in Urban Sociology*. Glencoe, Ill.: The Free Press, 1957.

An excellent collection of essays and research reports on the structure, function, and culture of the city.

Lowry Nelson. *Rural Sociology*, 2nd ed. New York: American Book Company, 1955.

A general textbook in the field, especially good on social processes and institutions.

James A. Quinn. *Urban Sociology*. New York: American Book Company, 1955.

Deals with basic characteristics of the city and with its chief institutions.

Robert Redfield. *Folk Culture of Yucatan*. Chicago: University of Chicago Press, 1941.

A sociological classic, excellent in both theoretical framework and content.

Irwin T. Sanders. The Community: *An Introduction to a Social System*. New York: The Ronald Press Company, 1958.

An analysis of the social and cultural characteristics common to all communities regardless of size. Contains a section on the major institutions.

Max Weber. *The City*, translated and edited by Don Martindale and Gertrud Neuwirth. Glencoe, Ill.: The Free Press, 1958.

Essays on the evolution of cities and city life, using historical and cross-cultural data.

James West, *Plainville, U. S. A.* New York: Columbia University Press, 1945.

A carefully documented cultural and social-psychological study of a community in rural Missouri. See also Art Gallagher, Jr., *Plainville Fifteen Years Later*. New York and London: Columbia University Press, 1961.

CHAPTER 17

Human Ecology

When a traveler arrives by bus in the center of a large city, he often finds himself in an area containing pawnshops, all-night theaters, and cheap bars, hotels, and restaurants. Bus stations are usually located in the section of the city with relatively inexpensive services for transients. If the traveler wants to find the largest theater or department store in the city, he can assume with confidence that it will be only a few blocks away, near the center of the city. If he is on the way to visit a schoolteacher who lives in a single-family house, he can assume that his destination will be a considerable distance from the bus station: middle-class single-family dwellings are ordinarily built farther away from the central business district, near the periphery of the city. Our friend can make all these predictions because human activities are patterned spatially as well as in other ways.

Human ecology is that part of sociology which studies the spatial distribution of human groups and institutions. Geography is not the only factor determining spatial distribution of a population. The north side of town may not be topographically different from the south side, but if early settlers on the north side are or become wealthy and influential, certain other people will want to live near them and be associated with them, and property on the north side will become culturally desirable. Poor factory laborers, ethnic minorities, and other lower-status people will not be able to afford homes on this side of town. Nor will they have enough influence to keep dirty factories from being built in their south-side neighborhood. Being a resident of the south side will determine many things, from the quality of the public schools one's children will attend to the likelihood of being invited to join an exclusive club. The cultural character of the north and south sides will determine social space: residence within these geographic boundaries will be taken as a status symbol and will be a factor in defining social relations.

Ecologists are interested in the spatial distribution of any social phenomenon: what part of the community has the most suicides, where the areas of high and low economic status are located, where minorities live, whether people go to church in the neighborhood where they live, and so on. The ecologist regards spatial relations as an index of social relations. He is interested in the spatial structuring of human activities in order to learn about the social structure.

Ecologists, like other sociologists, are concerned with both structure and

265

process.[1] Ecological structure is represented by a map showing the distribution of some social activity, such as gambling or fertility or wholesale trade. Ecological processes are changes in the ecological structure, such as the expansion of the area devoted to retail trade or the invasion of a Polish-American neighborhood by Puerto Ricans.

We shall deal first with the ecology of the rural or primary community, which precedes the urban community historically and is simpler.

RURAL ECOLOGY

Because rural areas emphasize primary rather than secondary group relations and because they have fewer people and more homogeneous groups, the ecology of the rural community is affected by fewer factors, and its analysis is a less complex task. Nevertheless, primary communities are not identical. Indeed, they are alike only insofar as the forms of association between their people and groups are of the face-to-face type. The institutions and organizations found in primary communities vary widely in their ecological setting and culture.

Ecology and Land Settlement The family has traditionally been the basic social unit in all agricultural societies, but the spatial distribution of farm families has varied greatly. In some regions farm families are dispersed throughout the entire area. In others

1 · In a single chapter we can do no more than summarize the major findings of human ecology. For more detailed treatments of the field, see Amos H. Hawley, *Human Ecology: A Theory of Community Structure* (New York: The Ronald Press Company, 1950); and James A. Quinn, *Human Ecology* (Englewood Cliffs, N.J.: Prentice-Hall, Inc., 1950).

they live in a hamlet or village and work the adjoining land. Probably most of the world's farmers follow the latter pattern. While the concentrated village is the principal dwelling place of farmers in Europe and the Orient, exceptions are found in Great Britain, France, Germany, the Low Countries, the northern part of Scandinavia, and sporadically in southern Europe. Though the village is the chief pattern in India and China, there are variations. In Latin America and Africa, rural settlements are usually of the village type.

The United States illustrates how the reasons for the variations are historical. The nucleated or clustered-village type was brought to the colonies from England and the Continent. But local differences began to evolve as settlers moved into the interior. Individuals and single families crossed the Alleghenies and squatted on new lands, their claims later to be validated by legal action. In the Southern colonies the plantation system emerged out of commercial agriculture supported by slave labor.

Later, certain federal laws influenced the form of land settlement. In 1785 the rectangular survey was established, and public lands were divided first into townships of 36 square miles each. These were then subdivided into sections of 640 acres and quarter sections of 160 acres. In 1841 the requirement was made that, to obtain title to such land, the individual had to live on it. Still later the Homestead Act (1862) provided for settlement and payment for public lands at a low cost per acre.

The rectangular division of land made for a gridiron form of farms and fostered the separation of farmsteads from each other by considerable distances. As a matter of fact, much of the best agricultural land of the United States was settled under this pattern. It is a neat illustration of how a culture trait, in this case law, may influence the ecology of a community. However, there are some variations in the types of farm settlement.

The Primary Neighborhood and Community Since it rests on face-to-face relationships, the neighborhood is probably more primary than any other group except the family. The characteristic feature is that families live near one another and that they are bound together by intimate and personal relationships. The greater the number of bonds, the more distinctive the neighborhood. Frequently neighborhoods are built around a single organization, such as a country school or a mill. In contrast, the community is formed around common interests and the means of satisfying most human needs or interests.

Historically, neighborhoods have been basic social groups in rural America. In pre-industrial times the whole social life of open-country groups centered there. Most manufacturing was done at home, and the economic system was largely one of the direct exchange of goods and services. In these cases the neighborhood and the community were coterminous. Today many neighborhoods have disappeared as wider ranges of interaction have developed. They are, of course, by no means extinct. The traditional rural neighborhood is changing its function, however, as the bonds of mere locality are being replaced by urban special-interest groups which have reached out to serve rural areas. Wherever good

highways and proximity to trading centers permit, urban services, such as commercial baking, laundering, dry cleaning, and the like, are affecting the patterns of both family and neighborhood life.

To distinguish primary and rural communities from urban communities is not always easy. For many decades the United States census classified all incorporated places of over 2,500 residents as urban. All others were called rural. For the sociologist interested in the primary-group ways of life, this is an inadequate division between rural and urban communities. Some help was provided when, in 1930, the Bureau of the Census began designating localities under 2,500 population as rural-non-farm or rural-farm residency. This at least gave a more accurate figure for those who actually engage in farming. In 1960 the rural-farm people made up 12 percent of the country's total population. About one-fifth were reported as rural-nonfarm residents. Many of the latter are closely associated with agriculture, since they live in small communities which provide various services to farm families, and their ways of life have much in common with those of the farmer.

American primary communities, as they relate to agriculture, may be divided into four kinds: the open-country, the village or town-centered, the agricultural village, and the plantation.[2]

2 · Writers on rural sociology differ as to just how to classify rural communities. But this classification, suggested by Allen D. Edwards, will serve our purposes. His inclusion of the plantation—often neglected by rural sociologists—is a helpful addition. See his "Ecological Patterns of American Rural Communities," *Rural Sociology*, 1947, 12:150–161.

The Open-country Community Ordinarily we think of a community as composed of more or less definite institutions and organizations located within some relatively defined space. Yet there are some communities where the stores, garages, schools, and churches are dispersed rather widely. The people who live in such an area and trade in these stores or send their children to the schools or attend the churches do, however, regard themselves as members of a community. It might be debated, of course, whether these should not be thought of as extended neighborhoods rather than as genuine communities. The point is that, though widely diffused, these communities—if we may call them such —have names. They are thought of by the inhabitants as distinct communities, within which are to be found neighborhoods of the traditional type. Such communities are common in the South and in some parts of the Great Plains, and are found sporadically elsewhere.

Landaff, New Hampshire, for example, is largely of this type. Landaff has a church, a garage, a school, and some scattered service agencies, but it has no nucleus, no fixed center. Yet there is no doubt that, in the thinking of its residents, Landaff is a community and not just a neighborhood.[3] Like Landaff, most communities of this kind consist of farmsteads dispersed throughout the area, with various service agencies located at more or less convenient points.

However, unless they are bound

3 · See Kenneth MacLeish and Kimball Young, "Culture of a Contemporary Rural Community: Landaff, New Hampshire," *Rural Life Studies*, No. 3, Bureau of Agricultural Economics (Washington, D.C.: Department of Agriculture, 1942).

together by some emotional tie, such as a common religion or a common ethnicity, most of the open-country communities have a limited sense of unity and less sense of belonging together than do many primary communities. In short, identification with the community is not very strong. Furthermore, most of these open-country communities are far from self-sufficient. As good roads have been built, people in these places go to larger localities to satisfy most of their economic and recreational needs.

There are scattered examples of open-country communities which are closely integrated by religious, kinship, linguistic, and ethnic subcultures. Such are the Amish in Lancaster County, Pennsylvania, or the Amana of Iowa. Somewhat similar are certain other pietistic denominations, such as the Mennonites. But for the most part, such integrating factors are not present in the open-country communities of the United States.

Town-country Communities Most rural inhabitants in the United States tend to be oriented toward a village or town. But the degree of centralization and the ratio of open-country to actul village or town members are highly variable. Where the gridiron land survey made for dispersal of farmsteads on rather widely scattered farms, the village may have grown up at an important railroad stop or at the junction of two important lines of traffic, rail or highway. The villagers may be both farmers and others occupied with giving services connected with the rural economy.

Everywhere the earlier relations of farm families to village or town centers have undergone many changes.

The coming of the automobile and hard-surfaced roads made it possible to buy goods and services at longer distances from the farm than formerly. So, too, the development of mail-order buying enabled farm families to get things which might not be easily available nearby.

Yet the school, the church, the grocery store, and the garage continue to provide important services within easy reach. Some believe that in time the shift to larger centers will eliminate the need for these smaller places near the farmstead. While the relative importance of the hamlet and small village is declining, these centers will probably long continue to provide many goods and services for the farm family.

Agricultural Villages The settlement of farmers into more or less compact villages is not as usual in most of the United States as it is in so much of the world elsewhere. Yet the main features of the agricultural village deserve brief comment. The best-known instances of agricultural villages in the United States are those established by the Mormons when they settled in the Great Basin—western Utah, southern Idaho, and parts of Nevada.

The basic pattern was developed by Joseph Smith and first used in Nauvoo, Illinois. A community was arranged on the gridiron pattern, with streets 8 rods wide at right angles and square blocks of 10 acres each, divided into half-acre lots for single dwellings. The plan was later applied when Salt Lake City was laid out by Smith's successor, Brigham Young. And as other communities were established up and down the central valleys of Utah, the same general pattern was followed,

though the street widths and size of blocks were often modified.

The necessity for protection against hostile Indians and the co-operative effort to obtain water for the farms by irrigation were not the determining factors, for the farmers lived in the village or town and the farm properties which they worked were adjacent to it. Rather, this was an interesting example of deliberate community planning. Between 1847 and 1877 more than 360 such communities were established, reaching from southern Idaho through Utah into Arizona.

In keeping with the overall program for these communities, the Mormon Church set up a colonization plan to make sure that in each new community sufficient carpenters, blacksmiths, and other specialized workers would be available, as well as enough farmers. Since the entire orientation of these activities was to make the Mormons economically self-sufficient and independent of the "gentile" (non-Mormon) world outside, many communities were *instructed* to develop various industries in addition to their agriculture.[4] Iron works were built in some places, woolen mills in others, salt plants in still others—usually where the necessary raw materials were at hand. These local industries were to supplement the home manufacturing which—at least ideally—was as much a part of family life as farming itself. Actually, the Mormon communities were planned to be more than strictly agricultural villages. They were to be not only the centers of farming and local industry but the seats of all major religious,

4 · For a definitive study of this whole program, see Leonard J. Arrington, *Great Basin Kingdom: An Economic History of the Latter-Day Saints, 1830–1900* (Cambridge: Harvard University Press, 1958).

civic, and other noneconomic community affairs.

Another nucleated community
widely distributed throughout the
world is the "line village." This type is
common in southern Louisiana, where
French influence has remained great.
Among the rivers where frontage is
particularly valuable, houses occupy
small areas near the river, with the accompanying farmlands extending back
in narrow strips.

It is worth noting that there have
been many attempts to establish agricultural villages in the course of American history. Most of them were born
of the utopian socialistic or co-operative
movements of the nineteenth century.
Few remain.

Certainly so far as the Mormon
villages are concerned, they are marked
by a high degree of community solidarity and integration. Here it is not
farming but religious and other elements in the culture which furnish the
basis for a strong sense of belonging.
Of the socialistic or co-operative settlements in this country, it is worth
noting that most of them failed because those who took part in them
lacked or lost the moral and religious
zeal that inspired the founders and
leaders.[5]

The Plantation As a system of agricultural production, the plantation is
widespread. It is found in parts of
Latin America—as in sugarcane production in Cuba and in coffee-growing
parts of Brazil—and in the production
of rubber in Malaya and Africa. Allen D. Edwards defines a plantation as
a "form of social organization in which
labor, under unified direction and control, is engaged in the production of an
agricultural staple which is usually sold
on a world market."[6]

The plantation pattern was introduced into the United States from the
West Indies. Before the Civil War,
cotton and tobacco cultivation in the
South was largely organized under this
system. The center of the large hold-
ings consisted of the master's house,
houses for his supervisors, outbuild-
ings, and huts for slaves. And the
whole economy more or less revolved
around this nucleus. Even at this late
date, many of the earlier managerial
features remain. Sometimes the plantation is organized under the sharecrop-
per system. In other cases the work is
done by hired laborers.

In the South, smaller plantations
often operate as parts of a larger plantation community. But whether large
or small, the plantation is still the focus
and center of life for many white and
colored people in the South. Moreover, the influence often reaches beyond the plantation itself. Woofter
says, "Plantation customs and ideology
set the pattern for relationships in small
farm units. . . . Large planters persistently emerge as the political and
economic leaders of the cotton areas
. . . and the plantation stands out as
the basis for a hereditary oligarchy in
southern community life."[7]

Modifications of the plantation
system are found in some of the large-
scale corporation farms of California

5 · See Arthur E. Bestor, *Backwoods Utopias: the Sectarian and Owenite Phases of Communitarian Socialism in America, 1663–1829* (Philadelphia: University of Pennsylvania Press, 1950).

6 · Edwards, "Ecological Patterns," p. 158.

7 · T. J. Woofter, "Landlord and Tenant on the Cotton Plantation," *Research Monograph*, 1936, Vol. 5 (Washington, D.C.: Works Progress Administration, Division of Social Research).

and elsewhere. These are what Carey McWilliams has called "factories in the fields." The vast vegetable acreage of the Imperial Valley is owned largely by corporations. The farms are operated by managers and supervisors, who hire laborers to do the work. The aim is high profit, and farming is made into as efficient a business system as possible. Certainly the primary-group organization tends to disappear under such circumstances, except insofar as it continues in the noneconomic aspects of the lives of workers and managers. So too, the collective farms of the Soviet Union are adaptations of the plantation system.

URBAN ECOLOGICAL STRUCTURE

Before discussing specific ecological processes in urban life, let us see (1) the ways in which sites for cities are chosen and developed and (2) the usefulness of census tracts in the study of ecology.

The Location of Cities Cities tend to grow up on trade routes, and trade tends to follow the topography of least resistance. Men float their goods down streams to remote markets. Land routes along valleys, over low passes in mountains, by way of a chain of oases in a desert—all represent man's efforts to overcome nature's obstacles with the least expenditure of energy and time. Wherever there is a break in this flow, cities are likely to arise: where the sea trade must be transferred to river travel, or where there is a break in land travel because of topography, political barriers, or other factors. Paris, France, grew up where trade routes north and south met the Seine River. As C. H.

Cooley phrased it, "Population and wealth tend to gather wherever there is a break in transportation." Usually the larger the tributary or supporting area, the larger the central city. But factors of topography, population density, and political and economic organization also influence the pattern of location and growth.

If we examine a large map of any city, we note at once how its structure and growth are first of all dependent on the nature of the site itself. Richard M. Hurd remarks:

The first step in studying the ground plan of cities is to note the topographical faults which normally control the shape of cities, by interfering with their free growth in all directions from their points of origin. These are of two kinds: water surfaces, such as harbors, lakes, rivers, creeks, and swamps, or sharp variations from the normal city level, such as steep hills, deep hollows, and ravines.[8]

Where the land is flat, with no marshes or interfering contours, a city will tend to grow outward from the original center unless man-made factors, such as highways, defense walls, and railroad trackage, interfere. Topography gives the most obvious structure to a city. The towns and cities located on waterways must follow the lines of growth laid down by the water barriers. In hill-and-valley topography, the valley tends to be the seat of easiest communication and of industrial and commercial locations, while residential sections are found on higher ground. If the hills are too steep, travel between homes and work is difficult, so that even residential growth tends at the outset to follow the line of

8 · Richard M. Hurd, *Principles of City Land Values*, 4th ed. (New York: Real Estate Record and Guide, 1924), p. 33. By permission.

Aerial view of a planned community: a housing development in Los Angeles.

least resistance. Hurd summarizes the major influences of topography: "Level land attracts business, moderate elevations attract residences, land below the normal level attracts transportation lines, and filled-in land is generally used for warehousing, manufacturing, and cheap tenements." [9] Of course, the longer man has been settled in a locality, the less the influence of the natural topography becomes and the more important the man-made "cultural landscape." Man levels or cuts through hills, drains and fills swamps, builds dikes, dredges river mouths and harbors, constructs canals, and otherwise alters the natural landscape.

The site of a city soon develops a

9 · *Ibid.*, p. 36. By permission. However, in Chicago, filled-in land along Lake Michigan has been used for high-rent residences, parks, and schools.

structure or form, with the layout of streets playing the determining part. Unless there is a definite plan, when a city is founded the streets are laid out in conformity with natural topography, and the best available land is taken for retail stores and residences. The ground plan is thus settled, more or less, once and for all. Thenceforth streets tend to become obstructions to further development. Cities with narrow or winding streets, like Boston, Massachusetts, or cities with many diagonal streets, like Washington, D.C., or Madison, Wisconsin, produce unusually serious traffic problems.

Unless modified by plan or unusual topography, cities tend to develop in either axial or radial fashion. Where the streets are laid out with regularity, in squares or rectangles, the city's growth is usually restricted to the direction determined by two main intersecting streets or thoroughfares. There are some advantages and some disadvantages in the rectangular form. It allows the plotting of about equal-size blocks, makes easy the division of the city into administrative districts, and permits more adequate police or military control. The disadvantage of rectangular blocks is that there are no main thoroughfares to facilitate circulation between the center and the periphery, although within the center itself movement may not be difficult.

The radial pattern arises when there is a natural center at the end of a number of converging thoroughfares. As the city grows, it tends to follow these major traffic lanes, producing star-shaped cities like Tokyo, Nuremberg, and the older sections of London. This is perhaps the most efficient form of development.

Sometimes we find a combination of rectangular and radial patterns. Often there were originally a number of highways leading to the village or town, and as the city grew it was laid out in regular rectangular form superimposed on this system of highways. Washington, D.C., was deliberately planned to combine the radial with the rectangular scheme.

In Europe, some streets were developed around certain sections of cities as walls were torn down, moats filled in, or parks cut up. In Paris there are at least four sets of circular streets which arose as old walls were torn down and new ones were built farther away, only to be razed and themselves turned into streets. The beautiful Ringstrasse in Vienna was cut out of a series of public parks which had replaced older fortifications.

While the streets provide the basic ground structure of a city, railroad lines also contribute to it. In Chicago, for example, rail lines have tended to break up and isolate certain districts from others, though for the most part the lines have followed either the lake shore or the Chicago River and its branches. Wholesale trade areas and, more particularly, industrial sites call for much trackage, and in these areas slums or disintegrated neighborhoods are likely to develop. Often railroad tracks located on the outskirts of a city later become a barrier to further growth.

Social Area Analysis Several sociologists have employed a new method for the analysis of urban social structure by spatial units. Social area analysis, as the method is called, is a technique for the study of social and economic data in the local sub-areas of a city through the use of data collected by the United States Census Bureau on census tracts within the city.[10]

Census tracts are combined into neighborhoods on the basis of their similarity in three factors: social rank,

10 · See Eshref Shevky and Marilyn Williams, *The Social Areas of Los Angeles: Analysis and Typology* (Berkeley and Los Angeles: University of California Press, 1949); Eshref Shevky and Wendell Bell, *Social Area Analysis: Theory, Illustrative Application and Computational Procedures* (Stanford: Stanford University Press, 1955). See also Maurice D. Van Arsdol, Jr., Santo F. Camilleri, and Calvin F. Schmid, "The Generality of Urban Social Area Indexes," *American Sociological Review*, 1958, 23:277–284. A recent criticism of the method can be found in Van Arsdol, Camilleri, and Schmid, "An Investigation of the Utility of Urban Typology," *Pacific Sociological Review*, 1961, 4:26–32. For a reply, see Wendell Bell and Scott Greer, "Social Area Analysis and Its Critics," *Pacific Sociological Review*, 1962, 5:3–9. A cross-cultural application of the method has been made by Dennis C. McElrath, "The Social Areas of Rome," *American Sociological Review*, 1962, 27:376–391.

urbanization, and segregation (or, as Bell prefers to call them, economic status, family status, and ethnic status). The social rank of a neighborhood is computed on the basis of two measures: 1. the proportion of people in white-collar jobs and 2. the proportion of the population over 25 years of age with more than eight years of schooling. Social rank therefore is based on two major stratification variables: occupation and education. Three measures are used in calculating the index of urbanization: 1. fertility, 2. the proportion of adult females in the labor force, and 3. the proportion of dwelling units which are single-family houses. Segregation is measured by the percentage of the population which is nonwhite or foreign-born from countries of eastern and southern Europe.

Social area analysis has enabled the sociologist readily to relate divorce rates, suicides, voting behavior, church attendance, or any other factor for an area to the basic structural variables of economic, family, and ethnic statuses in that area.

URBAN ECOLOGICAL PROCESSES

In this section we shall examine the principal ecological processes, with particular reference to American cities.

Concentration of People The massing of people into a limited area is a distinctive feature of the urban community. While for statistical purposes the United States Bureau of the Census counts as urban all incorporated places of more than 2,500,[11] with regard to

ecology and culture cities must be examined in the light of both varying size and function.

We have noted that from the time of our first census in 1790 to the present, our urban population has become increasingly dominant. Figure 11 gives a graphic presentation of this shift in 170 years of the country's history. Other countries have also witnessed a rapid, though less phenomenal, growth in cities since 1800.

The geographical distribution of cities over the world reflects various developments in commerce, industry, transportation, government, religion, and agriculture. Those cities most fortunately located have flourished and today stand as large metropolitan centers more or less dominating a surrounding hinterland area. For the most part, such growth has been a concomitant of industrialization. The percentages of population which fall into the urban category vary widely, from Great Britain, with 80 percent, West Germany, 72 percent, and the United States, 64 percent, to countries showing little urbanization, such as Pakistan, with 11, and Thailand, with 10 percent.[12]

inhabitants or more incorporated as cities, boroughs, and villages; (b) incorporated towns of 2500 inhabitants or more except in New England, New York, and Wisconsin, where 'towns' are simply minor civil divisions of counties; (c) the densely settled urban fringe, including both incorporated and unincorporated areas, around cities of 50,000 or more; and (d) unincorporated places of 2500 inhabitants or more outside any urban fringe. The remaining population is classified as rural." From *U.S. Census of Population: 1950.* Vol. II, *Characteristics of the Population,* p. vi, Part 1, U.S. Summary, Chapter B (Washington, D.C.: U.S. Government Printing Office, 1952).

12 · Percentages from Jack P. Gibbs and Kingsley Davis, "Conventional Versus Metropolitan Data in the International Study of Urbanization," *American Sociological Review,* 1958, 23:504–514. For other discussions

11 · Under a new definition, adopted for the 1950 census, "the urban population comprises all persons living in (a) places of 2500

FIGURE 11 · Increasing Dominance of Urban Population in the United States *

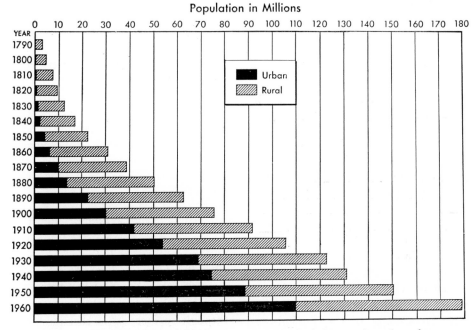

Population in Millions

* Data from various census reports. "Rural" includes both farm and rural nonfarm populations.

In the United States the 1950 census listed 48 urbanized areas of more than 250,000 population. Twenty-three are found in 11 of the Northeastern and East-North-Central states. These 11 states have more than five times as many large cities in proportion to their land areas as does the rest of the nation. A number of cities of between 100,000 and 500,000 population are found in the industrialized South, from North Carolina to Alabama. Other important concentrations are found in the Midwest, in Texas, and along the Pacific Coast. In contrast, seven states of the Great Plains and intermountain sections and the three northern New England states have no urbanized areas of more than 100,000 population.

More than one-third of our 48 large industrial-commercial cities are located on the seacoasts or the Great Lakes, a fact indicative of the importance of accessibility of water transportation to the development of cities. With the completion of the St. Lawrence Seaway, the Great Lakes industrial cities should expand further.

Concentration is measured by density per square mile. When individuals are scattered over a wide area, there is less probability of direct contact. Yet mere massing does not lead to intimate social relations, as every student of urban life knows. Urban life represents not only a certain massing of people but a different kind of interaction. As Louis Wirth put it, "The

of this topic, see Jack P. Gibbs and Leo F. Schnore, "Metropolitan Growth: An International Study," *American Journal of Sociology*, 1960, 66:160–170; and Philip M. Hauser, ed., "World Urbanism," *American Journal of Sociology*, 1955, 60:427–503 (a special issue devoted to various aspects of urbanization).

city is not merely the point at which great numbers are concentrated into limited space, but it is also a complex of human beings exhibiting the most extraordinary heterogeneity in almost every characteristic in which human beings can differ from one another." [13]

Cities have a small share of persons under 20 years of age; this is probably partly because of the tendency of persons with children to move to the suburbs. There are slightly more women than men in urban centers, but the differential is very small. About 10 percent of the urban population in the United States is nonwhite. Since there is discrimination against Negroes in many suburban areas and small towns, Negroes are over-represented on farms and in central cities and under-represented in rural nonfarm areas. Most of the foreign-born population live in cities. The proportion of the population who are married is about the same in cities as elsewhere, but a higher proportion of the farm population are single, while a higher proportion of the urbanites are widowed or divorced. Urban people have more formal education than rural, and twice as high a proportion of urban females as rural are found in the labor force. [14]

Centralization of Services The concentration of services in strategic places is an important ecological aspect of urban life. These services satisfy such common interests as work, education, government, religion, and recreation. Centralization is directly related to transportation and communication: service centers are located where these intersect. The focal point of most cities, or of any community for that matter, is the retail shopping center. Many additional services are provided in this central area. Large cities in particular may provide centralized services for a wide hinterland. Organizational headquarters for a region, governmental offices for a state or nation, or other specialized functions may be located in a particular city.

Centralization may occur first by the sheer addition of activities in a common location, as when a rural trade center at a crossroads becomes, gradually, the locus of schools, churches, post office, garage, and bowling alley. Centralization may also take place through an increase in the number of individuals who find gratification of some interest at the same location. The foci of centralization are in constant competition for patronage, and changes in either the services or transportation facilities may upset any working balance that may have been attained.

People come to think of distance not in miles but in time required for movement. As concentrations persist along with population mobility, a kind of territorial specialization of activities follows. An urban community becomes studded with centers of varying sizes and degrees of specialization. These in turn act as magnets to attract the appropriate age, sex, economic, and class groupings. Specialization occurs in time as well as in space, as when an ice-skating rink is converted to a swimming pool or meeting hall during the summer. More frequently a specialized business might find it worth its while to remain open only during certain

13 · Louis Wirth, "The Urban Society and Civilization," in *Eleven Twenty-six: A Decade of Social Science Research* (Chicago: University of Chicago Press, 1940), p. 57.

14 · Donald J. Bogue, "Urbanism in the United States, 1950," *American Journal of Sociology*, 1955, 60:471–486.

months: note the proliferation of summertime custard and hamburger stands in the United States.

Decentralization There is, of course, a point beyond which concentration and centralization cannot go. Competition for space in the central section of a city leads to such high land values that further expansion of business or other services becomes impractical. And while the construction of more and more skyscrapers keeps adding space for offices, there are physical limits to such facilities. The most obvious fact is that the higher the building, the more the space that must be used for elevators and other service fixtures and the less for commercial purposes. Then too, traffic congestion reduces the gains which come from concentration of goods and services. Loss in time and patience is, in the end, not offset by advantages of shopping or doing business in such centers. As a result, an opposite process of decentralization may set in.

One of the first and most common forms of decentralization is the development of large retail stores, gas stations, and garages in or near residential areas. Large cities everywhere are characterized by such subcenters, which duplicate in many ways the structure and function of the original centralized area of the city. But there are other forms of decentralization. Industries may move out of a central position to the fringe of a city, or new industries may be set up on the urban periphery and thus foster a new subcenter.

Suburbs may grow up on the periphery of an expanding city as more desirable locations for families. Or as transportation lines are built nearby, smaller communities may become suburbs or satellite communities of a larger community. (See Figure 12, which shows this situation for Chicago.) Sometimes these outlying communities become a part of the larger municipality. Sometimes they continue for a long time as independent political units.

Segregation Almost every large American city has not only slums and wealthy suburbs but settlements of minority groups. These may carry such descriptive names as Little Italy, Little Harlem, or Chinatown. Areas given over to vice or occupied by transient laborers, like Chicago's Hobohemia, also have unique features. Such separated segments of the total ecological structure have been called "natural areas," to indicate that they are the outcome of competition, conflict, co-operation, and group differentiation and accommodation.[15] Similar variations are to be found in all great cities but may represent quite different culture groups: occupational, caste or class, religious bodies, or others.

Segregation is never complete as to culture group or occupation. There is usually a mixture of peoples, especially around the fringes of the area. Even where Negroes are an overwhelming majority, one finds a few scattered white families. In his study of what he termed "polyethnic" areas, Paul K. Hatt found Jews, white Christians, Chinese, Filipinos, Japanese, and Negroes living in close proximity.[16] In

15 · The term "natural area" has been variously used, but we have tried to limit it to a more specific meaning. See Paul K. Hatt, "The Concept of Natural Area," *American Sociological Review*, 1946, 11:423–427; Hawley, *Human Ecology*, Chapter 6; and Quinn, *Human Ecology*, Chapters 12 and 18.

16 · Paul K. Hatt, "Spatial Patterns in a Polyethnic Area," *American Sociological Review*, 1945, 10:352–356.

FIGURE 12 · Chicago Metropolitan Area, Showing Location of Outlying Communities along Railroad Lines *

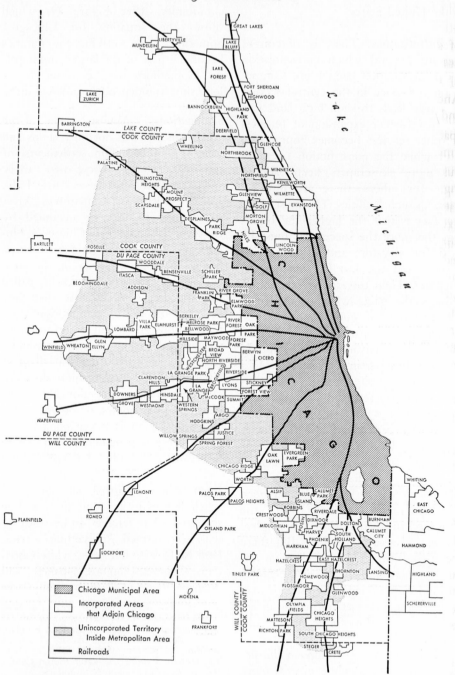

* From *Chicago Daily Tribune*, May 17, 1948. By permission.

some cities where many immigrants of like nationality reside, however, the areas tend to be more nearly homogeneous. Sometimes, as in New York City's Harlem, there is something akin to a self-contained community, with its own ecological structure along class and occupational lines.

The slum represents one extreme, the wealthy residential area the other extreme of an urban bipolarity. In the slum we find, as a rule, greater homogeneity of income than in the areas inhabited by the well-to-do. Yet in human activities the slum is often quite varied. Here are found all kinds of people who are compelled to live on a minimum income. The slum may be the hiding place for many practices which are forbidden by the mores but which satisfy the needs of persons who reside elsewhere.

This zone of slums may encircle the heart of the city. Interspersed throughout the zone are often light manufacturing and business concerns, which invade the area because of cheaper rents and the hope of an expanding central zone. There are high ratios of poverty, delinquency, and other indices of social disorganization, as well as many families of recent foreign extraction, high birth and death rates, and a high population density.

Between the upper economic and social classes and the slum and immigrant or Negro area there may be other examples of at least partial segregation. These are probably determined largely by economic factors. Workingmen's families tend to cluster in neighborhoods according to income level, occupational interests, and other cultural factors. Segregation by class can be just as real as segregation by race.

Assimilation and Segregation The processes of merging two or more deviant cultures may be helped or hindered by segregation. In a way, the immigrant area serves as a cultural island for the newcomers. It gives them a certain sense of security and so helps introduce them to the new culture. The effects of spatial segregation and retention of immigrant heritages may be characterized as follows: (1) Continuity with the old culture is maintained. (2) The immigrant sees the new country and its culture through the eyes of his own culture, especially as reflected in the ideas and attitudes of relatives and friends already settled there. Naturally, the newcomer accepts the definition of the American situation offered him by his fellow countrymen already here. (3) This continuity of the old and interpretation of the new through his fellow countrymen softens the severity of the change and profoundly influences the process of assimilation itself. (4) However, it is only as the immigrant is introduced into more and more of the features of American culture, and especially as his children come into contact with the school, with agencies of recreation, with American family life, and with other patterns, that the effects of the earlier culture wear off and assimilation really gets underway.

Of course, the reactions of the established population to the immigrant are often those of avoidance and prejudice. Fear of economic competition and misunderstanding of different culture patterns were common during the period when large numbers of immigrants were coming to the United States. But in time came various accommodations which were steps to assimilation.

The rates of assimilation have differed. Oriental immigrants for the most part have remained segregated, and their relations with the whites continue to be of an accommodative character. On the other hand, European immigrants, and especially their children and grandchildren, have gradually broken through the barriers of segregation to become assimilated. Public education, improvement in economic status, intermarriage, and moving out of the immigrant area itself have been most important factors in facilitating the process.

Invasion and Succession Population distributions seldom remain fixed: in a highly dynamic society, invasion and succession come into play. The invasion by one group of an area occupied by another leads to segregation and finally to displacement or succession by the intruding group. In some cases lower economic classes invade an area being abandoned by the well-to-do. Sometimes the reverse is true, as when apartment houses spring up in neighborhoods which have long been occupied by families of low incomes but which afford easy access to work or have other attractive features. Good illustrations of the latter are found along the East River in mid-Manhattan or in the "near-north side" in Chicago.

Succession tends to be marked by rather sharp changes in population types. Not infrequently in American cities there has been a long series of intrusions and displacements. The process is accompanied by continuous competition between groups.

Migration Population movement is closely related to the ecological processes just described. Mobility of this type refers to the actual movement in space of persons, not to social mobility, which has to do with changes in social status. Spatial movement is of three sorts: (1) the migration of people to a city, or away from it, to take up residence; (2) changes in residence within the community; and (3) the daily movement of people within the community.

The cityward migration of population is evident throughout recent history. As noted earlier in this chapter, the proportion of the population living in cities increased rapidly up to 1930. During the 1930–1940 decade, the urban increase was at a lower rate than the rural. Migration from farms to cities slowed down. In fact, in 1932, during the depression, there were actually more people moving to farms than from farms. But this was a temporary thing, and during World War II there was a strong cityward movement. At the end of the war there was a slight farmward mobility, chiefly by returning war veterans.

Residential movement follows the spatial expansion of the city toward its periphery. As one would expect, the rate of residential change is higher in hotel and rooming-house areas than in tenement sections, and higher in the latter than in districts farther out, where people own their own homes. There is a definite inverse relationship between home ownership and residential mobility. Among the many implications of high residential movement are lack of participation in community organizations, impersonal nature of human contacts, and high degree of occupational specialization, characteristics of the secondary-group organization of urban society.

The erection of skyscrapers increases congestion in movement by adding greatly to the number of persons and goods that must be moved into or out of an area and within the area itself. Some of the most striking facts about urban traffic congestion are these: (1) Between 1922 and 1944 there was an actual decline in the total passenger-carrying capacity of public utility equipment in the United States. It rose somewhat sharply in 1945 but decreased steadily through 1955. When we consider kinds of transit equipment, there are notable changes and variations. Thus from 1935 to 1940, surface railway cars declined from 40,050 to 5,300 units, while subway and elevated cars decreased from 10,416 to 9,232. In contrast, trolley coaches increased from 578 to 6,157 and motor buses from 23,800 to 52,400. (2) With these changes has come a decrease in the use of public urban transit facilities. From 1924 through 1955, this was about one-fifth. For suburban and related areas the drop has been greater, about one-half for the same period. (3) However, the larger the city, the higher the proportion of the total population that use various means of public transportation. This is graphically shown in Figure 13.

In addition to public transportation, privately owned automobiles carry thousands of people over our city streets. Every major city of the United States has been harassed by the problem of mounting congestion from such traffic. There have been many schemes for building multiple-deck expressways into and through the heart of our cities, some of which work, some of which are impractical. But even if all urban workers possessed and were to use their own cars on fast highways, they would have to find places to park them before they could "function at the point to which they . . . transported themselves." Modern elevator or ramp garages have limited possibilities. "Crediting each vehicle with the average loading in city traffic of 1.75 persons" and assuming that a modern office building allows an average of 150 square feet of floor space per worker, estimates show that it would take practically as much floor

FIGURE 13 · Ratio of Daily Transit Rides to Urban Population for 1956 *

POPULATION OF CITIES-1956	U. S. CENSUS	RATIO OF TRANSIT RIDES TO POPULATION
25,000 – 50,000	8,848,000	13%
50,000 – 100,000	8,931,000	30%
100,000 – 250,000	9,479,000	35%
250,000 – 500,000	8,242,000	59%
500,000 – Over	26,591,000	76%
TOTAL	62,091,000	

* Data from American Transit Association. By permission.

FIGURE 14·A Hypothetical Pattern of Urban Zones *

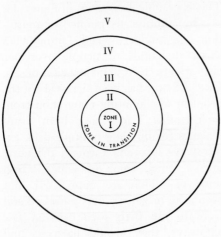

* Modified slightly from the original. See E. W. Burgess, "The Growth of the City," in *The City*, ed. R. E. Park (Chicago: University of Chicago Press, 1925), p. 51. By permission.

space to park a person's car as he has in which to do his work. To provide parking space for workers, not shoppers, under the assumptions stated, would mean doubling *"the cubage requirements of present central area buildings."* [17]

Congestion is evident also in pedestrian movement, as everybody knows. One has but to get into a mass of people on Broadway in New York at theater-closing time, at State and Madison at noon in Chicago or, for that matter, in the heart of any other modern city to realize this fact.

The solution to the problems of daily congestion is slowly being worked out, either by design or by chance, through the decentralization and dispersion of functions of the central areas of our cities. But the habits

17 · Quotations from "Moving the Masses in Modern Cities" (New York: American Transit Association, n.d.), pp. 24, 25 (pamphlet). By permission.

of man and the enormous amount of effort and capital invested in central areas preclude an easy solution.

THEORIES OF URBAN GROWTH

Various attempts have been made to formulate a systematic theory of ecological structure and process. In this final section of the chapter we shall summarize and comment on the more important of these.

The Concentric Zone Theory One of the best-known and most widely accepted theories is that of the concentric zone pattern. E. W. Burgess constructed a generalized hypothetical series of urban zones, as shown in Figure 14. According to this construct, the center of modern American cities is the point of chief concentration of specialized services. The center, Zone I, is characterized by skyscrapers, department stores, big hotels, motion-picture houses, transit lines, and daily mobility of population as it goes about its business or pleasure. In Zone II are found rooming houses, some light industry, and certain other services. In general, the second zone is characterized by rather rapid change or "transition." In Zone III are workingmen's homes, and shopping centers, schools, and occasional parks. In the fourth zone are better residences, and beyond this is Zone V, the suburban and commuter area. Ideally, there is an upward gradation in such features as income and status from the center to the periphery.

Burgess developed his theoretical construct from studies of urban communities, chiefly of Chicago. Actually, the distribution seldom conforms pre-

Urban societies have separate areas for different functions: an industrial district in Pittsburgh.

cisely to the hypothetical pattern. Topography, waterways, lakes, harbors, and so on all influence the direction and extent of a city's development. Certainly for Chicago, Lake Michigan cuts sharply through the middle of Burgess' circles, so that there we have a series of only half-concentric rings. Moreover, the Chicago River, the railroad lines, the highways, and the desirability of lake-front residences also affect the spatial distribution. (See Figure 12.)

The Sector Theory　A second formulation is the so-called sector theory, of Homer Hoyt.[18] This theory is, in brief, that the high-rent or high-income sec-

tions of a city tend to be on the outer fringes of one or more quadrants or sectors of the community. These areas also tend to be farthest removed from factory districts. The low-rent areas sometimes extend from the very center of the city to its periphery. The growth of population is marked by an outward movement of the high-rent areas along any given sector, which may be initially determined by topographic or other factors. The places left by the upper-rent families as they move outward are taken by families of lower economic status.

The Hoyt thesis describes radial growth, and the star-shaped city rather than one of concentric zones. Yet Hoyt's views and those of Burgess are not entirely incompatible. Much depends on the natural landscape and the

18 · Homer Hoyt, *The Structure and Growth of Residential Neighborhoods in American Cities* (Washington, D.C.: Federal Housing Administration, 1939).

Monkmeyer

Urban societies have separate areas for different functions: a residential suburb in Pennsylvania.

initial changes made by man. Where there are no serious natural or man-made barriers as in flat terrain—we do find cities which tend to conform to the Burgess theory.

Cultural Critique of Ecology Some criticism of both these theories has been made. Milla A. Alihan raised significant questions about the lack of clear-cut criteria in relating the concentric zones to various gradients, measured by indices of population, crime rates, and the like.[19] Her doubts about the assumed homogeneity of population and culture within the zones might be applied equally to Hoyt's views.

On the basis of a careful review of a number of studies of American cities, Maurice R. Davie also has raised some serious doubts as to the applicability of the concentric-zone theory. He says it "clearly does not apply to New Haven," nor to Greater Cleveland, studied by Howard W. Green, nor to sixteen "self-contained cities" examined by Harland Bartholomew. For Davie the Burgess thesis is too simple for the complex facts of urban development. He points out that it neglects the importance of man-made topography, which follows the building of railroads and industries.[20]

A more severe and far-reaching critique of both Burgess and Hoyt has

19 · Milla A. Alihan, *Social Ecology: A Critical Analysis* (New York: Columbia University Press, 1938).

20 · Maurice R. Davie, "The Pattern of Urban Growth," *Studies in the Science of Society,* ed. G. P. Murdoch (New Haven: Yale University Press, 1937).

been made by Walter Firey,[21] who stresses the need to recognize the place of sentiment as it affects urban growth and functions, and argues that economic competition for land is not the important variable in determining changes in business and residential locations. In his study of land use in Boston, Firey attempts to document his thesis. Actually, as John James has pointed out, his findings do not entirely refute Hoyt's thesis. And despite the topographical character of Boston, some features of poplation movement are not entirely incompatible with the zone theory. Certainly there are a nucleated center and certain gradients in social-culture features as one moves from this center to the suburban areas.[22]

21 · Walter Firey, *Land Use in Central Boston* (Cambridge: Harvard University Press, 1947).
22 · John James, "A Critique of Firey's *Land Use in Central Boston*," *American Journal of Sociology*, 1948, 54:228–234.

On the whole, the concepts and tools of ecological research have been an aid to our understanding of how cities arise, grow, and change their features. The importance of cultural factors must not be so overstressed as to lead us to ignore the place of either the natural or the man-made landscape of a given locality. The ecological and the cultural are intertwined at many points. As Richard M. Hurd, one of the initiators of modern human ecology, put it, "Underneath all economic laws, the final basis of human action is psychological, so that the last stage of analysis of the problems of the structure of cities, the distribution of utilities, the earnings of the buildings which house them, and the land values resulting therefrom, turns on individual and collective taste and preference, as shown in social habits and customs." [23]

23 · Hurd, *Principles of City Land Values*, 2nd ed., p. 18. By permission.

INTERPRETATIVE SUMMARY

The distinction made earlier between rural and urban communities is useful to ecologists, students of the spatial distribution of human groups and institutions. Primary agricultural communities are here again easier to describe, lending themselves to classification according to the degree of centralization of residential and service areas. The plantation and its variations are distinguished from other agricultural communities by their "big business" aspect, which leads to unique patterns of community contact and even whole stratification systems.

Cities tend to start at important trade crossroads and to develop in axial or radial fashion, following the natural topography unless man modifies the pattern. Well-located, industrialized cities grow especially quickly; for example, in our own country, a relatively small number of states have a high proportion of such large cities. Business and service areas in the city tend to become centralized until land in the main area becomes so expensive and access of commuters to the area so difficult that decentralization sets in. Industries, shopping areas, and whole suburbs may move to the periphery of the city, bringing the city's ways with them.

Social analysts speak of city neighborhoods, marking neighborhood divisions on the basis of homogeneity in economic status, in ethnic status, and in patterns of family living. Their research helps sociologists study the above processes, as well as intraneighborhood phenomena, and the way newcomers to a neighborhood establish accommodative relations with the older groups, become assimilated, or even push out the older groups. Various theories attempting to describe how cities grow and neighborhoods change, while not refuted, have been criticized as being limited in application and oversimplified in their generalizations about the cities they do cover.

REVIEW AND SUGGESTED READINGS

A · VOCABULARY

Ecology	Ecological structure	Rural nonfarm
Ecological process	Rural	Urban

B · QUESTIONS AND TOPICS FOR REVIEW

1. Illustrate each of the four types of agricultural communities in the United States.
2. Discuss the problem of traffic congestion in urban communities with which you are familiar. Discuss solutions, tried and untried.
3. Name outstanding examples of big cities which exist at unlikely places. How did they come to exist? How have the residents overcome topographical problems?
4. Give an ecological description of your home area, stressing
   a. the residential distribution of subgroups
   b. the location of business, industry, shopping and service facilities, and recreation
   c. patterns of migration—all three types
   d. ecological problems
   e. the prestige value associated with geographic space
5. Do you know any instances of *cyclical* invasion and succession? Under what circumstances would this occur?
6. Discuss your local shopping centers from the point of view of
   a. appropriateness for their location—economic success
   b. degree to which *novelty* is counted on to bring customers
   c. specialties offered

C · SUGGESTIONS FOR FURTHER READING

Otis D. Duncan and Albert J. Reiss, Jr. *Social Characteristics of Urban and Rural Communities*, 1950. New York: John Wiley & Sons, Inc., 1956.

An elaborate descriptive analysis based on census data.

Noel P. Gist and Sylvia Fava. *Urban Society*, 5th ed. New York: Thomas Y. Crowell Company, 1964.

A fresh, reorganized section on ecology in a standard text.

Amos H. Hawley. *Human Ecology: A Theory of Community Structure*. New York: The Ronald Press Company, 1950.

An elaboration of a work originally begun by R. D. McKenzie, one of the early contributors to the field of ecology. Deals chiefly with the nature and development of community structure.

Paul K. Hatt and Albert J. Reiss, Jr. *Cities and Society. The Revised Reader in Urban Sociology*. Glencoe, Ill.: The Free Press, 1957.

A collection of 62 papers covering a wide range of topics, among them the spatial and temporal patterns of cities.

J. H. Kolb and Edmund de S. Brunner. *A Study of Rural Society*, 4th ed. Boston: Houghton Mifflin Co., 1952.

Chapter 12, "Country Neighborhoods," and Chapter 13, "Agricultural Villages and Small Towns" provide excellent coverage of these topics.

Lowry Nelson. *Rural Sociology*, 2nd ed. New York: American Book Company, 1955.

Chapter 4, "Patterns of Land Settlement" contains some historical as well as sociological approaches to the topic. Chapter 5, "The Rural Community" deals with rural neighborhoods and various types of rural communities.

Thomas P. Peardon, ed., "The Urban Problems," *Proceedings of the Academy of Political Science*, 1960, 27:1-84.

A series of papers dealing with several of the basic problems of contemporary city life, political, economic, ecological, and urban renewal among them.

CHAPTER 18

Metropolis, Suburb, and Region

There have been two significant changes in urban communities in the United States: first, the clustering of central cities and their suburbs, and second, their steady expansion to form what are known as metropolitan areas. The first part of this chapter will deal with metropolitan areas: their structure, the functions of different types of suburbs, patterns of suburban social life, and the consequences of metropolitan expansion. The second part will treat regions: larger spatial units that are relatively homogeneous both geographically and culturally.

METROPOLITAN AREAS

By 1910 the growth of cities beyond their legal boundaries led the United States Bureau of the Census to establish the category "metropolitan districts." By 1950 such a large proportion of people were part of the social structure of cities while residing outside them in suburbs that the concept of Standard Metropolitan Area (SMA) was introduced. A Standard Metropolitan Area consists of a core or central city and all of the contiguous area meeting certain Census Bureau standards of density of population, specialization of labor force, and social and economic integration with the central city. In the 1960 census these areas were officially designated as Stan-

dard Metropolitan Statistical Areas (SMSA).

In 1950 there were 162 Standard Metropolitan Areas in the United States, with a total population of 85 million. A decade later there were 212 SMSA's, with a total of 112 million people. In fact, 97 percent of the population increase from 1950 to 1960 was in these areas. However, as can be seen in Figure 15, this phenomenal growth occurred primarily not in the central cities but in their suburbs. It is estimated that by 1970 there will be 214 such areas, with a population of 140 million, and the projection for 1980 is 260 metropolitan areas, with 177 million people.

In certain sections of this country, especially along the upper Atlantic seaboard, a great many metropolitan areas overlap or adjoin each other. This is particularly evident in the 600-mile stretch from Boston, Massachusetts, to the far tip of Fairfax County, Virginia. By 1960 this section had a population of around 40 million.[1]

Structure and Functions of Suburbs
Even casual observation reveals that not all suburban communities are alike.

1 · See Charles Grutzner, "Expansion of Cities Alters Patterns of Living in U.S," *New York Times*, January 27, 1957. This is the first of a series of eight articles dealing with problems associated with urban growth in the United States.

Various attempts have been made to work out a classification.[2] Schnore classifies suburbs of 10,000 population or more as either residential or industrial. Industrial suburbs, he finds, have the following characteristics: (1) they are "employing centers" which attract workers from other sections of the metropolitan area; (2) they are concentrated in the northeastern and north-central regions of the country; (3) they tend to be older than residential suburbs; (4) while they are found throughout the entire metropolitan area, they are often located beyond the limits of the densely populated urban core; indeed, (5) they are found in greater frequency as the distance from the central city increases; and (6) they are typically known as low-rent localities.

Residential suburbs of comparable populations are found in all metropolitan areas. They differ from industrial suburbs in that (1) their chief economic activity is retail trade, usually local in scope; (2) they tend to develop with increasing frequency as the size of the central city increases; (3) they predominate among the more recently incorporated communities; (4) very few of them are found outside the densely populated urbanized area or farther than 30 miles from the central city; and (5) they have higher rents than average among suburbs.[3]

The expansion of economic and other functions depends on changes in the central city as well as the suburbs. The residential populations of industrial

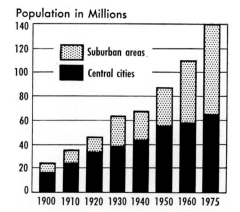

FIGURE 15 · Suburban Expansion as a Proportion of Metropolitan Growth *

Population in Millions

Suburban areas

Central cities

1900 1910 1920 1930 1940 1950 1960 1975

* Redrawn from *Better Living*, 1961, 15:24 (Wilmington, Dela.: E. I. du Pont de Nemours and Company, 1961). By permission.

suburbs grow less rapidly than those of residential suburbs, and this is directly traceable to the specialization of function in the industrial suburbs.

Residential suburbs are growing rapidly because they are becoming even more residential in character, by means of large increments of housing construction. At the same time, employing suburbs are growing less rapidly because they are becoming more exclusively devoted to industry and other employment-providing activities. In these employing places, the net effect of this increased specialization in production and employment is (a) to drive out pre-existent residential uses of land, and (b) to discourage new construction of housing.[4]

Such differentiation and specialization of land use in suburbs is but a part of the larger changes going on

2 · See, for example, Victor Jones, "Economic Classification of Cities and Metropolitan Areas," *The Municipal Year Book*, 1953 (Chicago: International City Managers' Association, 1953), pp. 49–57.

3 · Leo F. Schnore, "The Functions of Metropolitan Suburbs," *American Journal of Sociology*, 1956, 61:453–458.

4 · Leo F. Schnore, "The Growth of Metropolitan Suburbs," *American Sociological Review*, 1957, 22:165–173. Quotation from p. 171, by permission. In this article, the author uses the term "employing suburb" as practically synonymous with the "industrial suburb" of his earlier article cited above. See also Schnore's "Satellites and Suburbs," *Social Forces*, 1957, 36:121–127.

Central cities of metropolitan areas become more and more congested.

throughout metropolitan areas. In time some kind of working balance will probably arise between shifts in population in the central city and the suburban fringe and changes in the socio-economic functions.[5]

Patterns of Suburban Life What are some of the social and psychological elements in these shifts in residence? Why do families move to the suburbs? What satisfactions are there in being a suburbanite?

First, let us look at the subculture of the suburbanites. A high proportion of the urban workers who live in the suburbs came originally from rural areas.[6] Suburban residents engage in more "neighboring" than their urban counterparts, and there is considerable retention of the values and attitudes of small primary communities.[7] Suburbs differ in several ways, however, from small communities of similar size which are not part of a metropolitan area. Residential suburbs tend to show higher than average incomes per family and a higher proportion of persons in white-collar occupational statuses; they spend proportionately more on

5 · For rather exhaustive treatments of changes in metropolitan areas, see Donald J. Bogue, *Population Growth in Standard Metropolitan Areas, 1900–1950, with an Explanatory Analysis of Urbanized Areas* (Washington, D.C.: U.S. Government Printing Office, 1953); and Amos H. Hawley, *The Changing Shape of Metropolitan America: Deconcentration since 1920* (Glencoe, Ill.: The Free Press, 1956).

6 · Noel Gist, "Ecological Decentralization and Rural-Urban Relationships," *Rural Sociology*, 1952, 17:328–335.
7 · Sylvia Fleis Fava, "Suburbanism as a Way of Life," *American Sociological Review*, 1956, 21:34–37. This paper contains a good review of the literature on suburbia.

schools, and in general have a higher level of living than do nonmetropolitan communities of like size.[8]

Several studies indicate that migration to the suburbs is motivated by the desire to participate in this subculture, with its primary interaction and higher level of living, while still being able to work at urban occupations and procure urban services. A sample of informants who had moved from the central city of Milwaukee to unincorporated areas outside gave as the most important reasons the following, listed in order of their importance: "better for children," "less congested," "cleaner," "larger lot," "lower taxes," "forced to move," and "cheaper land." [9] From interviews with suburban dwellers in the metropolitan area of Chicago, Wendell Bell concludes

If anonymity, impersonality, defilement of air and land by industry, apartment living, crowding, and constant nervous stimulation are inherent in "urbanism as a way of life," as some writers say, then the findings of this study necessitate the conclusion that the suburbanite *is* seeking an escape from many traditional aspects of city life. The suburbanite seems to be seeking a way of life in which family, community, and immediate enjoyment through living the "good life" are dominant and interdependent ends.[10]

SOME CONSEQUENCES OF METROPOLITAN EXPANSION

A number of serious problems result from the expansion of metropoli-

8 · W. F. Ogburn, *The Social Characteristics of Cities* (Chicago: International City Managers' Association, 1937), pp. 47–55.
9 · Richard Dewey, "Peripheral Expansion in Milwaukee County," *American Journal of Sociology*, 1948, 54:118–125.
10 · Wendell Bell, "Familism and Suburbanization: One Test of the Social Choice Hypothesis," *Rural Sociology*, 1956, 21:276–283. Quotation from p. 283. By permission.

tan areas. Some, such as those concerned with highways, streets, and parking space, are physical; some, such as those involving industrial decentralization, are economic; others are governmental—taxation and schools; and some are sociological—housing and recreation problems, for example.

The Transportation Problem The automobile played a key part in the extension of suburbia and the development of metropolitan areas. Yet the automobile has created problems of congestion. These become steadily more serious, for both the population and the number of cars per capita are increasing. Since 1930 the number of motor vehicles has multiplied three times as fast as the number of people, from 26.5 million cars to 71.5 million in 1959. It is estimated that by 1975 there will be 100 million cars and trucks for an estimated population of 215 million. In 1930 there was one motor vehicle for 4.21 persons; in 1959 there was one for 2.46; and in 1975, by conservative estimates, there will be one for 2.15.

In an effort to improve the situation, tremendous road-building programs have been initiated. Superhighways facilitate the flow of traffic in the open country and usually bypass the core of the larger cities. Belt routes which circle downtown business districts also help. But the street congestion and the parking problems inside the central city are growing more serious. As one writer remarks, "The deficiency of parking space is more easily correctable than the acute highway congestion in and around urban centers. At the edge of the city limits the so-called modern highway degenerates, and the once broad expanse of adequate roadbeds narrows to nothing more than antiquated city streets." [11]

Economic Changes Accompanying the growth of the suburbs has been the decentralization of retail business and industry. Shopping centers have spread to the fringes of larger urban communities or into the suburbs themselves. Factories, too, are rising in the suburbs of many metropolitan areas, though some localities make strenuous efforts, chiefly through zoning, to keep industrial plants out. The metropolitan fringe is particularly desirable for manufacturers who use long assembly lines, since these require a great deal of space, and large tracts of low-cost land are not available in the central city.

The future advantages for industry and business in the suburbs are likely to be somewhat limited. The core cities tend to keep highly specialized services. Moreover, taxes in suburbia will rise as a result of increased demands for police and fire protection, utilities, schools, roads, hospitals, and recreational facilities. Nevertheless, it seems quite improbable that there will be any marked movement back to the central cities in the near future.

Educational Problems One of the strong appeals of suburbia has been the fact that, for the most part, these communities had better teachers, newer and more modern school buildings and, as a rule, higher educational standards than the central cities. Unfortunately, these very advantages have led to rapid growth in the suburbs, and this expansion has partially nullified the advantages. As suburban communities

11 · From Joseph C. Ingraham, "Autos in Urban Regions Rule and Frustrate Living," *New York Times*, January 28, 1957, p. 1.

have mushroomed in size, school costs have risen; it has been more and more necessary to set up double sessions of classes; and there has been a mounting shortage of good teachers. In some parts of the country these difficulties have been met, in part, by consolidation of two or more school districts and by centralizing school facilities at key points. The threat of increases in taxes needed, however, often blocks necessary programs for the extension of school facilities.

Housing Difficulties As metropolitan areas have continued to increase in population and expand in space, there have been widespread efforts to clear slums, stop neighborhood deterioration, and initiate programs for orderly urban development. Within the central cities this has meant replacing slums with housing projects, both public and private, of "vertical design"—that is, multiple-storied apartments which permit a considerable density of population per unit of ground space. Such a development is the Corlears Hook section of New York. At the time this project was undertaken, the existing tenements housed 878 families. The taller apartments which replaced them provide space for almost double that number of families. The vertical design in cities, however, is not without its limitations. For one thing, such construction invariably tends to aggravate traffic congestion.

In contrast with this type of new apartment housing found in the central cities is the "horizontal design"—that is, many one- or two-story single-family dwellings—found in the suburbs. One of the most serious aspects of rapid suburban growth is the fact that cheap construction and crowding of single-family dwellings create neighborhoods which in a few years may take on the features of village slums. As one observer puts it,

Assembly-line construction of thousands of one-family houses in a single development, smaller plots, increasing commutation rates, swamping of suburban facilities by newcomers, and poorly regulated commingling of residential and industrial use of former farmland has taken the promise out of the suburbs for many. . . .

When blight starts spawning in a suburb it may spread faster than in a central city. This is particularly true in suburbs lacking either the plan or governmental structures to support parks, transit, sanitation, and other services.[12]

Political Lag Our governmental units are largely the products of historical factors no longer applicable to the modern metropolis, and recent cultural changes have made their inflexibility more apparent than ever. The emergence of politically independent suburbs and satellite cities has resulted in overlapping and often competing governmental units. More than two decades ago, a government report stated

Overlapping . . . cities and suburbs of the metropolitan districts [areas] are several layers of different-sized, bewilderingly bounded governmental areas with separate legal and fiscal identities—counties, townships, school districts, and special districts of all kinds including sanitary, sewer, library, health, park, forest preserve, street lighting, utility, water and even mosquito abatement districts.

While metropolitan life overflows the artificial network of urban boundary lines, each little bailiwick of government preserves its independent island of author-

ity, with odd results . . . Criminals hop over jurisdictional lines which local police dare not cross without elaborate devices for administrative coordination which are only now beginning to develop.

Similarly, urban planning, highway construction, transport facilities, parks and recreational preserves too frequently must await the pleasure of minor suburbs . . . Equally serious is the political indifference and neglect arising from the retirement into the suburbs of large blocs of urban citizenry who . . . lose all civic concern in the city governing the core of their urban community . . .[13]

Various means have been used to eliminate at least some of the most flagrant overlapping. The interplay of state and federal rights has led to the setting up of joint boards for certain administrative functions. Such an agency is the Port of New York Authority, which has charge of the bridges and tunnels that connect New York and New Jersey. It also manages various airports, bus and motor-truck terminals, and certain shipping and storage facilities. In some instances—in Denver, Colorado, for example—city and county governments have been merged. Separate cities have been federated: the present City of New York came about from the unification of the five boroughs in 1898. No doubt the coming decades will see increased coordination among governing agencies in our metropolitan areas.

In many instances the metropolitan area reaches out to include a very extensive hinterland, so that the problems of the metropolitan areas—in the narrower sense of the census definition—merge into those of still larger and more extensive regions.

12 · Charles Grutzner, "Spread of Slums Arouses U.S. Cities and Suburbs," *New York Times*, January 31, 1957, p. 16. By permission.

13 · National Resources Committee, *Urban Government* (Washington, D.C.: U.S. Government Printing Office, 1939), p. 262.

FIGURE 16 · Relief Map of Continental United States *

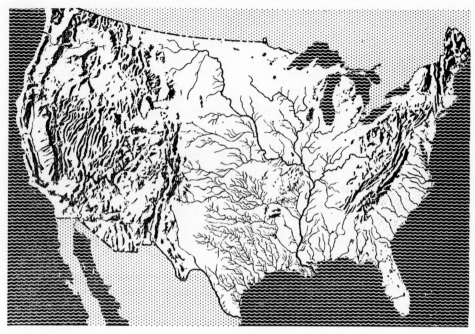

* U.S. Department of Agriculture, Washington, D.C.

REGIONS

Areas larger than folk societies or urban communities often possess considerable geographic and cultural unity. To the extent that there is a correlation between geographic homogeneity and patterns of culture or subculture, regions are of interest to the social scientist.

A region may be described as follows: (1) There is a physiographic foundation in climate, topography, natural resources, and plants and animals. (2) There are always basic economic patterns linked to these "natural" environmental elements: for example, the shipbuilding, importing, exporting, and fishing of the New England coast, or the cotton and rice economy of the Mississippi Delta. (3) The people in a region tend in time to take on certain distinctive patterns of thinking and behaving. Because of their shared experiences and activities, they develop a set of shared, learned behaviors peculiar to their area—a regional subculture.

There may or may not be some governmental counterpart to the region. In the United States, region is recognized only informally in politics, as when the "Southern bloc" of Senators holds a policy meeting, or when the governors of the Appalachian region discuss their common problems with the President. France, in contrast, is a country where, in spite of a strong central government, regions have been linked rather closely with provincial and local administrations.[14] On the in-

14 · See Hedwig Hintze, "Regionalism," *Encyclopedia of the Social Sciences*, 13:208–218 (New York: The Macmillan Co., 1934).

Figure 17 · Agricultural Regions of Continental United States *

* U.S. Department of Agriculture, Washington, D.C.

ternational scene, large "natural" regions have often been cut up by political states which have periodically struggled for full control of these areas. The Ruhr and Saar valleys in Europe are good examples.

Regionalism The word *regionalism* refers sometimes to a theory of, and sometimes to an action program regarding, the place of the region in national and international social structure and culture. Some persons concerned with national planning have characterized regionalism as "a clustering of environmental, economic, social, and governmental factors to such an extent that a distinct consciousness of separate identity within the whole, a need for autonomous planning, a manifestation of cultural peculiarities, and a desire for administrative freedom are theoretically recognized and actually put into effect." [15] Regionalism arose in France and elsewhere as a reaction to centralization of economic and political power. In the United States, on the contrary, it seems to have emerged in part from felt social differences, in part as a counteraction to the serious interstate barriers to economic and other unification of larger "natural" areas.

Viewed in this light, regionalism is a social-cultural movement involving a theory, a method of study and analysis of certain facts, and a plan for carrying out a political-economic program. Such movements have been confined chiefly to public and quasi-public agencies or associations within the national state.

15 · National Resources Committee, *Regional Factors in National Planning and Development* (Washington, D.C.: U.S. Government Printing Office, 1935), p. 138.

FIGURE 18 · Regional Distribution of Population by Decades, 1870–1950, and 1957 *

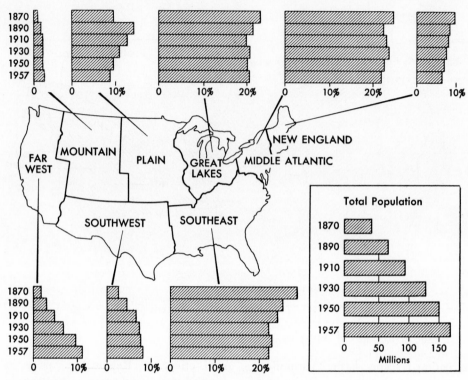

* From *Resources*, No. 4, June 1960 (Washington, D.C.: Resources for the Future, Inc., 1960). By permission.

American Regions Regional differences in the United States were apparent almost from the beginning of our country's history. The conflict between the South and the rest of the nation is often ascribed to political differences, notably to the degree of emphasis on states' rights, but this ignores other factors—geographic, economic, and cultural—which were correlated with political conflict. The climate which allowed a plantation economy to flourish in the South, the class structure of slaves and an ascribed aristocracy which accompanied that plantation economy—these regional differences divided the country, and the political views of the industrial North and the plantation South were more

symptom than cause of regional conflict. Important as political forces are, they do not operate independently of geography or of economic and other cultural conditions.

The United States has three large physiographic regions, as can be seen from Figure 16: 1.the rough mountains and desert of the West, 2.the Mississippi-Missouri-Ohio drainage basin, and 3.the lesser eastern mountains with their coastal plain. These three great regions subdivide into smaller agricultural regions determined by the length of the growing season and the amount of rainfall (see Figure 17). The principal industrial regions are in the Northeast, in the Great Lakes states, in scattered sections of the South, and increasingly in the Pacific states. Naturally, the economic attractiveness of a region for industry depends on a number of factors: availability of raw materials and labor, sufficient power, convenience of transportation, and accessibility to markets. The extension of commercialized and mechanized farming, the decrease in the proportion of the population engaged in agriculture and the concomitant increase in those employed in manufacturing and services, and the shifts of industries to new locations as new resources are found, all contribute to residential migration of the population.

Internal Migration Throughout the history of the United States, <u>the basic pattern of migration has been from east to west.</u> This was true when the early colonists landed on the East coast and moved inland; it was true when the pioneers pushed West to homestead land and, as Figure 18 shows, it is still true. We can understand the migration of pioneer days, but why are so many people moving around the country now? Who are these people, and where are they going?

    <u>People in early adult life constitute the most mobile segment of our civilian population.</u> They generally migrate to take advantage of job opportunities and to provide better living conditions for their families. In recent years there has also been an increasing tendency for people at the older ages to settle in areas with mild climates, particularly southern California and Florida.[16]

    <u>The other basic pattern of internal migration has been from farm to city:</u> the nation has become more and more

16 · From "Population Still Moving Westward," *Statistical Bulletin*, 1955, 36:8.

FIGURE 19 · Distribution of Negroes Among the Geographic Divisions of the United States, 1790–1950 *

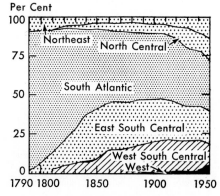

* From Donald J. Bogue, *The Population of the United States* (New York: The Free Press of Glencoe, 1959), p. 131. By permission.

urbanized. The extent of movement from farm to cities varies greatly from region to region, but in general it involves from one-fourth to one-half of all farm youth. For the country as a whole it has been estimated that about two-fifths of all individuals between the ages of 10 and 19 years who lived on farms in 1920 had migrated from there by 1930. The cityward drift of population continues as commercialization and industrialization of agriculture expands and as contacts between cities and farms continue to grow. A particularly interesting phase of this migration has been the steady shift of Negroes from the rural South to Northern industrial centers. Figure 19 shows the changing distribution of our Negro population from 1790 to 1950. With further mechanization of agriculture in the South, we may expect the northward shift to continue.

Differences in Regional Subcultures The economic status of the population in the several regions varies greatly, as

**Distinct Regions
Develop
Different Subcultures**

*New England
clambake*

Greater Providence Chamber of Commerce

*Midwest ice cream
social (or "sociable")*

Dale Humphrey, Galesburg (Ill.) *Register-Mail*

*New Orleans
Mardi Gras*

State of Louisiana, Dept. of Commerce and Industry

FIGURE 20 · The Reality of Regionalism: Per Capita Income by State *

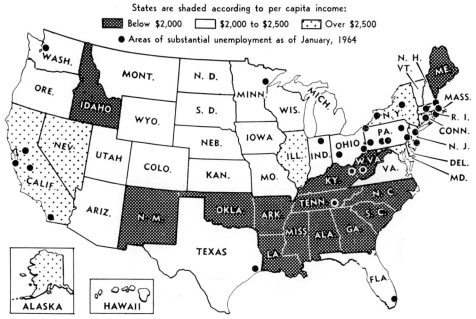

States are shaded according to per capita income:
▨ Below $2,000   ☐ $2,000 to $2,500   ▥ Over $2,500
● Areas of substantial unemployment as of January, 1964

* The *New York Times*, January 19, 1964, E7.

can be seen in Figure 20. In general it is low in the Southeast and Southwest, high in the Far West and Middle West, especially around the Great Lakes, and in the Northeast. The Northwest region falls in a median position. Variations in educational opportunities are also marked, as one can see from Figure 21. The Southeast has a high proportion of children to total population and to income, and its schools are understandably in the bottom category in per-capita expenditure and other items. On the basis of a very broad division of the United States into North, South, and West, certain differences in standards of living are apparent. Again the South shows a striking deviation from the other two large regions. And the contrasts are, for the most part, more striking in rural than in urban comparisons.

In considering these differences we must remember that the mere combination of statistics from various states is meaningless unless the facts indicate a solid basis of distinctive culture. In order to have a cultural region we need not only a geographic foundation but some common interest, some symbols of solidarity, some sense of belonging or in-group feeling. These intangible items are hard to identify and difficult to measure when they are discovered. Yet the New Englander does have a sense of difference from other Americans. And Southerners possess, in general, a certain pride and sense of group solidarity. But within these geographical and cultural regions, there is a loyalty to individual states which sometimes offsets regionalism. The states themselves often set up blocks to intraregional co-operation. The rise of what are in effect interstate tariff regulations is a case in point.

FIGURE 21 · State Spending for Education *

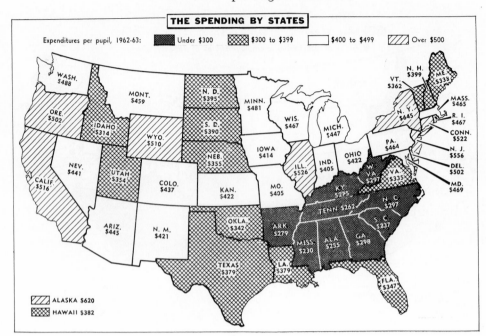

* The *New York Times*, September 1, 1963, E7.

State Barriers to Regionalism In spite of rapid changes in technology, reflected in mass production and in rapid transportation and communication, the separate states have tended in many matters to set themselves apart as virtually independent political-economic units. This trend toward state localism has occurred in spite of the fact that the federal Constitution explicitly prohibits the states from discriminating against or levying tariff duties on imports or exports from other states.

Among the most common state barriers are these: (1) Many states require that, whenever possible, public supplies be purchased from producers within the state. This includes such items as building materials, coal, butter, and public printing. Many states permit only bona fide residents of the state to be on their payrolls. (2) Another way to bolster state economic autonomy is an elaborate system of licenses and requirements for the sale and transportation of goods. All sorts of qualifications are put on the weight of truck loads, width of tires, use of trailers, and the like. (3) An elaborate system of quarantine laws has been used not only to keep out diseases and pests but to prevent competition in such goods as fruit and nursery stock. (4) Many states require various kinds of grading of products, packaging, and the like, measures devised in part to stimulate home-manufactured goods and keep out others. (5) All sorts of devices—licenses, excise taxes, restrictions on nonresident manufacturers, and others—have been used to stimulate state wine and liquor enterprises. On the other hand, some states exempt manufacturers who export to other

FIGURE 22 · Possible National Regions Based upon Composite Planning Problems *

Columbia Basin Region

Great Lakes Region

Northeastern Forest Region

Pacific Northwest Region

Great Plains Region

Midwestern Region

Eastern Region

California Valley Region

Intermountain Region

Ozark Appalachian Region

Southern Region

Gulf Coast Region

* From *Regional Factors in National Planning*, p. 166. Possible regional headquarters are indicated on the map by dots.

states. In this sense, the individual states imitate nations which subsidize exports and at the same time impede imports by tariffs, quotas, and other restrictions.

Regional Planning There has been continuous and at times bitter debate about the criteria to be used in setting up regional administrative agencies. Some experts have advocated that such regions be delimited around the major metropolitan areas. Others suggest that regions be delineated according to administrative convenience, such as transportation facilities or proximity to state institutions and federal administrative offices. This does not always create realistic regions.

Still another plan calls for combining groups of states. Actually, the earliest recognition of regional differences grew out of the traditional divi-sion of the country into such geographic divisions as the Northeast, Southeast, and North Central. While recent proposals would not follow the traditional combination of states, such a scheme would still be open to the criticism that states and combinations of states cut across too many regional differences in climate, soil, industry, and ways of life. As one commentator puts it, "States or groups of states are not particularly suited to function as planning regions." [17]

Another proposal is to base regions on single functions and then combine single-function areas when it is administratively feasible to do so. The division of the United States into drainage basins is one illustration of this approach. But here again, overlapping obviously would be increased.

17 · *Regional Factors in National Planning*, p. 163.

Perhaps the most practical plan, though not the easiest to draw up, would be to develop regions around a composite of physiographic and cultural data. Physiographic data include such things as climate, soil, topography, flora and fauna, and mineral resources. Cultural data includes population density, metropolitan influence, major types of productive operations, commerce, farm income, and the like. It is evident that the boundaries of such composite regions are not sharp, and certainly would not follow state lines (see Figure 22).

Setting up a specific regional area is clearly bound up not only with physiographic, economic, and political factors, but with the whole subculture of the area. If a region is to become a vital unit in social organization, it must be supported by a consciousness of shared subcultural patterns among its inhabitants. Unless regions develop the supporting attitudes and values of group solidarity and common action, the economic or political aspects will be largely superficial. A viable social structure requires the participation that stems from commitment.

INTERPRETATIVE SUMMARY

The United States is characterized by an increasing number of metropolitan areas and an increasing number of people in such areas. Most of the increase has been in suburban areas. Such areas may have an industrial, commercial, or residential orientation, but in any case the consequence is that the values and behavior patterns of city dwellers are extended to ever-widening areas.

Metropolitan expansion is inevitably accompanied by certain problems. Some of these are a simple consequence of increase in the city's members: traffic and parking became snarled in the central area, space for housing and business is limited. Other problems develop as people go to the suburbs to escape the city: the high-quality schools they build become overcrowded, and quality declines unless ever-increasing taxes can be met; the desire of low-income families for the better life of the suburbs may lead to the creation of city-like slums on cheap suburban land; conflict and confusion among various local administrative organizations may cause inefficiency or even impotence in law-enforcement.

Metropolitan areas, and indeed all areas in the United States, belong to larger areas called regions. America has three major regions, each having a distinct physical environment, economic patterns, and patterns of thought and behavior. In many societies, region is recognized as a basic political and administrative unit. In our country, while there have been and still are some attempts at regional administration, economic and other problems tend to be treated at the local, state, or federal level, state restrictions on interstate commerce in particular acting to discourage regional solidarity. However, people are conscious of differences among regions, particularly differences among regional subcultures. This is evidenced in the widespread migration of young people from certain regions to certain others which are known to have better educational and occupational opportunities, as well as in similar migrations of retired people to places renowned for high standards of living.

REVIEW AND SUGGESTED READINGS

A · VOCABULARY

Central city	Region	Standard Metropolitan Statistical
Industrial suburb	Regionalism	Area
Internal migration	Residential suburb	

B · QUESTIONS AND TOPICS FOR REVIEW

1. Discuss existing modifications of the typology of the residential suburb.
2. If you live in a residential suburb, give some reasons why you still have to go to the city on occasion.
3. Discuss some ways in which big cities attempt to get their inhabitants and fringe-area residents to continue to come downtown (or to the central area) for services.
4. Discuss the relation between the quality of a suburb's educational system and the physical proximity of the suburb to its city.
5. If you live in a suburb, what is the name and title of your area's main officer? When was he elected, and what are his duties? Can you give similar information about the mayor of the nearby big city?
6. Illustrate how the existence of overlapping and competing local governments can lead to inefficiency and even impotence in law-enforcement.
7. Why are rents in different regions sometimes drastically different?
8. Discuss the influence of location of colleges and universities on westward migration in the United States.
9. List some federal plans which are designed to help certain regions, as well as some regional self-help plans. In each case, are the inhabitants of the region involved conscious of the region's homogeneity?

C · SUGGESTIONS FOR FURTHER READING

Donald J. Bogue. *The Structure of the Metropolitan Community*. Ann Arbor: University of Michigan School of Graduate Studies, 1950.

Describes the use of ecological techniques and theories in study of metropolitan areas.

William Dobriner, ed. *The Suburban Community*. New York: G. P. Putnam's Sons, 1958.

Contains papers dealing with suburban social organization, style of life, and some suburban problems.

Otis Dudley Duncan, W. R. Scott, Stanley Lieberson, Beverly Duncan, and H. H. Winsborough. *Metropolis and Region*. Baltimore: Johns Hopkins University Press, 1960.

Studies, under the sponsorship of Resources for the Future, Inc., which provide some cross-sectional data on the metropolitan areas of the United States at mid-twentieth century.

Richard E. Gordon, Katherine K. Gordon, and Max Gunther. *The Split-Level Trap*. New York: Bernard Geis Associates, 1961.

An analysis by a psychiatrist and his wife, a social psychologist, of the stresses on suburban families resulting from two kinds of mobility, geographic and social.

International Urban Research. *The World's Metropolitan Areas.* Berkeley and Los Angeles: University of California Press, 1959.

A valuable reference work which marshals data making possible comparisons of urban phenomena across national lines.

Martin Meyerson, Barbara Terrett, and Paul N. Ylvisaker, eds. "Metropolis in Ferment," *The Annals of the American Academy of Political and Social Science,* November 1957, vol. 314, pp. vi + 1–231.

A series of papers on problems of metropolitan areas.

Howard W. Odum and Harry E. Moore. *American Regionalism.* New York: Henry Holt & Co., Inc., 1938.

The classic statement on regionalism as a theory of the place of the region in the social structure.

Harvey S. Perloff, R. F. Muth, E. S. Dunn, Jr., and E. E. Lampard. *Regions, Resources, and Economic Growth.* Baltimore: Johns Hopkins University Press, 1960.

A series of studies, under the sponsorship of the Resources for the Future, Inc., dealing with the interrelations of demographic problems, resources, and economic development.

John R. Seeley, R. Alexander Sim, and Elizabeth W. Loosley. *Crestwood Heights: A Study of the Culture of Suburban Life.* New York: Basic Books, Inc., 1956.

A report of research on a suburban community in central Canada. Part I deals with "structure and context": ecology, age and sex distribution, and so on. Part II discusses the family, the school, and the place of voluntary associations. Part III deals with the normative structure. A very stimulating study.

Robert C. Wood. *Suburbia: Its People and Their Politics.* Boston: Houghton Mifflin Co., 1959.

An incisive discussion of the current problems of American suburbs. In particular the author relates suburban values and practices to political institutions.

SUMMARY OF PART II

The basic units of which social structures are composed were discussed in Chapter 9, "Role and Status." Examples of both ascribed and achieved statuses and roles were presented. Chapters 10, 11, 12, and 13 dealt with aspects of differentiation and stratification systems. Chapter 10 discussed the division of labor, the process of differentiation, and the social bases of leadership. In "Class Structure and Its Functions," Chapter 11, we examined the caste system in India, stratification in modern Europe, and the class structure of the United States. The consequences of the stratification structure—differential life chances and varying styles of life— were shown. The process of movement within the social structure and the norms that encourage movement were treated in "Social Mobility," Chapter 12. The place of minorities in the social structure was described in "Racial and Ethnic Relations," Chapter 13.

Two chapters dealt with the relationship of demographic variables to social structures and functions: Chapter 14, "Population Pressures," presented demographic theories and trends in world population; Chapter 15, "Differentials in Population," discussed sex, age, and class distributions of population.

Chapter 16, "Folk and Urban Communities," was devoted to the characteristics of folk and urban social structures, the culture patterns that differentiate these two types of social organization, and the impact of urbanization on folk communities. The spatial distribution of human groups and institutions in folk and urban communities was treated in Chapter 17, "Human Ecology." Chapter 18, "Metropolis, Suburb, and Region," discussed suburbanization and the culture patterns associated with it; the larger ecological phenomenon of metropolitan areas was examined; and finally, regions were defined and their problems discussed.

We shall turn in Chapter 19, "The Structure and Functions of Social Institutions," to the universal social structures and functions first discussed in Chapter 6, and relate them to the concepts of norms and institutions. The succeeding five chapters will deal with each of the major social institutions: the different forms of institutional structures, the functions resulting from them, the culture patterns found in each of these institutions in the United States, and the norms surrounding each function.

PART III

SOCIAL INSTITUTIONS

CHAPTER 19

The Structure and Functions of Social Institutions

In ordinary, nonscientific speech or writing people often use the word *institution* to mean an organization with some specific purpose, usually a public or charitable one. Sometimes the building in which the organization is housed is also called an institution. Thus both the United States Senate and the Senate Building are referred to as institutions, and people call the First National Bank or the Second Congregational Church institutions.

For the purposes of social science, a more precise definition is required. Some sociologists have classified as institutions any set of people in organized interaction. With such a definition, any individual family or club or department store or prison or government is an institution. As we said in Chapter 5, we prefer the term *institution* to mean a set of norms integrated around a major societal function.

We have called a set of interacting people a group and classified them, according to the intensity, frequency, duration, and focus of their interaction, as families, congeniality groups, clubs, organizations, and so on.[1] Some

groups, such as the families or the governmental organizations in a society, are regulated by a related set of folkways, mores, and laws. This set of interrelated norms is an institution. In every state in the United States there is (1) a legislature (2) chosen by the residents of that state (3) on a competitive basis (4) with each adult citizen having one vote, (5) which he is not required to cast but can use or not as he sees fit. Each legislator (6) serves for a specified period of time, after which he must vacate his status or again compete for it, and (7) the legislature has certain specific powers and is denied certain others. Through this set of related norms, and many others specifying the roles of federal, state, and local executives, judges, policemen, and people in related statuses, the function of maintaining order in the society is carried out. This integrated set of norms is the American political institution. Neither the Senate Building nor the people in it are the institution; the institution is the complex of folkways, mores, and laws which determines the way order shall be maintained in the society.

A family, then, is not an institution; *the* family is. That is, our social norms call for a group whose members are to have certain behavior toward one another, and this group is responsible for the essential social function of the reproduction of new members.

1 · For a theoretical analysis of the relationship among the major structural concepts in sociology, see three papers by Frederick L. Bates: "Position, Status, and Role: A Reformulation of Concepts," *Social Forces,* 1956, 35:313–321; "A Conceptual Analysis of Group Structure," *Social Forces,* 1957, 36:103–111; and "Institutions, Organizations, and Communities: A General Theory of Complex Structures," *Pacific Sociological Review,* 1960, 3:59–70.

INSTITUTIONAL STRUCTURES

One cannot observe the values on which an institution is based. One can only observe human behavior; the norms must be inferred from the behavior. If, for example, one studies a society in which nearly all the adults are married but no husband has more than one wife and no wife more than one husband, he can conclude that the familial institution of that society calls for monogamy. It is the culture patterns, the regularities in shared behavior, which allow us to specify the content of institutions.

One of the first things a sociologist does in analyzing an institution, then, is to examine its structure. Since he cannot directly observe the norms themselves, he studies the interrelated roles of the people who are conforming to the normative structure. To return to the example from the preceding paragraph, the first step in studying familial institutions is the analysis of familial structures.

Every institution, in order for its functions to be performed, has a division of labor among its participants. Among the many norms making up the institution are those defining the various roles necessary to the performance of the institutional function. The familial institution, for instance, is responsible for the reproduction of new members for the society; it will therefore specify role behavior appropriate to the statuses of father, mother, son, daughter, suitor, husband, wife, and any other statuses, such as obstetrician or midwife, which are related to the reproductive function in the society.

Of course, not every person who participates in a given institutional structure has exactly the same behavior as every other person in the same role. For one thing, the expectations of one institutional role may interfere with those of another. The expectations of career woman *vs.* those of mother, for example, create role conflict for a person who tries to work and rear children at the same time. Trying to balance the requirements of sometimes conflicting roles, then, can lead individuals to behave differently within the same institutional framework. In addition, each of us brings his own personality to any group in which he participates; we may all conform to its major norms, but our behavior will vary in many small ways. It is obvious that two women who may be described as mothers may behave quite differently within this role. There are, however, certain major expectations laid down within the familial institutions which lead to a set of similarities in their behavior: the institutionalized role of mother.

Sociologists are especially concerned with the place of each institution in any society; indeed, an emphasis on any one institution or number of institutions is a good indication of the ethics of a culture. A society which demands that its members spend half their time in worship and contemplation leaves them less time for family life, business, and other pursuits than a society with religious requirements that are not so stringent. The dominance of a single institutional structure is less likely for most persons in an urban society, because the urban way of life requires specialization, and each of one's roles tends to be but a segment of his total social life. As Arnold M. Rose says,

Institutions vary in the degree of specialization expected of persons, and this

Ewing Galloway

Rainmaking ceremony in Zululand. Manifest function: to relieve drought. Latent function: release of emotional tensions, reinforcement of in-group solidarity.

is often related to the degree of control the institution has over the life of its members. The more specialized and segmentalized the relation of a given member to an institution, the less is its control over him. The teacher is associated with the school only in his occupational life, whereas the nun is associated with the church in most aspects of her life. Even within the same institution this holds true: the religious leader (rabbi, priest, minister) has a less specialized relation to his church than does the average member, and his life is much more controlled by the institution. To the extent that an individual's life is controlled by one institution, he must have fewer relationships to other institutions. A priest, for example, must even withdraw from family life.[2]

2 · Arnold M. Rose, *Sociology: The Study of Human Relations* (New York: Alfred A. Knopf, Inc., 1956), p. 131. By permission.

Both formal and informal institutional structures exist. The United States Army is a highly formalized part of our political institution. Its part in fulfilling the function of maintaining order is regulated by written rules that are very specific and complex. Congressional lobbies are also regulated by our political institution, but for the most part, the sanctions imposed on lobbyists and the code of what constitutes proper lobbying behavior are informally structured.

INSTITUTIONAL FUNCTIONS

The essential social functions which must be met in any society in order for it to survive were discussed in Chapter 7. Societies must reproduce

Ewing Galloway

Familial functions are universal; institutionalized norms vary from culture to culture: marriage ceremony uniting Zulu chief and his sixth wife.

new members, socialize them, give them a sense of purpose, and provide for the maintenance of order and the production and distribution of goods and services. Each of these major functions is performed through some social structure, and that structure is regulated through a set of related norms, an institution.

It is simple to diagram the necessary relationships between the structures and their functions: reproduction occurs in the familial structure; the economic structure implements the production and distribution of goods and services; the educational structure implements socialization; and so on. This, however, is an analytic exercise, not a total description of a society.

Responsibility for the major functions is usually divided among several structures. The school, the church, the family, the play group, the theater—all perform a part of the task of socialization. Similarly, the sense of purpose may be rooted in any one or several of the principal institutional structures. Moreover, each structure may have functions in addition to its intended, recognized one.

Every institution centers around a fundamental need, permanently unites a group of people in a cooperative task, and has its particular body of doctrine and its technique or craft. Institutions are not correlated simply and directly to their functions; one need does not receive one satisfaction in one institution.[3]

Functions which are intended and recognized are called *manifest func-*

3 · Bronislaw Malinowski, "Culture," *Encyclopedia of the Social Sciences*, 4:626 (New York: The Macmillan Co., 1931).

tions; unrecognized or unanticipated functions are called _latent functions._[4] Free public education, for example, is a value in our culture, and our society contains structures to provide for this value. These structures have several manifest functions: molding literate, politically conscious citizens; training for adult roles; preparing for some occupational roles; preparing for college. But they also have latent functions: keeping adolescents out of the labor force, for example, has not been deliberate.

An outside observer can sometimes perceive latent functions of which participants in the structure are unaware. A manifest function of large-scale auto races is the satisfaction of the participants' and spectators' interest in speed and skill. A latent function frequently commented on by those opposed to the sport is the provision of an opportunity to tempt death or, in the case of spectators, possibly to see death occur.

The significance of institutional analysis for sociology lies in the fact that the total social structure of a society and its functions, both manifest and latent, can be seen efficiently in a description of its major institutions and their interrelationships.

INSTITUTIONAL DEVELOPMENT AND CHANGE

Institutions are not static. Like any other part of culture, they change through time. Alterations in one institution invariably reverberate throughout the institutional structure of a so-ciety, with changes in one set of norms bringing changes in others.

Let us take, as an example of the way institutions change, our own culture patterns of courtship and the norms governing the selection of a husband or wife. Here we can see the impact of religion, economic changes, urbanization, and the mass media on familial institutions.

Source of Courtship Patterns Our present concepts of courtship and marriage derive mainly from the belief that romantic love is the true foundation of happy marriage. The sentiment involves several ideas, most of them mystical: the idea that one can tell when he is "in love," that such love is abiding, that it involves mutual sacrifices as well as satisfactions, that the prospective mate will fulfill an ideal, that sexual passion is beautiful when it is an expression of love.

The cultural root of Western ideas about romantic love is to be found in the latter Middle Ages, in the so-called Age of Chivalry. The notion of romantic love arose among the nobility and their literary protégés. Gallant knights and troubadours carried romantic love to great heights, in poetry and perhaps in life. However, the "amorous cravings," the romanticism, and the sentimentalism about women were expressed "outside the bonds of matrimony," [5] marriage being arranged by parents, who kept in mind matters of status and wealth. Ideally, at least, true love was chaste, the idea that sexual fulfillment is all right for those "in love" developing later. The rationale of

4 · Robert K. Merton, _Social Theory and Social Structure,_ rev. ed. (New York: The Free Press of Glencoe, 1957), pp. 21–82.

5 · For an account of medieval romantic love, see Henry Osborn Taylor, _The Mediæval Mind,_ 4th ed., Vol. I (New York: The Macmillan Co., 1925), pp. 586–602. Quotation from p. 587.

Familial functions are universal; institutionalized norms vary from culture to culture: Glasgow bride and groom being piped to car by members of the groom's regiment.

Black Star

medieval romanticism is described thus by Taylor:

> Love, with the Troubadours and their ladies, was a source of joy. Its commands and exigencies made life's supreme law. Love was knighthood's service; it was loyalty and devotion; it was the noblest human giving. It was also the spring of excellence, the inspiration of high deeds. This love was courteous, delicately ceremonial, precise, and on the lady's part exacting and whimsical . . .[6]

While such high-flown and extreme expressions of romantic love disappeared with the decay of feudalism, the ideas and practices were carried down in the courts of kings and nobles.

6 · *Ibid.*, pp. 588–589. By permission of The Macmillan Company, publishers.

Finally, in the last three centuries, the rich bourgeois class everywhere has imitated the nobility; and since the eighteenth century the petty bourgeoisie has taken over many romantic ideas from these other classes.

The idea of romantic love has conflicted somewhat with traditional religious doctrines which deny the flesh and emphasize the life to come. However, since the idea of romantic love is pleasant and moreover is compatible with the stress on individualism which accompanied the rise of Protestantism and capitalism, it has flourished. What has emerged is a combination of features of both the romantic and Judeo-Christian ideals: stress on free choice of mate, constancy in love and stability

Monkmeyer

Ewing Galloway

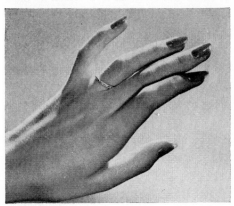
Ewing Galloway

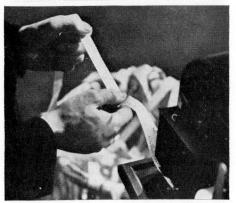
Ewing Galloway

Institutions—sets of norms—are represented by physical symbols.

of the family, disapproval but some sympathy for the wayward.

In colonial America, though the father continued to have chief control over the marriage of children, young people were allowed some freedom in the choice of a spouse. The colonies safeguarded marriage, however, by requiring that the consent of the parents be clearly expressed and that the marriage be recorded.

On the frontier and in rural America during the nineteenth century there was considerable freedom in the choice of mates. "Keeping company" was a folkway, though courtships tended to be brief. Romance in the rural community was usually but a prelude to a marriage and family life in which a wife and children were useful as economic assets, in addition to any affectional needs they might satisfy.

Courtship in the town life of the nineteenth century tended to be somewhat more prolonged. It was a period of testing and trying, in which "spooning" was tolerated but sex relations were tabooed.

Rapid urbanization since the opening of the present century brought further changes in courtship patterns. The high mobility of the population, the loss of primary-group controls, the increasing degree of specialization, the impersonal nature of many contacts, and other aspects of modern mass society have profoundly influenced courtship practices. For example, the sexual element in love-making has become rather openly recognized, both in communication and in overt conduct. Young people talk more freely about the biological foundations of mating. Advertisements carry material dealing with personal hygiene which would not have been tolerated a few decades ago. The automobile has permitted freedom of movement and thus helped do away with the former rigid control of love-making through community gossip. Young people are now able to escape the eyes and ears of parents and neighbors. The motion picture, television, and other media of mass communication have also helped alter the older family controls, as well as providing new romantic imagery.

Rapid Changes in Institutional Structure and Function: The Chinese Family The development of the set of norms governing courtship and marriage in American society illustrates institutional dynamics over a considerable period of time. An example of rapid institutional change can be seen in the Chinese family.[7]

For centuries, Chinese culture was characterized by a familial structure based on filial piety and extensive obligations to relatives. An individual's marriage was therefore a matter of great concern to his whole family, since it constituted a contract of mutual obligations among all those related to both spouses. Among the upper classes, the choice of a husband or wife lay with the parents and grandparents, since marriage was defined as an alliance between households. The most important criterion in the selection of a mate was the wealth and prestige of the family. Through shrewd marriage contracts a number of families of high status could be combined into a powerful group. Among the peasants, the principal factor to bear in mind in selecting a wife was her working ability. Her physical attractiveness or ability to inspire romantic inclinations was of no importance compared with her potential productivity as a field laborer.[8]

Even before the Communists achieved political dominance in China, the beginnings of "Westernization" of the family could be seen.[9] The traditional patriarchal, extended family was giving way to a smaller, husband-wife-and-child family unit, and mutual affection rather than family obligation was the rationale for mate selection. This change in familial institutions was still in process at the time of the Communist revolution.

7 · Hsaio-Tung Fei and C. Chang, *Earthbound China: A Study of Rural Economy in Yunnan* (Chicago: University of Chicago Press, 1945); M. H. Fried, *Fabric of Chinese Society: A Study of the Social Life of a Chinese County Seat* (New York: Frederick A. Praeger, 1953); Francis L. K. Hsu, "The Family in China," *The Family: Its Function and Destiny*, ed. Ruth N. Anshen (New York: Harper & Brothers, 1949), pp. 73–92; Francis L. K. Hsu, *Under the Ancestor's Shadow: Chinese Culture and Personality* (New York: Columbia University Press, 1948); Francis L. K. Hsu and J. H. Hu, "Guild and Kinship Among the Butchers in West Town," *American Sociological Review*, 1945, 10:317–364; Rose Hum Lee, "Research on the Chinese Family," *American Journal of Sociology*, 1949,

54:497–504; Marion J. Levy, Jr., *The Family Revolution in Modern China* (Cambridge: Harvard University Press, 1949).

8 · Hsaio-Tung Fei, "Peasantry and Gentry: An Interpretation of Chinese Social Structure and its Changes," *American Journal of Sociology*, 1946, 52:1–17.

9 · Olga Lang, *Chinese Family and Society* (New Haven: Yale University Press, 1946).

Since the revolution, the norms governing familial social relations have undergone another radical change. The government is making a deliberate attempt to exploit the familial institution for the benefit of political solidarity. The state urges young Chinese to select spouses with a view to founding a family that will contribute to the new order.

Marriage is no longer taken as a matter involving two families as in traditional China, nor between two individuals as in the Western world, but a spiritual union of two comrades of different sexes; and the first task of the couple is to strengthen and cherish their commonly shared belief of communism, and then to engage in production to build a new society.[10]

Contemporary China illustrates a deliberate attempt at institutional change. The familial norms were once *a*, if not *the*, dominant institution in Chinese society. The authorities are now trying to convert the family into an institution responsible for strengthening political consciousness and loyalty.

* * *

In the next five chapters we shall take up each of the major social institutions. It should be remembered that social scientists, like other scientists, interest themselves in general principles. The physicist is not interested in the behavior of *this* golf ball on *that* hill, but in the behavior of matter on an in-

10 · Shu-Ching Lee, "China's Traditional Family, its Characteristics and Disintegration," *American Sociological Review*, 1953, 18:272–280. Quotation from p. 280.

clined plane—any matter, on any plane, any time, anywhere. In the same way, the general sociologist is primarily concerned not with one family, nor with a set of families, nor with the twentieth-century American family. He is seeking generalizations about the social organization of human groups. His scientific commitment is to further the understanding of human social behavior. He does research on the American family to learn, for example, how socialization affects role definition, regardless of whether the socialization occurs among middle-class Americans, Chinese peasants, or Masai warriors in Africa. The ultimate goal of the sociologist is not to provide descriptions of social groups in some definite time or place but to make generalizations about social life. He studies institutions, therefore, because knowledge of the sets of norms which govern universal structures and functions in one society can be compared with that of institutions meeting the same needs in other societies, and such comparison will highlight the universal features of social life.

In these five chapters, we shall follow the order in which the universal social structures and functions were presented in Chapter 7: familial, educational, religious, economic, and political. Each chapter will have sections on the structures, the functions which they provide, and the patterns associated with them in the United States, and will close with a general section on the institutions as they are interrelated.

INTERPRETATIVE SUMMARY

The term *institution* is closely related to the word *structure*, the difference being that an institution is a set of *norms* which are embodied in specific structures. Institution is a key concept for both general sociologists and students of specific cultures. The latter examine the relative importance of institutions within a society and are thus able to tell what the society considers important. Their research on institutions leads to knowledge about all the structures and functions of the society.

Like structures, institutions may be formal or informal. While each institution has at least one avowed function, many have one or more functions which are unrecognized by some or even all participants. Finally, institutions are dynamic. They may change gradually or rapidly, as a result of conscious effort of participants or outsiders, or by the gradual falling off of outworn norms. The way in which the United States has modified and blended traditional standards concerning love and marriage is a good example of gradual, unconscious change in an institution. The change in China from the patriarchal, extended family unit to the westernized husband-wife-and-child pattern was also gradual and not conscious, while the later attempt by the Communists to change the pattern again to suit their own purposes was deliberate. As is the case with structures, functions, and other variables, a change in one institution will cause changes in other institutions, structures, and functions throughout the society.

REVIEW AND SUGGESTED READINGS

A · VOCABULARY

Division of labor	Latent function	Structure
Institution	Manifest function	

B · QUESTIONS AND TOPICS FOR REVIEW

1. *Structure* and *institution* are two closely related words. Pinpoint the differences between the concepts they represent.
2. "Sociologists are concerned, of course, with the place of each institutional structure in the ethos of a culture, since an emphasis on any one institution reduces the time and energy that can be allotted to the others." Which adult roles, and thus institutions, are considered most important by our culture?
3. To what extent are the norms of your religious group in conflict with romantic ideas about the institution of courtship and marriage?
4. Give an example of a group in which only some of the members, or none, were aware of latent functions. Give an example of one in which a latent function became a manifest function.
5. In what sense can latent functions be said to be good or bad?
6. What are some obstacles to deliberate change in the function or some of the norms of an institution?

C · SUGGESTIONS FOR FURTHER READING

James K. Feibleman. *The Institutions of Society*. New York: The Macmillan Company, 1957.

A study of various types of social institutions.

Neal Gross, Ward S. Mason, and A. A. McEachern. *Explorations in Role Analysis*. New York: John Wiley & Sons, Inc., 1958.

An example of the use in research and the interpretation of data of a conceptual scheme similar to that presented in this chapter.

Marion J. Levy, Jr. *The Structure of Society*. Princeton: Princeton University Press, 1952.

    An incisive analysis of how the parts of a society fit together.

Robert K. Merton. *Social Theory and Social Structure*, rev. ed. New York: The Free Press of Glencoe, 1957.

    Imaginative discussions of the structure of bureaucracy and the relationship between social structure and norms, and a provocative presentation of the case for functional analysis.

Talcott Parsons. *The Social System*. New York: The Free Press of Glencoe, 1951.

    A systematic, theoretical treatment of institutional structures and their functions.

Robin M. Williams, Jr. *American Society, A Sociological Interpretation*, 2nd ed. New York: Alfred A. Knopf, Inc., 1960.

    An examination of the institutional structure of contemporary United States from a functional point of view.

CHAPTER 20

The Family

The family is the basic primary group and the natural matrix of personality. A family is defined by the Census Bureau as "a group of two or more persons related by blood, marriage, or adoption and residing together." [1]

The precise facts about how the human family originated are unknown. Certain theorists contend that the original human grouping consisted of "group marriage," or a number of males and females living indiscriminately together, with the children of these unions considered the offspring of the whole group. Others have held that the original family was made up of only mother and children, the father, aside from his sexual function, playing a very insignificant role. Actually, no such condition as these theorists assume has ever been found, though in some societies male relatives in the mother's line have played a more important role than the biological father.

FAMILIAL STRUCTURES

In every society there is some form of regulation of family relations, fixing—within certain limits—not only the roles and statuses of the father and the mother but also making the child a legitimate member of the group. The

father or his surrogate normally has a family function, and the children have an approved role and status. This status carries over into the child's relations with the wider community.

Systems of Descent While biologically each individual is the product of two streams of genes—one from each parent—in many societies, lineage is counted in but one family line. When descent is traced in the father's line, or is *patrilineal*, the child takes the father's family name, becomes associated formally with the paternal family and clan, and has little or no relation with the mother's relatives. When descent is *matrilineal*, the child takes the mother's family name and is customarily more closely associated with her blood relatives than with the father's.

The *bilateral* family system, which we practice, seldom permits the solidarity and continuity possible in a unilateral scheme. Here the adults come together without the restrictions and binding influences found in the unilateral cultures. Although in our own bilateral system the children take their father's family name, both the mother's and father's relatives are considered kin of the child.

Lines of Control When the father or his family exercises control of the family, the organization is called *patriar-*

1 · Bureau of the Census, *Current Population Reports, Population Characteristics,* Series P-20, No. 17, May 19, 1948, p. 5.

chal. *Matriarchal* families are those where control is exercised by the mother or her relatives. Matrilineal families tend to be matriarchal in control, patrilineal to be patriarchal. Although in matriarchal families the mother has considerable power over the children, it is more often her family, rather than she alone, that regulates family contacts, as in the case of the Zuñi.

Familial Boundaries Particularly in folk societies, we find extended families, where the household unit consists of grandparents, married children, and grandchildren. (In patriarchal societies, such families are usually *patrilocal*—that is, a daughter lives with the family of her husband. In matriarchal societies, households tend to be *matrilocal*; the husband moves into the wife's home.) Such extended families are called *consanguine;* their boundaries are determined by blood relationship rather than by generations.

In our society the families are *conjugal*. An ordinary household consists of parents and their dependent children. When the children marry, they start separate households.

Types of Marriage Marriage is the institution or set of norms which determines the particular relation of parents to each other and to their children. The chief forms of marriage are monogamy, polygyny, and polyandry. (In popular usage *polygyny* is known as "polygamy.") Under any of these forms of marriage, the children's descent may be patrilineal, matrilineal, or bilateral, depending on the particular culture of the society.

Monogamy, the marriage of one man to one woman, is the most wide-spread form of mating. Since males and females are everywhere about equal in number—barring some special culture patterns such as infanticide—it is not surprising that monogamy is almost universal.

Polygyny is a type of marriage in which two or more women are legally mated to one man. The only extensive instance of polygyny in recent times in Western society was among the Utah Mormons, from about 1850 until 1890, when it was officially given up by the Mormon Church as a result of legal and moral pressures from the outside. It is estimated that about 5 percent of the marriages in this group were polygynous.[2]

It is a mistake to assume that polygyny arises from any marked sexual urges of the male. In most societies there is ample opportunity for sexual gratification outside conventional mating. Nor is there any society in which polygyny is widely accepted; monogamy remains the most common form of marriage.

Polygyny is really a form of multiple if interrupted monogamy. In most instances, each household is separate, and the husband rotates his attention among his wives. In some societies, however, there are joint households, where two or more wives and their children live together.

The most important motivations for polygyny are economic need and prestige. In Africa, for instance, wives are added to a household as the husband demands more help in order to

2 · For sociological accounts of Mormon polygyny, see Nels Anderson, *Desert Saints* (Chicago: University of Chicago Press, 1942); Kimball Young, *Isn't One Wife Enough?* (New York: Henry Holt & Co., Inc., 1954); and Thomas F. O'Dea, *The Mormons* (Chicago: University of Chicago Press, 1957).

An extended family in the United States.

Life Magazine

increase his wealth. In the Trobriand Islands of Melanesia, a chief's income consists of the annual endowments from the families of his various wives. Among the Tupis of South America, prominent men keep several wives for their prestige value, as well as for domestic service and labor in the fields. The same is true in Madagascar, in large sections of Africa, and among the Kai of New Guinea. Often the first wife urges the husband to take additional wives, each new one lightening the burden of the others, adding to the economic benefits, and improving the social status of the husband. The first wife frequently retains a certain position of favor and dominance over the other wives.

In polyandry several men are legally bound to one woman. This is the least common form of marriage, there being apparently but four or five localities in which it is found: in the Artic among certain Eskimo tribes; in Central Asia, especially Tibet; in the Marquesas; occasionally among the Bahima of Africa; among the Nayars of southwest and the Todas of southern India.

FAMILIAL FUNCTIONS

The family shares some of its functions with other social structures. For example, socialization is a consequence of the familial structure but it is a function which is also fulfilled by religious structures through Sunday School

*An extended family
in Africa.*

Life Magazine

classes, by formal educational organizations, by economic structures through on-the-job training programs, by informal neighborhood play groups, and so on. Conversely, the family participates in the maintenance of a sense of purpose, in the production and distribution of goods and services, and in other functions, even though it may not be the structure to which primary responsibility for these activities is assigned. We shall look first at reproduction, the one social function unique to the family in all societies, and then examine some of the other functions in which the family plays a part.

Reproduction The sexual life of man is not confined to the marriage situation, but all societies have norms attempting to guarantee that reproduction shall take place within a family framework. Everywhere there are variations in regard to premarital relations, and various extramarital patterns may be permitted along with more formalized family life.

In some tribes prenuptial intercourse is not only permitted but expected, though there is no evidence of complete promiscuity in any society. Everywhere incest taboos, kinship, age, and class rules limit the relations of the sexes both before and after marriage. While many peoples encourage, or at least tolerate, premarital relations, such relations are considered preparatory to marriage.

There is no uniformity in permissive premarital relations. In contiguous tribes, for instance, one group may put a high value on chastity, while their neighbors consider it of no consequence at all. Some folk societies, such as the Veddahs and other Negrito peoples, have as strong taboos against prenuptial sexual relations as our own Christian society, where chastity is a high virtue. In the Christian culture the sense of sin and guilt associated with sex affects not only premarital conduct but profoundly influences subsequent marital relations as well.

Among Christian peoples, however, rather striking differences often occur between ideal and practice. Kinsey's research indicates that a considerably greater amount of sexual activity takes place outside the marriage relationship than the ideal norms of our society would lead one to expect.[3] Since the patriarchal system, with all it implies for male dominance and female submission, was carried over into Christianity, it was very easy for the "double standard of morality" to arise. In many Christian communities the unmarried male is permitted prenuptial sexual freedom, but only with women whom he would not marry. The marriageable women of the community, in contrast, are held to strict taboos on premarital sexual relations. In such a society virginity is rated high, but male continence is neither expected nor often valued, in spite of theological taboos.

A study of 110 nonliterate societies around the world reveals that the

3 · Alfred C. Kinsey, W. B. Pomeroy, and C. E. Martin, *Sexual Behavior in the Human Male* (Philadelphia: W. B. Saunders Co., 1948); and Alfred C Kinsey, W. B. Pomeroy, C. E. Martin, and P. H. Beghard, *Sexual Behavior in the Human Female* (Philadelphia: W. B. Saunders Co., 1953).

least frequently and most lightly punished of deviations from the sexual mores is that of having premarital sexual relations. This is especially true when the partners are betrothed. The sexual offenses most frequently and severely punished are "incest, abduction, and rape." Moreover, the punishment increases with the likelihood of the offender's causing a child to be born outside the familial structure. Since a pregnancy arising from premarital sexual relations is likely to be followed by marriage, such relations are less severely punished than rape. In Western societies, the mother of an illegitimate child is scorned, and the child is often denied the right of inheritance. In all societies, some set of sanctions encourages the confining of reproduction to the family.

Socialization The basic socialization of the child takes place in the family. All the fundamental ideas, muscular skills, and norms are acquired in the home. Some of the things thus learned are deliberately and consciously taught the child by the parents, older siblings, and other close relatives. The child also learns a great deal nondeliberately—that is, unconsciously. This is especially true of basic attitudes and values.

The religious and moral training of children has always been bound up with the home; and though formal religious education has reached into the earliest years, the family still furnishes basic notions of God, of salvation, and of morality.

The home also provides the first recreational patterns for the child, though play groups furnish important connections with the wider world. In earlier times the family as a unit frequently participated in recreation together: games, picnics, family reunions. Today the individualized nature of recreation has tended to remove this function almost entirely from the home, though radio, television, and the automobile have done something to reunite the family in recreation.

As to education, the family provides the bases of all the child's later formal learning. In earlier societies the home furnished much of what is now in the hands of formal education; in spite of great changes, the family still gives the child his basic training in the social attitudes and habits important to adult participation in social life.

Habits of bodily care, of social relations, and of seeing the material world are learned in interaction with one's parents. Mother and father symbolize to the child forms of personal power. The child's own wishes must give way in the face of demands for obedience and conformity to these powers external to him. The manner in which he learns how to get along with his family will be carried over to interactions with school authorities, religious leaders, the police, and other agents of social control. So too, the way the child learns to look at the material forces around him will influence his future interests and attitudes toward science, religion, and art.

Normally, as the child grows up, he learns to manage situations outside the home and family; he extends his interests to other groups; his intelligence, his emotions, and his social habits develop until he weans himself from the original dependence on the mother, father, and other family members, who have served as his principal source of socialization.

Definition of Role Another important function of the family is to provide a sense of self for the child. Since the child is born helpless and incapable of managing his own behavior, it is highly important that he develop a sense of security out of his earliest social contacts in the family. The foundations of the sense of safety are laid as the child is shown love, care, and protection, and trained in regular habits of eating, sleeping, bodily care, and play. Consistency of training accompanied by love is of first importance; it provides the stability needed for further learning. It is basic to making the child's world friendly, understandable, and predictable. He must learn that his contacts with mother, with father, with brothers and sisters, and with others fall into more or less comprehensible and regular patterns—patterns marked by both affection and authority.

The sense of security is related to the child's definition of his own role. His assessment of his position in the family is fundamental to all his future relations in groups outside the home. Very often feelings of rejection, of difference, and of inferiority arise in the family and may carry over to later life. The self- or ego-ideal of the child will be affected at every point by his contacts with his parents. Parents may talk about honesty, truthfulness, perseverance, and other virtues of our culture, but it is their overt conduct, not their words, that provide the model.

The Economic Function Present-day American family life reveals changes in the relations of parents and children which grow out of current economic conditions. In urban communities par-

Ewing Galloway

Recreation has become one of the functions met by the economy.

ticularly, the absence of the father from the home for long hours leaves to the mother nearly all duties of child training and discipline, a condition not true of the earlier American family nor even now so true in rural America, where the father and children—at least those old enough to work—are often together for long hours daily.

The contrasts in the early and recent economy of the household are striking. In pioneer and early rural America, the husband and wife shared most economic activities. The household was the center of many work activities in which the wife played a definite role. Spinning, weaving, and making clothes continued for a long time to be her duty, and even when machine industry replaced a great deal of home manufacture, she made the clothes for the family. Then too, she took charge of curing meat, of preserving vegetables and fruit for winter use, and usually of the milk, eggs, and garden produce. The household members were concerned with *making a living* rather than with *earning wages*. Money economy had but slight place in the scheme of things.

Today the family is less and less an economic unit, especially in urban localities. In rural-farm families some of the older patterns remain. But the commercialization and mechanization of agriculture are dissolving the older rural home-centered economy.

Historically, the child has often been considered an economic asset. Among peasant peoples everywhere children are put to work at early ages in the fields and in the household. Even in some preagricultural societies boys are initiated early into fishing and hunting activities and girls into household duties. Today in the more industrialized societies child labor has pretty well disappeared.

The Conferring of Status One's position in the stratification structure is determined by the prestige of the statuses filled by his parents. As Winch says,

At birth one acquires a variety of initial statuses, and most of these are determined by the family and kinship organization into which he is born. As the individual passes through childhood into adulthood, he continues to possess some statuses which flow from his membership in a family group. Both child and adult, then, receive certain statuses because of their membership in a family. . . . Statuses conferred by the family consist of: (1) those which orient one in his relations with other members of the family (as designated by such kinship terms as brother, father, niece, etc.) and (2) those shared with the other members of the family which orient one with members of the society outside the family (urban, Protestant, middle-class, etc.).[4]

The achievements of one's parents can profoundly affect his life chances.

The Affectional Function It is easy to overemphasize the reproductive and socializing functions and to overlook the fact that the familial structure has functions as well for the many married couples who are childless. Some couples never have children; others live together for years before having children; in a society which has conjugal families, many couples live together for years after their children have left to found households of their own. What is the function of the institutionalized set of social relations between husband and wife?

4 · Robert F. Winch, *The Modern Family* (New York: Henry Holt & Co., Inc., 1952), pp. 83–84. By permission.

A strong need for dependency and security is present in every human being. This is built up in the child within the structure of the family. Adults carry over into later life this same need for confidence, reassurance, and emotional support from others. Today, with fewer children per family and with the disappearance of economic and educational activities from the home, husbands and wives are more and more dependent on companionship and sexual attraction to keep them together.

There is an especially important interaction centering in the sexual life. At the purely biological level this relationship among human beings is not far removed from that of the anthropoids. Actually, however, man's sexual activity is profoundly influenced by culture. While in some societies relatively little emphasis is put on the emotional aspects of sex, among many groups the act is bound up with mutual admiration, respect, and the desire of each mate to please the other in every way. As society removes from the family other functions, including much of the former heavy burdens in connection with child training, these more intimate relations may come to be more important.

FAMILIAL PATTERNS IN THE UNITED STATES

Our basic familial organization has its roots in the folk culture of western Europe, where family control was patriarchal in form. In addition to the major functions of childbearing and child rearing, the family was the important economic unit of the community. It also performed other important functions in education, religion, recreation, and the development of proper attitudes toward civic and other culture expectancies.

The Christian Church arose within the older primary-group organization of Europe. The church's position regarding family life was expressed in the doctrine of other-worldly asceticism, the doctrine of sexual sin, and ascription of low status to women. Christian taboos against sex were supported by all sorts of notions about its being sinful, lewd, nasty, and debasing. Women were thought chiefly responsible for man's downfall with the first instance. Marriage, while by no means man's highest state, was encouraged for the average person; and the church made marriage one of the sacraments in order to keep family life under its rule. This view continued for centuries, until disrupted by romanticism, individualism, and economic changes.

Romanticism, which we discussed in Chapter 19, fostered the idea of free choice of mates on the basis of love. The Renaissance, with its general enlightenment and criticism of tradition, influenced both theory and practice in regard to sex. Though the Protestant Reformation, especially its Calvinistic branch, laid heavy taboos on sexual freedom, its emphasis on individualism in other areas had the long-term effect of loosening the taboos. The Commercial Revolution furthered the trend, which expressed itself in business enterprise, in freedom of thought and expression, in the growth of the idea of the right of the individual to take part in the affairs of government, and in a general loosening of the older rigid class system. As individualism developed, as eighteenth-century rationalism began to have its effects, and as certain romantic notions persisted, the posi-

tion of women was somewhat improved.

Changes in familial patterns came slowly. Besides her major role of bearing and training children, the woman was obedient to her husband and a heavy contributor to the economic activities of the household, at least in all but the highest social class. She had no property rights of her own, and in law she was treated as a minor. She could not enter into a contract to do work or perform other services, and wages paid her went to her husband. She had no political rights or duties, such as voting or jury service. (In some parts of our country, women still are not subject to call for jury duty.)

With the Industrial Revolution came the gradual emancipation of women from complete dominance by father or husband; the attainment, finally, of political rights such as the vote; the gradual relaxation of the more severe Christian taboos on sex for both men and women; and the urbanization of population, with its effects on the economics of the household and on the decline of the importance of the home in education, religious training, and recreation.

In short, then, role expectations have altered and functions have changed in relative importance. Sexual relations, childbearing, and child rearing have proportionately a much larger place in total family life than they once had. In contrast, the economic function of the family and the home has become steadily less important. Comparable changes have occurred in other familial functions: religion and occupational training, for example.

Mate Selection Research indicates a strong tendency for people to select as spouses persons similar to themselves. That is, like marries like. (This is technically known as *homogamy*.) "Like" refers to all the sociological variables which we have studied: age, education, social class, race, religion, previous marital status, and area of residence.[5]

How mate selection is affected by residential propinquity, for example, is shown by a number of studies. When J. H. S. Bossard examined 5,000 consecutive marriage licenses issued in Philadelphia, he found that more than 17 percent of the couples gave residential addresses within one block of each other, 23 percent within two blocks, and over one-third within five blocks. More than half (52 percent) lived within 20 blocks of each other. Only 17 percent resided in different cities. Moreover, there is some evidence that the tendency of people to marry those in the same vicinity has actually increased, at least in certain cities. Ray H. Abrams found this to be true for Philadelphia, as did Ruby Jo Reeves Kennedy for New Haven.[6]

Apparently not only distance but also density of population influences the relative rates of selection of those nearby. On the basis of his studies in New England, John S. Ellsworth concludes tentatively, "Other things being equal, the possibility of marriage between persons living in different population groupings decreases as the distance between them increases but tends to increase with the number of persons available at given distances." [7]

It is not mere propinquity or density, however, which determines such assortative mating. Rather, it is that people of similiar race, nationality, occupation, religion, and social class tend to live in the same neighborhoods. In

5 · For evidence of homogamy in each of these areas, see: AGE: Paul C. Glick and Emanuel Landau, "Age as a Factor in Marriage," *American Sociological Review*, 1950, 15:517–29; August B. Hollingshead, "Age Relationships and Marriage," *American Sociological Review*, 1951, 16:492–499; A. Philip Sundal and Thomas C. McCormick, "Age at Marriage and Mate Selection: Madison, Wisconsin, 1937–43," *American Sociological Review*, 1951, 16:37–48; EDUCATION: Paul H. Landis and Katherine H. Day, "Education as a Factor in Mate Selection," *American Sociological Review*, 1945, 10:558–560; SOCIAL CLASS: Richard Centers, "Marital Selection and Occupational Strata," *American Journal of Sociology*, 1949, 54:530–535; August B. Hollingshead, "Cultural Factors in the Selection of Marriage Mates," *American Sociological Review*, 1950, 15:619–627; RACE: John H. Burma, "Research Note on the Measurement of Interracial Marriage," *American Journal of Sociology*, 1952, 57:587–589; R. Risdon, "A Study of Interracial Marriages Based on Data for Los Angeles County," *Sociology and Social Research*, 1954, 39:92–95; RELIGION: August B. Hollingshead, "Cultural Factors in the Selection of Marriage Mates," *American Sociological Review*, 1950, 15:517–529; Ruby Jo Reeves Kennedy, "Single or Triple Melting Pot? Intermarriage in New Haven, 1870–1940," *American Journal of Sociology*, 1944, 49:331–339; Kennedy, "Single or Triple Melting Pot? Intermarriage in New Haven, 1870–1950," *American Journal of Sociology*, 1952, 58:56–59; PREVIOUS MARITAL STATUS: Paul C. Glick, "First Marriages and Remarriages," *American Sociological Review*, 1949, 14:726–734.

6 · See J. H. S. Bossard, "Residential Propinquity as a Factor in Marriage Selection," *American Journal of Sociology*, 1932, 38:219–224; Ray H. Abrams, "Residential Propinquity as a Factor in Marriage Selection: Fifty-year Trends in Philadelphia," *American Sociological Review*, 1943, 8:288–294; Ruby Jo Reeves Kennedy, "Premarital Residential Propinquity and Ethnic Endogamy," *American Journal of Sociology*, 1943, 48:580–584. See also M. R. Koller, "Residential Propinquity of White Mates at Marriage in Relation to Age and Occupation of Males, Columbus, Ohio," *American Sociological Review*, 1948, 13:613–616; and J. R. Marches and G. Turbeville, "The Effect of Residential Propinquity on Marriage Selection," *American Journal of Sociology*, 1953, 58:592–595.

7 · From John S. Ellsworth, "The Relationship of Population Density to Residential Propinquity as a Factor in Marriage Selection," *American Sociological Review*, 1948, 13:444–448. Quotation from p. 448. By permission. Ellsworth's findings may be tied in with S. A. Stouffer's theory of "intervening opportunities." See the latter's "Intervening Opportunities: A Theory Relating Mobility and Distance," *American Sociological Review*, 1940, 5:845–867.

short, the ecological factors of segregation have a place in this process.

While homogamy governs mate selection so far as social characteristics are concerned, like does not always tend to marry like so far as psychological variables are concerned. For example, while a young man is likely to marry a young woman of the same social class, same religion, and comparable education, he may marry a girl whose personality tends to be opposite to his rather than similar in make-up. If a submissive man marries a dominant woman or a hostile man marries a deferent woman, we may say that their motivations or needs are complementary.[8]

The Measurement of Marital Adjustment. Various attempts have been made to determine the specific elements which make marriage a success or failure in this country. These studies deal chiefly with middle-class urban families.[9] They throw light on the possibility of predicting marital satisfaction on the basis of premarital experiences and situations, since they indicate some of the more important factors making for success or failure in wedded life. Of course, no one factor alone is significant.

The researchers report that a high degree of marital happiness between one's parents, absence of conflict with

8 · For a fuller explication of this theory, with illustrative cases, see Robert F. Winch, *Mate-Selection: A Study of Complementary Needs* (New York: Harper & Row, 1958).

9 · See E. W. Burgess and L. S. Cottrell, Jr., *Predicting Success or Failure in Marriage* (Englewood Cliffs, N.J.: Prentice-Hall, Inc., 1939); L. M. Terman, *et al.*, *Psychological Factors in Marital Happiness* (New York: McGraw-Hill Book Co., 1938); and E. W. Burgess and Paul Wallin, *Engagement and Marriage* (Philadelphia: J. B. Lippincott Co., 1953).

parents, and strong attachments to mother or father are predictive of success in one's own marriage. They find that having had firm but not violent discipline and parental instructions in sexual matters is important. Income, on the other hand, is not very significant. It must be stressed again that no one of these factors is crucially important in itself, but that combinations of them may be highly significant. Of all the factors, probably happy home life and likeness in socialization are the most important.

Size and Composition of the American Family In spite of some popular notions about the ill effects of divorce and the emancipation of women on the American family generally, not only is a high proportion of our population married but our young people wed at a relatively early age. In fact, the age at marriage has been dropping for some decades. The median age at first marriage for men declined from 26.1 years in 1890 to 22.8 in 1960. The corresponding figures for women were 22.0 in 1890 and 20.3 in 1960. (See Table 33.)

The early marriage age in the United States results in a high proportion of married persons in the total population. The situation is quite different in most other industrialized countries, where an aging population, less national wealth, and lower standards of living probably play a part in delaying entrance into matrimony. To cite a few comparative figures from the late 1940's: For males aged 20–24 and 25–29 who had ever married, the United States percentages were 28 and 64 respectively. For Eire, in contrast, the percentages for these two age groups were 3 and 17 respectively. In

TABLE 33 · Median Age at First Marriage, by Sex, for the United States: 1890 to 1960 *

Year	1890	1900	1910	1920	1930	1940	1950	1960
MALE	26.1	25.9	25.1	24.6	24.3	24.3	22.8	22.8
FEMALE	22.0	21.9	21.6	21.2	21.3	21.5	20.3	20.3

* *Current Population Reports: Population Characteristics*, Series P-20, No. 72 (Washington, D.C.: U.S. Government Printing Office, December 21, 1956), p. 3, and "U.S.A. Population Changes: 1950–60," *Population Bulletin*, 1963, 19:32.

England and Wales they were 14 and 53 percent; in France, 21 and 64 per-cent—much nearer our own. For fe-males aged 15–19 years and 20–24 years, the United States percentages were 12 and 55 respectively; for Eire, 1 and 12; for England and Wales, 2 and 26; for France, 6 and 49.[10]

Though the marriage rate has been high, the average size of the American family has been shrinking. At the time of our first census in 1790, the average number of persons per family was 5.7. A hundred years later it was 4.9. By 1940 it had fallen to 3.8, and by 1960 to 3.65.

The changes in family size are cor-related, of course, with (1) childless marriage, the extent of which is indi-cated by the fact that 15 percent of American women who marry bear no children; (2) an aging population, which means that more families with no minor children survive than for-merly; (3) an increase in the average span of time between marriage and birth of the first child; and (4) the gen-eral decline in the rate of population growth.

FAMILIAL INSTITUTIONS

Let us look now at the institution of marriage and the sanctions sur-rounding it.

10 · "Americans Marry Young," *Statistical Bulletin*, 1947, 28, No. 2, p. 9.

Marriage Sex relations and marriage must not be confused. Marriage is a group-sanctioned bond establishing the family relations, especially with refer-ence to offspring. Sex relations do not necessarily lead to marriage. Indeed, marriage in most societies is not gen-erally encouraged for sexual or ro-mantic reasons. It is not sexual gratifi-cation that is the primary purpose of marriage but rather the legitimacy of the offspring and their care and train-ing through the early years. In the words of Malinowski, "Marriage on the whole is rather a contract for the production and maintenance of chil-dren than an authorization of sexual intercourse."[11] As we have seen in our own culture, the sexual and affec-tional phases of marriage may become more important with the decline of ec-onomic and related functions in the family.

In most societies, marriage is a secular, not a religious, contract. Reli-gious sanctions, true enough, are often added, but marriage is not universally supported by religion. When religion has a part, as in Judeo-Christianity, it may serve to increase the emotional bonds and to put more weight be-hind the community controls over the family.

Marriage implies a welding of two

11 · Bronislau Malinowski, "Marriage," *Encyclopaedia Britannica*, 14th ed., 14:940–950 (Chicago: Encyclopaedia Britannica, 1929).

lives together in reference to certain obligations and duties. Since people think concretely, this union is usually expressed by a symbol. In various parts of the world one finds such rites as the bride and groom eating out of a common bowl, drinking from the same vessel, mixing clay or earth together from two separate lots, performed as symbolic of the union. Marriage symbolism is illustrated in our own society by, among other things, the use of engagement and wedding rings.

Marriage Sanctions No society permits absolutely free selection of mates. As we have seen, close degrees of blood relationship, age differences, class differences, and wider kinship relations limit this choice.

The *incest taboo* is without doubt the most nearly universal restriction on mating. It prohibits marriage chiefly between parent and child and between brother and sister. Yet it often reaches out to more remote blood relatives. The few historical instances of sanctioned incest, as among the ruling families of ancient Egypt, Peru, and Ireland, were not the result of primitive conditions but of a belief in divine powers that would be dissipated by marriage outside the royal line.

The intensity of the taboo is some indication that the rules are sometimes broken. Social workers, psychiatrists, lawyers, clergymen, and others dealing with more intimate family problems realize that incest is not unknown in present-day society; nor is it confined to any one class.

Exogamy is the type of union in which a person marries someone outside his own group, whether the group be family, clan, village, or other social unit. The opposite type of union, in which a man mates within his group, is called *endogamy*.

Tribal endogamy is almost universal. In the more rudimentary societies it is a natural outcome of isolation and strong in-group solidarity. Within the tribe or larger society, where a clan system develops or where professional or aristocratic ranking or economic status or a caste system arises, endogamy is generally required or at least strongly encouraged.

Exogamy arises wherever groups of persons are believed sufficiently related to be forbidden to marry, with a consequent insistence on their mating in other groups within the wider community. It is usually found in association with wider kinship and clan relations. In our own bilateral system, formal exogamy is in little evidence, marriages between distant relations not being considered incestuous.

Two factors govern the selection of a spouse: (1) the degree to which a society's normative structure allows one a free choice, on the one hand, or, on the other, allows his parents, priest, employer, or someone else to decide whom he should marry; and (2) the degree to which the norms rule ineligible some persons whom one might marry. Linton Freeman has cited four extreme situations which can arise from variations of these two factors.[12]

When a man from the Yaruro Indian tribe of Venezuela is of marriageable age, his mother's brother picks one of his daughters for the young man, and the bridegroom moves into his uncle's household. The only fe-

12 · This discussion is adapted from Linton C. Freeman, "Marriage Without Love: Mate Selection in Non-Western Societies," Chapter 2, in Robert F. Winch, *Mate Selection: A Study of Complementary Needs* (New York: Harper & Row, 1958).

males who are eligible brides are his mother's brother's daughters, and he does not even select the one he will marry. This would indeed indicate a rather narrow field of eligibles.

The Hottentots also marry within a small field of eligibles determined by kinship, but within the field one is allowed free choice of mates. In feudal Japan the field of eligibles was wide, but the participant had his spouse selected by his family. In the United States a situation opposite to that of the Yaruro prevails: an open field of eligible mates and the individual free to select his own spouse. Aside from the incest taboos concerning sexual relationships within the immediate family or between close cousins, which are enforced by custom and by law, people in the United States are not required to select their mates within determined limits.

Divorce In very few societies is marriage a contract terminated only by death; nearly everywhere there is provision for the dissolution of marriage under special conditions. When marriage is a religious rite or sacrament, however, divorce is often forbidden or extremely difficult to obtain. In many societies, when the family is an economic unit and offspring are economically valuable, a sterile wife may be returned to her family. If a bride-price

has been paid, this may be—often must be—repaid to the husband or to his father or family representative. Impotence in the husband is often recognized as a cause for marriage dissolution. Adultery is a widespread reason for divorce, though in societies dominated by patriarchal and masculine authority, adultery on the part of the husband is often condoned. Other grounds for divorce in some societies are economic insufficiency, emotional incompatibility, and insanity.

There has been a tremendous increase in the divorce rate in the United States during the past century. Such an increase is obvious evidence that the right to dissolve marriage by divorce has become more widely recognized and accepted both in the mores and in the law.

Almost everywhere, the presence of children acts as a deterrent to divorce, even though the customary or legal code permits dissolution. The tribe or state generally takes the view that the care of children is a primary obligation of the family, a fact which we have emphasized, of course, as basic to the whole historical function of the family. The economic value of children, as well as the difficulties involved in settling inheritance and financial questions when a family is dissolved, have also been important factors in keeping the family intact.

INTERPRETATIVE SUMMARY

The familial structure normally consists of a mother, a father, their children and, in some societies, certain members of one parent's extended kinship group. Where the system is patrilineal, control is likely to be patriarchal, and the wife may live with her husband's extended kinship group. In matrilineal societies, the reverse tends to be the norm. Bilateral structures have historically been patriarchal, though the household itself has tended to exclude all but the two parents and their children. Monogamy is the most common type of marriage. Polygyny and polyandry exist in some societies, an individual taking on multiple spouses for purposes of prestige and/or economic aid. All societies have some prohibitions involving mate selection. One almost universal prohibition is that against incest, within or without marriage; however, the definition of incest varies. Many societies further restrict eligibility along class or other in-group lines. Finally, a society may require that an individual's parents or some extended kinship group select his mate. Most societies have some provision for dissolution of marriage, though what constitutes justification for dissolution varies.

Reproduction is the one social function unique to the family in all societies, and all societies have more or less severe sanctions to ensure that reproduction does not occur outside marriage. Probably the next most important function is socialization of offspring. From early social experiences within the family, the child learns what his statuses and probable life chances are, and he develops a self-image. Historically, the family has been the basic economic unit, though this function has diminished in urban societies. As this and other functions have been removed from the family, the function of satisfying the basic human need for affection has become especially important.

The family in the United States is conjugal in nature. Descent is traced patrilineally, though the husband's and wife's kinship groups are both important, and the control of the father over the family is by no means absolute.

Most of the characteristics of the contemporary American family can be traced to economic upheavals such as the Industrial Revolution and to related ideational forces, particularly romanticism, the Renaissance, and the Protestant Reformation. For example, the emphasis on individualism has led us to leave mate selection largely to the individual, except for certain incest taboos. The belief in individual value has also led gradually to increased freedom and privileges for women. High standards of living, medical advances, and other factors have caused the marriage age to drop and the size of the average family to decline.

Researchers have found that the factors most responsible for happy marriages in our country are similarity of social background, previous happy family life, and healthy attitudes toward sex. Though individuals in the United States tend to marry people with socially similar backgrounds, the divorce rate in this century is high.

REVIEW AND SUGGESTED READINGS

A • VOCABULARY

Bilateral family	Matrilineal family	Polyandry
Endogamy	Monogamy	Polygyny
Exogamy	Patrilineal family	

B • QUESTIONS AND TOPICS FOR REVIEW

1. At present there are about 103 females per 100 males in the United States. What consequences has this situation already had, and what long-term consequences do you think will develop?
2. What sanctions are imposed in our country against (a) premarital sexual relations, (b) rape, (c) adultery, and (d) incest?
3. A young woman wrote to Ann Landers, a syndicated advice-to-the-lovelorn columnist, telling her that she was to be married in two months and that she had just discovered that she was pregnant. She asked the columnist whether

she should tell her parents immediately or simply go through with the planned church wedding, trusting that her condition would not be noticeable. The columnist's brief reply was that the parents should be told, since the young girl could not count on not appearing pregnant at the time set for the wedding. Discuss this answer in the light of American modes.

4. How do you account for the fact that Americans tend to marry young?
5. The American marital structure was described as *bilateral*. Qualify this statement.
6. At what stages in their lives do people tend to buy or increase their life insurance?
7. What are the strong and weak features of monogamy? How do you account for the high divorce rate in the United States? Is divorce common in all classes?

C • SUGGESTIONS FOR FURTHER READING

Jessie Bernard. *Remarriage: A Study of Marriage.* New York: Holt, Rinehart, and Winston, 1956.

A highly competent work which uses census data, case materials, and data on 2,009 marriages collected through interviews. Among other topics discussed are success or failure of remarriages, personality types of spouses in remarriages, intrafamily relationships, status of stepchildren, and the problems of aging.

E. W. Burgess, Harvey J. Locke, and Mary Margaret Thomes. *The Family: From Institution to Companionship*, 3rd ed. New York: American Book Company, 1963.

Provides broad coverage, chiefly from the standpoint of social psychology.

Harold T. Christensen. *Marriage Analysis*, 2nd ed. New York: The Ronald Press Company, 1958.

Part II, dealing with changes in family organization in the United States, is especially pertinent to this chapter.

E. Franklin Frazier. *Black Bourgeoisie: The Rise of a New Middle Class in the United States.* New York: The Free Press of Glencoe, 1957.

An excellent, objective treatment, both historically and sociologically.

Paul C. Glick. *American Families.* New York: John Wiley & Sons, Inc., 1957.

A very good description of the demographic and structural characteristics of the American family, based on data from the census.

William J. Goode. *After Divorce.* Glencoe, Ill.: The Free Press, 1956.

An empirical study of 425 urban mothers aged 20 to 38 at the time of divorce. Various cultural and personal background facts are analyzed, the conflict process leading to divorce is examined, and the post-divorce problems are discussed at some length.

Talcott Parsons and Robert F. Bales, with James Olds, Morris Zelditch, Jr., and Philip E. Slater. *Family, Socialization and Interaction Process.* Glencoe, Ill.: The Free Press, 1955.

A treatment of role differentiation in the family as an example of the working of universal processes in a primary group. Especially valuable are Chapter 5, by Bales and Slater, which reports research on role differentiation in small groups other than the family, and Chapter 6, by Zelditch, on a cross-cultural study of family structure.

Robert F. Winch. *The Modern Family*, rev. ed. New York: Holt, Rinehart and Winston, Inc., 1963.

Contains a nice contrast of the traditional Chinese peasant family with the family in an Israeli kibbutz, as well as an excellent analysis of the structure of the American family and its basic and derived functions.

Robert F. Winch, Robert McGinnis, and Herbert R. Barringer, eds. *Selected Studies in Marriage and the Family*. New York: Holt, Rinehart and Winston, Inc., 1962.

A collection of papers and chapters from various books covering a wide range of topics related to marriage and the family.

Gibson Winter. *Love and Conflict. New Patterns in Family Life*. Garden City, N.Y.: Doubleday & Co., Inc., 1958.

A discussion of cleavage between the demands for impersonal competition in the commercial world and the need for intimacy and love in the family.

CHAPTER 21

Sociology of Education

There is considerable variation in the make-up of societies, whether folk or urban. Some are small in numbers, some relatively large; some permit polygyny, others are strictly monogamous; some have a rather rigid class structure, in others the class system is loose and flexible; and so on. But regardless of size and the combination of choices from the cultural spectrum that prevails in any society, some structures to provide the function of socialization will be present. Each individual must learn the lore accumulated by his ancestors, must practice certain skills, must be indoctrinated with the values of his group, and must learn the expectations associated with the roles he will play.

EDUCATIONAL STRUCTURES

The transmission of culture can be only partially delegated to formal organizations, such as school systems or religious organizations. Much education always takes place in informal structures, such as play groups, where the child learns by imitating his older playmates. Even in structures specifically set up to perform the function of socialization, there is, in addition to conscious and formal transmission of culture, a great deal of nondeliberate and informal passing-on of knowledge, skills, and values. In American schools, for instance, we stress both competition and co-operation. The former is found in strong rivalry for rewards, such as grades for academic work or success in athletics. We train in co-operation through stress on group spirit and teamwork.

Informal Groups All nonliterate peoples have some form of transmission of culture, but the functions we think of as "educational" fall to the family, clan, or vocational or magico-religious guild. While there are many variations, the fundamental content of folk education is not unlike that of urban societies: folklore, mythology, history, manual skills, appropriate manners, and instruction and practice in the folkways and mores.

The differences in education among nonliterates rest, as they do with other peoples, on their views of the child. Some, like the Plains Indians, regard the child as a miniature adult, with much the same motives as an adult. Such tribes give much time to deliberate instruction in legends, moral tales, and religion. The Bantu-speaking Negroes of South Africa view the child as an irritating creature who is unaccountable in his conduct and subject, as are adults, to deception, threats, and intimidation. The Arapesh, in contrast, look on the child as one to be carefully guarded and gently in-

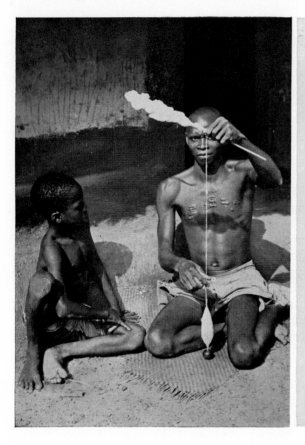

In a folk society, one is socialized into his occupational role by observing his parents: African boy watching his father spin thread.

Monkmeyer

structed, since his function will be to take over the care and protection of his elders.

Sometimes the work of teaching is done by the parents, with one or the other taking the main responsibility; sometimes it is in the hands of uncles or aunts or grandparents. Though formal schools as we know them are entirely lacking, some differentiation of specialists is present. Such are the craftsmen of certain guilds who teach the crafts, shamans or priests who instruct in magical or religious rituals, and war leaders who train youth in military skills.

Formal Organizations Education as a special function of a particular group or agency of society did not arise until mankind had invented writing and arithmetic and had advanced in agriculture, metallurgy, and commerce. All the ancient civilizations—Egypt, Babylonia, Assyria, Persia, India, China, Greece, and Rome—had systems of formal education. In all these, however, it was confined to the privileged and leisure classes, and much of what has now become a part of formal schooling, such as vocational and civic training, was left to other groups: familial, religious, political, and economic. The upper classes tended to stress philosophy and ethics, art and music, rhetoric, mathematics, and gymnastics and military arts—studies considered proper interests of the ruling classes.

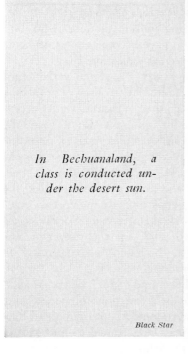

In Bechuanaland, a class is conducted under the desert sun.

Black Star

Education in the Middle Ages was in the hands of the Roman Catholic Church. At first it was rather meager, consisting of simple instruction of the illiterate masses in church regulations and intellectual and moral initiation of individuals into the priesthood and orders of the church.

The serious beginnings of modern education, both elementary and higher, had to await the Renaissance, the Reformation, and important economic changes. Protestantism, with its emphasis on individualism in religion, the rise of trade and city life, and the Industrial Revolution, which freed the individual from serfdom and the feudal mores, began to break the class and theological holds on education. It

became increasingly apparent that neither a sound representative government nor an efficient business or industry could be managed without literate and technically trained individuals.

Today all urban societies have extensive educational facilities: the school plant, a wide variety of curricula and methods of teaching, a specially trained personnel for management and instruction, and a rationale or philosophy of the aims, methods, and values of education.

Supplements to Formal Structures

The existence of schools, formal organizations which have as their principal function the education of the population, does not mean that all or even most socialization is provided by them. As we have seen, whether in folk or urban societies, most individuals receive their essential early training from their families. From parents and brothers and sisters people learn to walk and talk, and to distinguish the basic concepts of right and wrong which prevail in their societies. Even those of us who live in societies having elaborate formal educational systems get a large proportion of our knowledge and our ideas of good and evil outside the school— from our friends, our elders, and from observing people in everyday situations.

In addition to learning in primary groups and in school, the individual in a literate society is exposed to an enormous amount of facts and opinions through the mass media. It makes good sense to consider newspapers, radio corporations, book publishers, and similar organizations as supplementary educational structures.

The Press Books are pouring from American presses at the rate of about 15,000 titles a year. Nearly one-third of them are of a more or less technical character. These books furnish material for formal education, and the reading habits set up in school carry over to provide people a means of further acquisition of skills, knowledge, and entertainment. Perhaps even more important than books are magazines and newspapers, which have been increasing in circulation in recent decades.

Books, magazines, and newspapers flood us with a stream of words that cannot fail to leave their impression. This material is constantly providing not only facts but myths, legends, and stereotypes that are reflected sooner or later in political, economic, religious,

and moral attitudes and behavior. Reverence for the printed word is one of the reasons propaganda and advertising are very effective.

Movies, Radio, and Television In addition, the motion picture, radio, and television have become powerful media of mass communication.

These new visual and verbal stimuli constantly confronting our people influence their attitudes and habits, though in different ways than the press. For example, research into the effects of the radio shows that, for the most part, serious broadcasts reach chiefly the more educated groups, the very groups already under the influence of the printed page. For those less schooled and in the lower-income brackets, the radio is used mostly to give entertainment, relatively superficial advice, and "spot" news. In addition to their functions of newscasting and entertainment, both radio and television may be expected to find greater use in the school for more formal education.

Never before has the world had such an array of agencies for mass impression. Oratory, formal teaching, religious exhortation, and all other methods of arousing groups of people with the same stimuli at the same time pale into insignificance beside these mighty forces. Whoever controls these media will determine in large measure the direction our masses will go. In the capitalistic United States, while formal education is predominantly state-controlled, these other means of stimulation are, with few exceptions, in the hands of private enterprise. But to an increasing extent, other national states are taking over control of the newer devices, combining them with the tra-

Much socialization is accomplished informally.

ditional educational system, sometimes in order to bend them to the ends of their particular political and economic systems. This raises the profound question of the effect of propaganda, as well as of education, on thought and conduct.

Since the consequences of educational structures depend directly on the values embodied in the other institutions of a society, let us examine the contrast between two principal kinds of educational socialization found in contemporary societies: totalitarian and democratic.

EDUCATIONAL FUNCTIONS

While the modern world has seen the emergence of a variety of educational systems, the two modal patterns are those which center around the val-

ues and practices of representative democracy and those which are oriented toward totalitarian, authoritarian values and practices.

The aim of education, both formal and informal, in all societies is to socialize the young and old alike into the fundamental values, norms, and practices of the society. Each society justifies its kind of education as being "good" for the masses. The crux of the difference, of course, lies in what is considered good—that is, in what is defined as good by the culture.

Since the contrasts in values have bearing on both domestic and international affairs, it is important to know just what these differences mean, not only for political and economic institutions, but for such a powerful agency of cultural training as the school. Some of the important differences in the two social systems are reflected in the aims of education as related to the groups or classes which manage the social controls and sanctions, and especially to the larger purposes of the state.

Totalitarian Socialization

The aim and content of education are bound up with the theory of the interrelation of the society, the state, and the individual. Under totalitarianism, the state is considered to be coterminous and identical with the national society. In the words of Benito Mussolini, "Everything for the state, nothing outside the state, and nothing against the state." [1] Such a philosophy leaves no place for the rights and liberties of the individual as recognized under democracy.

Authoritarian states have a ruling elite which determines the basic philosophy of the state, its goals, and the methods of attaining those goals. Such a ruling group believes it has a mission. And the leaders provide the symbols of identification which help tie the masses to their rulers, all in the name of the larger totality.

In all authoritarian countries it is considered important to indoctrinate the young, through the schools and otherwise, with deference for and loyalty to the purposes of the ruling class. The methods of accomplishing such conformity and control take the form of regimentation of practically every aspect of the lives of the people. The stress on group solidarity is repeated in drama, song, literature, and in state-controlled organizations for all ages.

Under authoritarian rule, the control of the ruling class over the school is complete. The teachers are chosen in part because of their party loyalty, and are closely supervised; deviations from the "party line" are severely punished. The course of study is laid down by central authorities, and little or no modification at the local level is tolerated. Students of all ages must be given nothing but the "truth" prescribed by the ruling elite. An illustration from the Soviet Union is pertinent.

There was for a long time a bitter controversy among Russian scientists over the Mendelian principles of heredity. Marxist philosophers looked askance at genetics, since it does not appear to give sufficient weight to the role of the environment in making and remaking the individual. Periodically the debates of Russian biologists came to the attention of the Communist Party leaders. Lest such controversies undermine faith in the official Party views, pressure was exerted to enforce conformity. Thus in September, 1948, *Pravda*, the official newspaper of the Communist Party, published an open letter, addressed to Stalin and signed by the head of the national Academy of Medical Sciences of the Soviet Union, which said, in part, "We promise you, our dear leader, to remove the errors committed by us in the shortest time, and to reconstruct all our scientific work in the spirit shown us by the great party of Lenin and Stalin." [2]

In such authoritarian countries the idea of a free science and a free literature is no more to be tolerated than are conceptions and practices of free speech and free elections, if they run counter to the views of the ruling elite.

1 · Quoted in I. L. Kandel, "The End of an Era," *Educational Yearbook of the International Institute of Teachers College, Columbia University* (New York: Teachers College, Bureau of Publications, 1941), p. 71.

2 · Quoted in the *New York Times*, September 23, 1948, C8.

The controls are always rationalized, of course, as measures based on the sound views of the rulers.

Democratic Socialization In contrast to the patterns of authoritarianism under dictatorship are those traditionally associated with democracy. The ideal of a free man in a free society is so much taken for granted by individuals brought up under representative government that it is often difficult for them to comprehend any other scheme of life.

Democracy is more than a set of political institutions and processes. Under its philosophy the society is not considered to be coequal and coterminous with the national state. The latter is, rather, but an agency of the former and constantly under its control. As an old maxim has it, "The State is for man, not man for the State." Moreover, the basic philosophy rests on beliefs in natural rights to "life, liberty, and the pursuit of happiness." This implies, further, not only a jealous regard for one's own rights but a duty to provide and guard similar rights for others.

An examination of our Bill of Rights reveals a good foundation for the basic democratic philosophy that the state is the servant of the citizen, not his master. The Bill of Rights is a heritage from our British forebears, who opposed the monarchy, with its concept of divine right to rule, by setting forth—rather explicitly—what they regarded as their democratic rights. The chief items are to be found in the first ten amendments to the Constitution of the United States. Among the most important for us today are the provisions for free worship, for freedom of speech and writing, and for the rights of petition, private property, and trial by jury.[3]

It would be a mistake, of course, to assume that there are no class and other group controls in a representative democracy. There are. In some European countries the class structure is more rigid than it is in the United States. In Britain, for example, both the Anglican Church and the upper class have, in the past, largely determined policy and practice in education. While the Industrial Revolution brought an increasing extension of school opportunities for the middle and lower classes, the system itself changed very slowly toward a pattern more democratic in aim, content, and procedure.

In the United States, education was at first largely in the hands of the church and the local community; and it tended to be restricted to the financially abler classes. Free public education was not considered essential until it became clear to leaders and masses alike that universal literacy goes hand in hand with universal suffrage and participation in civil life. In most democratic countries the abolition of property qualifications for voting and office-holding is correlated with the demand for compulsory elementary education at public expense. In this matter the United States was far in advance of most other countries.

While the classroom subject matter has changed through the decades, American education has revolved around the concepts of sound knowledge, public welfare, training in basic

3 · Among college students, at least, there is great ignorance of the meaning of the Bill of Rights. See Raymond W. Mack, "Do We Really Believe in the Bill of Rights?," *Social Problems*, 1956, 3:264–269. See pp. 414–415 for pertinent data from this paper.

skills, and indoctrination in the fundamental values of democracy. An educated citizenry in a democracy means persons with not only sound knowledge and skill but also the ability to combine individual choice and freedom with a sense of personal and public responsibility for their judgments and actions.

This thesis does not imply that everyone will finish the same grade with the same education. Rather, it indicates that every means possible should be used to provide equality of opportunity in education for all the children of all the people, with due regard for individual differences. It is presumed that out of such a system will come intelligent citizens who will be capable of managing their own affairs and who at the same time will be voluntary participants in the larger concerns of the community and the nation. While we have not always been entirely clear as to the central theme of public education, for the most part we have been exceptionally successful in the diffusion of mass education.

Despite the many sharp and striking contrasts between education under representative democracy and under totalitarian systems, the aim of mass education is always to prepare the young for later participation in adult society. Hence the school will carry society's values to its charges. The aims and values may seem bizarre or dangerous to outsiders. For example, some nations which stress co-operation might be aghast at the degree to which we emphasize rivalry and competition in our schools; while most of us would certainly oppose the even greater degree to which competition is stressed in a country like, say, Japan, where suicides because of college failure are

common. But so long as a cultural system persists, the school will be its servant. Moreover, the moral principles of loyalty, obedience, patriotism, and a whole host of codes of good manners and mutual participation in group life have much in common in both systems. For example, many of the "Rules for School Children" adopted in 1943 by the Soviet leaders could fit, with slight modification, the democratic schools. The stress on diligence, obedience, personal cleanliness, good posture, use of proper language, and like matters is pretty much in the same general tradition as our own.[4]

Cultural variations are seldom completely distinctive and unique. So it is with matters of education.

Functions Other Than Socialization

Like any other structure, an educational structure can have *latent* functions—functions other than those for which it was created and intended. Formal school systems ordinarily have several latent functions.

For one thing, beyond the elementary grades, schools serve as a marriage market. People tend to select spouses of a class and educational status approximately equal to their own, and there is no more likely place to find them than at school. Both high schools and colleges afford opportunities to meet and get to know persons of the opposite sex in one's age category and educational status.

A related latent function of educational structures is to provide an op-

4 · See *I Want to Be Like Stalin* (New York: John Day Company, 1947), pp. 149–150. This book, from the Russian text on pedagogy by B. P. Yesipov and N. K. Goncharov, translated by George S. Counts and Nucia P. Lodge, is a mine of information about the content and method of teaching children in the Soviet Union under Stalin.

portunity to widen the student's circle of acquaintances. One usually leaves college, for example, with a set of friends different from and broader than the set with which he left high school. Related to this consequence is, for many, the function of forming relationships with people who will become business or professional contacts in the future.

The educational structure of the United States has an interesting latent function with respect to our economic structure: schools keep a sizable and fairly predictable proportion of able-bodied young people out of the labor force. Imagine the unemployment problem if we were suddenly to dump into the labor market the twelve million young people fourteen to eighteen years of age who are now attending school!

Other than socialization, probably the most important function of educational structures is conferring status. The amount of formal education one has is highly correlated with his class position. Research indicates that this is true not only in the United States but in Japan, Germany, the Soviet Union, and other societies.[5] Actually, education is related to one's position in the stratification structure in two ways: (1) a portion of people's evaluation of one's status derives directly from how much and what kind of education he has received, and (2) many of the other important criteria of class position, such as occupation, income, and style of life, are partially consequences of the type and amount of education one has had. Men who finish college, for example, earn two and a half times

as much as those who have only a grammar-school education.[6] Similarly, 55 percent of college graduates are professionals, while only 6 percent of high-school graduates attain such prestigious occupational statuses. And 25 percent of the people who get some high-school education but do not graduate are semiskilled laborers, whereas only 2 percent of the college graduates are found at this occupational level.[7]

Perhaps the surest indicator of the importance of education in the stratification system is the eagerness with which newly wealthy but relatively uneducated people surround themselves with the trappings of learning: a library, paintings, a symphony subscription, and so on. Nor is this deference to education confined to the wealthy. Fathers of moderate means who never graduated from high school see to it that their children attend college. Education, then, not only helps one acquire income and occupational prestige; the education itself confers status, as illustrated in the concept "educated person."

EDUCATIONAL PATTERNS IN THE UNITED STATES

Formal education in the United States has developed through three major phases. During colonial times and even during the first fifty years of our history as a nation, the support and control of education was almost entirely local. Between 1830 and 1880 the foundations of our modern school sys-

5 · Alex Inkeles and Peter H. Rossi, "National Comparisons of Occupational Prestige," *American Journal of Sociology,* 1956, 61:329–339.

6 · Elizabeth Hoyt *et al., American Income and Its Uses* (New York: Harper & Brothers, 1954), p. 103.

7 · Paul C. Glick, "Educational Attainment and Occupational Advancement," *Transactions of the Second World Congress of Sociology,* 2:183–94. London: International Sociological Association, 1954.

TABLE 34 · Per Cent of Population 7–24 Years of Age Enrolled in School, by Age, 1910–1960 *

Year	Age				
	7–13	14–15	16–17	18–19	20–24
1910	86.1	75.0	43.1	18.7	a
1920	90.6	79.9	42.9	17.8	a
1930	95.3	88.8	57.3	25.4	7.4
1940	95.0	90.0	68.7	28.9	6.6
1950	95.7	92.9	74.4	32.2	12 9
1960	99.5	90.3		38.4	13.1

a. Not available

* *Census of Population: 1950*, Vol. II, *Characteristics of the Population*, Tables 42 and 43; Current Population Reports, *Population Characteristics*, Series P-20, No. 107, January 16, 1961.

tem were laid down, paralleling in development the nation's expanding industrial life. During this period the states more and more assumed control over their educational systems.

After about 1880 there was growing recognition of the central importance of schooling. Child labor was gradually abolished, girls and women were afforded more educational opportunities, and the curriculum was broadened to include health and vocational education. There was a great increase in the total amount of time spent in school. There was even greater attention to high-school training; and there has come, in the last few decades, a great increase in enrollments in colleges and universities. Recently the belief has spread that education should be a continuous process from infancy throughout life, and there has been a tremendous growth in programs of formal adult education.

The Growth of Formal Education
That the people of the United States put great stress on education is shown by these few figures: The enrollment in schools and colleges in 1964 was over 52 million individuals. The full-time enrollees in 1947 accounted for 42 per-

cent of all individuals in the 5–34 age range; by 1964 the figure had risen to 58 percent. Of all American children between the ages of 7 and 14, more than 99 out of 100 were in school. An overall view of the changes is shown in Table 34, which reports the constantly increasing percentage of the population in school. In no other country in the world and at no other time in history has such a large proportion of a population been in school. There is reflected here an amazing faith in the value of formal education.

School opportunities have been constantly expanding for some decades. In 1880, of the 15 million individuals aged 5–17 years in our population, fewer than two-thirds were enrolled in school. By 1947, 85 percent, and by 1964 more than 95 percent of this age group were in school. By 1900 compulsory elementary education had become firmly established. And while secondary enrollments had been going up slowly since 1880, after 1910 they increased rapidly. In 1890 there were about 400,000 high-school students; in 1910 about 900,000. In 1940 there were 6.6 million; by 1964 there were more than 10 million. The growth of college and university enrollments has also

Monkmeyer

A traditional rural classroom with fixed desks and seats.

been impressive. In 1900 there were only about 200,000 students in this category. The next 40 years saw a million added to this number. In 1950 there were more than 2.2 million students in American colleges and universities; and in 1964 college and university enrollments reached a record high of over 4 million.

Changes in Curriculum Since what is taught in our schools is largely a reflection of the norms of the larger society, changes in the curriculum are indicators of trends in the total institutional structure of our society.

The main shifts in elementary-secondary education have been from curricula oriented around subject matter to those focused on the child as a growing personality. The former stressed content and capacity to repro-

duce what had been read or heard. Today the school is more and more child-centered, with stress on the self and on social development.

In methods, the shift has been from a rather severe authoritarian to a more permissive practice, in which the child has a larger degree of participation. "Progressive education," though now largely discarded as a formal technique, has influenced even the more conservative public and parochial schools. Motivation, co-operative learning, and mental hygiene are given much attention.

The rapid rise in high-school population, especially after 1910, led to a proliferation of separate courses and various groupings of courses of study, such as liberal or college-preparatory, commercial, vocational, and fine arts. There has been a drift away from

Black Star

A modern classroom with light chairs which can be turned toward the experimental tables or shifted to face the chalkboard.

courses designed to prepare the pupil for higher education to those which have a more practical usefulness in jobs or in the home and which give the future citizen some preparation for his public and political rights and duties. The ancient languages, algebra, geometry, trigonometry, and formal political history have tended to give way to modern languages, "modern" mathematics (with emphasis on understanding rather than mere mastery of operations), and social studies with emphasis on current problems. Intense competition with the Soviet Union has led to re-examination of the desirability of a stronger curriculum in science and mathematics. After Sputnik, it was contended in many high quarters of government and education that the Russian "superiority" or "success" was due to the fact that students in the USSR were far more thoroughly trained in the natural sciences, mathematics, and technology than those in the United States.

Along with these trends has gone considerable reorganization of the institutional framework. The secondary school is being extended downward to include the last two years of the traditional elementary program, and upward to cover the first two years of college. The former we know as the junior high school; the latter, the junior college. American junior colleges have grown rapidly. In 1927–1928 they had an enrollment of about 50,000; three decades later their enrollment had increased eightfold. Under the growing pressure for college education, many communities have established a two-year college course, sometimes in connection with their high schools. It may well be that these "community colleges" and the junior colleges will come to be the typical terminus of formal education for most of the population.

While development of high schools has been, to some extent, a hit-or-miss affair, and while there has been some confusion of purpose, the leaders of American education have come more and more to take the position that every normal person should have at least a high-school education, and an ever-growing portion of our young people at least two years of college. The trends in secondary education look largely to occupational preparation, but it is assumed that intelligent citizens must have some general education as well. Programs to meet this need include literature, history, and science and try to stress also social attitudes and values that make for a well-rounded personality.

Like the secondary schools, colleges have witnessed considerable changes in the course of study, though these have been less drastic than in the high schools. There has been a shift from classical courses to those of a more applied or "practical" sort. There has been a considerable increase in pre-professional and professional courses in medicine, engineering, journalism, art, agriculture, social work, and teaching. As new specialized vocations arise—for example, in personnel and other administrative work, in public relations for business and government, and in radio and television—the colleges and universities provide training for these new occupations.

Adult Education A public opinion poll reports that "more than two out of every five adults in the voting population expressed the desire to engage in some kind of study." The survey also showed that more women than men wanted adult education; that the 21–29 age group expressed the greatest demand; and that the more schooling a person has, the more additional education he wants. In subject matter, social science stood first, with professional fields second.[8]

There are various reasons for this interest in adult education. Desire to improve one's knowledge and skill with respect to job or profession is one. Wide public interest in domestic and foreign affairs, coupled with the growing belief that only through an informed citizenry can the country solve its problems, is another. Then too, people have much more leisure than formerly and want to take up reading, crafts, arts, or other activities to enrich their lives. The press, the radio, television, and the motion picture provide some of the needed information, but not enough. More formal school facilities are also required.

In the early days we had lecture series and the chautauqua, educational-recreational assemblies of several days' duration. Then came public forums and more formal adult education under both private and public sponsorship. Various universities set up extension and correspondence courses. Every state now has some facilities for extension work. While many students work for credit in these courses, many others

8 · See "A Report of the President's Commission on Higher Education," *Higher Education for American Democracy*, Vol. II (Washington, D.C.: U.S. Government Printing Office, 1947), p. 61. See also Howard Y. McClusky, "Adult Education," *Social Work Year Book*, 1957, ed. Russell H. Kurtz (New York: National Association of Social Workers, 1957), pp. 88–93.

enroll merely for the satisfaction of getting additional knowledge.

Another adult education effort has been the Americanization program, especially during the decades when this country was receiving thousands of European immigrants each year. More recently, various plans to combat discrimination against minority groups and to foster good will have been attempted under such titles as "Intercultural Education."

There is a wide variety of technical institutes, both public and private, which as yet have not been integrated into the formal educational system. In addition, many industrial and business firms have programs of apprentice and in-service training for specialized vocations.

Education and Stratification We have pointed out that one of the functions of educational structures is to confer status. When we examine the system of formal education in American society, we see that the amount and quality of education one receives will vary with income, occupation, race, and region. Each of these variables has consequences, therefore, for the stratification system, not only in its own right but to the degree that it influences educational opportunity and hence life chances.

Income As has already been noted, it can generally be said that the lower the income, the higher the fertility rate. This makes for a relative concentration of school-age children in low-income families. Thus the families which can least afford to send even one child through school are those most likely to have a number of children.

Not only is the family hard put to finance a college education for any of its members, but the children are likely to quit high school to earn money.

The family income is related not only to the amount but to the kind of education one is likely to receive. Students from higher-income families can afford more education and are hence more likely to aspire to the professions, which require more years of preparation and more expensive schooling. Students from families with lower incomes usually have little choice but to enroll in commercial and industrial courses.[9]

Occupation Since we know that income and occupational prestige are positively correlated, we should expect a direct relationship between the occupational status of the parents and the amount of education given the children. Indeed there is: the lower the occupational level of the parents, the less the educational attainment of their children. Research at Indiana University shortly after World War II revealed that 14 percent of the student body was composed of sons of professional men, although professionals constituted only 4 percent of the state's population. On the other hand, only 13 percent of the students were sons of semi-skilled and unskilled laborers, although such workers constituted 44 percent of the population. This situation existed despite the fact that government aid had greatly increased the number of students from lower-class homes attending college: the G.I. Bill of Rights

9 · See W. Lloyd Warner, Robert J. Havighurst, and Martin B. Loeb, *Who Shall Be Educated?* (New York: Harper & Brothers, 1944).

had nearly doubled the proportion of students from the lower occupational strata attending the university.[10]

These occupational and income data indicate, of course, that the class structure has functions for the educational institutions themselves. Studies have shown that most public-school teachers in the United States come from middle-class families. It is not surprising, then, that the schools are oriented to middle-class norms.[11]

Race From our immediately preceding discussions of income and occupational status, we should expect the Negro to be getting less education than the white, since Negroes have a lower median income than whites and are over-represented in low-prestige occupations. It is true that the Negro has improved his educational position vastly in this century. Almost half the American Negro population was illiterate in 1900; half a century later the fraction was down to about one-tenth. Despite this dramatic educational mobility of a whole category, the Negro has by no means achieved equality with the white. Among the population 14-24 years of age in 1960, a total of 37.4 percent of the whites, but only 22.6 percent of the nonwhites, had completed four years of high school or more. Even these figures represent rapid change, for a decade earlier the comparable percentages of those 14-24 completing four years of high school or more were

36.8 for whites and 15.7 for nonwhites.[12]

Under a system which forced Negroes to attend segregated schools, the quality as well as the quantity of education was lower than that for the whites. Since the ruling of the United States Supreme Court on May 17, 1954, which held racial segregation in the schools to be unconstitutional, there has been a steady—though still resisted—advance in integrating the schools. This should mean a gradual improvement in the education given the Negro pupils.

Region Even desegregation will not alone wipe out inequalities in opportunity according to race. Nearly one-third of all American Negroes still live in the South Atlantic states; almost another third live in the South Central states; and in the ranking of regions according to the quality of formal education, the South stands at the bottom. Figures 20 and 21 (pp. 299–300) show that the Southern states are, for the most part, least able to pay for schools, and that they do in fact invest less per pupil than most states in other sections. Figure 23, showing the distribution and trends in teachers' salaries, reinforces this point.

This situation exists in the South partly as a reflection of rural-urban differences. The South is heavily rural

10 · Raymond A. Mulligan, "Socio-economic Background and College Enrollment," *American Sociological Review*, 1951, 16:188–196.

11 · Probably the best sociological research on the functions of the stratification structure for the adolescent in school is August B. Hollingshead's *Elmtown's Youth* (New York: John Wiley & Sons, Inc., 1949).

12 · These figures are from the Bureau of the Census, *U.S. Census of Population: 1960*, United States Summary, Detailed Characteristics (Washington, D.C.: U.S. Government Printing Office, 1963), pp. 420–421. In the Census, nonwhites includes Negroes, Orientals, American Indians, and persons of Mexican ancestry who are thought to be Indian. But in general it is not misleading to think of nonwhites as Negroes, since more than 90 percent of the nonwhites in the United States are Negroes.

FIGURE 23 · Distribution and Trends in Teachers' Salaries *

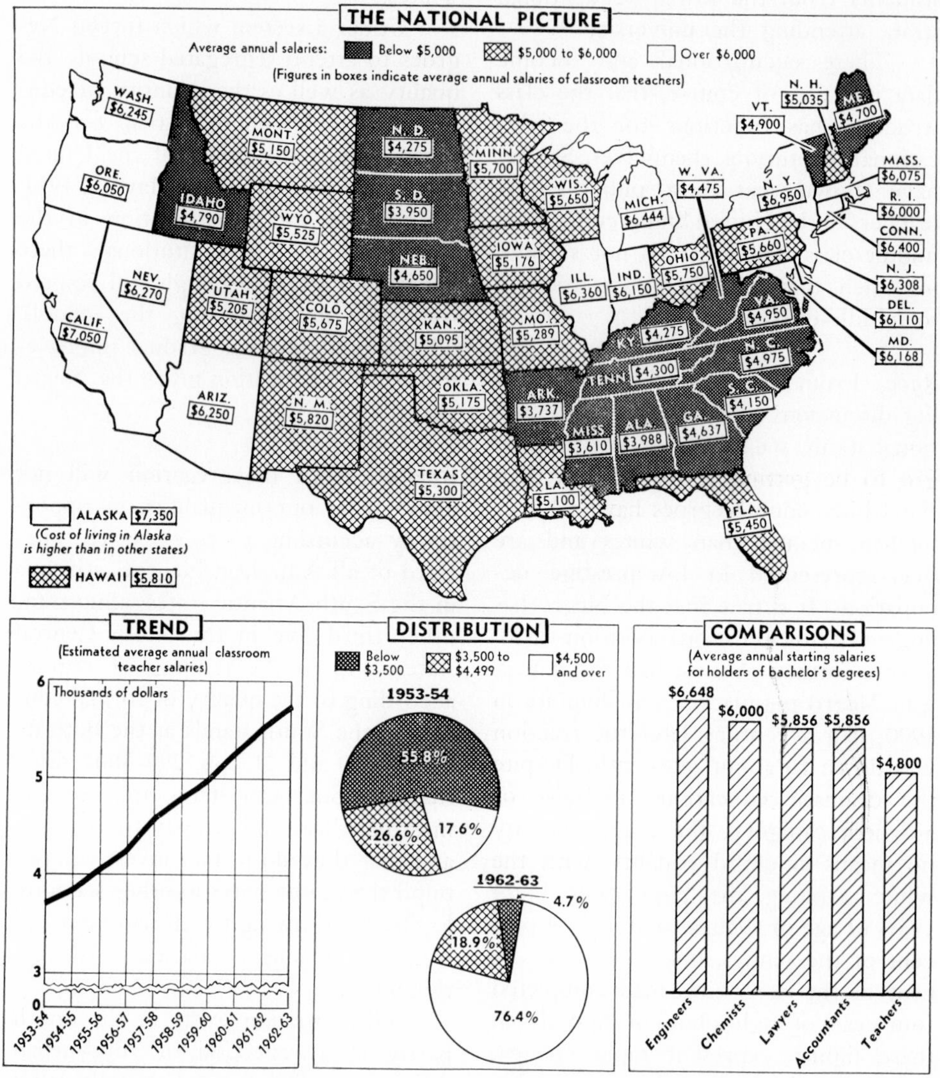

THE NATIONAL PICTURE

Average annual salaries: ▉ Below $5,000   ▨ $5,000 to $6,000   ☐ Over $6,000

(Figures in boxes indicate average annual salaries of classroom teachers)

WASH. $6,245
ORE. $6,050
NEV. $6,270
CALIF. $7,050
IDAHO $4,790
MONT. $5,150
WYO $5,525
UTAH $5,205
ARIZ. $6,250
N. M $5,820
COLO. $5,675
N. D. $4,275
S. D. $3,950
NEB. $4,650
KAN. $5,095
OKLA. $5,175
TEXAS $5,300
MINN. $5,700
IOWA $5,176
MO. $5,289
ARK. $3,737
LA. $5,100
WIS. $5,650
ILL. $6,360
IND. $6,150
MICH. $6,444
OHIO $5,750
KY. $4,275
TENN. $4,300
MISS. $3,610
ALA. $3,988
GA. $4,637
W. VA. $4,475
PA. $5,660
N. Y. $6,950
VA. $4,950
N. C. $4,975
S. C. $4,150
FLA. $5,450
N. H. $5,035
VT. $4,900
ME. $4,700
MASS. $6,075
R. I. $6,000
CONN. $6,400
N. J. $6,308
DEL. $6,110
MD. $6,168

ALASKA $7,350
(Cost of living in Alaska is higher than in other states)

▨ HAWAII $5,810

TREND
(Estimated average annual classroom teacher salaries)

Thousands of dollars

6

5

4

3

0

1953-54 1954-55 1955-56 1956-57 1957-58 1958-59 1959-60 1960-61 1961-62 1962-63

DISTRIBUTION

▉ Below $3,500   ▨ $3,500 to $4,499   ☐ $4,500 and over

1953-54
55.8%
26.6%
17.6%

1962-63
4.7%
18.9%
76.4%

COMPARISONS
(Average annual starting salaries for holders of bachelor's degrees)

$6,648 $6,000 $5,856 $5,856 $4,800

Engineers   Chemists   Lawyers   Accountants   Teachers

* The *New York Times*, June 23, 1963, E7.

and, throughout the United States, the proportion of individuals enrolled in school for each age category is highest in urban and lowest in rural-farm areas.

Clearly, a sizable proportion of our population is capable of acquiring more formal education than it is now given opportunity to secure. The stratification system operates to remove some of these people from school before they have an opportunity to realize their educational potential.

EDUCATIONAL INSTITUTIONS

Teacher-Pupil Relations Teaching is a matter of social contact of pupils and teachers. While skills and the materials in books must be mastered, these do not exist without the interaction of teacher and pupil. Unfortunately, much of our earlier educational psychology failed to recognize that *all learning is essentially social.* If the social climate of learning is not conducive to efficient work, if the teacher sets up emotional resistances in the pupils or fails to present the material in such a way that they can comprehend it, learning is retarded or actually made impossible.

Contemporary teacher-training courses have stressed the social nature of learning, and the result has been a trend toward the "student-oriented" classroom, where healthy personality development is considered as important as the acquisition of knowledge. Particular attention has been paid to individual differences in learning, both by provision of separate classes for fast, medium, and slow learners and by means of day to day realization of such differences on the part of the teacher.[13] The prevalent, though by no means unchallenged, educational theory is that homogeneous ability groups not only expedite learning but foster security.

Pupil-to-Pupil Relations Pupils themselves build up distinctive patterns of action. They assist one another in the learning process, the superior boy or girl often helping the duller or lazier pupils. It is unfortunate that little use has been made of the natural social interaction of pupils in the teaching process. Formal provision might easily be made in many instances for the pupils to teach one another.

13 · For a discussion of this problem, especially as it concerns high-school students, see "Education of the Academically Talented," *Annual Report, 1958–59,* of the Carnegie Foundation for the Advancement of Teaching.

Just as the teachers acquire from the pupils such social designations as the "easy mark," the "old grouch," or the "swell guy," so do the pupils. There is the "teacher's pet," the athletic "hero," the "sissy," the "grind," the "grade-getter," and the "clown." Teachers as well as pupils are responsible for the development of these stereotypes.

The primary, spontaneous groups of pupils, exemplified in play activities, are not long left to carry on by themselves: the school provides formal control through athletics and clubs. In our increasingly complex society these more specialized secondary groups serve an invaluable function in helping direct play activities along lines which prepare the boy or girl for later participation in other groups and in the community.

The Family and the School The teacher assumes the role of a substitute parent in administering discipline and in exercising authority. Parents expect the teacher to assume such responsibility and frequently object if they imagine that the school is failing to carry over this pattern of authority. Parents are often really more concerned with the moral and social effects of education than with formal instruction, even though they hold dearly to the fetish of book learning.

The school affects the daily routine of the family in many ways: the hours when breakfast and lunch must be served; trips the parents must make on special occasions, such as school entertainments; and shopping tours. The family culture itelf is affected. Instruction in cleanliness, brushing teeth, proper diet, and even book knowledge reaches back into the home, perhaps challenging parental ideas and habits and sometimes creating conflict between the children and the parents, especially when the parents have a cultural background different from the American culture which the child gets from the school.

The Community and the School In spite of our faith in education, the function of teachers is limited largely to formal instruction of the children. In general, teachers are treated casually, are seldom brought into close contact with the families of their pupils, and are often looked on as "social" nonentities.

Certain phases of our American educational system make for this condition. For a long time nearly all elementary-school teachers were women, and even today the ratio of women to men teachers in elementary schools is about 3 to 1. Doubtless the lower social status of women generally reflects upon teachers. Mobility and early marriage make for temporary relations between the members of the community and the teachers, especially where school boards still do not employ married women as teachers. Another factor is the lack of formal organization of teachers. Without the advantages of group solidarity which would provide her with bargaining power, the teacher is nearly always dealt with as an individual. When she gets into any difficulty, she usually has to fight her battle with the community and the school board almost single-handed.

In moral conduct the teacher must conform to the code of the most conservative groups in the community. Even parents who themselves indulge in less traditional forms of conduct demand that the teachers of their children exemplify the highest virtue.

In instructional materials also, conservative beliefs predominate. No textbook is likely to be selected which contains material that will offend the prejudices of any group in the community sufficiently well organized to protest. When the American Legion, the Daughters of the American Revolution, chambers of commerce, political cliques, labor unions, religious organizations, and like groups object to a book or disapprove of a teacher, their protests are likely to be heeded. There is an orthodoxy in the schools not unlike that demanded by theology. Nor is it only in the lower schools that restrictions operate. Many colleges endowed by conservative churches restrict the teaching of science. Economic and political radicalism are also taboo in educational circles. In spite of their potential leadership, educational institutions tend to conform to conservative standards, and generally do not direct communities in new thought and action.

INSTITUTIONAL CONFLICTS

There are numerous conflicts in educational ideology that continue to be topics of public discussion.

Specialization vs. Liberal Arts What should be the optimum amount of specialization in the curriculum? At what point should highly specialized subjects be introduced, and how much should they be emphasized? Only a course of study focused on subject matter readily lends itself to specialization. As outside vocational demands have more and more influence on secondary and advanced education alike, it is easy to emphasize technical courses on the

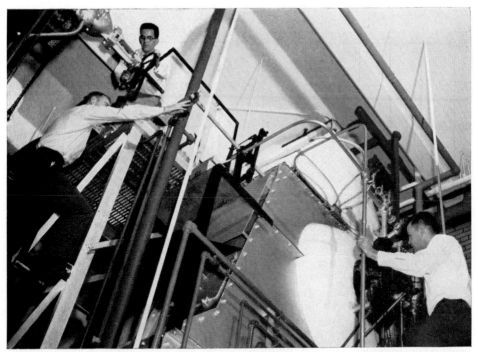

*In an urban society, many occupational roles require specialized training: engineering
students checking efficiency of a steam power plant.*

grounds that they fit individuals more adequately for their future occupations.

The bits-and-pieces character of much of our liberal-arts education is well-recognized, and various attempts have been made to develop some kind of "core of general education" for both high school and college. This core, which represents those parts of the total course of study that are considered basic for all students, consists of materials organized without regard to traditional subject-matter divisions. Various general orientation and survey courses in the sciences and humanities make up this approach at the college level. So too, the trend in some quarters to reduce the number of free electives and the number of different courses in the college curriculum is a reaction to what is seen as diffuseness and compartmentalization.

Social Action vs. Conformity In examining the place of the school in the community, there is the perennial question of the treatment of public issues in the classroom. The problem of academic freedom usually arises whenever special-interest groups in the community object to teachers' discussing topics which such groups consider either "dangerous" or none of the school's business.

In the matter of social action the taboo is even more severe. Direct participation in reform on the part of teachers usually meets with strong opposition from those who control the schools at every level. High-school or college students seldom take part in

Figure 24 · Trends in United States Education *

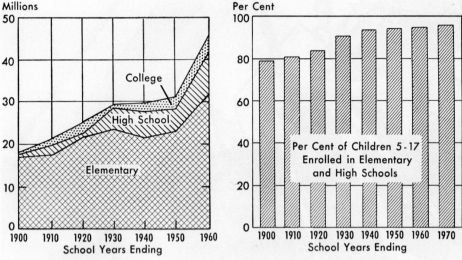

* The *New York Times*, March 30, 1958. By permission. 1960 data from *Current Population Reports*, Series P–20, No. 107, January 16, 1961.

conflicts between labor unions and employers or become active in political campaigns. This is not true, of course, in some countries, where the institutions of higher learning especially are often the seedbeds of progressive and even radical movements.

Federal Aid and Local Control Another problem has to do with the nature and kind of federal aid which public education may or should receive. In the past, the major support of education has come largely from local and state sources. While most states have tried to equalize educational opportunities within their own boundaries, marked differences between states and regions continue, as we have seen. Out of an awareness of this differential and out of general concern about further extension of schooling has come a growing pressure for more federal funds for the schools.

There has been much opposition to such proposals from business inter-

ests that object to further federal taxation and from many educators who believe that, if such aid were given, the federal government would play an ever larger part in the direct control of the schools. There is, in other words, some anxiety that further governmental control of the school might be a threat to traditional freedom of education. Nonetheless, the enormous growth in number of public school pupils, shown in Figure 24, exerts pressure for federal aid.

Public vs. Private Schools This last point brings up another. What about the relation of private to public education in a democracy? The courts have more or less consistently contended that education is a function of the nonpolitical groups of our national society, as well as of the government.[14] There can be no doubt that privately en-

14 · See Kimball Young, *Social Psychology*, 3rd ed. (New York: Appleton-Century-Crofts, Inc., 1956), pp. 554–555.

dowed institutions of higher learning have played an important part in our national life. Yet mounting costs of schooling have led some to argue in favor of government aid to such institutions. Again, the fear of direct control makes many people connected with privately supported schools hesitate to press for government help. Since a good deal of the private schooling in this country is in the hands of religious denominations, there is the further complication of government support for church activities.

Indeed, there has been a good deal of sharp public debate, as well as a number of court cases, dealing with tax aid to private schools. Such matters as teachers' salaries, provision of school buses, free textbooks, and free lunches are controversial. Many parents believe that since they pay taxes to support the public schools even though they send their children to private schools for which they must pay fees, it is only just and proper that aid be given to the private schools.[15]

In 1960, for the first time in American history, a Roman Catholic was elected President. This event may well symbolize and point up changes in some of our old beliefs regarding the relations of church and state.[16]

Closely associated with this problem is the matter of religious instruc-

15 · Regarding this discussion, see these editorials: "Christian and State in America," *The Christian Century*, 1959, 76:891–893; and "A Regrettable Revival," *The Christian Century*, 1961, 78:131–132. The latter discusses the views of Cardinal Francis Joseph Spellman in defense of public tax support for parochial schools.
16 · The following articles reflect various views on this matter: Winthrop S. Hudson, "The Religious Issues in the Campaign"; Charles A. Andrews, "A Catholic President: Pro"; and Harold A. Bosley, "A Catholic President: Con," *The Christian Century*, 1960, 77:1239–1247.

tion in the public schools, which we shall discuss in Chapter 22.

Relativism vs. Ethnocentrism As the United States comes to play an increasingly important part in international relations, there is certain to be public discussion as to what changes may and should be brought about in the teaching of American history and training in loyalty and patriotism. Any marked recurrence of isolationism as a reaction to extensive spending of funds for foreign aid is likely to lead to strong insistence on continuing the teaching of the traditional values associated with the nation-state. In general, the schools may be expected to remain conservative.

Education for the Masses Finally, against the background of modern mass society and its highly complex culture may be put the fundamental question of the educability of the masses. Are most people capable of acquiring the knowledge, skill, and moral responsibility to enable them to take part not only in choosing their leaders from among the most able but also of having a place in the management of human affairs? Or are they so limited in learning ability, so prone to emotional-wishful thinking rather than rationality that it is hopeless to expect much from more education or a different kind of education? Will there not always be a need for a special and distinctive elite to inform and especially to guide and direct the masses?

The democratic ideal rests on the affirmation of the first question. Authoritarianism affirms the other two. Certainly the stress on the authoritarian rather than on a more equalitarian principle fosters the belief that somehow the masses need a strong father-image as a focus of their identification and co-operation. There is no positive proof, one way or another, on this topic. It is a matter of faith which grows out of a given normative system.

INTERPRETATIVE SUMMARY

All societies have some provisions, formal or informal or both, for socialization of individuals. In totalitarian societies, a central purpose of education is to develop loyalty and subservience to the state. In democracies, the purpose of education is to develop individuals who are both self-sufficient and capable of making the democratic system work.

The American emphasis on individual worth has led to increased education for all classes. However, the situation even today, with a larger proportion of the United States population in school or part-time school than at any other place at any time, is still not ideal. Accessibility of education is still limited by one's race, region, and the occupation and income of his family. The fact is sobering when the latent functions of education, most of which are desirable, are considered.

Increased school enrollment is only one of the changes that have occurred in the American educational system. Many of these changes are related to the American belief in universal education. For example, the recognition that for many people high-school education is terminal education has led to emphasis on useful subjects, particularly vocational subjects, and on new methods which will help the average child understand his schoolwork more easily. Traditional liberal arts subjects have been revamped, and sometimes combined, with the average student in mind. The number of junior colleges and relatively inexpensive two-year community colleges is increasing. Other changes, such as the proliferation of ability-grouped classrooms, have been a result of current psychological emphasis on a secure, student-oriented atmosphere. Still other changes, such as increased specialization in curriculums and emphasis on mathematics and science, may be traced to specialization in all areas of American culture and to current competition with Russia.

One aspect of American education that has not changed substantially is its source of control, which has always been local and state. In fact, both teacher behavior and curriculum have historically been controlled by the more conservative elements in the community, and needed federal aid has been resisted on the grounds that it would lead to federal control. Certain sub-groups have set up private schools in order to increase control over their children; for them the dilemma posed by federal aid has been an especially difficult one.

REVIEW AND SUGGESTED READINGS

A • VOCABULARY

Democratic socialization   Totalitarian socialization

B • QUESTIONS AND TOPICS FOR REVIEW

1. Discuss the status of teachers in your home community.
2. What high-school subjects do you think particularly call for the student-oriented approach?

3. Explore probable motivations for learning among different age groups. Rank your present motivations in order of importance.
4. Discuss and qualify the assertion that most people who watch serious shows on television are those who have already thought deeply about issues as a result of reading.
5. Qualify: "A . . . latent function of educational structures is to provide an opportunity to widen the student's circle of acquaintances."
6. To what kinds of literature would you expose high-school students who were not going to college? Does your thinking follow the mainstream of current educational philosophy as it is described in this chapter?
7. What are some of the advantages of junior colleges?
8. Why do teachers generally not organize into units for bargaining purposes? To what degree have they so organized in the past few years, and how effective have they been?
9. Discuss specific instances in which teachers or professors have expressed unorthodox views or participated in "radical" social movements. In each case, what has been the outcome?

C · SUGGESTIONS FOR FURTHER READING

Jacques Barzun. *Teacher in America*. Boston: Little, Brown, & Co., 1944. (Reprinted, Garden City: Doubleday & Co., Inc., 1955.)

A delightfully written and incisive analysis of the role of the teacher in the United States.

Wilbur B. Brookover and David Gottlieb. *A Sociology of Education*, 2nd ed. New York: American Book Company, 1964.

A general text in educational sociology which draws on anthropology, sociology, and social psychology for both materials and points of view.

B. J. Chandler, Lindley J. Stiles, and John I. Kitsuse, eds. *Education in Urban Society*. New York: Dodd, Mead & Co., 1962.

A collection of papers by social scientists and educational administrators on problems facing educators in metropolitan areas.

Aaron V. Cicourel and John I. Kitsuse. *The Educational Decision-Makers*. Indianapolis: The Bobbs-Merrill Co., Inc., 1963.

A report of a research study on the processes of differentiation and mobility as they operate through parental guidance, peer-group pressures, and educational counseling in a suburban high school.

James B. Conant. *The American High School Today: A First Report to Interested Citizens*. New York: McGraw-Hill Book Co., 1959.

A discussion of the characteristics of American education, the purposes of the comprehensive high school, the matter of size and location of schools as they influence comprehensiveness, and some specific recommendations.

C. Wayne Gordon. *The Social System of the High School*. Glencoe, Ill.: The Free Press, 1957.

An analysis of the interrelation of the general status network in high school to the specific roles and norms as they operate in the classroom, in sponsored organizations, and in informal groups.

Neal Gross. *Who Runs Our Schools?* New York: John Wiley & Sons, Inc., 1958.

A study of teachers' beliefs about educational administration, educational goals, and of the conflict of values over organizational objectives.

Robert J. Havighurst and Bernice L. Neugarten. *Society and Education.* Boston: Allyn and Bacon, Inc., 1957.

A summary of how social scientists look at educational institutions.

Florence Greenhoe Robbins. *Educational Sociology: A Study in Child, Youth, School, and Community.* New York: Henry Holt & Co., Inc., 1953.

A general textbook in educational sociology which draws heavily on social psychology.

Bernard Rosenberg and David Manning White, eds. *Mass Culture: The Popular Arts in America.* Glencoe, Ill.: The Free Press, 1957.

Erudite discussions of the impact of the mass media on the socialization process. Comic books, magazines, detective fiction, movies, television, and advertising are analyzed as molders of cultural norms, attitudes, and social behavior.

Lawrence G. Thomas. *The Occupational Structure and Education.* Englewood Cliffs, N.J.: Prentice-Hall, Inc., 1956.

An examination of the socioeconomic significance of socialization with particular reference to its effect on the labor force.

Robert Ulich. *Philosophy of Education.* New York: American Book Company, 1961.

A masterly textbook by one of the twentieth century's great educators treating basic philosophical issues and their practical results in education.

Kimball Young. *Personality and Problems of Adjustment,* 2nd ed. New York: Appleton-Century-Crofts, Inc., 1952.

Chapter 15 deals with pupil adjustment in school, Chapter 16 with mental health problems of college students.

CHAPTER 22

Sociology of Religion

In the course of trying to satisfy the more immediate needs of sustenance, shelter, reproduction, and group and personal safety, prehistoric man found himself confronted with many forces in nature which he did not understand. He speculated, and that was the beginning of philosophy. He put forth a finger to investigate, and that was the beginning of science. He experienced awe and fear, and these were the beginnings of religion.

Religion concerns man's belief in supernatural forces which influence human events. Many societies have a wide range of organizations associated with religion, including special officials, forms of worship, ceremonies, sacred objects, tithes, pilgrimages, and the like. In literate societies, religious leaders have developed elaborate theories or theologies to explain man's place in the universe. Furthermore, the world religions—Hinduism, Buddhism, Confucianism, Judaism, Christianity, and Mohammedanism—are cores of elaborate cultural systems that have dominated whole societies for centuries.

RELIGIOUS STRUCTURES

Primitive religion rests on a belief in personal and impersonal powers which play a part in man's life. Belief in personal powers is called *animism*. It is illustrated by belief in

spirits, ghosts, and demons which bring good or bad luck. Impersonal power, called *mana* (Melanesian), *orenda* (Iroquois), *manitou* (Algonquian), or other names, manifests itself in natural objects, through men, or through spirits or ghosts. Whether the supernatural power is personal or impersonal, it is usually dealt with in the primary group. Folk societies do not typically set up special formal organizations, like our churches, for religion.

Informal Groups To the nonliterate, the various phases of life are not sharply divided, as they are with us. Work and art, play and religion, magic and toolmaking—all are closely interwoven. Economic activities are often surrounded by noneconomic rituals. Recurrent events in the life of the group, such as birth, death, illness, marriage, and seasonal changes, have special emotional significance. Ceremonies connected with these events become part of the folkways.

Surrounded as he was by forces of nature and of other men, forces which he did not fully understand, early man did not distinguish in any logical way between natural and supernatural elements. In fact, it is difficult to sort out primitive religion from the other phases of rudimentary culture. In particular, what we call magic permeates both religion on the

361

one hand and practical behavior on the other.

Magic is invented or discovered in the same way other techniques are invented or discovered. A certain act is performed, either accidentally or because imagination suggests that it might be successful. If it seems to work, it is adopted as a rule of action. If, for example, it is discovered that friction produces heat, this may suggest fire. The imagination furnishes a clue which proves valid in overt action. But imagination suggests also that if I burn a wax effigy of my enemy, I will be doing him harm. Or, as among the Batak of Sumatra, that if a barren woman has a wooden image of a child placed in her lap, she will bear a child. If the intended victim actually does fall ill or if the woman does conceive, the practice is regarded as successful. We call fire-making naturalistic or realistic because its action is fully explained by present-day physical science. We call effigy-making magic because any success it may seem to have is outside the cause-and-effect relations known to science.

Because members of nonliterate societies do not ordinarily organize secondary groups as a setting for religious interaction, there is seldom any sense of the separation of religious norms from other norms, of religious groups from other groups, or of religious activities from other activities. One would never hear in such a society the sentiment, often voiced in ours, that "we should bring business and religion closer together." In folk society they have never been separated.

Formal Organizations In our society religious belief and expression have become institutionalized into secondary groups which we call churches. In a broad sense a church is (1) a body of devotees (2) organized for a religious purpose and developing as an agency for this with (3) a hierarchy of officials and leaders and (4) a body of doctrine and philosophy which ties the whole together into a systematic unit. In popular speech, too, the term *church* is sometimes used to mean a unit of common religious beliefs and practices, as when we speak of the Christian Church. At other times, *church* refers to a more limited body of believers within this larger grouping, such as the Presbyterian or the Methodist Church. (These, properly speaking, are denominations.) In a fourth sense, *church* refers to a congregation or locally organized body of worshipers —and, of course, to the building where these people gather for religious services.

A *sect* is a body of believers that grows up within the larger church or denomination. Certain persons, often few in number at first, begin to disagree about points in the main ceremonials and doctrine of the parent organization. At the outset they do not think of themselves as outside their denomination: only as they come into conflict with the ecclesiastical officials of the principal body does the idea of separation arise. Often it is only after they have been expelled from the organized church that they formulate their own creed, their own official hierarchy, and take on a distinctive name and become a new "denomination."

The sect is at odds with the institutionalized church on almost every count: it is a primary group whose institutions refuse integration with the institutionalized church's social order and reject cultural values which are at

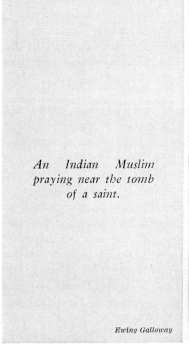

An Indian Muslim praying near the tomb of a saint.

variance with its religious ideology. Today's sect is quite likely to be tomorrow's church. The whole history of the development of the Protestant denominations, as indicated by their name, is a story of groups objecting to certain ways of a church and breaking away to start sects. In time, a sect makes its peace with the wider society and becomes a church itself; later, a new generation of people may break away from it and form another sect.

Participation in Formal Structures For several reasons, statistics on church membership are not a very dependable measure of the extent of participation in organized religious groups.

First, there is no adequate census

of church members throughout the world—nor, for that matter, in the United States. There has been strong opposition in the United States to a scientifically conducted census of religious membership. Religion, in our mores, is a form of individual and group activity which has no relationship to the government, except insofar as the state protects churches, like any other accepted institution, from interference in their activities. As a result, members of many denominations, as well as a number of citizens concerned with civil liberties, view an objective census of church membership as none of the state's affair.

Second, there is little agreement among denominations as to what constitutes membership. Some groups count anyone born or baptized into their fold as a member, even if he denies membership and has not participated in the group for years. Some churches count infants and children as members, while others count only adolescents and adults.

Finally, we are faced with the question of a measure of participation. Is the indifferent member to be equated with the ardent one? Just how real this question is becomes apparent when we realize that, though the most reliable estimates posit that well over half the people in the United States are church members, a public-opinion poll conducted by an independent commercial research firm indicates that slightly less than one-third of the people in the United States attend church regularly.[1]

With these reservations, one can get an approximate idea of the extent and distribution of church membership in the United States from Table 35. Uncertain as these figures are, they are nevertheless better estimates than are available for world religions. An educated guess as to the geographic distribution of the different faiths is reported in Table 36. Christians are the

largest single category, though they constitute only about 30 percent of the total.

About three-fourths of the church members in the United States belong to the half-dozen largest organizations. But it is worth noting that there are about 250 other denominations in the United States, many with fewer than 1,000 members.

Religious Roles Religious norms and practices give rise to distinctive social roles. As an elderly Maori remarked to a white man, "Gods die if there are no priests to keep them alive." [2] Social roles in religion fall into two general classes: the religious thinkers and mystics, found in both formal and informal religious structures, and executives or operators, who are by definition more prevalent in formal structures. The former class includes the mystics proper, the prophets, and the messiahs. The latter include the priests or pastors, formal teachers, missionaries, and various administrators. Mystics are likely to be innovators and disturbers of the established order. Religious executives are generally conservative, preferring the old and tried to the new.

1 · Reported in "Do Americans Go to Church?" *Catholic Digest*, 1952, 17:1–7.

2 · Quoted in W. I. Thomas, *Primitive Behavior* (New York: McGraw-Hill Book Co., 1937), p. 329.

TABLE 35 · Church Membership in the United States, 1956 *

Religious Group	Members
Buddhist	63,000
Old Catholic and Polish National Catholic	351,068
Eastern Orthodox	2,598,055
Judaism	5,500,000
Roman Catholic	34,563,851
Protestant	60,148,980
TOTAL	103,224,954

* *Information Please Almanac, 1958*, ed. Dan Golenpaul (New York: Information Please Almanac, 1957), p. 495. (Source: *Yearbook of American Churches.*) Compiled from figures furnished by 255 of 268 religious bodies in the United States.

TABLE 36 · Principal Religions of the World *

Statistics of the world's religions are only very rough approximations. Aside from Christianity, few religions, if any, attempt to keep statistical records; and even Protestants and Catholics employ different methods of counting members. All persons of whatever age who have received baptism in the Catholic Church are counted as members, while in most Protestant Churches only those who "join" the church are numbered. The compiling of statistics is further complicated by the fact that in China one may be at the same time a Confucian, a Taoist and a Buddhist. In Japan, one may be both a Buddhist and a Shintoist.

RELIGION	North America	South America	Europe	Asia	Africa	Oceania	TOTAL
Christian—Total	160,760,567	117,397,913	456,357,814	47,175,262	30,879,417	10,828,482	820,399,455
Roman Catholic	90,582,000b	111,922,000	230,338,000c	30,144,000	18,608,000	2,483,000	484,077,000
Eastern Orthodox	2,386,000	. . . .	112,447,669	8,106,071	5,868,089	. . . .	128,807,829
Protestant	67,792,567	2,475,913	113,572,145	8,925,191	6,403,328	8,345,482	207,514,626
Jewishd	5,430,000	632,362	3,442,627	1,684,454	660,750	58,250	11,908,443
Moslem	33,000	342,615	12,425,300	318,341,515	85,325,598	102,000	416,570,028
Zoroastrian	. . . .	. . . .	. . . .	140,000	. . . .	. . . .	140,000
Shinto	. . . .	. . . .	. . . .	30,000,000	. . . .	. . . .	30,000,000
Taoist	15,000	17,000	12,000	50,000,000	1,200	8,000	50,053,200
Confucian	86,000	95,000	50,000	300,000,000	7,500	52,000	300,290,500
Buddhist	165,000	135,000	10,000	150,000,000	. . . .	. . . .	150,310,000
Hindu	10,000	275,000	. . . .	318,467,610	300,000	100,000	319,152,610
Primitive	50,000	1,000,000	. . . .	45,000,000	75,000,000	100,000	121,150,000
Others or none	67,422,433	872,110	86,807,259	229,790,159	17,739,535	3,308,268	405,939,764
Grand Total	233,972,000	117,767,000	559,105,000	1,490,599,000	209,914,000	14,557,000	2,625,914,000

a Includes Australia, New Zealand, and Oceania.   b Includes Catholics in Central America and the West Indies. c Includes communist-controlled Eurasia.   d Includes Jewish population, whether or not related to the synagogue.

* *Information Please Almanac, 1958*, p. 494. By permission. Slight discrepancies in totals given for Eastern Orthodox and Jewish memberships in this table and in Table 35 result from the fact that these figures are estimates.

There is, in fact, a sort of continuing struggle in religious organizations between these two kinds of persons. Some would confine religious expression within rather definite limits set by symbols, rites, traditions, and established theology. Others would not unduly hamper religious experience by such established patterns of thought and action but would leave much room for the individual's unique experience.

The *priest* or *rabbi* or *pastor* fills the role expectations of carrying on the religious rituals and expounding theology. He is the special person who officiates at the church ceremonies and cares for both spiritual and temporal affairs.

Religious *teachers* or *philosophers* have played a central part in the rise of the great world religions. Jesus, St. Paul, Mohammed, and Buddha are all familiar instances. The *missionary* is a special teacher whose business it is to carry the message, rituals, and symbolism of an established religion to nonbelievers.

The *religious executive* may be, like St. Paul, both missionary and organizer. In many Protestant churches where a priestly hierarchy is not developed or is practically nonexistent, the affairs of the church organization are carried on by executives whose work combines that of priest or pastor with social-service activities and management.

The *mystic* plays a special part in the growth of religion. He identifies himself or comes into union with the god, or with the world-spirit, or with the Absolute—however the culture phrases the idea of supernatural forces. The mystic illustrates the place in a society of the divergent person who may initiate changes in culture. Mystics believe that, through their dreams, visions, and other unique mental experiences, they come into direct personal communication with divine powers.

The *prophet* is an important religious leader. While he may be a priest, often he is a mystic. He serves as spokesman for some divine power, issuing warnings, giving commands, and revealing the course of future events. Obviously, the prophet's role is set by the culture. When there is a strong priestly hierarchy, as among the Ekoi of West Africa or in the Roman Catholic Church, there is little opportunity for such persons to appear.

The *messiah* is the divine leader or prophet who is recognized as having supernatural attributes, who foretells some catastrophic end of the world and often assumes the role of final judge. The messiah ordinarily comes from among the people themselves, who in a time of crisis look to him to save their society from disaster. Mohammed, for example, was the messiah of the people who came to call themselves, after him, Mohammedans. Christ, of course, is the messiah of Christians.

Basic Religious Patterns The institutional practices and formal theories which have grown up about religion are many. The most important are ceremonials, symbolism, sacred objects and buildings, and creed and theology.

Ceremony or *ritual* is a standardized and accepted action directed toward some specific end. (Rituals and ceremonies are not confined, of course, to religion.) In religion, ritual is a settled manner of entreating or controlling the supernatural powers in regard to some particular situation. Ordination, the sacraments, various forms of sacrifice, and penance call for special rituals. In some churches, such as the Greek Orthodox or Roman Catholic, the ceremonials are elaborate. In other churches, like those of the Quakers or Calvinists, the forms play only a slight part in religious life.

Throughout religion, *symbolism* is important. Symbols are substitutes for or representations of objects or situations. They may be verbal or tangible. A commonly recognized religious symbol helps the person identify himself with his fellows and so promotes a sense of solidarity. Often it comes to stand not alone for the particular object or situation to which it was originally attached but for the whole group and its culture: the cross stands for Christianity, the crescent for Mohammedanism. We must recall that the symbol in the mind of the user may serve either an intellectual or an emotional purpose. For the religious worshiper, the object and its symbol are combined into an indivisible emotional experience, which asserts itself whenever the symbol is brought forth. The Eucharist, for example, symbolizes for the Christian the supreme sacrifice of Jesus, and in this ritual the worshiper identifies himself intellectually and emotionally with one of the main tenets of his theology.

Sacred objects associated with the various religions have symbolic power insofar as they evoke memories of a religion's history and traditions. The Hebrew ark of the covenant and the phylactery, the Christian candles, altar, and especially the cross play important parts in many religious ceremonials.

For their religious exercises people often repair to special sacred localities: mountaintops, mineral springs, groves of trees, river banks, seashores. Special *buildings* are erected, such as the tabernacle of the ancient Hebrews; the temples of ancient Babylonia, Egypt, Greece, and Rome; the synagogues of the Jews; and the cathedrals and churches of Christians.

Theology is the systematic explanation which religious leaders work out to show man's relation to his god and to the universe. Often this includes some account of the origin of the world and of man, like the stories of creation in the Bible. It represents the *creed*, or body of beliefs and doctrines of the church. The written words become the sacred scriptures.

RELIGIOUS FUNCTIONS

Religious structures exist in every society, and they function for the continuity of the society. The supernatural laws and beings around which such structures are oriented supply an ultimate idea of reality to which the cultural values and social norms can be related. Religion provides the individual with an institutionalized crystallization of his hopes and outlet for his fears. It offers a higher court of appeal when he feels that his fellows have treated him unjustly, and promises better things in the future.

Sanctions for the Mores Religion has frequently been a powerful factor in lending emotional support to the moral code. In all the great religions of civilized man there is an intermingling of religion and morals. There can be no question that the belief in a god influences moral conduct. Even among the Ekoi of West Africa, where magic is considered very powerful and where spirits are used for malevolent ends, men believe in benign spirits who counteract the evil ones and aid man

in more humane ways. So too, some nonliterates of relatively simple culture, such as the Australian Bushmen and the Andaman Islanders, believe in spirits that are considered guardians of morality.

As the concept of an ethical god develops, this relation of religion to morality becomes more important. By identifying himself with such a god, an individual may modify his conduct. Among the Hebrews, Jehovah, at first a tribal god of vengeance, gradually emerged as a universalistic god of high moral qualities.

In Christian theology the struggle between the forces of God and the forces of Satan symbolizes the conflict within the individual between the moral and the immoral, between the spirit and the flesh, between good and evil. Throughout Christian history the role of God and the saints as standards of virtue has been highly important. A personal deity becomes an ideal with which one may compare his own conduct.

Any scheme of otherworldly reward or punishment for conduct becomes a powerful aid to morality. But although the idea of continuity of life after death is rather widespread, not all groups have the notion of retribution or divine judgment. Indeed, this idea came rather late in cultural development.

In many religions the belief in a final judgment, with its terrible punishments for the evil and glorious rewards for the virtuous, is pictured in bold and striking manners. Without doubt, the fear of hell fire and damnation has been a powerful factor in the control of conduct. Associated with fear, systems of penance and absolution have been developed to remove or at least lighten the burden of future punishment.

The virtues of honesty, fair-dealing, conformity to sexual codes—in short, all the accepted details of moral conduct of the community or society—may become integrated with religious beliefs and practices. Today there is a tendency to integrate principles of social welfare, the morality of fairer distribution of wealth, of sound and honest politics, of high community standards of health and conduct into the religious ideals of the church.

Economic Motivation   In a nonliterate society nearly every feature of life is mixed with religion. This is clearly evident in economic life: food-gathering, hunting, fishing, herding, agriculture, trade, and barter—each is directly related to the gods. It is not always so apparent that religion also plays a part in our more complex capitalistic economy, but Max Weber, a German sociologist, R. H. Tawney, a British economist, and others have argued that there is a parallel between the development of Protestant ideas and practices and the rise of modern capitalism in Western Europe and America.[3] The individualism of Protestantism goes hand in hand with the rise of nationalism and the change from the relatively rigid class structure of the Middle Ages to the open-class system of our own time. The otherworldly as-

3 · See Max Weber, *The Protestant Ethic and the Spirit of Capitalism*, trans. Talcott Parsons (New York: Charles Scribner's Sons, 1930); and R. H. Tawney, *Religion and the Rise of Capitalism* (New York: Harcourt, Brace & Co., 1926). The whole notion of such a relationship is called into serious question by the work of Kurt Samuelsson, *Religion and Economic Action: The Protestant Ethic, The Rise of Capitalism, and the Abuses of Scholarship* (New York: Basic Books, Inc., 1961).

ceticism of Catholicism, in which emphasis was put on confession of sins and absolution as preparation for the hereafter, gave way to what Weber aptly calls "worldly asceticism," in which, while the moral virtues of hard work, honesty, truthfulness, and steadfastness of purpose are retained, activity is directed toward the affairs of this world as preparation for the hereafter. Assuming a method of salvation such as the Calvinist doctrine of predestination or the Lutheran doctrine of grace, the individual must fulfill his role in the world of everyday affairs in order to demonstrate his worthiness for membership in the Kingdom of God.

During the Middle Ages, money-making was considered distinctly secondary to godly pursuits. By the sixteenth century, material gain had assumed greater importance, and the profit system was well established by the time of the Reformation. The dogmas of the Protestant religious movement were, in part, an outcome of a more materialistic philosophy which was influencing business and statecraft, and these dogma, in turn, gave further support to capitalistic endeavor. Hard work, sacrifice of present pleasures for future profits in a business, honesty in business dealings, and other homely virtues became the daily morality of the pious Protestants, especially the Calvinists, the Quakers, and the Separatists. The individual, having religious assurance of salvation, practiced these virtues as evidence of his godliness. While these new ideas and practices had to fight their way step by step against religious tradition, in time they won wide acceptance.

Capitalism, Protestantism, and political democracy, bound together by certain accidents of history and certain similar ideologies, came to full bloom in America. The emphasis on religious piety, individualism, liberty and activity, and the worship of material success, coupled with almost unlimited natural resources, made early America a living example of this combination of the repression of pleasure-seeking and the direction of energy into hard work, success, and religious satisfaction. Nowadays, however, we cannot assume the existence of any direct cause-and-effect relationship between the Protestant and Catholic faiths and role behavior in contemporary American society. Research indicates that whatever influence these two religious subcultures have on their adherents in our society is overridden by the general ethos.[4] There is no evidence that the so-called Protestant ethic is participated in any less by Catholics than by Protestants or Jews in contemporary United States.

Yet institutions are interrelated, and there remains in our normative structure not only some connection between economic and religious institutions, but a belief on the part of many that such a relationship ought to exist. Expressing such a belief in the connection of business, religion, and certain moral virtues, Roger W. Babson says:

Statistics lead me to believe that the faith, industry, thrift, and enterprise in people are very largely due to religion. . . . Where the people are irreligious, are found indifference, wastefulness, and extravagance. . . . Ninety-five per cent of the people who do not get along well materially owe their misfortune to lack of these religious qualities of faith, industry, courage, imagination, and thrift. This means that the real great work of the church today lies in reviving these great productive qualities in the souls of the masses.[5]

It would be a mistake, however, to assume that all communicants and all church leaders agree with such views. Quite to the contrary, some believe that capitalism has been injurious to the true aim of religion. The inequalities of wealth and the exploitation of people, both as workers and as consumers, by business interests have led some church leaders and others to give thought to reforms in the economic order. In the early twentieth century there arose among certain American Protestant groups what was known as the "social gospel" movement, which contended that human rights should come before those of property; that mutual service, not profit, should be the chief economic motive; and that co-operation, not competition, should be the mode of economic production and distribution.

Yet so long as the church gets its chief support from the dominant capitalist class, it is not easy for it to go far in economic views from those who pay its bills. If the church, like the traditional school, continues to reflect the dominant economic and political views of those in power, it will consume much of its time and energy defending the prevailing economic and political order.

Other Functions of Religious Structures

Formal teaching has long been a prerogative of organized religion. In Christian history, the church has played a decisive part in education. The cathe-

4 · Raymond W. Mack, Raymond J. Murphy, and Seymour Yellin, "The Protestant Ethic, Level of Aspiration, and Social Mobility: An Empirical Test," *American Sociological Review*, 1956, 21:295–300.

5 · From Roger W. Babson, *Religion and Business* (New York: The Macmillan Company, 1920), pp. 97–99. By permission.

Ewing Galloway

Cross-cultural variation in institutional symbols: a church designed by Frank Lloyd Wright in California.

dral schools of the Middle Ages were used for religious and moral training, and early Protestantism fostered elementary learning so that members might read the Bible.

The Sunday School was established in 1780 by an Englishman, Robert Raikes, with a view to more formal religious and moral education. The movement soon spread to America. In the last religious census in the United States, about four-fifths of the congregations reported Sunday Schools.[6]

More influential even than the Sunday School has been the parochial school, organized to fulfill the legal demands for formal schooling but offering children of various churches religious and moral instruction not available in public schools. The philosophy underlying this form of education was set forth in the "Encyclical on Education" (1930) by Pope Pius XI:

It is necessary that all the teaching and whole organization of the school, and its teachers, syllabus and textbooks in every branch, be regulated by the Christian spirit, under the direction and maternal supervision of the Church; so that Religion may be in very truth the foundation and the crown of youth's entire training; and this in every grade of school, not only in the elementary but in the intermediate and the higher institutions of learning as well.[7]

Closely related to more formal religious education has been the development of such organizations as the

6 · *Summary and Detailed Tables, Religious Bodies, 1936*, vol. 1 (Washington, D.C.: U.S. Government Printing Office, 1941).

7 · See "The Pope's Encyclical on Education," *Current History*, 1930, 31:1101.

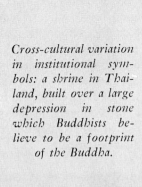

Cross-cultural variation in institutional symbols: a shrine in Thailand, built over a large depression in stone which Buddhists believe to be a footprint of the Buddha.

Black Star

Young Men's Christian Association, the Catholic Youth Organization, and the Young Men's Hebrew Association. There are, in addition, vacation schools, clubs, and forums, and the churches sponsor other activities in which more formal education is supplemented with opportunities for discussion of current moral, religious, and economic problems.

The Boy Scouts, Girl Scouts, and Camp Fire Girls, though not strictly religious organizations, have much in common with these other agencies. These groups carry on chiefly leisure-time activities, relating these activities rather definitely to the ethical and religious principles taught in the church. The Boy Scout, for instance, is taught

to respect his parents, to have reverence for God, and to play fairly.

It is significant that religious organizations are taking over some of the functions formerly located in the home, in the neighborhood, and even in the school. For many Americans, religious activity serves as a focus for the integration of a host of other activities.

RELIGIOUS PATTERNS IN THE UNITED STATES

Community and Church In the primary community of medieval Europe the church was the focus of much of the peoples' lives. In Protestant countries it continued to serve important functions, although where rival denominations and sects arose, the integrating benefits of religion and church organization were often lost in theological conflicts. In spite of the continuation of these divisive tendencies, churches in the United States have served the community as the center not only of religious thought and action but also of moral standards. Today the primary-community church reflects the changes which have gone on in the wider world outside. Open-country churches, for example, are declining, while village and town churches are becoming the center of both farm and village religious activity. The rural and village church has added educational, recreational, and social-service activities to its functions.

Formerly the church was the focus of much of the neighborhood life. The Catholic churches have continued to be particularly effective as neighborhood centers, since the membership is divided geographically into parishes, in the same manner as voting precincts or school districts are laid out. This gives the pastor a chance to serve the people who are themselves neighbors and who already have attitudes of solidarity growing out of common life. The urban Protestant parishes, for the most part, are not now divided on geographic lines, with the result that members are often drawn from widespread areas. So long as the population remained fairly stationary, this handicap was overcome by the fact that the church buildings were located in the residential sections in which most of the members lived. Today in our rapidly growing American cities the situation is quite different. Many church edifices are left stranded in the midst of retail or wholesale districts or in cheap rooming-house or emerging slum areas just beyond the retail business section. The members often live so far from the home church that they drift away to other parishes nearer by or give up their church affiliation entirely.

In other ways the city church is affected by changes, especially in the growing emphasis on secondary-group organization. Many sophisticated urban people are skeptical of what organized religion has to offer. There is frequently a conflict within the church body itself as to whether it should liberalize its dogma, taking up social-service and educational and recreational programs, or stick by the old and tried at the cost of younger membership and at the risk of slow decay and perhaps final disappearance.

Religion and Stratification A considerable body of research offers evidence that religious beliefs, as well as religious participation, vary from stratum to stratum in the class structure.[8] Dynes' research, for example, has shown that acceptance of the sect type of organization is associated with low socio-economic status, while acceptance of the church type of structure is more frequently found among those with more formal education who fill occupational statuses of higher prestige.[9]

Several studies report a direct relationship between incidence of church

8 · For an excellent summary of this literature, see Will Herberg, *Protestant — Catholic — Jew: An Essay in American Religious Sociology* (Garden City, New York: Doubleday & Co., Inc., 1956).

9 · Russell R. Dynes, "Church-Sect Typology and Socio-Economic Status," *American Sociological Review*, 1955, 20:555–560. For a critique of the church-sect typology, see Peter L. Berger, "Sectarianism and Religious Sociation," *American Journal of Sociology*, 1958, 54:41–44.

TABLE 37 · Class Composition of Selected Religious Denominations *

STRATUM	PER CENT DISTRIBUTION BY DENOMINATION					
	Congre-gational	Episco-palian	Jewish	Methodist	Catholic	Baptist
Upper	24	24	22	13	9	8
Middle	43	34	32	35	25	24
Lower	33	42	46	52	66	68

* Adapted from Liston Pope, "Religion and the Class Structure," *Annals of the American Academy of Political and Social Science*, 1948, 256:84–91. Table from p. 86. By permission.

membership and economic status or prestige.[10] Church attendance is highest among the middle class. One careful and detailed research project found that religious interest was related to social mobility—upwardly mobile people were more interested, downwardly mobile people less interested.[11] Certainly the denomination to which one belongs is a factor in his status in the stratification system, as is indicated in Table 37.

RELIGIOUS INSTITUTIONS

Religious bodies are usually no different from others in their jealous regard for power and control. Frequently, when a church group is threatened, it responds, as do other groups, by avoidance, escape, or some kind of aggressive counteraction. How violent religious conflict may become

10 · See Hadley Cantril, "Education and Economic Composition of Religious Groups: An Analysis of Poll Data," *American Journal of Sociology*, 1943, 48:574–579; Louis Bultena, "Church Membership and Church Attendance in Madison, Wisconsin," *American Sociological Review*, 1949, 14:384–389; August B. Hollingshead, *Elmtown's Youth* (New York: John Wiley & Sons, Inc., 1949), pp. 243–266.
11 · Gerhard E. Lenski, "Social Correlates of Religious Interest," *American Sociological Review*, 1953, 18:533–544. Lenski also found an association between degree of religious interest and amount of income, but did not find interest significantly related to occupational status or educational level attained.

is witnessed in Western history by the Crusades of the Middle Ages against the infidel, by the Thirty Years' War between Catholic and Protestant nations in Europe, and by the cruelty of sectarian strife in the British Isles during the seventeenth century. More recently the bitter conflicts between Moslems and Hindus in India and between Arabs and Jews in the Near East show that religion, when linked with economic and political aims and institutions, may be a powerful element in open conflict.

Given the numerous religious subcultures in the United States, the norms governing behavior in the religious realm are anything but universal. Sets of values have clashed in several areas, including the role of religion in socialization, the denominational differences in dogma, and the competition of religion and science as structures meeting the necessary function of providing a sense of purpose.

Religion in Education Historically, Christianity has frequently been involved in a conflict between church and state. The controversy over the claims of the Roman Catholic Church to temporal power—that is, political control—went on all through the Middle Ages. Protestantism arose, in part, out of this struggle. Today the separation of church and state is a basic tenet of all democratic countries. Yet difficulties arise from time to time regarding the place of the church in education. Many believe that all basic education in a democratic country should take the form of public schooling. But various churches have long contended that the home and the church are the essential and proper agencies of education. Efforts to close parochial schools by legislation have met with failure. For example, an Oregon law of 1922 provided that after 1926 all parents must send their children to public schools. Yet the Supreme Court held as follows:

As often heretofore pointed out, rights guaranteed by the Constitution may not be abridged by legislation which has no reasonable relation to some purpose within the competency of the state. The fundamental theory of liberty upon which all governments in this Union repose excludes any general power of the state to standardize its children by forcing them to accept instruction from public teachers only. The child is not the mere creature of the state; those who nurture him and direct his destiny have the right, coupled with the high duty, to recognize and prepare him for additional obligations.[12]

It is clear that education continues to be regarded in this country as a family and religious prerogative, in spite of the theory of public schooling for all. But the matter has not rested there. Since the Oregon case was settled, a number of problems regarding religion and education have arisen.

One of these has to do with provision for religious instruction. The system of "released time," as it is called, is an arrangement under which time is allowed from the regular school hours

for children to attend classes in religion taught by people from their respective denominations. In most states such instruction is not permitted in public-school buildings but must be elsewhere, in places determined by the churches concerned. Children are required either to attend or do their regular schoolwork in this period. In Illinois such instruction was permitted, for a time, in the school building. But in a test case, the Illinois enabling law was declared unconstitutional by an 8 to 1 decision of the United States Supreme Court.[13] The decision held that the Illinois law contravened the First Amendment to the Constitution, which had "erected a wall between church and state," as Justice Hugo Black put it in the majority opinion.

Aside from the legal aspects, there has been considerable controversy over the value of the released time plan of religious instruction. While there is much support for it from some leaders of all three major faiths, there is growing criticism from many educators who believe that such a program actually stimulates a sense of religious difference among children and thereby fosters prejudice.

More recently, in 1964, a case protesting the saying of prayers in public schools was brought before the Su-

12 · See *Society of the Sisters of the Holy Names of Jesus and Mary* v. *Pierce, Governor of Oregon.* 296 *Federal Reporter* 929. Case affirmed in 268 *US Reporter* 510.

13 · See *Illinois ex rel. McCollum* v. *Board of Education, School District No. 71, Champaign County, Illinois, et al.* Appeal from the Supreme Court of Illinois, No. 90, argued December 8, 1947; decided March 8, 1948. 333 *US Official Reporter* No. 2, pp. 203–256. For discussions of this problem, including reviews of similar cases, see Donald McDonald, ed., *Religion and Freedom* (New York: The Fund for the Republic, 1958, pamphlet); William Lee Miller *et al., Religion and the Free Society* (New York: The Fund for the Republic, 1958, pamphlet); and Robert Gordis *et al., Religion and the Schools* (New York: The Fund for the Republic, 1959, pamphlet).

preme Court and won. The decision is significant not only in that it upholds the fundamental separation of church and state, but in that it recognizes the rights of nonbelievers in American society: most prayers in the public schools had been short and nonsectarian, and only nonbelievers and those opposed on philosophical grounds had objected in the first place.

Yet the courts have approved legislation which provides for free textbooks and free bus transportation for children who attend parochial schools. Moreover, there is growing pressure from some Catholic leaders for federal and other tax aid for parochial schools, on the grounds that such schools deserve public aid, since they provide education for a large number of young people. To counteract this trend, many Protestant groups take a firm stand against any plan to permit the use of public funds for parochial schools.

The whole conflict reveals many of the basic difficulties in a highly diverse culture such as ours. The plea for cultural diversity must always face the counter-argument that, to survive, a culture system must also have a large degree of uniformity and agreement within its institutional systems.

Denominations and Dogma While conflict has marked the relations between many religious bodies, co-operation is by no means lacking. In American Protestantism there has been a trend toward consolidation and co-operation. That there is considerable support for such steps is shown in a 1948 poll of Protestant churchgoers, in which more than 40 percent of those asked favored a combination of all Protestants in the United States into one church. Denominations do feder-

ate for various purposes and for short or long periods of time. For example, the National Council of Churches of Christ, established in 1950, consists of 29 Protestant and certain Eastern Orthodox denominations. This organization represents about three-fifths of all Protestant church members. It has four divisions: Christian Education, Christian Life and Work, Home Missions, and Foreign Missions.[14]

Another instance of co-operation is the "community church" that emerges with the union of separate Protestant groups. Such action sometimes takes place, of course, when the separate denominations become too weak to keep going by themselves. But sometimes the union is born of a strong public view that a community-wide church will serve the religious needs of people more effectively than separate denominations. The community church often stimulates public forums, offers recreational facilities to boys and girls of the entire city, and undertakes preventive programs in health and delinquency. This is a far cry from the church which functioned only as the dispenser of dogma, moral advice, and unregulated charity.

Co-operation across the traditional barriers between Catholic and Protestant or between Christian and Jew is more difficult. Recent decades have seen a tendency toward certain joint action among these churches. The organization of local ministerial associations is a step in this direction. The National Conference of Christians and Jews, founded in 1928, has tried to de-

14 · Data from *The World Almanac, 1961* (New York: New York World-Telegram and Sun, 1961), p. 700. See also Purnell H. Benson, *Religion in Contemporary Culture* (New York: Harper & Brothers, 1960), pp. 656–667.

velop tolerance and co-operation. Yet all such efforts are limited by strong interfaith rivalry backed by prejudice.

The distinctive features of the major religions reflect the larger cultures of which they are a part. Yet, as some of the barriers of prejudice and isolation have disappeared, certain tendencies toward worldwide co-operation have arisen. Such gatherings as world religious conferences, in which representatives of all the major religions have participated, are evidence of a growing awareness of common problems in religion in spite of differences of creed. But such efforts must of necessity remain largely verbal so long as political conflict continues on the international scene.

Religion and Science There is still a widespread belief that religion and science are in fundamental conflict. Many feel that, as science is more and more applied to solving modern problems—both technological and social-psychological—there is less need for religion. When people talk about religion and science being in conflict, they usually refer to the fact that church officials have at various times opposed the findings of men of science, findings which the churchmen look on as contravening the long-established creed or dogma of their respective organizations. In this sense history is indeed full of conflicts between theology and scientific findings. For example, when Galileo was haled before the Court of Inquisition for his scientific work, he was indicted

. . . for holding as true the false doctrine taught by many—namely, that the sun is immovable in the center of the world and that the earth moves and also with a diurnal motion; . . . following the

hypothesis of Copernicus, you include several propositions contrary to the true sense and authority of the Holy Scripture. . . . The proposition that the sun is the center of the world and immovable from its place is absurd philosophically, false and formally heretical because it is expressly contrary to the Holy Scriptures. . . .

Galileo recanted and renounced his alleged heresy. But Bruno, who refused to renounce Copernican cosmology, was burned at the stake in Rome, and as late as 1819 the books of Galileo, Copernicus, and Kepler were on the Catholic *Index* of forbidden books. But it must be recalled that neither Martin Luther, whose break with Catholicism started the Protestant Reformation, nor the Orthodox Jews of the time were any more sympathetic toward the discoveries of science.

Since science depends on complete freedom of thought and since its findings run counter to many church dogmas, it was inevitable that conflict should arise. The Copernican system, which replaced the older view of the cosmos, reduced the earth to a mere speck in the total universe and robbed man of much of his former importance in his own eyes. Later, in the nineteenth century, the Darwinian theory of evolution placed man definitely in the animal kingdom. And during the past seventy-five years, psychology and the social sciences have shown that man's mental life and behavior can be studied and understood—in large part, at least—through the method of science.

There is no doubt that education and practical technology have altered many of man's views about God, sin, immortality, and other features of traditional theology. In 1948 a public opinion poll made in ten countries re-

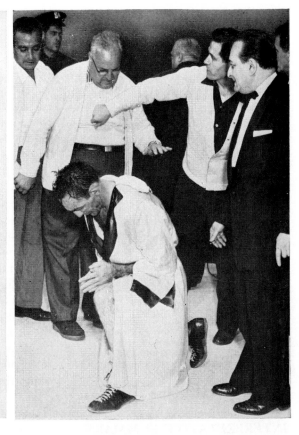

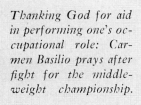

Thanking God for aid in performing one's occupational role: Carmen Basilio prays after fight for the middleweight championship.

United Press International

ported the answers to a question about personal belief in God. "Yes" answers ranged from 96 percent in Brazil and 94 percent in the United States to 66 percent in France. That skepticism is related to various political and other views is apparent. For example, in France the Communist part of the sample reported nearly two-thirds "No" answers.[15]

It is somewhat difficult to evaluate such findings, since people may be loath to tell exactly what they believe in matters they consider personal. Nevertheless, there are other evidences of loss of belief. James H. Leuba's studies show that between 1914 and 1933 there

was a decline in the percentage of scientists who declared a belief in God and immortality. Furthermore, scientists who dealt with the inorganic world reported a higher percentage of believers than did biologists, psychologists, and sociologists. The higher the eminence in science, the lower the proportion who reported such beliefs. In a companion study of student opinions, it was found that the proportion of believers decreased sharply as one moved from college freshmen to seniors.[16] While other studies have shown that students, for example, still feel the need for some kind of belief, it is also

15 · See *Public Opinion Quarterly*, 1948, 12:173–174.

16 · For a convenient summary of this work, see James H. Leuba, "Religious Beliefs of American Scientists," *Harper's Magazine*, 1934, 169:291–300.

clear that their views on specific doctrines are hazy and often nonexistent.[17]

Belief as a Universal Function   The mystic identification with power outside oneself may offset or balance the disappointments, heartaches, and pain of daily living, in which half-measures, compromises, and self-denials are common. It is easy for the critic of religion to point out that this sort of thing is "an escape from reality," a mass neurosis or, as Freud argued, a mere "illusion."[18] But this will hardly do. Cultural reality is not something material or made up of biological reactions to

17 · See Paul C. Glick and Kimball Young, "Justification for Religious Attitudes and Habits," *Journal of Social Psychology*, 1943, 17:45–68. See also Gordon W. Allport, James M. Gillespie, and Jacqueline Young, "The Religion of the Postwar College Student," *Journal of Psychology*, 1948, 25:3–33.
18 · See Sigmund Freud, *The Future of an Illusion*, trans. W. D. Robson-Scott (New York: Liveright Publishing Corp., 1928); and his *Civilization and Its Discontents*, trans. J. Riviere (New York: Random House, 1930).

food, drink, and sexual objects. It is a matter of socially learned beliefs, attitudes, ideas, meanings. It exists in the minds of men. One cannot, therefore, with Freud blandly dismiss religious experience as an unfortunate illusion without at the same time raising the question as to whether art, philosophy, and most of the other fundamentals of social organization and family life are not illusions also. Faithfulness to a mate, loyalty to a country, or belief in a bank note can be shown by this logic to be illusions too.

One need not affiliate himself with a religious organization in order to survive. But everywhere men believe in something which imbues them with a sense of purpose, be it science, religion, or philosophy. An explanation of reality is a part of every culture, and the student of society must take that explanation into account if he is to understand the social structure and its functions.

INTERPRETATIVE SUMMARY

Throughout history, religions have served the functions of explaining the unknown and making it less terrifying, of defining man's place in the universe and giving him a sense of purpose. Religions have provided man with standards of morality and, conversely, have frequently lent sanctions for already existing political, economic, and other mores of a society. Finally, in order to preserve their more general functions, religious organizations have increasingly entered the areas of recreation and social work.

Religions differ in theology. Many religions have tried to answer such questions as Is there one god, or more than one? If so, what is he like—good, bad; carnate, incarnate, etc.? Is there an afterlife? What is it like? Upon what is admission based? To what extent should I work now to gain entrance?

In folk societies, worship of intangible divinities tends to go along with belief in animism and magic. As might be expected, formal religious structures do not exist, though religion itself may pervade all areas of life. Religious leaders may be mystics or priests; in more complex societies, the former are generally outside the pale of the established churches, which tend to be conservative. All religions, folk and urban, rely on ceremonies, with their attendant symbols, sacred objects, special locales or buildings, for perpetuation.

Historically, religious conflict is more common than co-operation; in fact, the history of religion involves a series of bitter conflicts within established organizations, gradual splits, and emergence of sects into new denominations. More recently there has been a trend toward consolidation of similar groups and there has even been limited co-operation among dissimilar national and international organizations for specific purposes.

In the United States, the influence of religion on man's behavior is especially difficult to assess, since the "Protestant ethic" is by now firmly a part of the ethos. Figures concerning the number of individuals participating in each church are also inexact, since individuals are reluctant to give "private" information about their religious habits, and since churches differ on the question of what constitutes membership. However, what statistics we have show that the United States has hundreds of denominations, that Christianity is the largest single category, and that middle-class individuals and upwardly mobile individuals tend to be the most avid participants. As for location of churches, Protestants have discarded the "community church" of former days in favor of denominational churches, though lately this trend has reversed itself somewhat. Catholics have retained the community church, as well as church-run community schools. Though the Supreme Court has banned prayer in public schools and the use of public-school facilities for sectarian religious training, the right of private groups to build private schools which include religious training has been considered basic; and particularly bitter arguments have arisen concerning financial responsibility of the federal and state governments for these parochial schools.

REVIEW AND SUGGESTED READINGS

A · VOCABULARY

Ceremony (in religion)	Protestant ethic	Theology
Magic	Symbolism (in religion)	

B · QUESTIONS AND TOPICS FOR REVIEW

1. Religion has been called the "opiate of the people." Certainly the special need of the poor for religion is understandable. How do you account for the fact that in the United States there is a correlation between interest in religion and upward mobility?
2. Was *animism* ever widespread in Western culture? Explain.
3. Name two *Western* plays which assume in the audience a widespread belief in *animism*.
4. Characterize the Salvation Army as church, denomination, sect, or something else; and classify its leadership. Do the same for the Black Muslims.
5. What does your religious denomination say about immortality? What effect do you think that belief has on the day-to-day lives of members of your congregation?
6. What are some of the specific problems of the parochial schools in your community?
7. How do you account for the fact that among scientists who deal with the inorganic world there is a higher percentage of believers than among biologists, psychologists, and sociologists?
8. Do you think that the present Supreme Court ruling which outlaws prayer in the public schools will extend to the singing of Christmas carols? Why or why not?

9. Discuss recent political, social, and religious achievements of consolidated religious organizations.

C · SUGGESTIONS FOR FURTHER READING

Thomas F. Hoult. *The Sociology of Religion.* New York: Henry Holt & Co., Inc., 1958.

A general textbook with an institutional approach.

W. W. Howells. *The Heathens: Primitive Man and His Religions.* New York: Doubleday & Co., Inc., 1948.

A study by an anthropologist of religion among nonliterates.

Richard D. Lambert, ed. "Religion in American Society," *The Annals of the American Academy of Political and Social Science,* November 1960, vol. 332, pp. viii + 220.

A series of 14 papers dealing with past and present trends in church membership and religious interest, the new role of the laity, the church and secular affairs, and problems of division and unity.

Gerhard Lenski. *The Religious Factor.* Garden City, N.Y.: Doubleday & Co., Inc., 1961.

Based on empirical findings of the Detroit Area Study. Describes and analyzes how white Protestants, Negro Protestants, Catholics, and Jews differ in political and economic values and practices.

John B. Noss. *Man's Religions,* rev. ed. New York: The Macmillan Company, 1956.

A very sound survey of the chief religions of the world.

Rudolf Otto. *The Idea of the Holy,* 2nd ed. Trans. J. W. Harvey. New York: Oxford University Press, 1950.

A philosophical discussion of the nonrational foundations of religion.

Bertrand Russell. *Religion and Science.* New York: Oxford University Press, 1935.

Discusses, among other topics, the grounds for the conflict of religion and science, and most of the classic events connected therewith, such as the Copernican revolution, biological evolution, modern psychology, and the doctrine of the soul. There is a stimulating chapter on science and ethics.

Louis Schneider and Sanford M. Dornbusch. *Popular Religion. Inspirational Books in America.* Chicago: University of Chicago Press, 1958.

A sociological analysis of 46 books characterized as "inspirational religious literature," among them the works of Bruce Barton, Russell H. Conway, Harry E. Fosdick, Emmet Fox, E. Stanley Jones, Norman Vincent Peale, Fulton J. Sheen, and Ralph Waldo Trine.

Joachim Wach. *Types of Religious Experience, Christian and Non-Christian.* Chicago: University of Chicago Press, 1951.

A collection of the author's previously published papers written with appreciative insight.

J. Milton Yinger. *Religion, Society, and the Individual. An Introduction to the Sociology of Religion.* New York: The Macmillan Company, 1957.

The first half of this book discusses various sociological and social psychological facets of religion. The second half consists of a wide selection of material from various publications on religion.

CHAPTER 23

Sociological Aspects
of the Economic Order

In primary-group societies there is often no formal organization of economic endeavor. That is, there are no secondary groups, such as labor unions or manufacturing corporations, whose chief reason for being is related to the production and distribution of goods and services. In a tribal society, it is more likely that the economic function will be performed by a group already in existence than by one created especially for that purpose. Ordinarily, the economic institution is just one of the many sets of norms which define the familial roles. A father fishes because one of a father's duties is to provide food for his family, not because he is an employee of the Apex Seafood Corporation.

The type of ownership of property varies with the culture. In some societies it may be divided among members according to individual needs or according to some ranking system by age, sex, and social position. In other societies, individuals considered responsible for creating an item may be recognized as entitled to own it. The development of Western capitalism has gone through certain phases which reflect the whole shift from a primary-group organization of society to industrialized, impersonal mass society and culture.

Capital is wealth devoted to the production of commodities or services. The accumulation of capital depends on some form of abstinence, some restraint of the impulse to consume goods at once. Long ago man learned to forego immediate consumption so that he might secure more goods at a later time. Even in primitive economies, men save meat they might otherwise eat in order to use it for bait to trap more meat.

Whether or not an item is capital is determined by the use to which it is put. Coal burned in a grate to heat a living room is a consumers' good; used in a blast furnace in making steel, it is a capital good. Capital or producers' goods are easily distinguishable in machines, plants, railroad equipment, and the like. A box of breakfast cereal and a dress are obviously consumers' goods when they are in the hands of those who actually will make use of them.

ECONOMIC STRUCTURES

The economic institutions of modern states are labeled "capitalist" or "socialist" according to whether individuals or the state controls the capital goods. A society in which most of the capital goods are owned and controlled by individuals is called capitalist; when the state takes over ownership and control of capital goods, the economic structure is said to be socialist. Naturally, the two may be mixed in any number of proportions.

Formal Structures The first and still highly important form of ownership and control is *individual* (or *sole*) *proprietorship*. As capitalist enterprises expanded, one man joined with another and systems of partnership arose. This enabled two or more individuals to pool their natural resources, capital, and labor with a view to making a profit. Sociologically, a *partnership* represents a particular form of co-operation.

In time, a third kind of ownership, the economic *corporation*, emerged. As a kind of secondary group, the corporation enables individuals to act under a common name in order to own, hold, and manage property or an enterprise. The benefits of such operation are distributed among the associated stockholders. The corporation operates under a charter from the state which defines its rights, duties, and obligations. The individual stockholder ordinarily is not liable for the debts of the corporation, and the life of the corporation is independent of the lives of those who own the stock.

No other phenomenon of our time typifies mass society more adequately than the corporation. Although recognized in law as a legal personality with many of the rights and duties of an individual, it operates in complete anonymity and impersonality. While it may enter into a contract, the controls which may be exercised over it are not exactly those which society may exercise over an individual. A corporation may be fined or enjoined by the courts, but it cannot be put in jail, nor can it suffer from a sense of guilt and conscience. Yet corporations are the property of multiple individuals, and particular men run them. (As we saw in 1961, though a corporation cannot be put in jail, the individuals who run it can, and several officials of General Electric were so punished for price-fixing.) They make decisions on policy and practice and hence affect the lives of workers, consumers, and others. In fact, present-day corporate organization influences our productive capacity, our financial system, the employment of labor, and the buying habits of everybody.

The corporation is not confined to capitalistic economies; it is found also under socialism. For example, the nationalization of banking and coal mining in Britain modified only slightly the essential corporate forms of organization and control of these enterprises. Soviet Russia has developed most of her state-controlled and state-managed economy along corporate lines.

The Dominance of the Corporation In the United States, 95 percent of the business firms have fewer than 20 employees. A glance at this statistic might lead one to the conclusion that small businesses dominate the economy, but this is not true. The firms with fewer than 20 employees account for less than one-fourth of the wage and salaried workers in the economy. The other three-fourths are employed by the corporate giants which comprise only 5 percent of the total number of firms. More than one-third of the workers are in firms which have 1,000 or more employees.[1]

The extent of corporate concen-

1 · U.S. Department of Labor, Bureau of Labor Statistics, *Economic Forces in the U.S.A. in Facts and Figures* (Washington, D.C.: U.S. Government Printing Office, June, 1955), pp. 62–63.

tration varies greatly among industries. It is greatest in manufacturing, transportation, and public utilities. In utilities, for example, more than two-thirds of the employees work for firms hiring 1,000 or more. On the other hand, in construction, service industries, and retail trade, from 40 to 50 percent of the workers are in firms employing fewer than 20 persons.

Evidence of the domination of the economy by large corporations can be seen in Figures 25, 26, and 27. Even if we define as "small" those companies with assets up to a million dollars, the small companies have less than 13 percent of the market. Furthermore, as shown in Figure 26, small companies operate on a smaller profit margin than large companies. Figure 27 illustrates the fact that companies with fewer

FIGURE 26 · Small Business' Share of Total Profits: 1947–1955 *

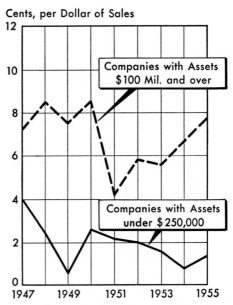

* From Federal Trade Commission, reprinted in the *New York Times*, January 15, 1956, E5. By permission.

FIGURE 25 · Small Business' Share of Total Manufacturers' Sales: 1952–1955 *

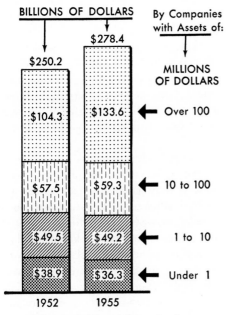

* From Public Affairs Institute, reprinted in the *New York Times*, January 15, 1956, E5. By permission.

FIGURE 27 · Small Business' Share in Military Contracts: 1951–1956 *

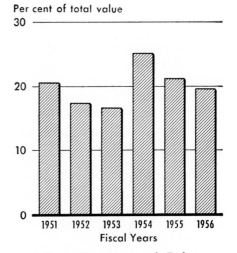

* From Department of Defense, reprinted in the *New York Times*, January 15, 1956, E5. By permission.

than 500 employees (and that includes over 99 percent of the firms) received less than 20 percent of the military contracts in the early fifties. Finally, the student of economic structure should note that, in all three of these figures, the trend seems to be running against the small firm.[2]

The Industrial Group as a Community

In economic organization as in other social life, it is not always easy to separate formal from informal structures. In industrial groups, as elsewhere, the people who come to fill roles in the formal organization soon develop informal social relationships, and congeniality groups, clubs, and other social structures emerge within the industrial plant.

A factory, department or other retail store, business office, or any other aggregate of individuals concerned with economic production or distribution develops many features of a community, though not all of them. Since the aim of the plant is narrower and more specialized than that of the true community, and since its population consists only of members of the labor force, it necessarily lacks the breadth and scope of the community as usually defined. Yet in many of its features the resemblance is close. The factory, like the community, is characterized by a given locus, and certain functions are

carried on by individuals in particular roles and statuses. In both cases—factory and community—some of the relations of individuals and groups are formal and institutionalized; others, of an informal sort, develop naturally from the very circumstance of people living or working together in close proximity.

The personnel have certain traditional or contractual relations to one another. The most obvious division is that between management and labor. The former may be the owner but under corporate organization is usually an agent of the owners. The relations of management to workers are those of graded authority and responsibility. Within this large framework there are stratified statuses. In management they range from the chief executive downward through subordinate management personnel to the foreman. Among the workers there are gradations in skill, seniority, and other accepted criteria of differentiation of role. These gradations are measurable not only in wages, working conditions, and various work privileges but in widely accepted social status. For example, among railroaders, engineers and conductors are at the top of the prestige pyramid, section hands and repair workers at the bottom.

Spatial arrangements are made in accordance with management's decisions as to what makes for highest industrial efficiency. Thus a plant has a certain ecology related to the roles of the various workers. To keep the plant operating successfully, all sorts of rules are laid down as to where to do one's job, skills expected, use of materials, avoidance of wastage and spoilage, compliance with safety measures, provision of light, ventilation, rest periods,

2 · The classic study of corporations reported that as of January 1, 1930, the 200 largest corporations (each with assets of 90 million dollars or more) other than banks controlled nearly one-half the total corporate wealth, two-fifths of total business wealth (other than banking), and somewhat more than one-fifth of all the national wealth. See A. A. Berle, Jr., and G. C. Means, *The Modern Corporation and Private Property* (New York: The Macmillan Co., 1933), p. 32. See also A. A. Berle, Jr., *Power Without Property* (New York: Harcourt, Brace & Co., 1959).

devices for handling grievances and suggestions for improvement of product or working conditions, and so on.

On the informal side, workers tend to develop cliques or groupings among themselves depending on spatial proximity, likeness of work done or level of skill, especially as related to the status factor, commonality of outside interests, and other situations or motivations which serve to bring about associations not recognized in the formal organization of the plant as an economic unit. Such groupings may and often do result in certain informal status systems that may influence the morale of the workers.

For example, in spite of the rapid development of mechanization and even automation in industry, there are certain sections in which hard physical work is performed today under almost the same conditions as a century ago. One of these sections is dock work. Helle worked among longshoremen in five major European seaports in order to study hiring practices and the formation of groups in relation to the danger of accidents on the job. He used multiple-choice questionnaires to collect comparable data on "organization," "attitudes" and "accident rates" in the five ports. Where hiring procedures disregarded both friendship and antipathy among longshoremen by assigning workers to gangs according to their registration number, attitudes toward the work environment were comparatively negative and accident frequencies were high. Conversely, where longshoremen themselves had the opportunity to choose gang members and foremen and where association with able and popular foremen was related to good work performance, work attitudes were compara-

tively positive and accident rates were lower.[3]

Thus failure of management to take informal associations into account by using them or breaking them up in the interest of efficiency may result in loss of efficiency. These informal groupings are often powerful factors in influencing the level and amount of production. There are mores of plant performance involving how much work to do for a day's pay, avoidance of speed-up which may affect other workers' wages, protection of one another from foremen in matters involving wastage and spoilage of machines or materials, and many other features of work activity. Failure to conform to these mores usually leads to various forms of punishment: ridicule, ostracism, and at times even bodily injury.

While such patterns, formal and informal, arise and continue in most plants, they are further influenced when labor unions are organized and collective bargaining comes into operation. Union contracts frequently not only act to modify the formal features of the plant in such matters as wage rates, hours, conditions of work, insurance benefits, amount of product to be turned out per worker per day, and so on, but also may influence the informal features of life in the plant by affecting status relations. And in plants not completely unionized, divisions of workers along lines of membership or nonmembership may make for conflict.

3 · Horst Jürgen Helle, *Die unstetig beschäftigten Hafenarbeiter in den nordwesteuropäischen Hafen: eine industriesoziologische Untersuchung in Antwerpen, Bremen, Bremerhaven, Hamburg und Rotterdam* [The unsteadily employed longshoremen in the ports of northwestern Europe: an industrial sociological investigation in Antwerp, Bremen, Bremerhaven, Hamburg and Rotterdam] (Stuttgart: G. Fischer, 1960).

Black Star

Getting food in a folk society: using water buffalo and wooden plows to work rice fields.

ECONOMIC FUNCTIONS

The essential function of the economic system is, of course, the production and distribution of goods and services. In even a very simple economy, such as one which requires only picking coconuts or catching fish, there is usually some organization in which roles are assigned. There must then be norms governing who gathers coconuts, who is responsible for dividing the catch of fish, at what age one is obligated or expected to enter the labor force and support himself, what is to become of persons who are too old to gather their own food, and so on. This is simply another way of saying that one function of the economic system is division of labor.

Stratification as an Economic Function

The restriction or expansion of role differentiation depends on the complexity of the economic structure. A society which depends solely on hunting for its sustenance will have a relatively small number of economic roles. Not much economic differentiation can take place in a community where every able-bodied person must devote most of his waking hours to throwing spears at rabbits in order to keep from starving. A sedentary agrarian culture frees more people from full-time food production, allows some members the leisure to become priests or craftsmen, and generally implements differentiation of roles. In an urban, industrial society, the economy requires so many specialists and provides so many differ-

FIGURE 28 · Union Membership as a Potential Political Factor *

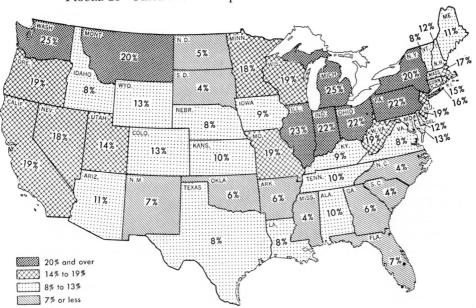

20% and over
14% to 19%
8% to 13%
7% or less

* The *New York Times*, September 23, 1956, E9. By permission.

ent roles that it becomes a major cri- terion for social stratification. One function of the economic structure, then, is to place people in social strata. While a small agricultural community is likely to rank its members on the basis of their family lineage, an indus- trialized society is more likely to rank them according to their occupational roles and resulting incomes.

The Distribution of Power   Like other structures, the economic order has many consequences in addition to its manifest function of producing and distributing goods and services. Im- portant among these is the effect which economic organization has on the dis- tribution of political power.[4] One ex-

4 · For two sociological discussions of this phenomenon, the first on the local level and the second on the national, see Floyd Hunter, *Community Power Structure* (Chapel Hill: University of North Carolina Press, 1953); and C. Wright Mills, *The Power Elite* (New York: Oxford University Press, 1956).

ample of the potential of economic status as a political factor may be seen in Figure 28, which shows the per- centage of potential voters in each state belonging to labor unions. Remember that where as many as 25 percent of the voters are union members, it is reasonable to assume that a comfort- able majority of all voters belong to families containing a union member. There is a high correlation between a state's having a low percentage of union members in its electorate and the like- lihood that the state has a tradition both of conservative state administra- tion and of sending conservative legis- lators to Congress.

The fact that there is a marked association between one's economic status and his political affiliation was documented by the subcommittee of the United States Senate which inves- tigated expenditures in the 1956 na- tional election campaign. People with corporate interests, as well as those with labor interests, seemed to have definite ideas as to which party best represents those interests. The Republican Party received donations largely from persons with big business investments, while financial aid from organized labor went almost entirely to the Democrats.

The fact that radio and television costs have constituted the largest single item of expenditure for both parties in recent Presidential election campaigns means that greater wealth gives greater opportunity to plead one's case before the electorate. To the extent that the mass media are molders of public opinion, wealth is political power.

The Interdependence of Economic Structures Another consequence of such complicated economic structures is that they are dependent on the existence of other similar structures for their own survival.

That modern nations can scarcely be economically self-sufficient is apparent to most of us. Such interdependence has been greatly increased by the rise and spread of industry, which requires raw materials from widely scattered sources. In fact, in the century preceding World War I a sort of economic world order had arisen despite the persistence in some nations of tariffs and other limitations on free trade. The restrictive nature of much of the world's trade today is related to shifts in the balance of political power which have been under way for some time. Nonetheless, economic interdependence is clear. We purchase and use articles of food, clothes, implements, tools, machines, and recreational objects that are made of raw materials from all over the world. Our breakfast

coffee, tea, or cocoa is imported, as are the tin and bauxite which go into kitchen utensils used in preparing the meal. People ride to work in motor vehicles that could not be made without imported tin, bauxite, chromium, and rubber. The automobile uses materials from 18 different countries; beauty shops need products from 17, clothing manufacturers from 21. The electrical goods industry imports from 17 countries, and the jewelers from 21. Radio is dependent on 18 items from abroad, the stationery-supplies industry on 24, and the telephone on 15 different outside sources.

The United States, in turn, exports great quantities of coal, copper, gypsum, lead, petroleum, phosphate rock, silver, and zinc. So too, meats, dairy products, apples, tobacco, wheat, and lumber are shipped abroad in large quantities. Of manufactured articles the most important exports are automobiles, electrical machinery, engines, hardware, farm equipment, sewing machines, firearms, cotton goods, motion pictures, and rubber products.

In order to move the needed goods and services from region to region and from country to country, the world has been covered with a network of land, sea, and air transport and communication lines. From the turn of the present century to the outbreak of World War II, the marine tonnage in the world increased 136 percent. To facilitate transportation, common navigation rules have been worked out by international agreements. Similarly, uniform freight rates on shipping lines operating in the same regions or between the same ports have been generally agreed upon. Long before the coming of the railroad, many of the larger rivers of the world were "inter-

Libby, McNeill & Libby

Getting food in an urban society: assembly line in a cannery.

nationalized" for traffic, and all sorts of provisions for the use of port facilities were made. In Europe particularly, international arrangements were developed to facilitate railway transport across the thousands of miles of political boundaries. Uniform bills of lading, reciprocal use of rolling stock, agreements fixing responsibility for damages, co-ordinated timetables, and many other common practices were set up. There were also agreements among European nations to aid in motor transport services.

The story of air transport is even more striking. In the two decades separating the two world wars, airplane lines reached into every part of the globe. Almost overnight the most remote regions came within relatively easy flying distance. In 1947 an aviation treaty established the International

Civil Aviation Organization, with 26 nations participating. This institution set up basic standards for global air traffic.

The international postal service, known as the Universal Postal Union, was established in 1874 and, except during wartime, embraces practically the entire habitable globe in a single worldwide postal area. The development of radio communication followed a somewhat similar course. After early monopolistic trends, international agreements were made regarding commercial radio and the use of radio in shipping. Since World War I, radio broadcasting has become not only commercially but politically one of the most important media of communication to the masses.

The telephone and, later, the radio-telephone have made possible worldwide conversation. The Americas have taken the lead in the international use of the telephone. As early as 1938, through a combination of radio, cables, and land transmission lines, the United States could reach every continent and the major islands of the sea by means of 74 different telephone circuits.

It is evident from all this that, in transportation of raw materials and manufactured goods and in communications, the world has moved toward an international order. In fact, we find a rather paradoxical situation in which we have international traffic and communication rules but national ownership and national control determining the final decisions. The isolationism which has become linked to nationalism stands in sharp contrast with the interdependence of economic structures and functions.

Other Functions We have discussed several of the major functions of economic organization. It should be remembered that integration of all institutions means that each has some consequences for all the others. Thus reproduction and socialization of new members must occur if there are to be persons ready to fill the roles in the economic structure, and goods must be produced and distributed if people are to live so that they can reproduce and socialize new members for the society.

ECONOMIC PATTERNS IN THE UNITED STATES

The labor supply of any society consists of all its potential workers, male and female. At what age an individual is counted as a potential worker is a matter of cultural definition. For example, adolescents under 14 years of age are not considered to be in our national labor force. Earlier, and still in some societies, younger children were considered part of the labor force. Figure 29 shows the composition, by age and sex, of the labor force in our society. The actual *labor force* may be defined as that fraction of a population which is engaged in producing or distributing goods or services. Those persons temporarily unemployed are also included.

Composition of the Labor Force The labor force of this country has grown steadily, in keeping with our rising population. In 1890 it consisted of 22.2 million persons, or about 23 percent of the total population. In 1940 it was 53 million, or 40 percent of the people. In 1950 it was over 63 million, and by 1960 it was over 70 million. The proportion of the total population represented in the labor force for the past few decades has remained slightly more than 40 percent. This leveling-off of the fraction of the total population in the labor force is due largely to the disappearance of child labor and to the increase in automation.

A second important feature of our labor force is the increasing number of women gainfully employed. Even more striking has been the increase in the number of married and divorced women in the labor force. Although half a century ago only a negligible proportion of the labor force was composed of married women, now nearly a third of the workers are women, most of them married women living with their husbands. The increase in the number of gainfully employed women, both married and single, is of course only one aspect of the

FIGURE 29 · Population and Labor Force *

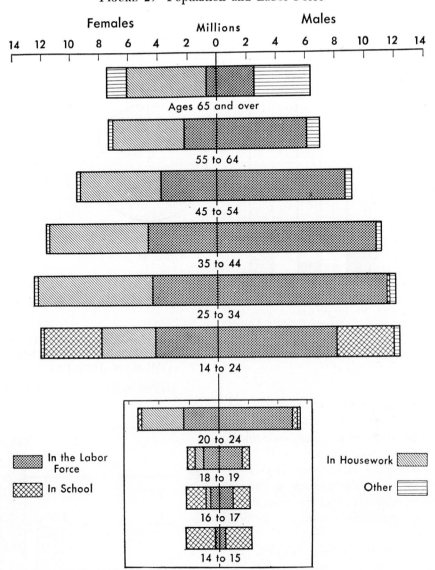

* U.S. Department of Labor, Bureau of Labor Statistics, *Economic Forces in the U.S.A. in Facts and Figures* (Washington, D.C.: U.S. Government Printing Office, June, 1955), p. 19.

changing status of women in our society.

Figure 30 shows how the labor force has grown. Figures 31 and 32 show the increasing proportion of women and the increase in earnings of workers.

The revolution in educational expectations has had its impact on the labor force, too. Whereas half the young men from 14 to 19 years old were in the labor force in 1890, only a third from this age group are job-seekers or job-holders today.

FIGURE 30 · The Growth of the Labor Force in the United States: 1930–1960 *

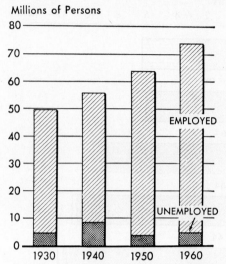

Millions of Persons

* Adapted from the *New York Times*, August 21, 1955, E7. By permission. 1960 data from *Health, Education, and Welfare Trends* (Washington, D.C.: U.S. Government Printing Office, 1960), p. 12; and *Current Population Reports*, Series P–60, No. 35, January 5, 1961.

The proportion of men 65 and older who are in the labor force has declined from more than two-thirds in 1890 to about 30 percent in 1960. This change is attributable largely to social security, the increase in private pension programs, and the practice of making retirement at a given age compulsory.

The total amount of time expended in work in our society is less than one might think. Not only do many of the added millions of workers in the labor force (especially the women) limit themselves to part-time work, but the length of the work week itself has been greatly reduced. The standard work week in 1900 was 54 to 60 hours or more. A person steadily employed in a manufacturing plant thus worked about 3,000 hours a year.

FIGURE 31 · Changes in the Proportion of Women in the Labor Force: 1900–1960 *

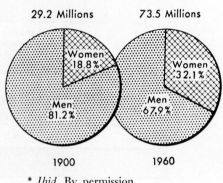

HOW MANY WORKERS ARE WOMEN
Per Cent of Labor Force

* *Ibid.* By permission.

FIGURE 32 · Changes in the Average Weekly Earnings of Production Workers: 1920–1960 *

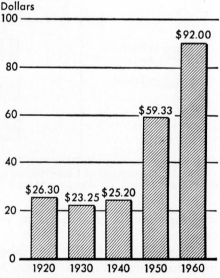

HOW MUCH THEY EARN

* The *New York Times*, August 21, 1955, E7. By permission. 1960 estimate calculated from *Current Population Reports*, Series P–60, No. 35, January 5, 1961.

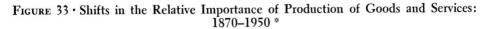

FIGURE 33 · Shifts in the Relative Importance of Production of Goods and Services: 1870–1950 *

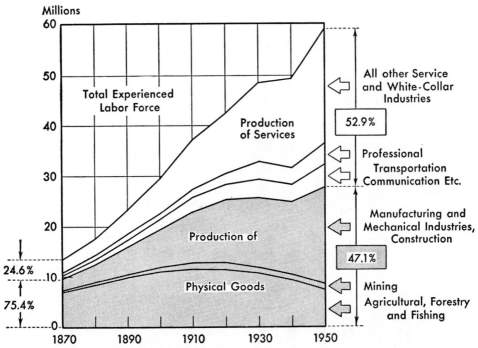

* U.S. Department of Labor, Bureau of Labor Statistics, *Economic Forces in the U.S.A. in Facts and Figures* (Washington, D.C.: U.S. Government Printing Office, June, 1955), p. 24.

Today such a worker averages less than 40 hours a week and receives a paid vacation, thus working only about 2,000 hours a year.

Distribution of the Labor Force In the last century there has been a major industrial shift from the production of goods to the production of services. In 1870 about three-fourths of the people in the labor force were engaged in producing tangible goods. As Figure 33 shows, by 1950 the proportion was less than half. The figures include employers and the self-employed, as well as wage and salary workers. This shift in the distribution of the labor force has been brought about largely by technological improvements. Heavy manual labor has given way to machine production, which has freed a larger portion of the labor force to run laundromats, rent out evening clothes, provide package delivery services, give pedicures to French poodles, be tree surgeons or public stenographers—in short, to enter service industries.

Of course, agriculture too has become more mechanized. At the time the United States was founded, farming was the most important income-producing activity, and as recently as 1870 more than half the labor force was engaged in agriculture. Today farmers comprise only 6.3 percent of the labor force. According to the Census of Agriculture, there were 600,000 fewer farmers in the United States in

FIGURE 34 · Changes in the Distribution of Skills in the United States: 1910–1960 *

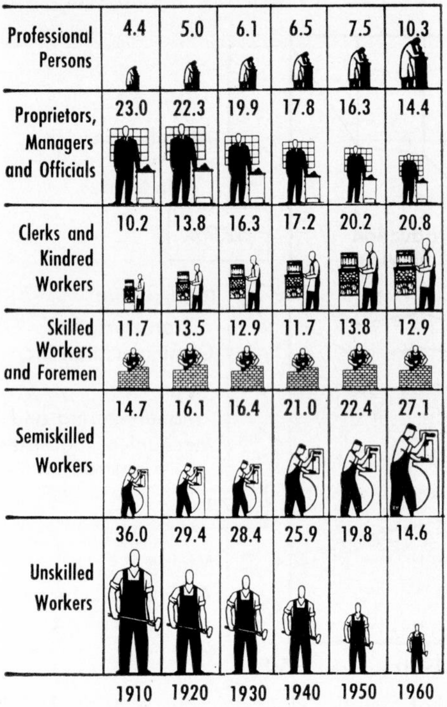

	1910	1920	1930	1940	1950	1960
Professional Persons	4.4	5.0	6.1	6.5	7.5	10.3
Proprietors, Managers and Officials	23.0	22.3	19.9	17.8	16.3	14.4
Clerks and Kindred Workers	10.2	13.8	16.3	17.2	20.2	20.8
Skilled Workers and Foremen	11.7	13.5	12.9	11.7	13.8	12.9
Semiskilled Workers	14.7	16.1	16.4	21.0	22.4	27.1
Unskilled Workers	36.0	29.4	28.4	25.9	19.8	14.6

* From *Economic Forces in the U.S.A.*, p. 29. 1960 data from Bureau of Labor Statistics.

1954 than in 1950.[5] Individuals who under other conditions might have been farmers are entering the urban labor force, particularly the service industries.

Figure 34 shows the dramatic growth in semiskilled labor and clerical occupations. Since 1890, clerical workers in the labor force have increased fivefold, professional and technical workers threefold, sales workers nearly twofold, and proprietors and managers by almost one-half. Household work-

5 · "Fewer and Larger Farms Shown in Latest Summary of Census," *Agricultural Situation*, 1956, 40:12. (Agricultural Marketing Service, U.S. Department of Agriculture, Washington, D.C.: U.S. Government Printing Office.)

ers declined 50 percent, but other service workers, such as barbers, beauticians, cooks, firemen, janitors, policemen, and waitresses, have doubled. On balance, service occupations increased by a third.

The growth of the semiskilled category is explained only partly by the fact that mechanization has led to the replacement of a large number of unskilled workers with a smaller number of semiskilled machine operators. In the past three decades, the labor movement itself, by the very success of its demands for increased salaries, has helped force employers to mechanize and save money on wages.

The nation's economy is less and less dependent on muscle power and more and more dependent on professional, technical, and clerical skills. The shift from brawn and manpower to education and brain power reflects a basic trend in American economic life.

ECONOMIC INSTITUTIONS

Competition is a basic value in our culture; we find norms structured around the value of competition in each of our basic institutions. In courtship, young people compete for dates with the members of the opposite sex considered to be the most desirable. Through missionaries and revivals, churches compete for members. Our major political offices are filled by the process of competition: office-seekers compete for popularity with the voters. In the area of socialization, we motivate children to learn by having them compete for grades.

Economic Competition Economic competition is rivalry and struggle to get possession of those things which a given culture considers wealth. It is but a phase of the larger universal struggle for goods, tangible and intangible. There exists, on the one hand, a limited resource, and, on the other, a population with an ever-increasing number of wants, both basic and culturally defined.

As for personal motivation, the traditional theory of economic competition assumes complete self-interest on the part of buyers and sellers. It takes for granted a rational judgment of wants and of the means of satisfying them. It postulates the principle that each man acts to get the most he can from others while giving as little as he must himself.

This view of competition clearly reflects the whole social-cultural period in which modern capitalism developed. Capitalism assumed a self-regulating interrelation of price, demand, and supply. This, in turn, rested on a simple psychology of rational motivation directed "to *economizing* or *utility-maximizing* behavior" believed to flow directly "from the fact that human wants are comparatively unlimited in relation to the resources available for the satisfaction of such wants." [6]

It was the contention of laissez-faire economists of the eighteenth and nineteenth centuries that the free flow of goods and services through rational and unhampered competition would result in the most efficient production and distribution of goods, capital, and labor supply—all to the ultimate benefit of the consumers. They fully believed

6 · See J. J. Spengler, "Sociological Presuppositions in Economic Theory," *Southern Economic Journal*, 1940, 7:131–157, quotation from p. 132, italics in the original. This is a thoughtful and stimulating paper on the limitations of classical theory.

in the competitive practice of their time—that the institutions of private property, contract, profit-making, and laissez-faire freedom of action were a true and objective operation of universal forces in nature and society.

Modern psychology does not support this view of human behavior. Men have impulses and interests that do not completely correspond to their rational needs. Political and religious views, class status, and life philosophy also influence economic behavior. Love, sympathy, hatred, anxiety, and indifference, tied to irrational attitudes and values, often enter into man's economic choices.

Norms Governing Consumer Patterns
Modern technology and complex business enterprise have profoundly altered the market situation in which the ordinary consumer finds himself. Such changes are due to mass production, to the disappearance of the earlier competitive pattern with the rise of many near-monopolies, to the shift from an agricultural to an industrial economy, to the high degree of division of labor, and to urban life. The consumer has become more and more dependent on the institutions of the market place. At an earlier date, say 1890, the ordinary buyer in a small town or rural trading center purchased goods that were usually of a quality not very difficult to determine. On the basis of what he could see, touch, or taste, he could decide whether or not to buy. Today in modern retailing the quality, durability, and utility of goods are not well standardized in relation to price. The research of consumers' testing agencies indicates that the less expensive of two competing products frequently is the one of higher quality. The more ex-

pensive product may capture a sizable share of the market, however, by skillful advertising and packaging.

Advertising profoundly influences consumer wants and habits of buying. Some advertising is useful in informing prospective buyers about available materials or services, but much of it is emotional and status-appealing. "Keeping up with the Joneses" is an old motive, and all sorts of advertisements stimulate people to buy so that they may have a product popular with the "best people."

The nature of retailing has changed greatly. The department store, the mail-order house, and the chain store all give witness to the growing complexity of the market, to alterations in the earlier competitive patterns, and to changes in the role of the ultimate consumer. The chain store is a good reflection of business enterprise in mass society. It is efficient—it eliminates the middleman and handles standardized goods—but its merchandising tends to be impersonal.

Finally, alterations have been made in the use of credit. Many consumers no longer pay cash or use an open charge account. Rather, they pay on some sort of fixed installment plan. Installment buying has become, indeed, a culture pattern for large sections of our population, and the charges for this service are passed on, in one form or another, to the consumer.

The difficulties for the consumer can be traced to the transition from an old to a new method of distributing consumption goods. While many critics decry advertising, chain-store, and other aspects of contemporary selling, it must be realized that all these are intimately interwoven with the whole fabric of modern business enterprise.

The government of the United States, acting as an agency for the consuming public, has taken increasing interest in consumer protection. There are laws providing for pure food and drugs, for standard methods of packaging and labeling, and for licensing and inspection—control over the conditions surrounding the production of a good or a service rather than over the nature of the product itself. Such regulations are found in public transportation systems, in restaurants, packing houses, and so on. So too, governments attempt to set up standards regarding such matters as weight, freshness, chemical composition, and quality. In addition to governmental aids, various private consumer organizations have been set up to inform prospective buyers about quality and price. Such organizations often publish buyers' guides.

Sociological Aspects of Economic Institutions People are socialized to participate in economic activity in order to satisfy their basic needs—that is, to support themselves. But people are motivated to work for other reasons as well. If they were not, why would the man who earns fifty thousand dollars a year put in extra hours striving for a promotion and a raise, or why would the man who inherited enough wealth to live comfortably do the work necessary to get through professional school and then show up at an office every day? Why do sociologists who study industrial organization find it not unusual for a member of a small work group in a factory to turn down a chance for promotion to a job as foreman, accompanied by a raise in pay?

Both the wealthy man who continues to work and the worker who re-

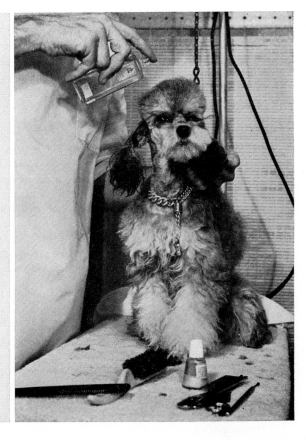

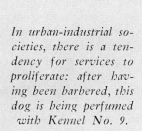

In urban-industrial so-
cieties, there is a ten-
dency for services to
proliferate: after hav-
ing been barbered, this
dog is being perfumed
with Kennel No. 9.

Black Star

jects a promotion illustrate the fact that there are incentives governing work which are not economic. People are motivated to pursue economic activity not only to make money but to gain power and prestige, to cultivate and maintain primary group relations, to contribute to a sense of purpose, and to fulfill the expectations of other social roles, such as husband or father. The worker who would rather stay with his production gang than be promoted is willing, perhaps, to forego economic gain for the feeling of "belonging" which he enjoys as a member of the primary group. Many people who have enough wealth to permit them to enjoy full-time leisure continue to work because they have been socialized in American society, where the norms of the culture have convinced them that healthy adult males ought to be engaged in something productive. It is common for people who have retired to complain of feeling useless; they have lost a sense of purpose which their work gave them.

Only by noting these sociological variables and by taking into account the interplay between the norms governing production and the other social institutions can one understand the institutions governing the economic structure and its functions.

INTERPRETATIVE SUMMARY

In mass societies, the production and distribution of goods and services tend to be handled by a few large corporate structures, state or private. These structures resemble community structure in several ways: individuals have roles and statuses, in this case related to the division of labor; informal groups supplement the formal structure; and both tacit and stated norms govern behavior.

Besides being a sort of community unto itself, the corporation has profoundly affected the larger community. For one thing, an individual's job status is likely to be the determining factor in his ultimate status in the community. Moreover, *he* will identify himself so strongly with members of similar occupational strata that he may vote for and help finance political figures and parties who seem sympathetic to that stratum; thus the economic institution influences the political institutions of a culture. Under systems of free enterprise, the existence of highly mechanized corporate giants has led to many minor culture patterns affecting consumers: the emergence of big retailing combines, the extension of advertising and credit, and even the extension of protective government control, an action that was not contemplated in the days of widespread trust in laissez-faire economics.

In the United States, both the composition and the distribution of the labor force have changed over the years, largely as a result of technological advances which were in turn made possible by the existence of large amounts of corporate capital. The labor force presently has more women than ever before, fewer young and very old people, far fewer people doing unskilled labor, and more occupied in performing services.

Paradoxically, on a world scale economic sophistication has led to increased economic interdependence. Though concern for the political balance of power has dictated caution, the general trend is toward increased co-operation, a co-operation which has been implemented by vast international communication and transportation networks.

REVIEW AND SUGGESTED READINGS

A • VOCABULARY

Competition	Labor force
Corporation	Technology

B • QUESTIONS AND TOPICS FOR REVIEW

1. In what ways besides those already mentioned is the economic structure of the United States related to political power?
2. What are some of the advantages of corporate ownership?
3. Trace the history of government control of one product or area.
4. What special goods and services does the "discount store" provide? What are its chief methods of retailing and advertising? What do you think is the future of such establishments?
5. Name some service industries which have emerged or expanded in your lifetime. In each case, how prestigious are the statuses involved?
6. Discuss recent changes in the international economic status quo.
7. Has work *per se* always been considered a value in Western culture? What about erudition?

8. Discuss overt attempts of labor or corporate interests to control distribution of political power.

C · SUGGESTIONS FOR FURTHER READING

Theodore Caplow. *The Sociology of Work.* Minneapolis: University of Minnesota Press, 1954.

Contains penetrating comments on occupational ideologies, some good data on the labor force, and an excellent discussion of occupational prestige.

Robert Dub'n. *The World of Work: Industrial Society and Human Relations.* Englewood Cliffs, N.J.: Prentice-Hall, Inc., 1958.

A fine treatment of the organization of work in contemporary industrial society.

William H. Form and Delbert C. Miller. *Industry, Labor, and Community.* New York: Harper & Brothers, 1960.

A discussion of the relations between the economic institution and other institutions in an industrial society, within the framework of community power structure.

John Kenneth Galbraith. *The Affluent Society.* Boston: Houghton Mifflin Co., 1958.

Poses the question of whether an economic theory based on an economy of scarcity is relevant to the problems of a society of plenty.

Alvin W. Gouldner. *Patterns of Industrial Bureaucracy.* Glencoe, Ill.: The Free Press, 1954.

A fascinating case study of the norms governing behavior in a mine and a factory, and a real contribution to sociological theory in the form of a typology of bureaucratic rules.

Scott Greer. *Last Man In: Racial Access to Union Power.* Glencoe, Ill.: The Free Press, 1959.

A report of research on the power structure of labor unions and its consequences for racial relations and the role of the leader.

Edward Gross. *Work and Society.* New York: Thomas Y. Crowell Company, 1958.

An analysis of man in the role of worker, with a cross-cultural comparison of economic institutions.

Edward S. Mason, ed. *The Corporation in Modern Society.* Cambridge: Harvard University Press, 1959.

A stimulating collection of readings on the corporation, its structure, and its impact on other organizations.

Paul Meadows. *The Culture of Industrial Man.* Lincoln, Nebraska: University of Nebraska Press, 1950.

An excellent analysis of the culture patterns peculiar to an industrial society and their implications for the individual.

Wilbert E. Moore. *The Conduct of the Corporation.* New York: Random House, 1963.

A sensitive observer's report on the inside workings of a large-scale modern business bureaucracy.

Eugene V. Schneider. *Industrial Sociology*. New York: McGraw-Hill Book Co., 1957.

Contains a good section on rules in industrial bureaucracies and an excellent treatment of the social structure of trade unionism. Valuable also for its extensive bibliography.

Harold L. Wilensky. *Intellectuals in Labor Unions: Organizational Pressures on Professional Roles*. Glencoe, Ill.: The Free Press, 1956.

Essentially a study of decision-making as it is determined by the varied norms shaping the role of the staff expert.

CHAPTER 24

Political Sociology

All societies have some sort of larger, overall regulations dealing with the general welfare of the tribe or the community. Usually there are designated groups or persons who set up the rules and act to see that they are enforced. In its broadest sense, this wider regulatory force may be called the government. In more rudimentary societies such controls are largely informal. In more complex societies they are both informal and formal. Generally, the more complex the community, the more formalized the controls. More definite organization is reflected in special personnel—legislative, administrative, and judicial—whose roles are to operate the various control agencies. In the strict sense, the concept of political order or government refers to these special regulations and the operating personnel.

Political scientists specialize in the study of the structure and processes of government. Yet some political data have considerable interest to sociologists. These include the relationship of the society to the nation-state, the way in which the mores and public opinion influence political interaction, the place of political revolution in social change, and the functions of political structures for other institutions.

We shall examine the structures, functions, patterns, and institutions of these aspects of government.

POLITICAL STRUCTURES

In ancient Greece a citizen was a full member of the city-state, with a certain role and status in public life. These stood in contrast with his culturally deep-rooted relations with his family, kin, and occupational or other associations. The distinction between public and private matters is historically important because it indicates the shift from a kinship to a territorial basis of control, from private vengeance to public punishment, from small, primary-group obligations to larger obligations based on secondary contacts.

In modern times the political order is centered in the sovereign state. As a social myth and as a set of practices, the state is the core of contemporary nationalism. The sovereign state has become the principal instrument of public order and reflects, in fact, the continuing need for some overall agency of control in an industrialized mass society.

We may look on the *state* as an organized power structure the functions of which are the management and control of the society. This involves such things as external and internal security, justice, and welfare, and varying provisions for individual freedom, depending on the nature of the state and the national society. The state also

Different ways of achieving power: a political convention.

has sole power to levy taxes to pay for these services.

In the simplest society a separate governmental structure may be barely discernible. In such a society, where the social structure is practically coterminous with a few families or clans, most matters of social control are handled within the family structure. Even in such a situation, there is usually a chief or council of elders in whom ultimate authority for major decisions resides. But let us remember that, regardless of how elaborate the machinery of government may become, some of the norms are always decided and enforced through informal structures, Behind the formal organization of the state there are always folkways and mores supported by informal sanctions.

Formal Structures The state is, of course, a historical product. As populations grew, increasing differentiation of roles led to a breakdown of controls and the need for extension of regulations to new areas of conduct. This meant a shift from a family or kinship basis of social control to one founded on the larger community, with particular individuals, groups, or classes setting down the rules and putting them into effect. More integrated forms of government tended to arise as groups or societies were threatened by, or fell into conflict with, other societies. This tendency was most important in the rise of more complex states: warfare between groups makes for stronger in-group solidarity.

It seems a far cry from the simple tribal or village council of older men to the elaborate operations of modern government, and yet these institutions have much in common. They both revolve around a power structure and its functions. First, someone or some group makes the rules and laws or at least standardizes those at hand, without which there could be no social order. This is the legislative structure. Second, somebody or some group enforces the regulations. This is the executive or administrative structure. Third, some group is responsible for settling controversies where the meaning and application of the laws or codes are in question. This is the judicial structure.

Bureaucracy Growth of government has meant an increase in the relative importance and role of the administrative structure in comparison with the legislative and judicial branches. This shift has brought with it increased public concern over the nature of the executive structure.

Originally the term *bureaucracy* referred to the administration of government by means of bureaus—that is, special units to care for such matters as taxation, police protection, communications, foreign relations, and military defense. Today the term has come to include certain unintended but nonetheless important features of administration. The most striking of these is the development of a set of self-perpetuating culture patterns in which the means of public service often become ends in themselves and in which the power interests of the administrative personnel are directed to their own protection rather than to satisfactory operation of the governmental agency as a public service.

The structure of administrative roles—the "table of organization," as military parlance has it—becomes so sacred that no deviation from it is permitted. The fixed rules designed to facilitate decision tend to predominate at the expense of variable situations. As bureaucratic members of the military are fond of saying, "You can't go wrong if you stick to the book"—that is, to the rules and procedures laid down by those in the higher echelons of authority. Such emphasis means a tendency to view various activities as fitting neatly into predetermined and rigid categories. Everything has to be labeled, acted on, and reported in formalist fashion, with no deviations. The flow of decisions may become so intricate that the purpose or intent of the action becomes secondary to the proper fulfillment of the procedural rules. This means a high degree of impersonality in handling cases requiring administrative decision. The bureaucrat is symbolic of his organization: he has no power to make personal decisions.

Black Star

Different ways of achieving power: the dictator's method, as used by Hitler.

Such stress on "the book" and on cautious following of the rules results in what Veblen aptly called "trained incapacity"—that is, loss of flexibility to meet new situations. Personnel are chosen by examinations to prove their preparation or competence for the job; but once past a usually short probation period, they are protected by various regulations concerning tenure, recurrent promotion, and seniority, whether their competence is maintained or not. The whole structure is a fixed and safe world, marked by rigid rules, methodical and impersonal execution of the rules, and hence a predictable outcome. Once such a scheme gets into operation, it resists modification.

The regimen set down in institutions has its counterpart in the human beings who operate the system. There is no neater illustration of the interplay of culture and personality than in the field of bureaucratic administration. The competence needed for a job will vary with what is expected, and the incumbent in a given office must come up to certain standards. But once he is on the job, there is pressure to be prudent, methodical, and precise in carrying on his work. One needs little or no initiative or imagination, and one avoids responsibility by passing difficult questions on to a higher authority or by hiding behind the rules. In fact, to demonstrate such qualities will usually lead to punishment of some kind, not reward. Innovations are not welcome in a bureaucratic world. Rather, this world encourages and rewards conformity, timidity, and deference to higher authority and regulations.

Yet, living in a safe world, bureaucrats often show arrogance or indifference to their clientele. The officeholder can compensate for his enforced conformity by showing his power over others. This is a feature of bureaucracy which those conditioned to a culture of individualism, personal give-and-take, and flexible decisions find so frustrating in military service and in dealing with governmental bureaus generally. While bureaucratic features may arise in the economic order, at least under free enterprise individuals can "take their business elsewhere." But if you do not like the service at the United States Post Office, you cannot decide to patronize some other firm. There simply is no place else to go for most governmental services. This absence of choice is one of the most striking features of life in a highly planned society.

Some believe there is a drift toward administration by professional bureaucrats in government, just as there

is in private enterprise. This drift may be even stronger in totalitarian societies than in representative democracy, because public service there is a means of rewarding party members for their political adherence. It is, in effect, a spoils system on a vast scale.

In short, once the administration of government—or of business, for that matter—becomes encrusted with bureaucracy, the system tends to perpetuate itself, unless some devices are set up to prevent its doing so. Cautious and "safe" men pick men like themselves for the jobs. There is a kind of empire-building of the timid to protect themselves from the strong. The bureaucrats fear any inroads on their role and status by bold and ingenious people. Officialism, like extreme ecclesiasticism in the church, means that the form of the law remains, but the "spirit," the dynamic function, soon disappears.

POLITICAL FUNCTIONS

We have mentioned three major types of formal political structures: legislative, executive, and judicial. These need not, of course, be operated by separate or distinct groups. In a totalitarian society, one man and a handful of subordinates can make the laws, enforce them, and arbitrate disputes about them. In our society, we insist that roles in the three structures be mutually exclusive. One cannot at the same time fill the status of a Senator who makes laws and that of a Supreme Court Justice who adjudicates disputes about those laws, nor can one assume the role of a Representative who makes laws and simultaneously be the Attorney General charged with enforcing them. What political scientists call the system of checks and balances in the government of the United States is an arrangement whereby the three major functions of government are the responsibility of three separate groups, each of which exercises some limitation on the powers of the others.

The three principal internal functions of government (as opposed to its external function, the protection of the society against other societies) are (1) the institutionalization of norms, or decreeing the rules under which the society shall operate; (2) the adjudication of conflicts, or settling disputes between groups within the society about the application of institutionalized norms and their sanction; and (3) the planning of the state's operation and the enforcement of its institutionalized norms.

The Institutionalization of Norms
The central role of legislative bodies is to make the laws which become the governmental controls of the society. Other chief functions are taxation and investigation of administrative personnel to see that they carry out the mandates of the legislature. In some systems legislators may act, on occasion, as a judicial body, as in the impeachment of public officials. The legislative group—parliament, assembly, congress—set up to make the laws usually does so in accordance with some written or unwritten constitution. Law-making, however, need not be confined to the legislative structure. In our system, law is also made by judges in rendering court decisions, by administrative action, and by a machinery of initiative and referendum which permits direct legislation by the voters.

In democratic countries, legislators are elected by various systems of voting, sometimes directly and sometimes, as when one legislative body chooses the members of another, indirectly. Representation is usually on the basis of territory, such as the precinct, county, or other geographic district. And in this country at least, prospective legislators must live in the local residential area where they stand for office, for it is traditionally held that persons who live in a neighborhood, city, or region will serve its interests best. The British hold a different view and nominate and elect men to the House of Commons regardless of their home address. Despite practice in the United States, there is little doubt that the older theory of geographic locus breaks down under modern conditions. It reflects the primary-group culture from which it sprang. Today individuals and groups believe they should also be represented in accordance with the secondary-group interests of their professions, businesses, labor unions, and the like. The lobby and the pressure group show the extent to which modern legislatures must deal with problems other than those which are confined to primary groups living in limited localities.

The Soviet system of representation on the basis of one's being a worker in a plant, or in a railroad system, or a member of a labor union, or a farmer illustrates a shift from a strictly territorial to a more functional basis of representation. And indeed, our own pressure group or lobby is a kind of unofficial functional representation.

The Adjudication of Conflicts While the law—constitutional, statute, or judge-made—fixes the rules of human conduct, conflicts of interest constantly require some adjudication. Hence courts are set up, usually at two levels: those of original jurisdiction and those for appeal, the latter culminating in

American society in the United States Supreme Court.

The selection and qualifications of individuals to operate the courts vary with the culture. In Anglo-American practice, judicial functions have been divided between those of jury and those of judge. The jury system goes back to the primary-group theory of democracy, that an individual accused of crime has the right to be tried by his equals—his "peers," as the legal language puts it. Though our jury system has been much criticized and though there has been a trend to abandon trial by jury except in more serious criminal cases, it still represents an important link between citizenry and government.

The Administration of the State and the Enforcement of Norms

A third basic function of government is to put into effect the "will" or laws of the state. Where government is at all complex there are usually several levels of administrative power and function. First, there is the *head of state*. He may be elected by popular vote, or he may derive his role and status from being a member of a ruling family or from his headship of a dictatorial clique or party. He is charged with the responsibility of enforcing the power of the state. The dictator-head may be both lawmaker and law-enforcer, though this situation exists less often than popular notion imagines.

The head of the state usually has some kind of council or cabinet to advise him. Sometimes the council itself is the head of the state in the sense that its decisions are binding, as in Britain. Sometimes it is only advisory, as in the United States. In Soviet Russia the real head of the country is the Politburo of the Communist Party, although it is not even mentioned in the published constitution. This is a case of single-party dominance of the executive and legislative functions. The various congresses and presidia are largely window-dressing for the real control exercised by the Communist Party.

The second-level administrators are the heads of major governmental departments or bureaus. They are charged with carrying out the executive policies determined by the head of the state and his advisors. Below this second level are several other layers of administrators: division and bureau chiefs, and a mass of specialists of various qualifications, duties, and responsibilities.

In democracies it was once common to draw practically all administrative personnel from the membership of the political party in office. (This "spoils" system, as it is called, has also been used under authoritarian and dictatorial forms of government.) But as the duties of administrators became more complex and required special skills and experience, and as the abuses of patronage mushroomed, devices such as the civil service were set up to limit the spoils system. The function of the civil service is to take much public administration out of the hands of politicians and set up professional standards for the selection, continuity, and promotion of most government personnel.

The Protection of the Society against Other Societies

The first three functions of government are necessary to the preservation of order within the society. But it is also essential that the society defend itself against outside attack. The two principal means for accomplishing this end are war and diplomacy. The accommodation of conflicts

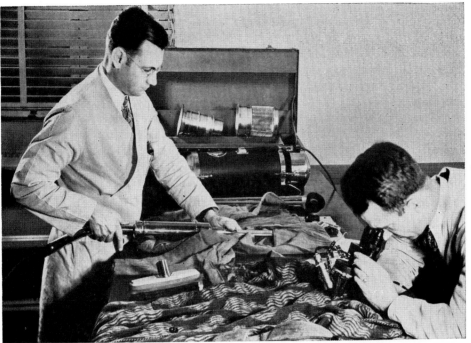

Ewing Galloway

The maintenance of order, too, is specialized in an urban society: FBI experts collecting hidden dust from clothing for microscopic study.

with other societies can be implemented by bargaining, compromise, or threats, or the societies can attempt to subjugate or destroy each other through warfare.

Despite modern communication, the spread of technology, and the exchange of goods and ideas from country to country and region to region, the world is marked by a high degree of cultural diversity. Take but the matter of language, the principal carrier of cultural diversity. Including all the local and regional variations, there are several hundred languages. There are 284 million people who speak English, 161 million who speak Russian, 598 million who speak Chinese, and more than 200 million who speak Hindustani. These make up about half the world's population. Moreover, the first three of these languages are the core of rather distinctive cultural systems. In the rest of the world are other nations not far removed from the cultural systems of, say, the English- or the Russian-speaking peoples. Yet there are still other linguistic groups with rather sharp cultural differences. Facile solutions of the problems of war and peace too frequently neglect the fact of peoples' intolerance of those who are different.

Mankind is not only intolerant but inconsistent. Many may desire a world order based on law or rule of reason; but countering this, as always, is the play of nationalist myths and legends which may serve to block movements to establish a global legal system with one central structure for enforcing norms. It is very doubtful that the masses of men in the countries with a high standard of living will voluntarily submit to plans which would take from them what they now hold. Given what we know about the distribution of population and resources in the world, we can expect competition and conflict among states to continue. Each society, therefore, must have some structure with the function of protecting it from external threats.

POLITICAL PATTERNS IN THE UNITED STATES

In highly dynamic periods such as the present, political patterns do not remain static. They are influenced by technological inventions, the breakdown of primary-group forms of living, and the related extension of secondary and mass-society patterns of action. These changes have been associated particularly with an extension of governmental controls, especially in the area of the planning function of the executive structure.

The Growth of Government One of the most striking changes in modern life is the expansion of the government into areas of action long considered outside the direct scope of the state. This is particularly true with reference to economic institutions, but it is evident in almost all other important phases of our society. The manner in which a state tends to become the all-embracing, controlling agent depends on the cultural values and practices of the time and place. In most democratic countries the trend has been chiefly in the direction of administrative regulations of capitalistic enterprises and of furnishing certain public services. On the whole, such trends have not as yet disturbed very greatly the familial, re-

ligious, and economic institutions of democratic societies. In authoritarian countries the state has taken over property and economic enterprise almost entirely, with more and more regimentation and planning of nearly every aspect of both public and private life.

There are various ways of measuring the expansion of functions in the political order. The most obvious are increases in the cost of government and in number of public personnel. Others are the growth in services and regulations.

The extension of the political structure is easily seen in the increasing proportion of the labor force employed by the government. As is shown in Table 38, the portion of the labor force employed by the government has increased in the past century nearly five times as fast as the number of privately employed workers.

A further indication of the trend toward government's taking responsibility for many aspects of social life is revealed in patterns of taxation. A quarter of a century ago, 14 percent of the national income went for taxes. Today 31 percent of the national income is taken by taxes. (These figures include all taxes: federal, state, and local.) The centralization of government is shown by the growing proportion of taxes collected by the federal government. Twenty-five years ago the federal government received only one-fourth of all taxes collected in the United States. That fraction has grown to three-fourths.[1]

It is true that our society is much larger in population and in geographic

1 · These figures are from an address by former Secretary of Agriculture Ezra Taft Benson before the American Association of Land Grant Colleges and Universities, Washington, D.C., November 15, 1956.

TABLE 38 · Increase in Proportion of Government Workers in Total Working Force
in the United States: 1850–1960 *

YEAR	TYPE OF WORKER (Millions)		Per Cent
	Privately Employed	Government Employee	Government Employed as of Total Employed
1850	7.2	.2	2.8
1870	12.0	.4	3.2
1890	21.0	.9	4.1
1910	32.1	1.9	5.6
1930	42.4	3.4	7.4
1950	54.0	7.5	12.2
1960	58.2	11.0	15.9

* Adapted from J. Frederic Dewhurst and Associates, *America's Needs and Resources: A New Survey* (New York: The Twentieth Century Fund, 1955), pp. 40–41. By permission. 1960 data from Department of Labor, Bureau of Labor Statistics, *Employment and Earnings.*

area than it used to be, but the major share of governmental expansion in personnel and budget is attributable to increases in services provided by the government. The state now takes at least some of the responsibility for caring for the aged, the mentally ill, and the unemployed, as well as providing all of the citizenry with postal service, highways, schools, parks, and many other services. It also regulates the currency, the mass media of communication, interstate transportation, the quality of foods and drugs, and numerous other enterprises regarded as needing supervision in the public interest.

The single largest expenditure of government in the United States is for the preservation of external order through the diplomatic and military structures. In addition to financing our own military forces, we spend billions of dollars annually helping support the military forces and economies of other societies. The economic aid which we furnish to other countries accounts for considerably less than half our foreign expenditures, the bulk of which go to military aid. Too, there has been a trend in the past decade to broaden the geographic distribution of our foreign expenditures. One result of our efforts toward the maintenance of external order is that our political structure has a new posture in relation to the political and economic institutions of many other nations in the world.

The Party System Those who want power have two simple but basic aims. The first is to get into office—legislative, administrative, or judicial. The other is to stay in office. In democratic societies these purposes are institutionalized in the multiple-party system. In authoritarian societies either a ruling class or a single party, which soon takes on the features of a stabilized ruling class, retains this power by various devices, such as physical force and propaganda.

Under the democratic system, parties seek election by a plurality of the citizens under certain rules laid down in the law and the mores. As a means of securing the general support or popular "will," political parties become organized in a hierarchal fashion and develop codes, leadership, tactics, and strategy for capturing elections, including membership drives, propaganda, and "getting out the vote."

While parties struggle in the larger

FIGURE 35 · Lifespan of French Premierships since World War II *

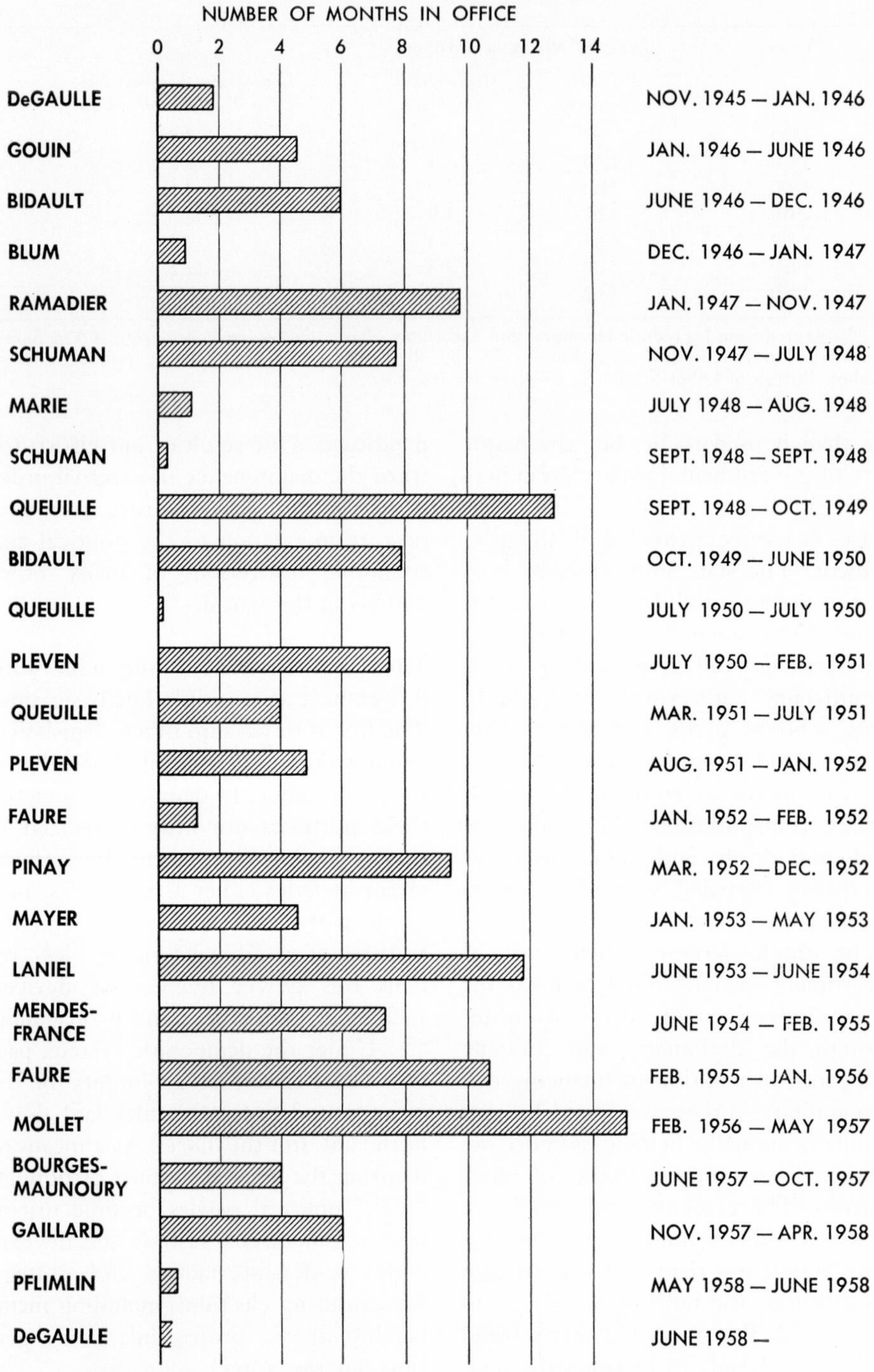

NUMBER OF MONTHS IN OFFICE

DeGAULLE	NOV. 1945 — JAN. 1946
GOUIN	JAN. 1946 — JUNE 1946
BIDAULT	JUNE 1946 — DEC. 1946
BLUM	DEC. 1946 — JAN. 1947
RAMADIER	JAN. 1947 — NOV. 1947
SCHUMAN	NOV. 1947 — JULY 1948
MARIE	JULY 1948 — AUG. 1948
SCHUMAN	SEPT. 1948 — SEPT. 1948
QUEUILLE	SEPT. 1948 — OCT. 1949
BIDAULT	OCT. 1949 — JUNE 1950
QUEUILLE	JULY 1950 — JULY 1950
PLEVEN	JULY 1950 — FEB. 1951
QUEUILLE	MAR. 1951 — JULY 1951
PLEVEN	AUG. 1951 — JAN. 1952
FAURE	JAN. 1952 — FEB. 1952
PINAY	MAR. 1952 — DEC. 1952
MAYER	JAN. 1953 — MAY 1953
LANIEL	JUNE 1953 — JUNE 1954
MENDES-FRANCE	JUNE 1954 — FEB. 1955
FAURE	FEB. 1955 — JAN. 1956
MOLLET	FEB. 1956 — MAY 1957
BOURGES-MAUNOURY	JUNE 1957 — OCT. 1957
GAILLARD	NOV. 1957 — APR. 1958
PFLIMLIN	MAY 1958 — JUNE 1958
DeGAULLE	JUNE 1958 —

* The *New York Times*, February 10, 1957, E6. By permission.

public arena in an effort to best their opponents through elections, there is also frequent competition and factional conflict within the party organization itself, aiming at domination of policy. Inner cliques or "rings" develop, which furnish continuity between one campaign and the next. These political factions are usually more thoroughly organized than the party itself.

It is generally believed that the most successful parliamentary governments have operated through the two-party system. In countries of many political parties, the conflicts for power are often hard to resolve by compromise and other accommodations. This is particularly true in periods of grave crisis, such as prolonged economic depressions or war. Figure 35 shows the executive instability which, in France, was a consequence of a multiplicity of political parties, no one of which was able to attain a majority. De Gaulle's ascendancy was made possible in part by the fact that only one French Premier lasted longer than a year in the troubled decade following World War II.

Under ordinary conditions of stable society, election of a party to manage the government does not mean that the party defeated at the polls has no influence. Rather, it represents an important minority for the period—"His Majesty's loyal opposition," as the British phrase it. It influences public opinion in favor of its countersuggestions to proposed legislation. It acts as a balance to and an alert critic of the party in power. Under democratic political structures, defeated parties, then, do not take up arms to start a revolution, nor does the majority suppress the minority by violence. Both operate under mutually accepted rules of the political code. In time the parties have to face the national community again to see which will be elected for a new term of office. It is typical of our society that the citizenry awards control of the government first to one party, then to the other. Never in our history has one party kept control of the national government for more than twenty consecutive years.

The political institutions of the United States are unlike those of the French and British, as well as most other representative systems, in that they do not guarantee a legislature with a majority from the same party which elects the executive. A president from one party may stay in office even when the other party wins control of the legislative branch or branches.

Politics and Stratification One would expect that, under a system such as ours, parties would tend to come to represent the interests of certain secondary groups and, indeed, the voters apparently feel that they do. Table 39 shows the answers concerning which of the two major parties better serves their own interests.

There is a direct relationship between the status one occupies in the stratification structure and the party which he feels best serves his interests. In general, the higher one's occupational prestige, the more likely he is to favor the Republican Party; the lower his occupational prestige, the more likely he is to believe that his interests are best represented by the Democratic Party.

This set of beliefs is carried into the polling booth. Table 40 indicates that people tend to vote by stratum as well: Republican if upper class, Democratic if lower class.

TABLE 39 · Occupational Status and Definition of Political Interest Group *

OCCUPATION OF HEAD OF FAMILY	POLITICAL PARTY BELIEVED BEST TO SERVE THE INTERESTS OF PEOPLE IN THAT OCCUPATION		
	Per Cent Choosing Republican	Per Cent Choosing Democrat	No Difference or No Opinion
Business and Professional	62	21	17
White-Collar Workers	51	32	17
Farmers	23	57	20
Skilled Workers	18	58	24
Unskilled Workers	11	65	24

* From the *Chicago Sun-Times*, February 28, 1955, p. 21.

TABLE 40 · Occupational Status and Voting Behavior, 1952 *

OCCUPATION OF HEAD OF FAMILY	PER CENT VOTING:			
	Republican	Democrat	Other†	Not Voting
Professional or Managerial	59	27	2	12
Other White Collar	52	28	1	19
Farm Operators	42	24	1	33
Skilled and Semi-skilled Workers	34	39	1	26
Unskilled Workers	19	40	1	40

† Includes third party votes and respondents whose vote is unknown.
* Adapted from A. Campbell, G. Gurin, and W. E. Miller, *The Voter Decides* (Evanston, Ill.: Row, Peterson, 1954), p. 72. By permission.

It is possible that there is a trend away from voting by stratum. Figures from recent elections indicate that income, occupation, religion, and education are less directly related to voting behavior than they have been in the past. But the phenomenon has by no means disappeared: in the 1956 election, only 23 percent of the people with incomes of more than $10,000 a year voted Democratic, while 77 percent in this income bracket voted Republican.

POLITICAL INSTITUTIONS

The relation of the national community or public to the party system and government—at least under a democracy as we know it—is characterized by a number of important theories and practices. The core of these is stated in what we call the "Bill of Rights," including such items as the rights of free speech, free assembly, petition, trial by jury, the writ of habeas corpus, and a number of others.

Mores and Law The mere fact that the Bill of Rights is the law of the United States does not mean, of course, that its provisions are known and accepted by all citizens. As a matter of fact, research indicates that even most college students are not familiar with its provisions. Furthermore, when students were given an opinion questionnaire about the provisions of the first ten amendments to the Constitution without being told the source of the questionnaire items, most of them indicated disagreement with some of the provisions, and a majority disagreed with several of the amendments. (See Table 41.) Despite

TABLE 41 · Extent of Agreement with the Bill of Rights Among 560 University Students *

AMENDMENT	PROVISION	PER CENT INDICATING		
		Agree	Disagree	No opinion
I	Freedom of speech, press	82.5	14.3	3.2
I	Freedom of religion	77.1	13.6	9.3
I	Peaceable assembly	56.8	35.7	7.5
II, III	Bear arms, quartering of troops	63.6	20.3	16.1
IV	Search and seizure	81.8	14.6	3.6
V	Self-incrimination	56.1	33.2	10.7
V	Due process	70.0	25.7	4.3
V	Double jeopardy	23.6	71.8	4.6
VI	Public trial	54.3	34.3	11.4
VI	Confront accuser	23.9	67.5	8.6
VI	Informed of accusation	94.8	2.3	2.9
VI, VII	Trial by jury	89.6	9.3	1.1
VIII	Excessive bail and punishment	61.4	32.2	6.4
IX, X	Reserved rights of people	44.3	51.1	4.6

* Raymond W. Mack, "Do We Really Believe in the Bill of Rights?" *Social Problems*, 1956, 3:267. By permission. This research, originally done at Northwestern University, has since been replicated by J. Harold Ennis at Cornell College, Linton C. Freeman and Sherwin J. Feinhandler at Syracuse University, Robert McGinnis at the University of Wisconsin, and Paul Lasakow at the University of Alabama. See also Hanan C. Selvin and Warren O. Hagstrom, "Determinants of Support for Civil Liberties," *British Journal of Sociology*, 1960, 11:51–73.

this demonstrated lack of information about the Constitution, when these people were asked whether or not they agreed with all of the provisions in the Bill of Rights, an overwhelming majority said yes.

What is the sociological significance of widespread ignorance of a statute basic to the governing of our society? The traditional position of sociologists has been that the mores and community opinion precede law; and the classic illustration has been the Eighteenth Amendment—"You can't legislate morality." Many in the present generation of sociologists have moved to the position that, while morality cannot be legislated in a democracy through the enforcement of law to which the majority stands opposed, legislation *can* guide the development of community opinion on matters regarding which the bulk of the citizenry

have not taken a strong stand one way or the other. An act outlawing reading cannot be enforced and will not be obeyed, because most people believe that they have a right to read. On the other hand, a law forbidding the manufacture, sale, or use of sulphur matches could probably be enforced simply because of the indifference of public feeling in the matter of sulphur matches. In other words, most people tend to obey the law if it does not run counter to some strongly held value. The majesty of the law can be employed to create and strengthen community mores and is, for that reason, of sociological significance.

The Spread of Self-Government The diffusion of Western European patterns of culture around the world has had political consequences. The colonial patterns of the eighteenth and nineteenth centuries brought more than technology to Africa, Asia, and Latin America; they also brought ideas.

Intentionally or unintentionally, the colonial administrators, the missionaries, the traders, and the settlers taught the natives of these continents many of the values of European cultures. We know enough about the integration of institutions not to expect Asians or Africans to learn our economic institutions, adopt Western notions of education, and so on, without changing their political norms. The colonial powers may have done a better job than they intended of convincing their subjects that Western culture is superior to that of the natives; throughout Asia and Africa today there is a remarkable enthusiasm for adopting not only our technology but our political institutions as well.

Africa especially has been a continent of extreme change. Since as recently as 1950, when there were only four independent states in Africa, it has developed into a complex of independent countries and countries moving toward self-rule. Change has been effected through referendums, war, U. N. intervention, and realignment.

The Separation of Society and Government The norms of representative democracy prescribe that the state shall not be identical or coterminous with the society in which it is embedded. Under this theory, in the words of the usual Fourth of July oration, "The state is the servant, not the master, of the people." The theory means, in brief, that ultimate power in a democratic society rests with the citizens, not with the state.[2] When we call a democracy "representative," we mean just that. Individuals "represent" the members of the national society and, in the last analysis, are responsible to them. The party system is but a convenient device to implement this basic relationship.

The theory of representative government is not, of course, uniformly and universally accepted. But that is not to say that dictatorships neglect the matter of support from the wider national society. Certainly modern dictators attempt to win popular support and conformity by education and propaganda, as well as by coercion. Stable society and governmental order rest on human acceptance and expectations; and skillful masters of men realize that to get this in revolutionary times, changes in attitudes, values, and habits in the masses must occur. Although concentration camps, machine guns, and the secret police are effective as controls, nothing but minimum participation in government can be expected unless people learn the political norms and accept them as part of the society's institutional structure.

2 · See Kimball Young, "Society and the State: Some Neglected Areas of Research and Theory," *American Sociological Review*, 1946, 11:137–146.

INTERPRETATIVE SUMMARY

Most societies have some structure which is responsible for maintaining internal order. Historically, the same structure or groups of structures has been responsible for protecting the society from outside attack; and this function will undoubtedly be necessary as long as people remain nationalistic and mistrustful of cultural differences, and as long as the needs of certain societies outstrip their resources.

In modern times, the political order is typically centered in the sovereign state. There are two main types of states: the authoritarian state, in which a dominant minority imposes its will on the people; and the democratic state, in which elected officials serve the people. Both types of government have gradually become more complex and even bureaucratic in administration: orders filter down through a chain of command, decisions tend to be inflexible and conversative, and administrators, especially at the middle and lower levels, tend to be individuals who are interested in keeping their jobs.

While authoritarian governments tend to centralize all functions in the hands of a small group, modern democracies have generally divided the three main internal functions of government—the creation of law, administration of law, and judging of disputes involving law—among three structures, though functions of the three structures may overlap somewhat. The legislative branch codifies existing mores into law and, less frequently, may initiate legislation for the purpose of changing mores. It usually acts under some sort of constitution. The executive branch consists of an elected chief executive, various advisers, the extent of whose influence varies among countries, and various administrative sub-heads. It is this branch of democratic governments that is generally criticized for being bureaucratic. Judicial systems show variations in number of authority levels, as well as in provisions concerning who shall be judges.

Democratic officials are elected by plurality, after first being nominated by parties. The two-party system, in which the minority retains considerable influence, has generally been the most stable form of parliamentary government.

The United States has a three branch government with some overlap of functions among the branches. The system contains some checks against bureaucracy and "spoils" appointments. One unique feature of the system is that the election of a chief executive from one of the two major parties does not guarantee a majority of that party in the legislature. Another pattern involves the extension of government control to new areas, especially the areas of economics and welfare. A final feature is the American emphasis on defense spending. Defense is the United States' biggest single expenditure, enormous sums going for economic and military aid to allies as well.

A world trend toward self-government is now in progress; note especially the patterns in former colonies of the huge European empires. Even in authoritarian countries, dictators who would remain in power generally cannot rely on coercion, but must give some attention to indoctrinating people into at least *thinking* they are getting what they want.

REVIEW AND SUGGESTED READINGS

A • VOCABULARY

| Bill of Rights | Executive structure | Legislative structure |
| Bureaucracy | Judicial structure | |

B • QUESTIONS AND TOPICS FOR REVIEW

1. We have noted that there may be a trend in the United States away from voting in accordance with one's occupational affiliation. What criteria might override an individual's class-consciousness in a given election?
2. Is bureaucracy inevitable in modern society? Discuss.

3. What are some frequent complaints about the Civil Service?
4. Describe an instance in which you were frustrated by the inflexibility of a bureaucracy.
5. Using recent issues, show how the functions of the three governmental branches overlap.
6. Do you predict a counter-trend in the near future away from increased government control? Give reasons for your answer.
7. Discuss some specific points about the Civil Rights Bill of 1964 which were raised by supporters of the bill who apparently thought that morality *can* be legislated in some instances.

C • SUGGESTIONS FOR FURTHER READING

Gabriel A. Almond and James S. Coleman, eds. *The Politics of the Developing Areas.* Princeton: Princeton University Press, 1960.

A five-year progress report by the Social Science Research Council Committee on Comparative Politics, attempting a systematic framework within which empirical studies may be made.

Reinhard Bendix. *Nation Building and Citizenship: Studies in a Changing Social Order.* New York: John Wiley & Sons, Inc., 1964.

An examination of the emerging non-Western nations against the backdrop of Western experience.

Peter Blau. *Exchange and Power in Social Life.* New York: John Wiley & Sons, Inc., 1964.

A fascinating attempt to blend interactionist social psychology with the sociology of political and economic organization.

Theodore Caplow. *Principles of Organization.* New York: Harcourt, Brace & World, 1964.

Uses an analytical model to develop the thesis that human organizations comprise a single natural class, and to examine their nature and effectiveness.

Robert Dubin, ed. *Human Relations in Administration. The Sociology of Organization.* Englewood Cliffs, N.J.: Prentice-Hall, Inc., 1951.

A well-selected and wide range of materials bearing on various aspects of organizational behavior.

Heinz Eulau, Samuel J. Eldersveld, and Morris Janowitz, eds. *Political Behavior: A Reader in Theory and Research.* Glencoe, Ill.: The Free Press, 1956.

A collection of papers and sections of books which covers a wide range of topics bearing on political structure and function.

Scott Greer. *Governing the Metropolis.* New York: John Wiley & Sons, Inc., 1962.

An inquiry into the functions of metropolitan social structure for political systems.

Scott Greer. *Metropolitics: A Study of Political Culture.* New York: John Wiley & Sons, Inc., 1963.

An empirical description and comparison of metropolitan political reform campaigns in St. Louis, Miami, and Cleveland.

Arthur Kornhauser, Harold L. Sheppard, and Albert J. Mayer. *When Labor Votes: A Study of Auto Workers.* New York: University Books, Inc., 1956.

A study of the voting behavior of union members and of the factors which affect their vote; a discussion of the union's role in politics as seen by union members.

Robert K. Merton, Ailsa P. Gray, Barbara Hockey, and Hanan C. Selvin, eds. *Reader in Bureaucracy.* Glencoe, Ill.: The Free Press, 1952.

A selection of writings on the theory, growth, power relations, and structure of bureaucracy.

David B. Truman. *The Governmental Process. Political Interests and Public Opinion.* New York: Alfred A. Knopf, Inc., 1951.

An incisive analysis which deals with groups and group organization in the political process, with leadership, and with the tactics of influence with regard to political parties and to the legislative, administrative, and judicial operations of government.

Roland Young, ed. *Approaches to the Study of Politics.* Evanston, Ill.: Northwestern University Press, 1958.

Twenty-two essays exploring the nature of politics and methods by which it can be studied. There are several contributions by sociologists, including Gordon W. Blackwell, Scott Greer, Harold Guetzkow, Floyd Hunter, Marion J. Levy, Jr., Talcott Parsons, and Peter H. Rossi.

SUMMARY OF PART III

We have dealt in this section with the analysis of social institutions, or sets of norms for the major societal functions. Chapter 19, "The Structure and Functions of Social Institutions," provided a general discussion of institutional forms and their consequences, both manifest and latent. It also offered two illustrative cases of institutional development and change: courtship patterns in America, and the role of the family in the Chinese social structure.

Separate chapters were devoted to the analysis of each of the major social institutions. These chapters followed the order in which the universal social structures and functions were presented in Chapter 7: familial, educational, religious, economic, and political. Each chapter opened with an explanation of the various structures which perform the necessary functions. This was followed by a section on the functions, both manifest and latent, which are the consequences of these structures. Next we examined the patterns of behavior associated with the particular institution in the United States. Each chapter in Part III closed with a general section on the set of norms built around the basic functions and the processes effecting change in that institution. Particular attention was paid to intra-society conflicts concerning norms.

In Part IV, we shall turn to an examination of deviant behavior and social change.

SOCIAL DYNAMICS

CHAPTER 25

Deviant Behavior

We live in a world of order, which means that norms or standards of conduct are set up to guide and control us. As we have seen, norms are group-shared expectations. Yet the fact that a social group expects certain behaviors from an individual or from another group does not always mean that its expectations are met. No norm is *always* obeyed; individuals do not *always* conform to every set of expectations. In this chapter we shall examine the nature of deviance from social norms.

There are several reasons why the behavior of a large number of people never conforms perfectly to the norms of the society in which they live. For one thing, norms are general, while an individual's behavior in any situation is specific. An expectation, if it is to apply to different people in varying situations over a period of time, must be conceived in quite general dimensions. It is therefore always possible for situations to arise in which the norm is not applicable. Each of us learns the rules of his society as a set of broad (and usually flat) generalizations: " You should eat meat with a fork, not with your fingers," or "Honor thy father and thy mother." But there are situations in which deviation from the norms is tolerated. One can eat meat with his fingers at a picnic, and no one would expect a starving man to eschew food because he did not have a fork. Indeed,

there are situations where violation of the norm becomes itself an expectation: in many societies, the son whose father commits treason is expected to reject, not honor, his father.

The generalized nature of norms is only one factor which can help us explain deviation. Another is variation among individuals and groups in their perception of what the norms are and their interpretation of what they mean. It is possible, for reasons ranging from mental incompetence to geographic (and hence social) isolation, for a person to be unaware of some of the norms of his society. In American society, for example, an illiterate is cut off from an important source of information about what is expected of a citizen. Many Americans are aware of the norm "Keep the sabbath day to sanctify it, as the Lord thy God hath commanded thee," but there is widespread variation in the interpretation of this rule.

Then too, norms differ in the degree to which they are considered obligatory. Considerably weaker sanctions are imposed on a person who deviates from a folkway, such as a clothing fashion, than on one who violates one of the mores. As one moves down a scale of tolerance toward the point where a custom passes from a folkway to a cultural alternative, deviance becomes more and more likely.

Finally, one cannot understand the

amount of deviance in a mass society without noting the extent to which it is the product of differing subcultures. As we have seen in Chapters 11, 13, 16, and 18, normative standards vary by social class, by ethnic group, by degree of urbanization, and by region. A group-shared expectation in a company store patronized by sharecroppers in rural Arkansas may be a violation of the norms in a Park Avenue gift shop catering to wealthy New Yorkers. Taking a hubcap from an automobile in a lower-class slum area is stealing; taking a piece of the goal posts (much more expensive than hubcaps) after a football victory at a college stadium is only a high-spirited prank. In this case, class position determines what is or is not criminal. In a multi-group society such as that of contemporary United States, with its host of racial, ethnic, class, occupational, and regional subcultures, deviance is more than a little in the eye of the beholder.

From the sociologist's point of view, it is useful to analyze deviant behavior as a function of the social structure. Rather than assuming that rural areas have a different proportion of innately deviant personalities than urban centers, or that lower-class people are more pathologically inclined than middle-class, the sociologist asks what it is about the social structure that produced different consequences in, say, rates of deviance for laborers and professionals. In one sense, of course, this places behavior that is a consequence of mental subnormality outside the province of the sociologist. However, a moron or imbecile is deviant precisely because he is unable to conform to socially defined standards. In a society which honored the capacity to remove oneself from the reality known to others and to experience supernatural visions, the person we call a schizophrenic might be highly esteemed as a mystic.

Let us deal first with mental subnormality and mental disorders, both organic and functional. We shall then move from these somewhat bio-social cases of deviance to more strictly social violations of norms: suicide, drug addiction, alcoholism, and crime.

MENTAL SUBNORMALITY

At the opening of the present century the school authorities in Paris, France, concerned with the problem of retarded pupils in their public schools, asked a psychologist, Alfred Binet, and a medical specialist, Thomas Simon, to look into the matter. These men devised a test to measure individual differences in ". . . memory . . . , power to reason, ability to compare, power of comprehension, time orientation, facility in the use of number concepts, power to combine ideas into a meaningful whole, the maturity of apperception, wealth of ideas, and knowledge of common objects, etc." [1] The test consisted of 54 questions or problems "arranged in the order of difficulty" and designed to measure intelligence from age three to an assumed adult level. Binet and Simon developed certain criteria of normal intelligence for each year of age.

The test, first published in 1911, was translated, revised, and expanded by Lewis M. Terman, an American psychologist, and became widely known as the Stanford-Binet test. Terman also devised a convenient index of mental

1 · Lewis M. Terman, *The Measurement of Intelligence* (Boston: Houghton Mifflin Co., 1916, p. 36). For many years this book was the accepted explanation of the Stanford Revision of the Binet-Simon intelligence scale.

maturity known as the Intelligence Quotient. It was derived by dividing the mental age by the chronological age:

$$\frac{MA}{CA} = IQ$$

In 1917 Arthur S. Otis, who had been a student of Terman's at Stanford University, developed an intelligence scale which could be given to groups. The content was drawn from individual tests, but Otis invented a system of alternative answers—probably suggested by then-current educational tests—which made possible the use of true-false and multiple-choice questions. During World War I a group of psychologists used Otis' scheme in constructing the Alpha and Beta group tests, which were given to thousands of troops as an aid in job classification. Today many types of intelligence tests are used in education, industry, the military, and correctional and penal institutions.

In the earlier decades of mental testing there was considerable controversy as to the relative importance of heredity and environment in determining the IQ. Most scholars today recognize that, while IQ tests are a good indicator of individual differences in innate ability to learn, one's performance on such a test is influenced to some extent by his environment, by what he has already learned.

Mental tests have been used widely in determining degrees of subnormality in intelligence, especially in school populations. After all, it was the problem of school retardation which led, in part, to the development of these tests.

The population can be divided according to level of intelligence into categories called feeble-minded, normal,

and superior. The feeble-minded, in turn, are usually subdivided into three levels: idiot, imbecile, and moron. The *idiot* has only the most rudimentary capacity to learn; he remains throughout life unsocialized and incapable of caring for himself. A large number of those in this category need institutional supervision. The *imbecile* may acquire simple motor skills, modest facility in speech, and certain elementary social habits. But he is not able to manage his own affairs, take responsibility, or participate in normal society. On the other hand, the *moron* is capable of a good deal of motor learning and of mental training through the elementary grades. Moreover, he may be sufficiently socialized to enable him to take a minor and unobtrusive place in the social order. Thousands of people in this category are law-abiding and useful members of society.

The *normal* person, as measured by adequate tests, will attain a mental age somewhere between fourteen and sixteen. He will be able to complete high school, but most people at this level will have difficulty getting through college. To get a bachelor's degree, most students must have mental ability beyond that of the average normal person. The *superior* are those with IQ's of 120 or more, as measured by standard tests.

It should be borne in mind, however, that social adjustment depends on social-emotional qualities or traits as well as on degree of intelligence. Some individuals of normal or even superior intelligence have difficulty adapting themselves to the values and norms of their society because they are emotionally unstable. Many neurotics are in this category. Such people deviate from the norms not because of intellectual subnormality but because of mental disturbance.

MENTAL AND EMOTIONAL DISORDERS

As he matures, the individual is provided with a host of patterns or "copies" of thought and action that are defined for him as proper and good by parents, playmates, teachers, employers, and others. Even mood, temperament, or disposition—whatever term one uses to describe fundamental and persistent patterns of feeling-emotional responses —must be considered, like other behavior, in the light of societal or cultural conditioning. Temperamental qualities fully accepted in one society may be considered pathological in another.

Norms are always relative, so far as the individual is concerned, first to those of the larger community, and second to those of subgroups to which he owes allegiance or with which he has a feeling of solidarity. The "normal" act or thought rests on general consensus in some particular group. This does not mean absolute conformity. All societies take cognizance of individual variations. Moreover, deviations in thought and words are often permitted so long as overt conduct conforms fairly well to the accepted and proper patterns. Usually it is only when the number of divergent features in behavior is believed excessive or when some unaccepted activity is so intense or violent as to be considered detrimental to others that it is dealt with as abnormal.

Nature of Neuroses Let us look at those forms of divergent thought and conduct which are defined in American society as neurotic or psychotic.

A *psychoneurosis,* or *neurosis,* is a form of mental and behavioral divergence from the normal which tends to make the individual less efficient socially and personally but which does not completely incapacitate him for social participation in everyday group life. Neurotic persons may express undue worries, obsessive fears, or extreme fatigue, or show hysteric responses which keep them from effective, emotionally and intellectually satisfying lives. With neurotics there is usually no need for special hospital care; many of them, however, seek help from clinical psychologists or psychiatrists. They represent a borderline type of behavior and mentality between the normal and the psychotic.

There are various subcategories of neuroses. The three most common types are anxiety neurosis, obsessional-compulsive neurosis, and hysteria. The first may be characterized by a sense of fatigue, by fears, irritability, imaginary ailments, pessimism, and hypochondria. The second shows such symptoms as obsessive thoughts, suicidal and other compulsions, manias such as pyromania, or the impulse to set fires, and extreme fears such as claustrophobia, or fear of closed places. The third includes forms of dissociation of thought and action, of which the dual or multiple personality is the classic model.

Psychosomatic Disorders In addition to the long-accepted classification of neuroses, there are a number of visceral and other bodily maladjustments of psychological rather than organic origin. These are known as psychosomatic disorders.

The close interplay between fear, anger, and other emotions and certain bodily disturbances has long been recognized. But it is only in recent decades that specific psychogenic factors, such as frustration, anxiety, hostility, and dependency, have been positively correlated with various visceral and other bodily disorders. Obviously, not all visceral and other bodily ailments are psychosomatically induced, but it is becoming increasingly clear that a great many such disorders have a distinctly psychological foundation.

Let us look at one illustration of the impact of the emotions on the body. Miller and Baruch compared the hostility feelings of a group of allergic children with those of a nonallergic group. The latter children showed much more direct and indirect hostility to others and to themselves, and less "blocking" or restraint of overt hostility than did the allergic children.[2]

From data collected in Great Britain, J. L. Halliday has reported some interesting facts about age, sex, and class differentials and changes in the incidence of certain psychosomatic disorders. For example, during the latter part of the nineteenth century peptic ulcers and essential hypertension were predominantly female disorders. At the midpoint of the twentieth century these had become increasingly more evident in males. It is interesting also to note that exophthalmic goiter and hysteria, both of which have emotional components, have shifted to higher incidence among men. Moreover, the age incidence of gastritis, peptic ulcers, cardiovascular disorders, and anxiety states has dropped. Halliday has further shown that gastrointestinal disorders, essential hypertension, exophthalmic goiter, and rheumatism occur more frequently in urban than in rural areas. The rate of deaths from peptic ulcers is higher for both sexes in the lower occupational groups than in the professional and well-to-do classes. In hypertensive cardiovascular disorders, the death rate for males is highest in well-to-do classes but is highest for females in the poorest classes.[3]

Halliday believes that these changes indicate a neutralization of former and culturally determined sex differences, but more particularly that they typify an increased complexity in modern urban living.

The Nature of Psychoses A *psychosis* is a more severe mental and behavioral disorder, involving such divergence from normal conduct as to require medical and even institutional care, and often marked by disorders of mind and conduct which involve the entire make-up of the personality.[4] The psychotic frequently loses his orientation to the world around him. His acts become dangerous to others or are so divergent as to demand severe control by his fellows. He frequently lacks insight into his conduct. In short, the psychotic individual becomes so unlike those around him that he loses practically all the so-

2 · Hyman Miller and Dorothy W. Baruch, "A Study of Hostility in Allergic Children," *American Journal of Orthopsychiatry*, 1950, 20:506–519.

3 · J. L. Halliday, *Psychosomatic Medicine: A Study of a Sick Society* (New York, W. W. Norton & Company, Inc., 1948).

4 · For attempts to get at correlates and causes of mental breakdowns, see H. Warren Dunham, "Social Structure and Mental Disorder: Competing Hypotheses of Explanation," *Milbank Memorial Fund Quarterly*, 1961, 39:259–311; Dorothy S. Thomas and Ben Z. Locke, "Marital Status, Education, and Occupational Differentials in Mental Disease: State Patterns in First Admissions to Mental Hospitals for All Disorders and for Schizophrenia, New York and Ohio as of 1950," *Milbank Memorial Fund Quarterly*, 1963, 41: 145–160; and Alexander H. Leighton and Jane M. Hughes, "Culture as a Causative of Mental Disorder," *Milbank Memorial Fund Quarterly*, 1961, 39:446–488.

cially accepted forms of interaction. The word *insane* is applied properly to those psychotics who are considered by legal definition to need institutional care. There are many psychotics, of course, who never reach the courts and who are not sent to public or private establishments for treatment.

The psychoses are traditionally divided into two large categories: the functional and the organic. Functional psychoses are those for which no obvious and easily detectable constitutional condition can be found responsible. The inception and development of this type of psychosis are considered to be largely psychological—that is, related to some inability to meet the adaptive demands of the social environment. Organic psychoses, in contrast, are those which have a detectable neurological lesion or some other physical condition as the foundation.

The Functional Psychoses The functional psychoses have been traditionally divided into schizophrenia, paranoia, and manic-depressive disorders. The first is characterized by extreme dissociation of components of the personality. (The word *schizophrenia* comes from the Greek and means a split mind.) The most distinctive feature of this disorder is gradual and insidious development of inattention and emotional indifference to the world outside the individual and growing incoherence of ideas, ending in deterioration of normal mental life. Fantasy often blossoms into most bizarre forms. Hallucinations of sight and hearing are common; delusions often appear.

The second type, *paranoia*, is marked by conceit, extreme suspiciousness, feelings of persecution, egocentricity, and projection of false ideas and intentions on other persons. The delusional system may become very elaborate, and persons and events in the paranoiac's world become misconstrued, twisted, changed, and falsified to fit into his delusions.

The third type of functional psychosis is sometimes called the cyclic or *manic-depressive*. Unlike schizophrenia and paranoia, there is no fundamental change in the personality but rather an exaggeration of tendencies already at hand. Sense of selfhood is retained, but there is marked extension of mood and emotion. There are two phases, the manic and the depressed. The former is characterized by distractibility of ideas, flightiness, and a great pressure to be doing things. In this stage the patient seems to have boundless energy; at times there are delusions of grandeur and momentarily great rage. In contrast, the depressive phase is marked by inattention or conflict of attention and a gloomy and anxious outlook on life. The patient may attempt suicide to escape his anxiety and sense of guilt. Melancholy may be so extreme as to be marked by delusions that are sometimes paranoid in character.

The Organic Psychoses Those mental disorders in which there is some detectable brain or other neurological defect or in which there is some toxic or other physiological basis are called organic psychoses. We shall take note of the four most common: paresis, epilepsy, toxic psychoses, and senile dementia.

Paresis is the result of brain tissue injury caused by syphilitic infection. It is marked by gradual deterioration: loss of sound judgment, loss of insight, and development of delusions. The paretic may make foolhardy business deals, show no regard for the canons of conventional morality, and even commit serious offenses against persons and property quite out of keeping with his previous behavior. In the later stages of paresis there may be definite clouding of consciousness and a dreamlike disorientation to time and place.

Reports indicate that only 4 or 5 percent of those known to be infected with syphilis become paretic. Moreover, it is said that one-fifth of those diagnosed as paretic show no sign of syphilitic infection. The immediate background of this mental breakdown may be any one or a combination of the following: emotional stress, overwork, alcoholism, sexual excess, and other highly deviant behavior manifestations. Here, as in other organic disorders, we must reckon with both constitutional and social-psychological factors.

Under the term *epilepsy* are grouped a number of somewhat diverse sets of symptoms. There are periodic seizures of two kinds: *grand mal*, marked by sudden and violent tonic contractions of the muscles, falling down as a result, loss of consciousness, foaming at the mouth, and changes in respiration. After a minute or two of the attack there is relaxation, and the individual often falls into a deep sleep. The second type of attack is the *petit mal*, which is a mild attack, characterized by giddiness, momentary loss of consciousness, and mild muscular disturbance.

The *toxic psychoses* cover a wide range of mental disturbances derived from fever, nutritional deficiencies, lead poisoning, carbon-monoxide poisoning, and overdosage of alcohol. The symptoms differ with the particular cause. For example, those arising from fever often show severe delirium, with which are associated nightmares, rest-

lessness, and excitement. The symptoms of alcoholism are discussed in another section.

Senile dementia is by definition the psychosis of old age. It may be marked by loss of memory, of ability to concentrate, and by egocentricity, insomnia, often hostility, and occasionally some paranoidal reactions.

Let us now turn to examine a type of deviant behavior which is linked directly to the degree of participation in the social structure.

SUICIDE

The frequency and meaning of suicide vary from society to society. The rate of suicides in the United States has generally declined since the turn of the century, but with some fluctuations. For example, in 1900 it was 11.5 per 100,000 population; it rose to 17.8 in 1908, dropped to little more than 10 during and after World War I, but rose to 17.4 in 1932. Since 1940 it has remained at about 10 or 11 per 100,000 (1950: 11.4; 1961: 10.4).

Suicide, at least in our Western world, is popularly thought to reflect the stress of urban living. Certainly for decades the urban rate was higher than the rural, though in recent times there is some evidence of a reversal.[5]

Some Differentials in Rates Suicide rates differ considerably according to such sociological variables as age, sex, race, marital status, social class, and religion.

Older people have a higher inci-

5 · See W. Widich Schroeder and J. Allan Beegle, "Suicide: An Instance of High Rural Rates," in *Mental Health and Mental Disorder*, Arnold M. Rose, ed. (New York: W. W. Norton Company, Inc., 1955), pp. 408–419.

dence of suicide than younger. Although people over 45 years make up only one-fifth of the population, 60 percent of the suicides come from this group. For those 65 years or more the rate is three times as high as for those under 45. Taking one's life in later years may well be the result of weariness, ill-health, and disillusionment. When an adolescent or a lovesick young man destroys himself, it often gets great public attention, but actually the rate for young people is very low.

In our Western society suicide is much more frequent among men than among women: the ratio in the United States is approximately four to one. In older age groups the ratio of male to female incidence is even greater. It is interesting to note, however, that the rate of attempted suicide is higher for women than for men.

In the United States the rate for whites is about three times that for nonwhites. This difference is somewhat complicated by the fact that a high proportion of our Negro population lives in the rural South, and rurality is probably a hidden variable.[6] With further increase in the number of Negroes in urban centers and with mobility pressures for status, we may witness an increase in the suicide rates for nonwhites.

Among people 20 years of age and over, the rate for married persons is much lower than that for either the single, widowed, or divorced. Further evidence of the protective function of the family is shown by the fact that the suicide rate among childless couples is higher than among those who have children.

The rates of suicide also vary with religious affiliation, at least in the Western world. In both Europe and America the rate for Roman Catholics is much lower than for Protestants. This may reflect the higher degree of group integration among Catholics. But for both groups the rates have tended to increase somewhat in recent decades.

Social-cultural Setting The classic study of suicide was made by Émile Durkheim, the French sociologist.[7] Durkheim classified suicide into three types: anomic, egoistic, and altruistic. The first occurs among individuals who are not closely integrated into group life, who experience a sense of what Durkheim, as we have seen, called *anomie*—that is, a feeling of living in a world where the norms and values have broken down, a world lacking the cohesiveness and solidarity associated with an integrated society. The second type occurs among individuals who are not bound or integrated into a group. This is what Ruth Cavan calls "secret, personal suicide."[8] In sharp contrast, the altruistic suicide is a high expression of group membership, solidarity, and identification with the expected norms and values. This was amply illustrated in Ancient Rome, where it was regarded as honorable for a defeated general to fall upon his sword; in medieval Japan, where hara-kiri was both approved and expected; and in India where, until fairly recently, a widow

6 · See Jack P. Gibbs, "Suicide," in Robert K. Merton and Robert A. Nisbet, eds., *Contemporary Social Problems* (New York: Harcourt, Brace & Co., 1961), p. 244.

7 · Émile Durkheim, *Suicide*. trans. John A. Spaulding and George Simpson (Glencoe, Ill.: The Free Press, 1951. Original French edition, 1897).

8 · See Ruth Cavan, *Suicide* (Chicago: University of Chicago Press, 1928), pp. 3ff.

was supposed to throw herself on her husband's funeral pyre (the suttee).

For years there was a difference of opinion about the occurrence of suicide among primitive peoples. Some anthropologists contended there was little suicide; others believed it to be very common and widespread. Today most anthropologists agree with Paul Bohannan that "primitive societies vary as widely in matters of suicide as do record-keeping societies." [9]

The Jews, Moslems, and Christians have long been conditioned to regard suicide as a sin, as a form of murder. The sacredness of human life and the doctrine that only God can give life or take it away are strongly held beliefs in these religions. When some of the teachings of the Catholic church were legalized in Europe, suicide became a crime as well as a sin. The first civil laws against suicide in England, which date from the eleventh century, provided that the offender's property be confiscated and the body denied a Christian burial.

The variation in cultural patterns, values, and norms of different countries is reflected in their suicide rates. Suicide is high in Denmark, Austria, Switzerland, Japan, and West Germany. It is very low in Eire, Northern Ireland, Scotland, Spain, Italy, the Netherlands, and Norway. The United States, England and Wales, The Union of South Africa (whites only), France, and Finland fall in the middle range.

Some writers believe that most suicide among nonliterate peoples is altruistic. This they conclude from noting practices in tribes where it is expected that the old and infirm will take their own lives. In other tribes wives kill themselves on the death of their husbands. In warring tribes the fighters may commit suicide to avoid capture or as a face-saving device. Then too, suicide may take place as expiation for the violation of some taboo or other prohibition in the mores. [10]

Psychological Factors As a behavior manifestation, suicide has much in common with homicide. The Freudian interpretation links suicide to the "death instinct," or man's innate tendency to self-destruction. Karl Menninger says that psychologically the act reveals three elements: a desire to kill, a desire to be killed, and a desire to die. [11]

Other psychological approaches have related suicide and homicide to the frustration-aggression hypothesis. A sense of blockage, stress, and tension arising from the frustration of some motive, drive, or wish may lead to an outlet through aggression. The most severe forms of this are obviously homicide and suicide.

Certainly there are many specific psychological as well as circumstantial factors that play a part in motivating an individual to take his own life. Among others, ill-health, deep-seated anxieties, humiliation, feelings of inferiority, unrequited love, hostility, and guilt may contribute to the decision. Yet, as Bohannan remarked, ordinarily suicide is "not an act which occurs on the spur of the moment, but rather one

9 · Paul J. Bohannan, ed., *African Homicide and Suicide* (Princeton: Princeton University Press, 1960), p. 23. The editor's review of the theories of homicide and suicide provides an excellent foundation for the specific discussion of these two closely related behaviors in seven African tribes.

10 · For a convenient summary of the relation of suicide to type of society, see Marshall B. Clinard, *Sociology of Deviant Behavior*, rev. ed. (New York: Rinehart & Company, Inc., 1963), pp. 408–412.

11 · Karl Menninger, *Man Against Himself* (New York: Harcourt, Brace & Company, 1938), p. 71.

which has a long explanatory history." [12]

Efforts to understand motivation meet with obstacles. For one thing, it is difficult to get valid first-hand information: suicide notes are not much help. For another, survivors' explanations may be inaccurate and therefore useless. However, the cause assigned by the survivors may be a useful clue to what is considered worth living or dying for.[13] That is, it provides us insight into the values and norms of a given group or society.

DRUG ADDICTION

The federal statutes define a drug addict as any person who "habitually uses any habit-forming narcotic drug as defined . . . so as to endanger the public morals, health, safety, or welfare, or who is or has been so far addicted to the use of such habit-forming drugs as to have lost the power of self-control with reference to his addiction." [14] The chief drugs used are morphine and heroin, derived from opium, and cocaine, which comes from the coca plant. From the physiological and psychological standpoint, these drugs fall into two categories: depressants and stimulants. The former decrease mental and physical activity; the latter facilitate and excite responses and reduce symptoms of fatigue. The chief depressants are morphine and heroin; the best-known stimulant is cocaine.

Judging by medical information found on Assyrian tablets, opium was widely used for therapeutic purposes as early as 4000 B.C. Its use spread throughout the Near East and later

into the Classical World (Greece and Rome). During the Middle Ages, Arab physicans made extensive use of opium, and Arab traders of the time of Mohammed carried it to India. By the seventh century it had reached China. (This is a nice illustration of cultural diffusion, a topic we shall discuss in the next chapter.)

In Europe opium was widely used in various disguised forms in medicine and confections from at least the fifteenth century. At the beginning of the nineteenth century, various European chemists succeeded in extracting certain alkaloids from the crude opium. The first was morphine, then narcotine, and finally codeine. In 1898 heroin, which is three times as potent as morphine, was produced. Throughout the nineteenth century in both Europe and America opium was used for almost every known malady. The invention of the hypodermic needle in 1845 facilitated its use in both medicine and addiction.

Nonmedical Use of Opium The personal and social problems associated with the nonmedical use of opium first appeared in those countries which cultivated the poppy: Persia, Turkey, and Arabia. Later the growing of poppies spread to India and China. The first forms of opium were the seeds of the capsule of the poppy. These were eaten or used to make a paste. Later, juice of the capsule was extracted. Smoking opium began with the Dutch in Formosa about 1800. From there it spread to China; later, Chinese laborers carried it with them wherever they migrated as a labor force.

It is not always easy to tell just when a person becomes a drug addict. Certainly the habit grows apace, but

12 · Bohannan, p. 25.
13 · Bohannan, p. 26.
14 · Quoted by Clinard, p. 293.

there are probably both physiological and psychological factors which make for differences in tolerance. There are physicians known to have used opiates for years without its ostensibly affecting their health or practice. Surely this too must be true of many users in the entertainment world. However, stress, tension, inner conflict, and other personality disturbances may facilitate more and more involvement in addiction until the personality disintegrates.[15]

When the individual attempts to give up the habit or does cease its use altogether, there follow what are known as withdrawal symptoms. Their nature and the order of development have been stated as follows: "restlessness and depression, followed by yawning, sneezing, excessive mucous secretion, sweating, nausea, uncontrolled vomiting and purging, twitching and jerking, intense muscular cramps and pain, abdominal distress, marked circulatory and cardiac insufficiency and irregularity, face drawn and haggard, pallor deepening to grayness, exhaustion, collapse and in some cases death."[16]

Morphine and heroin account for about two-thirds of all the drug addiction in the United States. The number of addicts, according to the Federal Bureau of Narcotics, was 46,798 as of January 1, 1962. Public health doctors estimate a much higher incidence. It is said that the number of drug addicts has declined in recent times. However, various governmental agencies and committees report that there is an increasing number of young addicts, many of whom begin with marihuana and pass on to the opiates.

The sex ratio is about that of adult crime, nine men to every woman. The practice of drug addiction is particularly prevalent in large cities. Slightly more than half those treated at the federal hospital at Lexington, Kentucky, ranged between five and twenty years of addiction.[17]

ALCOHOLISM

As noted above, alcoholism is a form of toxic psychosis. Because it has become such a serious worldwide problem, however, it is discussed in this separate section.

Someone has argued that alcoholic beverages probably came into use soon after prehistoric man invented a cup, beaker, bowl, or other vessel. Be that as it may, the antiquity and wide dispersion of the consumption of alcohol, in one form or another, is generally recognized. (The cultural significance of this kind of drinking varies from society to society.) Whether alcoholism in our modern sense is found among primitive peoples is not certain. Certainly many tribes periodically indulged in heavy drinking on various festive occasions.[18]

Among literate societies there is a wide range, as illustrated by the sobriety of the Orthodox European Jews

15 · A telling description of the process of drug addiction is to be found in Alexander King, *Mine Enemy Grows Older* (New York: Simon and Schuster, Inc., 1958).

16 · From E. C. Terry, "Drug Addiction," *Encyclopedia of the Social Sciences,* 1931, 5:246 (New York: The Macmillan Co., 1931). A literary but accurate picture of withdrawal symptoms is found in Nelson Algren, *The Man with the Golden Arm* (New York: Doubleday & Co., Inc., 1949).

17 · Much of the factual material cited in the last two paragraphs is from Clinard, pp. 295–297.

18 · See Donald Horton, "The Functions of Alcohol in Primitive Societies," in *Alcohol, Science, and Society* (New Haven: Quarterly Journal of Studies on Alcohol, 1945).

and the high incidence of drinking among the Irish. Too, shifts in the cultural climate and definition, such as accompany immigration to the United States, may result in changes in drinking patterns.[19]

Our concern here is with the deleterious effects of excessive consumption of alcoholic beverages—in other words, with alcoholism. Alcoholics are excessive drinkers. The World Health Organization of the United Nations defines them as those "whose dependence upon alcohol has attained such a degree that it shows a noticeable mental disturbance, or an interference with their bodily or mental health, their interpersonal relations and their smooth social and economic functioning; or who show . . . signs of such development."[20] The riddle of why some heavy drinkers become alcoholics while others do not has not been solved. There are a number of facts, however, which should be examined.

First, there is some evidence that the incidence of alcoholism has declined in the past century. Certainly there is evidence in this country that the consumption of distilled liquors has decreased, while the drinking of beer and wine has increased. For example, in 1850 the annual per capita consumption of distilled spirits was 2.24 gallons; of malt liquors, 1.58 gallons; and of wines, 0.27 gallons. The corresponding figures for 1962 were 1.23, 15.29, and 0.91.[21]

For the population over 21 years of age, estimates of those who drink range from 57 to 65 percent. And of these the ratio of men to women is 3 to 2. There is more drinking in the younger decades than the older.

As with other forms of addiction, it takes time to become an alcoholic, sometimes as long as 20 years. Clinard states that what he terms "the alcoholic process" goes through four stages: (1) Early moderate drinking, usually in the company of other people. (2) Excessive drinking, in which the drinker begins to lose control of his consumption. Sometimes this begins with heavy drinking on weekends or vacations. (3) The relatively uncomplicated alcoholic stage. The individual now seems incapable of daily functioning without liquor. While he may promise over and over again to give up the habit, he is unable to do so. He resorts to lying, staying away from home at taverns and other places which dispense liquor, and spends more and more of his income to satisfy his craving. He begins to be a "lone drinker," to avoid his former friends. (4) The chronic stage, marked by intense craving for liquor. As Clinard aptly puts it, "The alcoholic now drinks to live and lives to drink." He eats very little. He develops a real anxiety neurosis that he will "run short" of a supply of drink. His body must have a quota of alcohol at all times. He is a sick man.[22]

Efforts to cure alcoholism have been going on for decades. Today, Alcoholics Anonymous is the best-known organization making a serious attempt to help alcoholics give up drink.

19 · For a review of some of the literature on this topic, see Clinard, pp. 357–359.

20 · Expert Committee on Mental Health, Alcoholism Subcommittee, "Second Report," Technical Report Series, No. 48 (Geneva, Switzerland: World Health Organization, August, 1952), p. 16.

21 · Data from Statistical Abstract of the United States, 1963 (Washington, D.C.: U.S. Government Printing Office, 1963), p. 796.

22 · Some of the data here are drawn from Clinard, pp. 341–346. See also Jessie Bernard, Social Problems in Midcentury, Chapter 11 (New York: The Dryden Press, 1957).

CRIMINAL BEHAVIOR

If sociologists are to explain the consequences of social structure, they must understand patterns of deviation from society's norms as well as patterns of adherence. A theory which accounts for conformity to the folkways and mores as a function of the way society is put together ought also to treat violation of norms as a consequence of the social structure.

Crime To maintain internal order, modern societies have developed written codes specifying what must or must not be done by an individual to another individual or to the state. Rules regarding wrongs committed against another individual are called torts. Taken together, they are known as civil law. Legal rules dealing with wrongs committed against the society as a whole are called criminal law; violation of one of these is a crime. Obviously, there is considerable overlap here. Some crimes are acts committed against an individual—for example, rape—but, because such crimes are considered threats to the social order, they are treated in criminal law. In the United States, crimes are divided into relatively serious violations, called felonies, and less grave offenses, known as misdemeanors.

Violation of a criminal law does not in itself constitute a crime. With few exceptions, the perpetrator of an act in violation of the criminal code must have *intended* to violate the law for his act to be considered a crime. It is this provision concerning criminal intent that is important in the definition of juvenile delinquency. In many states it is assumed that a person under a certain age (usually sixteen) is in-

capable of having criminal intent, and hence cannot commit a crime.

Patterns of Criminal Behavior Statistics on crimes are not complete indicators of criminal activity. A number of crimes committed never come to the attention of law enforcement authorities. Considerably fewer than half the crimes reported to the police result in arrests. Many persons who are arrested are dismissed without ever being prosecuted in court. Of those prosecuted, many are acquitted. Given the steady filtering process between the commission of a crime and the conviction of a criminal, studying people in prison in order to learn about criminal behavior is like studying people at bankruptcy proceedings to learn about business. You can learn something about the world of business by observing the failures, but your picture will be warped; in the same way, you can learn something about crime by studying convicts, but you should bear in mind that your picture is distorted and incomplete.

Crimes involving physical violence, while the backbone of the mystery novel trade, are relatively rare. In the United States, assault is the most frequent of those crimes committed against the person. Rape is second (if we count both forcible and statutory), and the least common is felonious homicide. The Federal Bureau of Investigation lists as "major" crimes aggravated assault, auto theft, burglary, larceny, manslaughter by negligence, murder and non-negligent manslaughter, rape, and robbery. Of these, crimes against the person constitute a very small proportion, usually only about 5 percent.

Far more numerous than assaults, rapes, or murders are crimes against property, of which the most frequent are auto theft, burglary, and larceny. Note that these crimes, unlike offenses against the person, do not necessitate face-to-face interaction beetween the criminal and his victim. As we have learned, one strong pressure to conformity, internalized through the process of socialization, is the guilt an individual may feel at violating a norm in the presence of another. Thus it is not only safer but probably easier psychologically for most people to violate a social expectation when the victim is absent and anonymous.

A type of crime somewhat different from crimes against the person or against property is the crime against public safety and morals. It is in this realm that we find organized, or corporate, crime. Organized crime includes such offenses as gambling, selling narcotics, and prostitution. The peculiar features of these crimes is that the victim sides with the criminal—the man who runs the gambling establishment, the drug pusher, or the prostitute—against the police and courts. Society, in such cases, is trying to protect people who do not want to be protected. For organized crime to exist, large numbers of people must patronize the criminals, and people charged with finding, arresting, prosecuting, and convicting must be failing to carry out their responsibilities.

Not all the crimes against public safety and morals occur as organized criminal activity, but probably most such offenses are in this pattern. It is easy to see a similarity between criminal activity and other economic activity: organized crime imitates in its organization the legitimate means of producing and distributing goods and services. The top executives in an ille-gal gambling operation engage in occupational role behavior not unlike that of the managers of a legitimate corporation.

The Criminal as a Social Type Sanctions, or rewards and punishments, exist to inhibit the commission of crimes. When such social controls are relatively weak, we can expect more violations of the law. As we have noted, differences among subcultures may account for variations in how seriously people view the norms. There is some evidence that crimes of violence, for example, differ by social class: middle-class people may abuse one another verbally in situations where lower-class people would use blows. There are also regional variations in the United States in crimes against the person: the South has significantly higher rates of felonious homicide, rape, and aggravated assault than the rest of the country. There are facile explanations for these regional differences: the South has a high proportion of Negroes, and a high proportion of low-income, poorly educated people. All three of these variables correlate with the incidence of crimes of violence. But it seems reasonable that the whole subculture can be a major explanatory factor, in that it exhibits a tradition more tolerant than the rest of the society of the expression of physical violence.[23]

Regional variation aside, Negroes commit more crimes than whites in the United States. Rather than merely noting this generalization uncritically, however, one should evaluate it in the light of the fact that it may reflect dif-

23 · Earl R. Moses, "Differentials in Crime Rates Between Negroes and Whites, Based on Comparisons of Four Socioeconomically Equated Areas," *American Sociological Review,* 1947, 12:411–420.

ferences in socioeconomic status more than differences in racial subculture. We know that police overestimate arrest rates among minority groups.[24] Certainly the pressures of minority status include many of the same social characteristics known to be associated with criminal behavior: poverty, a low level of formal education, inadequate housing, and other features of lower-class life chances.

It is widely believed that young people are more likely to be criminal than old people, but this is another generalization that requires cautious evaluation. In the first place, amateur or inexperienced criminals are more likely to be arrested, and hence influence crime statistics, than are older, professional criminals. Second, it is true that most persons arrested in the United States are under thirty-five years of age, but then, most people in the United States are under thirty-five years of age.

Too, nearly 90 percent of the persons arrested in the United States are men. This sexual difference in criminality, like race and age, seems more reasonably attributable to social than to biological factors. Sykes notes:

[I]t would follow that as the social status of men and women became more nearly alike, their crime rates would become more nearly alike. And, indeed, a number of comparisons bear out this line of reasoning. During the years of the Second World War women in the United States came to hold a social position more nearly like that of men, and the difference between their crime rates decreased accordingly. There is good evidence to indicate that in certain ethnic subgroups, such as Negroes in the United States, equality between the sexes is much increased; and

among Negroes the difference between the crime rates of males and females is less than in the case of whites. It has long been argued that in large cities women play a less subordinate role than they do in small towns; and it is true that the crime rates of men and women are more alike in the former than in the latter.[25]

Probably the best predictor of criminal behavior is social class status. As we saw in Chapters 11 and 12, occupation, education, income, and other indicators of one's position in the stratification structure are closely correlated with life chances. Among the functions of low status is, for example, more frequent and direct contact with criminality.[26] It is perhaps not the years of schooling, the amount of money, or the standing of the job itself which is so important here as the intervening variables: the social factors which are themselves a consequence of low socioeconomic status, such as overcrowded housing in blighted neighborhoods; loss of self-respect; inadequate parental discipline by an immature, poorly paid, frequently unemployed parent; or the squelching of ambition in a bright child attending a badly equipped, poorly staffed school.

A GENERAL THEORY OF DEVIANT SOCIAL BEHAVIOR

Following Durkheim's theory of *anomie*, or lack of normative cohesion, and its relationship to suicide, Robert K. Merton has formulated a general theory of rule-violating behavior. Mer-

24 · William M. Kephart, "Negro Visibility," *American Sociological Review*, 1954, 19:462–467.

25 · Gresham M. Sykes, *Crime and Society* (New York: Random House, 1956), p. 65. By permission.

26 · This is the point of Sutherland's theory of differential association. See Edwin H. Sutherland and Donald R. Cressey, *Principles of Criminology*, 6th ed. (Philadelphia: J. B. Lippincott Co., 1960).

FIGURE 36 · A Typology of Modes of Individual Adaptation *

Modes of Adaptation	Culture Goals	Institutionalized Means
I. Conformity	+	+
II. Innovation	+	−
III. Ritualism	−	+
IV. Retreatism	−	−
V. Rebellion	+ −	+ −

* Robert K. Merton, *Social Theory and Social Structure*, rev. ed. (Glencoe, Ill.: The Free Press, 1957), p. 140.

ton contends that *anomie* is likely to be most severe when the culture, while prescribing certain ends or goals, leaves many individuals in positions where they do not have access to legitimate means for achieving these ends. If, for example, the culture holds that all participants should be literate but the economy is such that many people must work most of their waking hours to stay alive and the state does not provide schools, books, or teachers, the consequence is severe stress for impoverished persons trying to reach the goal of literacy. The lack of integration of the means and ends in such a society would lead to *anomie*.

Merton suggests five ways in which an individual can deal with the goals of his culture and the institutionalized ways of reaching them. (See Figure 36.) He can accept both the ends and the means for reaching them, *conformity;* he can be satisfied with the goals but reject the accepted ways of achieving them and invent methods of his own, *innovation;* he can cling to the institutionalized means as ends in themselves while forgetting the goals for which they were originally in-tended, *ritualism;* he can reject both his cultural goals and the forms appropriate to them, *retreatism;* or he can abandon both the cultural goals and means but take the position of a revolutionary and try to introduce new ones, *rebellion.*

While the first type is the true conformist, the third usually passes for one. Many people looked on in their society as deviants—the racketeer seeking upward mobility, for instance—constitute the second type. Retreatists include tramps or bohemians, and the fifth type is characterized by the rebel with a cause.

We should remember that deviant behavior has impact on the social structure far beyond the deviant act itself. The process of dealing with deviants has its own consequences (latent functions): jobs are created for policemen; undercover agents serve as role models for children; reformers meet their own emotional needs by ministering to others. The social structures created for the control of deviance evolve their own norms and ultimately leave their mark upon the culture in which they originate.

INTERPRETATIVE SUMMARY

No society expects all members to conform to all of its norms. Norms are general; they do not apply to all situations. Norms vary in importance; some may almost be alternatives. And powerful subcultural norms often conflict with those of the wider society.

Finally, an individual may for some reason be unaware of a norm or all norms. Individuals who are mentally deficient are not expected to know the norms. This aggregate, as defined by the authors of the IQ and related tests, consists of individuals having eighth-grade mental age or less at adulthood. Similarly, people with mental disorders may deviate. Neurotic individuals are those who are disturbed to the point of crippling their own effectiveness; such persons are still able to participate in society. Psychotics are those who are so severely disturbed, whether for organic or socio-psychological reasons, that they cannot carry on everyday interaction.

Widespread patterns of deviant behavior include suicide, alcoholism, drug addiction, and crime. Émile Durkheim has noted two extremes in suicide patterns: suicide by individuals who feel alone or confused and suicide by individuals who feel so closely integrated in their society that they are willing to kill themselves if the norms so dictate. Suicide rates and motivations vary among and within societies. In the United States there are age, sex, racial, religious, and other differentials.

Drug addiction and alcoholism are similar in several ways. Neither is of recent origin; both are widespread. In each case, addiction is gradual; in each, tolerance varies among individuals. In the United States, more men than women are addicts or alcoholics, and more young people than old.

Crimes which are considered serious in the United States are those involving violence against individuals, crimes against property, and crimes threatening the public safety and morals. However, criminal behavior as a wider society defines it may be accepted behavior in a subculture. In the United States, for example, there are class and regional differences in rates and kinds of crimes. Statistics concerning age differentials are necessarily inaccurate, but again men seem to engage in this type of behavior more than women.

Robert K. Merton has developed a theory of deviant behavior which seems applicable to those situations in which an individual is mentally and intellectually capable of recognizing society's goals. He says that, while conformists work for accepted goals in accepted ways, deviants either use unacceptable tactics, or refuse to try, or actively attempt to change the goals themselves.

REVIEW AND SUGGESTED READINGS

A • VOCABULARY

Anomie	Mental disorder	Psychosomatic
Deviance	Neurosis	Subnormality
Intelligence quotient	Psychosis	

B • QUESTIONS AND TOPICS FOR REVIEW

1. Are there any psychosomatic disorders which are common in people of your age group and social class?
2. Who is the most idiosyncratic person you know? To what degree has his nonconformity handicapped him?
3. Illustrate: "Deviance is in the eye of the beholder."

4. What norms, small and large, of college students tend to be different from those of the wider culture?
5. Why is a play, film, or novel about a case of functional psychosis likely to be better than one concerning a case of organic psychosis?
6. Which of the three types of functional psychoses is *least* likely to appear, even in modified form, among normal people? Why?
7. What specific sanctions does the United States employ to guard against suicide?
8. Is altruistic suicide ever considered praiseworthy in the United States? Is altruism a common motive for suicide here?
9. Why is organized crime hard to fight?
10. Why is it difficult to think of a crime that is not an *intentional* violation of a norm?
11. What crimes are most prevalent among the upper and middle classes?
12. How does Merton's definition of the term *innovation* differ from the popular definition?

C · SUGGESTIONS FOR FURTHER READING

Daniel Bell. *The End of Ideology*. Glencoe, Ill.: The Free Press, 1960.

Contains three excellent chapters for the student of crime in the United States: "Crime as an American Way of Life"—on organized crime as a route to social mobility for the members of immigrant minorities; "The Myth of Crime Waves"; and "The Racketridden Longshoremen"—on the symbiotic relationship between legitimate businessmen and labor racketeers.

Herbert A. Block and Gilbert Geis. *Man, Crime, and Society*. New York: Random House, 1962.

An objective analysis of delinquency and crime in modern society.

Daniel Glaser. *The Effectiveness of a Prison and Parole System*. Indianapolis, Indiana: The Bobbs-Merrill Company, Inc., 1964.

A report of a five-and-one-half-year research study of recidivism.

August B. Hollingshead and Frederick C. Redlich. *Social Class and Mental Illness: A Community Study*. New York: John Wiley & Sons, Inc., 1958.

The report on one part of a large research project, carried on by a team of social scientists and psychiatrists, in interrelations between social stratification and mental illness in New Haven, Connecticut.

Salvator F. Lucia, ed. *Alcohol and Civilization*. New York: McGraw-Hill Paperback Series, 1962.

From a symposium at the University of California Medical School in 1961. Covers the effects of alcohol on the body, alcohol in our society, and the interdisciplinary standpoints of the symposium speakers.

Richard L. Masland, Seymour B. Sarason, and Thomas Gladwin. *Mental Subnormality: Biological, Psychological, and Cultural Factors*. New York: Basic Books, Inc., 1958.

A survey and interpretation of research sponsored by The National Association for Retarded Children. There is a list of references covering 631 titles.

David Matza. *Delinquency and Drift*. New York: John Wiley & Sons, Inc., 1964.

A fascinating and controversial theoretical contribution to the understanding of juvenile delinquency.

Arnold M. Rose, ed. *Mental Health and Mental Disorder*. New York: W. W. Norton & Company, Inc., 1955.

A collection of papers dealing with such topics as social psychiatry, social characteristics of the mentally disordered, community problems and mental breakdown, some material on personality organization and disorganization, sociological approaches to specific mental diseases, problems of marginality to mental breakdowns, and a final section on contributions to mental health.

Thorsten Sellin and Marvin E. Wolfgang. *The Measurement of Delinquency*. New York: John Wiley & Sons, Inc., 1964.

A thorough historical review of techniques and problems in crime measurement.

Alfred H. Stanton and Morris S. Schwartz. *The Mental Hospital: A Study of Institutional Participation in Psychiatric Illness and Treatment*. New York: Basic Books, Inc., 1954.

A report of a three-year study of a psychiatric ward, dealing with roles, the formal and informal organization, and the power structure.

Edwin H. Sutherland and Donald R. Cressey. *Principles of Criminology*, 6th ed. Philadelphia: J. B. Lippincott Co., 1960.

A standard textbook in the field, containing Sutherland's theory of differential association, chapters on the various correlates of criminal behavior, and an extensive section on penology.

Lewis Yablonsky. *The Violent Gang*. New York: The Free Press of Glencoe, 1962.

Based on a four-year study of youth killer gangs in New York City's upper West Side. Focuses on two particular gangs: the Balkans and the Egyptian Kings.

CHAPTER 26

Social and Cultural Change

Stable and permanent though structures and functions or norms and their sanctions may appear to be, they are subject to change through time. As a matter of fact, when sociologists describe a social structure, they deliberately stop all normal social processes in order to get a clear view of society and its culture at a given point in time. Such a description bears exactly the correspondence to social reality that a photograph bears to life. It may be a true picture at the moment of description, but it tells the observer nothing about the conditions that obtained in the past, the processes that were in motion at the time the picture was taken, or the probable alterations of the structure in the future.

Every society is characterized by an interplay of those forces that make for cultural stability and those that make for change. Culture is never really static. Yet, for purposes of indicating broad differences, we say a culture is *stable* when a condition of equilibrium of patterns and processes is its basic feature. In contrast, a culture marked by rather extensive alteration of its patterns and resulting disequilibrium is said to be *dynamic*. Many nonliterate peoples, especially those living under conditions of isolation, have remained relatively unchanged for long periods of time. Such were the Australian aborigines before the arrival of the white man. Even under conditions of civilization, certain relatively complex cultures continued a long time without any striking changes. This was the situation in Egypt during long periods of its ancient history. Yet it would be a mistake to assume that the culture of any society, large or small, is ever completely stable and static.

Cultures may be modified in two ways: by diffusion—that is, by borrowing traits or patterns from other cultures—and by the invention or discovery of new cultural elements within the society. In either case, social change will be the result: the addition of traits or patterns to the culture will produce modifications in the social structure. We shall deal first with invention and discovery, and then turn to diffusion.

DISCOVERY AND INVENTION

It is not always easy to draw a distinction between discovery and invention. The former represents perception of relations between elements not previously recognized or understood. The relationship may have been deliberately sought or it may have been found accidentally. On the other hand, invention is a combination of known elements or devices into some new form. In a sense, discovery is fundamental to invention, since man must have certain knowledge and skill regarding things, people, and situations before he can put his knowledge and skill to work to produce something novel. Yet the discovery of new facts or relations may depend on the invention of new methods of thinking or acting. For our purpose, the term *invention* will serve both for the discovery of some fact or principle and for the creation of a new device or pattern.

Since technology has made a striking impression on daily life in our time, people sometimes get the notion that invention involves only mechanical devices. But inventions occur in both material and nonmaterial phases of culture. The automobile and the telephone seem—and are—highly significant inventions. But so, too, are the Australian ballot, intelligence testing, and chainstore merchandising.

Basic Features of Invention Inventions may be classified into two sorts: empirical and planned. Until the rise of modern science, most inventions were of the former type. Empirical invention generally grows out of trial-and-error attempts to improve some device or institution already at hand, or out of accidental discovery of a technique. Science has now provided us with the means of planning or directing and even predicting many of our inventions.

We may well ask what stimulates inventiveness. The old saying that "necessity is the mother of invention" requires qualification. Recurrent need may or may not induce inventiveness. Primitive man needed means to relieve pain and to counteract disease. His magic was an attempt at such a device, but only modern anesthetics and medicines have met these needs successfully. The long-continued use of old and in-

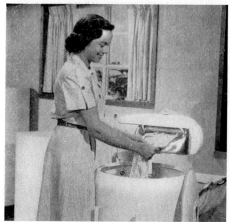

Technological changes resulting from the application of science.

effective ways of doing things is ample evidence that sheer necessity does not always give birth to efficient invention.

The truth is that very often, in the words of Thorstein Veblen, "Invention is the mother of necessity." That is to say, once an invention has become accepted as a new element in a culture, it may set up wants and motives not previously present in the society. The whole expansion of human needs under conditions of modern industry and merchandising is evidence enough of this fact.

It is the cultural and social situation that makes invention possible. The existence of sufficient leisure for calm and deliberate examination of various possibilities is important. An element of curiosity must be present. Without doubt, "just monkeying around" with mechanical devices or ideas has brought about valuable new combinations. In trial-and-error invention, as in all hit-or-miss learning, accidental combinations are often significant. False combinations may even suggest correct solutions later. Musing or daydreaming is also important. Getting "hunches" or making guesses is as necessary, especially in the early phases, as actual manipulation of physical objects or of social situations.

Yet neither pressing necessity nor mental reverie alone, nor the two together, fully account for invention. Such advances depend on two major factors: culture and the individual. These are closely interrelated, but for purposes of discussion we shall deal with (1) the general cultural base; (2) the culture's values and attitudes toward invention—that is, the interest or run of attention; and (3) the place of special and high intellectual abilities.

The Cultural Base With reference to the effect on culture and society, inventions may be classed as primary or basic, and as secondary—that is, derived, or "improving," as Ralph Linton calls them.[1] Primary inventions are illustrated by such things as the discovery of the use of fire, the discovery of ultraviolet rays, and the invention of the phonetic alphabet; the wheel; the means of smelting iron ore; and the zero, negative numbers, and calculus. Secondary inventions are those which have to do with improving or modifying other inventions, such as air conditioning or the introduction of the automatic transmission in the automobile.

An invention, if it is to survive, must have relevance to the existing culture. There is, in fact, a selective process going on at all times with reference to inventions in any society. If there is strong intellectual or emotional resistance to change, an invention may be dropped before being tried out. If, on the other hand, a society is receptive, the invention may effect profound changes. So too, the use of an invention in the total culture is important. The Greeks, for example, invented a steam engine but limited its use to religious rituals. Their culture was not ready for its application to modes of transportation or machine production.

Both basic and improving inventions depend on the state of knowledge and skill in a given society. The effect of the lack of scientific knowledge and techniques is illustrated in the work of Leonardo da Vinci. Certainly he was intellectually capable of inventing a

1 · Ralph Linton, *The Study of Man* (New York: Appleton-Century-Crofts, Inc., 1936), pp. 316–317.

successful flying machine—in fact, he did construct some interesting models of airplanes. But they were not workable, because he lacked the necessary tools of modern mathematics and mechanics. As a painter, however, Leonardo was one of the greatest masters of all time, and his contributions to the study of human anatomy and to military techniques were outstanding. For these attainments there was an adequate cultural foundation.

Not only do potential inventors sometimes lack the mechanical principles or methods, but the essential materials may not be at hand. The lack of essential materials usually reflects cultural retardation in some related skill or knowledge. Thus hard steel could not be produced until certain alloys were developed.

In our society, extensions of inventions depend on the ever-larger cultural base from which they emerge, on cultural acceptance of inventions in general, and on the stimulation of capitalistic enterprise which seeks to apply inventions in order to make greater profits. We cannot ignore the importance of capitalism as a stimulant to both science and technology, though in recent decades such socialistic states as the Soviet Union have encouraged inventions in the name of the state and public welfare. The Russian successes in rocketry and missiles dramatize her great strides in science.

Planned Invention and Science As we have noted, until the rise of modern science, most inventions were empirical. Science now provides us with a means of directing and even predicting many inventions. Of course, one discovery or invention often has to wait for another. The photoelectric cell, for example, long known to physics, was not perfected for practical use until the invention of a vacuum-tube amplifier.

The planning of inventions for the larger needs of society has only begun. An early example was the designing and testing of the Liberty motor during World War I. Under a governmental directive, a number of engineers and other experts cooperated to develop a more satisfactory airplane engine. The development of the submarine detector during the same war was another case of necessity followed by planned and cooperative research. During World War II there was much more of this sort of thing. The outstanding example was the Manhattan Project, out of which came the atomic bomb.

Such planned invention is not the product of wartime needs only. In agriculture, too, there are a considerable number of planned inventions. One of the most striking is the development of hybrid corn, which has made possible an increase in yield of nearly 30 percent. This new corn was developed by controlling the process of pollination so as to secure vigor, uniformity, and other desired characteristics. So far, most of our planned inventions have had to do with mechanical and biological problems.

Attitudes, Values, and Run of Attention Along with the necessary cultural base in knowledge and skill, the social attitudes and values regarding invention are important. From our standpoint, nonliterate man had a real need for public health measures to prevent disease, reduce the death rate, and improve his physical well-being. That he did not get these measures was partly because he lacked information and techniques but partly also because his ideas and values regarding birth, death, and disease were vastly different from our own. What a culture demands and what it values highly will help direct its inventors. For further example, among the Crow Indians there was considerable stress on individual visionary experience, which encouraged the introduction of a new religious cult. In Samoa there is some allowance for innovation in ritual and decorative arts, yet "in the decorative arts, the freedom given to the individual is rendered nugatory by the absence of cultural recognition of the innovator and by the strong prejudice against active imitation so the gifted individual receives but passing praise for his work."[2]

The Samoan attitude grows out of the general cultural patterning which stresses individual conformity to tradition and cooperative relations. We, in contrast, put much emphasis on interpersonal competition for attainment, especially in mechanical invention and business enterprise. On the other hand, we do not reward with either money or honor those who suggest sharply different institutional norms.

It is evident, then, that what W. I. Thomas calls "the run of attention" in a society has much to do with the particular direction that inventions will take. Our entire matrix of technology and money-making sets the framework within which potential innovators growing up in our society will operate. Were we to fix our present material culture at about its present level and turn our inventive attention elsewhere,

we might experience greater and more numerous changes in patterns of political, religious, artistic, or recreational activities.

Intellectual Ability and Inventiveness
To recognize that the particular run of attention will be determined by culture does not deny the importance of persons of superior mental endowment in producing new inventions. We may well ask what place special ability or so-called inventive genius has in invention. It is very easy to assume that inventions are the result of the innate ability of a few chosen persons. There is no doubt that, given the proper cultural stimulus, the stratum of superior individuals will furnish the inventors. Yet what the superior person will do with his capacity depends on the society and its culture. It is hardly conceivable that the genius of the jungle would become a great physician, though he might well become a military leader or the inventor of a new religious ritual.

The absolute and relative number of first-rate minds will always be a factor, also, in scientific advancement. Suppose that all the Class A nuclear physicists—men of superior native ability—should be wiped out at one stroke, with no replacements available. The Class B men would still be capable of continuing important research and invention because, with present techniques, worthy discoveries and valuable applications would still be made. But there is little doubt that long-range advances in physics would be slowed down so as to affect all scientific progress related to it.

The relation of culture to individual ability raises the question of the "great-man theory" of history—that is,

2 · Margaret Mead, "The Role of the Individual in Samoan Culture," *Journal of the Royal Anthropological Institute of Great Britain and Ireland*, 1928, 58:481–495.

does history make great men or do great men make history? Confining ourselves only to the matter of invention, the particular direction of inventions and their nature are determined by culture. Often we forget the slow accumulation of basic knowledge by less well-known men who made possible the more spectacular work which we hear about. The inventions of Thomas A. Edison in electricity, for instance, would have been impossible without hundreds of researches in the century before him.

The close relationship between cultural base, values and attitudes, and high abilities is well demonstrated by the large number of duplicate inventions and discoveries during the age of modern science. Some years ago W. F. Ogburn compiled a list of 148 important inventions and discoveries made independently by two or more persons. Some of the more striking examples from this list follow: [3]

1. Discovery of sun spots by Galileo (1611), Fabricus (1611), Scheiner (1611), and Harriott (1611).
2. Decimal fractions by Stevinus (1585), Bürgi (1592), and possibly by Rudolff (1530) and Beyer (1603).
3. Logarithms by Napier-Briggs (1614) and Bürgi (1620).
4. Calculus by Newton (1671) and Leibnitz (1676).
5. Law of gases by Boyle (1662) and Marriotte (1676).

6. Discovery of oxygen by Scheele (1774) and Priestley (1774).
7. Molecular theory by Avogadro (1811) and Ampère (1814).
8. Photography by Daguerre (1839), Niepce (1839), and Talbot (1839).
9. Law of conservation of energy by Mayer (1843), Joule (1847), Helmholtz (1847), Colding (1847), and Thomson (1847).
10. Telegraph by Henry (1831), Morse (1837), Cooke-Wheatstone (1837), and Steinheil (1837).
11. Spectrum analysis by Miller (1843), Stokes (1849), Angstrom (1854), Kirchoff-Bunsen (1859), and Draper (1860).
12. Telephone by Bell (1876) and Gray (1876).
13. Phonograph by Edison (1877) and Cros (1877).
14. Relations of microörganisms to fermentation and putrefaction by Latour (1837) and Schwann (1837).
15. Theory of natural selection and variation by Darwin (1858) and Wallace (1858).
16. Sewing machine by Thimmonier (1830), Hunt (1840), and Howe (1846).
17. Stereoscope by Wheatstone (1839) and Elliott (1840).
18. Reaper by Hussey (1833) and McCormick (1834).

3 · For the entire list, see W. F. Ogburn, *Social Change with Respect to Culture and Original Nature* (New York: The Viking Press, Inc., 1922), pp. 99–102. For a critical comment on duplicate inventions, see Tertius Chandler, "Duplicate Inventions?" *American Anthropologist*, 1960, 62:495–498. See also "Comment" by A. L. Kroeber, p. 498.

Clearly, inventions and discoveries do not depend on one particular exceptional person alone but also on the nature of the culture out of which the new elements in the invention arise. True, if there are few superior persons available to make inventions, the rate of invention will be retarded. But since advances in invention depend so much on minor accretions to the total body of knowledge, it is indeed doubtful that any one particular inventor is essential at a given time. Great men alone do not make inventions, but neither can culture as a body of knowledge alone induce them.

Particular societies, of course, need not produce their own inventors and scientists; the advancement in one country or region may pass over to another. The larger effects of invention and technology can be discussed only when we have examined the features of diffusion, or borrowing.

DIFFUSION

Culture grows not only by invention or discovery but also by diffusion. *Diffusion* is the borrowing and adopting of cultural traits or patterns from other social units or individuals. Ordinarily, diffusion is thought of as a movement of traits through *space*. In this sense it is not to be confused with *transmission* of culture, which has to do with passing traits and patterns through *time*—that is, from generation to generation. Thus, formal education is not diffusion but transmission.

The Spread of Culture The elements of culture may diffuse between nations and regions, from class to class, from community to community, and between any other association of men, or merely from man to man. For example, Christianity and, later, industrialism spread from Europe and the United States to Japan and China.

Much of our American system of education was borrowed from nineteenth-century Germany. As a rule, fashion spreads from the upper to the lower classes. Urban ways are diffused to rural localities.

Diffusion can be either direct or indirect. Direct diffusion occurs when persons or groups have physical contact. Indirect diffusion is the spread of traits without personal or group contact. The first is illustrated by migration and colonization, by contact through war and trade, and by the work of religious missionaries. The second is witnessed in the spread of printed materials, by radio and television, and by the infiltration of ideas and goods in commerce carried on without direct personal contact. Indirect diffusion accompanies the development of secondary-group organization.

The spread of culture is not always just from more-advanced to less-advanced groups. It is often reciprocal. While Western man has diffused his culture, especially the material phases, over most of the earth, nonliterate peoples have contributed heavily to civilized societies. The contribution of this kind most obvious to Americans is, of course, the large number of cultural items which we received from the native Indian. These include, among many others, maize or Indian corn and many methods of its cultivation, the potato, beans, tomatoes, and tobacco. The Indian also gave us the game of lacrosse, and he taught colonists new methods of stalking game and the enemy in dense woods.

In turn, the white man brought the Indian the horse and saddle and firearms. These items produced great changes in the culture of the tribes on the Great Plains, giving them mobility, adding to their efficiency in game hunting, and stimulating their interest in warfare. On the other hand, these very alterations probably retarded any incipient tendencies toward more settled community life and agriculture. The whites also brought Christianity to the American Indian but, as elsewhere, it tended in many instances to be fused with the native religion, an indication that the items which are diffused sooner or later merge with the indigenous culture patterns if they do not replace them.

War and conquest have been important factors in diffusion. The Roman legions spread Latin culture around the Mediterranean and beyond. Not only new political systems but also new economic organization and religion have followed in the wake of war.

It is generally accepted that diffusion is more important than invention in the total building of any culture; of all the items in any given culture, more are borrowed from other peoples than are invented. Very often culture traits which are thought to have arisen from geographical conditions or from crises actually have come from other culture groups. Some anthropologists go so far as to lay down a kind of rule that, other things being equal, it is easier to borrow than to invent. Perhaps because of the inertia of habit and man's lack of originality, it seems more common to look around and find some method already in use than to think up an entirely new device to meet the situation.

Rates of Diffusion Culture traits and patterns diffuse at different rates. As a rule, material traits spread much more quickly than those which have to do with forms of the family, political organization, art, religion, or recreation. Native peoples, for example, often readily accept firearms, utensils, tools, and cloth, but at the same time retain their own language, kinship organization, religion, and art. The diffusion nearly always involves some modification. Rarely is any trait, unless it is of a material nature, borrowed by people without some modification at their hands.

Diffusion may go on in an informal and almost unconscious way, or it may be the result of a conscious attempt to foist an alien culture on another society. Spreading by trade and migration is often of the first sort; that fostered by organized religion or by a conquering state usually is more deliberate.

There are also certain hindrances to diffusion, such as inadequate transportation and communication, complete isolation, taboos on change, and resistance to foreign ideas and techniques. So too, displacement of one pattern by another prevents the further spread of the pattern displaced. The practice of drinking coffee is not likely to spread in a country such as China, long addicted to tea.

The factors affecting rate of diffusion may be summarized as follows: (1) availability of transportation and communication, including distance and barriers to travel such as mountains or sea; (2) resistance to culture changes, such as taboo, sense of superiority, and general cultural inertia; (3) prestige of the lending culture and its people; (4) conquest of one people by another; (5) migration, especially when *en masse*, as in the Teutonic invasions of the Roman Empire, in modern immigration, or in enforced moving of large populations from one region to another; (6) the need for some new element to meet a critical situation; and (7) adaptability of the recipients of the new culture, as in the ready adoption of Western industrialism by Japan.

As a matter of fact, the cultural and psychological elements operating in diffusion are not unlike those which more or less determine invention. That is, the broad cultural base of prior skill and knowledge must be taken into account. So too, the basic values and attitudes of potential recipients are important. Individual capacity is of some significance—persons of high ability, scholars, political and industrial leaders, war chiefs, and religious functionaries will usually be in the vanguard of reception. Finally, since nearly all borrowed traits are subject to some modification in their new setting, special ability will play a part in adapting the item to the new situation.

FACTORS INFLUENCING INNOVATIONS

The acceptance of innovations is qualified by the nature and extent of the changes, by the rate at which they are introduced, and by the degree of readiness of groups. This last will be affected by the existing ideas, attitudes, and habits of individuals.

We have already indicated that societies differ in their receptiveness to change. In a society oriented to modern technology, new cultural elements that contribute to further technology are more acceptable, on the whole, than radical innovations in institutions that support the moral system of the society. So too, changes of wide scope will tend to induce more reaction than will minor changes. One factor con-

tributing to present-day anxieties is the fact that people cannot readjust themselves fast enough to the large number of innovations to which they are exposed. In psychological terms this means that individuals cannot do the "unlearning" necessary to the acquisition of the many new habits and attitudes without becoming confused and distressed in the process.

Cultural Lag Whether induced by political revolution or by slower methods, changes in one field often induce dislocations in another area of behavior. For example, the last 150 years have seen a tremendous burst of material inventions in western Europe and America which have altered the nature of technological culture the world over. In sharp contrast, corresponding modifications in the nonmaterial culture have been slow, halting, and ineffective. Often new needs arising from rather sudden material changes have not been adequately satisfied. In other words, the previous integration of the major parts of a total culture has been disturbed by these changes.

This differential in the rate of change W. F. Ogburn termed *cultural lag,* which he defined in these words:

The thesis is that the various parts of modern culture are not changing at the same rate, some parts are changing much more rapidly than others; and that since there is a correlation and interdependence of parts, a rapid change in one part of our culture requires readjustments through other changes in the various correlated parts. . . . Where one part of culture changes first, through some discovery or invention, and occasions changes in some part of culture dependent upon it, there frequently is a delay in the changes occasioned in the dependent part of the culture.[4]

4 · *Social Change,* pp. 200–201. By permission.

It is now generally accepted that many of the contemporary problems of society result from this lag. There is today a wide range of new habits, attitudes, and ideas fostered by material alterations which society did not anticipate and for which there has been no preparation. This dislocation is largely a result of differentials in rates of change. In fact, *social disorganization* refers to the breakdown of the societal order to such an extent that the former controls are dissipated, and a certain chaos or disorder arises from the fact that the old ways of doing things have not yet been replaced by adequate new ways.

Few people would deny that advantages have accrued from technological innovations: lessening of the severity of work and hours of labor, increase in leisure for all classes, widespread education, mobility and travel, increased "animation" of life, extension of contacts, and a higher standard of living for millions. But it is also true that many dislocations have arisen from the failure of the nonmaterial culture—especially that connected with societal organization—to keep pace with these new material culture patterns. Mobility has broken down the neighborhood and primary community, weakened social controls, and fostered certain types of crime. Changes in industrial production have caused technological unemployment, depressed the position of skilled workers, and increased the number of semiskilled workers.

The political order, too, is marked by many dislocations: the continuance of outworn political units of voting, the restriction of residence for office-holders, and the persistence of many governmental forms that belonged to the horse-and-buggy era. The lag in laws and administration of justice and in the correction and care of dependents, defectives, delinquents, and criminals is compounded by the lack of personnel adequately trained for work in a complex society.

When new patterns are believed to threaten old values and long-accepted ways of doing things, resistances are bound to arise. The receptivity of the individual to modifications in habits and attitudes is qualified by habits and attitudes already in existence. In our own society change has at times been resisted by business, labor, class and community interests, as well as by government bodies and even by scientific experts.

Capitalistic Enterprise and Changes in Technology There are hundreds of instances of opposition to technological improvements in the history of modern capitalism and industry. The major aim of profits often blinds entrepreneurs to new opportunities to make money and to serve the public more efficiently at the same time. The major consideration is often not "Will it work?" but "Will it pay?" Various factors enter into this inertia. Among others may be mentioned these: the large capital investments in going concerns already providing goods and services; the cost of putting new plants into operation and of selling the product or service; the desire to maintain a dominant position over existing or potential competitors; the somewhat unwieldy nature of large corporate enterprise, which makes for disinclination to modify ways and means; and the trouble smaller businesses have securing capital to start new enterprises. There are almost endless illustrations of such resistance; we shall select but

Ewing Galloway   *Ewing Galloway*

Technological Inventions Allow Changes in Culture Patterns

The pony express was considered a rapid means of communication in the early days of the nineteenth century. Western life reflected its influence.

Earlier means of communication are rendered obsolete by inventions such as these parabolic antennas atop the Federal Telecommunication Laboratories.

a few from the history of transportation.

The introduction of the railroad into the United States met with great opposition. In 1812 John Stevens' proposal to introduce railway lines into New York State was flatly turned down by such leaders as DeWitt Clinton, Gouverneur Morris, and Robert R. Livingston. When later—1815 in New Jersey and 1823 in Pennsylvania—Stevens obtained charters, he had difficulty persuading capitalists to invest in his enterprises. The owners of canal barges and of stagecoach lines were particularly bitter about the railroads. The rationalizations of potential investors who objected to the railway were many and ingenious: fear of speed, of setting fire

to towns, of disrupting the local life, and so on.

Once the railroads had become fairly well established, moreover, a process of crystallization set in. Owners and investors opposed further advances. Commodore Cornelius Vanderbilt, one of the early railroad magnates, dismissed George Westinghouse and his air-brake invention with the remark that he had no time to waste on fools. Eli J. Janney, the inventor of the car-coupler, had to wait ten years before he could get a foundry to manufacture it for him. Until very recently, the design of the Pullman sleeper was pretty much the same as it was in 1859. Electric locomotives, streamlined trains, and other improvements were adopted very slowly. When the auto-bus came into use, railway executives and employee unions alike opposed the extension of bus lines because it was felt that their competition would ruin the railroads.

The automobile presents another story of long, slow development. As early as 1769, Nicholas Joseph Cugnot invented a three-wheeled vehicle powered by two steam cylinders. But he got no popular support for his device. Other steam-propelled carriages were tried out with only limited acceptance. When the internal-combustion engine, in combination with other inventions, made the automobile practicable, years went by before the new vehicle was accepted. The automobile was "a rich man's toy" which would never have any practical use. The first American automobile manufacturers got a cool reception from the Wall Street bankers. In 1908, John Pierpont Morgan and his partners refused to buy a block of securities priced at $5,000,000 in a concern that was later consolidated into General Motors.

As with the railroads, improvements in the automobile were opposed by corporate owners, although the lag in accepting what people called "refinements" was less than with many other mechanical devices. Yet the self-starter, six- and eight-cylinder engines, four-wheel brakes, balloon tires, and automatic transmission were slow to be adopted. To this day, the placing of the motor in the rear of the automobile has been limited to buses and a few types of stock-model cars.

The story of the airplane parallels these others. This radical departure in the means of transportation and communication seemed fantastic even to a generation already attuned to rapid technological changes, and all the early airplane manufacturers had difficulty financing their inventions.

The Prejudice of Workers Laborers, like investors, have often been slow to accept new technologies. The factory system in England and elsewhere met with much opposition from the workers. The most recurrent opposition to modifications in industrial processes has come from labor unions. In the 1870's, the introduction of labor-saving devices in the boot-and-shoe industry was bitterly opposed by the workers' unions. Silk workers went on strike against the three- or four-loom system. Building and construction workers have fought a steady battle against the introduction of machine processing into their work. Agreements with union painters have dictated the width of brushes so that workers would not be able to cover more surface than the unions considered fair. Union painters have long opposed the introduction of spray guns. The history of trade unionism is filled with such cases.

The introduction of the Diesel locomotive was opposed by the railroad unions because it threatened the fireman's job. Indeed, it was only after the railroads agreed to keep firemen on the engine crews that Diesels were put into wide use.

Political Resistance Political factors have also played a part in retarding industrial advancement. Public officials have felt pressures of two sorts: from the people in general, and from vested interests of business or labor. Public opposition to the railroad as dangerous and disruptive of custom and tradition delayed legislation that would have facilitated the railroad's development.

Some states even passed laws against this new form of transportation. For example, since the state of New York had gone into heavy public debt to subsidize the Erie canal, it wrote into early railroad charters and franchises restrictions that made it practically impossible for the railroads to compete with the canal barges. A tonnage tax so high as to make it impossible for railroads to carry freight was one of these restrictions. When the railroad unions became strong, they agitated in Congress to limit the length of trains and to determine the size of train crews—at the very time when improved roadbeds, more powerful locomotives, and safety devices made possible longer trains and smaller crews. This is a kind of socially induced cultural lag.

So too, all sorts of local and state restrictions have been put on automobile operators. Many towns and cities have opposed plans for through highways that would bypass them and thus cause them to lose business.

Even when it is in the interest of the state, there may be much opposition to an improvement. United States naval officials were highly skeptical of John Ericcson's screw propeller, and at first they flatly rejected his plans for the famous *Monitor*. The submarine was considered an insane invention; and though the first successful undersea craft was built for the United States in 1898, it was not until World War I that submarines came into general use. During the time between the two world wars, the French General Staff consistently refused to take seriously the airplane, the armored tank, and other mechanical means of military offense and defense—this despite the fact that the Germans not only were making great strides in these mechanized instruments

of warfare but were in many instances making no secret of their progress. The French military leaders developed what has been called "the Maginot Line psychosis"—they considered their major preparation for war the Maginot defense system.

Through patent laws, the government gives legal protection to patentees. A patent is regarded as private property by the law, and there is nothing to force a person or corporation holding a patent to make use of it. Thus, by developing new products and processes themselves and then storing them away, corporations have been able to prevent technological advances in the interests of their prior investments, a frequent pretext being that the novel product is not worth what it would cost to make.

In nonmechanical fields, political opposition has been even more striking. Statutes in dairy states often forbid the sale of colored oleomargarine, and chain stores are often highly taxed, on the theory that this will keep the independent grocers going. The dissemination of knowledge of birth-control methods is still a crime in some states.

Inertia Among the Experts   A most interesting aspect of this entire subject is the frequent resistance of experts themselves. Scientific training is highly specialized; and men who for years have done work in one particular line, especially if they have obtained high prestige, often oppose changes if these run counter to their professional or other beliefs.

In 1826 an engineer said of the railroad that "a rate of speed of more than six miles an hour would exceed the bounds of providence," and the suggestion of John Stevens that trains might travel 20 miles an hour was met with derision. A notable instance of scientific authority invoked against an invention was the astronomer Simon Newcomb's criticism of the airplane. In 1906 Newcomb publicly declared that neither the laws of physics nor the state of the industrial arts made it practicable for man to "fly long distances through the air."

The history of modern medicine is replete with illustrations of hostility to innovations. Opposition greeted the pioneer work of Louis Pasteur in the field of bacteriology and immunology. In the study of mental diseases an interesting instance is the ridicule which greeted Dr. Sigmund Freud when, before a distinguished group of neurologists in Vienna, he reported a case of male hysteria. He was informed in no uncertain terms by the most eminent neurologists of the day that this was impossible, since hysteria was associated only with female physical functions. Freud lived long enough to see complete verification of his contention and recognition of his competence in the field of mental disease.

Class and Community Resistance Not only do vested economic interests, political bodies, and even experts often resist cultural change, but the general population also frequently does so, often, of course, taking its justification for opposition from these other groups.

Class factors enter very thoroughly into resistance. An amusing and revealing class attitude was expressed in the English Parliament by Craven Fitzhardinge Berkeley in these words: "Nothing is more distasteful to me than to hear the echo of our hills reverberating with the hissing of railroad engines runing through the heart of our hunting country, and destroying that noble

sport, fox hunting, to which I have been accustomed from my childhood." [5] The royalty of Europe long opposed the substitution of automobiles for horse-drawn carriages on state occasions.

Class resistance to institutional modifications is well-known. Attempts to modify the system of private enterprise have met with recurrent criticism from the propertied classes, and agitation to abolish the capitalistic system has led to legal and violent extralegal means to silence such ideas.

The opposition of the general public is often no less vigorous than that of the privileged classes. When the railroads first came into rather general use, preachers, merchants, and the man in the street often denounced them as instruments likely to destroy their way of life. There are numerous examples in the history of education of negative reactions to new pedagogical practices. In one community the system of staggering the time for recess so as to allow more play space for the children had to be abandoned because some parents who saw children on the playground all through the day spread the word that this "new-fangled" plan meant all play and no work. The introduction of a course of study which would lessen the emphasis on such subjects as Latin and incorporate vocational subjects, art, music, and the like had to overcome opposition in community after community before being accepted.

Of course, the student should not imagine that every innovation is met by strong resistance. Many changes are

5 · Quoted by B. J. Stern in "Resistances to the Adoption of Technological Innovations," Part I, sec. 4, *Technological Trends and National Policy* (Washington, D.C.: U.S. Government Printing Office, 1937), p. 40.

facilitated by the pressure of grave economic-political crises. The establishment of the Securities and Exchange Commission, following the stock market crash of 1929, is a case in point. But on the whole, the more drastic the change, the more intense the emotional opposition is likely to be. In spite of the American belief in progress and the stress progress gets in both formal and informal education, alterations which touch our more basic values, attitudes, and habits arouse anxiety, hostility, and negative feelings. The most acceptable changes are those which are in line with principles already taken for granted. The knowledge of science remains far in advance of application.

There are some critics of technology and science who agitate for a moratorium on mechanical inventions, in the belief that mankind has suffered more than it has benefited from technological changes. So far most of this opposition has been confined to talk and writing. Yet it is within the bounds of possibility that, following continued disasters of war, famine, disease, and other social ills, some leader or group of leaders might actually set about putting a legal and moral taboo on science, invention, and technology, on the theory that these cultural elements do more harm than good.

TECHNOLOGY AND INSTITUTIONS

New technological or other devices, whether originating within a society or borrowed from outside, obviously set up a network of effects. In closing this chapter we shall discuss some of the ways in which innovations influence one another and constantly affect the culture and the social structure.

Culture and Technology The influences of innovations are both direct (primary) and indirect (secondary). Direct or primary influences are evident in such an invention as the cotton gin, which almost completely replaced former production techniques. So too, if a state changes from a representative democracy to a totalitarian, one-party system, many former institutions will be liquidated and replaced by others, although some old ways of doing things may continue alongside the new.

The secondary or derivative influences are even more striking. These have to do with the extension of effects to other technologies and institutions or associations. For example, the cotton gin stimulated cotton raising and the large plantation system; it influenced slavery and so had a great effect on political and everyday life, not only of the South but of the North as well.

In recent decades we have witnessed profound modifications in life as a result of the introduction of motor vehicles. The automobile, at first considered a luxury, soon became a routine necessity. To mention only a few of its more obvious effects: It led to the building of hard-surfaced, all-weather roads, which permitted higher speeds. This in turn led to further improvement of highways: the elimination of sharp turns, the construction of superhighways, and so on. And the position of the driver was changed from the right to the left side of the car to permit better control.

New elements in a culture often have far-reaching effects. The automobile may reduce the revenue of the

With muscles, many men: building a dam in China.

railroads and hence influence the consumption of coal. On the other hand, the automobile "causes" an extension of pipelines for oil and increases the consumption of gasoline. The introduction of two items serving the same end, such as gas and electricity for household use, sets up a struggle for dominance. Such competition serves a selective function.

The motor vehicle influenced still other activities. For example, the displacement of draft animals on the farm and in our cities altered the importance of forage crops and pasturage in the rural economy. And the automobile has increased the mobility of people—daily, seasonally, yearly. Because it increased congestion in urban centers, it has encouraged decentralization of population and so affected the growth of suburbs. It has influenced home life, made union school districts possible, and so on and on.

Or take the changes brought about by the radio. As early as 1933, W. F. Ogburn and S. C. Gilfillan indicated at least 150 definite effects of the radio in such categories as uniformity of programs—especially those originating in urban centers—recreation and entertainment, transportation, education, the spread of information, religion, industry and business, occupations, government and politics, and other inventions.[6] Radio and, more recently, television have also brought in new words: *broadcast, newscaster, shortwave, fre-*

6 · W. F. Ogburn and S. C. Gilfillan, "The Influence of Invention and Discovery," *in Recent Social Trends in the United States* (New York: McGraw-Hill Book Co., 1933), pp. 153–157.

Courtesy Jim Jackson

With applied mechanics, a single machine: a road-repairing machine handled by one man to plane rough surfaces, fill in holes, and roll paving smooth in one operation.

quency modulation, televise, high fidelity, and *Telstar.*

With regard to advances in communication and transportation, modern man has not yet fully understood what increased speed through space may mean for future economic and political organization or for human personality itself. Certainly the contraction of space as measured by time may bring about great changes in many of our institutions. One can only imagine the political and social changes that simultaneous worldwide telecasting may bring.

Advances in the biological sciences have also been striking. Medical research, coupled with public health programs, has eliminated contagious and infectious diseases to a degree un-

dreamed of a century ago. The changes influence the age distribution of our population and hence affect our entire social structure.

Nonmaterial changes are also important, because institutional inventions have widespread effects. For example, the juvenile court system, set up in this country about 1899, has had far-reaching influence not only on the care of young delinquents but also on public attitudes toward the delinquent boy or girl. As a result, too, schools are learning to recognize misconduct among their pupils with a view to prevention of delinquency, and parents are changing their attitudes toward control of children. The juvenile court has also broadened the field of social work and instilled new ideas regarding the causes of crime in the minds of many judges and attorneys.

Material and nonmaterial changes influence one another. The nonmaterial effects of mechanical inventions are of varying degrees and kinds. The introduction of the typewriter first changed the habits of clerks, who had formerly used pen and ink. Later, it gave rise to a class of special operatives, mostly unmarried women, many of whom still lived with their parents. This in turn influenced the habits of the family in the home: housework, control of the income of children, and matters of freedom of mobility and outside contacts.

Lag in Application These examples are striking but, again, we must not assume that invention necessarily means use. New devices often fail to become part of our technology or institutions. For example, the recall of judges, which once attracted great public interest, did not persist. So too, as noted above, resistance may long delay otherwise useful changes. With regard to technology, there are other factors to be taken into account. A new instrument or machine must be durable, simple, safe, and economical to install, operate, and repair. Then, also, there must be the materials needed for its manufacture, and nowadays it must be capable of mass production.

The application of knowledge of nuclear physics is an interesting case in point. Its first use in war was not followed by any rapid application to peacetime industry, partly because of its possible use in future wars and partly because of the high cost of building plants and of switching over to this form of power.

In our final chapter, we shall look at the process of social change in American society. We shall attempt to project current institutional patterns into the future and analyze the major social trends of our time, using the framework introduced earlier.

INTERPRETATIVE SUMMARY

No society is completely static. Of course, a culture never accepts all potential innovations, and those that are used enter at varying rates. Need is not the only factor affecting acceptance. Material innovations are always accepted more readily than concomitant changes in basic values and beliefs, regardless of need. Both material and ideological innovations may be resisted because the "run of attention" of the society lies elsewhere. Vested interests, such as business, labor, scientific groups, social classes, or communities, may resist change. In such cases, frequent motivations are fear of losing an investment, prestige, or other security, or simple inability to see that a "farfetched" idea might work. A society's political structures, also having investments to protect or not wishing to alienate the public for other reasons, may resist change. Of course, an innovation may also be rejected because it really is not practical or relevant to a culture!

Cultures are modified in two ways: by invention and by diffusion, wholesale or modified adoption of elements from outside cultures and from subcultures within the society. Invention is stimulated or discouraged by the factors above, as well as by the "cultural" base, which includes the cumulative knowledge, skills, and materials present in a culture at a given time. The scientific method is now an invaluable part of the cultural base of many societies. Diffusion, which is responsible for most cultural change, is affected by the basic factors influencing all innovation and by certain other factors, notably prestige of the lending culture and immigration.

Innovations are likely to have more widespread effects than those that were specifically intended. For example, one material change may cause far-reaching changes in a culture's basic institutions and structures. Conversely, when a material innovation is accepted but necessary changes in institutions are resisted or people are unable to carry out institutional changes quickly enough, a society may undergo a long period of deleterious cultural lag or even become seriously disorganized.

REVIEW AND SUGGESTED READINGS

A · VOCABULARY

Cultural base	Discovery	Run of attention
Cultural lag	Duplicate invention	Technology
Diffusion	Invention	

B · QUESTIONS AND TOPICS FOR REVIEW

1. Show how the following innovations had *indirect* effects in the United States:
   a. paperback book industry
   b. civil rights law of 1964
   c. changes in draft quotas
   d. proliferation of teachers' colleges
   e. increased availability of low-priced American and foreign cars
2. Whose fault is cultural lag?
3. Discuss recent instances of business, labor, or scientific opposition to innovation.
4. Can you think of a recent discovery or invention that was empirical rather than planned? Why are empirically derived innovations rare in the United States?
5. Relate the term *diffusion* to concepts learned in earlier chapters about social processes.
6. Name some material innovations that were not successful in our culture, and discuss reasons for their failure.

C · SUGGESTIONS FOR FURTHER READING

Francis R. Allen, Hornell Hart, Delbert C. Miller, William F. Ogburn, and Meyer F. Nimkoff. *Technology and Social Change*. New York: Appleton-Century-Crofts, Inc., 1957.

A timely discussion of the impact of technology and applied science on social institutions.

Egbert De Vries. *Man in Rapid Social Change*. Garden City, N.Y.: Doubleday & Co., 1961.

A brief, well-organized treatment of a wide range of changes, especially economic modernization. Written for the World Council of Churches, 1961.

Theodosius Dobzhansky. *Mankind Evolving*. New Haven: Yale University Press, 1962.

A sophisticated discussion linking biological and social evolution.

Bert F. Hoselitz and Wilbert E. Moore, eds. *Industrialization and Society*. Paris and The Hague: UNESCO and Mouton, 1963.

A number of sound papers prepared for the UNESCO Conference, 1963.

Ronald Lippitt, Jeanne Watson, and Bruce Westley. *The Dynamics of Planned Change*. New York: Harcourt, Brace & Co., 1958.

A discussion of personal and group planning with strong emphasis on actionism.

Margaret Mead, ed. *Cultural Patterns and Technical Change*. New York: The New American Library of World Literature, Inc., 1955.

A manual prepared by The World Federation for Mental Health for UNESCO. It deals with problems of mental health as related to the impact of modern technology on peoples who have been living in nonindustrialized societies. The basic question, as the editor puts it, is "How can technical change be introduced with such regard for the culture pattern that human values are preserved?"

Wilbert E. Moore. *Social Change*. Englewood Cliffs, N.J.: Prentice-Hall, 1963.

A concise, scholarly discussion of the normality and quality of change. Attention is given to the extent of change and to the process of modernization. Finally, there is an excellent, brief analysis of the long-standing problem of social evolution.

John Eric Norkskog, ed. *Social Change*. New York: McGraw-Hill Book Co., 1960.

A collection of readings on population growth, culture change, and changes in major institutions.

W. F. Ogburn and M. F. Nimkoff. *Technology and the Changing Family*. Boston: Houghton Mifflin Co., 1955.

A descriptive analysis of the impact of technology on familial institutions. The authors state that "a surprisingly large number of changes in family living in the past century or two in the United States can be traced to three clusters of inventions and discoveries, those centering around steam and steel, contraceptives, and scientific discoveries affecting forms of religious beliefs. There are, however, ideological forces producing changes in the family that cannot be adequately traced to technological or scientific origins." (p. iii.)

M. B. Sahlin and E. R. Service. *Evolution and Culture*. Ann Arbor: University of Michigan Press, 1960.

The authors see the long-range view of social evolution as useful background for the study of economic modernization.

W. L. Thomas, Jr., ed. *Man's Role in Changing the Face of the Earth*. Chicago: University of Chicago Press, 1956.

An extensive symposium—there are 52 contributors—covering a wide range of topics, from the biological and physiographic aspects to the social and cultural. The papers were originally given at an international symposium held in June, 1955, at Princeton University under the joint sponsorship of the Wenner-Gren Foundation for Anthropological Research and the National Science Foundation.

George K. Zollschan and Walter Hirsch, eds. *Explorations in Social Change*. Boston: Houghton Mifflin Company, 1964.

Original papers by 31 contributors from several disciplines.

CHAPTER 27

Some Major Social Trends

This book has been devoted to a study of the structure of societies and the consequences of social structure. In closing we come to an analysis of some of the major trends in American society. Many, though not all, of the features of the social structure and culture of the contemporary United States stem from the Industrial Revolution. To the extent that these trends are consequences of the Industrial Revolution, the society we are describing is typical of industrial societies generally.

For a framework useful in examining trends in a large-scale society, we shall employ the universal social functions introduced in Chapter 6: replacement of population, socialization of population, maintenance of sense of purpose, production and distribution of goods and services, and maintenance of order. First, however, let us look briefly at the context in which these trends occur: the reorganization of human society that has come about with industrialization.

A SOCIOLOGICAL VIEW OF THE INDUSTRIAL REVOLUTION

Throughout the greatest part of human history, most workers secured their own raw materials and owned their own tools. They worked under their own roofs on their own time, and themselves gauged their market—that is, they made the decisions as to both the quality and the quantity of what they should produce and sold the finished product to a consumer. Let us look at a worker living before the Industrial Revolution, a guildsman, say, in medieval Europe, a man who lived in a commercial town and made linen.

Such a man secured his own raw materials; he grew flax on the land adjacent to his cottage; he spun the flax into thread on his own spinning wheel and wove the thread into linen cloth on his own loom, under his own roof; he gauged his own market, deciding whether it was better to establish a reputation as a man who made the best linen and got a good price for it but sold only a little or a man from whom you could get linen tomorrow if you needed it at once (and you were likely to need frequent changes because of the quality of the merchandise he turned out). Within limits, he set his own pace; when he was through making his linen, he sold it. Some people came to his shop for purchases. Occasionally he went around the countryside to trade fairs, set up a stand, and marketed his product. He took the money he made, spent it for food and his other needs, grew more flax, spun more thread, wove more linen, and sold it.

This social structure began to

change when an entrepreneur, an individual capitalist, took over some of these operations. What such a man did was to acquire a good deal of raw materials, more than he himself could work on. Instead of growing flax outside his house and owning his own spinning wheel and loom, for example, he purchased more flax than he could possibly process by himself. He then made agreements with a number of cottagers around the countryside, took the flax around and deposited a certain amount of it with each of them, picked up linen they had finished, took it to town, and sold it. And he came back the next week, having taken the proceeds, the money from selling his linen, and bought more flax; he passed this out to his cottagers and picked up what linen they had finished that week, took it to town, and sold it. In other words, the entrepreneur greatly altered what had been the universal system of human work throughout history. Now it was the entrepreneur, not the worker, who secured the raw materials, gauged the market, determined the quality and the quantity of the product. It was he who brought the flax, took the linen, and paid off the workers. He told them whether to produce a great deal of cheap linen or a little excellent linen. And he sold the finished product.

The domestic system (that is, the system under which goods were made in homes) did not last very long—for a very good reason: the entrepreneur was an intelligent, ambitious man. And since he was both intelligent and ambitious, it soon occurred to him that in running from cottage to cottage he was spending a great deal of time that could be spent more productively. So he moved into town. There he took workers from under their own roofs into a big barnlike structure that he had built. This move had certain advantages for the entrepreneur: he could keep his eye on the worker, he could put pressure on him, and he could see that a little more was produced when he needed a little more. Eventually, as the system prospered, a last step was taken. The entrepreneur bought some spinning wheels, put the spinning wheels in the barn, and went out into the country to get more cottagers. They didn't even have to have their own spinning wheels.

Here are many of the essentials of mass production. There are factories, with all the people in one building. A capitalist owns the tools they work with, the roof they work under, and the raw materials. He takes the product and sells it. A labor force in the modern sense of the term has been created. This is what Karl Marx referred to as "the separation of the worker from the means of production."

As a result of this economic revolution, several important alterations occurred in the social structure. For efficiency, people were aggregated. This was the beginning of modern urbanism. Then, with fixed capital, the entrepreneur had money tied up in one place. This cut down his mobility in a way that the domestic system did not. Formerly, if it was not a good year for linen, the entrepreneur who had been running around the countryside picking up his linen and leaving his flax with a cottager had only to take what capital he had accumulated and go into something else. But as soon as he bought the building in town and filled it with spinning wheels, the entrepreneur of the eighteenth century may not have had a great deal of fixed capital by the standards of General Motors, but he had a great deal for those days. He had the beginning of the kind of fixed capital we know today.

With the factory system and fixed capital came another crucial change in the social structure: free labor. Back in the guildsman's day, most of the people in medieval Europe were not free. True, they were not slaves in the sense that we use the term, but they lived under a system of mutual obligation. Serfs belonged to a manor; they had rights in the land. Everybody lived under this obligation system. The baron could not drive the serfs from the land, because they had always lived there. The serfs had to give a certain portion of their labor or produce to the baron because they were allowed to live on the land and got protection from him.

This kind of social order was foreign to a mass-production, fixed-capital economy. In a mass-production economy, people must be able, when the linen business gets bad, to move somewhere else. When there are too many people working in one place and not enough in another, they must be able to go elsewhere. A free laborer is free to work for an employer of his choice. When another entrepreneur offers him more money, he is free to move; he is free to quit—and he is free to starve. This is an essential part of free labor, because the entrepreneur has his money tied up in fixed capital. With money tied up in fixed capital, the easiest cost to reduce is labor cost. The employer can lay off people until he needs more productivity, and then he can hire them again.

Factory production, fixed capital, and free labor—all are characteristics of the industrial revolution; all have consequences in an industrial social order. Against this background, let us examine some of the trends in our industrial society.

REPLACEMENT OF POPULATION

One problem we do *not* have in American society is replacement of personnel. If we have a problem, it is

FIGURE 37 · U.S. Census—20 Year Forecast *

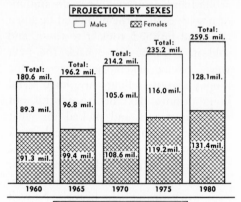

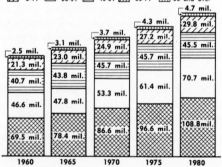

* The *New York Times*, August 12, 1962, IV, 9. By permission.

The United States Census Bureau has issued new predictions for 1980, by which time it sees a population of 259, 584, 000 if the present fertility rate continues—as it has for five years—at 179 births a year for every 1,000 women of childbearing capability. The charts above are based on this rate and show projections by sexes and age groups. Should the fertility rate drop to 154 per 1,000 women, its 1949–51 level, the prediction is for an increase in the population to 245,736,000.

TABLE 42 · Population Growth by Age Groups in the United States, 1955–1970 *

July 1	MILLION PERSONS								
	Under 5	5 to 9	10 to 14	15 to 19	20 to 24	25 to 34	35 to 44	45 to 60	60 & Over
1955	19.1	17.2	13.3	11.2	10.8	24.2	22.8	26.8	20.8
1960	20.8	19.2	17.2	13.4	11.3	22.8	24.0	29.2	23.0
	Projections								
1965	22.0	20.8	19.2	17.3	13.5	22.5	24.3	31.5	25.4
1970	25.0	22.1	20.9	19.3	17.3	25.2	23.0	33.6	28.2

July 1	PER CENT INCREASE IN 5 YEARS								
	Under 5	5 to 9	10 to 14	15 to 19	20 to 24	25 to 34	35 to 44	45 to 60	60 & Over
1955	11.6	29.0	19.7	4.8	−7.3	+0.9	+5.8	8.3	12.8
1960	8.8	11.7	29.0	19.8	5.0	−5.5	+5.1	9.2	10.9
	Projections								
1965	6.0	8.8	11.6	28.8	19.4	−1.3	+1.3	7.7	10.3
1970	13.4	6.0	8.7	11.6	28.4	+12.0	−5.3	6.7	11.2

* Adapted from *Population Changes in the Coming Decade* (pamphlet published by Sears, Roebuck and Company, based on data from the United States Bureau of the Census), October 25, 1960, pp. 6, 8. By permission.

whether the *production and distribution* of goods and services can keep up with our population growth—or how to maintain order if we fail to sustain the level of living our citizenry has come to expect. As can be seen in Figure 37, the rate of increase in population in the United States is running 8 to 9 percent for a five-year period. Also pertinent to the projected rate of growth is the fact that the largest percentage of increases during the past decade have been in the age categories that will comprise people entering childbearing age during the coming two decades (see Table 42). Unless some factor causes a delay in the number of marriages, as World War II did, the number of marriages per year is directly related to the proportion of the total population entering childbearing age.

Such a rate of increase doubles a population within four decades, which means that we are doing so well at the replacement of population that unless everything we do in the production and distribution of goods and services is doubled within forty years, we will lower our level of living.

SOCIALIZATION OF NEW POPULATION

The growth of population is impressive, but we are increasing even more dramatically the amount of formal education we give to people and the number of people to whom we give it. The best index we have of this

FIGURE 38 · Growth of School-age Population in the United States, 1960–1969 *

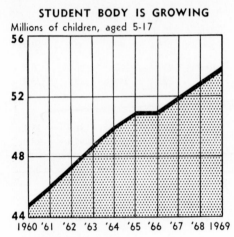

STUDENT BODY IS GROWING

Millions of children, aged 5-17

* The *New York Times*, February 26, 1961, E7. By permission.

FIGURE 39 · Increase in Number of Teachers Needed in the United States, 1960–1969 *

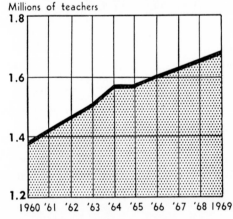

MORE TEACHERS ARE NEEDED

Millions of teachers

* *Ibid.* Projection is by Committee on Economic Development. It assumes teacher-pupil ratio will remain constant.

is the proportion of the population aged eighteen and nineteen that are in school. This was 19 percent in 1920—with a much smaller population. It was 25 percent in 1930, a fast rate of growth even in comparison with the rate of

FIGURE 40 · Increase in Cost of Education in the United States, 1960–1969 *

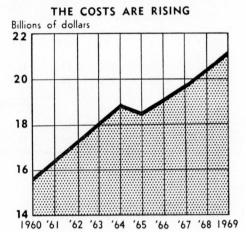

THE COSTS ARE RISING

Billions of dollars

* *Ibid.* Projection is based on the assumption of a 2 percent annual increase in teachers' salaries and stable prices.

population increase. By 1940, 29 percent of the people aged eighteen and nineteen in the United States were enrolled in school. By 1950 the percentage was 32, and now it is 35.

In 1900 one person out of twenty-five who was of college age was in college. Now it is one in four. More than half the high-school graduates in the United States now go on to college.

The consequences of this enormous increase in formal education can be seen in Figure 38, which indicates that the number of children in school will increase by nearly ten million during the 1960's. This will be accompanied, of course, by an increased need for teachers (Figure 39) and increased expenditures for education (Figure 40).

A college education is no longer considered merely polish for an elite minority (see Figure 41). It is a requirement for a middle-class member of the labor force. With automation, this will be even more true. Automation cuts the need for some kinds of

FIGURE 41 · Distribution and Trends in Bachelor's Degrees Awarded *

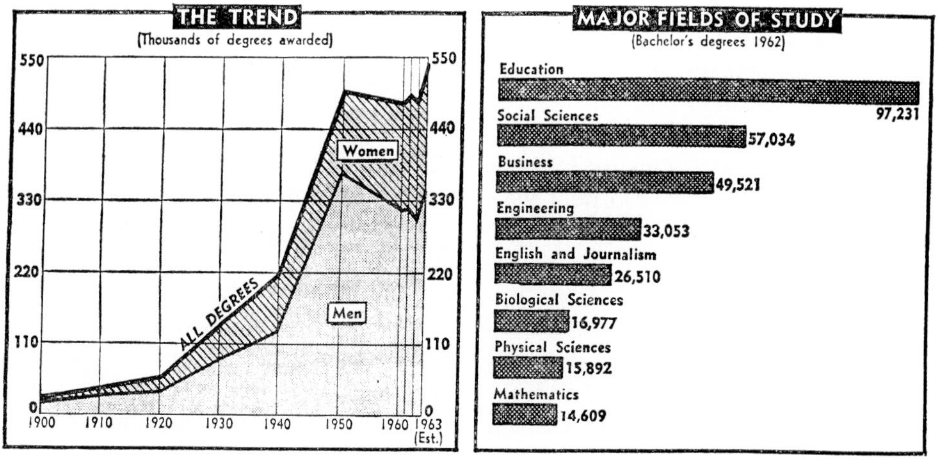

* The *New York Times*, June 16, 1963, E9.

workers in the labor force, but it increases the need for others. What we need less and less is unskilled laborers. What we need more and more is white-collar workers. In other words, a large proportion of the labor force may be composed of minor managers and executives. Certainly automation is not going to reduce the trend toward more education for a larger proportion of the population.

MAINTENANCE OF A
SENSE OF PURPOSE [1]

In a large-scale economy, as in a small one, early socialization, crucial to the development of a sense of purpose, is a function primarily of the familial structure. Young people must learn what is right and wrong, what the social expectations are, and a large share of this socialization occurs in the fam-

1 · An earlier form of this section appeared in an article by Raymond W. Mack, "Social Consequences of Occupational Specialization," in *The National Elementary Principal*, May, 1961, 40:10–13. The material was first used as part of a speech.

ily. But one consequence of the Industrial Revolution is that, while mothers and fathers still provide models for much behavior, children no longer learn the norms of work in the family. The separation of place of work from place of residence (a consequence of the requirements of a mass production line, with the resulting fixed capital) removes working fathers from the view of their children. In the English textile mills in the early days of the Industrial Revolution, when workers and their families lived beneath the factory roof, children learned to spin and weave from their parents. But the boy who helped his father homestead a farm now has a grandson majoring in soil chemistry at Iowa State.

"Daddy goes to work." In most societies throughout most of human history, Daddy didn't go to work, because work was right there where Daddy was. The reason he goes to work now is that he is a specialist who contributes his knowledge or his acquired skill to making one part of one part of a product. Few people in our labor force can point to a finished product and say, "I made that." So Daddy's skill can be used only on an assembly line, whether it is a production or an intellectual staff line, and he has to go join other men in a work environment separated from their places of residence where they can pool their skills. Most children do not see their fathers earning a living, because "Daddy goes to work."

Contrast this with a nonindustrial society, where the men get up every morning and go out to fish and the women get up and garden. What happens to little boys or little girls in such a society? They play until they are four or five years old, as little boys and girls should. When a boy is about six years old, he starts going out on the boat with his father and his uncles as a general handyman. He gets in the way, as six-year-old boys will, but he helps a little, too. He can hand them this or that, and he watches what is going on. By the time he is eight years old he knows enough to help mend nets. By the time he is ten years old, he is beginning to learn where the good fishing spots are and to be able to tell what kind of weather is good for fishing. At twelve he not only knows how to repair his father's boat, but he has worked on it enough to know how to build one himself. At about fourteen he goes through a ceremony at the end of which he is told, "You are now a man!" He is ready to get on the boat the next morning and go to work with the other adults. He doesn't have to be sent to a naval college; he doesn't take any courses in bait-cutting. He already knows the job. He has been living with it for years.

His little sister, meanwhile, is helping sweep the hearth when she is seven.

She helps grind the maize by the time she is nine and prepare food by the time she is twelve. She knows about planting seasons and harvesting seasons. By the time she is fourteen and old enough to get married, she is long past the need for a course in home economics. She has had that course at home.

These things do not happen in our society. Most children in our society have very little idea of what Daddy does when he goes to work. They just know that he goes and he comes back. As a matter of fact, not only do most children not know what their fathers do, but neither do many wives know exactly. When sociological research involves interviews in a district where factory workers live, it is not at all unusual to have something like the following conversation between interviewer and housewife:

"What does your husband do?"

"He's at the Ford plant."

"What does he do there?"

"He works over at the Ford plant —you know."

"Is he on the assembly line, is he a machine operator, is he a supply man?"

"I don't know. He's worked over at the Ford plant for ten years now."

Under such circumstances, one can hardly expect the youth in a specialized economy to be able to walk out of adolescence into an adult occupational role; they have had no chance to learn how to be adult members of the labor force in practice or in imitation.

Similar, if less striking, is the impact of occupational specialization on educational institutions, particularly on the functions of formal educational structures. The same thing is happening in the school that has happened in the family. The school is an important factor in socialization, of course, but there seems to be a trend away from, rather than toward, its being a finishing school in *occupational* socialization. Our lawyer friends tell us that they *really* learned their profession in their post-graduate stints as clerks in law firms. What happens to the boy who graduates from the shop curriculum in a technical high school? He becomes, not a welder, but a welder's *apprentice* on a construction gang. Often we praise corporations that encourage students to get a broad general educational base and let the company teach them the details of the job. We laud such firms for their enlightened dedication to the liberal arts, when what they are really dedicated to is the quite rational assumption that, given the complicated network of social expectations engendered by pooling the skills of specialists in a complex organization, the agency best equipped to socialize one into that network is that organization.

To the extent that one gains a sense of purpose from his work, then the family and the school in an industrial society have lost the function of providing a sense of purpose. The large organizations which provide "on the job" socialization are now responsible for that function to some extent. Two questions are pertinent: (1) to what extent *does* one rely on his work to give him a sense of purpose? and (2) just how well has the industrial system succeeded in providing a sense of purpose?

The answer to the first question is that occupational specialization contributes a good share to what we call the impersonality of urban life. People in urban-industrial societies have seg-

mentalized roles. One may be an assembly-line worker, a Methodist, a Grand Vizier at the lodge, a father, a member of the bowling team. No one of these bears the same necessary relationship to another that the roles filled by a tribesman in an unspecialized society do. In a society which has not felt the impact of technology, one need only know a man's clan membership to predict his occupation, his religion, or his educational attainment. Among the roles which a man plays in an urban-industrial society, occupation is crucial. It is more specialized than most of his roles; he has an enormous investment in it. An adult male in our labor force spends more of his waking hours at work than at home; his work is likely to be a powerful factor in shaping his view of the world. Moreover, his community judges him largely according to the prestige of his occupation; he *is* what he *does*.

In order to answer the second question, let us look at the structure of large organizations. Whether they are voluntary associations, business firms, or whole societies, groups reach a critical point beyond which face-to-face communication and differentiation without stratification are no longer possible. As groups pass this critical point of complexity, they must assume formally organized hierarchical structures. Such structures, of course, make for more rigidly specified roles.

Recently Adolph Berle, Jr.,[2] called attention to a social problem that occurs when a conflict in values leads to friction between the economic institution and the maintenance of a sense of

2 · See *Power Without Property: A New Development in American Political Economy* (New York: Harcourt, Brace & Co., 1959).

purpose. Ownership and proprietorship, which have traditionally been parallel, are becoming separate occupational specialties. This trend is probably the source of much of the complaining about "the organization man" —when a complex organization has socialized replacements to perform its specialized roles, it is not likely to be tolerant of deviance. While such a man has the prestige that goes along with wearing a white collar, there are plenty of white collars above him.

Such a situation, if unrelieved by compensations, would not seem to lead to a sense of purpose. However, individuals have a way of "building in" compensations. Such a bureaucratic division of labor through a whole society leads to what some sociologists have called *situses*—sets of related occupational specialties arranged hierarchically and separated from other sets of related roles, which also are arranged in hierarchies. Each situs or family of related occupations builds up a set of norms peculiar to it. These occupational subcultures insulate their participants from the members of another situs. Doctors and nurses hold values not shared by railroaders and truck drivers; the occupational norms of longshoremen are not those of laboratory workers.

Societies with elaborate occupational differentiation, therefore, while bound together by a common culture, are at the same time fragmented by occupational subcultures. People who share an occupational history develop norms, enforce an in-group ideology, and come to serve as a reference group for one another. We see this at its extreme when physicists from the Soviet Union and from the United States have more to talk about with one another than either group has with the farmers from its own country.

But let us remember that role segmentalization is not synonymous with a fragmented social structure. The stuff of occupational subcultures can serve as the specialized urban-industrial worker's social substitute for community. Occupational codes can contribute to what Durkheim called organic solidarity; they can help replace the mechanical solidarity of the rural village. Occupational groups, with their shared values, can contribute to the sense of purpose which formerly was a function of the small community.

PRODUCTION AND DISTRIBUTION OF GOODS AND SERVICES

Consider the following office rules, posted in this country in 1872 by Zachary U. Geiger, sole proprietor of the Mount Cory Carriage and Wagon Works.[3]

1. *Office employees will daily sweep the floors, dust the furniture, shelves and showcases.*

2. *Each clerk will bring in a bucket of water and a scuttle of coal for the day's business.*

3. *Clerks will each day fill lamps, clean chimneys, trim wicks. Wash the windows once a week.*

4. *Make your pens carefully. You may whittle nibs to your individual taste.*

5. *This office will open at 7 A.M. and close at 8 P.M. daily, except on the Sabbath, on which day it will remain closed.*

6. *Men employees will be given an evening off each week for courting purposes, or two evenings a week if they go regularly to church.*

3 · "So you think you'd prefer the GOOD OLD DAYS," pamphlet published by State Farm Mutual Insurance Co., Bloomington, Ill., 1960. By permission.

7. *Every employee should lay aside from each pay a goodly sum of his earnings for his benefits during his declining years, so that he will not become a burden upon the charity of his betters.*

8. *Any employee who smokes Spanish cigars, uses liquor in any form, gets shaved at a barber shop, or frequents pool or public halls, will give me good reason to suspect his worth, intentions, integrity, and honesty.*

9. *The employee who has performed his labors faithfully and without fault for a period of five years in my service, and who has been thrifty and attentive to his religious duties, is looked upon by his fellowmen as a substantial and law abiding citizen, will be given an increase of five cents per day in his pay, providing a just return in profits from the business permits it.*

Certainly the Industrial Revolution has brought drastic changes in economic institutions. With 7 percent of the world's land area and only 6 percent of its population, the United States produces more than one-third of the world's goods. The average work week has been reduced by about one-third in this century, while production per man hour has tripled. Women constituted about 20 percent of the labor force in 1900; they now account for one-third. During the past sixty years, family income has increased two and a half times in purchasing power. During the same period, the proportion of Americans who own their own homes has increased from one in three to three in five.

These changes have been accompanied by corporate concentration, by the separation of ownership from control in American industry. Most of the functions which used to be performed by an entrepreneur—an owner-proprietor—are now performed by a salaried manager. The large individual business is owned, not by one man who can run it but, as some of the institutional advertising tells us, by millions of people. The stockholders among whom this diversified ownership is spread do own their companies. But they delegate control of the corporation to salaried management. The *owners* of the corporation do not dominate it as individuals. As a matter of fact, we have here a sort of collectivization of ownership. It is voluntary and so is extremely different from state collectivization; but it is collectivization nonetheless. In some respects, the differences in the occupational role of the manager of a Russian factory and of an American factory are not as extreme as they seem at first glance. The difference is in the position of the citizenry so far as freedom is concerned. But modern industrial systems, no matter what their economic norms and political goals, are staffed and run by salaried managers.

Another economic trend with implications for the labor force is automation, which we may define as mechanization to the point where machines run other machines. Most of our engineering technology in the last century and a half has been put to inventing and perfecting machines that produce a product—that is, production machines. It is only recently that we have developed machines that will do such formerly expensive and time-consuming tasks as quality testing and readjustment of the production line machine. With a whole factory automated, fixed capital will take on new meaning.

By the standards of an automated economy, our present fixed capital is inadequate. The Industrial Revolution is just beginning. The concept of fixed capital brings to mind huge factories, with big steel machines that cannot be picked up and moved. Think of the meaning of fixed capital when one machine is running another machine, so that the greatest expense is not turning out the product but stopping the machine. Here fixed capital reaches the point where the costliest thing one can do is cease production. A stable market, a steady demand, become essential.

MAINTENANCE OF ORDER

Finally, and perhaps most important for an understanding of industrial society, is a trend that sociologists describe as movement from status to contract. In medieval times the serfs had the land because of their status, because of who they were. A baron was a baron for the same reason: his grandfather had been a baron, and it was his right. The serfs owed him certain obligations and he owed them certain obligations, not because of some peculiar training they had had, not because of achievement, but because each man was born into his status. The whole society was structured on ascribed statuses.

By the time the cottagers were moved into town to work in factories, this structure was crumbling. No longer did people owe these kinds of obligations simply because of the positions they occupied. The nearest thing to the old system in an industrial situation is the small one-company town that survives for generations. Here the owner is the grandson of the original owner; the odds are that the foreman is the grandson of the original foreman and that many of the laborers are grandchildren of the original laborers. Everybody knows everybody else;

people speak to one another on the street; and everybody knows what church everybody goes to and whose daughter is being courted by whose son. Suppose a worker in this kind of situation falls ill. There is no unemployment compensation. But none is needed, because a system of mutual obligations exists. When a man is ill, the owner's wife comes by with a basket of groceries and asks if there is anything she can do to help, and a couple of people who work with him will have their wives or daughters over helping nurse him. People will send him pies and cakes, and a month later, when he has recovered, he returns to his job. This is a status system, a system of mutual obligations. In a larger economy, in which most people work for big organizations, contracts are substituted for this kind of status system. We do not expect Mrs. Henry Ford to be running around with a basket of groceries to the home of an unskilled laborer who is sick. Instead, the government arranges a contract substitute.

Wherever there is a social need which the baron would have met for the serfs or the serfs would have filled for one another, the trend is toward having the government contract an obligation.

We are no longer a society of rural villages and independent entrepreneurs. The economic and political institutions of an urban-industrial society are inextricably interwoven because, in the shift from status to contract as a principle of social organization, a wage contract alone replaces only a small part of the total system of mutual obligations. The history of our learning to live with urbanization and industrialization is a history of the process of negotiating supplementary contracts. We start with a wage contract, but we supplement it with a Social Security contract, an unemployment insurance contract, and so on. This is the method which industrial societies—democratic or totalitarian, capitalist or socialist—have devised as a substitute for the mutual-obligation system found where institutions tend to be coterminous—where familial, economic, and political functions derive from the same group.

The question is not whether such supplementary contracts will exist in an industrial social order, but how to maintain a maximum of individual freedom in the context of the change from status to contract.

INTERPRETATIVE SUMMARY

The Industrial Revolution has had a profound effect on the major social functions. First, obviously, it has influenced the production and distribution of services. As domestic industry gave way to the entrepreneur and finally the corporate system, in which ownership and management are separated, productivity per man and employee income have increased and working conditions have improved, while hours in the work week have gradually decreased. Automation, the industrial system in which machines run machines, is already demanding increased amounts of fixed capital and bringing further changes in the way this basic function is carried out.

Next, paradoxically, the free enterprise system has led to increased government control over employer-employee relations. Though workers are free to leave a job and employers free to make dismissals, for the term of employment the two interests are required to make contracts for every obligation which in earlier times would have been fulfilled by each as a matter of status.

In an industrial-urban economy, where the father works away from home, individual sense of purpose or lack of it is greatly dependent on how one views himself as worker. The hierarchical structure of large corporations, especially the management structures, would seem at first glance to stifle creativity, freedom, and thus dignity. However, stratification has also led to the development of situses, occupational "in-groups."

The Industrial Revolution has even affected the function of socialization of population. The United States has more of its population in school than ever before, despite the fact that the population itself is growing larger. The increase in numbers attending college is especially striking, and is undoubtedly partly accounted for by the fact that large organizations want and are in a position to demand white-collar workers who have college educations.

REVIEW AND SUGGESTED READINGS

A · VOCABULARY

Automation	Entrepreneur
Domestic system	Industrial Revolution

B · QUESTIONS AND TOPICS FOR REVIEW

1. What does the word *entrepreneur* popularly mean today? Does the word have a good or a bad connotation?

2. One problem that has been a result of our expanding population is the shortage of teachers. What incentives have been provided by school districts to make teaching attractive?

3. What may be the future of an individual who graduates from college with a liberal arts degree?

4. Why are many college students unsure about what "major" to choose, even when such a choice is imminent?

5. Discuss specific ways in which workers—on any level—go about developing a sense of purpose. How do employers try to foster this feeling in their workers?

6. Discuss the pros and cons to the question of lowering the hours in the "work week" still further. What are some of the arguments presented by various unions? Have any groups of laborers succeeded in lowering the work week? Do you think that this is the start of a trend?

C • SUGGESTIONS FOR FURTHER READING

Lyman Bryson, ed. *An Outline of Man's Knowledge of the Modern World.* New York: McGraw-Hill Book Co., 1960.

A fascinating compilation of summaries of knowledge in various disciplines, including an excellent analysis by S. M. Lipset of trends in American society.

Clifford Geertz. *Old Societies and New States.* New York: The Free Press of Glencoe, 1963.

A fine theoretical analysis of the sociology of emerging nations.

William J. Goode. *World Revolution and Family Patterns.* New York: The Free Press of Glencoe, 1963.

An important contribution to the sociological understanding of institutional change.

Seymour Martin Lipset. *The First New Nation.* New York: Basic Books, Inc., 1964.

An excellent analysis of the roots and consequences of tension in American culture between the values of individual liberty and equality of opportunity.

Robert K. Merton, Leonard Broom, and Leonard S. Cottrell, Jr., eds. *Sociology Today: Problems and Prospects.* New York: Basic Books, Inc., 1959.

A collection of papers by leading sociologists on the major issues and prospects in each of the several specialties in sociology.

Robin M. Williams, Jr. *American Society: A Sociological Interpretation,* 2nd ed. New York: Alfred A. Knopf, Inc., 1960.

A survey of major groups and institutions of American society.

SUMMARY OF PART IV

In the final section of this book we have discussed deviant behavior, social change, and some major social trends. Chapter 25 presented a brief discussion of deviations from the norms in our contemporary society. These range from problems of mental deficiency and mental disorders which involve both hereditary and environmental factors—that is, which are biosocial in origin—to the more strictly socially and culturally determined, such as suicide, drug addiction, alcoholism, and crime.

The process of social change was the topic of Chapter 26, where the place of invention, discovery, and diffusion of new elements in culture was examined.

The last chapter took a look into the future. Using the five universal functions introduced in Chapter 7 as our framework, we have attempted, within the context of the Industrial Revolution, some projections of the social order in the United States for the next few decades.

Glossary

Accommodation Used in two senses: As a condition, a state of equilibrium between individuals or groups in which certain working arrangements have been agreed on or accepted. As a process, the social adjustment between individuals or groups, aimed at the temporary suspension of conflict. Also called "antagonistic co-operation." Some common forms of accommodation are tolerant participation, compromise, arbitration, and conciliation.

Acculturation The merging of two or more cultures, ranging from accommodative arrangements to full assimilation or synthesis of cultures. The entire sequence of processes involved in the contact and subsequent intermixture of the traits and patterns of two or more cultures.

Aggregate A number of persons who are classified together because they share some characteristic, but who do not necessarily interact with one another.

Alternatives, cultural Various possibilities of action with reference to the same object, situation, or problem, all of which are approved by the society in question. In other words, the individual has a choice among a number of permitted courses of action.

Amalgamation The biological union of previously distinct racial or subracial groups.

Animism The belief that all things, animate and inanimate, are endowed with personal power or souls.

Anomie A condition of society marked by normlessness or lack of values and goals; characteristic of some members of mass society.

Assimilation The fusion of divergent habits, attitudes, and ideas of two or more groups or societies into a common set of habits, attitudes, and ideas.

Association A general term to describe a group of interacting persons; sometimes used to mean a consciously formed group, usually of a secondary sort. Also used to designate a special-interest group—for example, a trade association.

Attitude The predisposition or tendency to react typically towards an object, situation, or value; usually accompanied by feelings and emotions.

Audience A group in physical contiguity all of whose members are subject to the same stimuli. (*See* Crowd.)

Bureaucracy An organization for administering a formal structure, characterized by rules, a hierarchy of offices, and centralized authority.

Capital goods Those economic goods or forms of wealth used in the production of consumer goods.

Caste A closed, endogamous category resulting from stratification in which status in a hierarchy of power relations is defined and permanently fixed by ancestry.

Caucasoid race One of the three major biological divisions of man (*homo sapiens*), commonly known as the white race.

Censorship The regulation and control of writing, speaking, or any other form of communication according to group-accepted codes.

Class A category resulting from stratification in which the status, while often determined at birth or during early life, is not so completely or irrevocably fixed as in caste.

Club A formally organized congeniality group.

Community A group living in a given locality or region under the same culture and having a distinctive geographical focus for their major activities.

Competition The act of striving for some object that is sought for by others at the same time; a contention of two or more persons or groups for the same object or goal.

Conflict Direct and open antagonistic struggle of persons or groups for the same object or end. The aim of the conflict is the annihilation, defeat, or subjection of the other person or group as a way of obtaining the goal.

Congeniality group A group which is formed and persists simply because friendships arise out of repeated association and shared interests or experiences.

Conjugal family A form of family organization in which the typical household consists only of parents and their dependent children.

Consanguine family A form of family organization in which several generations make up a single household.

Consensus General accord or agreement in matters of opinion, belief, values, and attitudes.

Consumers' goods Economic goods or wealth produced for direct consumption, not for the production of other goods.

Co-operation Joint action or working or playing together for an object or end which may be shared; mutual aid.

Crowd A number of persons whose interaction is of brief duration and low intensity. The members are in physical contiguity but seldom share the specific focus typical of an audience. (*See* Mob.)

Cultural lag A condition of disequilibrium arising out of an unequal or uneven rate of change in two or more cultural elements which are functionally interrelated.

Cultural learning Learning which is predetermined by the culture patterns of a group or society.

Culture The shared, learned behavior patterns which are a precipitate of social interaction.

Culture pattern Two or more separate units or traits of culture organized into some more or less constant form of configuration.

Culture system Those larger and more or less integrated patterns of culture which characterize a given society or civilization—for example, Oriental as contrasted with Occidental, or Classical as compared with Medieval.

Culture trait A unit or feature of a culture pattern used in the description and analysis of that culture.

Definition of the situation An individual's perception of an object or feature of the environment which influences his attitudes, ideas, emotions, and actions. It is related to anticipatory reactions or expectancies. Such a prior definition may be culturally or individually determined.

Demography The statistical study of human populations with particular reference to birth and death rates, age and sex composition, and economic, educational, class, and other distributive aspects of the members of a society.

Deviant behavior Action or response which departs from or runs counter to the norm and the accepted and expected ways of a group or society.

Differentiation The process of developing different sets of rights and duties associated with various statuses. These rest on differences in age, sex, class, intelligence, occupation, and so on.

Diffusion The spread in space of culture patterns from one society to another.

Discovery The perception of relations among elements not previously recognized or understood.

Division of labor A concept used in the discussion of social organization to refer to the differentiation of roles.

Ecology The study which deals with the mutual and interacting relations of organisms and their environment. Human ecology deals with the spatial distribution of populations and their culture as these are affected by invasion, succession, segregation, centralization, and related processes.

Elite The dominant, prestige-bearing and prestige-receiving group or class within a larger society.

Endogamy Marriage within the tribe, class, or group.

Esteem The evaluation of an individual's role behavior in a given status; the judgment of his fellows of how well he fulfills the expectations of his role.

Ethnic category A number of people originally associated with a particular geographic area and sharing a common cultural heritage.

Ethnocentrism Belief that one's race, society, or culture is superior to all others; the tendency to judge other cultures by the standards prevalent in one's own.

Ethos Those predominant characteristics of a whole culture system which distinguish it from other culture systems.

Exogamy Marriage outside the tribe, class, or group.

Fecundity The potential capacity for reproduction.

Fertility Indication of the actual use of powers of fecundity; measured by the rate of reproduction.

Folk society A social structure characterized by a small number of people living in relative isolation; the entire society tends toward being a primary group, with such cultural features as familism, a strong sense of unity, and informal sanctions.

Folkways Norms which can be violated without stringent punishment; minor rules of behavior.

Function The activity or consequence associated with a structure.

Group Two or more people in a state of social interaction.

Headship A position of dominance and control of a group or organization which is conferred by some outside power and usually associated with some predetermined office.

Heredity Transmission of physical traits from parents to offspring through biological mechanisms, involving genes and chromosomes.

In-group Any group or society toward which a person has a strong sense of belonging and of common ends; developed by identification. The opposite of out-group.

Institution A set of related folkways and mores integrated around a principal function of the society.

Intelligence quotient An index of intelligence or learning ability which is computed by dividing the mental age—as determined by a standardized test of intelligence—by the chronological age.

Interaction Action and/or communication between individuals involving reciprocal stimulation and response. Relationship set up between two or more people in regard to each other or in regard to some object or situation.

Invention A combination of known elements or devices into some new form.

Isolation State of separation, segregation, or detachment. May be geographic, cultural, or psychological.

Labor force That fraction of a society's population which is engaged in producing and distributing goods and services for remuneration.

Laissez faire Literally, to let people do as they please or choose. In economics, a theory that economic behavior should not be regulated by governmental or other community controls or interferences.

Leadership A status of dominance and prestige acquired by ability to control, initiate, or set the pattern of behavior for others.

Legend A form of social myth based, in part, on historical fact, dealing chiefly with heroes and events related to the successes and failures of a group or society.

478 · Sociology and Social Life

Lethal selection The differential selectivity of certain diseases or conditions with respect to the death rate.

Life chances The odds for or against an individual's having any given experience, as they are influenced by his class status.

Longevity Length of life, determined by both hereditary and environmental conditions. Demography is concerned chiefly with variations in the average longevity of given groups, not with the *span of life* of any particular individual.

Magic A practice believed to produce effects by the assistance of supernatural beings or by a mastery of secret forces in nature.

Marginal man A person who participates in two different cultures without being totally accepted in either.

Mass society Modern populations which are characterized chiefly by secondary-group contacts, by high specialization of role and status, by anonymity, high mobility, and impersonal relationships generally. (*See Anomie;* Urbanism.)

Matrilineal The family form in which descent is traced through the mother's lineage.

Maturation Changes in tissues and organs of the body which take place as the individual gets older and which occur without learning or conscious effort.

Migration The movement of individuals or groups in space.

Minority A number of persons defined as a social category and excluded from full participation in the culture.

Mob An emotionally aroused crowd with some purpose such as attack on a person, a group, or property; or such as escape from danger—for example, a panic crowd.

Mobility, social Movement from status to status within the social structure.

Monogamy The marriage form in which the norms require the union of one man and one woman.

Mongoloid race One of the three major biological divisions of man (*homo sapiens*), commonly known as the yellow race.

Mores Norms the violation of which results in severe sanctions; rules which have strong moral meaning.

Mortality The death rate; usually computed as the number of persons per thousand who die in a given year.

Myths Stories and descriptions, largely of an imaginative nature, which provide a group with the meaning of their life and culture. Myths represent the fundamental beliefs, convictions, and values of a group.

Negroid race One of the three major biological divisions of man (*homo sapiens*), commonly known as the Negro race.

Neolithic age Literally, "new stone" age; the period of polished stone implements and domestication of plants and animals.

Neurosis A mild mental disorder which interferes with effective and normally expected behaviors. It is illustrated by compulsive habits, undue anxieties, and dissociative responses.

Nonliterate A term applied to a level of culture marked by simple technologies, relatively simple social organization, and lack of written language.

Norms Group-shared expectations. (*See* Social control.)

Opinion Conviction, not necessarily based on positive knowledge, about some person or object.

Organization A formally ordered group which differs from a club in being deliberately formed with reference to a specific goal.

Out-group Any group or society toward which a person feels a strong sense of avoidance or opposition. Opposite of in-group.

Paleolithic age Literally, "old stone" age; the earliest period of man and culture, usually divided into Lower and Upper. Corresponds roughly to the Pleistocene of geology.

Particularism The tendency to explain complex events or situations by some single, particular cause.

Patrilineal The family form in which descent is traced through the father's lineage.

Pattern The recurrent regularities in behavior on which prediction rests.

Personal-social learning Learning from social interaction which is not predetermined by culturalized habits and attitudes but which grows out of more or less natural interactions of persons.

Personality Totality of habits, attitudes, ideas, and characteristics of an individual which grow out of the interplay between his constitutional make-up and his role and status in the various groups of which he is a member and which determine his sense of self.

Pleistocene The geological period just before the present, or Holocene, in which are found the beginnings of man and his culture. Marked by successive glaciation and retreats of the ice in the Northern Hemisphere.

Polyandry The marriage form in which the norms permit the union of one woman with two or more men.

Polygyny The marriage form in which the norms permit the union of one man with two or more women. (Popularly known as "polygamy.")

Power structure The distribution and use of power in a given group or society.

Prejudice Culturally predetermined, biased attitude toward or conception of a person or group.

Prestige The evaluation of a status; the judgment within a society's norms of the desirability of a given status.

Primary group Basic social group operating through intimate, face-to-face contacts. The source of the early personal-social and cultural training which the individual receives from others; for example, the family, neighborhood, and play group.

Process A series of changes taking place through time in a definite manner; the dynamics which occur in a structure, function, or pattern.

Propaganda Open or veiled suggestions and other means of inducing modification or acceptance of certain beliefs, attitudes, and practices.

Psychosis A severe and usually specific mental disorder which so seriously interferes with normal behaviors as to warrant nursing or medical care, either enforced or voluntary.

Psychosomatic Referring to neurotic responses characterized by both psychic and somatic features, the latter being revealed in malfunctions of various organs or parts of the body, as in hypertension, peptic ulcers, skin allergies, and so on.

Public An aggregation of individuals, not necessarily contiguous in space or time, held together through some more or less common interest or common stimulus.

Race A main biological division of the human species the members of which have several physical traits in common. There are usually a number of "composite" and sub-races with somewhat distinctive physical characteristics within the larger categories. Race is often confused with society and culture.

Region A large area possessing considerable geographic and cultural unity.

Regionalism A theory of, as well as a program regarding, the place of the region within the larger society of which it is a part.

Resource A potential good or service, determined largely by the state of the culture and the social expectancies.

Role The function of a status; the expectations which are a consequence of occupying a given position in a social structure.

Sanctions The rewards or punishments used to enforce the norms in a society.

Secondary group Group founded on conscious common interest, not necessarily dependent on face to-face relations. Many secondary groups are related to institutions—for example, state, church, and education.

Self The sense of individuality built up from drives and cycles of activity as they become associated with role-taking, with getting status, and with learning to view one's habits, attitudes, and ideas as other people do. (*See* Personality.)

Sibling One of two or more children of the same parents; not necessarily of the same birth or sex.

Social category A number of persons sharing some innate characteristic which is socially defined and which, therefore, alters their life chances.

Social class *See* Class.

Social control Power over members of a group through group-accepted codes, or power over a smaller group by a larger, more inclusive group.

Social distance Term to express the idea of gradation of one's own group and its values with respect to those of another group; measured by the degree of acceptance and intimacy of contact.

Social expectancy The belief or expectation that another or others will perform a certain act or take a particular attitude; developed from anticipatory responses built up in social interaction.

Social mobility *See* Mobility.

Social norms *See* Norms.

Social organization More or less standardized or conventionalized form or structure of group life.

Social process Mode of action, operation, or interaction among individuals or groups.

Social role *See* Role.

Social status *See* Status.

Socialization The interactional process by which the individual learns the social-cultural qualities (habits, ideas, attitudes, and so on) that make him a member of society and hence a human being. (*See* Cultural learning; Personal-social learning.)

Society The general term for men living in social interaction. More specifically, the largest social group or aggregate in which more or less common culture patterns are found, covering the fundamental institutions.

Sociology The scientific study of the social aspects of human life; the analysis of the structure of social life—the way in which groups are put together—and the way in which they function.

Specialization A differentiated role based on special knowledge and skill.

Specialties, cultural Particular aspects of behavior which characterize members of special-

ized groups within a larger society; an aspect of complex division of labor.

Status A position in a social structure.

Stereotype A group-accepted but logically false image or concept, usually expressed as a cliché, with which is associated a strong feeling-emotional tone.

Stratification Both the process of ranking differentiated categories into classes and the resulting hierarchy of classes.

Structure The way the parts of a whole are put together; the relationship of the parts to one another.

Subculture Shared, learned patterns of behavior common to a specific group or category within the larger society.

Subnormality A deviation from a norm or normative expectation; usually applied to intelligence levels below the normal.

Symbol Any object, picture, gesture, sign, mark, printed or written matter, or sound which stands for another or serves to recall another, and which directs mental and actional associations.

Trends, social Changes or modifications in society and culture which are characterized by directionality but not necessarily by improvement.

Universals, cultural Those reactions and beliefs expected of every member of a society and supported by its mores and value systems.

Urban society A social structure characterized by large size and great density of population, heterogeneity, a complex division of labor, much relatively impersonal interaction, formal sanctions, and a proliferation of secondary groups. (*See Anomie;* Mass society.)

Urbanism Culture patterns associated with urban society.

Urbanization The process of becoming urban.

Value The quality of desirability (or undesirability) believed to inhere in an idea, object, or action. Values are accepted, in time, by the group in certain orders of priority.

Index of Names

Index of Subjects